Handbook of Indo-Pacific Studies

This handbook explores the significance of the Indo-Pacific in world politics. It shows how the re-emergence of the Indo-Pacific in international relations has fundamentally changed the approach to politics, economics and security.

The volume:

- explores the themes related to trade, politics and security for better understanding of the Indo-Pacific and the repercussions of the region's emergence;
- studies different security and political issues in the region: military competition, maritime governance, strategic alliances and rivalries, and international conflicts;
- analyses various socio-economic dimensions of the Indo-Pacific, such as political systems, cultural and religious contexts, and trade and financial systems;
- examines the strategies of various states, such as the United States, Japan, India and China, and their approaches towards the Indo-Pacific;
- covers the role of middle powers and small states in detail.

Interdisciplinary in approach and with essays from authors from around the world, this volume will be indispensable to scholars, researchers and students in the fields of international relations, politics and Asian studies.

 Handbook of Indo-Pacific Studies has two companion documents available that provide additonal tools for Indo-Pacific Studies: "The Didactic Companion" and the "Guide for Curriculum for Indo-Pacific Studies". Both are available on the Routledge website as well as under the QR code to the left.

Barbara Kratiuk currently works at the Faculty of Political Science and International Studies, University of Warsaw, Poland.

Jeroen J.J. Van den Bosch currently works as an editor and project coordinator at Adam Mickiewicz University in Poznań, Poland.

Aleksandra Jaskólska currently works at the Faculty of Political Science and International Studies, University of Warsaw, Poland.

Yoichiro Sato currently teaches at Ritsumeikan Asia Pacific University, Japan.

Indo-Pacific in Context

This series brings together topical research on contemporary and long-standing issues encompassing the Indo-Pacific region.

With countries steeped in history, communities diverse in cultures, developing economies and emerging markets, Indo-Pacific has emerged as the key stakeholder in a world order in flux. The region has solidified its presence in the global political discourse through multilateral initiatives, defence agreements, and strategic partnerships. It has emerged as a zone of contestations, conflict, and cooperation.

The works published in this series showcase interdisciplinary research in the arts, the humanities, and the social sciences, including a range of subject areas such as politics and international relations, international economy, sociology and social anthropology, women, gender and sexuality studies, history, geo-politics, military studies, area studies, cultural studies, environment and sustainability, development studies, migration studies, urban development, digital humanities, and science and technology studies.

Works in the series are published simultaneously in UK/US and South Asia editions, as well as in e-book format. We welcome a range of books aimed at furthering scholarship and understanding of the Asia-Pacific region. Authors and researchers interested in contributing to this series may get in touch with rioeditorial@tandfindia.com

Handbook of Indo-Pacific Studies

Edited by Barbara Kratiuk, Jeroen J. J. Van den Bosch, Aleksandra Jaskólska and Yoichiro Sato

For more information about this series, please visit: www.routledge.com/Indo-Pacific-in-Context/book-series/IPC

Handbook of Indo-Pacific Studies

Edited by Barbara Kratiuk,
Jeroen J. J. Van den Bosch,
Aleksandra Jaskólska and Yoichiro Sato

Routledge
Taylor & Francis Group
NEW YORK AND LONDON

Cover image: Getty Images

First published 2023
by Routledge
4 Park Square, Milton Park, Abingdon, Oxon OX14 4RN

and by Routledge
605 Third Avenue, New York, NY 10158

Routledge is an imprint of the Taylor & Francis Group, an informa business

British Library Cataloguing-in-Publication Data
A catalogue record for this book is available from the British Library

ISBN: 978-1-032-35928-1 (hbk)
ISBN: 978-1-032-37272-3 (pbk)
ISBN: 978-1-003-33614-3 (ebk)

DOI: 10.4324/9781003336143

Typeset in Sabon
by Deanta Global Publishing Services, Chennai, India

DISCLAIMERS

This handbook is created within the framework of the Eurasian Insights: Strengthening Indo-Pacific Studies (EISIPS) project (2019-1-PL01-KA203-065644), an Erasmus plus Strategic Partnership in Higher Education, and realized with co-funding from the Erasmus plus program of the European Union.

The European Union cannot be held responsible or liable for the contents of this work.

Barbara:
To AK, GK, BK and MK. And to KB. Thank you.

Aleksandra:
To those who are always hungry for knowledge. Use your knowledge to make the world a better place.

Jeroen:
To Zuzanna and new beginnings.

Yoichiro:
To my dear friend, Professor K.V. Kesevan.

Contents

Figures

Maps

Tables

Contributors

Barbara Kratiuk is a Research Fellow at the University of Warsaw, Poland. She studied at the University of Freiburg, Germany, and the London School of Economics and Political Science, UK. Before academia, Barbara worked as a journalist and independent researcher with a short stint in diplomacy. She focuses her research on power distribution, Southeast Asia amidst great power rivalry and the impact of the Vietnam War on regional dynamics and pop culture in international relations.

Jeroen J.J. Van den Bosch has a background in Area Studies (Slavonic Studies) and Political Science (International Relations) and currently works as an editor and project coordinator at Adam Mickiewicz University in Poznań (AMU), Poland. His research fields encompass theories of dictatorships, their classification, autocratic cooperation and transitions.

Aleksandra Jaskólska is Assistant Professor at the Faculty of Political Science and International Studies, University of Warsaw, Poland. Since 2010, she has been involved in the activities of the Centre for Contemporary India Research and Studies University of Warsaw. Her research interests include the role of domestic actors in shaping foreign policy, India's foreign policy, political systems in countries of South Asia, regional parties in India, cultural diversity in the countries of South Asia and demographic challenges faced by South Asia.

Yoichiro Sato currently teaches at Ritsumeikan Asia Pacific University, Japan. His major works include *The Rise of China and International Security* (co-edited with Kevin Cooney, Routledge, 2008), *The U.S.-Japan Security Alliance* (co-edited with Takashi Inoguchi and G. John Ikenberry, 2011), *Re-Rising Japan* (co-edited with Hidekazu Sakai, 2017) and *Identity, Culture and Memory in Japanese Foreign Policy* (co-edited with Michal Kolmaš, 2021).

Andrea Carteny is Associate Professor of History of International Relations, as well as director of CEMAS (Centro di Ricerca Cooperazione con l'Eurasia, il Mediterraneo e l'Africa Sub-sahariana), an interdepartmental research centre, at the Sapienza University of Rome, Italy. Andrea's research focuses primarily on the concept of national identity, nationalism and ethnocentrism, as well as Eurasian History and pan-Turanism.

Astha Chadha is a Japanese Government MEXT PhD scholar at Ritsumeikan Asia Pacific University, Japan, and Non-resident Lloyd and Lilian Vasey Fellow at the Pacific Forum, Hawaii. Astha holds an MSc in International Relations and MA in Economics. Astha has published research on India–Japan relations, religion in international relations, regional powers in the Indo-Pacific and South Asian rivalries.

Elena Tosti Di Stefano is a PhD candidate in "History of Europe" at Sapienza University of Rome, Italy, and Research Fellow of the Research Centre "Cooperazione con l'Eurasia, il Mediterraneo e l'Africa Sub-sahariana" (CEMAS).

Karina Jedrzejowska is Assistant Professor at the University of Warsaw, Poland, Faculty of Political Science and International Studies (Department of Regional and Global Studies). She is a graduate of the University of Manchester, UK, Warsaw School of Economics, Poland, and the University of Warsaw. Since 2017, she has been a governing board member and the treasurer of the World International Studies Committee (WISC). Her primary research areas include global financial governance and economic development.

Catherine Jones is Senior Fellow at the University of St Andrews, UK. She was a visiting researcher at the University of Columbia, Nanyang Technological University in Singapore and at the University of Waterloo. She is a recipient of a Korea Foundation grant. Her main research areas are the nexus between security and development in East Asia, security challenges presented by North Korea and East Asian states in international institutions.

Tomasz Łukaszuk is a political scientist-orientalist by education, a diplomat by experience and researcher by passion. He is an author of articles on maritime governance in Asia and Europe as well as a former Polish Ambassador to Indonesia and India.

Chris Ogden is Senior Lecturer/Associate Professor in Asian Affairs at the University of St Andrews, UK, where he researches the global rise of China, India and Asia, contemporary great power politics, and national security dynamics across East Asia and South Asia. In order to transmit his authoritative expert knowledge into the public domain, he delivers many invited public talks, is regularly interviewed by global media organizations, and frequently writes op-ed and analysis pieces.

Przemyslaw Osiewicz is Associate Professor at Adam Mickiewicz University in Poznań, Poland and FULBRIGHT Senior Award Visiting Scholar at Georgetown University, Washington DC, USA (2016–2017); He is Non-Resident Scholar at the Middle East Institute, Washington DC, USA and a member of the Polish Accreditation Committee (2020–2023).

Stefano Pelaggi received an MA in Sociology and a PhD in History, both from Sapienza University of Rome, Italy. He is currently Adjunct Professor at Sapienza University, Senior Fellow Researcher at Centro Studi Geopolitica.info. His research field is mainly focused on the concept of soft power and public diplomacy in the Asia-Pacific region, particularly in Taiwan and in the Chinese projection in Europe and Italy.

Paolo Pizzolo is Research Fellow in International Relations and Geopolitics. He graduated in Political Science and International Relations and holds a PhD in Political Science, Political Theory and Political History from Luiss Guido Carli University,

Italy. He looks at key interpretative paradigms of IR theory such as realism, liberalism, Marxism and constructivism, as well as analytical approaches to international politics.

Gulshan Sachdeva is Jean Monnet Chair; Coordinator, Jean Monnet Centre of Excellence; and Professor at the Centre for European Studies, Jawaharlal Nehru University, India. He is Book Series Editor, Europe-Asia Connectivity (Palgrave). Some of his recent publications include *Challenges in Europe: Indian Perspectives* (Palgrave 2019) and *India in a Reconnecting Eurasia* (2016) (Washington: CSIS).

Bhaswati Sarkar is Assistant Professor at Jawaharlal Nehru University, India. She is a political scientist by training and her main areas of interest are ethnicity, nationalism, minority rights, multiculturalism in the context of Europe, politics of citizenship, terrorism and Europe's response at state and union levels. She previously taught at the erstwhile Centre for Russian, Central Asian and East European Studies. In the Centre for European Studies, she currently offers a course on identity issues in Europe.

Jayati Srivastava is Professor of International Politics at the Centre for International Politics, Organization and Disarmament (CIPOD), School of International Studies (SIS), Jawaharlal Nehru University (JNU), India. Her areas of research include global civil society; legitimacy of global governance; global justice; southern perspectives on IR, aesthetics and international politics; and international environmental politics

Shankari Sundararaman is Professor of Southeast Asian Studies at Jawaharlal Nehru University, India. She was a Visiting Fellow at the Asia-Pacific College of Diplomacy (APCD) at the Australian National University (ANU), where she worked on the trilateral relations between India, Indonesia and Australia. She was also a Visiting Fellow at the Centre for Strategic and International Studies (CSIS), Jakarta in 2006–2007. She is also a columnist with *The New Indian Express*.

Lorenzo Termine is currently a PhD Candidate at Sapienza Università di Roma, a Research Fellow of a Rome-based think tank and author for several Italian and English magazines and journals. His areas of study include International Relations theories and Strategic studies. His research focuses on hegemony, revisionism, US-China relationship, and China's defense strategy and nuclear policy.

Tran Phuong Thao holds an MA in International Relations. She attended the PhD program of Ritsumeikan Asia Pacific University, Japan, in 2018 and is still pursuing her PhD. Her current research is a comparative study on the role of collective memory in conflict resolution and peace-making.

Rafał Ulatowski is Assistant Professor at the Faculty of Political Science and International Studies, University of Warsaw, Poland. He has been awarded scholarships by the Konrad Adenauer Foundation, the German Academic Exchange Service, DAAD (2013 and 2014–2015), the German Institute of Polish Culture (2015) and the French government (2015). His research focuses on international political economy, energy security and German foreign policy.

Jitendra Uttam is currently Assistant Professor at New Delhi's Jawaharlal Nehru University, India. He holds a PhD from Seoul National University, Korea. He is the author and co-author of two books – *The Political Economy of Korea: Transition,*

Transformation and Turnaround (2014) and *Varieties of Capitalism in Asia: Beyond the Developmental State* (2017).

Rafał Wiśniewski is Assistant Professor in the Strategic Studies Department, Faculty of Political Science and Journalism, Adam Mickiewicz University, Poznań, Poland. His research interests revolve around international security in the Indo-Pacific, great power rivalry and military strategy.

Anna Wróbel is Assistant Professor at the Faculty of Political Science and International Studies University of Warsaw, Poland. She completed her postgraduate studies in Foreign Trade at the Warsaw School of Economics (2004) and obtained her PhD in Political Science from the Institute of International Relations, University of Warsaw, Poland (2007). Her expertise lies in global trade governance, international trade in services, common commercial policy and trade regionalism.

Hidetaka Yoshimatsu is Professor of Politics and International Relations at Ritsumeikan Asia Pacific University, Japan, as well as Visiting Research Fellow, University of Adelaide, Australia. He has published articles that focus on Japan's external relations and regionalism in Asia in numerous journals, including *The Pacific Review*, *Asian Survey* and *Journal of Contemporary China*.

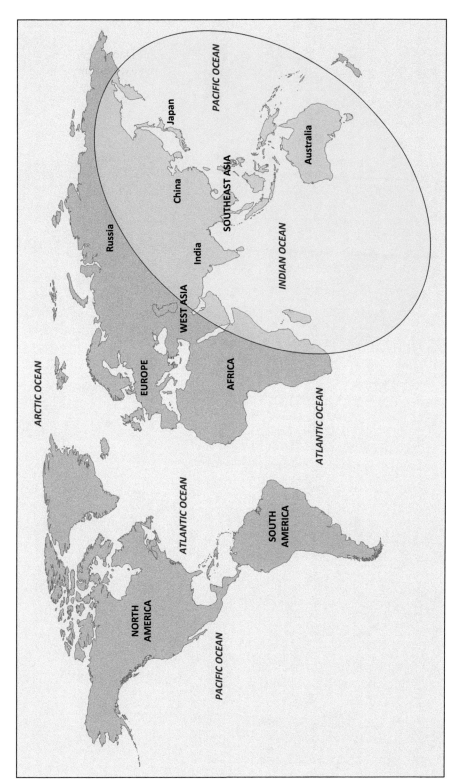

Map 1 Scope of the Indo-Pacific. *Source: Gurpreet Khurana*

Introduction

This handbook came about from a desire for a comprehensive, student-centred handbook. Aleksandra, Jeroen, Yoichiro and I have often spoken about the fact that, especially in Europe, these are few and far between, very often difficult to obtain for an average student. Some of the best books on East or South Asia, like the ones by Michael Yahuda and Donald Weatherbee or the ones by Sumit Ganguly are not widely available. For this reason and also because we believe in popularising science and helping people understand the increasingly complex world we live in, this handbook is available in open access to anyone who wants it, courtesy of both the Erasmus+ grant and our publisher. We can only hope the readers will find it useful and informative and as much of a pleasurable read as we editors have when we received all the chapters.

With co-funding of the Erasmus+ grant of the European Union[1] we were able to bring together brilliant people, who are passionate about both teaching and the subject matter: the Indo-Pacific region, which encompasses a vast area that has been mostly analysed in separate fragments. We tried to bring it together not only for students wanting to specialise on this region or educators planning to adjust the focus of their courses but also for anyone who is doing research or is otherwise interested in this topic for professional or personal reasons.

What is worth noting regarding the Indo-Pacific is that the concept has seen a resurgence. In politics, the term has been in use since Karl Haushofer, who talked about the "Indo-Pacific space." As Gurpreet Khurana noted, in geography this is a term that has been used widely to denote ecosystems in the tropical areas of the Indian and Pacific Oceans.[2]

What is the Indo-Pacific now? As the Indo-Pacific is a concept established largely through strategies of different states, it is important to note that the geographic limitations vary depending on where the given strategy originated from. While Kaplans' definition of Indo-Pacific is very broad, the nucleus of the meta-region, as defined by Peter Cozens, is smaller: starting in the west at the edge of South Asia with Pakistan, through India, then expanding to North and Southeast Asia all the way down to New Zealand and the Pacific Islands.[3]

This geopolitical mindset has been around for a while, but of late the Indo-Pacific has seen a resurgence and seems to encompass a more permanent conceptual shift.

Of course, the Indo-Pacific existed long before Haushofer. The area, as mentioned by Kaplan, was connected by the flow of trade, people and ideas long before modern states put a label on it. We can note that the Indo-Pacific has evolved

DOI: 10.4324/9781003336143-1

through multiple stages: from the bilateral structure of Antiquity and the Middle Ages through a period of fragmentation that lasted from the mid-19th century to the end of the Cold War right to the multipolar world structure of the late-20th and 21st centuries. It is important to note that in each of those periods, the Indo-Pacific experienced both dynamics of cooperation and rivalry. The connections were there, but they were not as dense as they are in the 21st century, therefore any previous (Indian-Chinese) bipolarity was not characterised by rivalry, rather by two vying civilisational gravity centres.

The Indo-Pacific of the past, before the colonial race of the 19th century, was largely bipolar, by which we mean there existed two centres of power, located in the cyclical civilisations of India and China. Most of the flows of trade, people and knowledge revolved around those civilisations in the Indo-Pacific connected with less populous sub-regions. This period is characterised by a lack of large-scale rivalry. Neither Indian nor Chinese civilisations sought to expand their influence far beyond their established spheres of influence. At rare times they fought each other but always had consideration for each other while making foreign policy decisions. Most states at the time were focused on trade and exchange of knowledge, not so much on conquest, at least not toward the Indo-Pacific.

The colonial period and the Second World War and its aftermath, led to a fragmentation of the region: individual states had fewer connections to their neighbours than with their imperial metropoles. India no longer extended influence over South and Southeast Asian kingdoms, China was no longer the centre of a tributary system that spanned most of East Asia. Different Indian kingdoms found themselves beholden to the British government. Lao, Cambodia and the Vietnamese kingdoms were no longer able to trade with their neighbours, but rather forced to trade with their metropole. The Philippines were dependent on and fully controlled by the United States. While Great Britain would be the dominant power in the Indian Ocean reaching to the Malacca straights, considerations had to be made for other colonial powers in the region like France, the Netherlands and, to a degree, Germany. This dynamic only changed once Japan became a regional power by the turn of the 20th century. Those connections between regional powers, colonies and metropoles included the flow of trade, people and knowledge, as well as political relations.

The Second World War and Cold War further fragmented the Indo-Pacific, as the US-USSR rivalry was complemented by the Non-Alignment Movement. Multiple conflicts in the Indo-Pacific, from the partition of India through the Korean war to the Indochina wars meant that most of the connections that existed before became disrupted by political struggles.

The current reincarnation of the Indo-Pacific is yet again different – more multilateral – and multiple states are centres of power and influence, each trying to mould the Indo-Pacific into what they see as beneficial, but also cooperate based on common interest and historical connection. Some of the historical connections, disrupted by the last century, have been re-established. New ones were forged, especially when considering the United States' entry into the Indo-Pacific space.

The Indo-Pacific now includes states that previously were either not interested in participating, preferring their isolationist policies (Japan) or did not exist for a long time (the United States). This means that for the first time in history, China and Japan are powerful states at the same time, making them natural rivals. The arrival of the United States in the Pacific through colonisation (the Philippines) and later by establishing military presence in Japan and the Korean Peninsula, rendered the United States a new actor that rocked the previously stable and established dynamics of India-China considerations. Coupled with the rise of regional middle powers, it is clear that the modern Indo-Pacific is to be a different space than before the Second World War.

The recurring theme of a "free and open Indo-Pacific" that appears in the strategies of the United States, Japan, India and Australia is largely about trade, connectivity and regional security. In many ways it echoes elements of an Indo-Pacific that existed before. We are therefore talking about a resurgence of the Indo-Pacific, not its origin, when we talk of the strategies individual states introduced in the region.

The concepts of the Indo-Pacific by individual states, while based around the idea of "free and open Indo-Pacific" have included other aims and agendas. For the United States, the Indo-Pacific was necessary to connect India to the Asia-Pacific and help guard the existing regional order and US interests. For Japan, this is a network that "will allow people, good, capital and knowledge to flow freely,"[4] which is a clear indication that Japan sees the Indo-Pacific as a frame to respond to the growing role of China and its Belt and Road Initiative.

An Australian White Paper of 2013 mentioned two key factors: India's emergence and the growing trade and investment flows in the region. Australia's approach and interests are largely identical to Japan's. Echoes of those same considerations could be found in India, as from New Delhi's perspective the Indo-Pacific is "a new phase of engagement to bridge the distance of geography through shared interests and actions."[5] Yet for China, the Indo-Pacific is a concept that can threaten the security of its trade routes and block Chinese economic growth by focusing on the transformative Japanese-Indian and Indian-US relations that inform the region.

There are therefore recurring themes in the Indo-Pacific. Some like openness, connectivity, flow of goods and people echo the traditions of the Indo-Pacific. Others, like the scrutiny of China's role in the region are new – China naturally had a place in the Indo-Pacific as one of the two most important actors and now is largely considered a revisionist power for wanting to reclaim that spot. The Indo-Pacific thus can be many things to many states and people, albeit with common characteristics: it is a polycentric structure based around flow of trade, people and knowledge.

With this short review we aim to give the broad strokes of a definition of what we understand by the Indo-Pacific. Details differ from chapter to chapter, depending on the authors' personal take and their needs to explain the phenomena they discuss.

The handbook itself is divided into four parts: theory, socio-economic issues, security and politics. The first part, consisting of two chapters, brings closer the different understandings of Indo-Pacific from different schools of thought and the evolution of the term. There, in the first chapter Shankari Sundararaman traces back in history the Indo-Pacific idea, its development and importance to the modern day. Professor Sundararaman shows in her chapter how Indo-Pacific has always really been there in the minds of politicians and strategists but perhaps it was simply not verbalised. In the next chapter Stefano Pelaggi and Lorenzo Termine put the Indo-Pacific in the context of hotly contested geopolitical theories to see how those ideas influenced the modern thinking about the Indo-Pacific and its importance for the great powers and their strategies.

The second part, focusing on socio-economic issues, tackles such topics as democracy and authoritarian rule, cultural aspects, trade, economic integration and financial institutions. There, in paired Chapters 3 and 4, Karina Jędrzejowska and Anna Wróbel respectively wrestle with the idea of integration and trade and financial interactions within the region. They show tremendous diversity in institutions, approaches and policies among all the involved states.

In the fifth chapter Aleksandra Jaskólska looks at the influence of religion on international relations in the Indo-Pacific region. The hypothesis that assumes that religion is one of the factors which affects international relations in the Indo-Pacific region and cannot be treated as only a minor or irrelevant factor as it is widely seen in the West (mostly European countries).

The sixth and seventh chapters are again complementary. Written by Jeroen J.J. Van den Bosch and Bhaswati Sarkar respectively, they delve into political systems of the Indo-Pacific. Both democratic and authoritarian regimes that exist in the region have a huge impact on security, connectivity and politics. The democratic slide towards more authoritarian rule is also important for understanding the specifics of the region and the states within.

Finally, the eighth chapter in this section was authored by Gulshan Sachdeva. Gulshan looks at connectivity in the Indo-Pacific. The connections between states that have existed for centuries and are being reinvented and rediscovered now play an important role in the shaping of both the region and of regional relations.

The third part covers security of the Indo-Pacific, along various dimensions, ranging from maritime governance, environmental issues and arms races to international conflicts.

The ninth chapter of the handbook deals with military build-up in the Indo-Pacific. Rafał Wiśniewski analyses the importance of arms and perception of threat as well as use of military in international relations in the Indo-Pacific. The rivalry between the United States and China informs a lot of this competition that might prove to impact stability in the region.

Rafał Ulatowski analyses security from a different perspective: energy in Chapter 10. China, Japan, Australia and India are all huge energy consumers. They are all, along with the United States, also huge oil and gas consumers. This competition for resources and the need to secure trade routes to ensure steady flow of fossil fuels are important considerations for all the regional players.

In Chapter 11, Jayati Srivastava explores the environmental issues in the Indo-Pacific. She analyses the problems, the environmental security and the approaches different states in the Indo-Pacific take to these pressing problems.

The regional players often engage not only in competition but also cooperation. I write in Chapter 12 about the different types of cooperation between states, from alliances to alignments. I also point out how many of those partnerships are driven by very practical considerations.

In a mirror chapter, Chapter 13, Astha Chada looks into strategic rivalries. The competition between states has been increasing steadily over the last decade, and it has impacted all of the states within the Indo-Pacific. What is important to note is that the US-China rivalry is only one of those and that other rivalries have almost as much impact on the Indo-Pacific.

Chapter 14 is dedicated to what sometimes happens when the rivalries cannot be contained. Przemysław Osiewicz looks at all conflicts in the Indo-Pacific and their typology and causes to find commonalities and differences, and analyses how they shape and impact the region.

In Chapter 15, Tomasz Łukaszuk looks at maritime governance in the Indo-Pacific. He looks at the institutions and actors involved in attempts to regulate the sea lanes of communication, maritime conflicts and issues that arise from increased sea activity in the Indo-Pacific.

Finally, the fourth part is dedicated to foreign policy and international politics: the United States, Japan, India and China, middle and small powers all have their approaches and strategies relating to the Indo-Pacific shown here. First, in Chapter 16 Yoichiro Sato looks at the United States, one of the states that promoted the idea of the Indo-Pacific. He puts forward a hypothesis that the United States has become too overstretched and that it needs regional allies to maintain the leading position.

In Chapter 17, Chris Ogden and Catherine Jones look at China and China's approach to the region. While Beijing rejected the Indo-Pacific as a strategy aimed against China, its own strategy toward the region is being implemented to increase the Chinese sphere of influence and bring it back to its traditional place in Asia.

Chapter 18 was authored by Jitendra Uttam, who looks at India's tryst with the Indo-Pacific. The rejuvenation of the Indo-Pacific brought forward the realisation of how important India is for regional stability, cooperation and politics. All of this is analysed in this chapter.

Hidetaka Yoshimatsu in Chapter 19 looks at the Japanese approach towards the Indo-Pacific. From the confluence of the two seas to the increased presence in the Pacific Ocean, Japan has become an active player in the region, pragmatically approaching the situation to realise its own interests.

Chapter 20 is dedicated to the EU approach to the Indo-Pacific. In this chapter, Andrea Cartegny and Elena Tosti di Stefano look at the strategies of individual European states as well as their often difficult history with the region as well as the general strategy of the European Union, which is largely focused on trade and stability.

In Chapters 21 and 22, Tran Phuong Thao and Paolo Pizzolo together with Stefano Pelaggi respectively look at middle and small powers in the Indo-Pacific. These smaller states have become very important for the Indo-Pacific in a time of increased great power rivalry. They employ many different strategies to ensure their survival, which is what the three authors analyse in their chapters. These two chapters conclude the handbook.

Since this book project has been both a scholarly and a didactic mission, students and educators can consult our tailor-made didactic companion, listing learning outcomes and presenting various (classroom) assignments to aid them in their study or coursework planning. On behalf of the editors and authors, we hope that all readers will enjoy this handbook and that both new and experienced scholars find it useful to discover new dimensions of this geopolitical region.

Barbara Kratiuk
University of Warsaw

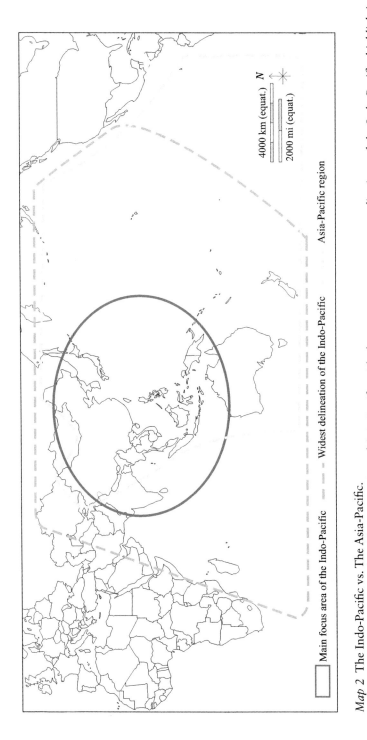

Map 2 The Indo-Pacific vs. The Asia-Pacific.
This map contrasts the older conception of Asia-Pacific with the contemporary conceptualisations of the Indo-Pacific, highlighting its core region of focus according to most current approaches. There is a clear shift putting Southeast Asia at its core and decoupling Latin America from this frame in order to balance China in a more multipolar setting, including India. Map created by editors, adapted from: https://d-maps.com/carte.php?num_car=3503&lang=en in line with terms and conditions of use, designed by Typeface NV.

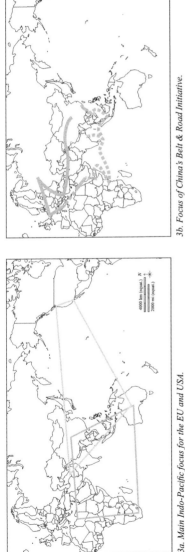

3a. *Main Indo-Pacific focus for the EU and USA.*

3c. *India's 3 spheres of influence in the Indo-Pacific.*

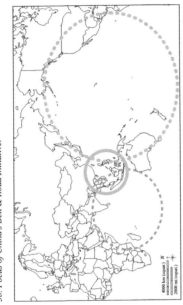

3b. *Focus of China's Belt & Road Initiative.*

3d. *Japan's "Free and Open Indo-Pacific".*

Map 3 Different Strategic Priorities in the Indo-Pacific.

While all actors define the Indo-Pacific as the area encompassing both oceans, this map shows the contrasting areas of strategic focus by the United States and EU that are each limited rather to one ocean mostly (the US on the Pacific and the EU on the Indian), even though the US (Indo-)Pacific command has always included the whole region. India's approach puts itself at the core, while Japan aims to work with existing frameworks (ASEAN) to connect both oceans. Australia, like Singapore, Malaysia, Indonesia and Thailand, have their own two-ocean worldviews more in line with Japan's approach. China altogether counters the Indo-Pacific concept with its Belt and Road Initiative, including other areas not specific to the Indo-Pacific. **Sources:** J.S. Gill & R. Mitra, "India's Indo-Pacific Strategy: Understanding India's Spheres of Influence," *Sigma Iota Rbo Journal of International Relations*. 2018. R. Medcalf, "An Australian Vision of the Indo-Pacific and What It Means for Southeast Asia, *Southeast Asian Affairs*, 2019. "Free and Open Indo-Pacific," Ministry of Foreign Affairs, Japan. (www.mofa.go.jp/files/000430632.pdf) Map created by editors, adapted from: https://d-maps.com/carte.php?num_car=3503&lang=en in line with terms and conditions of use, designed by Typeface NV.

Notes

1 This book project was co-funded in the context of the *Eurasian Insights: Strengthening Indo-Pacific Studies in Europe* project (EISIPS – No. 2019-1-PL01-KA203-065644), a strategic partnership for higher education Erasmus+ programme of the European Union.
2 G. Khurana, "What Is the Indo-Pacific? The New Geopolitics of the Asian-Centred Rim Land." In *Geopolitics by Other Means Indo-Pacific Reality*, ed. A. Berkofsky, S. Miracola. ISPI, 2019, p. 16.
3 P. Cozens, "Some Reflections on Maritime Developments in Indo-Pacific," *Maritime Affairs*, vol. 1, nr 1 (2005).
4 Shinzo Abe, "Confluence of the Two Seas," speech in India's Parliament, 22 August 2007.
5 Narendra Modi, "Prime Minister's Keynote Address at Shangri La Dialogue," 1 June 2018.

Part I
Theory of the Indo-Pacific

1 Understanding the Indo-Pacific

Historical context and evolving dynamics

Shankari Sundararaman

Introduction

Over the last decade there has been a predominant shift in the use of the terminology of the Indo-Pacific, which has become a part of the foreign policy lexicon of several states that earlier referred to this region as the Asia-Pacific. This shift in terminology is not merely a change in nomenclature but represents the expansion of a region into a mega-region. The Asia-Pacific emerged as a post-Cold War concept driven from the factors of economic integration which also allowed for closer security level ties. On the other hand the Indo-Pacific refers to a region that transcends the tradition understanding of a region as being geographically "contained" but is more of a mega-region as a result of two factors. First, it implies a critical shift in the maritime extents that link the Indian and the Pacific Oceans as a singular maritime unit. And second, it also links the territorial extents that encompass the littoral states of these oceanic extents as these states have an increasing stake in maintaining the rule-based order in the maritime regions that surround them. Today even as the countries of the region are trying to address what constitutes the definitional conceptions of the Indo-Pacific, it is imperative to understand how the Indo-Pacific differs from the Asia-Pacific

In order to understand the concept of the Indo-Pacific, it is necessary to recognise that the huge transitions shaping the Asian context have led to the evolution of this concept. While arguably some states still prefer to maintain the erstwhile conceptual understandings of the Asia-Pacific and both terminologies are used interchangeably, it is important to understand that the Indo-Pacific refers to a mega-regional identity, and any efforts to club this conceptual framework into a kind of "regionalism" is inherent with its own challenges. Many of the interpretations by various countries that have now begun to unveil their own approach to the Indo-Pacific show a great degree of differences in the geographical scope and extent of this concept for each country. That ambiguity adds complexity to the definitional scope and extent of the concept itself. Therefore, it is imperative to recognise that each country that is now formulating a distinct approach to the Indo-Pacific is doing so from the compulsions of their own foreign policy perspectives. On the one hand, as a factor of these divergences, the focus on converging views among countries is more upon the normative principles of a rule-based order and how each state needs to engage with the normative order in the wider region. On the other hand, the *fluidity* of how each country defines its context leads to a greater degree of *flexibility* based on the individual needs of each country's foreign and security policies. This shapes the current discourse on the Indo-Pacific and how states are approaching the context from their own dynamics.

DOI: 10.4324/9781003336143-3

For much of the post-Cold War period, the region has been known by the earlier *avatar* which is the Asia-Pacific. This same region is today undergoing a significant shift with the structural rise of China, both economically and politically, shifting the influence and position that it plays in regional and global affairs. As this shift has been evolving over the past three decades, there are increasing implications of the rise of China both at the regional and systemic levels. Simultaneously, the rise of India is also occurring leading to a greater emphasis on how India's foreign policy is also shaping the region. This has led to two important dynamics that have emerged – the focus on the Indian Ocean and its linkages to the Pacific Ocean are clearly indicating the significant maritime interconnectedness of these two regions. With India's rise, the context of the territorial limits of the erstwhile Asia-Pacific has evolved to give greater emphasis to the Indo-Pacific. As these two terms are increasingly being used interchangeably, it brings the focus back to the huge transitions shaping this region. Any efforts to answer the question as to what kind of "regionalism" is implied by the term Indo-Pacific is fraught with challenges, especially since the term indicates a region in which competing and contradictory visions of what this region actually represents are different for different countries. In a recent study by Heiduk and Wacker the reference to the Indo-Pacific is used to identify "various, sometimes divergent concepts. These in turn are based on very different ideas on regional order. What they all have in common is the reference to the importance of a rules based international order" (Heiduk et al. 2020).

One of the clearest arguments put forward by Jeffrey Wilson is that the Indo-Pacific represents a shift from an "economic to a security-driven process." Wilson argues that the Indo-Pacific represents an example of what is known as "rescaling." He defines this as a practice in which the political processes are reshaped on the basis of the spatial scale that these processes seek to include. Wilson identifies three clear forms of rescaling to address the shift from the Asia-Pacific to the Indo-Pacific – these include geographic rescaling which brings several other countries into the context of the region's identity. How the Indo-Pacific is defined clearly indicates a minimalist and a maximalist approach – the minimalist approach looks at the erstwhile Asia-Pacific and includes the rise of India, making it the region eastwards from India to cover the expanse of the Asia-Pacific (Wilson 2018). This, however, limits the extent of the Indian Ocean, particularly the western Indian Ocean and does not include the littoral states of the Indian Ocean that expand West Asia and Eastern Africa. The maximalist approach to defining the Indo-Pacific is to include the entirety of the Indian Ocean (both west and east) and western Pacific (Wilson 2018). The work of eminent scholars such as Rory Medcalf too supports this argument. The erstwhile understanding of the Asia-Pacific left India out of the regional focus. This was untenable because India too needs to be given its rightful place in the emerging geopolitical landscape where several countries are changing the nature of global interactions among states as the region shows profound structural power shifts which need to be addressed (Medcalf 2020).

Further, Wilson also states that two other types of rescaling are critical when trying to understand the emergence of the Indo-Pacific. First, is *institutional rescaling* which Wilson states refers to the extent to which institutions will be extended to incorporate new members. Second is the *functional rescaling* that is shifting the raison d'etre for the emergence of the Indo-Pacific. The Asia-Pacific was driven by an economic integration approach, particularly in how the regional free trade agreements were to be seen in terms of their compatibility with the norms of the global trading arrangements as enshrined in the processes of the World Trade Organization. In comparison, the

Indo-Pacific is driven by a security-led approach in terms of how regional states and extra-regional states could respond to the structural shifts in the region that bring with it security challenges to the existing normative order that governs the interstate system (Wilson 2018).

Historical relevance of the Indian and Pacific Oceans

Even as the contemporary relevance of the Indo-Pacific is gaining prominence, it would be imperative to look at this context from a historical perspective as it indicates the dynamism that this concept has even as it continues to evolve. From the Indian perspective, the reference to the Indo-Pacific always draws its origins from the famous speech made by Prime Minister Shinzo Abe to the Indian parliament where he highlighted the metaphorical reference to the "confluence of the two seas" as being indicative of the interconnectedness between the Indian and Pacific Oceans. This speech, however, drew inspiration and quoted the work of a book titled the *Majma-ul-Bahrain* by the Mughal Prince Dara Shikoh. The name of the same work was called *Samudra Samgamah*, a Sanskrit reference to the same title meaning the "confluence of the two seas." The original emphasis on this phrase was to indicate a spiritual synthesis between the philosophies of Sufism and Vedanta, bringing a cultural synthesis between Islam and Hinduism, this metaphor was used by Prime Minister Abe to refer to the singularity of the interconnectedness between the Indian and Pacific Oceans and the geopolitical factors that were driving the recognition of the Indo-Pacific concept (Abe 2007). Prime Minister Abe's analysis of the Indo-Pacific and the relevance of India in the context of the vision that the Indo-Pacific represented stemmed from two critical factors – first, India was a predominant power with the capacity to project its capabilities within the Indian Ocean region. Second, India's own economic growth and its rising potential made it a significant power with which convergences were emerging, particularly for Japan in terms of securing the increasingly connected extents of the Indian and Pacific Oceans. Both Japan and India found security convergences in this context due to increasing Chinese presence in the Pacific and the Indian Ocean regions, bringing the focus on maritime security concerns sharply into focus (Khurana 2007: 86). Prime Minister Abe's address also needs to be assessed within the background of the developments that were evolving in the maritime spaces linking these oceanic extents. In the aftermath of the 9/11 attacks on the United States and US engagement in Afghanistan, the Bush administration evolved the Proliferation Security Initiative (PSI) the track and halt the proliferation of weapons of mass destruction (WMDs), which brought the Indian and Pacific Oceans into a strategic unit to address the movement of fissile materials across the maritime extents. The PSI interdiction exercises launched through the early years were critical in linking these maritime spaces (Bergin 2005: 141). Gurpreet Khurana argues that the term Indo-Pacific, therefore, needs to be seen from a critical focus on what it entails as a vision for the wider region. According to him the term Asia was too focused on the continental aspects and was diverse in terms of the region it encompassed. Similarly, the term Asia-Pacific too did not represent the structural realities that were altering this vast region, while the combination of the oceanic extents of the Indo-Pacific was closer to the evolving realities that this regional expanse envisioned (Khurana 2020).

One of the first references to the Indo-Pacific concept emerged from German geopolitician, Karl Haushofer, later discredited for his links to the Reich. His works focused on the resurgence of Asia, wherein he referred to the term *Indopazifischen Raum* or the Indo-Pacific space. His core thesis argued India and China were separated by Tibet and therefore the interaction was through the seas, capturing the essence of the interactive ties through this oceanic extent even in the historical context (Khurana 2019). This interconnectedness of the oceanic extents is well emphasised in Robert Kaplan's *Monsoon: The Indian Ocean and the Future of American Power*, where he argues that the expansion of Islam from the Red Sea, through the Indian subcontinent and to the regions of Indonesia and Malaysia, represents a "map of these seas is central to a historical understanding of the faith" (Kaplan 2010). Kaplan also states that "this is a geography that encompasses, going from west to east, the Red Sea, Arabian Sea, Bay of Bengal, and Java and South China Seas" (Kaplan 2010: 5). Similar to the oceanic extents that were seen as one, there is also an increasing reference to the interconnectedness to the territorial extents of this region as well. Kaplan further argues that it was the Cold War that actually separated the territorial extents of this wider Indian Ocean region into various sub-units of the Middle East (West Asia), South Asia and the Pacific Rim. Historically this region was not divided into sub-units but was seen as an integrated region connected through the singularity of the Indian Ocean. As both China and India continue to rise, the linkage with West Asia and the regions of Southeast Asia will once again reduce the "separateness" of these sub-units, and its emergence as a singular unit will be emphasised by the singularity of the Indian Ocean itself.

Kaplan presents this view of an interconnected region in what he calls the greater Indian Ocean, which links the Horn of Africa; past the Arabian Peninsula to the Indian subcontinent, past the Indonesian archipelago and beyond. This reference by Kaplan to the extended region, today accounts for the geographic extent of what is referred to as the Indo-Pacific (Kaplan 2010).

Similar to these arguments of Kaplan, Southeast Asian historian Anthony Reid reiterates the importance of the maritime extents of the Indian and the Pacific Oceans, by tracing the history of *Nusantara* or Southeast Asia, as a region that witnessed vibrancy of trade and cultural exchanges even prior to the advent of the colonial powers. In two of his works titled *Southeast Asia in the Age of Commerce* and *A History of Southeast Asia: Critical Crossroads* he identifies the core region of what is today known as Southeast Asia and links the shifts that shaped this region particularly as it lay at the pivot of the Indo-Pacific region as it is known today. Of particular relevance to this trade was the region's spice trade which made it a prime focus for both traders and colonisers.[1] This region of Southeast Asia was known by other names: Europeans referred to this region as the Indian archipelago or what was called InsulIndia, depicting the island regions beyond the Indian subcontinent. Alternatively, some historians like Reginald May have referred to the region as Indochina denoting the region that lies between India and China, claiming this region to be influenced by a bamboo curtain where the cultural spread of both Indian and Chinese cultures are visible as the influence of these cultures waxed and waned depending on how stable and powerful the centre of these cultures were. Chinese and Indian cultural influences were not static but dynamic resulting in phases when the Chinese cultural imprint was stronger leading to the curtain moving westwards, and during times where Indian cultural influences were stronger the curtain moved eastwards (Sardesai 1997). Similarly, the works of Frecon and Meijer refer to the term Australasia which is the region that extends between India and Australia (Frecon & Meijer 2015).

As argued by Kaplan the movement of trade and cultural contact was done through the use of sailing with the monsoon winds of the Indian Ocean contributing to the capacity to travel these seas. Long before the introduction of the steam engine, the use of wind during the monsoon propelled a kind of linkage that spread across the entire region of the Indian Ocean and extended eastwards past the Indonesian archipelago through to the South China Sea and its littoral states. Historian Sugata Bose in his work *A Hundred Horizons: The Indian Ocean in the Age of Global Empire*, refers to the movement of trade between the regions linked together by the Indian Ocean, tying the main trading centres of India and China in the east to the Arab world and Persia in the west. Bose accounts the possibility of these connections only because of the close ties that were established as a result of the monsoon winds that propelled this movement across the region. For over 2000 years this region witnessed interactions through trade, and it lent the region a form of coherence that was visible regardless of the heterogeneity of the cultures and empires that mapped this region. He also states that there was a kind of "cosmopolitanism" that the region shared as a factor of these trade relations and cultural contacts, which also included the pilgrimage to the Haj as a contributing factor for developing such close ties among the communities that were part of this littoral region (Bose 2006).

India's historical interactions in the Indian and Pacific Ocean

A further understanding of the historical relevance also reveals that the region that covered this vast trade and cultural exchange was the home to several empires that had evolved a maritime consciousness. The term *thalassocracies* has been used by scholars like Frecon and Meijer to describe the empires that occupied this regional space such as the Sri Vijaya, Majapahit, Funan and others (Frecon & Meijer, 2015: 171). These empires were in the region of modern-day Indonesia and extended to the territorial extents of Cambodia and Vietnam on the mainland of Southeast Asia today. From the context of the empires in the Indian subcontinent the most well-known of the *thalassocracies* was the Chola empire from the southern part of the Indian peninsula. Foremost among the historians who have written on the Cholas (Cōlas) was Indian historian Nilakanta Sastri who refers to the close linkages between Chola empire and the Sri Vijaya empire, both of which had a strong maritime consciousness. Sashtri identifies that the empires of the regions traded with one another and that the Chola empire enjoyed dominance over the regions of the Bay of Bengal, which also extended to the regions of Sri Lanka and Maldives, as well as the regions of the Malay peninsula and the eastern archipelago, indicating that the Cholas had a considerable maritime presence in the waters of the eastern Indian Ocean (Sastri 1935). Sastri also indicates that the trade between the Cholas and the Chinese as well as parts of Southeast Asia was a critical feature even as early as the 11th century (Sastri 2018). The works of both D.G.E. Hall and Hermann Kulke, clearly reiterate this view on the trading relations that sustained the commercial activities in this region. They indicate that till the 11th century the trade in the region was largely peaceful and smooth, but this period of peaceful trade ended in the 11th century giving way to a more competitive form of trade in these maritime waters. Hermann Kulke refers to the control that the Cholas had over this entire region and adds that from the period of the Song dynasty in China trade relations became more competitive in the region (Sastri 2018). Philip Bowring in his work, *Empire of the Winds: The Global Role of Asia's Great Archipelago*, refers to the Cholas in his chapter titled "Tamil Tigers of Trade," wherein he focuses on the 1025 AD attack by Rajendra Chola on Palmebang and Kedah, which is the "only known recorded military engagement of an Indian state in Nusantaria" (Bowring 2019). The increasing rivalry between the Cholas and the Sri Vijaya was predominantly due to the access to commercial trading interests in the region. By this time both the east and the west were re-engaging with the trading systems of the Indian Ocean – the Song dynasty in China was critical to this trading environment and in the western Indian Ocean, on the African continent the Fatimid caliphate remained a strong power with trading interests (Bowring 2019: 73). Bowring argues that this period in the region's history was a "multipolar world," an order where the control by the Chola empire over the Bay of Bengal region connected it to the Khmer empire which then covered some of the regions of modern-day Thailand – the region of the Chao Phraya basin. His emphasis on multipolarity emerges from the view that several empires dominated the trading systems in the region simultaneously even as no single empire had control over it. Around this time the empires in Burma, as well as Sri Lanka and the regions of modern-day Sumatra were all woven into an intricate link of trading systems through the wider Indian Ocean region linking them to the Song dynasty and its empire in China through the current areas of the South China Sea.

As the above section clearly highlights the vibrancy of this region even prior to the colonial period, it is still pertinent to understand how the colonial phase shaped this region and created largely what were a loose set of empires or *mandalas,* whose power waxed and waned as the centres of these empires became stronger or weaker, into the kinds of consolidated administrative zones that were transformed and shaped into the nations states of the 20th century. The colonial phase brought in traders from outside the region who carved out their individual areas of interest and expanded both control over economic assets and subsequently political consolidation in the region. The period of European consolidation was not a smooth process devoid of confrontation. For almost the first hundred years the region saw a monopoly by the Portuguese who had control over the Asiatic seas. From 1511 to around 1596 the period of Portuguese monopoly continued till the Dutch came into the region towards the end of the 16th century followed by the British at the turn of the 17th century. Initially, the rivalry between the Dutch and the British was excessive, but slowly as time proceeded the two colonisers clearly carved out their individual zones of interest which were further consolidated with the Straits Settlement Agreement of 1824. This agreement also known as the Anglo-Dutch Agreement of 1824 demarcated the areas of the British and Dutch into two distinct zones, virtually splitting the Malacca straits into the northern and southern areas, almost a horizontal divide with the British expanding north of the Malacca and the Dutch expanding southwards (Sundararaman 2018). As part of this arrangement, the British had to vacate the territory of Bencoolen on the tip of the Sumatran island and would move to Singapore which had been established in 1818. This allowed the British uncontested access to the Malay peninsula and the control over Singapore ensured control over the Malacca strait too. For the Dutch, it allowed expansion into East Indies. What remained critical to this settlement was that the British interests over its trade rights with both China and India were to be safeguarded.

While this historical detail brings to the forefront the kinds of early interactions which existed in the region, it also has relevance in understanding the concept of the Indo-Pacific as a mega-region in the dynamics of the current changes impacting the regional and global order. This region was a vibrant trading region that used the seas as a means by which trade in goods and cultural exchanges were carried out. It connected the eastern and western limits of the Indian Ocean to the western limits of the Pacific Ocean through the seasonal monsoons allowing for the flow of goods and people between these regions. The significance of the historical links between India and China, as well as between the regions that constitute the Middle East (West Asia) and the east coast of Africa critically tie this region together through the extent of the maritime expanses, and the territorial regions were linked together through the access to the Indian and Pacific Oceans. While the empires in the Indian subcontinent and China remained important trading centres then, as post-colonial nation-states they have today re-emerged as critical economies that are driving the engine of global economic growth outwards, re-impacting the shift or the relevance of this region once again.

Shift from the Asia-Pacific to the Indo-Pacific: Impact on multilateralism

As colonialism gave way to the rise of free and sovereign nation-states in the aftermath of the Second World War, the sub-divisions of this once-integrated region began to shape the interstate system as the Cold War emerged. The shifting of US foreign policy to focus on the containment strategies of the Cold War necessitated a division of the region into various sub-units such as South Asia, West Asia, Southeast Asia or East Asia. The term Southeast Asia emerged during the Second World War when the Southeast Asia Command was set in place under General Douglas Macarthur. As the post-colonial order set in the region that covered the eastern Indian Ocean, the western Pacific Ocean began to acquire a different term of Asia-Pacific. This concept of Asia-Pacific emerged as early as the 1960s but in terms of the consolidation of this identity it was the late 1980s that saw the formation of the economic grouping of the Asia-Pacific Economic Cooperation (APEC) that significantly placed the emphasis on the term Asia-Pacific. As a region, Asia-Pacific had a dominant presence of the United States that led the shaping of the regional architecture for the Asia-Pacific region. It comprised sub-units of Northeast Asia, Southeast Asia, Oceania (Australia) and the Americas. This construct of the Asia-Pacific had a dual approach – first, it reiterated the importance of the role and influence that the United States enjoyed in the region, which was primarily driven from an economic perspective. The US remained one of the largest trading partners of the countries of this region. Second, the economic integration reinforced the strategic relations that the United States had with this region making this an additional layer in the regional integration framework.

It is important, however, to remember that the Asia-Pacific also had a core security dynamic that was led by the United States. In the initial years of the United States' containment strategy for the Asia-Pacific region, the focus was on the creation of a region-wide approach that was similar in principle to NATO but was not the same form or substance as NATO. The only two countries that were from Southeast Asia and part of the Southeast Asia Treaty Organization (SEATO) were Thailand and the Philippines. Robert Yates identifies that the move towards a collective security approach for the region clearly stemmed from the manner in which the first Indochina war was concluded. While both Britain and France were keen on seeing how the negotiations were concluded, the US was keener on establishing a collective defence treaty for Southeast Asia. In order to make the SEATO seem more credible the United States attempted to bring in the Colombo Powers, which had been an informal grouping of regional states from South and Southeast Asia – and comprised of India, Indonesia, Burma, Sri Lanka and Pakistan (Yates 2019). But the appeal to move forward on the SEATO was not accepted by all the members of the Colombo Powers, and finally only Pakistan was part of SEATO and two Southeast countries were Thailand and the Philippines. This came into place with the Manila treaty or pact and the Pacific Charter of 1954. This however, did not emerge as the sustaining security arrangement for the region.

The major focus on the security architecture was achieved through the "hubs and spokes" arrangement that primarily focused on deployment of larger forces in Japan, followed by ties with critical states that the US considered vital to its interests in the region – in Southeast Asia this was Thailand and the Philippines, South Korea and Taiwan in East Asia and Australia and New Zealand in the Pacific. Two critical aspects are relevant in this context – the hubs and spokes arrangement was a part of the US containment strategy and in its initial years the containment was directed at the USSR at the systemic level and at the regional level in the Asia-Pacific China was part of this containment strategy. Following the Sino-US rapprochement, the US presence in the region under the "hubs and spokes" continued until the end of the Cold War (Huisken 2009). Ron Huisken draws a compelling argument on the interlinkages between the US forward deployment in the Asia-Pacific region and the manner in which this in turn supported the growth of the region's economic miracle. The argument states that the initial period of this security arrangement was clearly about the need to insulate the region from the effects of communism from both the Soviet Union and China; and also to ensure that Japan did not militarise again. However, the shift in Japanese focus to economic development which saw a huge spurt of economic growth also led to overall economic growth for the region. Interestingly it seems to suggest that the presence of the US military allowed states to focus less on their security concerns while pushing their economic growth forward in an unrestrained manner. This critical link allowed for the region's enormous economic potential to come through (Huisken 2021).

While this US-dominated security architecture for East Asia was basically founded on the core principles of bilateralism and how the United States tied itself into the regional architecture through these bilateral mechanisms, the efforts to formulate a regional cooperation grouping led to the formation of the Association of Southeast Asian Nations (ASEAN), which between 1967 to 1999 expanded to cover the ten countries of Southeast Asia. Robert Yates argues that the ASEAN represented a kind of regional-level architecture that supported the US-led hubs and spokes mechanism that prevailed at the next level, through a role bargain mechanism where it sustained the principles through which the United States sought to lead the regional security architecture in East Asia. Yates identifies that the ASEAN played a dual role – as a primary role manager of the region and a regional conductor of multilateral processes (Yates 2019). Understanding the shift in these two roles of ASEAN clearly indicates the shift of the ASEAN processes to engage the region-wide processes of the Asia-Pacific. Moreover, as the region-wide processes are clearly shifting in light of the emerging geopolitical shifts in East Asia, ASEAN too finds itself under pressure to reinvent itself to address the changing approaches to the Indo-Pacific.

Throughout the Cold War, the focus of ASEAN's approach to the maintenance of regional peace and stability revolved around three basic tenets: keeping the region free from major power interference; cooperation on issues relating to insurgency within the domestic level of the individual member states; and fostering economic cooperation. The most significant of these was to keep the region free from external interference as the Cold War raged and the Vietnam war was at its height. While these three principles were the core objectives of ASEAN, scholars like Mely Cabellero-Anthony identify that the ASEAN was founded on a particular model of regional cooperation that promoted the commitment to what it called "intramural peace and stability," which was to adhere to convergences among the member states that would allow them to approach a common focus towards regional stability based on common areas of concern (Cabellero-Anthony 1998). In keeping with this broad framework, two factors were critical to the evolution of the ASEAN which were to accept the diversity within states as a given and therefore work around this diversity to address issues. This led to the mechanisms of consultation and consensus which became ASEAN's core approach to regionalism. So while accepting this diversity among member states, ASEAN's focus was on convergence and the maintenance of the normative approach. Even as ASEAN expanded to include other countries Southeast Asian countries from 1995 to 1999, the principles of "intramural peace and stability" was once again applied, addressing the gaps between the original members and the new members, which included Vietnam (1995), Myanmar and Laos (1997) and Cambodia (1999) (Acharya 1997). In the aftermath of the Cold War, the expansion of ASEAN processes to include the wider Asia-Pacific region and countries such as India, as sectoral dialogue partners was a shift in the regional mechanism that was extended outwards. Over a period of time, ASEAN mechanisms extended to cover countries such as China, Japan, South Korea, India, Australia and New Zealand.

The core foundations of ASEAN's role as a regional grouping were based on a normative role which has been enshrined in the various concepts that it outlined as its principles for the maintenance of regional order. With regard to the original ASEAN members, this role was based on the view that the member states had emerged from their colonial legacies and the need for internal consolidation was a given, leading to the non-interference in the domestic affairs clause. This remained, and continues to remain, a critical issue as far as ASEAN is concerned. At the regional level, ASEAN spearheaded several initiatives such as the Zone of Peace, Freedom and Neutrality (ZOPFAN); Southeast Asia Nuclear Weapons Free Zone (SEANWFZ); and the Treaty of Amity and Cooperation (TAC). The establishment of these key aims was critical to the evolution and sustenance of maintaining a regional order that was free from external intervention and would sustain the normative principles as enshrined in the United Nations charter, which is the basis on which the TAC evolved. The importance of this revolved around the fact that the ASEAN sought to move beyond the issues of territorial conflicts and interstate rivalries which had been based on historical claims that existed even prior to the colonial period. As colonialism gave way to the independent states in the region, the revival of age-old tensions and rivalries initially impacted the formation of a regional grouping, but eventual willingness to set aside such claims and counter-claims led to the formation of the ASEAN. Moreover, by adopting the twin pillars of consultation and consensus, ASEAN was able to form a mechanism that sought to foster confidence building within the region of Southeast Asia and also expanded this to the Asia-Pacific in the aftermath of the Cold War. Those who were critical of the process stated that the limits of ASEAN were its relevance to just the processes of confidence building and that it could not achieve more due to the inability to move to areas of preventive diplomacy and conflict resolution. However, as a regional grouping that emerged and guided the regional processes, several saw it more as a "process" oriented mechanism and not one that is "product" oriented. In the aftermath of the Cold War the extension of the ASEAN processes led to the evolution of key mechanisms for the region such as the ASEAN Regional Forum (ARF); the East Asia Summit (EAS); the Shangri La Dialogue (ADMM+); ASEAN Expanded Maritime Forum (AEMF) which reflected the key shift of the ASEAN focus from a primarily Southeast Asian grouping to one that encompassed the entire Asia-Pacific. ASEAN's relevance was critiqued by both Realist and Constructivist scholars alike: while the realist approach predominantly focused on the question of regional stability and regional order, it vested the importance of those concepts on the basis of a balance of power approach. Constructivists, however, looked at the role of ASEAN as a norms builder, a grouping that exchanged ideational factors, developed a form of socialisation by which several diverse regional actors were able to foster an ASEAN way of interstate behaviour.[2] As a result of its ability to expand during the post-Cold War period, ASEAN was seen as being pivotal to the regional architecture, especially in terms of managing the great powers and creating a normative approach to the region, so much so that former ASEAN Secretary-General Surin Pitsuwan described the ASEAN as the heart of Asia-Pacific multilateralism (Pitsuwan 2011).

This role, however, lasted for about two decades. As the rise of China began to shape the regional and global order, the shifting capacity of the ASEAN to manage regional stresses began to be very evidently weak, especially within the grouping itself as member states began to take divergent views on the rise of China. The pulls and pressures within the ASEAN began to impact its cohesion, and nowhere was this more evident than in the context of the South China Sea dispute. In July 2012, the ASEAN was chaired by Cambodia, and during its ministerial summit, the members could not even agree on a Joint Communiqué which was the first such time in its 45-year history. Even as a coherent view on the South China Sea issue could not be addressed, it raised several debates about the ability of the ASEAN to maintain its unity and centrality in a fast-evolving region. This was further reinforced when the Philippines took its maritime dispute with China to the Permanent Court of Arbitration (PCA), the ruling of which came in June 2016. In the aftermath of the ruling, China categorically rejected the ruling stating that it did not agree to conform to the decision and that the regional states of the ASEAN would not use this ruling as leverage to address the South China Sea dispute. Both the 2012 incident and the inability to address a joint resolution on the 2016 ruling were clearly indicative of the divisions within ASEAN, bringing the question of unity and cohesion within ASEAN, or the lack thereof, to the forefront. The ability of ASEAN to manage regional tensions has repeatedly come under question, and as the Indo-Pacific concept has increasingly taken clear shape the ability of ASEAN to maintain regional stability in the face of increasing major power rivalry has come under constant scrutiny. The following section will look at the impact that major power rivalry has had on the erstwhile Asia-Pacific region. It will also identify the core drivers of the Indo-Pacific framework, particularly in terms of how major power rivalry is pushing regional states into a process of multi-alignments with states which share convergence of security interests, even as overlapping economic issues may at times be common or at variance with one another. Newer mechanisms and dialogue platforms have also emerged as a result of the nature of transition that the region is witnessing, leading to a mosaic of bilateral, bilateral 2+2 dialogues, trilateral and mini-lateral dialogues. These mechanisms are clearly the result of the incredible shift the region has witnessed while the larger mechanisms led by the ASEAN continue to remain in place.

US–China rivalry and impact on norms and multilateralism

For nearly a decade, the United States has been revamping its approach to the Asia-Pacific, which has seen tremendous transitions as a result of the rise of China. Prior to the ASEAN summit of 2012 mentioned above, the US unveiled its "Pivot to Asia" Policy which was part of the US rebalancing in the region after a period of what has been debated as US absence from the region. While this absence remains notional, it basically highlighted the inclusion of the United States in the EAS which had begun to assume importance among the various ASEAN-led mechanisms as a driver of the Indo-Pacific region. While the United States had never been absent from its security commitments to East Asia or the Pacific regions, particularly countries such as Japan, South Korea, Australia and New Zealand (through the Australia, New Zealand, United States treaty), its exit from the Philippines and its late entry into the EAS were seen as absence from Southeast Asia and the ASEAN-led mechanisms. The US rebalance was clearly articulated when Secretary of State Hillary Clinton stated at the ARF meeting in Hanoi in 2010 that the United was back in the region (Clinton 2011). The subsequent strengthening of the US ASEAN relations through the US signing of the TAC and joining the EAS brought the focus back on the region with the growing rift that began to emerge in the Sino-US rivalry. A close reading of some of the lectures delivered by Secretary of State Hillary Clinton highlights the clear shift to concerns over the maritime domain, in particular the assertions of Chinese claims in the East Sea and the South China Sea. The reference made in these lectures to the maritime commons and the need for a more formal and binding Code of Conduct were clear indicators of the US shift towards the maintenance and preservation of the normative order. Similarly, there was also increasing reference to the need for a more coordinated naval diplomacy for the region as the maritime zones around these areas were becoming contested due to the claims of China. During the Obama administration this shift was clear, especially reiterated in the Nation Security Strategy papers for the years 2010 and 2015, which reaffirmed the focus on the maritime commons. The papers also revealed the role of US leadership in promoting maritime security cooperation and building a more robust security architecture in the Indo-Pacific, while emphasising the importance of international norms and law for a rules-based approach to the Indo-Pacific(US National Security Strategy 2010) With the shift to the Trump administration, there emerged a bipartisan policy towards both China and the Indo-Pacific which has also been evident under the recent transition to the Biden administration. Under the Trump administration, the 2017 National Security Strategy paper was even more emphatic in its shift to the Indo-Pacific and the ensuing rivalry with China. The paper actually re-invoked the Cold War mentality by referring to the outbreak of a "new Cold War" and clearly articulated that both China and Russia were seen as rival powers that were "competitors to American influence and interests" (US National Security Strategy 2017). In June 2019, the Indo-Pacific Strategy Report from the US Department of Defence categorically stated that Chinese revisionist power transition was a critical factor that led to the current rivalry between the US and China (The Department of Defence 2019). The report stated that the People's Republic of China (PRC) under the leadership of the Chinese Communist Party (CCP) was undermining the international system. It identified that being within the international system had benefitted the PRC, which had exploited the advantage it got as part of the system, but it had eroded the values and principles of the rules-based order (The Department of Defence 2019: 7). Under the Trump administration, the focus given to ASEAN was less and did significant damage to the ASEAN-led mechanisms in the region especially as President Trump preferred to focus on individual countries of the ASEAN such as Thailand and the Philippines which were considered as allies. This division of ASEAN into various categories that suited US interests undermined the cohesion of ASEAN even further (The Department of Defence 2019: 39-42). This division of the ASEAN grouping into various states was also based on their individual responses to the United States' freely accessible Indo-Pacific Strategy; while it has undermined the oft-quoted principle of ASEAN centrality, the concept also evolves from the United States' perceptions of the changing realities of the regional situation and recognising the close economic ties that several individual countries of the ASEAN share with China. Several voices from within the ASEAN region have addressed the Trump administration's policy paper as being tantamount to the same practise that China applies in dividing the ASEAN. While this division allows the United States to leverage its own role in the region by choosing the regional states with which it seeks to align its regional role, it does not contribute to the ASEAN-led mechanisms as being central to the regional multilateral processes. In the immediate aftermath of the Biden administration coming into office, the focus on ASEAN was limited even as the emphasis on continuing the policy towards China remained in place. This clearly hinted at the bipartisan consensus within the United States on its approach to China and how this was to evolve in the context of the Indo-Pacific's evolution as a strategic concept. The Biden administration however showed a single point of departure in that it continued to endorse the relevance of multilateralism. While Trump had decidedly focused on an America-first approach, in several areas of international cooperation, the Biden administration clearly re-emphasised the return to multilateralism, particularly on the two core areas of climate change and public health in the aftermath of the pandemic. This has been identified as a clear contradiction in how the Biden administration will handle the fault-line that emerges from its reaffirmation of multilateralism to the hard-line posture it has taken on China which continues to reflect the continuity in the US foreign policy under Trump and Biden.

The impact of the Sino-US rivalry is best visible in the region of Southeast Asia. China's relations with the region have dramatically shifted since the end of the Cold War, increasing the degree of economic integration very deeply while growing security dynamics are emerging. Nowhere is this dilemma more visible than in the context of the South China Sea dispute which has six claimant states, of which four are members of the ASEAN. Over a period of 30 years, China's position *vis-a-vis* ASEAN claimants has taken a volte-face. While in the early nineties Chinese officials referred to the possibility of joint explorations in the South China Sea, by 2002 the move towards a Declaration on a Code of Conduct (DOC) was visible, even as the China ASEAN Free Trade Agreement (CAFTA) came into existence. The move towards a more binding Code of Conduct (COC) was to be evolved within a decade of the DOC, which remains inconclusive as Chinese assertions in the region have increased implicating the regional claimants and pushing the boundaries of normative conduct. The 2012 ASEAN summit's collapse further implicated the shifts within individual member countries, such as Cambodia and its ties with China, which were used as leverage to split the ASEAN further. As Chair of ASEAN for that year Cambodia did not allow any discussions on the South China Sea dispute, bringing the debates on cohesion to the forefront (Hunt 2012).

Probably the single best indicator of Chinese assertion was the response that China gave to the ruling of the PCA, which gave its verdict on the Philippines-China dispute over the claims to the South China Sea, particularly the Scarborough shoal. The ruling clearly indicated that China had violated the rights of the Philippines under the United Nations Convention on the Law of the Seas (UNCLOS), to which the Chinese response was that the PCA ruling was not binding and it refused to back down from its claims over the South China Sea (Glaser 2016). The ruling also refuted China's claims to the nine-dash line on the basis of history, but China continued to violate the principles enshrined through the UNCLOS on grounds that the ruling was "null and void" (Glaser 2016). It is important to recognise that even ASEAN, as a regional grouping trying to address the South China Sea dispute within the ASEAN framework failed to endorse the matter in favour of the Philippines. This was because the judgement is non-binding and as a result remains a matter of moral pressure upon China.

One of the challenges for many of the smaller states across the Indo-Pacific region has been China's offer of assistance for infrastructural development which spans the entire Indo-Pacific region as well as increasingly in Africa too. These cash-starved states in need of developing key infrastructure are often drawn to receive assistance from China which comes without many conditions attached to it. However, two challenges emerge from this form of infrastructure development: first, many states are caught in a debt trap as a result of these infrastructure needs; second, when they are unable to return the Chinese loans, the major stake in these infrastructure projects are owned by China which also has the potential for dual use that implicates both economic use and military use. This has a profound impact on the geopolitics that emerges in the wider region as it credibly reduces the strategic autonomy that individual states have *vis-a-vis* China. As a result of this multi-alignment has become increasingly evident as states are in a constant state of hedging against the major powers while trying to evolve foreign policy practises that preserve their sovereignty and also allow them to find convergence on key issues that support the existing normative order.

Evolving dynamics of multi-alignment

As the US-China rivalry has evolved further, there is increasing pressure on ASEAN cohesion which has been visibly under stress for several years now. Other mechanisms have emerged, including the Quadrilateral Security Dialogue or the QUAD, and more recently the Australia, United Kingdom, United States (AUKUS) treaty. The QUAD emerged as early as 2007 on the sidelines of the ASEAN summit when four countries – United States, Australia, Japan and India had informal talks on the ability to foster cooperation on areas of mutual concern. This actually emerged from their responses to the 2004 Indian Ocean tsunami in which the agencies of these four countries acted as the first respondents to the humanitarian crisis unleashed by the tsunami. The initial approach to the QUAD 1.0 was summarily dismissed when China raised objections to the formation of the QUAD and countries like Australia at that time pulled out in deference to the enhanced economic ties that Australia had with China. As a critical indicator of bilateral relations with China, the initial avatar of the QUAD did not find much acceptance. The 2017 re-emergence of the QUAD was more different and more protracted in its approach to identifying China as the main focus. While this was implicit in the formation of the QUAD 2.0, the reference to China was not made explicitly and it remained central to the evolution of the QUAD 2.0. Increasingly the QUAD has seen more robust participation from countries like India and Australia. Specifically for Australia and India, increasing bilateral tensions with China have been evident. With India, border tensions have been taking place since the 2017 Doklam stand-off and the subsequent conflicts over Ladakh and more recently in Arunachal Pradesh. The continued violation of the Sino-Indian border by the Chinese into Indian territory and China's unwillingness to resolve the border dispute through negotiations have been irritants in the bilateral ties between the two. This has led India's foreign policy, which over the past decade has followed a multi-alignment approach, to become even more focused on furthering its strategic autonomy with regard to other countries with which it shares convergence of interests. Similarly for Australia, the close economic relations with China were increasingly tested in the last nearly two years, after the outbreak of the Covid-19 pandemic. The deteriorating bilateral relations between the two countries and China's increasingly used punitive economic measures against Australia reinforced the dynamics of the QUAD leading to a more open and clear posturing from Australia that its core alliance with the United States would continue to take precedence over that with China. Japan, the other member of the QUAD already has a significant bilateral relations security arrangement with the United States. One of the profound changes in the case of Japan is the emerging dynamics of its shift to being a "normal" state wherein it seeks to change Article 9 of its constitution which commits Japan to remain a Pacific state.

As this shift gradually evolves the impact and focus on the QUAD will become even more pronounced. For now, the QUAD focus continues to remain on the matters that are in the domain of non-traditional security challenges and with the aim of preserving a normative order in the Indo-Pacific. Post-Covid-19 QUAD initiatives have also increasingly focused on issues of vaccine diplomacy and assistance to the smaller island states in the Indo-Pacific. More recently the QUAD has also begun to look at areas of convergence and cooperation in outer space which is increasingly viewed as part of the global commons. As a result of the pandemic, from around April 2020, the QUAD countries also engaged in consultative mechanisms with South Korea, Vietnam and New Zealand which led to the view that the QUAD could expand to the QUAD plus. However, this remains somewhat premature as the QUAD itself remains nascent and needs further institutionalisation before it can be expanded. It remains critical that the QUAD engagement is deepened, rather than a move towards broadening the dynamics of the QUAD. However, given the view that the QUAD is not compatible with the regional mechanisms led by the ASEAN needs to be viewed more carefully. The ASEAN Outlook on the Indo-Pacific (AOIP) which was evolved in June 2019 had three main areas of concern: first, it emphasised the need for "dialogue instead of rivalry"; second, it reiterated the need for "development and prosperity for all" and third it gave critical focus to the maritime domain and the importance of the regional security architecture (ASEAN 2019). However, it critically fell short in two aspects – first, it did not look at the region of the Indo-Pacific as a contiguous region but preferred to refer to it as the Asia-Pacific and the Indian Ocean region, two distinct but integrated regions (Sundararaman 2021). This is a critical flaw in the AOIP as it fails to clearly identify the dynamics evolving across the Indo-Pacific. Moreover, the AOIP does not acknowledge the emergence of multiple trilateral and mini-lateral mechanisms that are fostered on areas of convergence but continues to reiterate the reliance on the ASEAN led mechanisms.

Similarly, the recent move towards the formation of the AUKUS grouping is a clear shift in how the Indo-Pacific is being viewed by the western allies that form the AUKUS. Over the last few years, several European states, as well as the EU itself, have come up with their own foreign policy approach to the Indo-Pacific. This shift has basically been to address the reiteration of the existing normative order which has consistently come under challenge by the unilateral actions of China, especially within the maritime order. Moreover, as China has unveiled its Belt and Road Initiative (BRI) the geo-economic challenges and the geopolitical challenges have actually dovetailed into one another with implications for several countries. There is an increasing view that while the BRI is predominantly identified as a critical part of China's foreign economic relations, it nevertheless brings with it very significant geopolitical challenges as well. For the ASEAN region, the immediate neighbour remains critical as these ten countries are closely integrated with China economically. It is important to recognise that increasingly the ASEAN seems to be pulled in different directions as it is caught within a region that is impacted by great power rivalry. On the question of the AUKUS, the ASEAN response has been very diverse and varied. While ASEAN as a grouping had refrained from any reference to the AUKUS, individual countries have responded. Countries like Malaysia and Indonesia have been a bit concerned that the AUKUS deal will lead to an increased arms race for the region. Countries like Singapore and the Philippines have actually welcomed the AUKUS and clearly enunciated that is a means through which Australia can seek to achieve its strategic autonomy in a region where its relations with China have severely deteriorated over the past few years. At the most recent EAS meeting, the ASEAN upgraded its ties with Australia to the level of a Comprehensive Strategic Partnership (CSP) belying the view that ASEAN relations with Australia will dip following the AUKUS deal.

ASEAN has continued to evolve its relations with other regional actors too. In the recently concluded ASEAN plus one (China) meeting in November 2021, the ASEAN and China elevated their ties to the level of a CSP. This interestingly comes at a time when both Australia and China are seeing the lowest point in their individual bilateral ties. The Joint Statement on upgrading the ties to the level of a CSP is a reaffirmation of the evolving ties between China and ASEAN (Joint Statement ASEAN-China 2021). On the Indo-Pacific, this Joint Statement falls short of making any reference to the shift in the regional dynamics but vaguely assesses the ASEAN Outlook for the Indo-Pacific as an "independent initiative" of the ASEAN. The statement, however, addresses the question of resolution of the South China Sea dispute on the tenets of the UNCLOS. While the Joint Statement was issued on 22 November 2021, just six days prior to that Chinese were interfering in the Exclusive Economic Zone (EEZ) of the Philippines in the Ayungin Shoal and preventing Philippines ships from delivering supplies to the region. The Ayungin Shoal has been an area of contested claims between the Philippines and China for years, but even as the run-up to the dialogue anniversary with ASEAN is underway, the incursions in the EEZ leave little space for trust between the two. This makes the Joint Statement with China seem like a farce, particularly in light of repeated Chinese aggression in these waters (Strangio 2021).

Similarly, ASEAN-India relations too have been under strain since India's exit from the Regional Comprehensive Economic Partnership (RCEP). There are several areas of broad convergence between India and ASEAN, including robust naval diplomacy as a core part of the ties with ASEAN. India's engagement with individual ASEAN countries has however been on the rise, particularly with both Indonesia and Vietnam. There are areas of convergence between India's Act East-Link West policy and Indonesia's "dua samudera" (two oceans) policy and the global maritime fulcrum; however, very little movement in terms of implementation has been visible on both sides (Sundararaman 2018). India, however, has increased the pace of its integration in areas of common interest with several of the regional countries. With both Japan and Australia, India's relations have expanded including a core two-plus-two dialogue formulation that is significantly helping to broaden the bilateral ties. India has also evolved the Indo-Pacific Oceans Initiative (IPOI) which critically focuses on the key areas of maritime security, the sustainable use of maritime resources and disaster prevention and management. This finds some resonance with the AOIP too, increasing further areas on which India and ASEAN can cooperate.

Throughout the Covid 19 pandemic, the issues surrounding the security of the South China Sea have been crucial to the region. Even though China has provided maximum assistance to the ASEAN region, there have been repeated violations of the EEZ of several member states of ASEAN by China, and the conflict has only intensified. In June 2020, the ASEAN summit for the first time issued a Joint Statement that the South China Sea conflict must be resolved on the basis of UNCLOS (Gomes 2021). ASEAN's ability to assert this position remains key to the resolution of the South China Sea dispute which will remain a litmus test in the evolving dynamics between ASEAN and China, even as regional shifts will continue to be visible.

Conclusion

The Indo-Pacific clearly represents the shifting power equations and structural shifts in the regional and global order. While the Indo-Pacific in a geographic sense represents a mega-region, geopolitically it also needs to be seen as a vision, one that represents a rules-based normative way of understanding the world, as different from the reassertions of historical claims and how the world was prior to the colonial period. Therefore, the Indo-Pacific needs to be seen as both a vision of the global order and the shifts that are transforming it as well as a mega-region where the economic emergence of the region is bringing about profound political and security changes as well. Even as the region goes through various transitions the core focus on the normative order will remain critical as states vie and contend for a greater role. The distinctive shift that the Indo-Pacific brings in is a strategic one where the compulsions of geopolitics are driving the manner in which states arrange their responses both individually and collectively. This becomes even more critical as the structural shifts are also challenging the existing norms of interstate behaviour. The question of norms is critical as it defines the core processes through which states interact and strengthening these have been the focus of multilateralism. Interestingly as the "regional" dynamics of the Indo-Pacific evolve there will be multiple forms of interaction at the bilateral, mini-lateral and multilateral levels which will all contribute to creating a web of security arrangements. Even as the Asia-Pacific endorsed a web of such arrangements at the economic level, the Indo-Pacific will strengthen such a web of arrangements at the security level – integrating both the economic and security aspects into a more complex regional architecture.

Notes

1 For a detailed reading of the maritime trade in the region see Anthony Reid, *A History of Southeast Asia: Critical Crossroads* (United Kingdon: Wiley Blackwell, 2015).
2 A. Acharya, Ideas, Identity and Institution Building: From the ASEAN way to the Asia-Pacific Way, *The Pacific Review*, vol. 10, no. 3, 1997, p. 320.

References

Abe, S. 2007. Speech by Prime Minister of Japan Shinzo Abe at the Indian Parliament on 22 August 2007. http://www.mofa.go.jp/region/asia-paci/pmv0708/speech-2.html.

Acharya, Amitav. 1997. Ideas, Identity and Institution Building: From the ASEAN way to the Asia-Pacific Way. *The Pacific Review*, vol. 10, no. 3, 319–346.

ASEAN Secretariat. 2019. ASEAN Outlook for the Indo-Pacific. https://asean.org/storage/2019/06/ASEAN-Outlook-on-the-Indo-Pacific_FINAL_22062019.pdf

Bose, Sugata. 2006. *A Hundred Horizons: The Indian Ocean in the Age of Global Empire.* Cambridge: Harvard University Press.

Bowring, Philip. 2019. *Empire of the Winds: The Global Role of Asia's Great Archipelago*, Bloomberg and New York: I.B. Taurus.

Cabellero-Anthony, Mely. 1998. Mechanisms of Dispute Settlement: The ASEAN Experience. *Contemporary Southeast Asia*, vol. 20, no. 1, 38–66.

Clinton, Hillary. 2011. *Foreign Policy*, Washington Nr 189, pp. 56–63.

Frecon, Eric and Meijer, Hugo. 2015. The US Rebalance in Southeast Asia: Maritime Security, Non-Traditional Security Threats and "Bamboo Diplomacy". In Hugo Meijer (ed.), *Origins and Evolution of the US Rebalance in Asia, the Sciences Po Series in International Relations and Political Economy*. New York: Palgrave Macmillan, 171–196.

Glaser, Bonnie, S. 2016. Shaping China's response to the PCA Ruling. *The Interpreter*, 18 July 2016, The Lowy Institute, Sydney. https://www.lowyinstitute.org/the-interpreter/shaping-china-s-response-pca-ruling.

Gurpreet, S. Khurana 2007. Security of Sea Lines: Prospects for India–Japan Cooperation, *Strategic Analysis*, 31:1, 139–153

Heiduk, Felix and Wacker, Gudrun. 2020. From Asia Pacific to Indo-Pacific: Significance, Implementation and Challenges. SWP Research Paper 2020/RP09, Stiftung Wissenschaft und Politik German Institute for International and Security Affairs. https://www.swp-berlin.org/en/publication/from-asia-pacific-to-indo-pacific.

Huisken, Ron. 2009. The US Role in the Future Security Architecture for East Asia. In Ron Huisken (ed.), *The Architecture of Security in the Asia-Pacific*. Australian National University E Press, Canberra, 67–84.

Huisken, Ron (ed.). 2021. *CSCAP Regional Security Outlook 2022*. Canberra: Council for Security Cooperation in the Asia-Pacific.

Hunt, Luke. 2012. ASEAN Summit Fallout Continues. *The Diplomat*, 20 July 2012. https://thediplomat.com/2012/07/asean-summit-fallout-continues-on/.

Kaplan, Robert, D. 2010. *Monsoon: The Indian Ocean and the Future of American Power*. New York: Random House.

Khurana, Gurpreet S. 2007. Security of Sea Lines: Prospects for India–Japan Cooperation. *Strategic Analysis*, vol. 31, no. 1, pp. 139–153.

Khurana, Gurpreet S. 2019. What is the Indo-Pacific? The New Geopolitics of the Asia-Centred Rim Land. What is the Indo-Pacific? The New Geopolitics Of the Asia-Centred Rim Land, 13–32.

Medcalf, R. 2020. Balancing Act: Making Sense of the Quad. *Australian Foreign Affairs*, (10), 30–48.

Pitsuwan, Surin. 2011. The ASEAN Heart of Asia. *The Jakarta Post*, 15 June 2011. http://www.thejakartapost.com/news/2011/06/15/the-asean-heart-asia.html.

Sardesai, D. R. 1997. *Southeast Asia: Past and Present*. Boulder, CO: Westview Press.

Sastri, Nilakanta K.A. 1935. *The Cholas*. Madras: The University of Madras.

Sastri, Nilakanta K. A. 2018. *Writings in the Hindu*, The Hindu History Series.

Strangio, Sebastian. 2021. Chinese Navy Harasses Boat Carrying Filipino Journalists: Report. *The Diplomat*, 9 April 2021. https://thediplomat.com/2021/04/chinese-navy-harasses-boat-carrying-filipino-journalists-report/.

Sundararaman, Shankari. 2018. India-ASEAN Relations: 'Acting' East in the Indo-Pacific. *International Studies*, vol. 54, no. 1–4, 67–78.

Sundararaman, Shankari. 2018. Understanding the Indo-Pacific: Why Indonesia Will Be Critical? In Satish Chandra and Baladas Ghoshal (eds.), *The Indo-Pacific Axis: Peace and Prosperity or Conflict*. Routledge, Abingdon, Oxon, p.

Sundararaman, Shankari. 2021. ASEAN, QUAD and AUKUS: Reinventing Centrality in a Multi-Layered Indo-Pacific. Kalinga International Foundation. https://kalingainternational.com/Shankari-Sundararaman13.html.

The Department of Defence. 2019. Indo-Pacific Strategic Report: Preparedness, Partnerships and Promoting a Networked Region. June 1 2019. https://media.defense.gov/2019/jul/01/2002152311/-1/-1/1/department-of-defense-indo-pacific-strategy-report-2019.pdf.

United States National Security Strategy. 2010. Office of the President of the United States of America. *The White House*. https://obamawhitehouse.archives.gov/sites/default/files/rss_viewer/national_security_strategy.pdf.

United States National Security Strategy. 2017. Office of the President of the United States of America. *The White House*. https://www.whitehouse.gov/wp-content/uploads/2017/12/NSS-Final-12-18-2017-0905.pdf.

Wilson, J. D. 2018. Rescaling to the Indo-Pacific: From Economic to Security Driven Regionalism in Asia. *East Asia*, vol. 35, no. 2, pp. 177–196. http://doi.org/10.1007/s12140-018-9285-6.

Yates, Robert. 2019. Understanding ASEAN's Role in the Asia-Pacific Order, Palgrave Macmillan Critical Studies of the Asia-Pacific, New York.

2 Understanding the Indo-Pacific

Geopolitical context

Stefano Pelaggi and Lorenzo Termine

As growing tension between the United States and China agitates Asia, a new analytical framework has gained attention in the study of regional geopolitics: the Indo-Pacific (IP). As formulated thus far, the IP appears a challenging concept for understanding politics and security in Asia for at least three reasons. Firstly, from a geographical standpoint, it is rather ambiguous as it encloses an exceedingly wide region and a still vague number of countries. Combining two geographical regions – the Indian Ocean region and the Pacific Ocean region – the concept has been targeted by harsh criticism of being shallow and pointless for the study of regional politics. Secondly, it includes countries that might not have a historical pattern of amity or enmity such as India and Japan. Since the risk of being dragged into a war with your neighbours is both in geopolitics and in international relations theory the most urgent danger for states' national security and thus the primary shaping factor for their foreign policies, two distant and mutually non-threatening countries are not likely to influence each other's international behaviour. Lastly, it is today a politically-loaded concept reflecting multiple actors' endeavours to frame two security environments together for specific strategic purposes. The IP is the product of an increasingly multipolar regional system where the rise of China appears as the major engine of competition and the main push factor behind regional states' alignment or distancing. Facing such a monumental ascent, different US administrations have advanced the IP as a new security framework serving American interests in Asia. The previous administration led by Donald Trump (2017–2021) has infused new lifeblood to the concept and pioneered a "free and open Indo-Pacific" strategy which pivots on strategic partners such as Japan, Australia and India. The Biden Administration has echoed the same considerations stating that the "ensuring" of "peace and stability in the Indo-Pacific over the long term" (Biden 2021) is crucial to the United States' national security.

Different names, same region? The scholarly birth of the Indo-Pacific

The Indo-Pacific region is still a misconceived geopolitical notion, as it has suffered from several setbacks and misunderstandings. This section will clarify whether the IP is a long-standing concept in the literature on geopolitics or if it has informed the political debate only in more recent times. To address this issue, the section will proceed by first delving into the established works by classical geopoliticians Halford J. Mackinder, Alfred T. Mahan, Karl E. Haushofer and Nicholas J. Spykman.

Before digging into the topic, it must be noted that geopolitics has frequently been a politically-loaded discipline, earning the accusation of being a mere justification of

DOI: 10.4324/9781003336143-4

power politics, expansionism and even – the German and Italian schools of geopolitics – of Nazi-Fascism (See also Box 2.1). Moreover, it is extensively debated whether classical geopolitics can provide a useful lens for today's international politics given its strong Western – European and North America – origin and bias (See also Box 2.2).

The first geopolitical analysis relating to the IP was presented by Halford J. Mackinder who talked of Eurasia as a "continuous land, ice-girt in the north, water-girt elsewhere" spanning between proper Europe and proper Asia. "To east, south, and west of this Heartland" are "marginal regions" which are "accessible to shipmen" (Mackinder 1904: 431). Hence, Mackinder blended India and China together as off-shoots of a single continental mass or what he calls "inner (or marginal) crescents" (Mackinder 1904: 435). However, more ambiguously, he explicitly separated the two as land regions, even though they share common climate features such as monsoons, belonging to different civilisations: the former Brahmanist, the latter Buddhist. In contrast, whatever lies beyond the crescents and the seas, such as Japan, Australia, United States, forms the "outer (or insular) crescent." His concept of IP then entailed a single continental shoreline comprising India and China – even though it is not clear if they formed a single, united region to Mackinder – and an entirely separated area including the archipelagos, islets, and the wide sea and ocean regions around them. No proper IP is thus traceable in Mackinder's work and his reasoning is of no use for understanding the origins of the notion. However, he was the first to devise a certain geopolitical continuity in those littoral regions that he conceived as advantageous to the Western powers and deserves the credit of imagining a merge of two previously divided regions – those dominated by India and China.

The second perspective on the IP was advanced by Alfred T. Mahan, United States Navy captain, strategist and father of the modern geopolitics of the sea, who argued that mastery over the seas and the oceans, which he labelled "Sea Power," is the cornerstone of the rise and fall of powers in history. For the control of large masses of water, and thus of the lanes of commerce and communication transiting through them, nations fought wars, ascended, or perished. The most pressing factor in the distribution of resources is access to the sea and the capacity to trade outward. Looking at the historical commercial routes in his classic "The Influence of Sea Power Upon History," Mahan then spoke of the "East Indies" and "Far East" and thus seemingly distinguished the region of India and Southeast Asia from that of China and Japan (Mahan 1965). This is clearly because his is a historical account of Sea Power until 1783 and thus long before the forced opening of China (1842) and Japan (1854) to foreign trade. As a result, Mahan's masterpiece's sections on Asia are strongly focused on the activities of the East India Company and the Seven Years Wars (1756–1763) and thus narrowed to the Indian Ocean as a geostrategic environment per se and the Far East as a separate – not friendly and not even fully disclosed – entity. India as a colony and contested territory at the core of several actors' claims – France and Great Britain – was then the heart of Mahan's depiction of the Indo-Pacific region. Within "The Influence" – it is worth saying – this strong India-centred perspective is confirmed by the almost complete oversight of China and Japan as geopolitical – i.e. sea – actors. Mahan devotes only two mentions to the former and one to the latter while India is named at least 130 times. His Indo-Pacific region would be thus composed of an Indo region, a Far East region and a Pacific region. No trace of a single, geopolitical entity called IP is thus found in Mahan's "The Influence." However, quite interestingly, Mahan's later work "The Problem of Asia" points at a region spanning between the possessions of the two major powers – Great Britain and Russia – and thus from Siberia to India. Mahan explicitly contends that "it is no longer consistent with accuracy of forecast to draw a north and south line [in Asia] of severance," "to contemplate eastern Asia apart from western," "to dissociate, practically, the conditions and incidents in the one from those in the other" (Mahan 2003: 67). Asia is indeed composed of "living parts" among whom "the relations" – as well as the relationship "to the whole" – must, therefore "be considered." Mahan even warns that should "the vast mass of China [...] burst her barriers eastward [towards the Pacific]" the "momentous issues dependent upon a firm hold of the Sandwich Islands" would require "a great extension of [US] naval power" (Mahan 2003: 10). This is the understanding of Asia hitherto closest to the contemporary notion of IP since it entails a regional interstate system where interdependence and mutual influence – hence the risk of war ("incidents") – reign supreme. This is of utmost importance for understanding the roots of the contemporary notion of IP because of the timing of Mahan's argument in "The Problem of Asia" – right after Japan's expansion onto the continent at the expense of China (1895) and shortly before Russia's debacle against Japan (1905) – and with a strong policy-oriented ambition of reorienting US policy towards the region.

Geopolitics as a field of study thrived also in Europe and in particular in Germany where Karl Ernst Haushofer, professor at the University of Munich, was active and put forward a different understanding of Asia, one that is particularly interesting for analysing the roots of the IP. In the 1920s and 1930s, Haushofer was one of the leading theorists behind the study of States as a living organism and researched the entanglement between geography and politics also in that region he labelled as "Indopazifischen" [Indo-Pacific]. This "political living space" was a sea-driven organism because no interaction between the Indian subcontinent (Haushofer 2002: 3), East Asia and the Western Pacific could be possible on land as Tibet and Himalaya were too insurmountable a barrier for human crossing. The Indo-Pacific, on the contrary, was a natural geopolitical unity according to Haushofer because of the binding role of the sea. Furthermore, after having lived in Japan, he thought that the rise of such a powerful country was leading "the Far East opening out into the greater living space [Lebensraum], the Pan-Pacific[1]" (Haushofer 2002: 10) which he imagined led by the Japanese Empire. According to Haushofer, the melding of the two oceans – the Indian and the Pacific – provided the Asian country with the most powerful instrument of power, "the arsenal of a Pacific geopolitics" (Haushofer 2002: 35). Haushofer's IP is then strongly centred on Japan as a rising, expansionist, hegemony-seeking country that had the resources and the spirit to unite politically what the German thinker saw as geographically coherent space. Even though his analysis is not as articulated as Mahan's, Haushofer deserves the credit of putting forward the first explicit mention of IP in the literature on geopolitics.

Fourth among the fathers of modern geopolitics, Nicholas J. Spykman gave birth to the theory of the Rimland, conventionally opposed to Mackinder's Heartland. Acknowledging that geography is "the most fundamentally conditioning factor" for states' conduct (Spykman 1938a: 29), Spykman points at the "world-location" and the "regional location" as sorting factors among nations. States' localisation and size are the most pressing elements shaping their foreign policy and their perceptions of the strategic environment they operate in. For instance, Japan "lives in deadly fear of a future in which China and Russia" will develop "the power potentials inherent in their gigantic size" (Spykman 1938a: 32) as his insularity no longer provides "the almost perfect defence it once offered" (Spykman 1938b: 216). The greatest concern for Tokyo is a Russia pushing "southward in search of ice-free ports" towards "Manchuria and Korea," and a China undergoing "westernization [i.e. development] (Spykman 1938b: 216). East Asia is thus Spkyman's horizon when he writes about China's and Japan's foreign policies while a different "world of the Indian Ocean" extends between "the connecting links" of "the Straits of Malacca and the Suez Canal" (Spykman 1938a: 42). For instance, according to Spykman, China's projection outwards is severely bound both by land as "the Himalayan range blocks the direct way from China to India more effectively than any fortification that man could devise" (Spykman 1938b: 235) and by sea since Beijing is "entirely without a navy" even if it faces "one of the major Sea Powers of the world five hundred miles" away (Spykman 1938b: 222). In conclusion, there is no such single entity as IP in Spykman's analyses.

As analysed above, among the classical geopoliticians only Karl Haushofer explicitly mentioned the IP as a geopolitical unit. However, his notion of IP is deeply rooted in his appreciation of the Japanese ambitions of expansion and conquest. Conversely, Mahan's later works addressed the matter in a more comprehensive fashion and with a perspective that suggested that the historical boundaries of Asian geopolitics were about to vanish as Japan's rise unfolded, the United States gained Hawaii, Guam and the Philippines, global trade reached a peak, and if China was to develop fast in the coming decades.

Box 2.1 The invention of geopolitics: geopoliticians as advisors to the Prince

The origin of geopolitics must be traced to the socio-political context of late-19th century Germany, England and the United States. The new ideas on States' natural external projection put forward by scholars such as Rudolf Kjellén, Karl Haushofer, Alfred Mahan, Nicholas Spykman and Halford Mackinder often served as a conceptual justification of their State's power politics. Karl Ernst Haushofer (1869–1946) was a leading proponent of geopolitics and a tragic figure. After a long stay in Japan (1908–1910) as an Army officer, he retired disillusioned after Imperial Germany's defeat in WWI and dedicated his energies to teach on the Far East and design Germany's future role in world politics, becoming a principle contributor to Western Academic geopolitical thinking. Later, many of his ideas and theoretical adaptions found themselves written in the racist Nazi worldview. Rudolf Hess was his student and friend, and through him Haushofer actually met Adolf Hitler in 1924, who later applied several of his ideas (like *Lebesraum* – living space) in Mein Kampf. Still teaching, Haushofer, refusing to divorce his Jewish wife, had to tread carefully in the new Nazi state: His son was implicated in the 1944 assassination attempt on Hitler and executed by the regime in late 1945. After being accused of collaboration by the Allies, he and his wife committed suicide in 1946 (Herwig 2016; Encyclopaedia Britannica 2020). When it did not take the form of full-blown support for an expansionist, aggressive foreign policy like in the case of Haushofer, the relationship between geopolitics and political power was always unbalanced in favour of the latter. As a naval officer, Mahan's views were specifically intended to provide the United

States with the right theoretical framework for waging 20th century power politics and, as a result, exerted a great influence over the Assistant Secretary of the Navy – and later US President – Theodore Roosevelt. Karl Haushofer is the example *par excellence* of a geopolitician advising the ruling power as he mentored Hitler's designated successor Rudolf Hess. His ideas of a State's *Lebensraum* (living space) and a German-Japan axis against the Anglo-American hegemony made him the harbinger of the Nazi foreign policy vision. Albeit from a more independent standpoint, even Mackinder's and Spykman's arguments specifically addressed their national security communities and assumed national interests as baselines.

Given the strong political connotation of geopolitical discourse, critics have reasonably argued that geopolitics cannot be considered as an objective social science as it lacks the needed distance between the scholar and the examined subject. Its normative ambition made geopolitics earn the frequent accusation of being the intellectual apparatus for legitimising any sort of ruling power and decision.

Box 2.2 The West-centrism of geopolitics

Geopolitics is indeed a useful tool for examining international politics, but it must not be ignored that it suffers from heavy constraints due to its mostly Western-centric perspective. In fact, in 1987 authors had already noted that "Anglo-American political geography poses and pursues a limited and impoverished version of the discipline, largely ignoring the political concerns of four fifths of humankind" (Perry 1987: 6). From its very foundation, geopolitics was embedded in the European geographical matrix of competing, rivalling, adjacent states (Heffernan 2000). For instance, Karl Haushofer's "living space" (Lebensraum), largely shaped after the ideas of his inspirer Friedrich Ratzel, was strictly related to the German experience and fear of encirclement by France, Russia and Great Britain and thus represented the mere "Spatialization of [Germany's] Imperialist Desire" (Ó Tuathail 1996: 35). Similar imperatives gave form also to Mahan's, Mackinder's and Spykman's arguments. This urgency imprinted geopolitics with a strong Western-only bias since the peculiar pattern of international confrontation that had occurred in Europe did not have similarities in other continents or areas. Moreover, the high degree of geopolitics' Westness is also reflected in the usage of concepts and notions such as hegemony, empire, balance of power, integration and assimilation which do not have equals in non-Western political lexicons. For example, in Asia historical Chinese hegemony followed a distinctive and completely different path from e.g., British hegemony during the XIX century or US global hegemony after the end of the Cold War (Zhang 2015).

In reaction to the political (see Box 2.1), Western-centred conception of geopolitics, in the 1980s and 1990s a new debate on the correlation between politics and geography took shape and led to the development of so-called Critical Geopolitics.

According to this strand of literature, geography cannot be considered as a given factor but instead needs to be read as a socially shaped construct. Territory, then, is a causal variable of politics but not in a direct, deterministic manner as intervening elements such as culture, ideology, mindsets and values divert the causal relationship. With specific regards to China, a number of scholars have tried to de-Westernise geopolitics and distillate a more Chinese perspective on the influence of geography on human political actions. For example, a hybrid Confucian view on geopolitics has been advanced as an interesting starting point for eschewing Western preconceptions and biases (An et al. 2020).

The Indo-Pacific century? The rise of China and its implications for regional geopolitics

After 40 years of intensive growth since the start of the "reform and opening" process, the People's Republic of China (PRC) has now been recognised as a great power (Medcalf 2020). From a military point of view, if in 2000 Beijing's was 3.14% of the world defence spending, in 2010 this number had grown to 7.10% and in 2018 to 14.03% (SIPRI 2020). Similarly, at the dawn of the 21st century, China possessed 3.6% of global GDP while in 2019 it totalled 16.3%. At the same time, Beijing's share of global exports increased from 3.2% to 10.6% (World Bank 2020). Beijing is also a central diplomatic actor as it enjoys the official recognition of 179 out of the 193 member-countries of the United Nations and actively participates in all the main international organisations and fora, while only a handful of countries have chosen to recognise Taiwan's Republic of China and renounced relations with the PRC. In a massive effort of cultural diplomacy, the number of Confucius Institutes worldwide reached 541 in 2020 and they offer thousands of Chinese language and culture courses to hundreds of millions of people around the world.

From a regional point of view, the Chinese rise appears even more monumental. If in 2000, the Chinese economy made up 24% of that of neighbouring Japan and was seven times larger than that of Indonesia, in 2019 the gap reached 182 % with Tokyo while Beijing's GDP is almost 13 times bigger than Jakarta's. As a result, the relative weight of Chinese output in the East Asia and Pacific region went from 14.6% in 2000 to 53% in 2019 (World Bank 2020)[2]. Similarly, if in 2000, Chinese military spending was 20.3 times greater than Indonesia's and 12.2 times that of Thailand's, in 2018 this ratio increased to 33.6 times in the former case and 36.6 times in the latter (SIPRI 2020).

From a geopolitical standpoint, such a tremendous shift in the global and regional distribution of resources has produced crucial consequences.

Firstly, China's rise has fundamentally altered the balance of power in Asia and has alarmed several neighbouring countries which have started siding with each other to signal cohesion and resolve to Beijing. As a matter of fact, China's ascent is the main driver behind the formulation of the IP, as it is the common push factor behind alignment or dealignment in Asia. There is little doubt that the United States has arranged much of the regional effort to contain – or at least to shape – China's rise. In 2012, for example, Filipino naval forces approached eight Chinese fishing boats operating near the Manila-administered Scarborough Shoal in the South China Sea. Chinese law enforcement ships stood by to protect the fishermen and prompted a Filipino warship to intervene. At the end of this stand-off, which was resolved also by US mediation, Beijing refused to comply with the terms negotiated and retained the Shoal which passed under China's *de facto* control, exerted from then on with constant patrolling activity. Later that year, the Japanese government's purchase of three of the Senkaku islands, hitherto in the hands of Japanese citizens, sparked protests from the PRC which has since increased the number of ships in transit in disputed waters. In response, then US Secretary of Defense Leon Panetta felt obliged to reiterate directly to Xi Jinping the US commitment to the defence of Japan, confirmed also by Barack Obama in April 2014 and in the joint Donald Trump-Abe Shinzo press conference in February 2017. In 2017, China and India clashed over control of the Doklam bowl in the most serious military confrontation between the two countries on the border since 1986. India perceived the Chinese effort of enhancing a border road as a way to gain a fait accompli and extend its presence straight into New Delhi's territory. In 2020, a new dangerous military stand-off took place between China and India in Ladakh.

Secondly, the economy is still playing a key role in keeping countries tied together. As one of the most important financial and trading regions of the world, in fact, the IP experiences patterns of interdependence which often have the final word on amity or enmity. Beijing's massive economic build-up has wired the whole region to China and vice versa. Several Asian countries are now deeply embedded in regional and global value chains passing through or stemming from China and are financially tied to the PRC that has often played the role of "lender of last resort." For instance, China's deep economic and commercial penetration into the Philippines is today a strong driver for cooperation – or at least not belligerence – between the two countries. China's economic ascent has massively contributed to a bloated increase in regional trade and sea shipping, multiplying Beijing's over-reliance on sea routes it cannot directly control. For this reason, Beijing is very cautious in challenging the countries around its continental mass and along the sea lanes of communication and the shipping routes that supply China with oil and gas and allow it to trade outwards its massive industrial surplus.

The rise of China, together, of course, with other Asian countries such as India and Vietnam, persuaded several authors that the maritime world "from Africa to Indonesia and then northward to the Korean Peninsula and Japan" was to become "one sweeping continuum." Hence, the geography of "maritime Eurasia" was soon "destined" to become "whole and condensed" (Kaplan 2010: 303). A former United States top official in the State Department put it quite bluntly in 2011: "Asia is being reconnected at last" (Feigenbaum 2011: 25). China's "expanding economic, political and military presence in the Indian Ocean, South Asia, the South Pacific, Africa and beyond" has to be considered then the main trigger of the IP's reconceptualisation and diffusion (Medcalf 2020: 13). The remainder of the chapter will analyse how great powers in maritime Asia have conceptualised the Indo-Pacific and then how China reacted to this notion, whether accepting it – wholly or partially – or rejecting it and proposing an alternative vision. Before tackling the subject, a caveat is needed. Geopolitics has been a Western-centric framework to understand global politics for most of its history and especially classical geopolitics has ignored non-Western perspectives on the relation between politics and geography or spatiality at large (See also Box 2.2). This distortion has been clearly highlighted by the so-called "critical geopolitics," a strand of geopolitical literature that strived to self-consciously remedy the biased legacies of geopolitics (O'Tuathail 1996).

Convergence in the making: The IP in the strategic discourses of the United States, Japan and India

The Asia-Pacific largely dominated the 20th century – at least from the late 1960s – and the beginning of the 21st. This landscape was roughly understood as "connecting Northeast and Southeast Asia with Oceania (and therefore Australia) and the Americas" (Medcalf 2018a: 16). This denomination implied a US-centred alliance network and regional security architecture which was built from 1945. Featuring less institutionalisation and multilateralism than the European, the US-led order in Asia has mostly followed the pattern of a "hub-and-spoke system" (Ikenberry 2011), i.e. a network of bilateral relations with favoured regional players. During the 20th century, Washington committed to the defence of the Philippines, South Korea and Japan. Moreover, the US-Taiwan relationship is based on a limited but fundamental corpus of treaties and provisions that leaves few doubts about full US military assistance to Taipei in case of escalation or Chinese invasion. Moving beyond its Cold War preference for bilateralism, since 1991 Washington has made steps forward also in supporting multilateral security initiatives in Asia, backing regional institutions such as the Association of Southeast Asian Nations (ASEAN) and its network of organisations as well as the East Asia Summit (EAS), and it has sponsored a revival of a broad-Asian security arrangement called the Quadrilateral Security Dialogue which ties the United States together with Japan, Australia and India. After the end of the Cold War, the United States improved its security relations also with other regional actors such as Thailand, Vietnam, Pakistan, Singapore, India.

However, an explicit mention of the IP did not arrive until the late 2000s. In August 2007, Japanese PM Abe Shinzo visited India and addressed the Indian Parliament. Drawing from the message by an Indian spiritual leader of the XIX century, Abe Shinzo envisioned the future "confluence of the two seas" – the Pacific and the Indian Oceans. This confluence was pushing Tokyo and New Delhi to build an "Arc of Freedom and Prosperity" in what he labelled "broader Asia," a macro-region including also the United States and Australia and built around Japan-India strategic partnership and alignment. The total range of issues Japan and India were agreeing to cooperate on was broad: defence, economics, diplomacy, development, technology, education, energy, environment, culture and others. Even while not yet mentioning the IP, Abe's remarks provided many cues that later were integrated into the notion. Since 2007, the notion of the IP has slowly been brought to the forefront of political and strategic discourse by several actors in Asia even if sometimes with remarkable differences. Hereafter, the different interpretations of the IP by the United States, Japan and India will be outlined. For the sake of clarity, due to word length limits, no examination of other middle powers has been carried out here (See also Box 2.4 for more).

The United States

During the 1980s and the 1990s US strategic documents and officials often referred to the "Pacific Rim" and the 21st century as the "Pacific Century." The Pacific Ocean was to be the future highway of prosperity and development. Throughout the history of US foreign policy after the Cold War, a dramatic rift is acknowledged to have occurred in 2011–2012 when the Obama Administration advanced the so-called "Rebalance" or "Pivot" to Asia. Even though a "pivot before the Pivot" had already been outlined but never carried out by the Bush Jr. Administration due to 9/11 and the War on Terror, it was Barack Obama who pioneered such a strategic rebalance towards Asia. Explaining this new vision in her 2011 pivotal article on America's forthcoming Pacific century, Hillary Clinton mentioned the IP with regards to Washington's alliance with Australia writing that from a strictly Pacific region, it was to become an Indo-Pacific one (Clinton 2011). In 2011 the US Senate Committee on Armed Services also claimed that US-India joint "naval exercises have become a vital pillar of stability, security and free and open trade, in the Indo-Pacific region" (US Senate 2011: 211). In 2012, Assistant Secretary of State for East Asia Kurt Campbell spoke of a "linkage between the Indian Ocean and the Pacific" whose grasping and conceptualising was the "challenge of the next phase of American strategy" (Campbell 2012).

In 2017, the new Administration led by Donald Trump brought about some noteworthy changes to US foreign policy towards the PRC and led the White House to a steep turn towards a US approach to the IP. More specifically, after Donald Trump's first trip to Asia in November 2017, the IP started to take shape as the geopolitical and conceptual backbone of US security and strategic involvement in Asia. According to the *2018 National Defense Strategy*, in fact, "long term strategic competition" between powers has re-emerged as the principal threat to US national security (Department of Defense 2018: 2) since – the *2017 National Security Strategy* choruses – China – together with Russia – threatens to challenge "American power, influence, and interests, attempting to erode American security and prosperity" (White House 2017: 2). In short, China must be considered a "strategic competitor" and a "revisionist power" as it is promoting a worldview utterly "antithetical" to US values and interests (White House 2017: 25). In particular, in the "Indo-Pacific" China is seeking "regional hegemony in the near-term and displacement of the United States" (Department of Defense 2018: 2). Each subsequent strategic and operational document released by the Trump Administration since the National Security Strategy (i.e. *2018 Nuclear Posture Review*; *2018 Design for Maintaining Maritime Superiority 2.0*; *2019 Missile Defense Review*) has echoed those conclusions. In May 2018, the US Pacific military command was symbolically renamed the Indo-Pacific Command in recognition of the greater emphasis on South Asia, especially India, and consistent with the new strategy. Between 2019 and 2020 several strategic documents were released: the Department of Defense's *Indo-Pacific Strategy Report*, later the Department of State's *A Free and Open Indo-Pacific: Advancing a Shared Vision*, and lastly the White House's *United States Strategic Approach to The People's Republic of China*. In each document, the United States promoted a full-fledged "Free and Open Indo-Pacific" strategy based on some main pillars: "fair," "reciprocal" trade relations based on principles such as respect for intellectual property rights, free trade, protection of private property, fair competition and open markets. In addition, the United States is pursuing preparedness of its Armed Forces, security partnerships and the promotion of a networked region in the IP. For instance, the US support for Taiwan is a representative case of the US presence in the IP (See also Box 2.3 for more). The Biden Administration has reaffirmed the IP as the centre of US "national interests […] deepest connection" (White House 2021: 10).

From a geopolitical perspective, the analysis of each of these documents highlights the US perspective on the IP. First of all, the American IP is a rather Asian and Australasian IP including most of the Indian Region, South East Asia, North East Asia, the whole Pacific Ocean and Australasia. Its military command's area of responsibility – the INDOPACOM of the US Armed Forces – confirms this vista and then excludes the Western Indian Ocean, Africa's east coast, the Red Sea, Gulf of Aden, the Persian Gulf, and the Arabian Sea, the responsibility of AFRICOM and CENTCOM. In 2015 a naval strategic document clarified that the IP was gaining increasing importance and comprises "Australia, Japan, New Zealand, the Philippines, the Republic of Korea, Thailand, Bangladesh, Brunei, India, Indonesia, Malaysia, Micronesia, Pakistan, Singapore, and Vietnam" (Department of the Navy 2015: 3). In this light, the US understanding of the IP resembles both Mahan's and Haushofer's points of view on the region because it has a strong maritime focus and thus it is mainly centred on those littoral states influencing the freedom of navigation in the area.

Box 2.3 Taiwan: edge of the Indo-Pacific?

The strategic position of Taiwan and its role, practically unique in the world, as an autonomous entity within the international community, represents an interesting case study for understanding the geopolitical dynamics of the Indo-Pacific. The island lays in the Taiwan Strait which is one of the most important shipping channels in the world linking major economies such as China, Japan, South Korea, Southeast Asia and India. The position of the island at the intersection of all the main hubs of the region, 160 km east from China, 250 km from the Philippines, just over 1000 km from the island of Hainan and 1400 km from the Spratly Islands, constitutes an indispensable pivot for control of the Asia-Pacific and Taiwan represents an indispensable strategic node for the United States in the South China Sea.

Taiwan can be defined as a medium power, being the 20th-largest in the world by purchasing power parity and is one of the countries at the forefront of technological innovation, a world leader in the semiconductor sector. However, Taiwan's international projection is extremely limited by the coercion of the People's Republic of China which claims sovereignty over the Taiwanese territory. Nevertheless, the geostrategic balance does not allow the PRC to exert force and reclaim the Taiwanese territory due to Washington's support. Sino-Taiwanese relations (Cross Strait Relation) remain, in the interpretation of Alan Romberg, "the only problem in the world today that could realistically lead to war between two great powers" (Kastner 2018). The 2017 National Security Strategy confirmed the US commitment to economic and strategic competition with the Chinese rival. The document assumes a central role for Taiwan in the IP region and in the dispute with the People's Republic of China and, thus, Taiwan best represents the new assertive US role in the IP, a pledge to free trade, open markets and the defence of democratic rights.

Japan

The first designer of the IP, Japan, however, took time before detailing a clear vision for it. Mostly linked to the political success of Abe Shinzo, the IP was thus paused between 2007 and 2012 when he returned to the Kantei for his second term as Japanese Prime Minister.

In December 2012, Abe Shinzo authored an op-ed in the magazine *Project Syndicate* and proposed the creation of a "democratic security diamond" in the IP. In his opinion, Japan, the United States, India and Australia were supposed to "safeguard the maritime commons stretching from the Indian Ocean region to the western Pacific," defend the existing regional order, and tackle China's growing assertiveness (Shinzo 2012). This concept of a "security diamond" was the logical heir of the 2007 "confluence of the seas" speech and represented its advancement (Pugliese & Patalano 2020).

In 2016, the Japanese premier formally launched his "Free and Open Indo-Pacific" strategy during the Sixth International Conference on African Development in Kenya. Japan – he stated – felt the responsibility of "fostering the confluence of the Pacific and Indian Oceans" and of "Asia and Africa" under the guiding principles of "freedom, rule of law, and the market economy," freeing it from "force or coercion," and making it "prosperous" (Shinzo 2016). Since then, this strategy began to take a more concrete form by channelling a huge flow of resources and capital, leading multilateral security partnerships and drills, and taking part in others' initiatives in the region. One of the first, rudimental projects within this new IP focus was the Trans-Pacific Partnership Agreement, a trade agreement aimed to deepen economic ties, slashing tariffs, fostering trade to boost growth, sharing policies and regulation, that after several setbacks and modifications – not least the withdrawal of the United States – entered into force on 30 December 2018. From August to October 2018, Tokyo then deployed three warships in the South China Sea for a joint military exercise with five IP countries and the United States. The Japanese vessels made port calls in India, Sri Lanka, Singapore, Indonesia and the Philippines and during the exercise linked up with the US Navy in the disputed territorial waters of the South China Sea with a submarine and other warships, including the *Kaga* carrier.

From a geopolitical point of view, Japan's IP is twofold. On one hand, its security dimension is enclosed in the "diamond" and it easily overlaps with that of the United States. Tokyo, New Delhi, Canberra and Washington are identified as the main pillars of security and stability in the IP, and are the foundations for the confluence of the seas. On the other, its economic side is much more multifaceted. If we look at Japan's bilateral economic cooperation and partnerships since then, we see that Tokyo's diplomatic activism has been truly bicontinental, stretching from Asia to East Africa and promoting commercial and financial integration between the two sides of the Indian Ocean, across South and East Asia, and the Pacific. This is arguably related to Japan's deep reliance on Africa-East Asia and Middle East-East Asia sea routes. For example, 90 percent of Tokyo's oil imports are shipped from the Middle East and/or Africa through the Indian Ocean. The African trajectory of Japan's economic IP is completely unique as it is absent from US blueprints.

India

Considered one of the most important rising countries and member of the BRICS during the 1990s and the 2000s, India has been re-orienteering its security and defence policy during the 2010s and under the government of Narendra Modi, leader of the nationalist Bharatiya Janata Party. In particular, China's rise has been the major motive behind India's declining affection for BRICS and multilateral cooperation led by Beijing. New Delhi is in fact suspicious of its bulky neighbour. Modi's foreign policy has mainly been concerned by China's assertiveness with regard to border disagreements (Aksai Chin, Arunachal Pradesh and indirectly Doklam), by its growing trade and defence relationships with India's surrounding countries and primarily archenemy Pakistan, and by the expansion of the Chinese naval presence in the Indian Ocean, where New Delhi worries of encirclement. In 2013, a military stalemate trapped India and China in Depsang and in 2017 India was alarmed by Chinese movements across the Sino-Bhutanese Doklam border and felt pressured to intervene on Bhutan's side. The following dangerous military stand-off lasted for weeks but the two countries managed to maintain peace and there no reported casualties. Still in 2017, India also declared its non-participation in China's massive infrastructure Belt and Road Initiative (BRI). Initial hesitations then became open opposition to BRI when Delhi refused to attend, at any level, the BRI international forum in Beijing and aimed to showcase supporting countries. Major concerns for New Delhi regarding BRI revolve around the China-Pakistan Economic Corridor, which starts in China but crosses Delhi-claimed but Islamabad-controlled Kashmir. Predictably enough, India is highly uneasy about the Chinese purchase of the Pakistani Gwadar port which – New Delhi fears – could be easily turned into a military outpost and encircle the subcontinent. Quite interestingly instead, New Delhi expressed anxiety about the Chinese military base in Djibouti at the tip of the Horn of Africa.

Since 2014 Narendra Modi's government has extended the security dimension of the traditional Indian "Look East" policy to a newly established "Act East" policy. This blueprint is configured as a series of connectivity plans – both maritime and land – aimed at intensifying commercial relations with, first, Myanmar, the Bay of Bengal and Southeast Asia and then with East Asia and the Pacific Region. Constant engagement at bilateral, regional and multilateral levels are then the pillars of the "Act East" policy. Japan is regarded as one of the major partners in India's foreign policy. With Tokyo, for instance, New Delhi has launched the vision of the Asia-Africa Growth Corridor, which is not only economic but above all strategic, as it aims to replace China's BRI in Africa. The Arab Gulf nations – especially Saudi Arabia and the United Arab Emirates – are also central to India's West outreach because, besides energy, they occupy strategic location for India's maritime security and commercial interests.

Another cornerstone of Modi's foreign policy has been India's leaning towards the United States. In January 2015, the *US-India Joint Strategic Vision for the Asia-Pacific and Indian Ocean Region* reflected India's concern about the tension over the South China Sea, shaking off the long Indian silence on Chinese expansionism in the maritime sphere. This was one of the first steps in Indian alignment with the United States which has been deepened since. In June 2016, the United States recognised India as a "Major Defense Partner," pledging to facilitate the sharing of technologies on a par with its closest partners and allies. In 2019, Australia, India, Japan and the United States met for the first time as the Quadrilateral Security Dialogue group, or Quad.

Geographically speaking, India's IP is peculiar. According to the *2016 India's Maritime Security Strategy* national interests and linkages "have expanded" over the years, "from the Arabian Sea and the Bay of Bengal, to the Indian Ocean region, thence across the Indo-Pacific Region" (Ministry of Defence 2016: 30). According to the document, crucial national interests to India are located across the *Indian Ocean Region* (emphasis added) which is enclosed between the Cape of Good Hope, the Suez Canal and the Gulf of Aden, the Malacca, Sunda and Lombok Straits, and the Western coast of Australia. As noted later by India's External Affairs Minister S. Jaishankar, cooperation under the Indo-Pacific umbrella has been hampered by a problem of incongruence. "Building partnerships in the Indo-Pacific maritime region" is difficult due to "the lack of consensus on what such a concept meant or even its geographic extent" (The Hindu 2019). Because of this difference in strategic vistas, the US Navy's cooperation with the Indian navy was limited to the eastern part of the Indo-Pacific region – US Seventh Fleet's and INDOPACOM's area of responsibility – whereas at the Western end, where many of India's vital interests lie, India-US military cooperation is negligible. However, at the 2018 Shangri-La Dialogue, Modi explicitly endorsed the "shared vision of an open, stable, secure and prosperous *Indo-Pacific Region* (emphasis added)," a wider geopolitical region than previously referenced. Nonetheless, Modi was rather impatient to dismiss any anti-China understanding of the IP, which, in his words, is no means a vision "directed against any country" or advanced by who "seeks to dominate" (Modi 2018). From then on, India has been quite eager to promote the concept of the IP but fell short in defining the differences between the IP and Indian Ocean region. In a fit of bluntness, India's 2019 National Security admitted that the US "Indo-Pacific strategy" is meant "to contain China in East and Southeast Asia" (Hooda 2019: 3) but that there are still many "divergent definitions" of the IP that "should be harmonised as a priority" (Hooda 2019: 8).

Asia for Asians: China's geopolitical landscape facing containment

In October 2012, Wang Jisi, a prominent Chinese international relations scholar and formerly a top advisor to President Hu Jintao, delivered an important speech outlining how China should react to the Pivot to Asia. In his opinion, China had to follow the principle of "Marching Westward" as the United States was rebalancing toward the Asia-Pacific. The "March Westward" imperative is generally regarded as the baseline for the following major development in China's geopolitical projection: the Belt and Road Initiative. During his visit to the Nazarbayev University of Kazakhstan at the start of a Central Asian tour, President Xi Jinping proposed to build an "economic belt along the Silk Road" (Xi 2013a). In October 2013 before the Indonesian Parliament, Xi Jinping expanded the project, foreseeing also a "Maritime Silk Road of the 21st century" (Xi 2013b). After returning from the tour, Xi Jinping held the first work conference – attended by the whole Politburo and the highest cadres from the diplomatic, economic and military sectors – on "Peripheral Diplomacy" where he advocated the need of ensuring stability around and closer ties with Western neighbours. To this purpose, BRI involves the development of basic infrastructure along six major land corridors towards the west – the Economic Belt – and the expansion of sea routes – the Maritime Road – connecting China with South Asia, Africa and Europe. Since the unveiling of BRI, then, scholars have wondered whether China's purpose was to regain its historical continental geopolitical projection and eschew confrontation at sea where it knew the cards were not stacked in its favour. However, as soon as the Belt and Road project started to unfurl, it was clear that it had a significant maritime projection in Asia. The Maritime Silk Road entailed ports and facilities among others in Pakistan, Myanmar, Malaysia, Sri Lanka, Brunei, the Maldives and Djibouti all along the sea route to Africa and the Mediterranean. On 1 August 2017, China opened its first overseas military base in Djibouti in the Strait of Bab el-Mandeb at the opening of the Red Sea and between 2018 and 2019 a second outpost in Tajikistan close to the Afghan border.

In 2015, China's *Military Strategy* claimed that the crucial "geostrategic landscape" for Beijing's national interest was the "Asia-Pacific." In November 2017, after Trump's first tour in Asia and initial hints regarding the IP, a Chinese MFA spokesperson stated that "politicized and exclusionary [regional visions and proposals] should be avoided." However, the Chinese official did not completely reject the IP but argued that whatever vision is to be implemented – "be it the Asia-Pacific or others" – it "shall heed the call of the times for peaceful development" and foster "win-win cooperation" (Geng 2017). Possibly because of the tones of Washington's December 2017 National Security Strategy and January 2018 National Defense Strategy, in March 2018, short before the IP gained consensus at the Shangri-La Dialogue, China's Foreign Minister Wang Yi dismissed the "Indo-Pacific" as "an attention-grabbing idea" that would "dissipate like ocean foam" (ABC 2018). China is still reluctant to employ the concept as it perceives the IP as a non-neutral geopolitical landscape. Accordingly, in its 2019 White Paper on Defence, Beijing continues using "Asia-Pacific" to describe the geographical region where its interests are located. Stubbornly, Chinese officials have persisted "in referring to the 'Asia-Pacific region' even when they are responding to questions concerning the IP" (Feng 2020: 16). Interestingly, the US-Japan-India divergences over the boundaries of the IP are seen by Chinese scholars as a "weakness" of the coalition (Heiduk & Wacker 2020: 32). Nevertheless, in the 2019 white paper the PRC recognised that in time "the Asia-Pacific has become a focus of major country competition" (PRC SCIO 2019: 6).

No matter how it is responding rhetorically to the diffusion of the IP as a geopolitical region, China is in fact an Indo-Pacific power. Its massive economic and military build-up has made China a strong outward-looking country both for interests and challenges. For instance, China's need of the mastery over the South China Sea for its anti-access/area denial strategy aimed at offsetting potential rivals' military superiority has alarmed many South East Asian states such as Vietnam, Philippines and Brunei and dragged it into a tense stalemate where Washington is signalling resolve to defend the status quo. Moreover, Beijing's energy security is greatly dependent on supplies from the Middle East and Angola. Almost 80% of China's energy imports transit through Malacca in what former President Hu Jintao defined the "Malacca dilemma," the over-reliance on chokepoints China cannot control directly. China's historical and recent antagonism with India and amity with Pakistan is further evidence that Beijing has a strong security connection with the subcontinent also via land. China's trade relation with the major Anglophone powers in the Pacific – the United States, Australia and New Zealand – drags it towards the Ocean. The history of the Maritime Silk Road is further evidence of the Indo-Pacific nature of China's geopolitical projection. In 2017, a white paper stated that the purpose of the Road was to realise the "China-Indian Ocean-Africa-Mediterranean Sea Blue Economic Passage," to link "the South China Sea to the Indian Ocean" through the "China-Indochina Peninsula Economic Corridor," to connect the "China-Pakistan Economic Corridor" and the "Bangladesh-China-India-Myanmar Economic Corridor." Moreover, efforts will also be made to build the "blue economic passage of China-Oceania-South Pacific, travelling southward from the South China Sea into the Pacific Ocean" (Xinhua 2017).

However, there is a major difference between China's interpretation – even if not explicit – of the IP and others': the absence of the United States. Responding to the new diplomatic activism in Obama's Pivot to Asia in the 2010s, China advanced the New Asian Security Concept (NASC), an architecture proposal for regional security and the only proposal of a Chinese-designed security institution. Initially mentioned by Premier Li Keqiang during the 2013 East Asia Summit and later relaunched by Xi Jinping in 2014, the NASC is meant to let the "people of Asia run the affairs of Asia, solve the problems of Asia, and uphold the security of Asia" (Xi Jinping 2014: 392). This proposal has been interpreted as challenging the security order backed by the United States in the IP as it is inspired by the Chinese long-standing mantra that security should be based not on "outmoded Cold War alliances and military blocs" (Larson & Shevchenko 2010: 82). China's intent, then, is to "establish a security architecture that is more exclusively "Asian," free of alliances, more attendant to its domestic security concerns, less liberal, and solidly rooted in Chinese economic power" (Ford 2020: 1). The Chinese IP would be then US-less and, according to many, increasingly Sino-centric (Gungwu 2013).

Box 2.4 Australia and Canada

The geopolitical framework of the IP has also gained attention in the political debate of middle powers such as Australia and Canada. Australian and Canadian commentators and politicians have expressed the need for their countries to be increasingly involved in Asian security and economic arrangements.

Australia has always been interested in Asia's security and economic dynamics. Given its geographical location at the opening of the wide Asian seas and continental mass, Canberra is greatly impacted by the cooperation-competition patterns in the region. Since 2013, and thus preceding the United States, Australia has leaned towards the new notion of the Indo-Pacific proposed first by Japan and has adopted it in official documents. The Australian Defence White Paper of 2013 mentioned the concept 56 times and even devoted an entire chapter to it. The usage is echoed also in the Defence White Paper of 2016 and the Foreign Policy White Paper of 2017. It is not just a matter of semantics. Australia has demonstrated a strong resolve to pursue the US-Japan-sponsored view of the Indo-Pacific and its security and economic implications. Thus, Canberra «views East and South Asia as an interconnected geopolitical space» where the Australian security and economic interests are increasingly dwarfed by China's monumental rise (Medcalf 2018b: 133).

Canada, for its part, was not always concerned about the dynamics affecting the Indo-Pacific region's security and economy. However, as the Asian economy grew and seized the largest share in the global GDP and commerce, Ottawa begun looking at the region with increasing interest. Nonetheless, Canada long refrained from adopting the term, signalling a more cautious stance on China than the United States. The only relevant debate on Canada and the Indo-Pacific took place in January 2020 when the Canadian Asia-Pacific Foundation gathered numerous speakers from Australia, Canada, China, India, Indonesia, Japan and the United States to present their views on the idea of Indo-Pacific. The roundtable was concluded by Jeffrey Reeves, Vice-President of the Foundation. Reeves argued that Canada should continue ignoring the Indo-Pacific geographic construct and prioritising the "Asia-Pacific" which leaves ample space for Ottawa to pursue its strategic interests. The strong anti-China rhetoric behind the "Free and Open Indo-Pacific" is, in Reeves' opinion, too constraining for Canada (Reeves 2020). Ottawa's reluctance to endorse the Indo-Pacific framework was confirmed again in 2020 when the Canadian Government issued a statement on "Canada and the *Asia-Pacific*" (emphasis added) and made no mention of the merging of the Indian and the Pacific regions (Government of Canada 2020).

Conclusion

Before dwelling on the findings of the chapter, omissions call for clarification. In the chapter no space has been given to regional middle powers' formulations or reactions to the rise of IP as a geopolitical horizon (see also Box 2.4). This is mainly because we have decided to focus on great powers' geopolitical competition. We are aware though that middle powers – both advocates and opponents of the concept – play a crucial role in international politics and in shaping the IP as the case of Australia clearly demonstrates. Canberra is indeed one of the leading middle powers advancing the IP and an in-depth analysis of its understanding would have proved useful to understand regional geopolitics. Moreover, no room has been left for non-regional powers – e.g. European – that are contributing to the ascent of the IP in political discourse. For instance, the United Kingdom, France and Germany are participating in the definition of the IP, its boundaries, challenges and actors.

The chapter has summarised several crucial facets when we deal with the Indo-Pacific from a geopolitical approach. First, the IP is a geopolitical landscape that still need a conclusive definition. It has been outlined – more or less explicitly – by two of the four major geopoliticians, namely Alfred T. Mahan and Karl F. Haushofer who clearly linked the emergence of this mega-region to the development of trade and navigation, the former, or the rise of an expansionist power, the latter. However, a clear-cut geopolitical perimeter was not set. Second, it is in the political – better strategic – domain that the recent origins of the IP must be traced. In particular, it was China's ascent on the regional stage during the 1990s and the 2000s that pushed the United States, Japan and India among others to feel the urgency of a new conceptualisation of Asia. Japan first, the United States and India later then started reconfiguring the geopolitical horizon of their regional policies in order to check Beijing's rise. Nonetheless, the three have not yet devised a single understanding of the IP but rather they are advancing different extensions of the concept. For instance, Japan and India, given their over-reliance on the Indian Ocean and the Gulf of Aden share a common African-Middle Eastern trajectory in their views on the IP whereas the United States puts forward a more Pacific-centric IP. Third, the lowest common denominator between the three visions is their strong maritime – very Mahanian – orientation of the IP. The notion of the IP in fact revolves around sea routes and navigation because the three powers feel that the worst-case scenario would be China threatening their national security interests by enjoying dominance over the seas: the East China Sea for Tokyo, the Indian Ocean for New Delhi, the whole of maritime Asia for Washington. Fourth, the chapter found that Beijing has not surprisingly perceived the IP as a politically charged concept and thus has refrained from not only endorsing but even mentioning it. Instead, China has doggedly kept on advancing the landscape of the Asia-Pacific in speeches and white papers. Lastly, the chapter argues that even though China is eschewing the IP as a geopolitical landscape, the IP is still real for its national interest. China is in fact an Indo-Pacific power because its economic, energy, political and security interests lie in the Indo-Pacific. Furthermore, China is expected to be increasingly an Indo-Pacific power because *rebus sic stantibus* the coalition the United States is forming to keep China in check spans across the Indo-Pacific region, uniting Australasia, East Asia, the Pacific and the Indian Ocean.

Notes

1 Quite confusingly, Haushofer also uses the term "Pan-Asia" extensively to describe Japan's natural sphere of influence.
2 World Bank taxonomy.

References

An, Ning, Jo Sharp, and Ian Shaw, "Towards A Confucian Geopolitics." *Dialogues in Human Geography*, 2020, doi:10.1177/2043820620951354.
Biden, Joseph, Jr., "Remarks by President Biden, Prime Minister Morrison of Australia, and Prime Minister Johnson of the United Kingdom Announcing the Creation of AUKUS." *White House*, (15 September 2021). https://www.whitehouse.gov/briefing-room/speeches-remarks/2021/09/15/remarks-by-president-biden-prime-minister-morrison-of-australia-and-prime-minister-johnson-of-the-united-kingdom-announcing-the-creation-of-aukus/.
Campbell, Kurt M., "Campbell Joins Bloomfield at Stimson's Chairman's Forum." *Stimson Center*, (19 January 2012). http://www.stimson.org/spotlight/asst-secretary-for-east-asian-affairs-kurt-campbell-speaks-at-stimsonschairmans-forum/.
"China mocks Australia over 'Indo-Pacific' concept it says will 'dissipate'." *ABC*, (8 March 2018). https://www.abc.net.au/news/2018-03-08/china-mocks-australia-over-indo-pacific-concept/9529548.
Clinton, Hillary R., "America's Pacific Century." *Foreign Policy*, (11 October 2011). https://foreignpolicy.com/2011/10/11/americas-pacific-century/.
Department of Defense of the United States, "Summary of the National Security Strategy." (2018). https://dod.defense.gov/Portals/1/Documents/pubs/2018-National-Defense-Strategy-Summary.pdf.
Department of the Navy of the United States, "A Cooperative Strategy for 21st Century Seapower." (2015). https://www.globalsecurity.org/military/library/policy/navy/21st-century-seapower_strategy_201503.pdf.
Feigenbaum, Evan A., "Why America No Longer Gets Asia." *The Washington Quarterly* 34, no. 2 (2011): 25–43.
Ford, Lindsey W., "Network Power: China's Effort to Reshape Asia's Regional Security Architecture." *Brookings*, (14 September 2020). https://www.brookings.edu/wp-content/uploads/2020/09/FP_20200914_china_network_power_ford.pdf.
Geng, Shuang, "Foreign Ministry Spokesperson Geng Shuang's Regular Press Conference on November 13, 2017." (2017). https://www.fmprc.gov.cn/mfa_eng/xwfw_665399/s2510_665401/t1510216.shtml.

Government of Canada, "Canada and the Asia-Pacific." (2020). https://www.international.gc.ca /world-monde/international_relations-relations_internationales/asia_pacific-asie_pacifique/ index.aspx?lang=eng.

Gungwu, Wang, *Renewal: The Chinese State and The New Global History*, Hong Kong: The Chinese University of Hong Kong Press, 2013.

Haushofer, Karl E., *An English Translation and Analysis of Major General Karl Ernst Haushofer's Geopolitics of the Pacific Ocean: Studies on the Relationship*, Lewiston: Edwin Mellen Press, 2002.

Heffernan, Michael, "Fin de Siècle, Fin du Monde: On the Origins of European Geopolitics," in David Atkinson, and Klaus Dodds, *Geopolitical Traditions: A Century of Geopolitical Thought*, 27–51, London: Routledge, 2000.

Heiduk, Felix, and Gudrun Wacker, "From Asia-Pacific to Indo-Pacific: Significance, Implementation and Challenges." *SWP Research Paper*, (9 July 2020). https://www.swp -berlin.org/fileadmin/contents/products/research_papers/2020RP09_IndoPacific.pdf.

Herwig, Holger H., *The Demon of Geopolitics: How Karl Haushofer "Educated" Hitler and Hess*, Lanham: Rowman & Littlefield, 2016.

Hooda. Lieutenant General Deependra Singh Hooda, "India's National Security Strategy." (2019). https://manifesto.inc.in/pdf/national_security_strategy_gen_hooda.pdf.

Ikenberry, G. John, *Liberal Leviathan: The Origins, Crisis, and Transformation of the American World Order*, Princeton: Princeton University Press, 2011.

"Indian Ocean Region Nations Should Build a Common Vision for Indo-Pacific: Jaishankar." *The Hindu*, (15 December 2019). https://www.thehindu.com/news/national/indian-ocean-region -nations-should-build-a-common-vision-for-indo-pacific-jaishankar/article30307459.ece.

Kaplan, Robert D., *Monsoon. The Indian Ocean and the Future of American Power*, New York: Random House, 2010.

"Karl Haushofer," *Encyclopaedia Britannica*, (last accessed on 11 November 2020). https:// www.britannica.com/biography/Karl-Ernst-Haushofer.

Kastner, S., "International Relations Theory and the Relationship across the Taiwan Strait." *International Journal of Taiwan Studies* 1, no. 1 (2018): 161–183.

Larson, Deborah W., and Alexei Shevchenko, "Status Seekers. Chinese and Russian Responses to US Primacy." *International Security* 34, no. 4 (2010): 63–95.

Liu, Feng, "The Recalibration of Chinese Assertiveness: China's Responses to the Indo-Pacific Challenge." *International Affairs* 96, no. 1 (2020): 9–27.

Mackinder, Halford J., "The Geographical Pivot of History," *The Geographical Journal* 23, no. 4 (1904): 421–444.

Mahan, Alfred T., *The Influence of Seapower Upon History*, London: Methuen & Co., 1965.

Mahan, Alfred T., *The Problem of Asia: Its Effect Upon International Politics*, Piscataway: Transaction Publishers, 2003.

Medcalf, Rory, "Australia," in Jeff M. Smith, *Asia's Quest for Balance. China's Rise and Balancing in the Indo-Pacific*, 133–152, Lanham: Rowman & Littlefield, 2018.

Medcalf, Rory, "Reimagining Asia: From Asia-Pacific to Indo-Pacific," in Gilbert Rozman and Joseph Chinyong Liow, *International Relations and Asia's Southern Tier*, 9–28, Singapore: Palgrave Macmillan Series, 2018.

Medcalf, Rory, *Contest for the Indo-Pacific. Why China Won't Map the Future*, Carlston: La Trobe University Press, 2020.

Ministry of Defence of India, "Ensuring Secure Seas: Indian Maritime Security Strategy." (2016). https://www.indiannavy.nic.in/sites/default/files/Indian_Maritime_Security_Strategy _Document_25Jan16.pdf.

Modi, Narendra, "Prime Minister's Keynote Address at Shangri La Dialogue." (2018). https:// www.mea.gov.in/Speeches-Statements.htm?dtl/29943/Prime+Ministers+Keynote+Address +at+Shangri+La+Dialogue+June+01+2018.

O'Tuathail, Gearoid, *Critical Geopolitics: The Politics Of Writing Global Space*, Minneapolis: University of Minnesota Press, 1996.

Perry, Peter, "Editorial Comment. Political Geography Quarterly: A Content (But Discontented) Review." *Political Geography Quarterly* 6, no. 1 (1987): 5–6.

PRC's State Council Information Office, "China's National Defense in the New Era." (2019). http://english.scio.gov.cn/node_8013506.html.

Pugliese, Giulio, and Alessio Patalano, "Diplomatic and security practice under Abe Shinzō: the case for Realpolitik Japan." *Australian Journal of International Affairs*, doi: 10.1080/10357718.2020.1781790.

Reeves, Jeffrey, "Canada and the Free and Open Indo-Pacific: A Strategic Assessmen." *Asia Policy* 15, no. 4 (2020): 1–64.

Shinzo, Abe, "Asia's Democratic Security Diamond." *Project Syndicate*, (27 December 2012). https://www.project-syndicate.org/onpoint/a-strategic-alliance-for-japan-and-india-by -shinzo-abe?barrier=accesspaylog.

Shinzo, Abe, "Address by Prime Minister Shinzo Abe at the Opening Session of the Sixth Tokyo International Conference on African Development." (27 August 2016). https://www.mofa.go .jp/afr/af2/page4e_000496.html.

Spykman, Nicholas J., "Geography and Foreign Policy, I." *American Political Science Review* 32, no. 1 (1938): 28–50.

Spykman, Nicholas J., "Geography and Foreign Policy, II." *American Political Science Review* 32, no. 2 (1938): 213–236.

Stockholm International Peace Research Institute, "SIPRI Military Expenditure Database." (2020). https://www.sipri.org/databases/milex.

US Senate, Committee on Armed Services, "National Defense Authorization Act for Fiscal Year 2012, Report." (22 June 2011). https://www.congress.gov/congressional-report/112th -congress/senate-report/26/1.

White House, "National Security Strategy of the United States." (2017). https://www.whitehouse .gov/wp-content/uploads/2017/12/NSS-Final-12-18-2017-0905.pdf.

White House, "Interim National Security Strategic Guidance." (2021). https://www.whitehouse .gov/wp-content/uploads/2021/03/NSC-1v2.pdf.

World Bank, "World Development Indicators." (2020). https://data.worldbank.org/.

Xi, Jinping, "Promote Friendship Between Our People and Work Together to Build a Bright Future." (2013a). https://www.fmprc.gov.cn/mfa_eng/wjdt_665385/zyjh_665391/t1078088 .shtml.

Xi, Jinping, "Speech by Chinese President Xi Jinping to Indonesian Parliament." (2013b). https:// reconasia-production.s3.amazonaws.com/media/filer_public/88/fe/88fe8107-15d7-4b4c -8a59-0feb13c213e1/speech_by_chinese_president_xi_jinping_to_indonesian_parliament .pdf.

Xi, Jinping, *The Governance of China*, Beijing: Foreign Language Press, 2014.

Xinhua, "Vision for Maritime Cooperation under the Belt and Road Initiative." (2017). http:// www.xinhuanet.com/english/2017-06/20/c_136380414.htm.

Zhang, Feng, *Chinese Hegemony. Grand Strategy and International Institutions in East Asian History*, Stanford: Stanford University Press, 2015.

Part II

Socio-economic issues in the Indo-Pacific

3 Political economy of the Indo-Pacific development

Karina Jędrzejowska

Introduction

From an economic perspective, the Indo-Pacific constitutes a highly diversified territory with countries facing numerous development challenges. It is also a region where political and economic tensions intertwine and set directions for potential cooperation in terms of politics, security, economy and broadly defined development. As the political dimension of the Indo-Pacific appears to be the one that attracts greater academic attention, this chapter looks at selected economic developments within the region by pointing out its diversity.

The aims of the chapter are as follows: 1) to highlight the developmental heterogeneity of the Indo-Pacific and its economic dimension, 2) to review the selected socio-economic indicators for the Indo-Pacific and 3) to present major efforts to institutionalise economic cooperation and boost development in the region. Upon completion of the unit, students will have the knowledge and skills that enable them to: 1) have empirical knowledge of a variety of Indo-Pacific socio-economic issues and challenges, 2) show how heterogenous development of the region affects cooperation and potential economic integration within the Indo-Pacific, 3) generate ideas for credible policy options in managing complex development challenges in the Indo-Pacific, with special attention given to the implementation of the 2030 Agenda for Sustainable Development. In addition to the subject-specific learning outcomes, on successfully completing the chapter students will be able to use selected World Bank and United Nations (UN) resources for bibliographical searches, data acquisition and analysis.

The structure of the chapter follows its objectives. The first section provides the introduction to the Indo-Pacific from the perspective of political economy, while the second section focuses on the heterogeneity of development in the region. The third section gives an overview of major developmental challenges within the Indo-Pacific, including poverty and inequality, economic challenges and economic vulnerabilities in the region. In the fourth section, the focus shifts towards Indo-Pacific regional development cooperation. The final section concludes.

The chapter is based mostly on the review of statistical data. The primary source of data for the analysis constitute databases provided by the World Bank, World Development Indicators (WDI) in particular. In addition to data analysis, the chapter refers to numerous reports and policy papers prepared by international organisations as well as Indo-Pacific-oriented papers in research journals.

Politico-economic conceptualisation of the Indo-Pacific

As noted in the earlier chapters of this handbook, the origins of the concept of the Indo-Pacific can be traced back to geography and – to a lesser extent – geopolitics

DOI: 10.4324/9781003336143-6

and security studies (Chen 2018; Galloway 2021). As such, the region in question is primarily a politically and security-oriented construct that focuses on the multifaceted political, security and maritime interdependencies within the Pacific and Indian Oceans. The prevailingly political nature of the region is confirmed in several Indo-Pacific strategies formulated by countries of the region along with their partners such as the European Union with its 2021 Strategy for Cooperation in the Indo-Pacific (Pascal 2021: 2). An exception of sorts constitutes the Japanese notion of the Free and Open Indo-Pacific (FOIP) in which the Indo-Pacific region is regarded as both political and economic system. The economic dimension of the region can also be seen in the conceptualisation of the Indo-Pacific provided by the members of the Association of Southeast Asian Nations (ASEAN). ASEAN countries stress the relevance of economic development of the area by underlying the need to achieve greater economic prosperity in the region as the purpose for enhanced regional cooperation (Heiduk & Wacker 2020: 2). A similar path was more recently followed by the United States (US) with the introduction of an "Indo-Pacific Economic Framework for Prosperity" (IPEF) as the new vehicle for the US economic engagement in the region (Goodman & Reinsch 2022; US Department of State 2019; The White House 2022).

Yet despite its gradually growing recognition, the economic dimension of the Indo-Pacific appears underdeveloped – both at the institutional level as well as in terms of research (Wilson 2017: 1). Evan A. Feigenbaum of the Carnegie Endowment for International Peace in his recent testimony in front of the US House of Representatives referred to this phenomenon as to the story of two Asias, in which the analysis and awareness of economic challenges are somewhat obscured by security issues (Feigenbaum 2022). Furthermore, most economic analyses interpret regional economic developments in the area through the lenses of a broader concept of Asia-Pacific. This is also the path followed by major international financial institutions such as the International Monetary Fund (IMF) or the members of the World Bank Group. Even though Indo-Pacific economic cooperation is yet to take the more formal shape of regional bloc(s), the economic potential of the region justifies interest in its economy. Moreover, social, economic and environmental challenges in the region affect the political and security interdependencies in the area (Rahman et al. 2020).

As already indicated, the Indo-Pacific is highly heterogeneous with regard to the level of development of individual countries. The region also seems divided into two halves marked by relatively wealthier and prevailingly more developed Pacific countries on one side and their less developed Indian Ocean counterparts on the other. Trade and investment ties between these two subregions continue to be relatively weak, and there are only limited options for institutionalised economic cooperation. Simultaneously, most countries of the region appear to be relatively well integrated into the global economy. It is the intra-regional economic architecture that remains underdeveloped where, yet again Pacific countries (East Asia in particular) boast a greater level of integration compared to the Indian Ocean area (Medcalf 2019: 54; Medcalf 2012).

Any attempt at analysing and understanding the political economy of the Indo-Pacific requires setting the borders of the region. From the general understanding of the "Indo-Pacific" as a combination of the Indian Ocean and the Pacific Ocean, it is natural to interpret the "Indo-Pacific" as consisting of the two oceans and the surrounding countries. However, not all countries use the term to describe the whole area. As the Indo-Pacific is perceived differently depending on the who and for which purpose refers to the concept, the selection of countries for analysis constitutes a challenge on its own. Almost every country provides its own geographical definition of the "Indo-Pacific" that at times has been evolving along with regional policy development. As such, the number of countries incorporated into the individual visions of the Indo-Pacific can vary from less than 20 to short of 40 (Haruko 2020: 2; CeoWorld 2022). This variation, in turn, contributes to differing perceptions and assessment of the relevance of the region for the global economy.

Some policymakers and researchers consider the above-mentioned ambiguity and – simultaneously – flexibility of the term "Indo-Pacific" as an advantage. The relative "fluidity" of the concept allows countries with strategic interests in the area to adjust the definition depending on the situation in the region. Australia – by whose reckoning the Indo-Pacific ranges from the eastern Indian Ocean to the Pacific, connected by south-east Asia – is the only country that in the process of delineating the Indo-Pacific puts forward economic ties within the region by underlying that the region encompasses nine of Australia's top ten trading partners (Galloway 2021). The United States and India use a broader definition by depicting the Indo-Pacific as the entire Indian Ocean region, extending its borders to the east coast of Africa. In the case of the EU, the regional boundaries are even broader, including the west coast of Africa and wrapping up in the South Pacific. Yet those interpretations of the Indo-Pacific seem to be driven more by geographical and political concerns than economical (Galloway 2021).

No matter what the exact definition of the region would be, at the very roots of the proliferation of the concept are economic factors related to China's economic expansion (Pascal 2021: 6–7). Moreover, the shift towards the Indo-Pacific indicates the fact that the Indian Ocean has replaced the Atlantic as the world's busiest and most strategically significant trade corridor. The emerging and developed economies of East Asia depend heavily on commodity transport routes across the Indian Ocean from the Middle East and Africa (Medcalf 2019: 54; Medcalf 2013). The region not only encompasses the world's most significant sea routes, but it is home to at least half the world's population and possibly two-thirds of the global Gross Domestic Product (GDP). Moreover, it comprises some of the fastest-growing economies. As such, the Indo-Pacific is deemed to be the centre of the globe not only politically, but economically (or rather geoeconomically) as well (Das 2019). Moreover, the economic and political interests and rivalries in the region are intertwined and fuel its conceptualisation.

For the purpose of the consecutive sections of the chapter, the Indo-Pacific countries are identified based on the most common concepts and their implementation in individual countries' policy papers. As such, geographical boundaries of the Indo-Pacific in the chapter are limited to 26 economies of the Western Pacific and Indian Ocean. In effect, the region consists mostly of representatives from East Asia, Southeast Asia and South Asia. The countries included in the analysis are Australia, Bangladesh, Bhutan, Brunei, Cambodia, Fiji, India, Indonesia, Japan, Laos, Malaysia, Maldives, Myanmar, Nepal, New Zealand, Pakistan, Papua New Guinea, Philippines, Republic of Korea, Singapore, Sri Lanka, Taiwan,[1] Thailand, Timor-Leste, United States and Vietnam. This list includes South Korea and Pakistan as they are usually incorporated by regional strategies set by other countries. However, neither of the two countries uses the term in its policies and official speeches by central authorities. The list focuses on the "core" Indo-Pacific countries and as such excludes African economies as well as the Caribbean islands states, even though they are occasionally considered part of the region.[2] An exception here constitutes Fiji – a country that often identifies itself with the concept of the Indo-Pacific and whose support for the concept has been recently confirmed by its declaration to join the US-led IPEF. A significant exclusion in the analysis constitutes the driving force behind the rise of the Indo-Pacific – China. It is not considered part of the region in the chapter based on the fact that the regional construct appears to be created in order to contain Chinese political and economic expansion, and possibly circumvent Chinese efforts for institutionalisation and domination of economic cooperation within its Asian trading partners. As such, China is simultaneously both present and absent in the region, as most regional developments happen either because or in spite of being the world's biggest exporter.

Heterogeneity of economic development in the Indo-Pacific

The economic potential of the Indo-Pacific constitutes the main justification for its global political and economic relevance. Depending on the definition applied, the Indo-Pacific is inhabited by up to five billion people, produces between 40% and 60% of the global GDP and incorporates some of the fastest-growing economies in the world as well as global economic powers. Moreover, the majority of the world's goods and energy supplies are transported via Indo-Pacific maritime routes. Simultaneously, the Indo-Pacific is the primary arena where economic rivalry between the United States and China is playing out. Considering that political and economic engagement in the region and support for the notion of the Indo-Pacific are often seen as an alternative to the China-centric economic perspective on the area marked by initiatives such as the Belt and Road Initiative (BRI) or the Regional Comprehensive Economic Partnership (RCEP). Both initiatives can be to an extent interpreted as manifestations of Chinese imperialism in the Global South (Beeson 2018). Therefore, it comes as no surprise that major actors' economic priorities for the Indo-Pacific region revolve around trade and – to a in some way lesser degree – the relatively new concept of connectivity (Calleja et al. 2021: 4–5).[3]Another increasingly important factor remains the economic prosperity of the region and its development, and this is also the point where regional differences within the Indo-Pacific show the most.

In brief, the Indo-Pacific is a highly diversified area in terms of socio-economic development encompassing countries at all stages of development. Even though the majority of the region's representatives can be classified as developing countries, the region comprises also some of the most advanced economies, such as the United States, Japan and South Korea. Concurrently, among the developing countries of the region, there are those included on the United Nations' Least Developed Countries (LDCs) List, as well as major emerging markets constituting the driving force of today's global economy. To complicate matters more (and potentially impede institutionalisation of regional economic cooperation), countries of the Indo-Pacific are characterised by highly differentiated development strategies and socio-economic systems varying from transitioning post-socialist countries through developmental states of East Asia and major free market capitalist economies (see Box 3.1 – Developmental State of East Asia).

On the other hand, however, there are also some similarities in the regional development patterns. Over the last four decades, the Indo-Pacific has undergone a remarkable transformation with reference to economic growth and development. As hundreds of millions of people climbed out of poverty, the region has become home to world-class companies and an important engine of global economic growth. According to the US narrative, this transformation was possible due to a "free and open regional order" (FOIP: 5). Since the 1980s both in the area of the Pacific and Indian Oceans most countries have undergone reforms encompassing liberalisation and opening of their economies that enabled their gradual integration into global economic structures, inclusive global supply chains. Even though the pace and scope of economic liberalisation might have differed, the transition boosted economic growth rates in the region and its development. Nonetheless, economic opening came with a price in the form of contagion and greater propensity to economic crises, as evidenced during the 1997–1998 East Asian crisis and a decade later in the time of the 2007–2009 Global Financial Crisis (GFC).

Yet in spite of impressive growth numbers, numerous challenges typical for the representatives of the Global South remain across the Indo-Pacific. These include poverty, growing levels of inequality (gender and income inequality above all) and severe economic vulnerabilities linked with environmental threats. More recently, the COVID-19 pandemic has exposed new development issues such as supply chain crisis or vaccine inequality, by simultaneously deepening existing problems such as high levels of sovereign debt or financial instability. An overview of selected problems is presented later in the chapter.

As stated before, the Indo-Pacific as a region combines countries at all levels of development. This fact to a degree affects potential cooperation and economic integration. Table 3.1 presents the diversification of the region in terms of GNI per capita

Table 3.1 Indo-Pacific economies: GNI per capita and corresponding income groups, 2021

Country	GNI per capita (2020. Current USD)	Income group (2021)	Status
Australia	53680	high income	developed
Bangladesh	2030	lower middle income	LDC
Bhutan	2840	lower middle income	LDC
Brunei Darussalam	31510	high income	developed
Cambodia	1500	lower middle income	LDC
Fiji	4890	upper middle income	developing
India	1920	lower middle income	developing
Indonesia	3870	lower middle income	developing
Japan	42330 (2019)	high income	developed
Lao PDR	2520	lower middle income	LDC
Malaysia	10570	upper middle income	developing
Maldives	6490	upper middle income	developing
Myanmar	1350	lower middle income	LDC
Nepal	1190	lower middle income	LDC
New Zealand	42870 (2019)	high income	developed
Papua New Guinea	2720	lower middle income	developing
Pakistan	1270	lower middle income	developing
Philippines	3430	lower middle income	developing
Korea. Rep.	32930	high income	developed
Singapore	54920	high income	developed
Sri Lanka	3720	lower middle income	developing
Taiwan	27844 (2019)	high income	developed
Thailand	7040	upper middle income	developing
Timor-Leste	1990	lower middle income	LDC
United States	64140	high income	developed
Vietnam	2650	lower middle income	developing

Source: World Development Indicators 2022.

and corresponding income groups for the Indo-Pacific countries. It is worth noting that according to the World Bank country classification by income groups the vast majority of the representatives of the region can be listed as developing countries. Only eight countries in the region are usually considered developed as reflected by their high-income status. Even though there is no Indo-Pacific country that would fall into the low-income category (unless the geographical coverage is extended to include all South Asian countries), there are seven countries listed as the LDCs. This status indicates major developmental drawbacks, including relatively low income and high levels of economic vulnerability, in addition to comparably weak human assets as measured by the Human Assets Index (HAI).[4]

In 2020 the range of income per capita in the region varied from the level barely reaching the World Bank's middle-income criteria (1190 USD – Nepal) to almost 65000 USD in the United States. Such an income variation confirms deep intra-regional inequalities, and – even though the average income per capita for 26 Indo-Pacific countries in this analysis is close to 16000 USD – the income differentiation brings about deep social and economic problems. The divergence in the region is further confirmed when looking at the values of the Human Development Index (HDI) for the Indo-Pacific (Table 3.2). Although there are countries whose HDI levels position them in the highest human development group (very high human development), the majority of the sample falls into medium and high human development categories. It seems somehow reassuring that

Table 3.2 Human development in the Indo-Pacific, 2020

Country	HDI (2019)	Category of human development
Australia	0.944	very high
Bangladesh	0.632	medium
Bhutan	0.654	medium
Brunei Darussalam	0.838	very high
Cambodia	0.594	medium
Fiji	0.743	high
India	0.645	medium
Indonesia	0.718	high
Japan	0.919	very high
Lao PDR	0.613	medium
Malaysia	0.81	very high
Maldives	0.74	high
Myanmar	0.583	medium
Nepal	0.602	medium
New Zealand	0.931	very high
Papua New Guinea	0.555	medium
Pakistan	0.557	medium
Philippines	0.718	high
Korea, Rep.	0.916	very high
Singapore	0.938	very high
Sri Lanka	0.782	high
Thailand	0.777	high
Timor-Leste	0.606	medium
United States	0.926	very high
Vietnam	0.704	high
Taiwan	0.916	very high

Source: United Nations Development Programme 2020.

analogically to the World Bank classification there is no Indo-Pacific country in the low human development category. Yet given that HDI is an aggregate index incorporating indicators of a long and healthy life, quality of education and the level of wealth, values of individual indicators may vary and often fall below the regional average. This is the case mostly for the Indian Ocean countries majority of whom are at the medium human development level with Myanmar and Nepal achieving the lowest scores.

Despite intra-regional development discrepancies, high rates of economic growth have been a quintessential feature of most of the Indo-Pacific region for the last few decades. If this trend continues, in addition to the United States (and of course China), India, Indonesia, Japan and South Korea should be among the ten biggest economies in the world by 2030. It is worth noting that not even the East Asian financial crisis, the GFC or the current COVID-19 pandemic have prevented Indo-Pacific economies from registering high rates of economic growth. Whereas developed economies such as Japan, South Korea and Taiwan have seen their growth decline in recent years, emerging and developing countries such as India, Indonesia, Malaysia, Philippines, Thailand and Vietnam appear as major drivers of growth in the region. Here, it is also worth stressing the impressive development of China that allowed the country to claim economic leadership in Asia and move at least 400 million of its citizens out of extreme poverty.

Table 3.3 presents the latest economic growth rates for the region. As the growth rates for most economies of the region were positive in 2019, the data for 2020 shows

Table 3.3 Economic growth in the Indo-Pacific, 2019–2020

Country	GDP growth (annual %. 2019)	GDP growth (annual %. 2020)
Australia	2.1	0.0
Bangladesh	8.2	3.5
Bhutan	5.8	−10.1
Brunei Darussalam	3.9	1.1
Cambodia	7.1	−3.1
China	5.9	2.3
Fiji	−0.4	−15.7
India	4.0	−7.3
Indonesia	5.0	−2.1
Japan	0.3	−4.6
Lao PDR	5.5	0.5
Malaysia	4.4	−5.6
Maldives	6.9	−33.5
Myanmar	6.8	3.2
Nepal	6.7	−2.1
New Zealand	1.6	1.9
Papua New Guinea	4.5	−3.5
Pakistan	1.1	−0.9
Philippines	6.1	−9.6
Korea, Rep.	2.2	−0.9
Singapore	1.3	−5.4
Sri Lanka	2.3	−3.6
Thailand	2.3	−6.1
Timor-Leste	19.5	10.4
United States	2.2	−3.4
Vietnam	7.0	2.9

Source: World Development Indicators 2022.

a sharp drop in growth rates, with the average value for the region being negative at −3.5%. The COVID-19-induced economic crisis seems to have hit developing countries of the region the hardest, with the LDCs being most vulnerable. The World Bank estimates for 2021 and 2022 indicate that the economic contraction was temporary, and most Indo-Pacific economies are about to bounce back to a positive trend. The problem however constitutes the fact that the economic recovery in the area is uneven and unequal, with only advanced economies and emerging markets regaining high economic growth rates. Yet even those countries have experienced negative consequences of the crisis in form of the rising inflation and income inequalities.

Box 3.1 Developmental state of East Asia

Over the last three decades, the debate within development studies has shifted from the question of whether the state is an important element in the development process to the question of what type of state is the most fitting one for supporting economic development. The answer to this question might constitute the concept of a developmental state, a strategy that helped achieve the current high level of development by many Indo-Pacific countries.

The concept of the developmental state emerged to explain the rapid growth of a number of countries in East Asia in the postwar period. Following the Japanese growth miracle, by the mid-1970s, South Korea, Hong Kong, Singapore and Taiwan were experiencing double-digit growth rates. The governments of these countries directed the economy and deliberately disrupted the market mechanism in favour of economic planning. State intervention was not limited to the macro level, but also included measures aimed at individual private enterprises. The successes of these countries, which in a short period of time transformed from relatively weakly developed traditional economies into the most innovative and prosperous areas of the world, directed the interest of researchers towards their state-led development strategies.

A developmental state can be defined as a state defining economic development as its primary goal and ensuring the implementation of this goal through the use of appropriate tools. Chalmers Johnson, in presenting a pioneering study of Japan, identified the developmental state as one that gives priority to economic growth, productivity and technological competitiveness. It is a state conducting an active economic policy aimed at accelerating economic development. What is important here is the combination of economic planning and private ownership. Hence alternative terms often used are developmental or planned capitalism. A developmental state strives for macroeconomic stability and creates effective structures of public administration and judiciary ensuring respect for property rights and efficient conflict resolution. It combines a specific mix of industrial and trade policies based on the interplay of import substitution and export orientation. At the same time, such a state makes infrastructure investments and supports the development of human capital. Moreover, it creates an alliance between politics and the economy, which materialised in the establishment of a specialised bureaucratic apparatus that had ample powers and coordinated developmental efforts. The implementation of this concept seems to be most conducive to the accumulation of wealth, acceleration of economic growth and transformation of social structures in developing countries. As such, a developmental state is not so much a specific economic system as a tool for achieving the goal of catching up with developed economies.

Even if Japan's and East Asian Tigers' development strategies seem barely replicable under the current settings, some of their elements, inclusive industrial upgrading and infrastructural investment can be recognised in the developmental policies of China and numerous Indo-Pacific economies, along with India. As such, state-led development appears to remain a significant feature of Indo-Pacific development.

Suggested readings:

- M. Beeson, Developmental States in East Asia: A Comparison of the Japanese and Chinese Experiences, "Asian Perspective," 33(2), 2009: 5-39.
- Kholi, State-Led Development. Political Power and Industrialization in the Global Periphery, Cambridge University Press, Cambridge 2004
- Y. Chu (ed.), The Asian Developmental State. Reexaminations and New Departures, Palgrave Macmillan 2016.
- Ch. Johnson, Japan: Who Governs?: The Rise of the Developmental State, W.W. Norton & Company 1996.
- M. Woo-Cumings (ed.), The Developmental State, Cornell University Press 1999.

Selected development issues and challenges in the Indo-Pacific

Relatively lower levels of human development and disparities in economic growth rates in the Indo-Pacific reflect major developmental problems of the region. Though the rapid economic growth and spectacular poverty-alleviation successes in individual Indo-Pacific countries over the last four decades are well known, large variation in poverty rates persists both within and across countries. Moreover, yet again major progress was made in the Pacific area, East Asia to be precise, with South Asia lagging behind. The current problems in the region include a full spectre of development issues, most of which were aggravated in the last two years. These include social problems such as poverty, hunger, and growing income and multidimensional social inequality. Economic issues in the region comprise problems caused by high sovereign debt levels, expansion of the informal sector, numerous supply-chain-related risks as well as deficits in financial stability. Moreover, most Indo-Pacific countries are falling behind the goals and targets set by the 2030 Development Agenda.

Poverty and inequality

One of the major challenges for developing countries of the Indo-Pacific constitute high levels of extreme poverty. Even though most World Bank and UN reports focus on Asia-Pacific, a look at the data allows some conclusions about the Indo-Pacific to be drawn. In 2017, a little above 200 million people, or about 5% of developing Asia's population, lived in extreme poverty – on less than 1.90 USD per day. Before the pandemic, that number was estimated to decline to about 2.6% in 2020. Yet an estimated 75 to 80 million more people in Asia and the Pacific were pushed into extreme poverty because of disruptions in economic activity caused by the COVID-19 pandemic (Jerving 2021). Even with the regional data coverage being incomplete, Table 3.4 provides an insight into the situation in individual Indo-Pacific countries. On the positive side, a look at non-income indicators of poverty and well-being, such as access to electricity and drinking water shows that the situation in the region is in most cases not as bad as income levels might suggest.

Looking at poverty indicators, it is apparent that South Asia is home to a significant share of the global poor with four out of five extreme poor in the South Asia region residing in India. According to the Poverty and Shared Prosperity Report (2020), the number of extremely poor in South Asia dropped to 216 million people in 2015, compared to half a billion in 1990, and this number was expected to be further reduced below 200 million people by the end of 2020. In spite of a relatively lower poverty rate of around 13.5%, India's large population of 1.3 billion results in a high absolute number of poor (175.7 million poor people). Next, Bangladesh has made remarkable

Table 3.4 Poverty and inequality in the Indo-Pacific, 2019–2020

Country	Poverty headcount ratio at $1.90 a day (2011 PPP) (% of population. 2015	Gini index. 2019	People using at least basic drinking water services (% of population. 2020)	Access to electricity (% of population. 2020)
Australia	–	–	100.0	100.0
Bangladesh	–	–	97.7	96.2
Bhutan	–	–	97.3	100.0
Brunei Darussalam	–	–	99.9	100.0
Cambodia	–	–	71.2	86.4
Fiji	–	30.7	94.3	100.0
India	–	–	90.5	99.0
Indonesia	5.8	37	92.4	96.9
Japan	–	–	99.1	100.0
Lao PDR	–	–	85.2	100.0
Malaysia	0	41.1 (2015)	97.1	100.0
Maldives	–	29.3	99.5	100.0
Myanmar	4.8	38.1 (2015)	83.7	70.4
Nepal	–	–	90.1	89.9
New Zealand	–	–	100.0	100.0
Papua New Guinea	–	–	45.3	60.4
Pakistan	3.8	31.3 (2015)	90.1	75.4
Philippines	6.1	44.6 (2015)	94.1	96.8
Korea, Rep.	–	–	99.9	100.0
Singapore	–	–	100.0	100.0
Sri Lanka	–	–	92.2	100.0
Thailand	0	34.9	100.0	100.0
Timor-Leste	–	–	85.5	96.1
United States	1.2	41.5	99.9	100.0
Vietnam	–	–	96.9	100.0

Source: World Development Indicators 2022.

progress in reducing poverty, but its large population still maintained it in second place within the region in terms of an absolute number of poor (24.4 million extreme poor). The third place is Pakistan, which has a larger population than Bangladesh, but a smaller number of extremely poor (almost ten million extremely poor). Bhutan and Sri Lanka are considered development success stories where extreme poverty has become rare, although a large share of the population subsists on slightly more than the extreme poverty line. Out of all Indo-Pacific Indian Ocean economies, only in the Maldives, extreme poverty is nearly nonexistent.

Inequality remains a persistent human rights challenge and a critical barrier to economic development in the Indo-Pacific. And for a combination of cultural, political, social and structural reasons, women are the group hit the hardest. Gender inequality in the Indo-Pacific is visible both in health and educational sectors (Wong 2018). The region is also affected by high income inequality, with Gini coefficients for numerous countries in the region exceeding 40. Even though these numbers are far from the world's highest levels of income inequality recorded in South Africa and its neighbouring countries, income inequalities in the Indo-Pacific are on the rise. Together with the rising poverty levels, unemployment and lack of progress in eradicating of gender inequality, this factor might contribute to broader social tensions in the region.

High levels of poverty are closely followed by hunger and malnutrition. In the Indo-Pacific this is yet again the Indian Ocean area that faces major challenges. Out of all Indo-Pacific countries, in 2021 only the South Asian ones had the Global Hunger Index (GHI) scores indicating serious levels of hunger (2021). Simultaneously, South Asia also has the highest rate (around 15%) of undernourishment and the highest number of hungry in Asia. Looking at the broader area of Asia-Pacific, an estimated 375 million people in the region faced hunger in 2020, which is over 50 million more people than in 2019. Food security is a persistent problem facing millions of people across the region. Much progress has been made to reduce the number of undernourished people, but the region is still home to over 60% of the undernourished people in the world (UNESCAP 2017: x; UNESCAP 2018).

Selected economic tendencies

As the Indo-Pacific has developed close ties with global economies, major global developments are adversely affecting the economic conditions of the region. The COVID-19 pandemic, the war in Ukraine, a structural slowdown in China and fiscal tightening in the United States are currently having a negative impact on Indo-Pacific economies. According to the World Bank's predictions, the region's struggling firms, more than 50% of which reported payment arrears in 2021, will be hit by new supply and demand shocks. Households, some of whom fell back into poverty during the pandemic, will see real incomes shrink further as prices rise. And with debt as a share of GDP increasing by double digits since 2019, some governments may struggle to provide economic support for their citizens (World Bank 2022). Yet a closer look at economic trends for the region reveals that the general outlook might not be as negative.

Table 3.5 presents selected economic indicators for the Indo-Pacific in 2019 and 2020: the year preceding the pandemic and the first year of the COVID-19 crisis. Contrary to the situation in most European economies, the rise in inflation appears somewhat lower than expected. According to JP Morgan analysts, zero-Covid policies and rapid initial lockdowns have allowed the region to avoid even greater economic

Table 3.5 Selected economic indicators for the Indo-Pacific, 2019–2020

Country	Inflation. Consumer prices (annual %. 2019)	Inflation. Consumer prices (annual %. 2020)	External debt stocks (% of GNI. 2019)	External debt stocks (% of GNI. 2020)	Total reserves (% of total external debt. 2019)	Total reserves (% of total external debt. 2020)	Foreign direct investment. Net inflows (% of GDP. 2019)	Foreign direct investment. net inflows (% of GDP. 2020)
Australia	1.61	0.85	–	–	–	–	2.81	1.48
Bangladesh	5.59	5.69	18.06	19.99	57.27	63.72	0.63	0.35
Bhutan	2.73	5.63	17.25	132.05	45.80	52.64	0.51	-0.12
Brunei Darussalam	-0.39	1.94	–	–	–	–	2.77	4.71
Cambodia	1.94	2.94	60.06	70.82	122.45	121.45	13.52	14.04
China	2.90	2.42	14.85	16.07	152.44	142.90	1.31	1.44
Fiji	1.77	-2.60	25.64	35.68	77.62	–	5.86	5.28
India	3.72	6.62	19.73	21.41	82.63	104.62	1.76	2.42
Indonesia	3.03	1.92	37.06	40.54	32.13	32.55	2.23	1.81
Japan	0.47	-0.02	–	–	–	–	0.78	1.24
Lao PDR	3.32	5.10	93.96	94.78	6.65	8.11	4.00	5.06
Malaysia	0.66	-1.14	–	–	–	–	2.51	1.28
Maldives	0.22	-1.37	53.07	96.91	28.12	29.39	17.14	11.78
Myanmar	8.83	–	16.75	17.18	52.38	57.46	2.53	2.30
Nepal	5.57	5.05	18.86	23.21	133.77	145.07	0.54	0.38
New Zealand	1.62	1.71	–	–	–	–	1.37	1.93
Papua New Guinea	3.93	4.87	79.37	73.66	12.48	–	-3.64	-3.79
Pakistan	10.58	9.74	39.46	45.31	15.37	15.90	0.80	0.80
Philippines	2.48	2.64	20.17	25.30	107.05	111.69	2.30	1.82
Korea, Rep.	0.38	0.54	–	–	–	–	0.58	0.56
Singapore	0.57	-0.18	–	–	–	–	32.17	25.72
Sri Lanka	3.53	6.15	68.73	71.78	13.63	10.05	0.89	0.54
Thailand	0.71	-0.85	34.22	41.89	124.80	126.43	0.88	-0.97
Timor-Leste	0.96	–	7.45	9.73	322.62	283.23	3.64	3.81
United States	1.81	1.23	–	–	–	–	1.41	1.01
Vietnam	2.80	3.22	47.87	48.93	66.76	75.84	6.15	5.83

Source: World Development Indicators 2022.

disruption. Simultaneously, consumption patterns have remained broadly unchanged, mitigating the impact of higher prices for consumer durables. Another positive factor constituted the export orientation of the region (Shevlin & Lam 2021). Yet the initial World Bank estimates for 2021 and 2022 indicate that this tendency has little chance to hold, and central banks in the Indo-Pacific will be faced with monetary policy challenges caused by inflationary pressure.

Already the first year of the pandemic revealed that in order to tackle the crisis governments need to increase spending on healthcare. Together with costly efforts to avoid deepening recession, it led to increases in the sovereign debt in the region. Debt indicators vary across the Indo-Pacific (Table 3.5), but the increase in debt to GNI ratio in just one year indicates an increased risk for sovereign defaults in the area in the years to come. One factor that could possibly partially offset the risk is the relatively high level of foreign exchange reserves in the region. After the 1997–1998 Asian financial crisis, most countries in the region started building up their reserve holdings. Yet again export-oriented development policies were a conducive factor in building up the resilience of the region's economies.

Another positive development in the region constitutes the inflow of foreign direct investment (FDI). After the liberalisation of investment policies, introduction of investment incentives and lowering or removal of capital controls, the FDI inflow to most Indo-Pacific countries has been on the gradual rise since the 1990s. As FDI can play a vital role in development, especially in the context of the transfer of capital from developed countries to developing countries, most developing countries in the region have been continuously improving their policy framework for attracting investment. The pandemic-induced drop in FDI in the area (Table 3.5) seems to be only temporary. In the case of FDI, it is worth noting that this is the sphere where the Indian Ocean subregion has been catching up quickly. In 2020, according to UNCTAD's World Investment Report (2021), there has been an increase in FDI inflow of 20% to 71 billion US dollars in South Asia and the rapid rise has seen mainly in India by 27% to 64 billion US dollars.

(Un)sustainability of Indo-Pacific development

No matter whether considering Asia-Pacific or Indo-Pacific, as of mid-2022, the area is prevailingly off-track to reach the majority of the Sustainable Development Goals (SDGs) by 2030 (Calleja et al. 2021: 4–5). According to the Economic and Social Survey of the United Nations Economic and Social Commission for Asia and the Pacific (2019): "developing countries in Asia and the Pacific would need USD 1.5 trillion annually to end extreme poverty and ambitiously move toward universal health coverage, quality education and infrastructure while staying on track to limit climate change."

Over the recent decades developed countries of the Indo-Pacific – such as Japan, South Korea and Taiwan – have been shifting their thinking away from economic growth at all costs and towards sustainable development – or growth. This line of thought seems to be gaining momentum as a result of the COVID-19 pandemic. Simultaneously, developing countries of the Indo-Pacific are counted among the strongest advocates of sustainable development principles among emerging and developing countries worldwide. Many governments across the region have undertaken substantial efforts to achieve SDGs such as no poverty, zero hunger, good health and well-being, or quality education (Sustainable Development Report 2022).

Yet, as noted in the earlier section of this chapter, the Indo-Pacific region lags in areas such as gender equality or – in some cases – poverty eradication. Further problematic areas include sustainable cities and communities. This is a direct consequence of the Indo-Pacific being home to around 60% of the global population and 20 of the world's 33 megacities. As such, it is also the source of more than half of all global carbon emissions. This positions the Indo-Pacific in the very centre of global efforts to tackle the climate crisis. At the same time, it appears that in spite of numerous strategies focused on the implementation of sustainable development in the region, the situation is barely improving and even those countries that make major progress towards achieving the SDGs do not seem capable of doing it. An example of such a country constitutes India – simultaneously the regional leader in SDGs' implementation, as well as one of the world's biggest emitter of carbon dioxide (see Box 3.2 – Sustainable development in India).

Moreover, the Indo-Pacific as well as the broader area of Asia-Pacific are considered the most disaster-prone region in the world. In the last decade, over 1500 natural disasters were reported in the area, which affected 1.4 billion people. The most frequent disasters are floods and storms, while earthquakes and tsunamis are the deadliest. The growing severity of storms, floods and rising waters due to climate change is an additional factor that is contributing to potential major debt crises in the Indo-Pacific, and it can be expected that this trend will continue (Fletcher & Yeophantong 2019: 6).

Moreover, climate change brings numerous transboundary and multisectoral risks, exacerbating the existing risks posed by natural disasters. It affects agriculture, livelihoods and infrastructure. While the Indo-Pacific's large population fuels high energy demand and makes significant contributions to the global carbon budget, most Indo-Pacific countries are already grappling with the adverse effects of climate change. The Indo-Pacific is the most highly represented region within the Global Climate Risk Index, with a cluster of high vulnerability appearing yet again around the Indian Ocean (Calleja et al. 2021: 4–5).

With climate change constituting a substantial problem for the region, an increasing number of countries are rethinking their economic growth models and shifting towards green economy models. Japan, South Korea and the United States were among the Indo-Pacific countries that first announced green growth plans, based on the principle of sustainability. Yet, the focus on the green economy continues to be secondary to economic growth per se for the least developed countries in the region. For these countries, their objective continues to be to lift their citizens out of extreme poverty and eliminate hunger. Given that, it seems that economic growth will continue to be a bigger priority than green growth for most Indo-Pacific developing economies. And similarly, to the case of green growth, many countries across the Indo-Pacific are likely to continue to prioritise "traditional" economic growth policies over sustainable development.

Table 3.6 shows the progress towards achieving the SDGs measured by the SDG Index Rank and Score. The overall SDG Index score measures the total progress towards achieving all 17 SDGs. The score can be interpreted as a percentage of SDG achievement. A score of 100 indicates that all SDGs have been achieved. Yet again the split between the Pacific and Indian Ocean subregions is visible with many countries of the region ranked in the second hundred. An interesting case constitutes the "Spillover Score." As each country's actions can have positive or negative effects on other countries' abilities to achieve the SDGs, the Spillover Index assesses such spillovers along three dimensions: environmental

Table 3.6 Progress towards achieving the Sustainable Development Goals (SDGs)

Country	SDG Index Rank	SDG Index Score	Spillover Score
Australia	38	75.6	64.9
Bangladesh	104	64.2	97.9
Bhutan	70	70.5	93.4
Brunei Darussalam	93	67.1	67.3
Cambodia	107	63.8	97.6
Fiji	52	72.9	95.8
India	121	60.3	99.3
Indonesia	82	69.2	97.6
Japan	19	79.6	67.3
Lao PDR	111	63.4	90.2
Malaysia	72	70.4	79.2
Maldives	67	71	94.8
Myanmar	103	64.3	99.2
Nepal	98	66.2	98.5
New Zealand	26	78.3	67.2
Papua New Guinea	144	53.6	97.8
Pakistan	125	59.3	99.4
Philippines	95	66.6	97.2
Korea, Rep.	27	77.9	74.2
Singapore	60	71.7	33
Sri Lanka	76	70	93.7
Thailand	44	74.1	86.7
Timor-Leste	...	...	...
United States	41	74.5	64.4
Vietnam	55	72.8	95.3

Source: United Nations. Sustainable Development Report 2022.

and social impacts embodied into trade, economy and finance, and security. A higher score means that a country causes more positive and fewer negative spillover effects. The least developed countries of the Indo-Pacific appear to have the highest scores in this category. Paradoxically, these values often reflect a rather negative trend to neglect sustainable development as well as the low-level economic integration with the global economy of the countries in question (UN SDG Report).

Box 3.2 Sustainable development in India

India is a country of diversity and contradictions, also in the sphere of sustainable development. It is one of the fastest-growing economies in the world and one of the leaders in achieving the goals of the Agenda 2030. At the same time, this fifth-largest world economy in terms of GDP is characterised by the largest number of people living below the international poverty line (1.9 USD per day). India's per capita greenhouse gas emission rates may be among the lowest in the world, but India ranks third in the world in total greenhouse gas emissions, and three of the world's most polluted cities are in India. Moreover, individual Indian states vary in terms of development level, with the northern states being the least developed ones.

Simultaneously, the idea of sustainability constitutes an integral part of Indian culture, whose philosophy and values emphasise a sustainable way of life. The need for conservation and sustainable use of natural resources has been expressed in Hindu scriptures dating back as far as over three thousand years ago. *Vasudhaiva Kutumbakam*, an ancient Sanskrit maxim meaning "the world is one family," seems to summarise the Indian approach to socio-economic development.

However, despite its rich tradition and culturally ingrained respect for the natural environment, India has only relatively recently taken up the fight against increasing air and water pollution, land and forest degradation, and loss of biodiversity. After independence in 1947, the main objective of successive Indian governments has been to modernise the economy. Despite the presence of the idea of sustainable development in the teachings of Mahatma Gandhi, a more pragmatic approach to development, largely based on state-led industrialisation, prevailed.

Between 1951 and 2014, India's Planning Commission was responsible for preparing five-year plans that set goals for the Indian economy. Elements of the concept of sustainable development appeared in these plans gradually. The last plan – the twelfth – covered the period 2012–2017 and identified as priorities for India, among others, the elimination of poverty and social inequality, the fight against social exclusion or improving the availability of drinking water. In 2014, the Planning Commission was replaced by the government think tank NITI Aayog, which was given the task of coordinating the implementation of the SDGs in India through its development strategies. The first program prepared by NITI Aayog covered the period 2017–2020. In December 2018, NITI Aayog released the medium-term action plan Strategy for New India @75. Based on this document, a new long-term strategy for India's development will be prepared, which is scheduled to be announced in August 2022, the 75th anniversary of India's independence.

Yet despite the regular progress recorded by India in the various dimensions of sustainable development, much remains to be done. India's most significant problems include environmental degradation and persistently high poverty rates. According to the World Bank, nearly 30% of the population was below the poverty line, which translates into nearly 370 million people living in poverty. In the Human Development Report (HDR) for 2021 published by UNDP, India was ranked 131st, positioning it as a country with a medium level of human development. Additionally, inadequate resources to achieve the SDGs remain a problem for India. Reports prepared by a number of Indian think tanks estimate the gap for 2015–2030 at around $2.64 trillion. For climate change prevention measures alone, India needs about $170 billion more annually.

Suggetsed readings

- B.N. Patel, R. Nagar (eds.), Sustainable Development and India: Convergence of Law, Economics, Science, and Politics, OUP India 2017.
- NITI Aayog's SDG's Progress Reports: https://www.niti.gov.in/reports-sdg (last accessed 10.06.2022).
- A. Mathur, M.K. Shrivastava, The Pursuit of Sustainable Development in India, in: R.K. Pachauri et al. (ed.), Building the future we want, AFD, IDDRI & TERI, New Delhi, 2015.

- P. Sharma, A. Chaturvedi, The performance of India in the achievement of sustainable development Goals: A way forward, International Journal of Modern Agriculture, 9(4), 2020.
- P. Mohandas, Sustainable Development Goals (SDGs) – Challenges for India, Indian Journal of Public Health Research and Development, 9(3):1, January 2018.

Geoeconomics of Indo-Pacific development cooperation

Cooperation and regional economic integration of Indo-Pacific countries have been often quoted as a potential remedy to alleviate the region's development challenges and counteract potential Chinese domination in the region. In recent decades, the political economy of Indo-Pacific economic cooperation seems to have been dominated by the tendency towards deeper integration with major areas of cooperation including trade, infrastructure and sustainable development. Although both state-led and market-let regional economic cooperation have some tradition in the region, it can be said that economic cooperation and integration in the Indo-Pacific is driven mostly by development of regional trade and investment linkages. Trade agreements, investment treaties and political treaties only supported and to some extent accelerated market trends (Pardo 2021: 1–2; Bhaskar 2021; De 2020; Saeed 2017: 511).

While there is a high density of trade links within the Asia-Pacific and Indian Oceans, the connections spanning the two subregions are comparatively less developed (Wilson 2017: 4–5). The low density of economic ties joining the two halves of the Indo-Pacific has implications for institution-building and intergovernmental cooperation, also in the sphere of development cooperation. This is also reflected in the relatively underdeveloped institutional architecture for development and economic cooperation in the region (Wirth & Jenne 2022).

The first efforts to bring together the Indo-Pacific countries can be traced back to the aftermath of World War II when Japan together with the four East Asian tigers (Hong Kong, Singapore, South Korea and Taiwan) strengthened economic links among themselves and the United States. This cooperation was later extended when Indonesia, Malaysia, the Philippines and Thailand in the 1980s started joining regional manufacturing and investment networks. The development continued with the end of the Cold War, which brought the incorporation of post-communist Southeast Asian economies (Vietnam) into regional networks. This was also the time when Australia and New Zealand started strengthening trade and economic links in the region as well as offering more developed assistance targeted for the area. Simultaneously India's economic liberalisation and opening led to the development of trade and investment linkages between the Pacific and Indian Ocean economies (Pardo 2021: 2).

Yet the multilateral architecture for promoting development cooperation at the regional level in the Indo-Pacific is yet to be designed. The Asia-Pacific Economic Co-operation (APEC) is often perceived as the first regional multilateral framework for promoting economic development in the Indo-Pacific. Yet its focus is on the broader area of Asia-Pacific and mostly excludes India from its proceedings (Pulipaka & Musaddi 2021: 6). Much later, the East Asia Summit (EAS) became one the few multilateral fora incorporating India into an Asian multilateral structure, but the organisation has a very limited ability to promote economic cooperation and development. The Indian Ocean Rim Association (IORA) has a clear agenda on development cooperation, but – contrary to other institutions in the region – lacks connection with East Asia (Bhaskar 2021; Wilson 2017: 8).[5] A shift towards institutionalisation of development cooperation in the Indo-Pacific might constitute the US proposal for an "Indo-Pacific economic framework" (IPEF). The initiative appears to be not a single undertaking, like a trade agreement, but rather a broader platform for cooperation, but it is too early to predict its final shape (Goodman & Reinsch 2022).

An important factor in a region with prevailingly developing countries constitutes mechanisms of development financing. Development finance – both private resources as well as official development assistance (ODA) – contribute to poverty alleviation and help boost economic development of the region. With this in mind, it is worth noting that ODA flows are gradually becoming Indo-Pacific in character (Table 3.7). The region is home to four Organisation of Economic Cooperation and Development's (OECD) Development Assistance Committee (DAC) providers – Australia, Japan, Korea and New Zealand – each of which prioritises development cooperation with neighbouring countries to support regional stability. At the same time, other large

Table 3.7 Official development assistance (ODA) in the Indo-Pacific, 2019

Country	Net ODA received per capita (current USD. 2019)	Net ODA received (% of GNI. 2019)	Net ODA provided. total (% of GNI. 2015)
Australia	–	–	0.29
Bangladesh	27.49	1.42	–
Bhutan	237.73	7.87	–
Brunei Darussalam	–	–	–
Cambodia	59.69	3.86	–
Fiji	156.27	2.76	–
India	1.91	0.09	–
Indonesia	–2.33	–0.06	–
Japan	–	–	0.20
Lao PDR	88.08	3.55	–
Malaysia	0.19	0.00	–
Maldives	135.75	1.43	–
Myanmar	38.48	3.13	–
Nepal	47.56	3.94	–
New Zealand	–	–	0.27
Papua New Guinea	76.04	2.81	–
Pakistan	10.02	0.79	–
Philippines	8.37	0.22	–
Korea, Rep.	–	–	0.14
Singapore	–	–	–
Sri Lanka	9.05	0.24	–
Thailand	–4.86	–0.06	0.02
Timor-Leste	182.45	8.64	–
United States	–	–	0.17
Vietnam	11.35	0.45	–

Source: World Development Indicators 2022.

providers including the United States, France, Germany and the EU have pivoted towards the Indo-Pacific (Calleja et al. 2021: 1, 25–26).

Conclusion

This chapter has shown that the Indo-Pacific as an economic region is characterised by a high degree of diversity and complexity. It connects the most advanced and biggest economies in the world with a predominant number of developing countries, some of whom are classified as LDCs. A look into socio-economic indicators reveals that the region appears to be divided into two halves marked by the areas surrounded by the two Oceans. These subregions not only differ with regard to development levels, but they also lack substantial institutional ties as the intra-regional economic ties appear to be relatively weak. Moreover, it is uncertain whether the present institutional arrangements are adequate to meet development challenges in the Indo-Pacific and boost the economic prosperity of its representatives.

Yet despite numerous development challenges, both the Pacific and Indian Ocean subregions are amongst the most dynamic in the world and can be regarded as centres of economic growth. Yet the region representatives continue to experience geopolitical and geostrategic shifts. Following the ASEAN outlook on the Indo-Pacific:

> On the one hand, the economic growth of the region opens up possibilities of cooperation to alleviate poverty and elevate living standards of millions of people. On the other hand, the rise of material powers, i.e., economic and military, requires avoiding the deepening of mistrust, miscalculation, and patterns of behaviour based on a zero-sum game.
>
> (ASEAN 2021)

Notes

1 Statistical data on Taiwan is mostly missing from the World Bank and UN databases.
2 An alternative list provided by Calleja et al. (2021): Australia, Bangladesh, Brunei, Bhutan, Cambodia, China, Cook Islands, Democratic People's Republic of Korea, Fiji, India, Indonesia, Republic of Korea, Kiribati, Japan, Laos, Malaysia, Marshall Islands, Maldives, Micronesia, Nauru, Nepal, Niue, New Zealand, Palau, Pakistan, Papua New Guinea, Philippines, Singapore, Samoa, Solomon Islands, Sri Lanka, Tokelau, Thailand, Timor-Leste, Tonga, Tuvalu, Vanuatu, Myanmar, and Vietnam.
3 On trade and connectivity in the Indo-Pacific see chapters by A. Wróbel and G. Sachdeva in this handbook.
4 For more information on the LDC eligibility criteria: UNOHRLLS 2022.
5 The area of the Indo-Pacific is home to numerous institutions aimed at improving macroeconomic and financial surveillance, providing emergency liquidity support and protecting economies from excessive financial market and capital flow volatility. Examples include the ASEAN+3 Economic Review and Policy Dialogue, the Chiang Mai Initiative Multilateralization or the Eurasian Economic Community Anti-Crisis Fund (Jędrzejowska 2020: 103–118).

References

ASEAN, ASEAN Outlook on the Indo-Pacific, 2021, https://asean.org/asean2020/wp-content/uploads/2021/01/ASEAN-Outlook-on-the-Indo-Pacific_FINAL_22062019.pdf (Accessed 4 June 2022).

Beeson, M. Geoeconomics with Chinese Characteristics: The BRI and China's Evolving Grand Strategy. *Economic and Political Studies* 6, no. 2 (2018), pp. 1–17.

Bhaskar, N. India's Developing Economic Ties with the Indo-Pacific, 26 April 2021, https://www.orfonline.org/expert-speak/india-developing-economic-ties-indo-pacific/ (Accessed 4 June 2022).

Calleja, R., Hughes, S., Cichocka, B. *Two Birds, One Budget: Using ODA for Influence and Development in the Indo-Pacific?*, CGD Policy Paper 247, December 2021.

CeoWorld Magazin, Indo-Pacific Region, https://ceoworld.biz/indo-pacific/ (Accessed 4 June 2022).

Chen, D. The Indo-Pacific Strategy: A Background Analysis, 04 June 2018, ISPI, https://www.ispionline.it/it/pubblicazione/indo-pacific-strategy-background-analysis-20714 (Accessed 4 June 2022).

Das, U. What Is the Indo-Pacific?, *The Diplomat*, 13 July 2019, https://thediplomat.com/2019/07/what-is-the-indo-pacific/ (Accessed 4 June 2022).

De, P. Driving Indo-Pacific in an Uncertain World, *The Economic Times*, 06 September 2020, https://economictimes.indiatimes.com/blogs/et-commentary/navigating-indo-pacific-in-an-uncertain-world/ (Accessed 4 June 2022).

Feigenbaum, E.A. An Indo-Pacific Economic Framework, *Testimony before the U.S. House of Representatives Foreign Affairs Commmittee*, 01 March 2022, https://carnegieendowment.org/2022/03/01/indo-pacific-economic-framework-pub-86564 (Accessed 4 June 2022).

Fletcher, L., Yeophantong, P. *Enter the Dragon. Australia, China, and the New Pacific Development Agenda*, Australia Research Centre, Caritas Australia and the University of New South Wales, March 2019, joint report.

Galloway, A. What's the Indo-Pacific – and How Does the Quad Work?, *The Sydney Morning Herald*, 16 September 2021, https://www.smh.com.au/national/forget-asia-pacific-it-s-the-indo-pacific-we-live-in-now-where-is-that-exactly-20210810-p58hku.html (Accessed 4 June 2022).

Global Hunger Index, 2021, https://www.globalhungerindex.org/ (Accessed 4 June 2022).

Goodman, M.P., Reinsch, W. *Filling In the Indo-Pacific Economic Framework*, CSIS, January 2022.

Haruko, W. *The "Indo-Pacific" Concept. Geographical Adjustments and their Implications*, RSIS Working Paper, No. 326, 16 March 2020.

Heiduk, F., Wacker, G. *From Asia-Pacific to Indo-Pacific. Significance, Implementation and Challenges*, SWP Research Paper 9, July 2020, Berlin.

Jędrzejowska, K. From Global to Regional Financial Governance? The Case of Asia-Pacific, in M. Rewizorski, K. Jędrzejowska, A. Wróbel (Eds), *The Future of Global Economic Governance. Challenges and Prospects in the Age of Uncertainty*, Eastbourne: Springer, 2020, pp. 103–118.

Jerving, S. Extreme Poverty Rose by 80 Million in Asia and Pacific due to COVID-19, Devex, 30 August 2021, https://www.devex.com/news/extreme-poverty-rose-by-80-million-in-asia-and-pacific-due-to-covid-19-100672 (Accessed 4 June 2022).

Medcalf, R. Pivoting the Map: Australia's Indo-Pacific System, in *The Centre of Gravity Series 1*, Canberra: ANU Strategic and Defence Studies Centre, 2012.

Medcalf, R. The Indo-Pacific: What's in a Name, 2013, https://www.lowyinstitute.org/publications/indo-pacific-whats-name, https://www.the-american-interest.com/2013/10/10/the-indo-pacific-whats-in-a-name/ (Accessed 4 June 2022).

Medcalf, R. An Australian Vision Of The Indo-Pacific And What It Means For Southeast Asia, *Southeast Asian Affairs* (2019), pp. 53–60. https://www.jstor.org/journal/soutasiaaffa.

Pardo, R.P. Geo-Economic Megatrends in the Indo-Pacific: Integration or (partial) Decoupling?, CSDS Policy Brief, 17/2021, Special Edition.

Pascal, C. *Indo-Pacific Strategies, Perceptions and Partnerships. The View from Seven Countries*, Chatham House Research Paper, March 2021.

Pulipaka, S., Musaddi, M. In Defence of the 'Indo-Pacific' Concept, ORF Issue Brief, No. 493, September 2021, https://www.orfonline.org/research/in-defence-of-the-indo-pacific-concept/ (Accessed 4 June 2022).

Rahman, M.M., Kim, Ch., De, P. Indo-Pacific Cooperation: What do Trade Simulations Indicate?, *Journal of Economic Structures* 9, Article No. 45 (2020), pp. 1–17.

Saeed, M. From the Asia-Pacific to the Indo-Pacific Expanding Sino-U.S. Strategic Competition, *China Quarterly of International Strategic Studies* 3, no. 4 (2017), pp. 499–512.

Shevlin, A., Ram, C. Inflation in Asia Pacific – A Different Phenomenon, 02 Decemebr 2021, JP Morgan Asset Management, https://am.jpmorgan.com/sg/en/asset-management/liq/insights/liquidity-insights/updates/inflation-in-asia-pacific-a-different-phenomenon/ (Accessed 4 June 2022).

Sustainable Development Report, Country Profiles, 2022, https://dashboards.sdgindex.org/profiles (Accessed 4 June 2022).

The White House. Fact Sheet: Indo-Pacific Strategy of the United States, 11 February 2022, https://www.whitehouse.gov/briefing-room/speeches-remarks/2022/02/11/fact-sheet-indo-pacific-strategy-of-the-united-states/ (Accessed 4 June 2022).

The World Bank, The World Bank In East Asia Pacific, April 2022, https://www.worldbank.org/en/region/eap (Accessed 4 June 2022).

UNCTAD, World Investment Report, 2021, https://unctad.org/webflyer/world-investment-report-2021 (Accessed 4 June 2022).

UNESCAP, Enhancing Regional Economic Cooperation and Integration an Asia and the Pacific, United Nations, Bangkok, 2017.

UNESCAP, Key Social Development Challenges in the Asia-Pacific Region in the Context of the 2030 Agenda for Sustainable Development, Note by the Secretariat, Bangkok, 2018.

United Nations, Sustainable Development Report 2022, Country Profiles, https://dashboards.sdgindex.org/profiles (Accessed 4 June 2022).

United Nations Development Programme, Human Development Report 2020, https://hdr.undp.org/en/content/human-development-index-hdi (Accessed 4 June 2022).

UNOHRLLS, Least Developed Countries Category, 2022, https://www.un.org/ohrlls/content/ldc-category (Accessed 4 June 2022).

US Department of State, A Free and Open Indo-Pacific: Advancing a Shared Vision, 4 November 2019, https://www.state.gov/wp-content/uploads/2019/11/Free-and-Open-Indo-Pacific-4Nov2019.pdf (Accessed 30 November 2022).

Wilson, J.D. *Investing in the Economic Architecture of the Indo-Pacific*, Perth USAsia Centre, Indo-Pacific Insights Series, Vol. 8, August 2017.

Wirth, Ch., Jenne, N. Filling the Void: The Asia-Pacific Problem of Order and Emerging Indo-Pacific Regional Multilateralism, *Contemporary Security Policy*, 2022, DOI: 10.1080/13523260.2022.2036506, To link to this article: https://doi.org/10.1080/13523260.2022.2036506 (Accessed 4 June 2022).

Wong, P. Aid, Poverty, and Gender Inequality in the Indo-Pacific, 08 March 2018, https://www.lowyinstitute.org/the-interpreter/aid-poverty-and-gender-inequality-indo-pacific (Accessed 4 June 2022).

World Bank Group, Poverty and Shared Prosperity Report, 2020, https://www.worldbank.org/en/publication/poverty-and-shared-prosperity (Accessed 4 June 2022).

World Development Indicators, DataBank, 2022, https://databank.worldbank.org/source/world-development-indicators (Accessed 4 June 2022).

4 Trade regionalism in the Indo-Pacific

Anna Wróbel

Introduction

In addition to the quasi-global multilateral institution of the World Trade Organization (WTO), the architecture of the contemporary global trade governance system also includes preferential trade agreements (PTAs) created on the basis of Article XXIV of GATT (General Agreement on Tariffs and Trade) and Article V of GATS (General Agreement on Trade in Services).[1] The multilateralism (globalism)–regionalism relationship is evolving depending on the internal and external factors shaping countries' trade policies. In principle, regionalism can be seen as complementary or competitive to the GATT/WTO trading system. In the first case, regionalism is regarded as an endogenous element of the global system, complementing the commitments made in the WTO. In the second case, regionalism is seen as a competitive option to the non-discriminatory global system.

Analysing the trade policies of the major economies since the creation of the GATT system, it can be concluded that for many years multilateral negotiations were the most important platform for pursuing trade interests, with preferential agreements complementing the GATT-based strategy. A gradual change in this approach can be observed from the Uruguay Round onwards, when the North American Free Trade Agreement (NAFTA) was created following an impasse in negotiations in this forum. The signing of NAFTA can be seen as a competitive solution to the protracted GATT negotiations, providing the United States with access to important markets (Krugman 1991: 7–42). At the same time, NAFTA became an important instrument of pressure on the other participants in the GATT negotiations, showing that the United States could pursue its trade interests outside the multilateral system in an alternative way, which consequently facilitated breaking the deadlock in the GATT negotiations (Brown & Stern 2011; Lee 2011).

This time, due to the lack of progress in the Doha Round negotiations, the number of preferential trade agreements being negotiated by WTO members is increasing. Analyses of this phenomenon even speak of a proliferation of preferential trade agreements. Initially, the process of trade liberalisation within preferential trade agreements was relatively slow. It has been particularly intense since the mid-1990s. Throughout the GATT system (1948–1994), 124 different types of preferential trade arrangements were notified by the parties to the agreement (WTO 2011: 47). According to WTO data contained in the Regional Trade Agreements Database; the number of PTAs in force currently stands at 355 (25 May 2022). A particular intensification of WTO members' activities concerning the conclusion of PTAs has been observed since 2006, which was related to the suspension of the Doha Round negotiations in June that year. This time, however, PTAs have not become a factor

DOI: 10.4324/9781003336143-7

dynamising multilateral negotiations. On the contrary, the growing number of such agreements deepens the crisis of the WTO negotiations. In fact, PTAs are beginning to play the role of an alternative platform to the WTO for working out trade rules (Abbott 2007).

Preferential trade agreements are concluded by countries with different levels of economic development and are established in all regions of the world. They are created both by countries and by already existing integration groupings.

The aim of the chapter is to analyse trade regionalism[2] in the Indo-Pacific in order to identify changes in the characteristics of this process. The nature of cooperation within the framework of trade regionalism in the Indo-Pacific, the reasons and scope of this cooperation and the types of agreements defining it will be analysed. The main subject of consideration is intra-regional trade agreements concluded by the Indo-Pacific countries. The study was based on World Trade Organization data contained in the Regional Trade Agreements Database covering trade agreements notified by the WTO. The analysis covers intra-regional trade agreements concluded by the following countries: Australia, Bangladesh, Bhutan, Brunei Darussalam, Cambodia, Fiji, India, Indonesia, Japan, Lao PDR, Malaysia, Maldives, Myanmar, Nepal, New Zealand, Pakistan, Papua New Guinea, the Philippines, Republic of Korea, Singapore, Sri Lanka, Taiwan, Thailand, Timor-Leste, United States, Vietnam (Tables 4.1, 4.2).

The chapter draws on the author's previous research on discriminatory trade liberalisation and trade regionalism in the Asia-Pacific region (Wróbel 2016a, 2016b, 2019).

Characteristics of trade regionalism in the Indo-Pacific

One important side effect of the protracted negotiations in the WTO under the Doha Development Round (DDR) is the proliferation of bilateral trade agreements as an alternative global trade system. Many states, dissatisfied with the course of the DDR

Table 4.1 List of the Indo-Pacific countries considered in this chapter

Indo-Pacific countries	Australia, Bangladesh, Bhutan, Brunei Darussalam, Cambodia, Fiji, India, Indonesia, Japan, Lao PDR, Malaysia, Maldives, Myanmar, Nepal, New Zealand, Pakistan, Papua New Guinea, the Philippines, Republic of Korea, Singapore, Sri Lanka, Taiwan, Thailand, Timor-Leste, United States, Vietnam

Source: The author's own elaboration.

Table 4.2 Number of intra-regional preferential trade agreements in the Indo-Pacific (May 2022), by type

	Bilateral agreements	*Plurilateral agreements*	*Agreements in which at least one party is a preferential trade agreement (PTA)*
Intra-regional agreements	39	2	4
North–North agreements	14	0	0
North–South agreements	15	1	4
South–South agreements	10	1	0

Source: The author's own elaboration based on WTO Regional Trade Agreements Database.

negotiations and striving to deepen the multilateral liberalisation-related commitments adopted in the WTO, express the conviction that because of the limitation of the number of states participating in the negotiation process, greater progress in liberalisation of trade can be achieved under regional or bilateral negotiations. Another argument is that bilateral talks usually provoke much less interest and opposition from the objectors to free trade and various interest groups, which significantly shortens the period of negotiations and translates into a higher number of such agreements. Almost every member of the WTO is party to at least one PTA (Wróbel 2020).

By the end of May 2022, Indo-Pacific countries had notified 45 intra-regional preferential trade arrangements to the WTO. Given the significant number of intra-regional PTAs in the region, their analysis should take into account at least several criteria (Table 4.3). In the WTO World Trade Report 2011 on the role of preferential trade agreements, in order to characterise these structures, attention was paid to the geographical coverage, the level of economic development of the parties to the agreement, the type, the scope of the agreement and the degree of integration (WTO 2011: 54). Taking into account the criterion of geographical coverage, preferential trade agreements can be divided into intra- and inter-regional agreements. Due to the aim of the study, only intra-regional agreements concluded by Indo-Pacific countries will be analysed using the other criteria indicated in the WTO report (Table 4.4).

Due to the level of economic development of the parties to the agreement, PTAs are classified as North–North, South–South or North–South. Analysing the general trends regarding the process of proliferation of preferential trade agreements, it can be stated that in recent years the number of agreements concluded by developing countries has been steadily increasing in the world economy. This is evidenced by the change in the share of South–South agreements in the total number of preferential agreements. In the late 1970s, North–South agreements dominated, accounting for about 60% of PTAs, while the share of South–South agreements was only 20%. Today, this trend has been reversed. South–South agreements account for two-thirds of the total number of preferential trade agreements. In contrast, agreements between countries with different levels of economic development account for a quarter of all PTAs. The share of North–North agreements in the total number of PTAs has declined steadily since the 1960s and now stands at 10% (Wróbel 2013: 621). The Indo-Pacific region is not a good illustration of these trends. In the case of intra-regional PTAs, the countries there in force are also dominated by South–South agreements, largely due to the numerical advantage of these economies over the region's highly developed countries (UNCTAD 2008). North–South and North–North agreements prevail over South–South agreements due to the significant trade negotiating activity of developed countries in the region. In May 2022 North–South agreements accounted for more than 44% of intra-regional PTAs. The number of North–South PTAs is slightly lower: 31%. South–South relations accounted for over 24% of all intra-regional agreements in the Indo-Pacific (Table 4.5).

The WTO distinguishes between three types of preferential trade agreements: bilateral, plurilateral and those concluded by already existing PTAs. In particular, the intensive development of bilateral trade agreements can be observed in recent years. In the Indo-Pacific region alone, the number of intra-regional bilateral free trade agreements is 39. These agreements can be differentiated by the criterion of the level of economic development of the parties to the agreement used above. According to WTO data, 14 of these are North–North, 15 North–South and 10 South–South PTAs.

Table 4.3 Intra-regional preferential trade arrangements in the Indo-Pacific region

PTA Name	Coverage	Type	Notification	Date of entry into force	Signatories
ASEAN–Australia–New Zealand	Goods & Services	FTA & EIA	GATT Art. XXIV & GATS Art. V	1 January 2010	Australia; New Zealand; Brunei Darussalam; Myanmar; Cambodia; Indonesia; Lao People's Democratic Republic; Malaysia; the Philippines; Singapore; Vietnam; Thailand
Australia–New Zealand Closer Economic Relations Trade Agreement (ANZCERTA)	Goods & Services	FTA & EIA	GATT Art. XXIV & GATS Art. V	1 January 1983 (G) / 1 January 1989(S)	Australia; New Zealand
Australia–Papua New Guinea (PATCRA)	Goods	FTA	GATT Art. XXIV	1 February 1977	Australia; Papua New Guinea
Indonesia–Australia	Goods & Services	FTA & EIA	GATT Art. XXIV & GATS Art. V	5 July 2020	Australia; Indonesia
Japan–Australia	Goods & Services	FTA & EIA	GATT Art. XXIV & GATS Art. V	15 January 2015	Australia; Japan
Korea, Republic of–Australia	Goods & Services	FTA & EIA	GATT Art. XXIV & GATS Art. V	12 December 2014	Australia; Korea, Republic of
Malaysia–Australia	Goods & Services	FTA & EIA	GATT Art. XXIV & GATS Art. V	1 January 2013	Australia; Malaysia
Singapore–Australia	Goods & Services	FTA & EIA	GATT Art. XXIV & GATS Art. V	28 July 2003	Australia; Singapore
Thailand–Australia	Goods & Services	FTA & EIA	GATT Art. XXIV & GATS Art. V	1 January 2005	Australia; Thailand
United States–Australia	Goods & Services	FTA & EIA	GATT Art. XXIV & GATS Art. V	1 January 2005	Australia; United States of America
India–Bhutan	Goods	PSA	Enabling Clause	29 July 2006	Bhutan; India
South Asian Preferential Trade Arrangement (SAPTA)	Goods	PSA	Enabling Clause	7 December 1995	Bangladesh; Bhutan; Sri Lanka; India; Maldives; Nepal; Pakistan

Table 4.3 (Continued)

PTA Name	Coverage	Type	Notification	Date of entry into force	Signatories
ASEAN–India	Goods & Services	FTA & EIA	Enabling Clause & GATS Art. V	1 January 2010 (G) / 1 July 2015 (S)	India; Brunei Darussalam; Myanmar; Cambodia; Indonesia; Lao People's Democratic Republic; Malaysia; the Philippines; Singapore; Vietnam; Thailand
ASEAN–Japan	Goods	FTA	GATT Art. XXIV	1 December 2008	Japan; Brunei Darussalam; Myanmar; Cambodia; Indonesia; Lao People's Democratic Republic; Malaysia; the Philippines; Singapore; Vietnam; Thailand
ASEAN–Korea, Republic of	Goods & Services	FTA & EIA	GATT Art. XXIV, Enabling Clause & GATS Art. V	1 January 2010 (G) / 14 October 2010 (S)	Korea, Republic of; Brunei Darussalam; Myanmar; Cambodia; Indonesia; Lao People's Democratic Republic; Malaysia; the Philippines; Singapore; Vietnam; Thailand
ASEAN Free Trade Area (AFTA)	Goods	FTA	GATT Art. XXIV	17 May 2010	Brunei Darussalam; Myanmar; Cambodia; Indonesia; Lao People's Democratic Republic; Malaysia; the Philippines; Singapore; Vietnam; Thailand
Brunei Darussalam–Japan	Goods & Services	FTA & EIA	GATT Art. XXIV & GATS Art. V	31 July 2008	Brunei Darussalam; Japan
India–Japan	Goods & Services	FTA & EIA	GATT Art. XXIV & GATS Art. V	01-Aug-2011	India; Japan
India–Malaysia	Goods & Services	FTA & EIA	Enabling Clause & GATS Art. V	1 July 2011	India; Malaysia
India–Mauritius	Goods & Services	FTA & EIA	Enabling Clause & GATS Art. V	1 April 2021	India; Mauritius
India–Nepal	Goods	PSA	Enabling Clause	27 October 2009	India; Nepal

Agreement	Coverage	Type	Legal basis	Date	Members
India–Singapore	Goods & Services	FTA & EIA	GATT Art. XXIV & GATS Art. V	1 August 2005	India; Singapore
India–Sri Lanka	Goods	FTA	Enabling Clause	1 March 2000	Sri Lanka; India
India–Thailand	Goods	PSA	Enabling Clause	1 September 2004	India; Thailand
Korea, Republic of–India	Goods & Services	FTA & EIA	GATT Art. XXIV, Enabling Clause & GATS Art. V	1 January 2010	India; Korea, Republic of
Indonesia–Pakistan	Goods	PSA	Enabling Clause	1 September 2013	Indonesia; Pakistan
Japan–Indonesia	Goods & Services	FTA & EIA	GATT Art. XXIV & GATS Art. V	1 July 2008	Indonesia; Japan
Japan–Malaysia	Goods & Services	FTA & EIA	GATT Art. XXIV & GATS Art. V	13 July 2006	Japan; Malaysia
Japan–the Philippines	Goods & Services	FTA & EIA	GATT Art. XXIV & GATS Art. V	11 Dec 2008	Japan; the Philippines
Japan–Singapore	Goods & Services	FTA & EIA	GATT Art. XXIV & GATS Art. V	30 November 2002	Japan; Singapore
Japan–Thailand	Goods & Services	FTA & EIA	GATT Art. XXIV & GATS Art. V	1 November 2007	Japan; Thailand
Japan–Vietnam	Goods & Services	FTA & EIA	GATT Art. XXIV & GATS Art. V	1 October 2009	Japan; Vietnam
Lao People's Democratic Republic–Thailand	Goods	PSA	Enabling Clause	20 June 1991	Lao People's Democratic Republic; Thailand
New Zealand–Malaysia	Goods & Services	FTA & EIA	GATT Art. XXIV & GATS Art. V	1 August 2010	Malaysia; New Zealand
Pakistan–Malaysia	Goods & Services	FTA & EIA	Enabling Clause & GATS Art. V	1 January 2008	Malaysia; Pakistan
Korea, Republic of–New Zealand	Goods & Services	FTA & EIA	GATT Art. XXIV & GATS Art. V	20 December 2015	Korea, Republic of; New Zealand
New Zealand–Singapore	Goods & Services	FTA & EIA	GATT Art. XXIV & GATS Art. V	1 January 2001	New Zealand; Singapore
Thailand–New Zealand	Goods & Services	FTA & EIA	GATT Art. XXIV & GATS Art. V	1 July 2005	New Zealand; Thailand
Pakistan–Sri Lanka	Goods	FTA	Enabling Clause	12 June 2005	Sri Lanka; Pakistan

(Continued)

Table 4.3 (Continued)

PTA Name	Coverage	Type	Notification	Date of entry into force	Signatories
Korea, Republic of–Singapore	Goods & Services	FTA & EIA	GATT Art. XXIV & GATS Art. V	2 March 2006	Korea, Republic of; Singapore
Korea, Republic of–United States	Goods & Services	FTA & EIA	GATT Art. XXIV & GATS Art. V	15 March 2012	Korea, Republic of; United States of America
Korea, Republic of–Vietnam	Goods & Services	FTA & EIA	GATT Art. XXIV & GATS Art. V	20 December 2015	Korea, Republic of; Vietnam
United States–Singapore	Goods & Services	FTA & EIA	GATT Art. XXIV & GATS Art. V	1 January 2004	Singapore; United States of America
New Zealand–Chinese Taipei	Goods & Services	FTA & EIA	GATT Art. XXIV & GATS Art. V	1 December 2013	Chinese Taipei; New Zealand
Singapore–Chinese Taipei	Goods & Services	FTA & EIA	GATT Art. XXIV & GATS Art. V	19 April 2014	Chinese Taipei; Singapore

Source: The author's own elaboration based on WTO Regional Trade Agreements Database.

Table 4.4 Classification of preferential trade agreements

Classification criteria	Classification of PTAs
Geographical coverage	• intra-regional agreements; • inter-regional agreements (cross-regional).
Level of economic development of the parties to the agreement	• North–North agreements; • South–South agreements; • North–South agreements.
Type	• bilateral agreements; • plurilateral agreements; • agreements concluded by the already existing PTAs.
Degree of market integration	• FTA (free trade agreement); • EIA (economic integration agreement); • FTA & EIA; • PSA (partial scope agreement); • CU (customs union).
Substantive scope of the agreement	• goods; • goods and services; • services.

Source: The author's own elaboration based on WTO 2011.

Table 4.5 Number of intra-regional preferential trade agreements in the Indo-Pacific by parties' level of economic development in May 2022

Total intra-regional agreements	45
North–North agreements	14
North–South agreements	11
South–South agreements	20

Source: The author's own elaboration based on WTO Regional Trade Agreements Database.

Today, plurilateral relations are developing somewhat less intensively in the global economy compared to bilateral agreements. Such agreements usually cover countries located in the same region. The process of creating plurilateral trade links was particularly intensive within the framework of previous waves of regionalisation. In the course of these waves, integration agreements were formed, covering the economically most important regions of the world. At present, the countries forming these structures focus on strengthening economic cooperation within their frameworks rather than on creating new regional trade agreements, hence the aforementioned slowdown in the dynamics of development in the area of plurilateral preferential trade agreements. This general trend does apply to the Indo-Pacific region, where, in addition to intensive bilateralisation of trade relations, we have only two intra-regional plurilateral PTAs, namely South Asian Preferential Trade Arrangement (SAPTA) and ASEAN Free Trade Area (AFTA). As with bilateral agreements, these agreements can be differentiated according to the level of economic development of the parties. In this case, SAPTA is classified as a South–South agreement and AFAS as a North–South. In the Indo-Pacific region, as in other ones, what is emerging, in addition to bilateral and plurilateral agreements, are agreements concluded by existing PTAs with countries that are their important trading partners. The agreements negotiated by ASEAN with other economies in the region are an example of this type of relationship: ASEAN–Australia–New Zealand, ASEAN–India, ASEAN–Japan, ASEAN–Republic of Korea.

In addition to the level of economic development of the parties and type of agreement, the characteristics of PTAs should primarily take into account the degree of market integration and the substantive scope of the agreement. These two criteria allow the level of the economic integration process within the discussed structures to be assessed. The majority of preferential trade agreements in the world take the form of free trade agreements (FTAs), containing numerous exclusions concerning the preferential treatment of goods indicated in the agreements (Damuri 2009). There are also many agreements in which commitments characteristic of free trade areas are supplemented by disciplines to remove barriers to trade in services. Slightly less numerous are agreements that liberalise the parties' trade flows with respect to specific goods or product sectors (partial scope agreement, PSA). The share of customs unions in all PTAs is around 5%. Customs unions, deepened with commitments in the services sector, account for around 2% of all PTAs. The least numerous are agreements that only liberalise trade in services (WTO 2011: 62).

When analysing the substantial scope of the PTAs, it is important to stress that, especially since the 1990s, many of them have set ambitious liberalisation targets not only for trade in goods but also for trade in services. This is related to the progressive "servitisation" of national economies; the inclusion of the issue of services in the GATT Uruguay Round negotiations and the creation of a legal framework conducive to the abolition of protectionist barriers to trade in services in the form of the General Agreement on Trade in Services (GATS), and the desire of countries to deepen multilateral commitments in services adopted at the WTO, which seems to be easier to achieve in the PTAs due to a reduction in the number of countries participating in the negotiation process (Wróbel 2009). Today, almost one-third of PTAs worldwide contain commitments to liberalise trade in services (Adlung & Molinuevo 2008: 366). In addition to disciplines to reduce tariffs and liberalise trade in services, the substantive scope of preferential trade agreements increasingly includes investment, intellectual property protection, technical barriers and dispute settlement. Some PTAs, moreover, contain provisions on labour standards and environmental protection – as the scope of the agreements is extended beyond the tariff reduction of the constituent countries even when the agreement is referred to as a free trade area in its name. In relation to these agreements, the term economic integration agreements (EIA) is used in this study (Table 4.6).

Given that most intra-regional PTAs in the Indo-Pacific region were concluded after the GATT Uruguay Round, it is not surprising that the analysed agreements in most cases cover not only trade in goods but also other issues, especially trade in services. Of the 45 Indo-Pacific intra-regional agreements analysed, 34 were classified by the WTO as EIA and thus contained at least commitments to liberalise trade in goods and services, and often also provisions on investment and regulatory issues. In particular, the most comprehensive liberalisation disciplines characterise North–North agreements and, although to a somewhat lesser extent, North–South agreements. There are 11 agreements with provisions only on trade in goods in the region, of which 5 are FTAs and 6 are PSAs. Free trade areas include one plurilateral agreement (ASEAN Free Trade Area (AFTA)) and one concluded

Table 4.6 Number of intra-regional preferential trade agreements in the Indo-Pacific (May 2022), by integration model

	FTA	*FTA & EIA*	*PSA*
Intra-regional preferential trade agreements	5	34	6
North–North agreements	0	14	0
North–South agreements	3	17	0
South–South agreements	2	3	6
Bilateral agreements	3	31	5
Plurilateral agreements	1	0	1
Agreements in which at least one party is a preferential trade agreement (PTA)	1	3	0

Source: The author's own elaboration based on WTO Regional Trade Agreements Database.

Table 4.7 Number of intra-regional preferential trade agreements in the Indo-Pacific (May 2022), by substantive scope of the agreement

	Goods	*Goods & services*	*Services*
Intra-regional preferential trade agreements	11	34	0
North–North agreements	0	14	0
North–South agreements	3	17	0
South–South agreements	8	3	0
Bilateral agreements	8	31	0
Plurilateral agreements	2	0	0
Agreements in which at least one party is a preferential trade agreement (PTA)	1	3	0

Source: The author's own elaboration based on WTO Regional Trade Agreements Database.

by an already existing PTA (ASEAN–Japan). There is one plurilateral PSA in the region – SAPTA. As with the previous criteria, bilateral agreements dominate. For example, out of the 34 EIAs, 31 are bilateral agreements (Tables 4.6 and 4.7).

WTO crisis and the Indo-Pacific trade regionalism

The crisis of the basic function of the WTO as a negotiating forum has fundamentally changed the strategy of pursuing trade interests by the countries of the Indo-Pacific region. Those of them that previously treated PTAs as complementary, deepening liberalisation disciplines worked out in the GATT/WTO forum, intensified actions leading to the conclusion of further preferential agreements with important trading partners (e.g. the United States). In turn, countries that until recently based their trade policy on multilateral commitments within the WTO system, have changed their strategy, undertaking bilateral or plurilateral negotiations with important economic partners.

Such an example could be the Republic of Korea, which, unlike the United States, does not have such a long tradition of bilateral FTAs. The Republic of Korea has been relatively late in its efforts to strengthen bilateral economic relations with its major trading partners. Until the notable failure of the WTO conference in Seattle, South Korea was limited to participating in multilateral trade negotiations. With growing dissatisfaction with the way this system was operating and facing difficulties starting and continuing the DDR of negotiations, Korea made efforts to liberalise trade within intra- and inter-regional PTAs (Scott et al. 2006: 1). Currently, according to WTO data, the Republic of Korea is party to 21 PTAs, among which seven are intra-regional agreements concluded with other Indo-Pacific countries. Of which three are North–South agreements (ASEAN–Korea, Republic of; Korea, Republic of–India; Korea, Republic of–Vietnam), and the remaining four North–North agreements (Korea, Republic of–United States; Korea, Republic of–Singapore; Korea, Republic of–New Zealand; Korea, Republic of–Australia). Apart from the agreement with ASEAN, they are bilateral. All agreements concluded by the Republic of Korea with Indo-Pacific countries liberalise trade in both goods and services and are therefore classified as economic integration agreements (FTA & EIA).

A similar turn in trade policy to that of the Republic of Korea is also discernible in Japan's strategy of opening markets for goods and services produced in that economy (Fukunaga 2020). The first FTA negotiated by Japan entered into force in 2002. This was an agreement with Singapore (UNCTAD 2008: 159). In the following years, 17 further agreements were notified to the WTO: with Mexico (2005), Malaysia (2006), Chile, Thailand (2007), Brunei Darussalam, Indonesia, the Philippines, ASEAN (2008), Switzerland, Vietnam (2009), India (2011), Peru (2012), Australia (2015), Mongolia (2016), European Union (2019) and United Kingdom (2021). In 2018, the WTO was notified of the Comprehensive and Progressive Agreement for Trans-Pacific Partnership (CPTPP), to which Japan is a party.[3] Japan is currently negotiating PTAs with Turkey and Colombia. Trilateral Economic Partnership Agreement talks are also underway with the Republic of Korea and China. Previously held negotiations with the Gulf Cooperation Council and Canada were suspended. Among the eighteen PTAs notified to the WTO to which the Republic of Korea is a party, ten are Indo-Pacific intra-regional agreements, of which seven are North–South and three North–North. All these agreements except the ASEAN–Japan agreement cover trade in both goods and services. The agreement with ASEAN is the only PTA concluded by Japan that includes commitments relating only to trade in goods.

Conclusion

The Indo-Pacific region can hardly be considered a naturally distinct economic region in which economic integration processes are taking place. The concept is still largely political and strategic, although analyses of economic cooperation in the region and its potential economic impact are gradually emerging (Rahman et al. 2020; Goodman & Arasasingham 2022). The difficulty in analysing preferential trade agreements in the region is caused by the lack of a single definition of the region, an unambiguous geographical framework defining which countries and their trade policies should be included in the analysis of Indo-Pacific trade regionalism. The analysis identifies intra-regional preferential trade agreements in the Indo-Pacific and classifies them based on criteria identified in WTO reports. Many of these agreements were concluded prior to the spread of the Indo-Pacific concept, hence it is difficult to say that their original purpose was regional integration in this region. It seems that they can be seen more as agreements integrating the Asia-Pacific region.

Regardless of whether we adopt an Indo-Pacific or an Asia-Pacific perspective, it would appear to be true to conclude that the states of the region are not interested in a thorough process of regional integration manifesting themselves in the construction of supranational integration structures along the lines of the European Union. It is related to the different historical conditions of integration processes in Europe and the Indo-Pacific or Asia-Pacific region and, to the different (higher) level of trust in national governments in East Asia than in post-war Europe (Kozielski 2015: 175; Baldwin 2011). In addition, Asian states in the region are also characterised by limited trust in formal norms and greater attachment to custom. To some extent, the lack of supranational institutions for economic integration in the Indo-Pacific region is due to the absence of a leader who could induce Asian countries to give up some of their sovereignty. However, the likelihood of creating an integration structure with supranational institutions in the region is primarily ruled out by the policy of the United States, which, as a global power, will under no circumstances decide to limit its sovereignty within the framework of an EIA. This approach is well illustrated by the US policy of blocking the WTO dispute settlement system (Hoekman & Mavroidis 2019; Hoekman 2019). It therefore seems that what is to be expected in the Indo-Pacific trade liberalisation process is further preferential trade agreements in line with the global proliferation of such agreements as the WTO crisis deepens.

It is also worth stressing that preferential trade agreements in the Indo-Pacific region are a dynamic structure. They evolve under the influence of internal and external factors including, in particular, the changing economic situation in individual countries of the region and in the world economy, changes of strategy in the trade policies of economic partners and the condition of the WTO world trade system. Moreover, the Indo-Pacific is also an area of geo-economic rivalry, a struggle for influence in the region. In this context, Indo-Pacific countries are also building their position in the region using instruments of an economic nature, including trade policy tools, like preferential trade agreements which are the subject of this chapter.

In conclusion, it is also worth emphasising that the future evolution of trade agreements in the Indo-Pacific region should take into account the challenges that have arisen in the region and globally with the COVID-19 pandemic. The COVID-19 pandemic significantly disrupted trade and supply chains, with many countries implementing ad hoc trade-restrictive measures. The restrictions imposed have demonstrated the limitations of existing trade agreements, as well as multilateral trade rules, in providing guidance on how to respond to emergencies or crises in the least trade-restrictive manner possible. Current and future trade agreements should therefore include provisions on trade in times of crisis, pandemic or other emergencies, including, inter alia, rules on export/import restrictions to avoid serious shortages of essential goods and services as was the case in the COVID-19 pandemic. It is also a major challenge to increase transparency on the applicable safeguard measures taken in emergency situations and to exchange information on developments in crisis situations that may affect trade (Shirotori et al. 2021; Nicita & Saygili 2021). Further trade liberalisation in the framework of preferential trade agreements can also be seen as a tool to fight the economic crisis. Indeed, new trade flows in the Indo-Pacific can stimulate economic growth.

Notes

1 The term regional trade agreements (RTAs) or preferential trade agreements (PTAs) is used to refer to agreements created under Article XXIV of the GATT or Article V of the GATS. In this study, due to the classification of these agreements into intra-regional and inter-regional for stylistic reasons, it was decided to use the term preferential trade agreements.

Regional trade agreements occurs sporadically and is treated as synonymous with preferential trade agreements.

2 Trade regionalism expressed in the creation of preferential trade agreements can be defined "as a process of cooperation creating and implementing a regime of discriminatory trade liberalisation" (Śledziewska 2012). Indeed, PTAs imply, on the one hand, preferential trade liberalisation between a group of signatory states. On the other hand, the creation of such an agreement contributes to discrimination against countries that remain outside the trade agreement.

3 WTO Regional Trade Agreements Database does not contain information about the notification of the Regional Comprehensive Economic Partnership (RCEP).

References

Abbott F.M. (2007), A New Dominant Trade Species Emerges: Is Bilateralism a Threat?, *Journal of International Economic Law*, vol. 10, no. 3, pp. 571–583.

Adlung R., Molinuevo M. (2008), Bilateralism in Services Trade: Is There Fire Behind the (Bit-) Smoke?, *Journal of International Economic Law*, vol. 11, no. 2, pp. 365–409.

Baldwin R. (2011), Sequencing Regionalism: Theory, European Practice, and Lessons for Asia, Asian Development Bank Working Paper 2011, no. 80.

Brown A.G., Stern R.M. (2011), Free Trade Agreements and Governance of the Global Trading System, *The World Economy*, vol. 34, pp. 331–354.

Damuri Y.R. (2009), How Preferential are Preferential Trade Agreements? Analysis of Product Exclusions in PTAs, Swiss National Centre of Competence in Research, Working Paper, no. 30.

Fukunaga Y. (2020), Japan's Trade Policy in the Midst of Uncertainty, IFRI Centre for Asia Studies, Notes de l'Ifti, no. 112.

Goodman M.P., Arasasingham A. (2022), Regional Perspectives on the Indo-Pacific Economic Framework, CSIS Briefs, https://www.csis.org/analysis/regional-perspectives-indo-pacific -economic-framework

Hoekman B. (2019), Urgent and Important: Improving WTO Performance by Revisiting Working Practices, *Journal of World Trade*, vol. 53, no. 3, pp. 373–394.

Hoekman B.M., Mavroidis P.C. (2019), Burning Down the House? The Appellate Body in the Centre of the WTO Crisis, EUI Working Papers, RSCAS no. 56, Robert, Schuman Centre for Advanced Studies Global Governance Programme, https://ssrn.com/abstract=3424856

Kozielski P. (2015), Australia i jej rola w kształtowaniu procesów integracyjnych w obszarze Azji i Pacyfiku, Warszawa.

Krugman P. (1991), The Move toward Free Trade Zones, in: L.H. Summers (ed.), *Policy Implications of Trade and Currency Zones*, Kansas City: Federal Reserve Bank, pp. 7–42.

Lee Y.S. (2011), Reconciling RTAs with the WTO Multilateral Trading System: Case for a New Sunset Requirement on RTAs and Development Facilitation, *Journal of World Trade*, vol. 45, pp. 629–651.

Nicita A., Saygili M. (2021), Trade Agreements and Trade Resilience During COVID-19 Pandemic, UNCTAD Research Paper no. 70, UNCTAD/SER.RP/2021/13.

Rahman M.M., Kim Ch., De P. (2020), IndoPacific cooperation: what do trade simulations indicate?, *Journal of Economic Structures*, vol. 9, open access.

Scott J.J., Bradford S.C., Moll T. (2006), Negotiating the Korea-United States Free Trade Agreement, Policy Briefs in International Economics, no. PB06-4.

Shirotori M., Ito T., Duval Y., Du R., Marceau G. (2021), Readying Regional Trade Agreements for Future Crises and Pandemics, UNCTAD, https://unctad.org/news/readying-regional-trade -agreements-future-crises-and-pandemics.

Śledziewska (2012), Regionalizm handlowy w XXI wieku. Przesłanki teoretyczne i analiza empiryczna, Warszawa: Wydawnictwa Uniwersytetu Warszawskiego.

UNCTAD (2008), South-South Trade in Asia: The Role of Regional Trade Agreements, United Nations.

Wróbel A. (2009), *Międzynarodowa wymiana usług*, Warszawa: Wydawnictwo Naukowe Scholar.

Wróbel A. (2013), Preferencyjne porozumienia handlowe (PTA's): postęp czy blokowanie liberalizacji handlu, in: M. Chorośnicki, J.J. Węc, A. Czubik, A. Głogowski, I. Krzyżanowska-Skowronek, A. Nitszke, E. Szczepankiewicz-Rudzka, M. Tarnowski (eds.), *Nowe strategie na nowy wiek – granice i możliwości integracji regionalnych i globalnych*, Kraków: Krakowska Oficyna Naukowa TEKST, pp. 615–628.

Wróbel A. (2016a), Proces liberalizacji handlu wewnątrzregionalnego w regionie Azji i Pacyfiku, in: A. Jarczewska, J. Zajączkowski (eds.), *Region Azji i Pacyfiku w latach 1985–2015*, Warszwa: Wydawnictwo Naukowe Scholar, pp. 393–418.

Wróbel A. (2016b), Trade Regionalism in the Asia-Pacific, Trends in the World Economy, vol. 8, pp. 183–200.

Wróbel A. (2019), China's Trade Policy: Realist and Liberal Approaches, in: M. Grabowski, T. Pugacewicz (eds.), *Application of International Relations Theories in Asia and Africa*, Berlin: Peter Lang Verlag, pp. 173–204.

Wróbel A. (2020), The Functionality and Dysfunctionality of Global Trade Governance: The European Union Perspective, in: K. Jędrzejowska, M. Rewizorski, A. Wróbel (eds.), *The Future of Global Economic Governance. Challenges and Prospects in the Age of Uncertainty*, Eastbourne: Springer, pp. 161–175.

WTO (2011), *World Trade Report 2011, The WTO and Preferential Trade Agreements: From Co-existence to Coherence*, Geneve: WTO.

WTO (2022), WTO Regional Trade Agreements Database, https://rtais.wto.org.

5 Impact of religion on international relations in the Indo-Pacific

Aleksandra Jaskólska

Introduction

The aim of this chapter is to analyse the influence of religion on international relations in the Indo-Pacific region. Religion was chosen as a factor to be analysed for a few reasons. First of all, countries in the Indo-Pacific represent all major systems of religious belief: Christianity, Islam, Hinduism, Buddhism and folk religions. There is also a significant percentage of people who define themselves as unaffiliated. Second, there are countries that share a border whose citizens predominantly believe in a different religion. The same goes for organisations of regional integration in the Indo-Pacific. Third, the status of each religion is different among states in the Indo-Pacific. States may be secular or a religion may have the status of a state religion. Analysing the influence of religion on international relations in the Indo-Pacific region requires answering three research questions:

1 How does the level of religious diversity and status of the religion in a state influence a state's foreign policy?
2 What role does religion play in the context of political and economic cooperation between states or in solving border conflicts?
3 In what ways does religion influence the process of regional integration?

The answers to the questions serve to verify the hypothesis that assumes that religion is one of the factors which affects international relations in the Indo-Pacific region and cannot be treated as only a minor or irrelevant factor as it is widely seen in the West (mostly European countries). The chapter is divided into four sections. The first section focuses on an overview of the perception of religion in theories of international relations. In this section, definitions of religion and the evolution of the perception of religion by scholars are also presented. The aim of the second section is to show the religious structure of the Indo-Pacific. Sub-regions in the Indo-Pacific: South Asia, South-East Asia, Oceania and last but not least East Asia present various religious profiles. Special emphasis will be on India, Indonesia, Australia and South Korea as case studies which represent each of the sub-regions. The third section analyses the influence of religion on bilateral relations among countries in the Indo-Pacific, with a case study on India-Pakistan relations. The aim of this section is to analyse the role of religion in relations between countries in the context of border conflict, politics and economic cooperation. Finally, the fourth section focuses on analysing the influence of religion on the process of regional integration by using the South Asian Association

DOI: 10.4324/9781003336143-8

for Regional Cooperation (SAARC) and the Association of South-East Asian Nations (ASEAN) as examples. The chapter ends with conclusions in the form of answers to the research questions posed, making it possible to verify the hypothesis.

Religion and theories of international relations

Many scholars fail to agree on one definition of religion. One of the most popular is the one proposed by Émile Durkheim, who defines religion as "a unified system of beliefs and practices relative to sacred things, that is to say, things set apart and forbidden—beliefs and practices which unite into one single moral community called a church, all those who adhere to them" (Durkheim 2010). It is also interesting to have a look at Jonathan Fox's definition. He distinguishes four aspects of religion: belief system, rules and standards of behaviour derived from religious truths, religious institutions (organisational forms) and source and method of legitimacy (Fox 2004). And last but not least is Karl Marx's famous description of religion as the "opiate of the masses." Marx acknowledges religion's influence on the beliefs and behaviour of humans (McKinnon 2005). According to all three definitions, religion may influence our everyday life, so it means that it may also be seen as a factor in the internal and external policies of a state.

During the cold war, the role of religion in theories of international relations was hardly discussed (Jackson & Sorensen 2012). According to Zenderowski (2014), there are a few reasons for ignoring religion as an important factor in analysing international relations. First, it seems that the marginalisation of religion was partly contributed to by the belief of many scholars that the relegation of religion from the political sphere, symbolised by the Treaty of Westphalia (1648), gave secular states sovereignty over religions and rejected any supranational religious authority. A second explanation is the Western-centric nature of mainstream theories of international relations. Increasingly, the secular West (especially Europe) failed to recognise that much of the non-Western world took the opposite direction. A third explanation may be added as an addition to Zenderowski's list. Most Western scholars believe in theories of modernisation and secularisation, whose origins date back to the 19th century. According to these theories, religion was supposed to gradually die out as an anachronistic way of perceiving social reality. Indeed, the role of explaining the complexity of the world was taken on by modern ideologies (socialism, communism, liberalism, conservatism) that emerged in the 19th and 20th centuries (Fox & Sandal 2010).

The slow process of returning religion to the theory of international relations has been ongoing since the late 1970s, mostly because of the Islamic Revolution in Iran. It continued with the article by Samuel Huntington, "The Clash of Civilizations?" published in 1993 in *Foreign Affairs* (Huntington 1993). According to Huntington, post-cold war conflicts will be caused not by ideology but rather by culture. Civilisation will clash because of differences in values and politics. Religion was definitely seen as a part of culture/civilisation. The attack on the World Trade Center in 2001 was the next important event which brought the attention of the public to religion (Philpott 2002). It raised awareness of the importance of religion and marked the return of religion to world politics (Songbatumis 2021). In this context, its return is not to change the political paradigm, but instead to include it as a variable (Fox & Sandler 2004; Philpott 2002).

Let's have a look at the ways different theories of international relations approach religion. We can divide the existing theories of international relations into two main categories: materialist and non-materialist (Jackson & Sorensen 2012). Paradigms that we can write into the materialist current – realism, structural realism, liberalism and neo-Marxism – place more emphasis (or focus exclusively) on the material aspects of international relations, such as the state, military power, natural resources, the strength of the economy and its global linkages, etc. It is worth noting, however, that religion can enhance the strength of a given international relations actor, but it can also undermine the effectiveness of the actions taken by it. For a state building its regional or global power, it is not irrelevant whether the population of the countries subject to its hegemony generally follow the same or different religions. Religion often becomes an important factor in defining with whom it is worthwhile and with whom it is not appropriate to build political and military alliances (Zenderowski 2014). One of the representatives of the liberal theory, Andrew Moravcsik, even sees religion as an important source in the process of defining group preferences and interests (Moravcsik 2008).

In the second category, non-materialist theories, there are two major paradigms, constructivism and the so-called English School. They emphasise such factors of international relations as norms, values, beliefs, identity, etc. An especially interesting theoretical approach to analyse the problems presented in this chapter is constructivism, which frequently describes above meanings as "cultural" (Reus-Smit 2018). Constructivism, in opposition to realism which emphasises the centrality of the system (as an analytical category), focuses on the process, i.e. the dynamics of the transformation of international relations and their "social construction." Constructivists use a certain thought pattern, which in principle makes it possible to incorporate religion into constructivist conceptions of international relations. They much prefer to weave the issue of religion into more general considerations of the meaning of culture in international relations (Snyder 2011).

To sum up, as the West (mostly Europe) secularised, the processes of politicisation, deprivatisation of religion and desecularisation of politics intensified around the world. It is crucial to understand that modernisation does not necessarily mean secularisation and that there are several different "paths" of modernisation in the world that differ in their attitude to religion. Due to this it will be recommended to move away from the secularist model (Box 5.1) of understanding religion and politics as completely separate spheres of human activity, as it is perceived. Even though religion has been more present in the analysis of international relations since the beginning of the twenty-first century, there is still a lot of work to be done. Scholars who represent different theories of international relations should work on an approach in which religion can be understood as one of the factors which influence the dynamics of international relations.

Religious diversity in the Indo-Pacific: An overview

The population of the Indo-Pacific is ca. 4.5 billion out of the total population of 8 billion people living in 2022 (UNPF 2022).[1] The Indo-Pacific is one of the most religiously diverse regions in the world. Religion can be presented as a percentage of the global population living in the Indo-Pacific:

- 92 percent are Hindus and Buddhists;
- 80 percent are folk religionists (African traditional religions, Chinese folk religions, Native Americans and Australian aboriginal religions) and other religion followers

(Bahais, Jains, Sikhs, Taoists, followers of Tenrikyo, Wiccans, Zarotostrians and many others);

- 63 percent are those who identify as unaffiliated;
- 54 percent are followers of Islam;
- 12 percent are Christians;
- 1.3 percent are Jewish.

Each sub-region of the Indo-Pacific – South Asia (India, Pakistan, Nepal, Bhutan, Sri Lanka, Maldives and Afghanistan); South-East Asia (Brunei, Cambodia, Timor-Leste, Indonesia, Laos, Malaysia, Myanmar, Philippines, Singapore, Thailand and Vietnam); Oceania (Australia, Papua New Guinea, New Zealand, Fiji, Salmon Islands and other Pacific Islands); and East Asia (China, Hong Kong, Japan, Macau, North Korea, South Korea, Taiwan) have their own religious profiles (Table 5.1). In South Asia the dominant religion is Hinduism, with 68 percent of the overall population; next is Islam with 31 percent; 10 percent goes for Buddhists, Jains, Chrisitians, Sikhs and others. In South-East Asia the major religions are as follows: 38 percent of the entire population believes in Islam; 35 percent is Buddhist; 23 percent is Christian. In Oceania the biggest religious group is Christians with 74 percent of the total population; the second largest is the unaffiliated group, with 19 percent; and then Buddhism, Islam and Hinduism with 2 percent each. In East Asia more than half of the population (53 percent) categorised themselves as unaffiliated; 19.6 percent are Buddhist; 19.6 percent belong to folk religions; and 5.6 percent are Christian.

One country from each sub-region will be presented in the next part of the chapter. India, Indonesia, Australia and Japan had been chosen on the basis of the size of population, religious structure, and status of religion in their respective political systems (*de jure* and *de facto*) and its influence on foreign policy decisions.

Box 5.1 Secularism: Relations between religion and state

French historian and sociologist of secularism, Jean Baubérot defines secularism as:

- separation of religious institutions from the institutions of state, and no domination of the political sphere by religious institutions;
- freedom of thought, conscience and religion for all, with everyone free to change their beliefs, and manifest their beliefs, within the limits of public order and the rights of others;
- no discrimination against anyone on the grounds of their religion or non-religious worldview, with everyone receiving equal treatment on these grounds (Copson 2017).

This definition is widely accepted by many countries (mostly in the West). But within this political idea, there are many secularisms, both conceptual and practical. Their common ground (as presented above) is the separation of state authorities and institutions from religious authorities and institutions. But this separation can be to a different extent. It can refer to total separation of religion or state (as it is mostly done in the West) or there can be some influence of religion on state (but all religions are supposed to have the same possibility to

Table 5.1 Religious diversity in the Indo-Pacific

Country	Percent Christian	Percent Muslim	Percent Unaffilated	Percent Hindu	Percent Buddhist	Percent Folk Religions	Precent Other Religions	2022 Country Population
Australia	43.9	3.2	38.9	2.7	2.4	0.7	0.8	26,085,000
Bangladesh	0.2	89.8	<0.1	9.1	0.5	0.4	<0.1	167,750,000
Bhutan	0.5	0.2	<0.1	22.6	74.7	1.9	<0.1	780,000
Brunei	6.5	80.5	0.4	0.3	6.5	5.2	0.1	445,000
Cambodia	0.4	2.0	0.2	<0.1	96.9	0.6	<0.1	17,160,000
China	5.1	1.8	52.2	<0.1	18.2	21.9	0.7	1,440,000,000
India	2.5	14.4	<0.1	79.5	0.8	0.5	2.3	1,406,120,000
Indonesia	9.9	87.2	<0.1	1.7	0.7	0.3	0.1	279,050,000
Japan	1.6	0.2	62.0	<0.1	30	0.4	4.5	125,640,000
Laos	1.5	<0.1	0.9	<0.1	66.0	30.7	0.7	7,400,000
Malaysia	9.4	63.7	0.7	6.0	17.7	2.3	0.2	32,300,000
Maldives	0.4	98.4	<0.1	0.3	0.6	<0.1	<0.1	550,000
Myanmar	6.2	2.4	0.5	0.7	87.1	1.8	0.2	55,100,000
Nepal	0.5	4.6	0.3	80.7	10.3	3.7	<0.1	30,100,000
New Zealand	37.0	1.2	48.6	2.1	1.6	0.5	0.7	4,770,000
North Korea	2.0	<0.1	71.3	<0.1	1.5	12.3	12.9	25,950,000
Pakistan	1.6	96.4	<0.1	1.9	<0.1	<0.1	<0.1	229,100,000
Papua New Guinea	96.2	<0.1	<0.1	<0.1	<0.1	0.8	0.8	9,160,000
Philippines	92.6	5.5	0.1	<0.1	<0.1	1.5	0.1	112,260,000
Singapore	18.2	14.3	16.4	5.2	33.9	2.3	9.7	5,890,000
South Korea	27.4	0.2	53.4	<0.1	16.9	0.8	0.2	51,280,000
Sri Lanka	7.3	9.8	<0.1	13.6	69.3	<0.1	<0.1	21,460,000
Taiwan	5.5	<0.1	12.7	<0.1	21.3	44.2	16.2	23,620,000
Thailand	0.9	5.5	0.3	0.1	93.2	<0.1	<0.1	70,120,000
Timor-Leste	99.6	0.1	<0.1	<0.1	<0.1	0.1	<0.1	1,320,000
Vietnam	7.4	0.2	29.6	<0.1	14.4	45.3	0.4	98,890,000

Source: Own elaboration based on National Censuses, UN Population Division and Pew Research Centre.

influence state affairs). Examples of secular states in the Indo-Pacific: Australia, South Korea, Japan, India (only *de jure*). On the other hand, the constitution of Maldives designates Sunni Islam as the state religion and only Sunni Muslims are allowed to hold citizenship. Other countries in the Indo-Pacific with a state religion – Islam – are Brunei and Pakistan. There are also countries where being atheist is against the law, for example, Indonesia.

Suggetsed readings:

- Donald Eugen Smith, *Religion and Politics in South Asia* (Chicago: University of Chicago Press, 1963).
- Bipan Chandra, *India after Independence 1947–2000* (New Delhi: Penguin Books, 2000).
- Jean Baubérot, "French Secularism: Republican, Indivisible, Democratic, and Social," *Cités* 4(52), 2014: 11–20.
- Shu-Li Wang, Michael john Rowlands, Yujie Zhu (ed.), *Heritage and Religion in East Asia* (New York: Routledge, 2020).

India

The first case study is India with had a population of nearly 1.4 billion in 2022. The second most populous country in South Asia is Pakistan, which has a population of just over 229 million. India is one of two predominantly Hindu countries in the Indo-Pacific, the second country is Nepal (Bhatia 2020). The religious profile of India: Hinduism, which is practised by 79.5 percent of Indians; Islam, which is practised by 14.4 percent; Christianity, which is practised by 2.5 percent; Sikhism, which is practised by 1.7 percent. Followers of Buddhism, Jainism and Parsis constitute a total of about 3 percent (Census 2011).

India is a state built on the premises of "Unity in Diversity" which was promoted by Jawaharlal Nehru who was the first prime minister of India from 1947 to 1964 (Kieniewicz 2003). India was established as s democratic and secular republic. But only in 1976, with the 42nd Amendment of the Constitution of India, did the Preamble to the Constitution assert that India is a secular nation. However, India's secularism is understood differently than in the West and does not completely separate religion and state. All religions are supposed to have some influence on the state. The state subsidizes Hindu, Sikh and Muslim pilgrimages. Some religious groups, for example Muslims, have their own civil code. Blasphemy is prohibited by the penal code (Ganguly 2006).

Narendra Modi has been the prime minister since 2014 when the Bharatiya Janata Party (BJP) was elected to the Lok Sabha (lower house of the Indian parliament) and then re-elected in 2019 in both elections with a majority. The BJP promotes the ideology of Hindutva or Hindu nationalism. According to which, Buddhists, Jains and Sikhs are closely related to Hindus, so they are not treated as alien groups. The non-Hindus groups include Muslims and Christians, who are portrayed as enemies of Hindus (Jaskólska 2016). Due to the promotion of Hindutva in internal politics, India lost its status as a full democracy in 2020 and is categorised as having a flawed or hybrid democracy (Economist Intelligence 2022) (see Chapter 7). India can no longer be categorised as a secular state, even though it is written in the Constitution of India.

Discrimination policies towards Muslims had an impact on India's relations with countries with predominantly Muslim populations like Pakistan, Bangladesh and Gulf countries. One of the BJP government's discriminatory policies is the Citizenship Amendment Act (CAA) which was passed by the Indian government in December 2019 and implemented in January 2020. The CAA has expedited citizenship for Hindu, Sikh, Buddhist, Jain, Parsi and Christian immigrants from Afghanistan, Pakistan and Bangladesh who arrived in India before 2015 (Sufian 2022). However, it excludes Muslims, which has drawn not only criticism and protests from the government of Bangladesh and Pakistan, among others, but also internal instability (months of protests in major Indian cities).

The next example of promoting the ideology of Hindutva is a situation which happened in May 2022, when a BJP spokesperson, Nupur Sharma, made controversial comments about the Prophet Muhammad in a TV debate. It caused protests across the country against BJP and a diplomatic crisis with several Islamic nations, including the UAE, Saudi Arabia, Qatar, Iran, Pakistan, Indonesia and the Maldives. BJP decided to suspend Nupur Sharma from the party in June 2022, but the prime minister of India didn't provide any official statement regarding this issue (BBC 2022a). The internal and diplomatic crisis continued for several weeks. The influence of religion on India's relations with Pakistan will be presented in the next part of this chapter.

Indonesia

The second case study is Indonesia with a population of 279 million in 2022. The second most populous country in South-East Asia, the Philippines had a population of over 112 million (Britannica 2022a). Indonesia is one of the few countries in the Indo-Pacific (along with Bangladesh, Brunei, Maldives, Malaysia and Pakistan) where the majority of the population (in the case of Indonesia, 87.2 percent), are followers of Islam (Febrica 2021). Indonesia contains the largest Muslim population of all countries in the world. The second most popular religion is Christianity, 9.9 percent (mostly in Flores and Timor). The next is Hinduism, 1.7 percent (predominantly in Bali and Lombok). Followed by Buddhism, 0.7 percent (Ropi 2017).

Indonesia's national motto is "Bhinekka Tunggal Ika," which means "Unity in Diversity." It refers to the variety in the country's internal composition (ethnic, linguistic, cultural). Indonesia is somewhere between ideas of secularism and an Islamic state. Article 29 of the Indonesian constitution requires its citizens to "believe in the almighty God" but Indonesia is not an Islamic republic (like for example Pakistan). Islam, Hinduism, Buddhism, Confucianism, Roman Catholicism or Protestant Christianity are recognised and celebrated by the state (Hefner 2018). The Indonesian government obliges citizens to declare adherence to one of those recognised religions, being an atheist is against the law.

It is interesting to see how the perception of the role of Islam in both domestic and external politics is evaluated. During the Suharto period, when Suharto presided in Indonesia from 1967 to 1998, the government prohibited all advocacy of an Islamic state. Only after 1998, during the democratisation period, did Islam gain influence both in domestic politics and foreign policy. Aceh (located in western Sumatra) became the first (and the only one till now) province in Indonesia that since 1999 is authorised by the central government to implement Islamic sharia laws. The next example of the rising influence of Islam is the case of Basuki Tjahaja Purnama, known as Ahok, who is a Christian and was Jakarta's first non-Muslim governor (2014–2017) in 50 years. However, he was convicted of blasphemy in 2017. He was convicted and released early from his jail term after 20 months instead of 24 months (BBC 2022a). It is important to underline, the majority of the Indonesian Muslim community is highly supportive of a religious pluralist and peaceful society. But some decisions of the government are clearly antisecular.

To explore the role of Islam in Indonesia's foreign policy, three case studies will be presented: the Palestine-Israel conflict, the situation of Rohingya and Indonesia's relations with Pakistan (Songbatumis 2021). The Palestine issue has gone on continuously since its independence and the main foreign policy connection for Indonesian Muslims is that they demanded the government help Palestine's statehood. Indonesia refused to recognise the state of Isreal until the peace agreement between Palestine and Isreal was reached (Ng 2022). This position is contrary to Indonesia's stance towards solidarity with the Rohingya, a Muslim minority group from Myanmar. Rohingya suffered discrimination from the Myanmar government which the United Nations described as a textbook example of ethnic cleansing. Indonesia presents longstanding opposition to sanctions and has rejected policies that it believes would isolate Myanmar, jeopardise humanitarian relief and push it closer to China. The Rohingya case illustrates a commitment to the norm of non-interference which is more important to the government than protecting the interests of Muslims abroad (Murphy 2020).

Indonesia and Pakistan (the first and second countries in the world with the largest number of Muslim populations) had close relations even before Indonesia gained independence. Both countries are members of the Organisation of Islamic Cooperation. Indonesia supported Pakistan in 1965 during the war with India and even offered to militarily intervene in the conflict by attacking and seizing the Andaman and Nicobar Islands (located in the Bay of Bengal) which are Union Territories of India. Both countries have a long history of cooperation in the defence sector and exchange of military personnel for training. The countries also have a standing preferential trade agreement signed in 2012 which has an impact on more dynamic economic cooperation (George 2021). Indonesia is also lobbying for Pakistan to become a full dialogue partner of the Association of Southeast Asian Nations (ASEAN), which would increase political, commercial and economic links with ASEAN member states (*The Express Tribune* 2022).

Australia

The third case study is Australia with a population in 2022 of slightly over 26 million. The second most populous country in Oceania is Papua New Guinea, which has a population of 8.5 million (Britannica 2022b). In Australia, slightly more than 40 percent of the population are followers of Christianity. Unaffiliated is the fastest growing group in Australia which in 1960 was 0 percent, and in 2021 grew to nearly 40 percent. Muslims, Hindus and Buddhists each stand for around 3 percent (Table 5.1). It is worth mentioning that in contrast to Australians of European origin, Aboriginal communities are intensely spiritual (Barker 2019). Other countries in the Indo-Pacific with a majority of Christians (more than 90 percent) are the Philippines, Papua New Guinea and Timor-Leste (Table 5.1).

Section 116 of the Constitution of Australia states:

> The Commonwealth shall not make any law for establishing any religion, or for imposing any religious observance, or for prohibiting the free exercise of any religion, and no religious test shall be required as a qualification for any office or public trust under the Commonwealth.

It means that Australia does not have an explicit "separation of church and state," which is the essence of a secular state. State-religion relations in Australia can be described as liberal separation, pragmatic pluralism and non-establishment pluralism. All terms on the one hand involve separation between the institutions of state and religion, but on the other hand, allow religion and religious people to exist in the public square. The Religious Discrimination Bill is one of the ways to guarantee religious freedom, equality and protection from discrimination. In 2021 Prime Minister Scott Morrison introduced the bill to the federal parliament, its third iteration (Barker 2021).

In the 2017 Foreign Policy White Paper, the Australian Government declared "shared values" to be at the centre of its foreign policy and defined such values as "political, economic and religious freedom, liberal democracy, the rule of law, racial and gender equality and mutual respect" (Foreign Policy White Paper 2017). It seems that Australia's foreign policy is in a very limited way influenced by religion and its religious diversity. According to the Foreign Policy White Paper:

> Fundamentally important to our ability to navigate a world of dynamic change and uncertainty are our strength and resilience at home, the hard and soft power that give us influence internationally, and the values that reflect who we are and how we approach the world. We build our international engagement on these foundations
>
> (Foreign Policy White Paper 2017).

South Korea

The fourth case study is South Korea, with a population in 2022 of over 51 million. South Korea is the third most populous country in East Asia, after China (1.44 billion) and Japan (125.6 million). In South Korea, 53.4 percent identify themselves as unaffiliated to any religion. The second largest group is Christians at 27.4 percent. The third largest ground is Buddhists at 16.9 percent. In the case of other countries from East Asia, there is also a high percentage of unaffiliated in North Korea (71 percent), Japan (62 percent) and China (52 percent) (Wang et al. 2020).

Freedom of religion is constitutionally guaranteed in South Korea. Historically, Koreans lived under the influences of shamanism, Buddhism and Confucianism. Shamanism in ancient Korea was a religion which was associated with power and superstition. In the twenty-first century it is rather a colourful and artistic ingredient of their culture. Confucianism is more of a code of ethical conduct that emphasises the importance of loyalty, filial piety and ancestor worship than a religious belief. None of these religions/ways of life were abandoned (Kim 2002). Article 20 of the Constitution of South Korea provides that all citizens shall enjoy freedom of religion.

There shall be no discrimination in political, economic, social or cultural life on the basis of religion. No state religion shall be recognised. Freedoms provided for in the constitution may be restricted by law only when necessary for national security, law and order, or public welfare, but restrictions may not violate the "essential aspect" of the freedoms. The constitution mandates the separation of religion and state (*2021 Report on International Religious Freedom: South Korea*).

Religion, and to be more specific, shamanism, was involved in the impeachment of South Korean President Park Geun-hye. She was impeached in 2017 and 1 year later sentenced to 24 years in jail after she was found guilty of abuse of power and coercion (Shin 2020). She was released from prison in 2021, by the decision of the president of South Korea *Moon* Jae-in, nearly five years after being convicted (Shin 2021). Together with Park Geun-hye, Choi Soon-sil, her long-time friend (the daughter of Choi Tae-min, a shadowy quasi-religious leader who was closely linked to Park's father who was a president of South Korea) was also sentenced to prison but for 20 years. It was proven during the trial that Choi Soon-sil had access to government policy-making and used it to solicit donations to a non-profit fund she controlled. It was a huge scandal in Korean politics. The fact that former presidents Park and Choi were related to shamanism and other quasi-religious groups was perceived as politically incorrect by Koreans (Shin 2021).

As in the case of Australia, religion and religious diversity have a limited influence over foreign policy in South Korea. According to the Ministry of Foreign Affairs Republic of Korea (MOFA), its foreign policy strategy:

"has moved beyond the sphere of traditional government-oriented diplomacy by increasing its focus on public diplomacy, which includes reaching out to the foreign public through the arts, knowledge sharing, media, language, and aid" (MOFA).

Bilateral relations: India-Pakistan

The aim of this section is to analyse the impact of religion on relations between countries through a case study: India-Pakistan in the context of border conflict and political and economic cooperation. For the analyses, it is necessary to present the historical background of the creation of India and Pakistan, their religious structures and the status of religion in both countries.

The Indian subcontinent was colonised by the United Kingdom and British India was created. It had a very diverse religious structure with two dominant religions: Hinduism and Islam. During the decolonisation process in the 1940s, there were two main ideas about what British India should look like after the withdrawal of colonisers. The first option was to create one country, India (today's area of Bangladesh, India, Pakistan) which was supported by Mahatma Gandhi (one of the Indians involved in the independence struggle). The second option was promoted by Muhammad Ali Jinnah and his Two-Nation Theory (Box 5.2) by which followers of Hinduism and Islam could not live in one country. According to Jinnah, the only solution was to create a separate state for Muslims, Pakistan and for Hindus, India (Adeney 2007). Option number two was chosen by British colonisers in agreement with most of the Indian elite. The partition of British India was one of the most tragic events in the history of the subcontinent. Up to 2 million people lost their lives and approximately 14 million were forced to change their place of residence. It was one of the largest mass migrations in human history. Pakistan obtained independence on 14 August 1947 and India on 15 August 1947 (Akhter 2016). India according to its constitution became a secular state. The religious structure of India was presented above. Pakistan became an Islamic Republic, and Islam was recognised as a state religion. In 2022 Pakistan's religious structure: 96 percent of the population are followers of Islam; 1.9 percent of Hinduism; and 1.6 percent of Christianity (Table 5.1).

Relations between India and Pakistan are dominated by an unresolved border conflict, water sharing issues and, on top of that, the shadow of partition. As the aim of this part of the chapter is to analyse the impact of religion on relations between India and Pakistan, it is crucial to focus on the religious background of the border conflict in Kashmir. India and Pakistan fought three wars over Kashmir: in 1947, 1965 and 1971, which failed to establish a mutually acceptable border. The closest to it was the agreement in Shimla in 1972 which established the Line of Control (LoC). The LoC established a military controlled line between Indian and Pakistani controlled parts of Kashmir. The LoC serves as a border between India and Pakistan (Guha 2007). Why did this conflict start at the very beginning? Kashmir, officially known as Jammu and Kashmir was a princely state of Kashmir and Jammu during British rule. It was dominated by a Muslim population but it was ruled by a Hindu ruler, Maharaja Hari Singh. During the partition of British India, he wanted his princely state to remain an independent kingdom, but it was not possible at that time. In the end, Kashmir was divided between Pakistan and India. It caused not only a war but also mass migration and the division of families. One part of Kashmir became an autonomous territory in Pakistan, Azad Jammu and Kashmir, the second part, Jammu and Kashmir became one of the states in the Indian federation. Article 370 of the Indian Constitution gave it special status (autonomy) within the federation. On 31 October 2019, it became a union territory and lost most of its autonomy. It also caused serious tensions between India and Pakistan. According to Pakistan, the rights of the Muslim population living in Kashmir were violated because of this change of status of the state.

Religion doesn't need to be only a source of conflict. It may also be a way to establish relations. During and after the partition of British India many places of worship were destroyed or not accessible to worshipers. In 1974, India and Pakistan decided to sign a Protocol on Visits to Religious Shrines, to facilitate citizens of each country to travel to shrines and holy sites in the other country (Rajopadhye 2020). Unfortunately it doesn't work very well for the divided princely state of Kashmir because of the tensions over it, namely clashes on the border, in which both soldiers and civilians are killed, terrorist attacks and internal instability. But it works for another province Punjab, which was also divided during the partition of British India. The Kartarpur corridor (4.7 km long) connects the Dera Baba Nanak temples located in the Indian Punjab city of Gurdaspur with the Darbar Sahib gurudwara in Kartapur, Pakistan. It was inaugurated in November 2019. The ceremony was held on the 550th birth anniversary of Guru Nanak, the founder of Sikhism (Haidar 2019).

With reference to what was presented above, what is the impact of religion on India-Pakistan relations in the context of border conflict and political and economic cooperation? India and Pakistan have very different religious structures and different statuses of religions in the state. The countries have been in conflict over Kashmir since their creation in 1947, although they still manage to use religion as a tool to establish ties between divided provinces like in the case of the Punjab and Kartarpur corridor. Unfortunately, it is only a very minor improvement and because of a lack of trust, lack of willingness to end border conflict and misuse of religion by political leaders relations between India and Pakistan still remain tense. Leaders of both countries cancelled bilateral meetings and those that were to be held in international forums. In addition, both sides are imposing additional barriers and trade tariffs on each other. The leaders of the countries also decided to temporarily close border crossings. Such actions have a negative impact on the development of political, economic, scientific and cultural relations. They adversely affect the development of border trade and relations between communities living on both sides of the border. Lack of dialogue makes it impossible to resolve border conflicts and leads to their escalation.

Box 5.2 Two-Nation Theory

"Two-Nation Theory" refers to the thesis that Hindus and Muslims living in British India were two distinct communities that could not coexist within a single state without dominating and discriminating against the other or without constant conflict. The theory was proposed by Muhammad Iqbal (1877–1938) writer, philosopher and politician who was born in British India. In coming years theory was adopted and used by Muhammad Ali Jinnah (1876–1948) who was a leader of one of the political parties, the Muslim League. In 1940 in Lahore Muhammad Ali Jinnah gave a seminal speech setting out the need for a separate state for Muslims on the Indian subcontinent. Jinnad said: "Hindus and Muslims belong to two different religious philosophies, social customs and literary traditions. They neither intermarry nor eat together, and indeed they belong to two different civilisations which are based mainly on conflicting ideas and conceptions." According to Jinnah, the only solution was to create a separate state for Muslims, Pakistan and for Hindus, India. Mahatma Gandhi (1869–1948) who was also heavily involved in independence process was against it, and he believed that British India should not be divided. Leader of Indian National Congress, Jawaharlal Nehru (1889–1964) at the beginning opposed the idea of partition but at the end he accepted it. Two-Nation Theory was among the prime reasons for the partition of British India to India and Pakistan in 1947. After Bangladesh (East Pakistan) was declared independent from West Pakistan in 1971, then-Indian Prime Minister Indira Gandhi declared the Two-Nation Theory "dead." But the influence of Two-Nation Theory in the twenty first century is still discussed by scholars.

Suggetsed readings:

- Kathraine Adeney, *Federalism and Ethnic Conflict Regulation in India and Pakistan* (New York: Palgrave Macmillan, 2007).
- Zainab Akhter, "India–Pakistan Relations: Efficacy of Culture", *Millennial Asia* 7(2), 2016: 207–229.
- Clinton Bennett, "**Two-Nation Theory**," in: Kassam, Z.R., Greenberg, Y.K., Bagli, J. (eds.) *Islam, Judaism, and Zoroastrianism. Encyclopedia of Indian Religions* (Dordrecht: Springer, 2018).

Regional integration: SAARC and ASEAN

Regional integration in the Indo-Pacific is vibrant and dynamic but areas across the region do not possess the same characteristics (see Chapter 12). South Asia is one of the least politically and economically integrated regions of the world. On the other hand, South-East Asia is a champion of regional integration in the Indo-Pacific. What is the role of religion in this? The South Asian Association for Regional Cooperation (SAARC) and the Association of Southeast Asian Nations (ASEAN) will be used as case studies to represent two different models of regional integration. In the case of both organisations, a short historical background and the organisation's main goals will be presented. Then factors which had an influence on the level of regional integration with a special focus on the role of religion will be discussed.

The South Asian Association for Regional Cooperation (SAARC)

The South Asian Association for Regional Cooperation (SAARC) was established in 1985 at the initiative of Bangladesh. The member countries are India, Pakistan, Bangladesh, Sri Lanka, Nepal, Maldives and Bhutan and since 2007 Afghanistan (Michael 2013). The SAARC covers a population of ca. 1.7 billion and an area of a bit more than 5 million km^2. The main goal of the organisation according to the SAARC Charter is to promote the well-being of the peoples of South Asia; improve the quality of life of its people; promote economic growth, social progress and cultural development in the region; build mutual trust and understanding; promote economic, social, cultural, technical and scientific activities; strengthen cooperation with other developing countries; cooperate in international forums on matters of common interest; and cooperate with international and regional organisations with similar objectives (Saha 2005).

There are several factors that affected the lack of efficiency of the SAARC. First of all, India's conflict with Pakistan. Second, the lack of trust among member states, which is connected to the third factor, the unwillingness to transfer any state prerogatives to the organisation (Ahmed 2016). The fourth factor is the lack of economic cooperation.

The first factor, the longstanding India-Pakistan conflict, was presented above. Because of tensions between India and Pakistan, SAARCS's summits were held irregularly despite plans that they should be held annually (Bajpai 2021). The first summit was held in 1985 and only 18 meetings have been held up to 2022. The year 2014 was special because it was the summit of SAARC in Nepal and also a meeting in India. Narendra Modi invited all SAARC leaders to New Delhi for the swearing-in as prime minister ceremony. It was supposed to be a new beginning for the SAARC and a new chapter in India-Pakistan relations. Unfortunately it didn't happen. The next meeting was the SAARC emergency meeting because of the COVID-19 pandemic which was held virtually in 2020 but the prime minister of Pakistan was not present, only the special assistant on health (Pattanaik 2021).

The second factor is the lack of trust among SAARC member countries. It was caused not only by the India-Pakistan conflict but also by India's strategy towards South Asia since the beginning of the 50s in the twentieth century. India as a dominant power in the region wanted to dominate its smaller neighbours. It explains the third factor which is the unwillingness of member states to transfer any state prerogatives to the SAARC. States are afraid that they could be misused by other members of the organisation to interfere in their domestic politics and in the longer perspective their foreign policy.

The fourth factor is the lack of economic cooperation. According to World Bank data, South Asia is the least economically integrated region in the world (The World Bank 2018). Only 7 percent of the value of a South Asian country's trade is intra-regional trade. The South Asian Free Trade Area (SAFTA) has theoretically been functioning since 2006, but it has not increased trade in the South Asian region (Kathuria & Rizwan 2019).

What is the influence of religion on the factors presented above? The influence of religion on India-Pakistan relations was presented in the previous section of the chapter. Lack of trust among SAARC member countries is related to religion and religious diversity but this is not the main reason for it. India is the birthplace of Buddhism and Hinduism which are among the most popular religions in South Asia. This was used by the Indian government to promote the idea of India as a civilisation state and that the main power in the region should be a centre of cultural, political and economic cooperation. But it should be done on Indian terms which was not acceptable to SAARC member countries. Since 2014 when BJP came to power and Narendra Modi became the prime minister, the promotion of the ideology of Hindutva also had a negative influence on the level of trust among states. As factor two is related to factor three, the role of religion is very similar. What about the influence of religion on economic cooperation in the SAARC? Religion plays a role in different perceptions of values and ethics in business. For example the approach to loans and credits differs among Hinduism, Buddhism and Islam, three of the most popular religions in South Asia. Lack of economic cooperation is rather caused by the three factors presented above than by religion and religious diversity which may affect it in a limited way.

To support the above presented arguments it is useful to look at the Bay of Bengal Initiative for Multi-Sectoral Technical and Economic Cooperation (BIMSTEC) which is considered by some researchers as the successor of the SAARC. The BIMSTEC was established in 1997 by Bangladesh, India, Myanmar, Sri Lanka and Thailand. All member countries are located on the Bay of Bengal, except for Nepal and Bhutan which became members only in 2014 (Kundu 2014). The accession of these two landlocked countries has intensified the views of researchers and politicians that BIMSTEC is SAARC but without Pakistan. Behind the creation of BIMSTEC was the idea that the organisation was to serve as a bridge between South and South-East Asia as a platform for inter-regional cooperation between SAARC and ASEAN members. The religious profile of member countries is even more diverse than SAARC countries (Table 5.1) but it didn't stop those countries from political and economic cooperation.

The Association of South-East Asian Nations (ASEAN)

The ASEAN was established in 1967 by the governments of Indonesia, Malaysia, the Philippines, Singapore and Thailand. Currently the members include founding member countries and Brunei, Vietnam, Laos, Myanmar and Cambodia. The ASEAN covers a population of more than 600 million and a total area of 4.5 million km^2 (Acharya 2021). Under the banner of cooperative peace and shared prosperity, it brings together disparate neighbours to address economic and security issues. It also focuses also on scientific, technological and cultural cooperation (Roberts 2021). Religious harmony and social cohesion have always been high on the agenda of national, regional and global platforms.

What is the role of religion in the integration process of the ASEAN? In South-East Asia there is no dominant religion. The major religions are: 38 percent of the entire population of South-East Asia follows Islam; 35 percent is Buddhist; 23 percent is Christian. It means that reaching consensus is very important, there is no dominant group which would be able to impose its ideology, values and way of integration. This is one of the reasons why the ASEAN is not really highly institutionalised and still gives a lot of freedom to member countries. This approach is characterised by "non-legalistic style of decision making," in which "there is no transfer of national authority to a supranational" body, which is known as the "ASEAN Way" or "soft institutionalism." Political cooperation is limited to some extent, due to the rule of non-interface (Narine 2008).

In 1976, the members signed the Treaty of Amity and Cooperation in South-East Asia, which emphasises mutual respect and non-interference in other countries' affairs. It also relates to religion. Member countries need to reach a consensus through consultation to make important decisions. The ASEAN is headed by a chair, which is a position that rotates annually among all member states. It means that each member state may have a chance to present its own perception of further integration processes, which may be influenced by the country's religious profile. ASEAN summit meetings, which from 2008 occur semi-annually, bring together the heads of state of member countries. What is more, there are also annual conferences for foreign ministers who discuss the most current issues (Roberts 2021). From 1967 to 2022, 41 summits took place. Frequent and regular meetings make it possible to try to solve the challenges that arise on a regular basis.

The ASEAN managed to develop initiatives such as ASEAN Plus Three, an annual meeting of the heads of state of ASEAN members and the leaders of China, the Republic of Korea and Japan; ASEAN Plus Six, which includes ASEAN Plus Three and Australia, India and New Zealand; and the East Asia Summit (Nishimura 2017). Those initiatives are evidence that countries outside of South-East Asia are interested in cooperation with the ASEAN, which is recognised by them as one of the actors in international relations.

However, there remain major challenges to economic integration, such as non-tariff barriers, government-mandated investment prohibition areas and differences in GDP per capita. Domestic issues, such as instability (such as the political crisis in Myanmar) and corruption, have also hurt trade within the bloc. Those challenges are only partially related to religious diversity.

Indo-Pacific: Does religion matter?

An overview and evolution of the perception of religion in theories of international relations and answers to the research questions serve to verify the hypothesis that assumes that religion is one of the factors which may affect international relations in the Indo-Pacific region and cannot be treated as only a minor or irrelevant factor as it is widely seen in the West (mostly European countries). It means that scholars who represent different theories of international relations should pay more attention to creating theoretical approaches in which religion will be used in a more efficient way and is understood as one of the factors which influence the dynamics of international relations.

It is finally time to answer the research questions. The first question was about the ways in which the level of religious diversity and status of a religion in a state may influence a state's foreign policy. The religious structure of the Indo-Pacific is very diverse. Sub-regions in the Indo-Pacific South Asia, South-East Asia and East Asia present various religious profiles. India, Indonesia, Australia and South Korea were used as case studies which represent each of the sub-regions. India is a *de jure* secular state but *de facto* it is not. Even before BJP came to power with its ideology of Hindutva, India had its own definition of secularism where religion may play a role in politics but only if all of them can play it to the same extent. Anti-Muslim discrimination policies like the CAA had caused tension in relations with countries in the neighbourhood. Indonesia is somewhere between ideas of secularism and an Islamic state. Religion to some extent plays a role in foreign policy as Indonesia supports Palestine and has close relations with Pakistan. But on the other hand, it does not support the Rohingya minority in Myanmar. In contrast to India and Indonesia, religion has a limited role in the foreign policy of Australia and South Korea. In the case of those two countries, the level of religious diversity is high and there is no dominant religious group which may be strong enough to influence domestic and external politics.

The second question was about the role that religion may play in the context of political and economic cooperation between states or in solving border conflicts, using relations between India and Pakistan as a case study. India and Pakistan represent different religious structures as well as the status of a religion in a state. India is a secular state (at least *de jure*), Pakistan is an Islamic Republic. Religion used to play and still plays an important role in the unresolved border conflict over Kashmir which has a negative effect on political and economic cooperation. But there are also attempts to use religion as a tool to improve relations between states, as in the case of the Kartarpur corridor in Punjab.

The third question was about the ways in which religion may influence the process of regional integration, using the SAARC and the ASEAN as case studies. The SAARC, because of the India-Pakistan conflict, lack of trust and unwillingness of member states to transfer any state prerogatives to the organisation, didn't achieve any of the goals which were presented in its charter. Member states (except Pakistan) are looking for other possibilities for regional integration, such as the BIMSTEC. South Asia has a very diverse religious profile with the dominant religion being Hinduism at 68 percent of the overall population, followed by Islam with 31 percent of followers, and then Buddhists, Jains, Christians, Sikhs and others at 10 percent. India stands for most of the population which are followers of Hinduism and it sees itself as a leader of the region. But it doesn't exercise its potential in integrating South Asia. It rather focuses on securing its own position in the region.

On the other hand, the ASEAN is one of the most successful examples of regional integration in the Indo-Pacific. With relatively low levels of institutionalisation, the rule of non-interface and such so-called Asian values, proponents put forward a socio-economic, psychological and intellectual basis for regional cooperation. In South-East Asia there is no dominant religion. The major religions are: Islam, at 38 percent of the entire population, Buddhism, at 35 percent, Christianity at 23 percent. There is also no one dominant power like India in South Asia. The benefits and advantages of integration are bigger than the disadvantages or problematic issues which may be also related to religious diversity.

To sum up, religion is one of the factors which affects international relations in the Indo-Pacific region but not to the same extent in every country or organisation. Religious diversity differs among countries, and there are also different ways of understanding secularism and religious freedom https://www.bbc.com/news/world-asia-india-61701908. Due to this, religion influences the foreign policy of countries located in the Indo-Pacific to varying degrees. It is not possible to clearly determine whether the influence of religion is positive or negative. But what we know for sure is that religion can't be treated as only a minor or irrelevant factor in analysing international relations in the Indo-Pacific as it is widely seen in the West (mostly European countries).

Note

1 Population growth in the Indo-Pacific is relatively stable with a total fertility rate around 2.2. According to the United Nations, Department of Economic and Social Affairs, the population of earth in 2100 will be 11 billion and ca. 5 billion will live in the Indo-Pacific (UN DESA 2017). Population density in the Indo-Pacific region is ca. 150 per km², which makes it the most densely populated part of the world compared to Africa ca. 45 per km², Middle East and North Africa ca. 30 per km², Europe ca. 34 per km² , South America ca. 25 per km², North America ca. 20 per km².

References

2021 Report on International Religious Freedom: South Korea, Office of International Religious Freedom, 2022. https.//www.state.gov/reports/2021-report-on-international -religious-freedom/south-korea/ (accessed 16 April 2022).

Acharya, Amitav, *ASEAN and Regional Order Revisiting Security Community in Southeast Asia*, (New York: Routledge, 2021).

Adeney, Katharine, *Federalism and Ethnic Conflict Regulation in India and Pakistan*, (New York: Palgrave Macmillan, 2007).

Ahmed, Zahid Shahab, *Regionalism and Regional Security in South Asia: The Role of SAARC*, (New York: Routledge, 2016).

Barker, Renae, "Nothing Less than the Character of Australian Secularism Is at Stake in the Religious Discrimination Debate", *ABC*, 2021, https://www.abc.net.au/religion/australian-secularism-and-the-religious-discrimination-debate/13655762 (accessed 29 May 2022).

BBC 2022a, "Nupur Sharma: Prophet Muhammad Remarks Deepen India's Diplomatic Crisis", *BBC*, https://www.bbc.com/news/world-asia-india-61701908 (accessed 4 July 2022).

BBC 2022b, "Ahok: Former Jakarta Governor Released Early from Prison", *BBC*, https://www .bbc.com/news/world-asia-46982779 (accessed 29 May 2022).

Britannica a, *Indonesia*, Britannica, https://www.britannica.com/place/Indonesia (accessed 16 February 2022).

Britannica b, *Australia*, Britannica, https://www.britannica.com/place/Australia (accessed 16 February 2022).

Akhter, Zainab, "India–Pakistan Relations: Efficacy of Culture", *Millennial Asia*, 7(2), 2016: 207–229.

Bajpai, Lopamudra Maitra, *India, Sri Lanka and the SAARC Region: History, Popular Culture and Heritage*, (New York: Routledge, 2021).

Barker, Renae, *State and Religion the Australian Story*, (New York: Routledge, 2019).

Barker, Renae, "Nothing Less than the Character of Australian Secularism Is at Stake in the Religious Discrimination Debate", *ABC*, 2021, https://www.abc.net.au/religion/australian -secularism-and-the-religious-discrimination-debate/13655762 (accessed 29 May 2021).

Bhatia, Rajiv, *BIMSTEC or SAARC*, Gateway House, February 2020, https://www.gatewayhouse .in/bimstec-or-saarc/ (accessed 16 February 2022).

"Census of 2011". http://censusindia.gov.in/ (accessed 23 May 2021).

Copson, Andrew, *Secularism – Politics, Religion, and Freedom*, (Oxford: Oxford University Press, 2017).

Durkheim, Émilie, *Elementarne formy życia religijnego. System Totemiczny w Australii*,(Warsaw: Państwowe Wydawnictwo Naukowe, 2010).

Economist Intelligence 2022, Democracy Index 2021: Less than Half the World Lives in a Democracy. https://www.eiu.com/n/democracy-index-2021-less-than-half-the-world-lives-in -a-democracy/ (accessed 16 April 2022).

Febrica, Senia, "Indonesia and the Indo-Pacific: Cooperation, Interests, and Strategies", in L. Buszynski, and D. T. Hai (Eds.), *Maritime Issues and Regional Order in the Indo-Pacific. Palgrave Studies in Maritime Politics and Security*, (London: Palgrave Macmillan, 2021), pp. 233–255.

Foreign Policy White Paper 2017, https://www.dfat.gov.au/publications/minisite/2017-foreign -policy-white-paper/fpwhitepaper/index.html (accessed 23 May 2021).

Fox, Jonathan and Sandal, Nukhet A, "Integrating Religion into International Relations Theory", in J. Haynes (Ed.), *Handbook of Religion and Politics*, (London and New York: Routledge, 2010), pp. 270–284.

Fox, James, "Is Ethnoreligious Conflict a Contagious Disease?", *Studies in Conflict & Terrorism*, 27(2), 2004: 89–106.

Fox, James, and Sandler, Shmuel, *Bringing Religion into International Relations*, (New York: Palgrave Macmillan, 2004).

Ganguly, Sumit, "The Crisis of Indian Secularism", *Journal of Democracy*, 14(4), 2006: 11–25.

George, Justin Paul, "When Indian Navy Worried Indonesia Would Send Submarines to Aid Pakistan in 1965", *The Week*, https://www.theweek.in/news/india/2021/04/26/when-indian -navy-worried-indonesia-would-send-submarines-to-aid-pakistan-in-1965.html (accessed 23 May 2021).

Guha, Ramachandra, *India after Gandhi*, (New Delhi: Picador, 2007).

Haidar, Suhasini, *A Bridge across the India-Pakistan Abyss*, The Hindu, July, 2019, https://www .thehindu.com/opinion/lead/a-bridge-across-the-india-pakistan-abyss/article28691824.ece (accessed 23 May 2021).

Hefner, Robert (Ed.), *Routledge Handbook of Contemporary Indonesia*, (New York: Routledge, 2018).

Hidetoshi Nishimura, "Snapshots of the ASEAN Story: ASEAN's Strategic Policy Needs and Dialogue Partners' Contributions", *The ASEAN Journey: Reflections of ASEAN Leaders and Officials*, 1, 2017: 315–348.

Huntington, Samuel P., "The Clash of Civilizations?", *Foreign Affairs*, 72(3), 1993: 22–49.

"Indonesia Backs Pakistan's ASEAN Full Dialogue Partner Status", *The Express Tribune*, 2022, https://tribune.com.pk/story/2350800/indonesia-backs-pakistans-asean-full-dialogue -partner-status (accessed 16 February 2022).

Jackson, Robert, and Sorensen, Georg, *Wprowadzenie Do Stosunków Międzynarodowych. Teorie I Kierunki Badawcze* (Kraków: Wydawnictwo Uniwersytetu Jagiellońskiego, 2012).

Jaskólska, Aleksandra, "Sekularyzm versus Hinduski Nacjonalizm w Systemie Politycznym Indii", in M. F. Gawrycki, E. Haliżak, R. Kuźniar, G. Michałowska, D. Popławski, and R. Z. Zięba (Eds.), *Tendencje I Procesy Rozwojowe Współczesnych Stosunków Międzynarodowych*, (Warszawa: Scholar, 2016).

Kathuria, Sanjay, and Rizwan, Nadeem, *How South Asia Can Become a Free Trade Area*, https:// blogs.worldbank.org/endpovertyinsouthasia/how-south-asia-can-become-free-trade-area (accessed 14 April 2019).

Kieniewicz, Jan, *Historia Indii*, (Wrocław: Ossolineum, 2003).

Kim, Andrew Eungi, "Characteristics of Religious Life in South Korea: A Sociological Survey", *Review of Religious Research*, 43(4), 2002: 291–310.

McKinnon, Andrew M., "Reading 'Opium of the People': Expression, Protest and the Dialectics of Religion", *Critical Sociology*, 31(1–2), 2005: 15–38.

Michael, Arndt, *India's Foreign Policy and Regional Multilateralism*, (New York: Palgrave Macmillan, 2013).

Ministry of Foreign Affairs, Republic of Korea, https://www.mofa.go.kr/eng/wpge/m_5664/contents.do.

Moravcsik, A. A., "The New Liberalism", in Ch. Reus-Smit, and D. Snidal (Eds.), *The Oxford Handbook of International Relations*, (Oxford: Oxford University Press, 2008, 234–254).

Murphy, Ann Marie, "Islam in Indonesian Foreign Policy: The Limits of Muslim Solidarity for the Rohingya and Uighurs", *Asan Institute for Policy Studies*, p.1–15, 2020.

Narine, Shaun, "Forty Years of ASEAN: A Historical Review", *The Pacific Review*, 21(4), 2008: 411–429.

Ng, Jefferson, "Indonesia-Israel Relations: Is a Breakthrough Imminent?", *The Diplomat*, https://thediplomat.com/2022/01/indonesia-israel-relations-is-a-breakthrough-imminent/ (accessed 16 April 2022).

Pattanaik, Smruti S., "COVID-19 Pandemic and India's Regional Diplomacy", *South Asian Survey*, 28(1), 2021: 92–110.

Pew Research, *Global Religious Diversity*, 2014, https://www.pewresearch.org/religion/2014/04/04/global-religious-diversity/ (accessed 16 April 2022).

Philpott, Daniel, "The Challenge of September 11 to Secularism in International Relations", *World Politics*, 55(1), 2002: 66–95.

Philpott, Daniel, "The Religious Roots of Modern International Relations", *World Politics*, 52(2), 2002: 206–245.

Rajopadhye, Hemant, *India-Pakistan Peacemaking: Beyond Populist Religious Diplomacy*, ORF Issue Brief Nr 343, March 2020, https://www.orfonline.org/research/india-pakistan-peacemaking-62226/ (accessed 14 April 2022).

"Realizing the Promise of Regional Trade in South Asia", The World Bank, https://www.worldbank.org/en/news/feature/2018/10/09/realizing-the-promise-of-regional-trade-in-south-asia (dostęp, 03.03.2018).

Reus-Smit, Christian, *On Cultural Diversity: International Theory in a World of Difference*, (Cambridge: Cambridge University Press, 2018).

Roberts, Christopher B., *ASEAN Regionalism Cooperation, Values and Institutionalisation*, (New York: Routledge, 2021).

Ropi, Ismatu, *Religion and Regulation in Indonesia*, (Singapore: Palgrave Macmillan, 2017).

Saha, Santosh, "South Asian Association for Regional Cooperation (SAARC) and Social Development in South Asia: A Study of Some Successful Experiences", *Indian Journal of Asian Affairs*, 2, 2005: 1–44.

Sampa Kundu, S., "BIMSTEC at 17: An Assessment of Its Potential", *India Quarterly*, 3, 2014: 207–224.

Shin, Hyonhee"S Korea's Ex-President Park Freed after Nearly 5 Years in Prison", https://www.aljazeera.com/news/2021/12/31/s-koreas-disgraced-ex-president-park-freed-after-nearly-5-years-in-prison (accessed 29 May 2022).

Shin, Soon-ok, "The Rise and Fall of Park Geun-Hye: The Perils of South Korea's Weak Party System", *The Pacific Review*, 33(1), 2020: 153–183.

Shu-Li, Wang, "Michael John Rowlands", in Yujie Zhu (Ed.), *Heritage and Religion in East Asia*, (New York: Routledge, 2020).

Snyder, Jack, "Introduction", in J. Snyder (Ed.), *Religion and International Relations Theory*, (New York: Columbia University Press, 2011), pp. 1–23.

Songbatumis, Aisyah Mumary, "The Role of Islam in Indonesian Foreign Policy: A Case of Susilo Bambang Yudhoyono", *Polish Political Science Yearbook*, 2, 2021: 89–111.

Sufian, Abu, "Geopolitics of the NRC-CAA in Assam: Impact on Bangladesh–India Relations", *Asian Ethnicity*, 23(3), 2022: 556–586.

UNPF, "World Population Dashboard", United Nations Population Fund, 2022, https://www .unfpa.org/data/world-population-dashboard (accessed 14 April 2022).

World Bank, "Realizing the Promise of Regional Trade in South Asia", The World Bank, 2018, https://www.worldbank.org/en/news/feature/2018/10/09/realizing-the-promise-of-regional -trade-in-south-asia (accessed 3 March 2020).

World Population Dashboard, (United Nations Population Fund, 2022), https://www.unfpa.org /data/world-population-dashboard (accessed 14 April 2022).

World Population Prospects: The 2017 Revision, (Department of Economic and Social Affairs, United Nations), https://www.un.org/en/desa/world-population-projected-reach-98-billion -2050-and-112-billion-2100 (accessed 16 April 2022).

Zenderowski, Radosław, "Religia I Stosunki Międzynarodowe", in K. Kącka (Ed.), *Stosunki Międzynarodowe Wokół Zagadnień Teoretycznych*, (Toruń: Wydawnictwo Naukowe UMK, 2014), pp. 131–166.

6 Authoritarian regimes and their evolution in the Indo-Pacific

Jeroen J.J. Van den Bosch

"You can change friends, but not neighbours."

Atal Bihari Vajpayee (1924-2018)

The political regimes of the Indo-Pacific (IP) are under-studied for two reasons: traditionally, this macro-region has been carved up between South, Southeast, East Asia or the Asia-Pacific perspectives,[1] and no integrated comparative viewpoint exists so far. Secondly, because the (re)invented IP is rather an international relations (IR) phenomenon, the most common frames used today are foreign policy analysis (FPA) or structural IR theories. While FPA mostly compares or contrasts individual state policies, using state-centric frames, and perceives the world through the lens of interests, threats and alliances, this chapter's approach bridges domestic politics (*Innenpolitik*) and IR.

This chapter breaks open the "black box" of states and takes a closer look at the regimes behind them that operate the state apparatus. How does the leader with an inner circle staff the foreign policy executive and thus formulate policies, accounting for their legitimation strategies, power-sharing strategies and restrictions resulting from having to maintain (authoritarian) control? My point of departure thus lies within the domestic realm and differs from realist approaches and their inherit "competition bias" (ignoring areas of cooperation to focus on interstate rivalry).

The objects of this chapter are thus political regimes,[2] defined here as a group of people, together encompassing a network regulated by a set of (formal and informal) rules that identify who holds political power; how its members are selected and appointed; structure the hierarchy, relations and power division among them; and how the regime interacts with the society it rules (Skaaning 2006). To study these regimes, I apply theoretical frameworks grounded in research on democracies and dictatorships, their classifications, internal dynamics, survival strategies as well as modes of cooperation.

This chapter offers a diachronic approach: the vast available datasets of regimes (classification per country year) make it possible to track regime evolutions since the late 1940s, a time many of these states re-entered the international realm as independent states. Below, I start with a theoretical frame of how to classify regimes and explain why I start after colonialism. Then, I briefly set the stage of the IP in which these regimes emerged, before tracking regime evolutions over time and identifying key moments of change (junctures). The goals are to assess contemporary legacies derived from such changes, analyse how past regimes pressed their own institutions

DOI: 10.4324/9781003336143-9

and norms upon the states they rule, and how successive regimes (or governments) today are still constrained by such earlier path dependencies.

Colonial regimes and political regime classifications

Political regimes as research objects are located between the concept of the state and a government. They are more permanent forms of political organisation than specific governments but typically less permanent than the states they rule. States are more durable (normatively neutral) structures of domination and coordination including a coercive apparatus and the means to administer a society and extract resources from it (Fishman 1990: 428).

It is common to identify the following groups in any political regime.

- **Leadership** (incumbent): the paramount power holder(s) in the regime. They maintain their coalition of supporters through the allocation of public and private goods.
- **Ruling coalition**: a subset of the selectorate of sufficient size such that this group's support endows the leadership with political power over the remainder of the selectorate as well as over the disenfranchised members of the society (residents).
- **Selectorate**: the set of people whose endowments include the qualities or character-istics[3] institutionally required to choose the government's leadership and necessary for gaining access to private benefits doled out by the government's leadership.
- (**Residents**: this large group is not part of the regime, but encompasses the rest of the population that is excluded from the selectorate by the leadership and ruling coalition.)

(Bueno de Mesquita et al. 2003: 37–54; Van den Bosch 2021b: 398–399)

Sovereignty is a key characteristic of political regimes. For this reason, I start my analysis after the end of colonial rule. A colonial state cannot be considered a fully functional state, they differ from regular states because they routinely lack three important defining attributes: sovereignty,[4] a "nation" and external agency in foreign affairs. Colonies evolved at a time when the European kingdoms that created them were themselves transforming (at different speeds) into modern states. For this reason, their products, colonial states (as a type) are characterised by a lot of diversity (Young 1994: 43). Of course, before the creation of the UN, variations of statehood were much more common and prevalent, with protectorates, fiefdoms, vassal states, colonies, satellite states, etc. However, lack of sovereignty, representation and agency in foreign policy were the major hurdles for such colonial polities during and after their transformation to independent states.

Colonial states and political regime theory

Colonial bureaucracies had been primarily designed to manage or control popula-tions and oversee the extraction of resources, not to deliver services. Infrastructure was similarly designed to facilitate extraction and colonial control, creating a bias between wealthy, industrial, urban or strategic centres and remote, rural and impov-erished regions. The relative late colonisation of various parts of the IP, made this bias extremely pronounced in some regions, like the South Asian archipelagos.

In similar fashion, a colonial regime is not really considered a political regime. Such colonial regimes differ from most political regimes in the sense that the supreme powerholders are foreigners and part of an international network, often controlling other colonial polities. There is a surprising level of formalisation (for such autocratic polities), precisely stipulating and regulating the vertical power relations between the colonisers and the subjects or colonised (taxation, duties, liberties, judicial status, etc.), even when the latter is almost fully excluded from the regime's selectorate.

It is the horizontal dimension, or how power relations are structured with local elites, where colonial regimes differ most. However, the simple division between direct and indirect (colonial) rule does not suffice to capture this variety: colonial phases lasted for decades (if not centuries), and local institutions that collaborated or were forcibly co-opted did evolve over time – at times transforming their power bases and (regional) legitimacy patterns. In addition, sometimes "alien" institutions (e.g. churches) established by the coloniser to include native elites, did earn legitimacy in the eyes of the colonised. In the end, the moral bankruptcy of the colonial system led to more autonomy for subaltern organisations. Some would become important political organisations during transitions – ensuring their survival in some form or another, as well as the influence of its members in the new political dawn. Others would be branded as collaborators and dismantled post-independence.

Nonetheless, even when local elites (religious, political, regional) and their patronage networks (even entire previously autonomous kingdoms) were included in the selectorate of colonial regimes (and benefited from it), this regime type does not match all criteria to be considered a full-fledged political regime (on equal terms with those in independent polities.) Provincial, subaltern elites were kept from building up too much autonomy and concentrating power and did not control key military positions. They were often excluded from real foreign policy formulation. Their own subjugation to colonial law and their lesser legal status (e.g. *vis-à-vis* Western colonial residents) kept elites considered inside the "inner circle" actually too far from the locus of central power, unable to overthrow the real power holders. Nonetheless, the co-optation of old monarchic structures would matter for regime transformations after de-colonisation as I show below.

Classifying independent political regimes

In this chapter, I distinguish between the following regime types, following the typology of B. Geddes, E. Franz and J. Wright, used to classify authoritarian regimes. Their classification has been widely used by scholars since the early 2000s and is accompanied by a large dataset, used in this chapter (but is not the only classification of this kind) (Geddes 1999; Geddes et al. 2012a/b).

- **Monarchies** – A now "endangered" regime type, where a royal family are the powerholders, with a king, queen, sultan, shah or equivalent at the head of the regime and with extended family, aristocracy, business elites and top army officials making up the selectorate. Their small, exclusive, inner circle can be quite repressive in order to stay in power, because there is no good exit option other than handing over power and becoming a constitutional monarchy. In modern states, they are seldom divided because of their kin-network. As a type, they are resilient and have procedures for succession.

- **Military regimes** – Here a group of officers decides who will rule and exercises some influence on policy. Sometimes they rule directly (for short periods); sometimes they hide behind a technocratic government (or monarchy). When united, such regimes do not flinch from resorting to mass repression. When divided they prefer to return to the barracks instead of fighting amongst themselves. This is an exit option other regime types do not have.
- **Party-based regimes** – Here, access to political office and control over policy are dominated by one party, though other parties may legally exist and compete in elections. The military is controlled by a civilian apparatus (or its top leadership blended with it). There is a distinction between *single party regimes* (*de jure* or *de facto*) when there is no competition with other parties; *hegemonic party regimes* where elections take place, but they are neither free nor fair; and *dominant parties* where elections are free but not fair. Here the ruling coalition is the politburo or equivalent, and the rest of the selectorate are other party members and affiliates. Usually, succession is decided in the politburo, and when forced to democratise, these parties can continue to play a role in a post-transition order.
- **Personalist regimes** differ from both military and party-based regimes in that access to office, and the fruits of office depend much more on the discretion of an individual leader. The leader may be an officer or may have created a party to support himself, but neither the military nor the party exercises independent decision-making power insulated from the whims of the ruler. Without checks on the ruler by the ruling coalition, all decisions fall to the discretion of the leader, rendering policy unpredictable and making them resort to repression easily. Due to this form of extreme exclusion, using divide-and-rule tactics on the ruling coalition and selectorate, regime competition for rents is fierce. These regimes have no exit option, so they often cling to power by all means. They do not have procedures for succession but have a tendency for dynastism.

(Geddes 1999; Geddes et al. 2012a/b)

Setting the stage: Systemic evolution of the Indo-Pacific

Even in early modern times, the interconnectedness of the Asian sub-regions has often been highlighted by historians (even if they used an array of different concepts). The strong links between South and Southeast Asia with China (sometimes labelled as "Southern Asia") were very clear, and the foreign policies of all major regional actors were benchmarked toward this spatial continuum covering most of Asia.

Initially, this realm was bipolar and much of its territory constituted Western colonies and protectorates. British India was the central power in this proto-Indo-Pacific, then called the East Indies. India, as a semi-autonomous colonial state, rivalled Qing China and maintained direct diplomatic ties with other polities in the larger region as far as Japan. Of course, the Raj's India was a vehicle for British colonial interests, and upheld the latter's sway in Asia, particularly by providing manpower for colonial wars and acting as its main base of operations (Pardesi 2020: 127–129).

By the turn of the century, the weakening and implosion of Qing China and the ascendance of Japan and the latter's increasing imperial expansion would lead to fragmentation and a shift of the macro-region's gravity centre (from the Indian Ocean to the Western Pacific), which happened at first without much great power friction – at least until 1923 (the end of the Anglo-Japanese alliance) (Pardesi 2020: 130).

Interesting is the role of Tsarist Russia as a catalyst in this power shift (today equally often omitted in contemporary conceptions of the IP). Russia's expansion by the late 19th century pushed the British to rally with Japan. The ongoing British-Russian rivalry under the "Great Game" (1830–1907) did not stay confined to Iran or Afghanistan as Russia expanded and consolidated its influence in the Far East. Since Japan similarly felt threatened by the Russian refusal to acknowledge their possessions in the Korean peninsula, the alliance served to safeguard the mutual protection of British and Japanese interests in East Asia. This pact collapsed in 1923 under continuous US (and Canadian) pressure.

In the interwar years, the effects of the Great Depression were felt worldwide, and old power relations changed. British predatory fiscal policies in India became untenable, eventually reducing the empire to a second-rate great power by the 1930s. The ensuing power vacuum was then filled by Japan after its own military took over the reins of power, invaded Manchuria in 1931 under false pretences, and started its all-out conquest in 1937. With the spread of fascism in Europe, Britain was tied up there, and unable to halt a modernised Japan's military-propelled rise in the IP. Russia was still reeling from the October revolution and the Russian Civil War (fuelled and prolonged by the 1919 allied intervention in Siberia, including Japan). China had descended into civil war after the Qing dynasty was overthrown in 1911, and was still in disarray. The US was similarly unable to counter Japan militarily but actively pursued diplomacy aimed at isolating the now fascist regime by withholding any form of external legitimacy to the latter's conquests and annexations.

The attack on Pearl Harbor would be the turning point to draw the US in militarily. And after several years of heavy fighting, when the Japanese were pushed back and rallying to defend their homeland, it was again the Russian factor – Stalin's swift entry into the Pacific War theatre once the Soviet Army had taken Berlin – that pushed the US to accept Japanese conditional surrender and protect its own hard-fought influence in the region from Soviet encroachment.[5]

The emerging Cold War and bipolar order in this macro-region would carve up the concept of a united IP (into smaller sub-regions) and also set the stage for independence and statehood for the countries that currently inhabit the region. Most significantly these post war critical junctures[6] combined would fray the colonial order and influence political regime trajectories in ways that still matter today. This chapter thus starts at this point in time to analyse regime evolutions and identifies several important crossroads during and after the Cold War that triggered the regime change patterns in South, Southeast and East Asia, which later allowed a convergence of regimes leading to the reintegration of one larger IP region.

Monarchic survival in the Indo-Pacific

As elsewhere before the advent of colonialism, the largest polities in the IP were empires and kingdoms (with Rajahs, Sultans, etc.), which of course are both run by monarchic regimes. Smaller polities were city-states and chiefdoms (with indigenous princely rulers), who mostly also operated with hereditary monarchic dynasties (although not always patrilineal).

The survival chances of monarchic polities, both large and small, depended on their ability to resist colonisation, and also knowing when to cease resisting. After conquest, in all European colonies, there was actually only a thin layer of colonial cadres that had to manage newly incorporated territories.

True, larger, weakened empires were usually toppled by colonial powers supporting an opposing dynastic faction and putting a puppet ruler on the throne, or by decentralising power in former vassal polities and undoing the ruling dynasty. For instance, after the overthrow of the Qing dynasty in China, the Japanese imperial regime set up the "independent" Chinese **Empire of Manchukuo** (in the former disputed Manchurian territories) after 1934, nominally ruled by the reclusive, child-emperor Puyi (溥儀), the last crown prince of the Manchu branch – but fully controlled by the Japanese, encroaching ever deeper onto Chinese territories.

Smaller kingdoms were often incorporated intact into colonial structures. In contrast to Manchu rule, the **Korean Empire** befell such a fate in 1905 (indirect rule through a Japanese resident-general), but five years later it was already formally annexed to Japan and its dynasty abolished. Exceptions existed when local elites persisted so long in their resistance that colonial states did not want to empower them as their agents or where societies were so decentralised that no authority figure could be found, or thirdly, if the dominance of white settlers precluded the need for co-optation (Young 1994: 107). The latter two exceptions are very rare for the IP. Mostly remote tropical zones and small islands were directly incorporated, but real colonial control on the ground was tenuous. Pockets of white (plantation) settlements could be found in a few (smaller) provinces (e.g. Vietnam) but were usually displaced during decolonisation, unlike in Africa (Algeria, Kenya, South Africa), where entire regions were governed this way, just like in Oceania (Australia, New Zealand and New Caledonia).

Monarchic abolition and subjugation

Two examples of the first exception would be Aceh and Burma: the conquest of the Sultanate of Aceh (in today's **Indonesia**) by the Dutch during the "Aceh War" (Indonesian: *Perang Aceh*), officially from 1873 to 1904, was a protracted conflict, spanning decades, resulting in low-scale guerrilla warfare and even a holy war with suicide attacks, lasting until the Japanese occupation. The last sultan was captured and exiled, and selected aristocrats were co-opted to run the new "province." In contrast, the Sultanate of Mataram (on Java) was colonised by the Dutch and in 1755 split in two (later four) smaller polities, resulting in the Sultanates of Yogyakarta and Surakarta (Solo). Reduced in territory, they continued to exist as vassal states in the Dutch East Indies. After independence, they pledged allegiance to President Sukarno, but today, only one of them (Yogyakarta) survives as a special Indonesian province (even after reinstitution of some lost lands) with their sultan as governor, a hereditary position for the local dynasty.

In **Burma**, the initial hostility of the Konbaung dynasty and the ensuing bloody (first) Anglo-Burmese War (1824–1826) with Raj India, was followed by two more British-provoked wars (in 1852–1853 and 1885) concluding with the overthrow of King Thibaw Min and the annexation of Burma as a province of British India, making Rangoon its new capital. The country's turbulent post-independence history might have looked much different if the Konbaung had been allowed to continue under British rule and if there had been a central patronage network to rally around different groups for state-building.

Many monarchies survived the onslaught of colonialism (but not independence) by becoming sub-national polities and subordinating their patronage network to a larger colonial regime network. Colonial regimes used the traditional legitimacy of such monarchs to control (and tax) their populations, in exchange for some of the fruits of office. Monarchies had the best chance of survival if they collaborated early after takeover (and could prove their continued usefulness to the coloniser by maintaining law and order) like in India, Laos or Cambodia, or if their polity had inherent strategic significance (like the **Malay sultanates**).

As well-established patronage networks, such monarchies could exert quite some influence on the colonising power (e.g. the Sultanate of Johor as one of the Unfederated Malay States), but depending on the unification process, many would perish during centralisation and nationalisation processes after independence. The (over 550) princely states in **India** lost much of their real power, while some of the larger retained their splendour and (sometimes) their regional influence. Like in the federation of Malaysia, their inclusion (considering their former levels of autonomy) would form an effective counterweight against centralisation attempts by the new powerholders. Even if such princely states did lose out over time, the process required a lot of negotiation and consultation (especially in India) – making new regimes much more collegial (even if not necessarily democratic: e.g. Malaysia). The lack of princely states that joined Pakistan has been listed as one of several reasons for its structural autocratic predisposition (Roychowdhury 2021).

The kingdoms of **Laos** and **Cambodia** were kept intact by the French within their larger Indochina colonial regime, but not in **Vietnam**, where the Nguyễn dynasty resisted in 1885. In response, the French landed 42,000 troops and the annexation of inland Indochina happened in stages: first Cochinchina (with Saigon), later Annam and Tonkin, soon after turning Cambodia and Lao into protectorates. After razing the Nguyễn royal palace in Hue in 1888, direct rule was installed in Cochinchina, while the two other Vietnam protectorates were ruled indirectly through local ruling elites, Cambodia and Laos were managed through their kingdoms, which could regain a significant amount of autonomy under some kings (Schulte Nordholt 2016: 193–194). These last two monarchies would finally be undone in the revolutions of the 1970s, but lost their real grip on power in the civil wars before, mostly to renegade generals trying to stop a communist takeover. Only in Cambodia was the king reinstalled, in 1993, as a constitutional monarch.

Monarchic outliers

However, in some places decolonisation also brought opportunities for those monarchic polities that strategised a better future through continued alliance with the former coloniser or another foreign patron.

Brunei Darussalam (a gas and petroleum exporter since the 1960s) stayed in British orbit until 1984 but had been negotiating for more autonomy since 1959. A 1962 Brunei uprising was suppressed with British help and galvanised the sultanate to stay out of the Malay federation. Later it used British clout to have Malaysia and Indonesia respect its sovereign status after independence. Today, it is still an absolute monarchy and thus has a similar trajectory to other former kingly protectorates (e.g. Swaziland and Lesotho in Southern Africa), but due to its large natural resource wealth, the Sultan's grip on power is unchallenged, and he does not cede much power to "channel" discontent. Recently, the ageing Sultan Hassanal Bolkiah introduced Sharia Law, which paves the path for more domestic repression (against idling, discontent youth, excluded from government employment) and serves to attract investments from the Gulf states (Brennan 2014).

Bhutan switched its role from a British protectorate to a "protected state" of independent India, hoping to keep the ruling dynasty in power through isolation, banning foreign technology, and balancing its external diplomatic relations with powerful neighbours. Pressure through the "special relationship" with India and growing restlessness domestically did lead to soul-searching and finally increased democratisation, initiated by the last two kings of the Wangchuk dynasty itself, turning the country into a constitutional monarchy in 2005–2008, where most power resides in a parliament. The royal family maintains significant influence of course, especially in foreign policy, and this transformation is not considered a "selfless act" by scholars, but rather a strategic move to preclude a more violent ouster (Muni 2014: 159).

At the time of writing, **Nepal** has been the last monarchy in the region to fall. A British alliance had shielded them from intermingling with neighbours until Indian independence. What followed was a long tug-of-war of granting political freedoms to its diverse ethno-religious population and later reneging on promises by closing the legislative, arresting opposition leaders and upholding an "apolitical" government run by the monarch. A Maoist insurrection joined the fray in the 1990s, and Nepal slipped into a state of civil war soon after. A fatal blow to the coherence and legitimacy of the monarchy was the 2001 royal massacre, in which the crown prince murdered the king, queen and seven other members of his family, to succumb to his injuries from a suicide attempt soon after. Only UN intervention brought an end to the armed conflict, and the resulting interim constitution took away power from the royal family. Its fate – abolition – was decided in 2007 by the new democratic assembly.

To conclude, independent monarchies in the IP are now few and far between, but their legacy lingers beyond their imprint on national histories and cultures. The presence of several resilient monarchic networks within one polity can affect future regime formation. The impact of such sub-national monarchies on personalisation processes is quite clear, locking in governing cultures of decentralisation and collegiality, and thus slowing power centralisation (and the emergence of personalist rule). Clear examples are India and Malaysia.

However, the presence of a single monarchic regime within a polity yields a different dynamic. There seems to be a symbiotic relationship between military rule and a national monarchy, where the latter hides behind the former for legitimacy reasons: **Thailand** (Siam) – which was never colonised – is the best example that still functions in this fashion today (see below). But Laos and Cambodia befell the same fate during their civil wars starting in the 1960s with uniformed coup leaders hiding behind the façade of the traditional ruling family.

The crossroads of liberation and decolonisation (1945–1960)

For former colonies, the overlapping goals of communism and anti-Imperialism complicated the picture in the aftermath of World War II (until about 1955) and resulted in an ambivalent relationship toward the broad spectrum of domestic communists and socialist parties. These had appeared in the region, starting in 1920 with the Indonesian PKI (*Perserikatan/Partai Kommunist de India*). China (1921), India and

Vietnam (both 1925) were the other frontrunners. While the rise and fall of communist parties in the IP are important nuances for regime formation, for reasons of space I am unable to provide a detailed overview. Suffice it to say, during the interwar period (too) early armed uprisings resulted in fatal colonial crackdowns that often obliterated such parties for decades, forcing them to slowly recover underground. While the Bolshevik takeover was the major impetus and source of support and legitimacy, the geographical distance from Russia precluded the transfer of many logistical supplies. Therefore, the *Chinese Communist Party* (CCP) would take over that role but would only deliver effectively to Vietnam and North Korea after 1950 when their protracted civil war and WWII had ended. Most other communist movements received token aid, as the PRC was unwilling to provoke an outright US reaction or jeopardise its relations with friendly nations (e.g. Burma or Indonesia) (Wajid Ali 1975: vii–xvi).

Most of the smaller communist parties throughout Asia had been resuscitated during 1941–1945. Without much guidance from Moscow, they established working alliances with nationalists, united in a common anti-fascist, anti-colonial front. Alas, the different trajectories of individual parties are beyond the scope of this chapter. It was the struggle against the Japanese occupation (more than the failed attempt to restore colonial control) that had turned many of these nationalist and communist parties into effective, politically salient organisations, primed for guerrilla warfare with some preparing for large-scale armed struggle.

Between 1945 and 1960 regimes of the IP split up onto three distinct pathways to independence:

1. the frontrunner nationalist road;
2. the militant revolutionary road;
3. the default road to independence.

The undoing of the Japanese occupation (in its different forms) and the end of WWII is a major juncture that would affect decolonisation trajectories. The war's aftermath would empower a first generation of independent leaders able to break the shackles of colonial rule: North and South Korea (1945) were declared independent by their respective allied forces. Indonesia (1945) succeeded where Vietnam failed, pushing for independence before their displaced colonial rulers could regain control. Pakistan and India (1947) had (re)negotiated their conditions for independence during the war, and this included Burma/Myanmar (1948) and Sri Lanka (1948) soon after. Together with the Philippines and Thailand (which were not colonies), this would complete the list of countries that would reassert their sovereignty in the international system and thus did not need to ally with communist factions to obtain independence with violent means.

Nationalist frontrunners

Grabbing and not sharing independence

The Japanese occupation had displaced colonial regimes and fostered armed resistance by national and communist groups. As mentioned, they often collaborated in a united front and shared anti-colonial and nationalist aspirations, but this was an uneasy alliance, once independence was achieved.

The Japanese had supplanted colonial armies with their own creations, like Aung San's nationalists (**Burma/Myanmar**) or the Indonesian *Giyugun* and *Heiho* (volunteer and auxiliary). In these cases, nationalist elites could tap into this military potential to demand independence: Aung San joined the anti-Japanese struggle in 1944 and then rallied a coalition against the British to negotiate independence. In **Indonesia**, just after the Japanese surrender, nationalist leaders Sukarno and Hatta declared independence and enlisted radicalised youths into youth militias, integrating them into the recently disbanded and better-disciplined Japanese-formed organisations to defend their revolution (Van den Bosch 2021a: 265–267).

In the **Philippines** the landed elites bundled forces with US troops to eliminate the powerful *Hukbalahap*, its native anti-Japanese (communist) peasant army from central Luzon (in exchange the US would retain its military bases) (Francia 2014: Chapter 5). To **Taiwan**, the US ferried Chinese nationalist troops across the strait to accept Japanese surrender, and once they lost the war with the communists on the mainland, they would remain in charge on this archipelago. The **Thai** military had retained its own autonomy (switching sides against Imperial Japan only after the atomic bombings). Its military leaders withdrew to their barracks, granting political control to a civilian government (with communists free to operate without repression between 1946 and 1947), but biding their time to return (Ang Cheng Guan 2018: 37).

In all these four cases, nationalist forces got the upper hand. With independence achieved early, they would turn on their former allies and their revolutionary agenda as these became a threat to the elite-dominated status quo, their privileges and newly-gained spoils of office. This inevitably would lead down a path where communist elements would be persecuted and eradicated, entrenching conservative regimes that by default would side with the anti-communist bloc.

The Philippines was the first to violently eradicate their erstwhile communist allies. Already in 1945, they turned against the "Huks" and other communist movements. By doing so at the inception of their (renewed) full independence, they were able to uphold their civilian government in the process. Taiwan similarly rolled out the "White Terror" after 1947 (lingering until 1987), targeting intellectuals, "spies," dissidents, and anyone who was perceived to oppose the regime. By contrast, in Burma (1948), Thailand (1957) and Indonesia (1965) militaries would soon take over from nationalist ruling parties to deal with communists and other challengers.

Promised independence and structural dispositions

As soon as WWII broke out, politicians of the Indian National Congress enforced negotiations for independence with Britain. The fall of France (1940), every Japanese victory (e.g. in Burma and Singapore by early 1942) and every major crisis were used to negotiate a better deal until the British closed the talks. This radicalised into the "Quit India" movement and subsequent violent repression by Britain. In search of new allies during this deep crisis, the collaborating Muslim League received a seat at the table and thus also in the renewed post-war negotiations in 1945. By then, a weakened Britain could no longer control the negotiations, nor had the will or resources to keep their restive colony in check. After minor players were removed during the early talks, Congress and the Muslim League bargained hard, resulting in the two-state partition.

In the end, structural factors played a major role in the divergence of the Indian and Pakistani pathways. **India** was able to secure the central colonial bureaucracy, police force and army command. This led to tiresome negotiations and a lot of back-door arm-wrestling, but it did allow a collegial legislative branch to be formed (with Congress taking 45% of the votes and 74% of the seats), with a strong executive to reign in peripheral (centrifugal) regions and govern its large amount of princely states (Jalal 1995: 31, 37). This trend ingrained collegiality in politics, as it rolled out bureau-cratic patronage (bossism). The military, in these first decades, would remain firmly under civilian control (Van den Bosch 2021a: 266–267; Tudor 2013).

Quite the opposite happened in (West and East) **Pakistan**. The 1947 secession of Muslim Pakistan led to a stronger dominance of unelected elements from the onset, especially the military. While starting out with only 17.5% of the financial assets, it contained 30% of the defence forces of undivided India, but on a scope of only 23% of its land mass and 18% of the population (Jalal 1995: 22–23). The military protected its privileges and (due to the war with India) its defence budget in 1948 was higher than that of undivided India. Together with a Punjabi-captured bureaucracy, Western Pakistani landed elites and the military soon struck a deal to protect their position, resorting to violence (Jalal 1995: 54–55). The 1951 assassination of Liaquat Ali Khan, the first governor-general, heralded a long legacy of military domination in politics, formalised with the 1958 coup d'état. **Bangladesh** would fall victim to these same ills, exacerbated by its violent war for independence, obtained in 1971 (Van den Bosch 2021a: 266–267; Tudor 2013).

Hijacking independence and renegade regime change

The Korean War (1950) was the first proverbial pebble in the puddle that sent shock-waves throughout the IP, contributing to its carving up into smaller sub-regions. The Soviet advance into the northern part of the country, and the swift move by allied forces in the south to impede Soviet forces from controlling the whole peninsula had resulted in two respective (randomly) delineated zones of control, with no proper plan on either side how to proceed, let alone integrate these territories (Seth 2016: Chapter 3).

Both Moscow and Washington shifted through various options for installing local loyalists with enough legitimacy to govern these polities while various political experi-ments were considered to merge them. In both cases, the chosen "puppet" rulers went rogue. The US grudgingly embraced the authoritarian, strident nationalist Syngman Rhee that quickly became the "tail that wagged the dog" and personalised power right away with a brutal security service. The Soviets swiftly installed a rather effective sys-tem of communist governance, by setting up "soviets" (councils) for local governance, initiating land reforms, etc. – but their chosen peon, Kim Il-Sung, would personalise power *after* the Korean War (Van den Bosch 2017: 53–55; Oh & Hassig 2000).

In any case, both **Korean regimes** were frontrunners in using gatekeeping – manipu-lating foreign (geopolitical) leverage – to strengthen their own position by coaxing the great powers that supported them. After the "June 25 Incident" (or Korean War, 1950–1953) the US approach to communism changed, treating it as a globalised, rela-tively integrated and cohesive threat that must be contained. It boldened US support to work with/through the French in support of Vietnamese nationalists, despite their misgivings about French colonialism (Lee 1995: 114–116). As the US would be drawn into the Vietnam War (Second Indochina War, 1955–1975) and the ideological front-line would shift to Southeast Asia, so too would new regimes along this rift of great power proxy-conflict benefit from gatekeeping opportunities that would result in the consolidation of personalisation patterns in the anti-communist camp.

Militant revolutionary war

As mentioned, the coordinating role of Russia was small between 1942 and 1947 due to distance and communication issues, (Ang Cheng Guan 2018: 37) and in China a nationalist focus prevailed in the first decades after their communist takeover in 1949, providing merely token aid to other regimes (except to their neighbours, Korea and Vietnam).

The reoccupation of **Vietnam** by the French of course pushed the country into a second group of regime pathways. After having obtained "permission" from the Vichy-regime in Nazi-occupied France, the Japanese extended their hold over Indochina during WWII. By August 1940, they had set up bases in North Vietnam, and a year later had done the same in the south with the aim of advancing further into Malaya, Siam (Thailand) and Burma. By 1941, Ho Chi Minh had set up a Vietnamese armed national resistance, the Vietminh, who were violently suppressed by the Japanese until the very end of the war. The famines in (north) Vietnam in 1944 and 1945, claiming almost one million lives, led to an influx of recruits for the communist front. After Japan's surrender, the Vietminh were allowed to take over and declare independence (on 2 September 1945). Nationalist Chinese and nearby-stationed British troops swiftly re-occupied the northern and southern parts of Indochina, respectively, when instructed to disarm the Japanese. The south was lost for the Vietminh when the French returned and created the Cochinchina republic with help of the *Cao Dai*. (The *Đạo Cao Đài* were a syncretistic religious, nationalist sect that had its own militia). However, once the Nationalist Chinese forces retreated, Ho Chi Minh could re-establish control in the northern and central regions. By late 1946, the armed struggle had broken out against the French, and the Vietnamese communists would lead the anti-colonial struggle in Indochina (Schulte Nordholt 2016: 261–262; Ang Cheng Guan 2018: 35).

In different stages, this conflict would spill over into **Cambodia** and **Laos**, hardening US foreign policy and their containment policy. This revolutionary struggle and domestic civil wars swallowed the monarchies of Laos and Cambodia that had become independent polities in 1949 and 1953, respectively. Together with the PRC and North Korea, Indochina would become one large Asian communist bloc, linking up with Mongolia and the USSR. Although the latter would detach from the IP sphere for good after the Sino-Soviet split. Around 1956, Mao Zedong in China and Kim Il-Sung in North Korea – who had created their own regimes on Stalinist models – completely disapproved of Khrushchev's reforms (co-existence with the West, de-Stalinisation, the Hungarian crisis) and decided to erode linkages with the USSR. As a result, the PRC emerged as the default leader in the Asian communist bloc, although they kept collaborating with the USSR in Vietnam (Van den Bosch 2017).

Independence by default

In this period, there is a last group of regimes that established civilian regimes after their colonisation. These cases like Bhutan (1949) Malaysia (1957), Singapore (1965) and Brunei (1984) did not push for swift independence for strategic reasons. Bhutan and Brunei needed good relations with neighbours first and the support of their former coloniser to uphold their viable monarchic polities.

The newly created **Malay Federation** and **Singapore** underwent the traumatic "Malayan Emergency" in 1948–1960, a communist uprising in both countries (mostly the former and operating from southern Thailand), the eerie result of smouldering labour relations, rapid British economic policy for recovery, and long-term discrimination of ethnic Chinese. Because Malaysia and Singapore (and later Thailand) found themselves so near the Indochina front, they were guarded by the international embrace of SEATO (Southeast Asia Collective Defense Treaty, or Manila Pact). Their ruling elites thus achieved independence as anti-communist allies, tied to Western leverage, after having persecuted or at least contained their communist parties with allied help. Their late independence also precluded the need for a strong military build-up. Therefore, these regimes stayed civilian in nature. For instance, in Malaysia, the police force has more political influence and better training and weaponry than the army (Croissant & Lorenz 2018: 164–165).

To summarise, the brief interlude of Japanese control had an important long-run impact on regimes in the IP. Independence movements organised during the war, whether with inconsistent Japanese aid or in the face of Japanese repression, survived and determined the pathways. Nationalist frontrunners would break the shackles of colonialism and then turn on their erstwhile communist allies, retaining civilian regimes if they did so right away (Philippines, Taiwan) or radicalising into military regimes later if they let their communist parties rise in power first (Burma, Thailand, Indonesia). Attempts to restore pre-war colonial control led to disaster and violent struggle (Vietnam, Cambodia, Laos), and wars that would radicalise both ideological camps and break up the IP into sub-regions.

The Cold War divide and regime crystallisation (1965–1985)

The protracted war in Vietnam was the main course in a long banquet of appetisers that engulfed the IP with Cold War paradigms. Between 1965 and 1985, most regimes of the IP split up into two main distinct pathways, and a less-trodden third way for those regime types that were not compatible with said paradigms. In a way, regimes in the IP "crystallised" or took a more solid, durable shape in these decades.

1. the road of strategic opportunism;
2. the road of revolution and regime transformation;
3. the road of isolation and insulation (cf. section on monarchic survival).

The catalysers of this period where the all-in US involvement in Vietnam, and afterward, their protracted exit, which forced countries in the IP to work out a modus vivendi with the PRC.

Strategic gatekeeping and opportunist personalisation

During the 1970s and 1980s about one-third of all regimes in the IP turned personalist and locked their polities in consolidated one-man rule. A key pillar to achieve this was by gatekeeping their international relations. With Cold War-posing and oscillating threat levels, regimes negotiated aid, military hardware and training, foreign direct investment (FDI), trade agreements, etc. to boost their patronage networks, hone their secret services, increase vigilance and bolster their repressive apparatuses.

Those regimes that had potential alternatives to US and anti-communist support (and could play off great powers against one another) all turned personalist. Those that had no alternatives (like Taiwan and South Korea after Rhee) upheld authoritarian single parties (but de-personalised). The former group got unflinching support and survived for decades (**Indonesia, Philippines**) without external pressure to democratise before 1985. Those countries that received wavering or cyclical support (**Myanmar, Thailand, Pakistan**) were sometimes interrupted by short stretches of civilian rule.

Often such regimes became military-personalist hybrids, a rather uncommon form when compared to other continents. Here, the armed forces remained a cohesive force, even when they are commanded by a personalist ruler. To achieve this, top military officers shared in state patronage and were able to set up their own networks in exchange for loyalty. Unlike the regular type, these hybrid military tyrants do not drive wedges between army factions to achieve more control over them (Van den Bosch 2021a: 262, 268).

Initially, Vietnam, Cambodia and Laos also had personalist flare-ups. Dan Slater and S. Levitsky with L. Way find that when threatened, counter-revolutionary regimes merge the interests of their diverse elites. Because Leftist rebellions draw on urban dwellers to seize the capital and to plan the overthrow of power positions and property rights, conservative elites align and agree on this common threat, making economic and communal elites turn to protection pacts, ready to cede authority, tax revenue and other resources to strongmen to repel such existential threats (Slater 2018: 5–6; Levitsky & Way 2016: 216).

This resulted in (short-lived) personalist rule in regimes in **South Vietnam** (1955–1963), **Laos** (1959–1962) and **Cambodia** (1971–1975), that in the process all cast aside their inept monarchies to rally behind Cold Warriors. Even Rhee in **South Korea** (1948–1960) fits this mould; and partly Malaysia, although never personalist (due to its federative nature) (Van den Bosch 2021a: 265).

An important observation is that not only anti-communist regimes consolidated personalist rule. **North Korea** is quite the exception in this regard (see lower), but its extraordinary policy of extreme isolation, and by gatekeeping its relations with the USSR and the PRC after 1956, protected the regime from ideological erosion and turned it into a resilient, hereditary, communist personalist-single party hybrid.

Revolutionary regime transformation

Vietnam, Laos and Cambodia (until the fall of the Khmer Rouge) underwent deep structural change of their political and socio-economic systems, adopting and adapting Bolshevik or Maoist models to their own realities, while also learning from North Korea. Real revolutionary parties are hardened in the fires of a violent power seizure. A prolonged, ideologically-driven, violent struggle gives rise to a cohesive ruling party and a new coercive apparatus that is moulded and tightly controlled by the party. In the next step, these parties fend off counter-revolutionary challengers or have to deal with an external military conflict. Such threats reinforce elite cohesion, strengthen the coercive apparatus and facilitate the destruction of rivals (internal or external). Such revolutions tend to produce undisputed civilian authoritarian regimes and create states with far greater coercive capacity than the states they replace (Levitsky & Way 2016: 209, 211–212).

Their pre-established decision-making procedures can hinder brusque personalisation attempts. But, their specific civil-military relations make military coups unlikely and allow aspiring despots to foremost deal with civilian rivals when personalising power. Also, alternative centres of power are not tolerated after such parties come to power, justifying purges.

When personalisation takes place during the party-formation phase, a successful violent struggle will endow leaders with enormous charisma to complete this process (Castro, Khomeini, Lenin, Mao Zedong) and shape institutions to their bidding. Ideologically driven, their security forces are indoctrinated to serve the revolution. They are commanded by former revolutionary combatants, battle-hardened, and less likely to suffer problems of insubordination and rebellion than their non-revolutionary counterparts (Levitksy & Way 2016: 213). Very few such regimes succumb to military coups.

Even when personalisation has taken place during the party-formation phase (Lenin and Stalin in the USSR, Mao Zedong in the PRC), it is usually undone in subsequent leadership turnovers by the next generation, or it is an altogether temporary phenomenon (like with Lê Duẩn in Vietnam) (Levitsky & Way 2016: 209, 211–212; Van den Bosch 2021a). As mentioned, the Kim family in North Korea is a rare exception.[7] A clear example of the first group is the Russian Bolshevik party, which resorted to armed struggle under Lenin. Himself a personalist leader, he did favour unity in the politburo, thereby establishing clear collective decision-making procedures that would later be reinstated after the personalist escapades of Stalin.

When there is no personalisation during a revolutionary regime's formative phase it becomes very difficult to achieve such levels of personalist power. Political climbers first need to unravel pre-existing and tested collegial decision-making agreements of the ruling coalition and pry power from the top military officers united in a solid, cohesive fighting force. This is far from an easy task and many of these revolutionary regimes do not personalise: Angola (MPLA), Laos (LPRP), Mozambique (FRELIMO), Nicaragua (FSLN), Zimbabwe (ZAPU-PF). Still, these regimes enjoy exceptionally long lifespans. Once again, North Korea's experience is a rare exception because Kim Il-Sung managed to personalise the regime even when he himself did not create the Communist *Korean Worker's Party* (Brownlee 2007: 617).

To summarise, the 1965–1998 period saw a clear shift along both sides of the ideological frontier now stretching through the whole IP. With war-torn revolutionary regimes changing the very fabric of their societies, and on the other side, nationalist leaders of the "free world" reaching new pinnacles of personalist power by clamping down on communists in exchange for international patronage.

The revolutionary *tabula rasa* in one camp coincided with the large purge of communist parties in the non-communist bloc. The final result was a deep ideological rift between the PRC, North Korea, Vietnam and Laos that eroded their societies' geopolitical, economic, social, communication and transnational network linkages with the non-communist world, and on the other side, a fickle, heterogeneous coalition of nominally non-communist, opportunist regimes that cut off similar linkages with this bloc, but kept using their own strategic geopolitical leverage as a bargaining chip to keep their autocrats in powers, commit atrocities in the name of anti-communism and solicit aid from the West. Once the US pulled out of Vietnam, a normalisation phase could begin, in which economic linkages would soon be established between the two blocs in the IP. However, one has to wait until the official end of the Cold War for its ideological paradigm to lose salience and lead to increased integration.

The Cold War thus saw a regime crystallisation or "purification" of both blocs, but similarly to other world regions, once open warfare had abated, room for pragmatism returned, and in contrast to the US, located outside the region, the countries of the IP had to work out a *modus vivendi* with one another. The end of the Cold War thus only gave new impetus to processes that had started by the early 1980s. The US withdrawal from Vietnam also strengthened the official subdivision of the IP into sub-regions.

South Asia was made up of an isolated democracy unable to shed its socialist shibboleths (India) while at war with China, and the anti-communist, militarist US-ally (Pakistan), disconnected from ASEAN, and officially allied with the USSR (since 1971) (Pardesi 2020: 134). Southeast Asia was made up of a string of personalist, opportunist autocrats, pursuing high economic growth (and diversification) to rid themselves from US tutelage, opposed to a bloc of isolated people republics, increasingly desperate for new markets. Northeast Asia was cut in two at the 38th parallel dividing the Koreas, a disparity that deepened once the US-PRC normalisation led to a rapid economic boost for the US-strategic allies.

Russia, once having been so formative in the creation of the IP by the late 19th century and responsible for setting up the post-WWII ideological fault line, would slowly disappear from the macro-region. The Sino-Soviet split and the late Brezhnev stagnation nudged an increasingly assertive communist China to take its place. The end of the Cold War and the collapse of the USSR would remove most of the ideological tension and allow the IP sub-regions, each locked in with their own security dilemmas, to reintegrate into one larger macro-region once again.

Post-Cold War regime modernisation

Political "democratisation" was broad in scope, but not as in-depth as the IP. The economic liberalisation of the typical Asian "developmental" state (or state-led market) was the more significant post-Cold War shift and would result in autocratic modernisation rather than democratisation.

The end of the Cold War also meant the end of gatekeeping, until then a key technique for personalist rulers to hold on to supreme power. While the fall of personalist regimes brought back more collegial forms of authoritarian rule, and most regimes allowed elections as a tactic to channel popular discontent; this trend, in general, has been labelled the "democratisation" of Asia, but this observation only holds when one pertains a minimalist definition of democracy (the presence of elections and some regime turnover). However, where elections were often free and competitive, they were not fair and favoured incumbents. By 2020, most of these regimes have found a new equilibrium and should be considered stable and consolidated autocracies (Lee 2018; Policy Innovation Hub 2019).

The causes for such reform were a combination of factors, both external and internal pressures to "democratise," combined with elite splits and the fateful Asian financial crisis (1997), that forced elites to abandon their strongmen, state-led systems of governance, liberalise their markets, and open up the political scene. The lack of Cold War patronage let personalist rulers slip from power or forced their successors to

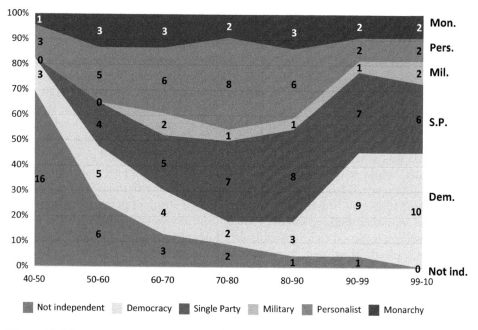

Figure 6.1 Most common regime types in the Indo-Pacific (1940–2010).

Source: Author's own work, based on Geddes et al. 2012a/b. Regime data shown for: Bangladesh, Bhutan, Brunei Darussalam, Cambodia, China (PRC), East Timor, India, Indonesia, Japan, Korea (North and South), Laos, Malaysia, Myanmar, Nepal, Pakistan, the Philippines, Singapore, Sri Lanka, Taiwan, Thailand and Vietnam (North, later coded as united; with South Vietnam coded separately until 1975)

reform. Those with a civilian base were ousted; those with a military base returned to the barracks (Genesan 2004; Schulte Nordholt 2016: 303–327).

In the Philippines, the ouster of Marcos in 1986 heralded a new path, followed by reforms in South Korea (1987), Pakistan (1989), Singapore (1990), Bangladesh (1991), Sri Lanka (1995), Thailand (1997), Indonesia (1998), Taiwan (2001) and Malaysia (2003) (Schulte Nordholt 2016: 305). A detailed close-up of the real nature of some of these new democracies, their civilian-military relations and the workings of party systems in the IP is beyond the scope of this chapter but is dealt with in the next chapter by Bhaswati Sarkar.

As Figure 6.1 shows, the most common regime type of the IP after 1990 became the heterogeneous group of **democracies**. Some like the Philippines or Indonesia still have entrenched, polarised and regional elites but succeed in keeping the military out of politics. Sri Lanka and East Timor still need to come to terms with their long civil wars. Others still deal with influential, former monarchic elite networks like recently reformed Nepal or Bhutan (the latter still listed as monarchic in the figure).

India, Japan, South Korea and Taiwan have matured as democracies despite some smaller shortcomings (e.g. on media freedom, accountability and representativeness).

They stand out because they were able to avoid Cold War personalisation because (after the initial strongman rule) none of these four polities could make credible overtures to communist countries to leverage more Western support, thus not allowing new leaders to strengthen their position *vis-à-vis* their inner circle. However, emboldened by populism in the USA (under Donald Trump) and in Europe, some of the region's democratic actors like India (or the Philippines) have recently embraced a nationalist, populist agenda that is swiftly eroding the (fragile) balance of their democratic institutions, and which in turn may trigger violent responses from or toward discriminated groups in society.

The graph groups together two forms of **single-party rule**: Singapore, Malaysia, Cambodia and Bangladesh still have hegemonic party systems, while a second group of communist, revolutionary parties (Laos, Vietnam, PRC) have proven equally resilient, with undisputed single-party rule (North Korea is the exception and is still listed as personalist). These states hold elections but with different functions. In Laos and Vietnam, elections are under the exclusive control of the ruling party and express its dominance, serve to mobilise voters and reinforce the unity of people and party. In Cambodia, Singapore and Malaysia, electoral competition is real but unfair. They provide ruling elites with information about the loyalty and policy preferences of the electorate, help mitigate conflict by channelling dissent through official regime channels, and co-opt elite actors with access to crucial resources. In all polities, elections serve to uphold a better image for foreign observers (Croissant & Lorenz 2018: 420).

Myanmar and Thailand are still listed as under **military** rule because their open intervention and dominance of politics have created an oscillating back-and-forth of veto coups in both countries, where officers lurk in the shadows and intervene every time an undesired civilian politician gets too much power or autonomy, or the latter try to set up control mechanisms for the military. In Thailand, the military has a long history of hiding behind the monarchy (Connors 2011). In both states, a rather unified, military regime has committed severe atrocities when repressing mass civilian protests, and political violence is thus a continuing reality. Pakistan and Bangladesh have a similar legacy of military involvement, and a return to military rule in these states remains a possibility.

Personalist rule has all but disappeared in the region. North Korea has remained its poster child with three generations of Kim rule, and Pakistan briefly relapsed under Musharraf (1999–2008). However, one should not ignore the long personalist legacies of others states (Indonesia, the Philippines, Myanmar, Thailand), which definitely have made their imprints on the current regimes, even if they have modernised into electoral regimes and try to channel discontent instead of repressing it.

Conclusion

This chapter discussed the most common forms of regime types in the IP since colonial times, highlighting several junctures: the Japanese occupation, the ideological proxy wars in Korea and Indochina and the end of the Cold War. This new order frayed the containment of the (divided) communist bloc in the IP. Vietnam and Laos, isolated and stagnating, changed course in 1986 and the early 1990s respectively, opening their controlled economies for much-needed FDI, especially after joining ASEAN (Schulte Nordholt 2016: 318–321; Creak & Barney 2018). Without the friction of the old ideological divide or the gains of anti-communist posturing by its neighbours (in exchange for Western patronage), the IP's party-based autocracies were able to make credible commitments to investors (Gehlbach & Keefer 2011). And with few obstacles left between the wide spectrum of regional authoritarian regimes to set up mutual trade relations, they mopped up old animosities with the goal of maintaining their respective domestic status quos, keeping ruling elites in power by recalibrating alliances internally and with new actors.

The final outcome is that party-based regimes are now the most common, of which about ten are multiparty and can be considered "democratic" only by minimalist standards, and even then, these cases differ quite significantly from one another. Another six are single-party regimes and have proven to be extremely resilient, especially those with a revolutionary origin. Still, the personalist, monarchic and military legacies of previous decades have left their imprints and may still affect regime behaviour and change well into the 21st century.

This overview of regime evolutions in this macro-region shows that there is no clean-cut democratic-autocratic divide running through the newly conceptualised IP. Democracies in the IP are often conflated with autocracies with free (but not fair) elections and have emerged from different pathways. This means they have different views on how to support or whether to promote democracy at all, while their diverse political cultures impede true democratic collaboration and integration schemes.

The peaceful rise of China, its takeover as the largest global economy (by GDP) and becoming the largest exporter since 2013 in combination with its recent personalisation under Xi Jinping is a worrying trend. Scholars are still assessing its current behaviour under personalist leadership and its potential to uphold and promote autocracy in the region (Kneuer & Demmelhuber 2021; Van den Bosch 2020).

Personalist legacies run deep and can re-emerge under increased great power rivalry (as before during the Cold War). In this regard, the current role of China (as a personalist great power) is very worrying and could lead to unpredictable and aggressive foreign policy actions, as the 2022 invasion in Ukraine by its Russian personalist counterpart has illustrated.

Notes

1 These viewpoints are a mixed legacy of strategic pragmatism (regional army commands) and area study traditions, petrifying older colonial divisions.
2 Political regimes differ from "international regimes," which are regulatory processes (characterised by principles, norms, rules and decision-making procedures) that function in the international realm, and cannot be equated with individual actors (even while they do possess agency as networks).
3 Virtually all societies in human history have used four criteria to sort people into or out of the selectorate: (1) personal origin: birthplace and lineage; (2) special proficiency: skills, beliefs and/or knowledge; (3) wealth; and (4) gender and/or age (Bueno de Mesquita et al. 2003: 43).
4 Sovereignty has two dimensions: a domestic one where supreme power resides within a political group derived from the polity, which has legislative, executive and judicial powers, and also maintains the monopoly on violence; the international dimension is engrained in the *de jure* equality between states.
5 The role of nuclear weapons in ending the Pacific War has also been questioned. Ward Wilson convincingly argues that it was once again the Russian Factor, not the bombings of Hiroshima and Nagasaki, that resulted in the acceptance of the terms of surrender by the Japanese (Wilson 2013).

6 A critical juncture is a key event that triggers structural change and puts actors on a new path-dependency.
7 For a detailed overview of how this personalisation process took place and was consolidated in this totalitarian regime, see: Van den Bosch 2017.

References

Ali, Niloufer Wajid, *Communist China and South a Southeast Asia (1949–1972)*, Lahore: Ferozsons Ltd., 1975.

Brennan, Elliot, "Three Reasons Brunei is Introducing Sharia," *The Interpreter* (www.lowyinstitute.org), 15 May 2014. https://www.lowyinstitute.org/the-interpreter/three-reasons-brunei-introducing-sharia

Brownlee, Jason, "Hereditary Succession in Modern Autocracies," *World Politics*, 59(4), 2007: 595–628.

Bueno de Mesquita, B., A. Smith, R.M. Siverson, J.D. Morrow, *The Logic of Political Survival*, Cambridge, MA-London: MIT Press, 2003.

Connors, Michael K., "When the Walls Come Crumbling Down: The Monarchy and Thai-style Democracy," *Journal of Contemporary Asia*, 41(4), 2011: 657–673.

Creak, Simon, Keith Barney, "Conceptualising Party-State Governance and Rule in Laos," *Journal of Contemporary Asia*, 48(5), 2018: 693–716.

Croissant Axel, Philip Lorenz, *Comparative Politics of Southeast Asia: An Introduction to Governments and Political Regimes*, Cham: Springer, 2018.

Fishman, R.M., "Rethinking State and Regime: Southern Europe's Transition to Democracy," *World Politics*, 42(3), April 1990: 422–440.

Francia, Luis H., *History of the Philippines: From Indios Bravos to Filipinos*, New York: The Overlook Press, 2014.

Ganesan, N., "The Collapse of Authoritarian Regimes in Indonesia and Thailand: Structural and Contextual Factors," *Asia Journal of Social Science*, 32(1), 2004: 1–18.

Geddes, Barbara, "Authoritarian Breakdown: Empirical Test of a Game Theoretic Argument," Paper prepared for the annual meeting of the American Political Science Association, Atlanta, 1999.

Geddes, Barbara, Joseph Wright, Erica Frantz, "Autocratic Regimes," Research paper, 4/5/2012a. Supported by NSF-BCS #0904463 and NSF-BCS#0904478

Geddes, Barbara, Joseph Wright, Erica Frantz, "New Data on Autocratic Breakdown and Regime Transitions," Research paper 8/9/2012b. Supported by NSF-BCS #0904463 and NSF-BCS #0904478.

Gehlbach, Scott, Philip Keefer, "Investment without Democracy: Ruling-Party Institutionalization and Credible Commitment in Autocracies," *Journal of Comparative Economics*, 39, 2011: 123–139.

Guan, Ang Cheng, *Southeast Asia's Cold War: An Interpretive History*, Honolulu: University of Hawai'i Press, 2018.

Jalal, Ayesha, *Democracy and Authoritarianism in South Asia: A Comparative and Historical Perspective*, Cambridge: Cambridge University Press, 1995.

Kneuer, Marianne, Thomas Demmelhuber, eds., *Authoritarian Gravity Centers: A Cross-Regional Study of Authoritarian Promotion and Diffusion*, New York-London: Routledge, 2021.

Lee, Johh, "Understanding Authoritarian Resilience and Countering Autocracy Promotion in Asia," *Asia Policy*, 13(4), 2018: 99–122.

Lee, Steven Hugh, *Outposts of Empire: Korea, Vietnam and the Origins of the Cold War in Asia, 1949–1954*, Montreal-Kingston: McGill-Queen's University Press, 1995.

Levitsky, Steven, Lucan Way, "Durable Authoritarianism," in: O. Fioretos, T.G. Falleti, A. Sheingate (eds.), *The Oxford Handbook of Historical Institutionalism*, Oxford: Oxford University Press, 2016: 209–220.

Muni, S.D., "Shifting Tides in South Asia: Bhutan's Deferential Democracy," *Journal of Democracy*, 25(2), 2014: 158–163.

Nordholt, Henk Schulte, *Een geschiedenis van Zuidoost-Azië*, Amsterdam: Amsterdam University Press, 2016.

Oh, K., R. C. Hassig, *North Korea Through the Looking Glass*, Washington DC: The Brookings Institution, 2000.

Pardesi, Manjeet S., "The Indo-Pacific: A 'new' Region or the Return of History?" *Australian Journal of International Affairs*, 74(2), 2020: 124–146.

Roychowdhury, Adrija, "Why Pakistan Ended Up with so Few Princely States," *The Indian Express*, 14 August 2021. https://indianexpress.com/article/research/why-pakistan-ended-up-with-so-few-princely-states-7453288/

Seth, Michael J., *A Concise History of Modern Korea: From the Late Nineteenth Century to the Present*, Lanham: Rowman & Littlefield, 2016.

Skaaning, S. E., "Political regimes and their changes: A conceptual framework," *Center on Democracy, Development, and the Rule of Law, Stanford University*, (55),(2006): 1–30.

Slater, Dan, "Violent Origins of Authoritarian Variation: Rebellion Type and Regime Type in Cold War Southeast Asia," *Government and Opposition*, 55(1), 2018: 1–20.

"The Rise of Sophisticated Authoritarianism in Southeast Asia," *Policy Innovation Hub*, 23 October 2019. https://medium.com/the-machinery-of-government/the-rise-of-sophisticated-authoritarianism-in-southeast-asia-a42742c4bdeb

Tudor, Maya, "How India Institutionalized Democracy and Pakistan Promoted Autocracy," in: *The Promise of Power: The Origins of Democracy in India and Autocracy in Pakistan*, Cambridge: Cambridge University Press, 2013: 1–43.

Van den Bosch, Jeroen J.J., "Irreversible Regime Transitions: The Impact of Hereditary Succession and Personalist Rule in North Korea," in: K. Kozłowski; K. Stüwe (eds.), *The Korean Peninsula Unification Trajectories: Insights from Poland and Germany*, Warsaw: Oficyna Wydawnicza SGH, 2017: 47–83.

Van den Bosch, Jeroen J.J., "Introducing Regime Cluster Theory: Framing Regional Diffusion Dynamics of Democratization and Autocracy Promotion," *International Journal of Political Theory*, 4(1), 2020: 71–102.

Van den Bosch, Jeroen J.J., *Personalist Rule in Africa and Other World Regions*, London-New York: Routledge, 2021a.

Van den Bosch, Jeroen J.J., "Political Regimes in Central Asia: Tracing Personalist Rule from the Khanates to the Present," in: Jeroen Van den Bosch; Adrien Fauve; Bruno De Cordier (eds.), *European Handbook of Central Asian Studies: History, Politics, and Societies*, Stuttgart: ibidem Verlag, 2021b: 387–446.

Wilson, Ward, "The Bomb Didn't Beat Japan … Stalin Did," *Foreign Policy*, 30 May 2013. https://foreignpolicy.com/2013/05/30/the-bomb-didnt-beat-japan-stalin-did/

Young, M. Crawford, *The African Colonial State in Comparative Perspective*, New Haven and London: Yale University Press, 1994.

7 Democracy in the Indo-Pacific

Bhaswati Sarkar

Introduction

The current attention of the West to the region is reflected in a series of documents by individual states like the USA, the UK, France, Germany and the Netherlands and organisations like the European Union elicited primarily by the rise of China and its challenge to the existing rule-based international order. The rule based international order and an emphasis on democracy defines all these documents. Global indices that measure both spread and quality of democracy clearly show that worldwide while the number of democratic countries has increased democratic erosion is also on the rise. The title of Freedom House "Freedom in the World 2021" report "Democracy Under Siege" is telling[1]. The report notes that this is the 15th consecutive year of decline in global freedom and warns that the long democratic recession is deepening. Much is also being written on democratic de-consolidation, a trend discernible in many of European Union's new member states inducted in the 2004 big bang enlargement and subsequent minor ones all having fulfilled the Copenhagen conditionality of democracy. It is against the backdrop of these developments and assessments that we focus on the Indo-Pacific which covers a huge land mass that is home of some of the world's oldest, largest and newest democracies. The primary question that the chapter explores – is how deeply committed are the countries of the Indo-Pacific to democracy, what position do they occupy in the democratic consolidation/de-consolidation binary. It specifically looks at countries like Indonesia, Philippines, South Korea, Malaysia, India and Sri Lanka[2], which started their democracy building and transition following decolonisation. But before this can be addressed the larger question of what democracy is and what democratic consolidation entails needs to be understood. Democracy popular as it is as a political system has no one clear definition. A rich body of research and diverse understanding has developed over a period of time with scholars stressing particular aspects – representation, participation, deliberation (Collier & Levitsky 1997 lists adjectives associated with democracy) as its defining characteristic. In the first section of the chapter democracy and democratic consolidation are discussed laying out the minimalist and maximalist positions. The post-colonial Indo-Pacific countries are then studied to show that they fulfil the minimalist democratic requirement but a number of factors like diversity management, corruption, increasing polarisation, weak opposition and onslaught on civil society prevent the improvement of democratic quality.

Democracy and democratic consolidation

The concept of democracy is ever expanding which also makes it difficult to find one definition of democracy. From its origin in ancient Greece it has evolved through

DOI: 10.4324/9781003336143-10

various routes over a period of time. The English, the American and the French revolutions represented different routes towards democracy which are reflected today in a number of different forms and practices. However they are subsumed in the notion of liberal democracy which became characteristic of "Western" societies in the nineteenth and twentieth centuries (Shell 1990). The literature on what constitutes democracy and democratic consolidation can broadly divided into the minimalist and maximalist positions.

The minimalist or procedural understanding of democracy focuses on the procedures or means in place to attain democracy. This position is reflected in the writings of Schumpeter, Huntington and Dahl. In his book *Capitalism, Socialism and Democracy* Schumpeter argued that democracy is an "institutional arrangement for arriving at political decisions in which individuals acquire the power to decide by means of a competitive struggle for the people's vote" (Schumpeter 1950). Similarly Huntington observed that "the central procedure of democracy is the selection of leaders through competitive elections by the people they govern" (Huntington 1991). Elections are also central to Dahl's understanding of democracy, and he holds that the twin principles of contestation and participation captures the essence of what political systems should minimally satisfy to be called democratic (Dahl 1982).What matters here is that elected officials regularly face election the end of their term and can be removed or re-elected. The expectation is that this fear of removal will motivate representatives to act responsibly and respond to the desires of the people they represent. Dahl argues that it is the political institutions that democracies develop that distinguish them from other political systems and identifies seven characteristics as "procedural minimum". Using these Kaldor and Vejvoda (1997) developed them as inclusive citizenship; rule of law; separation of powers; elected power holders; free and fair elections; freedom of expression and alternative sources of information; associational autonomy; and civilian control over the security forces. The "minimalist" definition of democratic consolidation by extension means meeting the minimal condition of a consolidated democratic system, which regularly holds a free and fair election regularly. The problem with this formalistic conception of democracy and democratic consolidation is that it does not focus on the democratic substance of government activity between elections. In a sense, democracy begins and ends with the act of voting.

Substantive democracy tries to overcome the shortcomings of the procedural. It argues for the need to evaluate the content or substance of government actions by evaluating how governments responses to the wishes of the public they represent. Substantive democracy can be understood as a process that regulates power relations in a way that maximises the opportunities for individuals to influence the conditions in which they live, to participate in and influence debates about the key decisions which affect society. It is a process that has to be continually reproduced (Kaldor & Vejvoda 1997). The "maximalist" definition of democratic consolidation signifies the existence of mature political institutions routinely practicing civil rights and the democratic rule of law. The need to move beyond the procedural has seen scholars focus on democratic quality emphasising the need to move beyond the question of whether a country is democratic to the degree to which it is democratic, and what kind of democracy it is (Diamond & Morlino 2004, 2005; Freedman 2006; Dressel et al. 2011; Morlino 2003, 2010). Freedman argued that it is not enough that "institutions and systems necessary for democracy exist because institutions and individuals can subvert, ignore, or flout the best-intended laws. Hence, it is important to see not just that institutions exist but whether they are functioning as intended" (Freedman 2006).

Beetham's argument that popular control and political equality are central to democracy and consolidation of democracy is a product of many factors or conditions like historical origins, economic and social structure, political agency and constitutional arrangements operating together is important in looking at democracies beyond the West (Beetham 1994). The institutions that democracy requires to ensure this popular control and political equality evolve differently in different settings influenced by the specific social order. In both India and the United States for instance, democracy grew in response to the challenge of colonial rule, but the responses were not the same in the two cases. America was a new nation characterised by social conditions that were very different from the social conditions prevalent since time immemorial in India (Béteille 2013). In the context of East Asian democracies the Asian value debate has been important. Essentially questioning the universalism of liberal democracy it articulates a relativistic understanding of the relationship between cultural values and systems of government. It argues that the state's view of what is good for the society is informed by its value system and is reflected in governance and in Asia "respect for authority, strong families, reverence for education, hard work, frugality, teamwork, and a balance between the individual's interests and those of society" were the guiding values. These values are not what informs the liberal democratic political system which has equality, freedom, recognition and accommodation of 'the fact of pluralism' at its heart (Bell et al. 1995).

In assessing the democratic trajectory of these Indo-Pacific states two categories of "majoritarian democracy" and "competitive authoritarianism" are useful. While fulfilling the procedural minimum of election they indicate erosion or un-realisation of the substantive aspect of democracy. In "majoritarian democracy" the polity is mobilised electorally around an agenda that benefits the majority and is essentially unfavourable to the interests of minorities, whether linguistic, religious, or ethnic. The minimal democratic standards that it fulfil makes it a low-quality democracy. It reflects a situation that Linz, in his famous essay "Totalitarian and Authoritarian Regimes," observed that Israel was democratic for the Jewish majority, but much less so for the Arab minority (Stepan 2015). In "competitive authoritarianism," while "formal democratic institutions are widely viewed as the principal means of obtaining and exercising political authority," the "incumbents violate those rules so often and to such an extent ... that the regime fails to meet conventional minimum standards for democracy" (Levitsky & Way 2002).

Satisfying the procedural minimum

Indo-Pacific democracies like India, Sri Lanka, Indonesia, the Philippines, South Korea and Malaysia started their democracy building and transition following decolonisation. At independence these countries chose to establish liberal democratic systems with political structures strongly influenced by the former colonizing state. India, Malaysia and Sri Lanka opted for parliamentary system. Indonesia, the Philippines and South Korea did debate about using a parliamentary system but in the end settled for a presidential one. Elections with contestation and participation we have seen are central to the procedural understanding of democracy to ensure this was the immediate challenge of these states. As colonies these countries had suffered centuries of economic exploitation which left them poor and underdeveloped and the majority of the population illiterate and in cases like that of India's independence was accompanied by the bloody violence of partition. To ensure the procedural minimum was for these countries under such circumstances challenging and met with varied success.

Indonesia, the Philippines and South Korea within years of democratic functioning collapsed into authoritarian rule. In Indonesia the 1950s were years of turbulence marked by violent demands for regional autonomy, regional military coups. The constituent assembly failed to agree on a draft constitution and President Sukarno used this as a pretext to terminate Indonesia's democratic regime in 1959 and initiate "Guided Democracy" (Horowitz 2013). Parliament was dissolved, new elections repeatedly postponed. The successful repression of the revolts by the army solidified the position of the military as the defender of the state, which in turn contributed to the strong place occupied by the armed forces for years to come. In 1967 Suharto usurped power and established the New Order, 'Pancasila Democracy' which led to further concentration of power, activities of parties were curbed, press freedom curtailed. There was no scope of any dissent to government, opponents particularly the Communists were jailed. Both Sukarno's "Guided Democracy"[3] and Suharto's 'Pancasila Democracy'[4] were dictatorships in practice. Democracy in the Philippines also collapsed into authoritarianism under President Marcos in 1965. South Korea experienced a similar collapse into authoritarianism in 1981.

India's early leadership was committed to building and strengthening parliamentary democracy. Aware of the challenges that the linguistic, ethnic, religious diversity posed in making this a reality an elaborate constitution was drawn up that opted for federalism and balanced individual rights with group rights. However, the initial years where years of one party dominance with the Indian National Congress enjoying complete sway. Though there was no democratic breakdown as in the East Asian counterparts Indian democracy did experience a reversal when Prime Minister Indira Gandhi declared an emergency in 1975 (Park 1975; Puri 1995). Malaysia like India opted for a parliamentary system. It too has strong ethno-religious divides that impacted the functioning of the new democracy. Politically and officially, the country's population is divided into two categories: Bumiputera and non-Bumiputera. Malays and other indigenous peoples make up the Bumiputera group while the non-Bumiputera group consists mainly of Chinese and Indians. Ethnic harmony characterised the initial post-independence years. The United Malays National Organisation (UMNO) as an ethno-nationalist party did defend special privileges for Malays but they joined forces with other political parties of the Chinese and Indian ethnic communities to lead the multiethnic national coalition, the Alliance, which later expanded and renamed itself the National Front (Barisan Nasional, or BN). Malaysia's first prime minister, Tunku Abdul Rahman, who led the Alliance, ensured that all ethnic communities had elite representation. All this changed after the racial riots in 1969. Eighteen months of emergency rule followed. Malay nationalism intensified and Malay special rights were promoted through the idea of *ketuanan Melayu* or Malay dominance. The political system did offer space for some political competition which was used by opposition parties like Islamist Parti Islam Malaysia (PAS), DAP and PKR but it was only in 2018 that they managed to end UMNO dominance (Welsh 2020). In Sri Lanka the initiation of a democratic system post-independence in 1948 was quickly embroiled in the politicisation of the ethno-religious-linguistic divide between the Sinhala Buddhist community comprising 75% of the population and the predominantly Hindu Tamil community making up the remaining 25% (Kadirgamar 2020). The majoritarian state policies like the disenfranchisement of the Up-Country Tamils immediately after independence, the unitary structure of the state, the privileged position of Buddhism and the Sinhala only language policy polarised the society (Kadirgamar 2020). The LTTE mounted a violent challenge to secure Tamil interests and the island was from the mid-eighties engulfed in civil war that left thousands dead (Ratner 2012).

Our discussion here shows that the immediate years of independence following decolonisation were years of extraordinary challenge for these new states as they set out to establish a democratic political system. Except for India, these countries failed to maintain the procedural minimum for democracies and collapsed into authoritarian/majoritarian rule. In the case of Indonesia, Sukarno and his advisors were far from convinced by liberal democracy as an appropriate blue print for their country's political system. Bouchier's work on Indonesia for instance clearly shows that in the constitutional assembly debates there was a sharp division between those who advocated the organic view of the state with no individual rights and others who favoured a strong interventionist welfare state balanced with citizens' rights (Bouchier 2015). The different "traditions, needs, and conceptions of human flourishing" in East and Southeast Asian societies were not hospitable to liberal democratic political system which emphasise on equality, freedom, recognition and accommodation of "the fact of pluralism" (Bell et al. 1995). In Korea the strong influence of Confucianism which values harmony of society as a whole more than individual preferences and emphasises top-down hierarchy, praises loyalty and respect toward those in a more senior position and acknowledges the strong responsibility of seniors towards their juniors was used as a political resource by the ruling elites for political purposes (Kim 2012). President of the first republic Syngman Rhee saw himself as the chosen one rather than an elected representative of one of three branches of government and adopted an increasingly authoritarian style. In 1954 he sought an amendment that would enable his re-election and help him continue in his position for life. Subsequently President Park Chung Hee (like his counter parts Chiang Kai-shek, Chiang Ching-kuo of Taiwan and Lee Kwan Yew of Singapore) benefited immensely from the instrumental use of Confucianism to bolster a strong state, ultimately replacing democracy with authoritarian rule (Kim 2012).

Democratic consolidation

As discussed in the first section, democratic consolidation can be understood as minimalist or maximalist. Here we will assess where these identified states of the Indo-Pacific lie on the minimalist-maximalist spectrum. In the Philippines, South Korea and Indonesia democracy was restored in 1986, 1987 and 1988 respectively. In Malaysia in the 2018 elections the opposition finally succeeded in removing the BN/UMNO from power. Sri Lanka post-independence quickly degenerated to a "majoritarian democracy". (see Box 7.1).

Box 7.1 Democratic setbacks in Sri Lanka

Sri Lanka is a special case where the turn to majoritarian democracy happened soon after independence which by the 1980s had plunged the country into a horrific civil war. At independence the Sinhalese-speaking, Buddhist majority resented the Christians and English speaking Tamils whom the colonisers had favoured. The Sinhala Buddhists were "a majority with a minority complex" whose sentiments were put to use by Sinhalese politician like Bandaranaike to win elections. He won the 1956 election promising to make Sinhalese the sole language to be used for civil-service exams and promotions as well as entry into the most prestigious professions. The slide towards majoritarianism had begun. This was resented by the Tamils who demanded devolution, federalism, or even independence for the portion of the national territory in which they were the majority. In 1978, a shift from a parliamentary to a semi-presidential system with a powerful executive presidency had been made resulting in further centralisation. Tamil resentment spilled into violent challenge by the Liberation Tigers of Tamil Eelam (LTTE) which was used by the regime to further cultivate majoritarian attitudes and pursue majoritarian policies. Subsequently after the resounding victory of the Rajapaksa government over the LTTE in 2009 the President instead of a push for reconciliation celebrated the victory of the Sinhalese community by making himself the focus of a personality cult and sealing his own and his family's iron grip on power so much so that the executive and legislative branches came to resemble a Rajapaksa family business. The government also used the military in the development and "Sinhalisation" of Tamil areas—particularly in the north. The weak and divided opposition, civil society clampdown and weakening of the judiciary meant that there was no check on the Rajapaksa government. Thus after the return of peace Sri Lanka which remained a democracy albeit flawed through the years of civil war degenerated to a "hybrid regime"[5] or "competitive authoritarianism."[6] Sri Lanka did see a democratic turnaround when in the 2015 elections President Rajapaksa lost to a united opposition coalition gathered and led by Maithripala Sirisena, in an election that had 82% voter turnout. Rajapaksa also failed to rebound in the parliamentary elections that followed. The Sirisena government while retaining the powerful presidency made some important amendments to secure balance of power – reinstated the two-term limit on presidents; the presidential term was reduced from six to five years; the president was barred from arbitrarily dissolving Parliament until at least four-and-a-half years have passed since its first sitting; a ten-member Constitutional Council including three civil society representatives was created; eleven independent governmental commissions were established; and the right to information was declared to be fundamental. But the gains did not last long and 2019 elections brought the Rajapaksa family back to power. Gotabaya Rajapaksa—the brother of the former president—was voted in as president almost exclusively with the backing of Sinhala Buddhist nationalist groups, retired military leaders, and parts of the business and professional classes. Mahinda Rajapaksa became the country's prime minister and once again the Rajapaksas sought to reconsolidate the majoritarian and militarized policies (Kadirgamar 2020).

At the minimum, political systems to be democratic must regularly hold free and fair elections and ensure associational autonomy. If elections are to be meaningful the electorate must be presented with alternatives to choose from. It is this that makes the presence of political parties critical for democracy. The literature on democracy stresses the important role political parties play in so far as they represent the people's will by performing the important tasks of interest aggregation and interest articulation. Democracy is a regime type in which there is an acknowledged role of the government as well as the opposition and this is accepted as normal and legitimate (Béteille 2013). Parties are therefore not just important in the context of elections but also equally important post-elections to hold governments accountable and in ensuring that they continue to represent the interests of the people.

Political parties

In Indonesia, the Philippines and South Korea the restoration of democracy opened up the political space for competition. However, the party system that developed suffers from issues that limit their capability to facilitate the democratic transit from procedural to substantive. In Indonesia when in 1998 the New Order's restrictive party and election laws were overhauled it was done through a compromise by parties in parliament at the time of the transition – Golkar, PPP and PDI and the demands expressed on the streets outside parliament. New laws passed in January 1999 while retaining the closed-list proportional representation (PR) system of the previous regime allowed for greater freedom for the establishment of new parties. As the new law required only 50 people as the minimum to form a new party it led to party system fragmentation which became one of the key features of the Indonesian party system (Tomsa 2010). Measures were introduced subsequently to check this tendency but other institutional changes like, the introduction of direct presidential elections in 2004, the extension of direct executive elections to the subnational level in 2005 and the switch from a closed-list PR system to a partially and eventually fully open-list system in 2008 created an electoral system heavily focused on individuals. Though political parties in Indonesia are relatively better institutionalized (Ufen 2008) and fulfil key functions such as political recruitment, interest articulation or political mobilization and participation (Mietzner 2013) they continue to suffer from many weaknesses that limit their effectiveness as electorate alternatives or a robust opposition. Party programmes lack substance and meaningful engagement with ordinary citizens, corruption is pervasive as is elitism. Fionna and Tomsa (2020) make a distinction between core parties and new parties in Indonesia. The core parties numbering six are the ones that have successfully competed in all democratic elections since 1999 and the new ones that only started to participate in elections in 2004 or afterwards. The new parties – the Democratic Party (Partai Demokrat, PD), the Greater Indonesia Movement Party (Gerakan Indonesia Raya, Gerindra), the People's Conscience Party (Partai Hati Nurani Rakyat, Hanura) and the National Democratic Party (Nasional Demokrat, Nasdem) have essentially been electoral vehicles to satiate presidential ambitions of major political figures and can thus be classified as "personalistic parties" (Gunther & Diamond 2003). Also, all of these parties were founded by or for ex-generals or tycoons formerly linked to Golkar (Aspinall & Sukmajati 2016). Patronage is the driving force of party politics and programmatic divisions have lost much of their relevance. Thus for instance despite there being an ideological divide between Islamic parties that seek a larger role for Islamic principles in public life and pluralist parties that advocate a multi-religious vision of Indonesia, parties and politicians across the divide collaborate regularly as their primary objective is to enter government and access the state's patronage resources. This has led analysts like Slater and Arugay to conclude that Indonesia is "one of the least polarized democracies in Asia" (Slater & Arugay 2018).The enthusiasm for parties following Suharto's ouster did not last long. Indonesia came to be characterized as an 'oligarchic democracy' with "unrepresentative and unresponsive parties" that worked for their own interests. Parties act like a "cartel" sharing power, decision making and spoils. The World Value Survey 2020 shows that in Indonesia only 8.4% have great confidence in political parties while 40.6% and 21.2% do not have much or any confidence in parties respectively (WVS Wave 7 2017-2022).

As in the case of Indonesia, political parties were banned under the authoritarian Marcos regime in the Philippines. However, at the same time Marcos created Kilusang Bagong Lipunan (KBL), which he used as his own electoral vehicle. Other parties like the Liberals and Nacionalistas were banned. In the years after independence political parties were essentially vehicles of competing and winning Presidential elections and the Marcos period further damaged prospects of a strong party system. Though many parties emerged in the post-Marcos period, they and old parties like the Nacionalistas and Liberals (functioning since 1907 and 1945 respectively) did not generate a robust party system. In elections of post-Marcos period a sizeable number of parties emerge and disappear each election contributing to electoral volatility (Hicken 2018). The party system in Philippines is under institutionalised and many like Hicken, Rocamora, Hutchroft argue that this is the outcome of both Philippines' colonial past and the way democracy unfolded in the colony. The return to democracy did not automatically ensure institutionalization of parties. On the contrary provisions like ban on presidential re-election, the requirement that voters vote not for the party but for the individual, mixed member system, peculiarity of party list adopted to prevent any authoritarian reversals and ensure representation of the historically marginalised and institutionally underrepresented groups and sectors, adversely affected the development of parties (Hicken 2018). Contrary to Indonesia, however, 13.6% have a great deal and 49.0% have quite a lot of confidence in political parties (WVS Wave 7 2017-2022).

In South Korea too democratisation opened up the political space for multiparty competition. But here also parties remain under institutionalised and personality centric. Steinberg and Shin argue that Confucianism has a very strong influence in Korea. The extension of this influence in the political realm has meant that the party system that developed functioned against at the backdrop of "entourage politics" where following the patriarchal family model the leader (father), as head, speaks and others follow. This was evident in the "three Kims' era" of Kim Jong-pil, Kim Young-sam and Kim Dae-jung as they established, dissolved, re-established, and renamed their parties at will and members faithfully followed (Steinberg & Shin 2006). The parties are thus mere clientelistic networks, with the leaders distributing material goods to select groups who voted for them (Diamond & Kim 2000). Political opposition had no legitimate place and its existence was considered to be immoral and illegitimate. Some attempts to tackle the influence of money in politics and clientelism were made. In 2004, Roh Moo-hyun government initiated reforms like making corporate contributions to electoral campaigns illegal, setting strict campaign spending limits and increasing the amount of public funding available to political parties (Hellmann 2011). The reforms did have some effect on clientelistic capacities but party organization continued to be weak continuing to function around the old "home boy" and "school boy" networks (Hellmann 2014). Parties are also inclined to deal with scandals by simply distancing themselves from outgoing governments and party leaders and rebranding themselves. For instance in 2012 before the presidential elections the Grand National Party distanced itself from the outgoing administration of President Lee Myung-bak as its approval ratings dipped, renamed itself Saenuri and adopted a new logo resembling an ear reiterating the "the party's determination to listen to the people's calls" and in 2017 it once again renamed itself the Liberty Korea Party to distance itself from the corruption and bribery scandal that led to the impeachment of the president (Hellmann 2014). While these strategies helped improve electoral fortunes of the parties in the short run, in the long run it affected democratic quality as scandals and corruption weakened peoples' trust on politicians. This lack of credibility and legitimacy gets reflected in the WVS report which shows 58.1% do not very much confidence in political parties and 17.4% have none at all (WVS Wave 7 2017-2022).

Given its ethno-religious demography what emerged in Malaysia post-decolonization was a party system dominated by these two factors resulting in the emergence of an ethnically dominated party system. Ethnic parties characteristically advocate the interests of a particular ethnic group and manipulate group identity generating fear of the "other" to ensure continued allegiance (Noh 2016). In this strongly divided ethnic society the United Malays National Organization (UMNO) maintained its dominance by appealing to Malay rights and also creating an agreement with the MCA (Malayan Chinese Association) and the MIC (Malayan Indian Congress) – to form the Barisan Nasional (National Front) that allowed for vote pooling from their respective ethnic group support. Using this formula the UMNO was able to maintain dominance since independence right up to 2018. The limited political space for competition was used by the opposition parties to challenge the UMNO.

Attempts to overcome the firmly entrenched ethnic politics have been unsuccessful. Early in the 1950s, Onn Jaafar made one such attempt forming the Independence Malaya Party (IMP) as a multi-ethnic alternative. However, it suffered heavy loss in municipal elections (1952-1953) and the national elections of 1954 when it won three seats in contrast to the UMNO-MCA alliance, which won 94 out of 119 (Noh 2016: 6). Other parties like Parti Gerakan Rakyat Malaysia (Gerakan), the People's Progressive Party (PPP) and Parti Socialist Malaysia (PSM) modelled after the IMP on non-communal grounds have had no success. Both Gerakan and PPP subsequently became part of the BN coalition The PSM ended up merging with Parti Keadilan to form Parti Keadilan Rakyat (PKR) (Noh 2016). Like in the other three countries discussed Malaysian parties are also plagued by corruption, scandal and vilification of opponents. During the 2008 elections, PAS made common cause with opposition parties DAP, PKR and formed the People's Alliance (Pakatan Rakyat, PR) focusing on fundamental issues of corruption, patronage, equality and governance. But for the Malay voters the PR campaign slogan "Anything but UMNO (ABU)" translated into "Anything but Malay rule" and moved Muslim votes away from PAS to UNMO (Noh 2016: 14). This forced PAS to re-focus on its core Muslim constituency. In 2015 PR was dissolved. A new coalition Hope Alliance/Pakatan Harapan (PH) was formed by PAN, DAP and PKR. The 2018 elections which ended BN dominance were held in the wake of 1Malaysia Development Berhad (1MDB), corruption scandal involving Prime Minster Najib Razak who was charged for stashing billions in overseas account for personal use. The PH gained from the electoral pact with former Prime Minister Mahathir's United Pribumi Party of Malaysia (Parti Pribumi Bersatu Malaysia, PPBM) and defeated BN. However, PH suffered a setback in 2020 when Prime Minister Mahathir precipitated a crisis refusing to step down and make way for Anwar as promised and the Malay nationalists of UMNO joined forces with their erstwhile Islamist foe PAS in the National Alliance (Perikatan Nasional, or PN) and formed the government in March 2020. The inability of the opposition coalition to hold together and make good of the opportunity to govern exposes the weakness of democracy building and consolidation in Malaysia. In general political parties suffer from lack of citizen's confidence, 50.2% do not have very much confidence on them and 18.2% have none at all (WVS Wave 7 2017-2022).

India's party system development can be understood in phases. In the first two decades after independence the Indian National Congress enjoyed complete dominance. This period was characterised as "one party dominance system" or the "Congress System" (Kothari 1964). The dominance of the Congress party did not mean an absence of competition, but the competition failed to essentially challenge its dominant position. Morris-Jones aptly described this phenomenon as 'dominance coexisting with competition but without a trace of alteration '(Morris-Jones 1978: 217). The second phase extended from 1967 to the defeat of the Congress party at the general election of 1977. Though the Congress retained power in the 1967 elections, power in eight out of seventeen states and its vote share registered decline from 44% in 1962 to 40% in 1967 (Chhuanawma 2020). Eventually in 1977 general election the Congress was defeated by the Janata Party. Morris-Jones characterized the new system as 'a market polity' where substantial number of participants are engaged in decision making but none strong enough to impose his simple wish. With the rise of regional parties and other national parties like Janata Party (1977), Janata Dal and the BJP a competitive multi-party system developed reflecting the change in the nature of the socio-economic profile of Indian polity and the assertion of these new socio-economic groups, mainly the middle peasantry, the backward castes and the Dalits of their rights. Post 1998 a 'loose bi-polar alliance system' developed. No party had the electoral strength to form a national government so coalition governments became the rule of the day. Two distinct alliances emerged at the national level, one led by the BJP called National Democratic Alliance and another led by the Congress called United Progressive Alliance. This phase has been characterized as a "loose bi-polar alliance system" or a 'multi-party loose bipolar alliance system' (Chhuanawma 2020).

While ideology defines some parties like BJP and the two communist parties (CPI and CPM), all other parties share ideological, policy and programme resemblance. Parties are engaged in "welfare populism" to garner support. Quite often, parties are known by their leaders rather than by their manifesto. If once the popularity of the Congress was mainly due to the leadership of Nehru, Indira Gandhi and Rajiv Gandhi, today the popularity that BJP enjoys and its electoral success revolves around the personality of Narendra Modi. This is also true of regional parties like All India Trinamool Congress (TMC) in West Bengal, All India Anna Dravida Munnetra Kazhagam (AIADMK) and Dravida Munnetra Kazhagam (DMK) in Tamil Nadu and Aam Aadmi Party (AAP) in New Delhi. Since the last two national elections of 2014 and 2019 which catapulted the BJP to power with a resounding majority and the important electoral gains it has also made in state elections, the opposition parties have been too weak and divided to mount any serious challenge to the government which has successfully used the "anti-national" narrative to deflect any criticism of its policies and delegitimise them.

The new parties that emerged in the 1990s and after, draw core leadership and electoral support principally from particular castes and other social groups. Using these social cleavages parties like Bahujan Samaj Party, Rashtriya Janata Dal, Samajwadi Party, Janata Dal (S), and others came to power in key states. While over-time the increase in number of parties strengthened democracy by including hitherto excluded castes and social groups they also suffer from weaknesses which limit their capacity to do so in a sustained manner. Parties in India are weakly institutionalized with frequent splits and mergers and the formation of new ones at regular intervals. Apart from using government programmes to maximize electoral support politicians increasingly rely on monetary incentives. Election campaigns and vote-gathering have thus become increasingly expensive, compelling political leaders to collect large donations for the party which they do by unduly favouring big business. Most parties are centered on one leader who exercises absolute control over the party. Leadership succession is often confined to the family members of the leaders, who see parties as personal property to be to be handed down to their children (Suri et al. 2016).

Our discussion here shows that political party competition in all these countries ensure that they satisfy the procedural minimum as democracies by participating in elections. However their continuing institutional weakness, lack of internal democracy, corruption and overriding concern to capture power negatively impact democratic consolidation.

Civil society

As discussed one criteria that democracy in its procedural minimum must satisfy is – freedom of expression and alternative sources of information; associational autonomy. Freedom of expression – the freedom to voice dissent through non-violent means – is indeed the foundation of democracy. The space that democracy provides for multiple voices is what sets it apart from dictatorship or authoritarian system that is run according to the wishes of a privileged few. Also for democracies to transit from procedural to substantive individuals need to have opportunities to influence the conditions in which they live, to participate in and influence debates about the key decisions which affect society. This is the avenue that civil society provides in democracies. Civil society consists of "sustained organized social activity that occurs in groups that are formed outside the state, market and family." Frank Schwartz and Susan Pharr (2003) observe that in forming civil society, state can possibly play four different roles – "inspire, enable, constrain and create". In the context of Indonesia, the Philippines, South Korea and Malaysia the role of civil society has been critical in democratic restoration and it has therefore been characterised as "movement driven transition". However, in the new democratic setup civil society has a chequered journey. Civil society activism helped Indian democracy to be more inclusive.

Marcus Mietzner (2021) in his study of Indonesian civil society and its capacity to contribute to democracy argues that the civil society, which was robust in checking government excesses, has weakened. In the initial years following democratic transition there were "principled defenders of democracy" in civil society cutting across the pluralist-Islamist cleavage. For instance, established in the early and mid-2000s, pluralist groups like the Wahid Institute or the Setara Institute, fought for civil, minority and women's rights. In the Islamist sphere, the youth wing of Muhammadiyah, which while becoming increasingly conservative in the 2000s, defended reformist political goals. There were also "cross-constituency groups" like the Legal Aid Institute (LBH), which had both pluralist and Islamist streams. Indonesia's growing pluralists/Islamists divide has also affected its civil society and thus though they grew in numbers they found it difficult to come together to promote and defend democracy (Mietzner 2021). The effect of this was clearly felt when in 2019 the Jokowi government succeeded in enacting a law on Anti-Corruption Agency (KPK) which arrested politicians. Such attempts to reign in KPK by removing its special investigative power had not succeeded earlier in the face of sustained mass, civil society and media criticism. The government also pushed through legislations criminalising extra-marital relations and law on prisons, which would allow corruption convicts to seek significant cuts to their sentences. It met with strong student opposition against which the government did not hesitate to use force (Mietzner 2021).

In the Philippines too civil society mobilization played a critical role in dismantling the authoritarian regime. The 1987 constitution formulated after the 1986 People Power Revolution recognizes the importance of civil society organisations. Article II, Section 23 states "The State shall encourage non-governmental, community-based, or sector organizations that promote the welfare of the nation." Further Section 15 and 16 of Article XIII directs the state to "respect the role of independent people's organizations…" and "by law, facilitate the establishment of adequate consultation mechanisms" respectively (ADB 2013:10). The first post-authoritarian presidency of Aquino between 1986 and 1992 passed several laws that created a favourable legal environment and civil society organisations mushroomed. These organisations were engaged in areas of education, human resource development, community development, health and nutrition, environment and sustainable development, law, advocacy and politics. However, civil society activism to a large extent appears to depend on the people in government, and the leadership of the President. Some presidents have been elected with the active support of civil society groups though recurrent corruption and cronyism which soon led to civil society disillusionment and opposition. This was the case with Joseph Estrada's election in 1998 and his removal in 2001 and the election of Gloria Macapagal-Arroyo following the People Power II protests (Arugay 2019). In 2010, civil society groups rallied behind Benigno Simeon C. Aquino's anticorruption and antipoverty presidential campaign. Aquino's presidency was receptive of the civil society organisations role as watchdog of government and their partnership with government to implement projects and provide services. Subsequently in 2016 the populist Rodrigo Duterte's campaign on a security and anti-drugs platform resonated with elite and middle-class voters worried about crime and corruption. He was also supported by several NGOs for his promised social reforms and pro-poor policies. Activists of National Democratic CSO joined his cabinet departments of social welfare, labour and agrarian reform. As the civil society organisations' support for the President gave way to criticism, Duterte clamped down on them. In 108 the Securities and Exchange Commission (SEC) the main national agency for regulating CSOs issued Memorandum Circular 15 categorizing CSOs as "low", "medium" or "high-risk" relative to their affinity to (communist) terrorism. The government also denounced foreign-funded CSOs as agents of the West, a trend in many countries in Europe and Asia (Lorch 2021).

In Korea the state – civil society relation has evolved over the years from one of confrontation and conflict during authoritarian rule to one of competition and co-operation under democracy. In 1989 the Citizens' Coalition for Economic Justice was a group formed by 1000 professionals – lawyers, professors, religious leaders and others to promote economic justice through the power of citizens. In 1994 the other important civil society organization, the People's Solidarity for Participatory Democracy (PSPD) was created. PSPD was active in monitoring and evaluating the performance of government ministers and members and filing lawsuits against corrupt public officials. The civil society groups continued to expand their influence under the successive governments of Kim Dae-jung and Roh Moo-hyun, Lee Myung-bak, Park Guen-hye and Moon Jae-in. They pursued a wide range of issues like voicing environmental concerns, registering protest against the Korea-US Free Trade Agreement. The state-civil society connect was evident in 2007 when following the victory of the conservative camp and Lee Myung-bak taking charge as President, conservative civil society groups gained prominence. The Lee Myung-bak and Park Guen-hye government's followed a hardline approach to civil society groups and anti-government demonstrations while maintaining a close connection with conservative groups (Jeong & Kim 2017). But governments have by and large refrained from intimidating CSOs as demonstrated during the Cheonan incident in 2010 when the PSPD and Solidarity for Peace and Reunification of Korea challenged the government claims or when civil society groups kept the Park government under pressure and once the media reported an illegal transaction by Park massive mobilization and protests followed till the President was removed and impeached in March 2017 (Suh 2015).

In Malaysia's long bout of authoritarian rule civil society groups like Bersih (Coalitions for Free and Fair Elections) and HINDRAF (Hindu Rights Action Force) were particularly active in mounting a challenge to UNMO's one party dominance. In 2007 Bersih and HINDRAF made common cause with the opposition and organised rallies to mobilise public support against UNMO. By and large governments viewed the activities of civil society organisations with suspicion and hostility. They were characterized as the "internal other". Prime Minister Mahathir argued that civil society organisations that tend to meddle in politics should be restrained, as their objective is to weaken government authority (Azizuddin 2011).

Notwithstanding this open distrust of civil society groups that challenge and criticize government, some collaborative state-civil society activity has developed with NGOs that are non-political working on the environment, welfare, women, youths, and child development like the Malaysian AIDS Council, the Malaysian Nature Society (MNS), and the World Wilde Fund Nature for Malaysia (WWF). The growing advocacy work of NGOs led to the enactment of the Domestic Violence Act in 1994 and the setting up of the SUHAKAM (the Human Rights Commission of Malaysia) in 1999. Organisations like the Peninsular Malaysia Orang Asli Association (POASM), have successfully represented the issues of Orang Asli (indigenous people) and their cultures to the government. Besides like in Korea there are civil society groups close to the government like Majlis Belia Malaysia (MBM, Malaysian Youth Council), Gabungan Penulis Nasional (GAPENA) focusing on the Malay language and literature activities and Gabungan Pelajar Melayu Semenanjung (GPMS) which have been involved in deliberation on issues of their own concern (Azizuddin 2011).

Civil society in India has played a critical role in strengthening the substantive aspect of democracy. Currently there are an estimated three million plus NGOs in India. The state and civil society relation in Nehruvian period constructive and cooperative. In 1977 the Gandhian activist Jayaprakash Narayan mobilised Gandhian workers, NGOs, students and trade union leaders to challenge the emergency imposed by

Prime Minister Indira Gandhi and bring political change. When the Janata Party came to power in 1977 it actively encouraged civil society work and NGO involvement in rural development programs. Funding for civil society organizations was increased and they were provided bureaucratic support. Once Indira Gandhi was back in power in 1980 the government civil society faced restrictions and repression. The Foreign Contribution Regulation Act (FCRA) was amended in 1984. It became mandatory for all NGOs getting foreign funds to register themselves with the Home Ministry. Successive governments have adopted a twin approach to civil society – encouraging those that could be partnered and restricting those that were "too political". For instance under Rajiv Gandhi's prime ministership NGOs and other civil society organisations were promoted to provide services and function as watchdogs and funds to civil society organisations that worked for social development were increased. In 1991 following liberalisation the state's withdrawal from many areas of social welfare increased scope of civil society activity. Once again aid and funding for NGOs that could help realise the development objectives increased while the forms of agitational civil society were limited. The Congress-led UPA government followed a rights-based approach and promoted state civil society relationship by forming the National Advisory Council (NAC). It was instrumental in drafting several key pro-poor laws like the Right to Information Act, the National Rural Employment Guarantee Act, the Forest Rights Act, the Right to Education Act and the Food Security Act. However, parallelly a new FCRA in 2010 replaced the 1976 Act to tighten its control over politicised elements within civil society that were perceived to be impeding the growth of neoliberal capital. This largely limited CSO activity to depoliticised service delivery sectors, resulting in what Neema Kudva calls the "NGO-ification of civil society" in India (Sahoo 2020).

Under the Modi government the FCRA continued to be used to tighten requirements that civil society organisations were required to fulfil. In 2016 for instance the Ministry of Home Affairs cancelled the registration of the Lawyers Collective, an NGO working on human rights issues (Bhatnagar 2016). A Civicus report shows that between 5 May and 9 June 2015, the MHA cancelled the registration of 4,470 CSOs for violating the FCRA. Furthermore, in 2016, the government cancelled licences of some 20,000 of 33,000 NGOs for violating FCRA provisions (Sahoo 2020). On the other hand the government has had no difficulty in working with those sections of the civil society that back its ideological project.

Our discussion shows that the role of civil society in ensuring democratic quality in these states by holding power accountable and empowering and including hitherto excluded groups has not been an unqualified success. In each country civil society groups engaged in these endeavour operate within increasing restrictions. Non-political organisations or organisations that share the agenda of the government in power, however, function with ease. World Values Survey (WVS Wave 7 2017-2022) shows some interesting results, on questions of confidence in environment and women's movements. In Indonesia and Philippines respectively, 52.2%; 51.65% and 47.3%; 48.3% indicated they had quite a lot of confidence in environment protection movements and 27.7%; 26.9% and 31.5%; 36.0% said they had a great deal of confidence in these movements. In Malaysia where only recently elections led to an end of UMNO dominance the percentage in these two categories are higher than even South Korea which has been functioning as democracy longer. 18.0% and 16.5% reposed a great deal of confidence and 59.3% and 57.4% had quite a lot of confidence in environment protection movements and women's movements in Malaysia while in South Korea 5.7% and 5.3% had great deal of confidence and 59.1% and 55.5% had quite a lot of confidence in these two movements respectively.

Democracy and diversity

John Stuart Mill observed that, "free institutions are next to impossible in a country made up of different nationalities. Among a people without fellow feeling, especially if they read and speak different languages, the united public opinion, necessary to the working of representative government, cannot exist" (Varshney 2015). This underscores the challenge that most highly diverse Indo-Pacific countries with multiple cleavages of geography, language, history, class and culture faced in building and consolidating a democratic system. It is of course not a challenge that escapes established democracies. In Europe, the Northern Ireland and the Basque challenge have involved violence and terror before being reasonably settled after years of negotiation. In recent years we have witnessed the demand for a Scottish independence referendum and the Catalan independence referendum from the United Kingdom and Spain respectively.

In the Indo-Pacific countries like India and Indonesia are amongst the world's most culturally diverse, encompassing hundreds of different languages and ethnic groups within their border. In Malaysia, the polarized social structure is a result of colonial labour migration and settlement. In Sri Lanka the Sinhala-Tamil cleavage plunged the country into years of civil war. Korea's common cultural foundations is affected by deep ethno-political divisions founded on historical legacies and exacerbated by political competition (Reilly 2006).

The capacities that these states develop to cope with such deep diversity has definite bearing on their democratic development and prospects. Four of them – Indonesia, Philippines and South Korea and Sri Lanka established unitary systems, India and Malaysia opted for federalism.

Indonesia's unitary state organization is based on the principle of "unity in diversity". At independence the Indonesian political elite's was averse to the idea of federalism associated as it was with the Dutch colonial experience. Further the perceived threat of dissolution of the country along ethnic lines from fierce separatists movements in Aceh, Papua (then Irian Jaya) and East Timor hardened the stance of policy makers on federalism. Thus even after the democratic transition in 1999 the devolution of power that followed did not create strong autonomous provinces (Hutchinson 2017). The two main laws – Law 22/1999 on Regional Autonomy and Law 25/1999 on Centre-Regional Fiscal Balance that were passed redesigned the organisation of the state and redistributed tasks by handing authority to smaller entities at local level – the 300 or so districts and not to the 26 provinces and also made provisions for the redistribution of fiscal resources (Hutchinson 2017). Arguably by devolving authority to entities that are too small, the central government wanted to stem both the federalist tide and ensure that separatist movements would not be able to garner the requisite strength to break away from the state (Neumeyer 2006).

The unitary Philippines state was challenged by mainly by separatists from the Moros of the Mindanao islands and the Sulu archipelago who feared the weakening of their religious, cultural, and political traditions by forced assimilation into a Catholic-dominated Philippine Republic and Cordillera in Northern Philippines. Conflict continued in Mindanao over five decades and the struggle for autonomy in Cordillera emerged in the late 1970s. The creation of autonomous regions in Muslim Mindanao and in the Cordilleras is enshrined in Section 15 of Article X of the 1987 Constitution. As part of a peace agreement to end conflict between the Philippine government and Moro secessionists The Bangsamoro Autonomous Region of Muslim Mindanao (BARMM) was formally established in early 2019. However, President Duterte, who is from Mindanao, came to office promising to end hyper-centralisation and to bring peace to Mindanao by establishing federalism which has not materialised (Breen 2019).

Malaysia unlike the other three, opted for federalism, governing power is constitutionally divided between national and state governments. Dominated by Barisan Nasional (National Front) there was no meaningful power sharing (Reilly 2006). However in practice Malaysia functioned as a highly unitary system with increasing centralisation backed by the argument of ensuring the nation's efficient development. Relations between federal and state governments are more akin to "intra- or inter-party relations" rather than conventional federal-state intergovernmental relations. The BN federal government has by and large succeeded in using intra-party control over BN state governments to function "more like branches than partners of the federal government" (Neo 2018).

The results of the 2008 and 2013 general elections changed this. Barisan Nasional (National Front) lost its two third majority in the Parliament and in the 2008 election it also lost five states to Pakatan Rakyat (People's Alliance) – Kelantan, Sabah, Terengganu, Penang and Selangor. In the 2013 general election, Pakatan Rakyat managed to hold on to three states – Kelantan, Penang and Selangor. The victory in Penang and Selangor, two of the richest states in Malaysia was particularly important (Muslim et al. 2015). As a result on a variety of policy issues, like demands for oil rights in Kelantan, Terengganu and Sarawak began to escalate. In 2018 Pakatan Harapan contested the general election on the promise to "revive the true spirit of federalism". On forming a government, the Pakatan Harapan-led federal government it did set up the Parliamentary Select Committee on Federal-State Relations in December 2018 but the government's lower allocations to opposition MPs and some opposition leaders not being allowed to attend state government events run contrary to power sharing. This was the trend on earlier instances when opposition parties gained power in the states. They faced federal government interference and encroachment into their policy areas of jurisdiction, and were also fiscally punished for not being aligned to the central party (Yeoh 2019).

India with its extraordinary diversity based on religion, language, caste and ethnicity, unlike Indonesia opted for federalism but like Indonesia unity was no less a concern for the political elite. In their reading a strong Union government was necessary for India's survival and political stability and this was reflected inherent bias for the Union government in the Indian Constitution. The term "federation" in fact finds no mention in the Constitution which in Article 1 describes India as a "Union of States". The working of Indian federalism can be understood through various phases of one-party federalism of early fifties to late sixties; bargaining or conflictual federalism from late sixties to late eighties; multiparty federalism from late eighties to 2014 and since then back to "dominant party" federalism (Ghosh 2020).

Regional assertions were present even in the in the first phase of one-party federalism. This came from one, the regional leaders within the overarching "Congress System" who had mass base, influence and power and two, from the rise of linguistic autonomy movement. The central government's initial reluctance to create linguistically organised states fearing disunity gave way to linguistic reorganisation of the states in the face of sustained regional movement (Sarkar 2014). In the second phase many regional parties and anti-Congress coalitions formed governments in the states, regional assertions followed from opposition party led states of Punjab, Andhra Pradesh, Tamil Nadu, West Bengal, Assam, Jammu and Kashmir. With federal power positions occupied by opposing political parties centre-states relation became increasingly confrontational. Article 356 and the office of the Governor was frequently used to impose centre's authority on opposition run states. The states pushed back and regional demands of Assam, Kashmir, Mizoram and Punjab escalated. In 1983, the centre appointed the Sarkaria Commission to look into the constitutional provisions on centre-state relations (Ghosh 2020).

Between 1989 and 2014, a number of regional parties emerged as important players ushering a new era of multi-party system and coalition politics which impacted the federal dynamics. This was a period of further decentralisation when the 73rd and 74th Amendments of 1992 created a third tier of Indian federalism at the Municipal and Panchayat level strengthening the empowerment of people at the grassroots (Ghosh 2020). With the victory of the BJP in 2014 and subsequent 2019 general elections by mustering a parliamentary majority, India shifted away from the era of coalition politics to one of a "dominant party" phase where the party system is now a BJP-led system (Chibber & Verma 2019). In 2018 the BJP was already in power in 21 states either on its own or with a strong regional ally. In this "dominant party" the centre-state relations have become more centralized and "competitive federalism" which in comparative literature is understood to have a decentralising effect works in the Indian context towards centralisation, where states ruled by the dominant party are advantaged as they compete for central funding and foreign investments. In effect "competition" results in "partisan federalism" rather than genuinely "competitive federalism" (Sharma & Swenden 2018).

The capability of institutional arrangements be it unitary or federal to accommodate diversity and strengthen democracy thus depends on how they are put to use and whether there is any genuine power sharing between diverse competing groups. In India for instance the linguistic reorganisation of states indicated accommodation but the centralising tendency also led to fresh escalation of regional movements. In Malaysia similarly opposition's electoral victories in states met with federal governments interference in their areas of jurisdiction.

Civil-military relations

Civilia in control of the military is understood to be a sign of consolidating, maturing democracies. It entails "that distribution of decision-making power in which civilians have exclusive authority to decide on national politics and their implementation. Under civilian control, civilians can freely choose to delegate decision making power and the implementation of certain policies to the military while the military has no decision-making power outside those areas specifically defined by civilians. Furthermore, it is civilians alone who determine which particular policies, or aspects of policies, the military implements, and the civilians alone define the boundaries between policy making and policy-implementation" (Croissant 2011). In the decolonised developing countries given the historical, economic, social and political conditions the military behaved differently and the civil-military dichotomy tended to blur. To understand civil-military relations in these countries we need to go beyond the conflictual zero-sum approach to one that emphasizes cooperation and harmony (Bilveer 2000).

In Indonesia, South Korea and Philippines the military's position has been strong *vis-à-vis* the civilian government. In Indonesia the turmoil of the 1950s and the inability of the civilian government to deal with it strengthened the role of the military. In 1958 General Nasution, argued that the military was "not just the "civilian tool" like in the Western countries, nor a "military regime" which dominates the state power but as one of the many forces in society, it would be involved in both security and non-security matters particularly in the social-political arena (Bilveer 2000). The Indonesian military believed that it was rightfully first a political and only then a military institution (Bilveer 2000). With the restoration of democracy this understanding has been challenged. The military's political role and representation in the national parliament (DPR) came under radar and it was argued that election by the people and not reservation that would determine the representation criteria. The reformers were pushing to reset civil-military relations. Even when the Indonesian military post-1998 agreed to switch to "indirect-role mode" and adopt a "constructive role sharing" approach it did not give up on the notion that partnership between the civilian and military sectors of society (Bilveer 2000).

In South Korea the military dominated the authoritarian regime and enjoyed extensive political privileges and institutional autonomy. Retired military officers with strong connections to the active officer corps (especially Hanahoe) were present in political institutions. The military controlled the internal security apparatus and military intelligence, and security agencies were involved in the supervision and suppression of political opposition and civilian influence on matters of defence and military policy was completely absent. Once democracy was restored civilian control over the military was established over a period of time under successive presidents. The military was first moved out of politics, and subsequently control over defence and military policy was established. The start was made during Kim Young-sam's Presidency (1993–1998) when he reduced the share of former military officers in the cabinet from 19.6%to 8%and recruited a large number of "progressive outsiders" and "reform-oriented men and women". A civilian became head of the National Assembly's defence committee for the first time and a parliamentary review of arms procurement processes was established. Further progress was made during Kim Dae-jung's presidency (1998–2003). Dae-jung introduced civilian experts into the Ministry of National Defence (MND); ensured the MND would publish defence white papers to make defence and military policy more transparent and also established the National Security Council (NSC) in 1998 (Kuehn 2016). However, civilian control of the military in the context of South Korea's threat perception has its limits. Since democratisation not a single civilian has been appointed Minister of Defence, 6 Vice Ministers were civilian but in practice, most of them are appointed to the post almost immediately after relinquishing military posts (Kim 2014).

In the Philippines since democratisation there have been several attempted military coups though they failed. To survive civilian governments developed "symbiotic relationship" with military elites demanding material rewards, exercising political influence on the government, and expanding decision-making powers in exchange for protecting its institutional well-being (Croissant 2011). The military has been involved in economic development programmes which increase their political autonomy and impacts civilian control. In 2007 the National Development Support Command (NADESCOM) was established. The Command consists of the Army's Engineering

Brigades and its' aim is to support and assist both the military as well as the civilian government to improve security and development conditions. The military thus plays a part not only in the internal security operations but also the anti-poverty programmes of the civilian government. This extended role of the military in internal security functions as a result of shortcomings in police capacity or in development tasks because of governance failures makes civilian control of military tenuous (Arugay 2012).

In Malaysia, the armed forces (MAF) are a defining symbol of Malay identity which since independence, has continued to be a predominantly Malay institution. Its upper echelons are occupied almost exclusively by the ethnic Malay. The military is subordinate to the civilian authorities but civil–military relations are governed by informal networking between them. The dominant party (UMNO) has rewarded the political loyalty of military officers (post retirement) with positions in state enterprises, public offices, and party politics (Croissant 2011).

In India the question of civilian control of the military was settled in the early years of independence. The world's fourth largest military, has since independence been under firm civilian control. Stephen Cohen writing in 1976 described this as "crushing civilian dominance over a very powerful and large military." Some important steps taken by the first Prime Minister Nehru, ensured this. The higher management of the military was reformed and Commander-in-Chief positions for the air force and navy were created which made the Commander-in-Chief of the army one of the three. Further all senior military officers were placed below elected ministers and senior civil servants. And more importantly unlike Malaysia, the Indian leadership worked to change the ethnic composition of the Indian army to make it more inclusive and reflecting India's democratic ethos. The government also set up paramilitary forces entrusted with internal security duties which ensured that the military was not involved in handling domestic agitations or civil disturbances (Joshi & Patil 2022). This strict civilian control had its own operational issues which were exposed in India's defeat in 1962 India-China War. Since then by and large the military, in return for maintaining its apolitical character, obtained considerable freedom in its own domain (Mukherjee 2021).

The discussion here shows that while civilian control of the military is taken to be the hallmark of matured democracies, the manner in and degree to which such control has been established in the countries in focus varies. The variations can be explained by initial starting conditions of decolonisation, failure of the civilian governments to deliver good governance or quest for ruling party to maintain hegemony. South Korea and Indonesia have managed to overcome past legacies of military intervention into politics, in the Philippines the inadequacies of the civilian government has given the military extended influence. In Malaysia the civilian control of the military has been used to perpetuate one party dominance and thus has not worked for overall strengthening of democracy. Interestingly the WVS shows that in Indonesia and Philippines, 18.6; 45.2 and 19.9; 43.5 percent surveyed indicated that 'having army rule' was very good and fairly good respectively (WVS Wave 7 2017-2021).

Recent trends

The various indices that measure democracy across the world indicate worrying trends in some of these countries that question their democratic consolidation. The most established and largest democracy has taken the biggest fall. In 2021 V-Dem characterised India as an "electoral autocracy" and in the Economist Intelligence Unit's Democracy Index, India slipped two places to the 53rd position. Indonesia and the Philippines are doing no better. South Korea is the only exception. The policies, vision and style of functioning of the popularly elected leaders of these states are seriously undermining democratic consolidation. In the plural and diverse setting of India and Indonesia the rise of ethno-nationalism limits the role of all citizens to participate equally. In India since the 2014 elections which catapulted BJP under Prime Ministers Modi to power the government has adopted policies to realise the party's vision of India as a Hindu nation. A slew of policies like the Citizenship Amendment Act 2019; proposal for the National Register of Citizens (NRC) to distinguish between illegal migrants and legal residents; a push for implementation of uniform civil code, abrogation of Article 370 ending the special status of the state of Jammu and Kashmir and creating two federally-ruled territories – Ladakh, and Jammu and Kashmir were initiated. The protests and agitations that followed was met with harsh response and all dissent delegitimised using the "anti-national" narrative. The majoritarian thrust of government policies coupled with diminishing space for freedom of expression, civil society and the media has seen India slide in democratic rankings (Khosla & Vaishnav 2021). Is India then on the road to being a "majoritarian democracy" like Sri Lanka? The Indian diversity embodies identities that are crosscutting, not cumulative system. Virtually all social identities – linguistic, caste, tribes are local or regional. Even the Hindu Muslim cleavage, the most problematic one in Indian politics, gets moderated because India's Muslims speak the language of the region in which they live. Language thus crosscuts religion. The same applies to India's tribes, castes, and linguistic groups (Varshney 2015). It does not provide a ready ground for pursuing majoritarian policies. Moreover the success of such policy will depend on the push back or lack of it from opposition parties and civil society. At the national level the Congress has weakened and opposition unity that could fill the void is fragile. However at the regional level there are strong political parties that have halted the electoral march of the BJP and are important players in India's federal set up. The Indian voter has also shown political maturity by voting for BJP at the Centre and regional parties in the states. Indonesia too like India under President Jokowi registered similar trends of democratic decline. On the question of commitment to civil liberties while the public attitude and commitment to civil liberties, including freedoms of speech, assembly, criticizing the government, and worship continues, the performance declined since the beginning of the Jokowi's term in 2014. In 2005 Freedom House raised Indonesia's rating from Partly Free to Free, and the country retained this rating through 2012. Since 2013, Indonesia has slipped back to Partly Free and following Jokowi's election in 2014 freedom conditions as measured by FH have worsened. The Jokowi government reigned in the Anti-Corruption Agency (KPK) by removing its special investigative power and pushed through legislations like criminalising extra-marital relations and amending the law on prisons, which would allow corruption convicts to seek significant cuts to their sentences. It met with strong student opposition against which the government did not hesitate to use force. Indonesia's polarisation between Islamists and pluralists is also growing. This had in 2017 led to the ouster and arrest of the then Jakarta governor Basuki Tjahaja Purnama (Ahok), a double minority as an ethnic Chinese Christian and a Jokowi protégé following massive protests (Bland 2019). In the 2019 election the reality of this polarisation made Jokowi chose powerful cleric Ma'ruf Amin as his running mate. Jokowi has also co-opted old ruling elite to neutralise their opposition, after his re-election, the party of his twice-defeated rival Prabowo, Gerindra, joined the government and Jokowi named Prabowo minister of defense. This effectively reduced the opposition to 104 seats to the government's 471 and weakened its ability to check government's power. In the Philippines Rodrigo Duterte came to power in 2016 on the promise of dealing with drug criminals and restoring law and order. He had his years in Davos as mayor to show what he could achieve. Duterte lived upto his promise and went after drug cartels. The war on drugs has seen an increase in role of coercive institutions of the state the police and the military which undermine the effort of democratic control over security forces. The government has also mounted attack on opposition, the judiciary and the media which weaken their capacity to check, balance and hold the government accountable. In addition control of information affects the citizen's capacity to make informed decisions (Curato 2021).

Conclusion

This chapter looked into the prospects of democracy in the Indo-Pacific by focusing on a host of countries that transited to democracy post-decolonisation. Democracy in these states is neither an unqualified success nor a complete failure. Between 1990 and 2019 all four countries have improved performance as reflected in the Human Development Index, Indonesia and Philippines are in the high human development category, Korea and Malaysia in very high category, India in the medium category (Human Development Report 2020). The trajectory of post-authoritarian democracy transition and consolidation in Indonesia, the Philippines and Korea show the situational complexity of democracy building in the initial conditions of decolonisation and indigenous values. The countries are more successful in meeting the procedural minimum of competitive elections than augmenting the substantive aspects of democracy by ensuring equality of participation, deliberation an inclusion of alternative views and opinions. Winning elections is the overriding concern that drives political competition of weakly institutionalised parties. Once in power elected governments push back all dissent and enact laws to control civil society and disregard opposition that is weak and divided. Sri Lanka and Malaysia's political development has prioritised the majority community which affected democracy building and its quality. India's development since 2014 shows weakening of political plurality and strengthening of majoritarian tendencies. However, aware that elections serve the useful purpose of legitimisation both internally and externally the political elite are unlikely to let go of fulfilling the basic minimum of procedural democracy.

Notes

1 Freedom in the World 2021 https://freedomhouse.org/report/freedom-world/2021/democracy-under-siege

2 For basic country information see Malaysia https://www.countryreports.org/country/Malaysia/government.htm; India https://www.countryreports.org/country/india/government.htm; Indonesia https://www.countryreports.org/country/Indonesia/facts.htm; Philippines https://www.countryreports.org/country/Philippines/facts.htm; Sri Lanka https://www.countryreports.org/country/SriLanka.htm South Korea https://www.countryreports.org/country/koreasouth/government.htm

3 Sukarno argued that Indonesia had its own "original form of democracy, which is not imported from abroad." It had its' own characteristics, "and therefore," Sukarno continued,

"there must be a guided democracy in this country, a democracy with a leadership." In 1955 he declared that Indonesia would not have a Western style democracy based on majority rule (which he termed as "majoricracy") but a *gotong rojong* democracy in which decisions are made on the basis of mutual agreement. For details see Justus M. van der Kroef (Aug 1957), ""Guided Democracy" in Indonesia" *Far Eastern Survey*, Vol. 26, No. 8, pp. 113-124

4 Suharto emphasized the close alliance between the New Order regime and the army (ABRI) under the banner of Pancasila, the first principle (or sila) is a belief in one supreme being; the second principle is described as a commitment either to a just and civilized humanitarianism (*Sila Kemanusian yang Adil dan Beradab*); the third Sila is a commitment to the unity of Indonesia (*Sila Persatuan Indonesia*); the fourth Sila stresses on the idea of a people led or governed by wise policies arrived at through a process of consultation and consensus (*Sila Kerakyatan yang Dipimpin oleh Hikmat Kebijaksanaan dalam Permusyawaratan/ Perwakilan*) and the fifth is a commitment to social justice for all the Indonesian people (*Sila Keadilan Sosial bagi Seluruh Rakyat Indonesia*). The New Order permitted only political activity consistent with the state ideology, political movements contrary Pancasila were viewed as a fundamental threat to the existence of the Indonesian state. See Michael Morfit (1981), "Pancasila: The Indonesian State Ideology According to the New Order Government", Asian Survey, Vol. 21, No. 8, pp. 838-851.

5 Larry Diamond (April 2002) "Elections Without Democracy: Thinking about Hybrid Regimes", *Journal of Democracy,* Volume 13, Number 2, pp. 21-34

6 In competitive authoritarian regimes, formal democratic institutions are essentially used to obtain and exercise political authority. Those exercising political authority flout rules so often and so extensively that the regime fails to meet conventional minimum standards for democracy (Steven Levitsky and Lucan A. Way (2002), "The Rise of Competitive Authoritarianism", *Journal of Democracy*, Volume 13, Number 2 April, pp. 51-65)

References

Aceron, Joy and Francis Isaac, "Contextualizing Vertical Integration in Philippine Civil Society", in Joy Aceron (ed.), *Going Vertical: Citizen-led Reform Campaigns in the Philippines (2nd Edition)*, Philippines: Government Watch, 2018: 34–39.

Adelman, Irma, "From Aid Dependence to Aid Independence: South Korea", *Comments at the Second Committee (Economic and Financial Committee's) 62nd Session*, UN General Assembly, 2007. https://www.un.org/en/ga/second/62/iadelman.pdf.

Arugay, Aries A., "Fall from Grace, Descent from Power? Civil Society after Philippine Democracy's Lost Decade", in Imelda Deinla and Björn Dressel (eds.), *From Aquino II to Duterte (2010–2018): Change, Continuity—And Rupture*, Singapore: Mainland Press Pte Ltd, 2019: 285–308.

Asian Development Bank, "Philippines Civil Society Briefs", February 2013, 1–12, https://www.adb.org/sites/default/files/publication/30174/csb-phi.pdf.

Aspinall, Edward and Mada Sukmajati, "Patronage and Clientelism in Indonesian Electoral Politics", in Edward Aspinall and Mada Sukmajati (eds.), *Electoral Dynamics in Indonesia: Money Politics, Patronage and Clientelism at the Grassroots*, Singapore: NUS Press, 2016.

Aspinall, Edward, Marcus Mietzner and Dirk Tomsa (eds.), *The Yudhoyono Presidency: Indonesia's Decade of Stability and Stagnation*, Singapore: Institute of Southeast Asian Studies, 2015.

Béteille, André "The Varieties of Democracy", *Economic and Political Weekly*, 48(8), 2013: 33–40.

Bedeski, Robert E., "State Reform and Democracy in South Korea", *The Journal of East Asian Affairs*, 6(1), 1992: 141–168.

Beetham, David, "Conditions for Democratic Consolidation", *Review of African Political Economy*, 21(60), 1994: 157–172.

Bell, Daniel A., David Brown, Kanishka Jayasuriya and David Martin Jones, *Towards Illiberal Democracy in Pacific Asia*, Great Britain: St Martin's Press, 1995.

Bhatnagar, Gaurav Vivek, "Suspension of NGO's FCRA Registration is Clampdown on Dissent, Says Indira Jaising", *Wire*, 2 June 2016. https://thewire.in/politics/mha-suspends-fcra -registration-of-indira-jaisings-ngo.

Billet, Bret L., "South Korea at the Crossroads: An Evolving Democracy or Authoritarianism Revisited?", *Asian Survey*, 30(3), 1990: 300–311.

Bilveer, Singh, "Civil-Military Relations in Democratizing Indonesia: Change Amidst Continuity", *Armed Forces & Society*, 26(4), 2000: 607–633.

Bland, Ben, "How President Joko Widodo is Eroding Indonesia's Democracy", *Italian Institute for International Political Studies*, 11 December, 2019. https://www.ispionline.it/en/pubblicazione/how-president-joko-widodo-eroding-indonesias-democracy-24587.

Bland, Ben, "Politics in Indonesia: Resilient Elections, Defective Democracy", *Lowy Institute for International Policy*, April 2019. https://www.lowyinstitute.org/publications/politics -indonesia-resilient-elections-defective-democracy.

Bourchier, David, *Illiberal Democracy in Indonesia: The Ideology of the Family State*, London and New York: Routledge, 2015.

Breen, Michael G., "The Philippines is a Test Case for Asia's New Federalism", *Humanities*, 6 May 2019. https://pursuit.unimelb.edu.au/articles/the-philippines-is-a-test-case-for-asia-s -new-federalism.

Bunte, Marco and Andreas Ufen (eds.), *Democratization in Post-Suharto Indonesia*, London: Routledge, 2009.

Caucus of Development NGO Networks (CODE-NGO) et al., *Assessment of the Enabling Environment for Civil Society Organizations in the Philippines*, CODE-NGO in Partnership with the Alternative Law Groups, Manila, 2016: 1–119.

Chandranegara, Ibnu Sina, Rantawan Djanim and Budi Astuti, "Managing Power Sharing of the State on Islamic Modern Society: A Case Study of Indonesia", *Journal Al-Azhar Indonesia Seri Humaniora*, 5(1), 2019: 38–47.

Chhibber, Pradeep and Rahul Verma, "The Rise of the Second Dominant Party System in India: BJP's New Social Coalition in 2019", *Studies in Indian Politics*, 7(2), 2019: 131–148.

Chhuanawma, L.H., "Evolution of Party System in India", *Mizoram University Journal of Humanities and Social Sciences*, VI(1), 2020: 105–115.

Chhibber, Pradeep and Rahul Verma, "The Rise of the Second Dominant Party System in India: BJP's New Social Coalition in 2019", *Studies in Indian Politics*, 7(2), 2019: 131–148, https://doi.org/10.1177/2321023019874628.

Cho, Youngho, "Appraising the Quality of Democracy as a Developmental Phenomenon: How South Koreans Appraise the Quality of Their Democracy", *Social Indicators Research*, 116(3), 2014: 699–712.

Chong, Chan Tsu, "Democratic Breakthrough in Malaysia – Political Opportunities and the Role of Bersih", *Journal of Current Southeast Asian Affairs*, 37(3), 2018: 109–137.

Collier, David and Steven Levitsky "Democracy with Adjectives: Conceptual Innovation in Comparative Research", *World Politics*, 49(3), 1997: 430–451.

Croissant, Aurel, "Civilian Control Over the Military in East Asia", *EAI Fellows Program*, 31, 2011: 1–56.

Croissant, Aurel, "Majoritarian and Consensus Democracy, Electoral Systems, and Democratic Consolidation in Asia", *Asian Perspective*, 26(2), 2002: 5–39.

Curato, Nicole, "Democratic Expressions Amidst Fragile Institutions: Possibilities for Reform in Duterte's Philippines", *Brookings*, 22 January, 2021. https://www.brookings.edu/articles /democratic-expressions-amidst-fragile-institutions-possibilities-for-reform-in-dutertes -philippines/.

Dahl, Robert A., "Dilemmas of Pluralist Democracy: Autonomy vs. Control", *Ethics*, 94(4), 1982: 701–710.

Diamond, Larry, *Developing Democracy: Toward Consolidation*, The Johns Hopkins University Press, Washington, 1999.

Diamond, Larry, "Elections Without Democracy: Thinking about Hybrid Regimes", *Journal of Democracy*, 13(2), 2002: 21–34.

Diamond, Larry and Byung-Kook Kim (eds.), *Consolidating Democracy in South Korea*, Lynne Rienner Publishers, Inc., 2000, Washington 1999.

Diamond, Larry and Leonardo Morlino, "The Quality of Democracy: An Overview", *Journal of Democracy*, 15(4), 2005: 20–31.

Dore, Giovanna Maria Dora, Jae H. Ku and Karl D. Jackson (eds.), *Incomplete Democracies in the Asia-Pacific Evidence from Indonesia, Korea, the Philippines, and Thailand*, Palgrave Macmillan, New York, 2014.

Dressel, Björn, "The Philippines: How Much Real Democracy?" *International Political Science Review*, 32(5), 2011: 529–545. https://doi.org/10.1177/0192512111417912.

Fionna, Ulla and Dirk Tomsa, "Changing Patterns of Factionalism in Indonesia: From Principle to Patronage", *Journal of Current Southeast Asian Affairs*, 39(1), 2020: 39–58, https://doi.org/10.1177/1868103419896904.

Freedman, Amy L., *Political Change and Consolidation Democracy's Rocky Road in Thailand, Indonesia, South Korea and Malaysia*, New York: Palgrave Macmillan, 2006.

Ghosh, Ambar Kumar, "The Paradox of 'Centralised Federalism': An Analysis of the Challenges to India's Federal Design", *Observer Research Foundation ORF Occasional*, 272, 2020.

Gunn, Geoffrey C., "Indonesia in 2012: An Electoral Democracy in Full Spate", *Asian Survey*, 53(1), 2013: 117–125.

Gunther, Richard, and Larry Diamond, "Species of Political Parties: A New Typology", *Party Politics*, 9(2), 2003: 167–199.

Hellmann, Olli, *Political Parties and Electoral Strategy: The Development of Party Organization in East Asia*, Basingstoke: Palgrave Macmillan, 2011.

Hellmann, Olli, "Party System Institutionalization Without Parties: Evidence from Korea", *Journal of East Asian Studies*, 14(1), 2014: 53–84.

Hicken, Allen, *The Political Party System From: Routledge Handbook of the Contemporary Philippines*, Routledge, 2018, Published online, https://www.routledgehandbooks.com/doi/10.4324/9781315709215-3.

Hooi, Khoo Ying, "Electoral Reform Movement in Malaysia: Emergence, Protest, and Reform", *Suvarnabhumi*, 6(2), 2014: 85–106.

Horowitz, Donald L., *Change and Democracy in Indonesia*, Cambridge: Cambridge University Press, 2013.

Huntington, Samuel, "How Countries Democratize", *Political Science Quarterly*, 106(4), 1991: 579–616, https://doi.org/10.2307/2151795.

Human Development Report, 2020. https://hdr.undp.org/sites/default/files/Country-Profiles/PHL.pdf.

Hutchinson, Francis E., "(De)centralization and the Missing Middle in Indonesia and Malaysia", *Sojourn: Journal of Social Issues in Southeast Asia*, 32(2), 2017: 291–335.

International Crisis Group, "Indonesia: Defying the State", *International Crisis Group Asia Briefing N°138*, August 2012. https://www.crisisgroup.org/asia/south-east-asia/indonesia/indonesia-defying-state.

Jati, Wasisto Raharjo, "The Situation of Declining Indonesian Democracy in 2021", *THC Insights*, June 2021. https://habibiecenter.or.id/img/publication/825aedece8d3ddbb46b5a4efb69dba59.pdf.

Joshi, Manoj and Sameer Patil, "Civil-military Relations in Independent India", 15 August 2022. https://www.orfonline.org/expert-speak/civil-military-relations-in-independent-india/.

Juan Vidal Aguas y Quijano, "The Philippines in the Twentieth Century: Social Change in Recent Decades", *College of William & Mary - Arts & Sciences: Dissertations, Theses, and Masters Projects Paper 1539625429*, 1987. https://scholarworks.wm.edu/cgi/viewcontent.cgi?article=4025&context=etd.

Kadirgamar, Ahilan, "Polarization, Civil War, and Persistent Majoritarianism in Sri Lanka", in Thomas Carothers and Andrew O'donohue (eds.), *Political Polarization in South and Southeast Asia: Old Divisions*, Carnegie Endowment for International Peace, 2018.

Kadirgamar, Ahilan, "Polarization, Civil War, and Persistent Majoritarianism in Sri Lanka" 53–66 in Thomas Carothers and Andrew O'Donohue (eds.), *Political Polarization in South and Southeast Asia Old Divisions, New Dangers*, Carnegie Endowment for International Peace, New York 2020, 1–108.

Kaldor, Mary and Ivan Vejvoda, "Democratization in Central and East European Countries", *International Affairs*, 73, 1997: 59–82.

Kang, WooJin, "Inequality, the Welfare System and Satisfaction with Democracy in South Korea", *International Political Science Review*, 36(5), 2015: 493–509.

Khosla, Madhav and Milan Vaishnav, "The Three Faces of Indian State", *The Journal of Democracy*, 32(1), 2021: 111–25.

Kim, Hakjoon, "The Influence of the American Constitution on South Korean Constitutional Development since 1948", *Asian Perspective*, 16(2), 1992: 25–42.

Kim, HeeMin, "Building a New Party System: The Case of Korea", *Asian Perspective*, 19(1), 1995: 195–219.

Kim, Ki-Joo "The Soldier and the State in South Korea: Crafting Democratic Civilian Control of the Military", *Journal of International and Area Studies*, 21(2), 2014: 119–131.

Kim, Soonhee, "Public Trust in Government in Japan and South Korea: Does the Rise of Critical Citizens Matter?", *Public Administration Review*, 70(5), 2010: 801–810.

Kim, Sunhyuk, "State and Civil Society in South Korea's Democratic Consolidation: Is the Battle Really over?", *Asian Survey*, 37(12), 1997: 1135–1144.

Kim, Sunhyuk and Jong-Ho Jeong, "Historical Development of Civil Society in Korea Since 1987", *Journal of International and Area Studies*, 24(2), 2017: 1–14.

Kim, Youngmi, "Confucianism and Coalition Politics: Is Political Behavior in South Korea Irrational?", *The Journal of Northeast Asian History*, 9(2), 2012: 5–32.

Kimura, Ehito, "Indonesia in 2010: A Leading Democracy Disappoints on Reform", *Asian Survey*, 51(1), 2011: 186–195.

Koo, Hagen, "Civil Society and Democracy in South Korea", *The Good Society*, 11(2), 2002: 40–45.

Kothari, Rajni, "The Congress 'System' in India", *Asian Survey*, 4(12), 1964: 1161–1173.

Kuehn, David, "Institutionalising Civilian Control of the Military in New Democracies: Theory and Evidence from South Korea", *GIGA Working Papers*, No. 282, 2016: 1–33.

Lee, Terence, "The Philippines: Civil-Military Relations, from Marcos to Duterte", https://doi.org/10.1093/acrefore/9780190228637.013.1845.

Lee, Yoonkyung, "Diverging Patterns of Democratic Representation in Korea and Taiwan: Political Parties and Social Movements", *Asian Survey*, 54(3), 2014: 419–444.

Levitsky, Steven and Lucan A. Way, "The Rise of Competitive Authoritarianism", *Journal of Democracy*, 13(2), 2002: 51–65.

Lewis, Glen, *Virtual Thailand the Media and Cultural Politics in Thailand, Malaysia and Singapore*, London: Routledge, 2006.

Lie, John and Andrew Eungi Kim, "South Korea in 2007: Scandals and Summits", *Asian Survey*, 48(1), 2008: 116–123.

Lim, Sojin and Niki J.P. Alsford (eds.), *Routledge Handbook of Contemporary South Korea*, London: Routledge, 2022.

Lorch, Jasmin, "Elite Capture, Civil Society and Democratic Backsliding in Bangladesh, Thailand and the Philippines", *Democratization*, 28(1), 2021: 81–102.

Mietzner, Marcus, *Money, Power, and Ideology: Political Parties in Post-Authoritarian Indonesia*, Singapore: NUS Press, 2013.

Mietzner, Marcus, "Sources of Resistance to Democratic Decline: Indonesian Civil Society and its Trials", *Democratization*, 28(1), 2020: 161–178.

Mietzner, Marcus, "Sources of Resistance to Democratic Decline: Indonesian Civil Society and its Trials", *Democratization*, 28(1), 2021: 161–178.

Morlino, Leonardo, "What is a 'Good' Democracy? Theory and the Case of Italy", *South European Society and Politics*, 8(3), 2003: 1–32.

Morlino, Leonardo, "What is a 'Good' Democracy?", *Democratization*, 11(5), 2004: 10–32.

Morlino, Leonardo, "Authoritarian Legacies, Politics of the Past and the Quality of Democracy in Southern Europe: Open Conclusions", *South European Society and Politics*, 15(3), 2010: 507–529.

Morlino, Leonardo, Björn Dressel, Riccardo Pelizzo "The Quality of Democracy in Asia-Pacific: Issues and Findings", *International Political Science Review*, 32(5), 2011: 491–511.

Mukherjee, Anit, "Civil-Military Relations and Military Effectiveness in India", in Rajesh Basrur, Ajaya Kumar Das and Manjeet Singh Pardesi (eds.), *India's Military Modernization: Challenges and Prospects*, Oxford Scholarship Online, Oxford, 2013: 196–229.

Mukherjee, Anit, "The Great Churning: Modi's Transformation of the Indian Military", *Texas National Security Review War on the Rocks*, 5 May 2021. https://warontherocks.com/2021/05/the-great-churning-modis-transformation-of-the-indian-military/.

Mundayat, Aris Arif, Pitra Narendra and Budi Irawanto, "State and Civil Society Relationships in Indonesia: A society-oriented Reading in Search for Democratic Space", *PCD Journal*, 1(1 & 2), 2009: 75–96.

Muslim, Nazri bin, Faridah Jalil, Nurhafilah Musa, Khairil Azmin Mokhtar, Rasyikah Md Khalid, "Malaysian Federalism – Issues and Acceptance", *Australian Journal of Sustainable Business and Society*, 1(1), 2015: 109–118.

Nadeau, Kathleen, *The History of the Philippines*, London: Greenwood Press, 2008.

Nam, Chang-Hee, "South Korea's Big Business Clientelism in Democratic Reform", *Asian Survey*, 35(4), 1995: 357–366.

Neo, Jaclyn L., "Malaysian Federal-State Relations Post GE14", *International Journal of Constitutional Law*, Blog, June 23, 2018, http://www.iconnectblog.com/malaysian-federal-state-relations-post-ge14.

Neumeyer, Hannah, "Unity in Diversity or Diversity in Unity: Indonesia's Process of Political Decentralisation and its Effects on Conflicts", *Law and Politics in Africa, Asia and Latin America*, 39(3), 2006: 292–305.

Noh, Abdillah, "Political Change and Institutional Rigidity in Malaysia: Is There a Way Out?" *ISEAS – Yusof Ishak Institute Working Paper*, 2, 2016: 1–26.

Overholt, William H., "The Rise and Fall of Ferdinand Marcos", *Asian Survey*, 26(11), 1986: 1137–1163.

Panda, Rajaram, "Elections in South Korea: Assessing Park's Victory", *Institute of Peace and Conflict Studies, Issue Brief # 201*, January 2013. http://www.ipcs.org/issue_briefs/issue_brief_pdf/IB201-CRP-Panda-Korea.pdf.

Park, Richard L., "Political Crisis in India, 1975", *Asian Survey*, 15(11), 1975, 996–1013.

Pietsch, Juliet and Marshall Clark, "Critical Citizens: Attitudes towards Democracy in Indonesia and Malaysia", *Japanese Journal of Political Science*, 16(2), 2015: 195–209.

Puri, Balraj, "A Fuller View of the Emergency", *Economic and Political Weekly*, 30(28), 1995: 1736–1744.

Rabasa, Angel and Peter Chalk, "Muslim Separatist Movements in the Philippines and Thailand", in Angel Rabasa and Peter Chalk (eds.), *Indonesia's Transformation and the Stability of Southeast Asia*, Santa Monica: RAND Corporation, 2001: 85–99.

Radon, Jenik and Lidia Cano Pecharroman, "Civil Society: The Pulsating Heart of a Country, its Safety Valve", *Journal of International Affairs*, 71(1), 2017: 31–50.

Ratner, Steven R., "Accountability and the Sri Lankan Civil War", *American Journal of International Law*, 106(4), 2012: 795–808.

Reilly, Benjamin, *Democracy and Diversity: Political Engineering in the Asia-Pacific*, Oxford: Oxford University Press, 2006.

Sahoo, Sarbeswar, "The Shrinking Democratic Space in India: Uncivil Society and an Illiberal State", *Melbourne Asia Review*, vol. 1, New York, 2020: 1–11.

Salleh, Badriyah Haji, "[Review of An Economic History of Malaysia, c. 1800–1990: The Transition to Modern Economic Growth by John H. Drabble]", *Journal of the Malaysian Branch of the Royal Asiatic Society*, 74(1), 2001: 111–114.

Sani, Mohd Azizuddin Mohd, "Managing the State-civil Society Relations in Public Policy: Deliberative Democracy vis-a-vis Civil Society Movements in Malaysia", *African Journal of Business Management*, 5(21), 2011: 8399–8409.

Sarkar, Bhaswati, "Unity and Diversity: India and Europe", in R.K. Jain (ed.), *Multiculturalism in India and Europe*, New Delhi: Aakar Books, 2014.

Satriawan, Iwan and Khairil Azmin Mokhtar, "Democratic Consolidation in Indonesia after Political Reform in 1998: Its Developments and Issues", https://www.academia.edu/16159758/Democratic_Consolidation_in_Indonesia_after_Political_Reform_in_1998_Its_Developments_and_Issues.

Schumpeter, Joseph, *Capitalism, Socialism and Democracy*, 3rd ed., New York: Harper & Row, 1950.

Schwartz, Frank J. and Susan J. Pharr (eds.), *The State of Civil Society in Japan*, Cambridge University Press, 2003.

Sharma, Chanchal Kumar and Wilfried Swenden, "Modi-fying Indian Federalism? Center–State Relations under Modi's Tenure as Prime Minister", *Indian Politics & Policy*, 1(1), 2018: 51–81.

Shell, Donald, "The Development of Democracy", *Transformation*, 7(4), 1990: 20–24.

Sidel, Mark and David Moore, "The Law Affecting Civil Society in Asia: Developments and Challenges for Nonprofit and Civil Society Organizations", *The International Center for Not-for-Profit Law (ICNL)*, 2019. https://www.icnl.org/wp-content/uploads/2019-Asia-Legal-Environment-Overview-final.pdf.

Slater, Dan and Aries A. Arugay, "Polarizing Figures: Executive Power and Institutional Conflict in Asian Democracies", *American Behavioral Scientist*, 62(1), 2018: 92–106.

Slater, Dan, "Party Cartelization, Indonesian-style: Presidential Power-sharing and the Contingency of Democratic Opposition", *Journal of East Asian Studies*, 18(1), 2018: 23–46.

Steinberg, David I. and Myung Shin, "Tensions in South Korean Political Parties in Transition: From Entourage to Ideology?", *Asian Survey*, 46(4), 2006: 517–537.

Stepan, Alfred, "India, Sri Lanka, and the Majoritarian Danger", *Journal of Democracy*, 26(1), 2015: 128–140.

Stone, Jason G., "Shifting Tides in South Asia: Sri Lanka's Postwar Descent", *Journal of Democracy*, 25(2), 2014: 146–157.

Suh, Jae-Jung, "Korea's Democracy after the "Cheonan" Incident: The Military, the State, and Civil Society Under the Division System", *Asian Perspective*, 39(2), 2015: 171–193.

Suh, Jae-Jung, Sunwon Park and Hahn Y. Kim, "Democratic Consolidation and its Limits in Korea: Dilemmas of Cooptation", *Asian Survey*, 52(5), 2012: 822–844.

Suri, K.C., Carolyn Elliott and David Hundt, "Democracy, Governance and Political Parties in India", *Studies in Indian Politics*, 4(1), 2016: 1–7.

Thoolen, Hans, *Indonesia and the Rule of Law Twenty Years of 'New Order' Government*, London: Frances Pinter Publishers, 1987.

Tomsa, Dirk, "Party Politics and the Media in Indonesia: Creating a New Dual Identity for Golkar", *Contemporary Southeast Asia*, 29(1), 2007: 77–96.

Tomsa, Dirk, "Indonesian Politics in 2010: The Perils of Stagnation", *Bulletin of Indonesian Economic Studies*, 46(3), 2010: 309–328.

Ufen, Andreas, "Political Party and Party System Institutionalization in Southeast Asia: Lessons for Democratic Consolidation in Indonesia, the Philippines and Thailand", *The Pacific Review*, 21(3), 2008: 327–350.

Varshney, Ashutosh, "Asian Democracy Through an Indian Prism", *The Journal of Asian Studies*, 74(4), 2015: 917–926.

Welsh, Bridget, "Malaysia's Political Polarization: Race, Religion, and Reform", in Thomas Carothers and Andrew O'Donohue (eds.), *Political Polarization in South and Southeast Asia*, Carnegie Endowment for International Peace, 2020: 41–53.

Wurfel, David, "Civil Society and Democratization in the Philippines", in Yoichiro Sato (ed.), *Growth & Governance in Asia*, Honolulu: Asia-Pacific Center for Security Studies, 2004: 215–225.

Yeoh, Tricia, "Reviving the Spirit of Federalism: Decentralisation Policy Options for a New Malaysia", *IDEAS*, Policy Ideas № 59 April 2019: 1–25.

You, Jong-Sung, *Democracy, Inequality and Corruption: Korea, Taiwan and the Philippines Compared*, Cambridge: Cambridge University Press, 2015.

8 Connectivity strategies in the Indo-Pacific and their geopolitical implications

Gulshan Sachdeva

Introduction

The current phase of globalisation is defined by geo-economics and geopolitics of connectivity. In the emerging Indo-Pacific economic architecture, almost every important country in the region has its own connectivity plans, either individually or part of multilateral frameworks. Many multilateral institutions like the World Bank and Asian Development Bank as well as think tanks like the Centre for Strategic and International Studies (CSIS) are tracking these designs systematically (CSIS n.d.). Within the changing geopolitical dynamics in the Indo-Pacific region, these connectivity strategies have also become an important part of national or regional strategies. Some of them have also competed for space and influence. Almost all connectivity initiatives in the region have both developmental and geopolitical dimensions. Some of them have also strong domestic political economy implications. Ultimately, some of these initiatives may lead to a new connectivity architecture in the Indo-Pacific. The chapter looks at the importance of connectivity in national and regional growth strategies and analyses development and geopolitical implications for the Indo-Pacific region.

China's Belt and Road Initiative

One of the major connectivity initiatives, which has dominated the discussion in the recent past is the Chinese Belt and Road Initiative (BRI). By March 2019, as per official Chinese information, 173 co-operation agreements with 125 countries and 29 international organisations concerning the BRI had been signed (China SCIO 2019). The initiative, which started earlier to cover Asia and Europe, has now been expanded to Africa, Latin America and the South Pacific. Between 2013 and 2018, the World Bank estimated that investment in BRI projects including energy projects was about $575 billion (World Bank 2019). As per the Organisation for Economic Co-operation and Development (OECD), BRI investment projects are estimated to add $1 trillion in funding between 2017 and 2027 (OECD 2019).

The Chinese President Xi Jinping announced Silk Road Economic Belt during his visits to Kazakhstan in 2013. The "Belt" plan has been to revitalise a series of trading and infrastructure routes between Asia and Europe. Connectivity through Central Asia was a key element of the initiative. Subsequently, President Xi announced a sea trade infrastructure "Road." This maritime "Road" would connect China with Southeast Asia, Europe and Africa. The major focus has been to build ports, bridges, industry corridors and other infrastructure throughout South-East Asia and the Indian

DOI: 10.4324/9781003336143-11

Ocean. For some time, together these initiatives were referred to as the One Belt One Road Initiative (OBOR). In March 2015, China's National Development and Reform Commission (NDRC) outlined the contours of the BRI. Since then it has been mostly referred to as BRI. Originally, the initiative proposed six international Economic Corridors (EC). These were the New Eurasia Land Bridge (NELB-EC); China–Central Asia–West Asia (CCAWA-EC); China–Mongolia–Russia (CMR-EC), China–Indochina Peninsula (CIP-EC), the China–Pakistan (CP-EC); and the Bangladesh–China–India–Myanmar (BCIM-EC). The initiative was based on the following five priorities (China SCIO 2019):

1 policy coordination (promotion of inter-governmental co-operation, macro policy exchanges);
2 infrastructure connectivity (improving connectivity infrastructure and coordination of technical standard systems);
3 unhindered trade (reduction in trade and investment barriers and promotion of regional economic integration);
4 financial integration (co-operation and coordination of monetary policy matters, setting up of financial institutions);
5 people-to-people contacts (cultural and academic exchanges, media co-operation).

Later, the sixth principle of "industrial co-operation" was also been added.

In May 2017, China organised the first BRI Forum for International Cooperation in Beijing (Xinhua 2017a). Twenty-nine heads of state and governments participated (Xinhua 2017b). In addition, 80 international organisations and 1600 representatives from about 140 countries participated. The forum produced more than 250 deliverables in five main areas (Xinhua2017c). Many MOUs were also signed with European countries, including Albania, Belarus, Bosnia and Herzegovina, Croatia, the Czech Republic, Germany, Greece, Hungary, Poland, Serbia and Ukraine. The Second BRI Forum was again held in Beijing in April 2019 (Belt and Road Forum 2019a) in which 37 world leaders participated. Instead of the original six EC, the Second Forum produced a list of 35 EC and projects (Belt and Road Forum2019b). Bilateral deals worth $64 billion were also announced. The emphasis was put on the consultative nature of the initiative and the quality of projects, including financial and environmental sustainability. For Europe, the list included China–Europe Land–Sea Express Line, the EU Trans-European Transport Networks, Europe–Caucasus–Asia International Transport corridor and Trans-Caspian International Transport Route, the Lake Victoria–Mediterranean Sea Navigation Line-Linkage Project (VICMED), and the Port of Piraeus. In both meetings, European participation was significant, including many leaders from important countries and representation from the EU. In the beginning, European policy-makers looked at the BRI in a positive manner. The EU strongly believes regional integration and the building of common regional infrastructure is generally useful for local and global political economy. The EU itself has been promoting regional integration initiatives throughout the world. In fact, under the EU–China strategic partnership, both also established a connectivity platform in 2015. The objectives of the platform included

> The objective of the platform has been to share information and develop synergies between European and Chinese initiatives. The idea has also been to identify areas

of cooperation between Trans-European Networks and Belt and Road Initiative as well as create a favourable environment for cross-border infrastructure networks between China and the EU.

(European Council 2015)

Initially, Chinese engagement with the EU evolved through bilateral interactions with Member States. In later years, there have been efforts to present a more common approach. At the First BRI Forum in Beijing in May 2017, Prime Ministers from Hungary, Poland, Greece, Spain and Italy and the Czech President participated. Broadly the EU welcomed China's initiative to bring investments in cross-border infrastructures "at the centre of the debate" (Sachdeva & Vergeron 2019). At the 20th EU–China summit in 2018, both agreed that "the two sides will continue to forge synergies between China's Belt and Road Initiative and the EU's initiatives, including the EU Investment Plan and extended Trans-European Transport Networks." In addition, they also agreed to "promote cooperation in hardware and software connectivity through interoperable maritime, land and air transport, energy and digital networks" (European Commission 2018b). After an initially positive approach, soon European policy-makers started looking at many of the BRI-related developments in Europe and elsewhere with some concern. There has been growing scepticism and apprehensions about Beijing's intentions and the way many of the projects are being implemented (Brattberg & Soula 2018). Because the EU and China are also very deeply engaged with each other economically, European perceptions of the BRI have also been linked to the depth and breadth of the EU's overall relationship with China.

Compared to the European approach, some important countries within the Indo-Pacific region for example India had reservations about the BRI project from the beginning mainly due to sovereignty-related issues concerning China–Pakistan Economic Corridor (CPEC) and geopolitical implications of projects in the Indian Ocean (discussed later). India also did not participate in any of the BRI meetings, though it is participating in Asian Infrastructure Investment Bank (AIIB).

Indian perceptions of the BRI have to be understood within the broader context of India–China relations which have been tense in recent years. Due to border clashes in 2020 and 2022 these relations have deteriorated further. The Indian government's position on the BRI project is more or less consistent since the initiative was first launched in 2013. The Ministry of External Affairs (MEA) has reiterated its stand through various official statements issued at different intervals. India has neither fully rejected the initiative nor endorsed it in a clear manner. At the same time, the government has clearly opposed CPEC activities (Sachdeva 2018).

In 2018, when India participated for the first time as a full member of the Shanghai Cooperation Organisation (SCO), it was expected that New Delhi might soften its position on the BRI. However, when the Qungdao Declaration was issued, India was the only member country, that did not endorse the BRI project (Qingdao Declaration, 2018). Before the announcement of Bangladesh–China–India–Myanmar (BCIM) Economic Corridor as one important component of the BRI, the four countries had already been working to materialise sub-regional co-operation for years. To integrate East and North-Eastern India with South-West China along with two of the least developed countries viz. Bangladesh and Myanmar, a Track II BCIM regional Economic Forum was established in 1999 in Kunming. In 2013, the concept was officially endorsed and participating nations agreed to establish a Joint Study Group (JSG) to strengthen connectivity, trade and other linkages through the development of a BCIM Economic Corridor (BCIM-EC) (MEA, 2013). Along with the CPEC, however, when the BCIM-EC was also declared as an important part of the BRI initiative by China, it created difficulties for Indian policy-makers (Uberoi 2016).

At the BRI-2 meeting in May 2019, China removed the BCIM-EC from the new list of 35 corridors. Instead, China–Myanmar EC and Nepal–China Multi-dimensional Connectivity Network (including railway project) are listed. Interestingly, the International North–South Transport Corridor (INSTC) became part of the new BRI list. Established much before the BRI in 2000, India along with Russia and Iran are founding members of the INSTC. If there were any alternative Indian plan to the BRI, the Chabahar port linked with the INSTC was going to be the central pillar of that strategy. Now the INSTC itself is listed as a BRI project. For India this is more serious than the BCIM listing. New Delhi will have to work with Moscow and Tehran to resolve this issue. In the current geopolitical framework, however, both of them may not have any problem with listing INSTC as a BRI project (Sachdeva 2019). Both India and Pakistan approach the BRI projects mainly through their geopolitical prism. The evolving engagement of smaller South Asian countries with China is mainly to profit from China's economic rise. The smaller South Asian countries continue to balance their relations between New Delhi and Beijing (Samaranayake 2019).

The BRI has also become a major part of China's development co-operation activities in the developing world. Through development projects, China is trying to connect six original corridors with transport routes. To support the CPEC, China has helped to upgrade and expand the Peshawar–Karachi Motorway and the Karakoram Highway in Pakistan. For the China–Indochina Peninsula Economic Corridor and the BCIM-EC, highways, bridges and tunnels are being constructed with Chinese help in Bangladesh, Myanmar, Laos and Cambodia. On the China–Central Asia–West Asia EC, Kyrgyzstan's North–South highway and Tajikistan's road renovation project are being supported. Similarly, over 100 cities in Europe and Asia are being connected by Chinese railways. China has also assisted Pakistan, Nepal, Maldives, Cambodia, Zambia, Zimbabwe and Togo in upgrading and expanding their airports (China SCIO 2021).

Since the BRI is a large programme concerning infrastructure, it may affect major economies even if they are not formally participating in the initiative. The World Bank studies have shown that BRI infrastructure projects could significantly improve trade, foreign investment and living standards of participating countries (World Bank 2019). At the same time, studies also assert that building infrastructure is not risk-free. To reduce risks, countries will require more transparency, especially regarding debt sustainability. These projects may also need open competitive procurement as well as higher social and environmental standards. Many developing countries also need to be concerned about corruption. Since a large part of the Indo-Pacific economies faces an infrastructure deficit, they could take advantage of BRI projects if accompanied by policies of openness and sustainability.

Connectivity initiatives from the European Union

One of the main features of the European integration project has been economic integration and interconnections. With its own successful experience, the EU has been promoting connectivity initiatives in neighbouring regions. Now it has the ambition of becoming a connectivity leader while expanding these initiatives within the Indo-Pacific region and other parts of the world.

In 1993, the EU started an interregional technical assistance programme called Transport Corridor Europe–Caucasus–Asia (TRACECA) (TRACECA n.d.). The aim was to develop transport corridors linking Europe with Central Asia through the Black Sea, Caucasus, and the Caspian Sea. It started with the involvement of eight countries viz. Armenia, Azerbaijan, Georgia, Kazakhstan, Kyrgyzstan, Tajikistan, Turkmenistan and Uzbekistan. Subsequently, Bulgaria, Romania, Iran, Moldova, Turkey and Ukraine have joined the initiative. With its permanent secretariat in Baku, the organisation provides technical assistance and promotes the development of regional transport dialogues on specified routes (TRACECA Route Map, n.d.). The officials of the participating countries develop co-operation through various working groups dealing with maritime transport, aviation, rail and road, transport security etc.

Although the EU has been active in providing connectivity finance and technical support to many courtiers in its periphery and Asia, its approach is changing since the launch of the Chinese BRI. There were internal discussions to present the EU's own approach to Asian and Indo-Pacific connectivity. It is becoming clear that Asia is growing fast, and its economies are integrating with each other. Asia has also become important for the EU economy. In 2019, Asia accounted for about 40 per cent of EU imports (about Euro 800 billion) and 28 % of exports (about Euro 620 billion). More than 90% of these flows were in industrial goods (European Parliament 2021). Not only China but also many other Asian economies have become an important part of the global supply chain. The 2016 EU Global Strategy had also called for increased economic diplomacy and security role in Asia (European Commission 2016).

The EU has engaged with Asia through Asia–Europe Meeting (ASEM), an informal platform for dialogue with Asian countries. It has also established strategic partnerships with China, Japan, India and South Korea. Similarly, it has signed trade agreements with Japan, South Korea, Singapore and Vietnam and negotiating with many others. Since connectivity was becoming an important theme in Asia, it wanted to bring the issue to the centre stage in Europe–Asia linkages. In 2017, the ASEM Foreign Ministers agreed on a common definition of connectivity. It involved

> improving political, social and security ties between Europe and Asia; bringing countries and societies together; establishing transport, digital, energy and educational connectivity; and contributing to the UN 2030 Agenda for Sustainable Development.
>
> (ASEM 2017)

In addition, there were also growing concerns within the EU Member States and institutions that through its BRI projects, China is promoting its version of globalisation rules with which Chinese companies are at the advantage over European firms. It was also felt that while funding many infrastructure projects in its periphery and in Central and Eastern Europe, China is also trying to break unity between EU nations, particularly through the 16+1 sub-regional format. The original initiative included eleven EU Member States from Central and Eastern Europe and five Balkan states – Albania, Bosnia and Herzegovina, Bulgaria, Croatia, Czech Republic, Estonia, Hungary, Latvia, Lithuania, Macedonia, Montenegro, Poland, Romania, Serbia, Slovakia and Slovenia. Briefly, it became 17+1 when Greece joined the group in 2019. In 2021, Lithuania dropped out of the group. There were also concerns about "debt trap diplomacy" by China in many countries in Asia and Africa. This type of diplomacy means burdening poor and vulnerable countries with unsustainable debt. It is alleged that China is supporting many unviable infrastructure projects in strategic developing countries. When these countries are not able to repay debt, they become vulnerable to China's geostrategic interests (Chellaney 2021; Jones&Hameiri 2020).

To deal with all these concerns, the EU presented its own "European way" of connectivity through its Europe–Asia connectivity strategy in September 2018 (European Parliament, 2021). The main features of the strategy included (European Commission 2018a):

- sustainable connectivity: economic, fiscal, environmental and social;
- comprehensive connectivity: transport (air, land, sea), digital, energy and human;
- international rules and regulations based connectivity.

The EU wants to engage Asia by (1) contributing efficient "connections and networks between Europe and Asia through priority transport corridors, digital links and energy cooperation" (European Commission2018a) (2) establishing connectivity partnerships (3) contributing towards investment gaps through resource mobilisation from the EU and global partnerships.

Building on its Europe–Asia connectivity strategy and other partnerships, the EU announced its wider and ambitious Global Gateway strategy in December 2021 (European Commission 2021c). The strategy is also linked with contemporary global challenges e.g. climate change, improvement in health systems, competitiveness and global supply chains. As per the plan, the EU will be mobilising major infrastructure funding up to EUR 300 billion between 2021 and 2027 in the areas of digital, climate and energy, transport, health, education and research. The Gateway is based on six principles viz. democratic values and high standards; good governance and transparency; equal partnerships; green and clean; security focused; and catalysing private sector investment. The strategy will be implemented together by the EU and its Member States, the European Investment Bank (EIB), the European Bank for Reconstruction and Development (EBRD) and the private sector. Various financial tools are also being developed to deliver the Gateway. The EU plan to provide finances as well as high environmental and social protection standards and strategic management. While outlining the strategy, Ursula von der Leyen, President of the European Commission asserted (European Commission 2021a):

> we will support smart investments in quality infrastructure, respecting the highest social and environmental standards, in line with the EU's values and standards. The Global Gateway strategy is a template for how Europe can build more resilient connections with the world.

Connectivity is also one of the seven main priority areas of the EU's Indo-Pacific strategy announced in September 2021 (European Commission 2021b). It intends to implement the strategy through strong connectivity partnerships, transport dialogues and helping partner countries in creating a regulatory and policy environment for public and private investment.

The US connectivity designs

The United States was the first to enter connectivity debates in the South and Central Asian region through its New Silk Strategy announced by the then US Foreign Secretary Hillary Clinton in Chennai in India in 2011 (Clinton 2011). The idea was to link Central and South Asian markets via Afghanistan through the network of trade, transit and energy corridors. Although the US idea did not work much due to uncertainty in Afghanistan and lack of funding, some of the concepts were later picked up by China in its OBOR programme. Now to deal with the Chinese connectivity challenge in the Indo-Pacific, the United States has again started working with other partners. To promote sustainable infrastructure and to mobilise $15 trillion infrastructure-related finance shortfall by 2040 in the developing and emerging world, the United States, Japan and Australia together initiated the Blue Dot Network in 2019. The Network will audit and certify quality infrastructure projects that meet robust international standards. The Network hopes that the certification "will serve as a globally recognized symbol of market-driven, transparent, Paris Agreement-aligned, and financially, socially, and environmentally sustainable infrastructure projects" (DOS n.d.). The OECD will provide technical support to the initiative (OECD n.d.). The OECD surveys have confirmed that a trusted certificate regime will increase private firms' participation in middle-income country projects. It will also increase their exposure to low- and middle-income countries (OECD 2021).

Japan, India and South Korea

Japan has been very active in infrastructure development in Asia for many decades through its development aid projects. It believes that investment in physical infrastructure leads to regional connectivity, the attraction of foreign direct investment and an increase in manufacturing capacity. Building on its earlier infrastructure-related investments in Southeast and East Asia, Japan under its Free and Open Indo-Pacific initiative is building new connectivity partnerships for "high-quality sustainable infrastructure" in the ASEAN, Bay of Bengal and South China Sea. It is also trying to improve its presence in Central Asia. Now, improving physical connectivity is an important part of the new initiative. As Japan is totally dependent on sea trade, its Indo-Pacific vision is largely linked through maritime routes. It has helped ASEAN connectivity programmes and is also keen to support linkages between East and South Asia. Table 8.1 explains Japan's approach to some of the regional connectivity initiatives.

Within the Indo-Pacific framework, it is also working with the EU through EU–Japan connectivity partnership and with India through Asia–Africa Growth Corridor (AAGC).

India has not announced any connectivity strategy but is trying to build its own connectivity narrative on the basis of many strategic partnerships and Free Trade Agreements (FTAs) it has signed in the last 15 years. It is also putting together its development co-operation engagements, Look East (now Act East) policy, Connect Central Asia, South Asian Association of Regional Cooperation (SAARC), Indian Ocean Rim Association (IORA), India–Africa Dialogues, engagements in Afghanistan and Middle-East into the narrative. These are linked with the International North–South Trade Corridor (INSTC), Asia–Africa Growth Corridor (AAGC), Security and Growth for All in the Region (SAGAR) initiative, Project Mausam, Make in India,

Table 8.1 Sub-regional connectivity initiatives and Japan's approach

	ASEAN	BRI	SASEC	BIMSTEC
	Ten ASEAN Member countries	Over 100 countries	Bangladesh, Bhutan, India, Maldives, Myanmar, Nepal, Sri Lanka	Bangladesh, Bhutan, India, Myanmar, Sri Lanka, Thailand, Nepal
Master Plan	Master Plan on ASEAN Connectivity 2025	Six Economic Corridors	SASEC Operational Plan 2016–2025	Master Plan for BIMSTEC connectivity
Japanese approach	Active engagement by identifying 70 flagship projects which Japan contributes to	Limited engagement, JBIC and CDB signed MOU for co-operation in third markets	Indirect engagement through ADB, ADB supports approx. 60% of funds and hosts the secretariat	Indirect engagement through ADB, bilateral partnerships with India and Bangladesh

Source: Yanagida (2020: 48)

Digital India etc (see Table 8.2). Russia, Iran and India are founding members of the INSTC. Later, many other countries joined the project, which provides a shorter route for trade to Iran, Russia and countries in Eurasia. There are many sectors, but for India the corridor facilitates the movement of goods via Iran, Caspian Sea and Astrakhan to Russia and adjoining countries of the Commonwealth of Independent States (CIS) including Central Asia.

India is also trying to improve its connectivity with the ASEAN region. Although FTAs in trade, services and investment is central to India's strategy, it is realised that infrastructure challenges could hamper growth in linkages. Emerging nodes of India–ASEAN connectivity, Myanmar and Northeast India, are both weak in infrastructure. At the same time, this is also an area which has difficult lands of many insurgencies. In the last 20 years, the Indian government has placed special emphasis on economic and infrastructural developments in the Northeast with many positive results. To enhance India–ASEAN connectivity two main routes are being connected. The sea route is the west link of the Mekong–India Economic Corridor (MIEC), and the land routes, with various optional routes, are along the trilateral highway between India, Myanmar and Thailand. The MIEC enhances the connectivity between Ho Chi Minh City, Phnom Penh, Bangkok and Dawei by road, and further to Chennai in India by sea route; the trilateral highway improves connectivity between Indian Northeast and ASEAN. These roads will be further connected to Indian Golden Quadrangle (GQ) project connecting major metros as well Delhi–Mumbai Industrial Corridor (DMIC).

Building connectivity has also become an important part of India's development co-operation activities abroad. The Indian development activities abroad broadly include lines of credit (LOCs), capacity-building programmes and grant assistance projects. By March 2020, the Exim Bank had signed 288 LOCs covering more than 60 countries in Africa, Asia, the CIS, and Latin America, with credit commitments of around US$ 29.6 billion (India Exim Bank 2019). Apart from LOCs, infrastructure support is also

Table 8.2 India's connectivity engagements

Name of the project	Countries involved	Details
International North–South Tarde Corridor (INSTC)	Founding Members: India, Iran and Russia Others: Armenia, Azerbaijan, Belarus, Kazakhstan, Oman, Syria, Tajikistan, Ukraine, Kyrgyzstan	7200 km long multi-model (ship-rail-road) transport network It mainly links India with Europe (Russia) via Iran/Caspian sea or Azerbaijan New Delhi is keen to add India built Chahbahar port in Iran into INSTC network
Bangladesh, China, India and Myanmar (BCIM) Economic Corridor	Bangladesh, China, India, Myanmar	Started from a second-track dialogue as part of Kunming Initiative in 1999 In 2015, China included it as one of the main BRI corridors. At the second BRI meeting it was not mentioned as a BRI project
India–Myanmar Thailand Trilateral Highway	India, Myanmar, Thailand	Connecting Moreh (India) to Bagan (Myanmar) and Mae Sot (Thailand)
Mekong–India Economic Corridor	Vietnam, Myanmar, Thailand, Cambodia	Connecting Ho Chi Minh City, Dawai, Bangkok, Phnom Penn and Chennai
Kaladan Multi-Model Transport Project	India, Myanmar	Connecting Kolkata (India) to Sitwe and Paletwa in Myanmar
Asia–Africa Growth Corridor	India–Japan (Asia, Africa)	Development co-operation projects, quality infrastructure and institutional connectivity, enhancing capacities and skills, people-to-people partnership
India–EU Connectivity Partnership	India–EU (Africa, Central Asia and the Indo-Pacific)	Digital, energy, transport and people-to-people connectivity
Chennai -(India) Vladivostok (Russia) Maritime Corridor	India, Russia	Announced in 2019 Covers sea of Japan, East and the South China sea through Malacca Strait to reach the Bay of Bengal

Source: Compiled by the author

extended under grant assistance projects mainly in the neighbourhood and Africa. With Japan, India has initiated an infrastructural project called Asia–Africa Growth Corridor (AAGC) (RIS n.d.). The AAGC will work through development co-operation projects, quality infrastructure and institutional connectivity, enhancing capacities and people-to-people partnerships. The project will be aligned with the development priorities of African countries. The priority projects will be in the areas of health and pharmaceuticals, agriculture, disaster management and skill development and connectivity

Because of its deep economic interests in China as well as the nuclear threat from North Korea, the **South Korean** leader is hesitant to openly endorse the Free and Open Indo-Pacific policy of the United States (Huynh 2021). Its connectivity vision has both northern and southern components. Its new Northern policy mainly focused on Russia. It also focuses on North Korea, Belarus, Mongolia, China and Central Asia. The policy aims to improve co-operation in building ports, railways, gas pipelines and shipping lanes. The Southern policy's objective is to improve connectivity infrastructure with

ASEAN countries (CSIS n.d). Despite reluctance to endorse Indo-Pacific approaches of the United States, recently South Korea and the United States agreed to align its New Southern Policy with the United States' vision of the Indo-Pacific (The White House 2021c).

ASEAN: Connecting the connectivities

ASEAN is an interesting case of a grouping trying to avoid competing visions of connectivity. It has its own Master Plan of ASEAN Connectivity (MPAC) 2025. The region has long been dependent on external financing for its infrastructural needs. It has benefitted greatly from infrastructure financing both from Japan and China. Unlike its earlier plans which focused more on individual projects, MPAC 2025 focuses more on enabling policies and other sectoral issues such as logistics system integration, trade facilitation, efficient urbanisation etc. To some extent, this has also been an attempt to keep ASEAN centrality relevant to competitive connectivity plans of its main partners. The MPAC focuses on five areas viz. sustainable infrastructure, digital innovation, seamless logistics, regulations and people mobility (ASEAN Secretariat2017).

Since ASEAN is central to the Indo-Pacific narrative, connectivity partnerships with the region are becoming central to many plans of Japan, India and the United States. Because of Japan's earlier engagements in ASEAN connectivity, connectivity partnerships with the region will create serious competition with the Chinese BRI. ASEAN leadership is fully aware of these competitive trends. Instead of becoming part of any competition between China and Quad nations, they are trying to engage with both sides. Muhibat and Kharisma (2019) argue that the infrastructural needs of the region are "too great for any major power to cover its own." Therefore, even in the presence of competing visions of connectivity, the region may actually gain from both sides.

By 2019, the value of China's BRI projects in the region was about $740 billion. These included about $170 billion in Indonesia, $150 billion in Vietnam, $ 104 billion in Cambodia, $100 billion in Malaysia, $70 billion in Singapore, $47 billion in Laos, $35 billion in Brunei, $27 billion in Myanmar, $24 billion in Thailand and about $10 billion in the Philippines. Most of this investment was in railways, roads or power plants. Chinese investment in infrastructure in the region looks impressive. However, due to decades of Japanese engagements in infrastructure projects its investments in infrastructure are also huge. Some estimates suggest that only in Indonesia, Malaysia, Malaysia, the Philippines, Singapore, Thailand and Vietnam, Japanese investment was close to $370 billion (Muhibat & Kharisma 2019).

In addition to Japan, now the United States, European Union and India are also further improving their connectivity-related linkages and investments in the ASEAN. Despite these developments, most ASEAN nations believe that they can concentrate on economic issues concerning connectivity partnerships and downplay geopolitical components of investment from both sides. This is the way they have been operating for many years with outside partners.

Still, the increasing competition has affected the preferences of individual ASEAN Member States. Traditionally Thailand and the Philippines were more sympathetic to the United States. In recent years, they have moved more towards China. Through infrastructure projects, Malaysia has also increased links with China. Chen (2018) categorises ASEAN countries' responses to China's BRI on the basis of the infrastructure projects into three broad groups:

1. Cambodia, Laos and Malaysia (very engaged with China);
2. Indonesia, Thailand, Myanmar, Brunei and Singapore (balanced position between different partners);
3. Vietnam and the Philippines (increasing engagements, with reservations).

In response to changing geopolitics and geo-economics in the region, the ASEAN nations, at the initiative of Indonesia ASEAN Outlook for the Indo-Pacific (AOIP) in 2019. Some of the ASEAN nations were also worried about losing ASEAN centrality in regional architectures in the wake of increasing activities of the Quad. As per the final AOIP Connectivity is one of the main important areas through which the ASEAN would like to co-operate with the Indo-Pacific region. It hopes that existing and future connectivity initiatives in the Indo-Pacific should complement its MPAC 2025. It also talks about "connecting the connectivities" of the Indo-Pacific initiatives with its own programmes (ASEAN Secretariat 2021). Through AOIP, it has emphasised "strengthening ASEAN Centrality, openness, transparency, inclusivity, a rules-based framework, good governance, respect for sovereignty, non-intervention, complementarity with existing co-operation frameworks, equality, mutual respect, mutual trust, mutual benefit and respect for international law" The AOIP also asserts that the "ASEAN also needs to continue being an honest broker within the strategic environment of competing interests" (ASEAN Secretariat 2021). Therefore, ASEAN is basically trying to benefit from competing connectivity designs rather than joining one side and losing its centrality.

Initiatives by the G7 and G20

As a part of its strategy to meet the strategic challenge posed by China, the group of seven (G7) countries announced a Build Back Better World (B3W) partnership in June 2021 (The White House 2021a). The idea is to counter Chinese connectivity designs and meet the infrastructure challenges of low and middle-income countries of the world. The guiding principles of B3W are being value-driven, having good governance and strong standards, being climate-friendly, having strong strategic partnerships, mobilising private capital through development finance and enhancing the impact of multilateral public finance. Its geographic scope is from Latin America and the Caribbean to Africa to the Indo-Pacific. The B3W envisages actions in the areas of climate, health and health security, digital technology, and gender equity and equality.

The issue of infrastructure funding has been a topic of discussion in many of the recent G20 summits. A Global Infrastructure Connectivity Alliance was also endorsed. The G20 has also agreed to the following guiding principles' quality infrastructure (The G20 n.d.):

1. maximising the positive impact of infrastructure to achieve sustainable growth and development;
2. raising economic efficiency in view of life-cycle cost;
3. integrating environmental considerations in infrastructure investments;
4. building resilience against natural disasters and other risks;
5. integrating social considerations in infrastructure investment;
6. strengthening infrastructure governance.

The G20 meeting in Saudi Arabia in 2020 further refined these guidelines for regional connectivity. It was agreed that quality infrastructure should be an integral part of the national development strategy. In addition, requirements of a cross-sectoral approach and international co-operation are crucial for regional connectivity (G20 2020).

Russia

Russia is also involved in some of the major connectivity initiatives in the Indo-Pacific. Its connectivity vision has a combination of hard and soft infrastructure connectivity within the former Soviet space and Eurasia. The Eurasian Economic Union (EAEU) provides the free movement of goods, services, capital and labour among its five Member States viz. Armenia, Belarus, Kazakhstan, Kyrgyzstan and Russia. In 2015, Russian President Vladimir Putin also announced coordination between EAEU and the Chinese BRI. The main coordination was expected to be in the areas of infrastructure development and trade facilitation. Later President Putin announced "Greater Eurasian Partnership" which would cover the EAEU, China, India, Pakistan, Iran and the CIS countries. Russia is a founding member of the International North–South Trade Corridor (INSTC) and is integrating with some Asian markets through energy pipelines. It is also advancing its energy and defence interests in the Arctic region.

Geopolitics of connectivity

Every major infrastructure can be looked at from various perspectives. The developmental aspect clearly highlights the economic benefits of the project for participating countries. Historically, many regional infrastructure projects within their regional co-operation or regional integration frameworks in Europe and Asia were primarily advocated for their economic benefits. Most multilateral institutions including the World Bank, Asian Development Bank and European Investment Bank financed these projects mainly for their economic benefits. In the last two decades, however, many of the large infrastructural projects of strategies have also been monitored very closely through the prism of geopolitics. This has clearly been the case with the United States' New Silk Road Strategy (NSRS), Russian-dominated EAEU and China-led BRI. The NSRS was clearly objected to by Russia and China. Similarly, the BRI has been looked at primarily from a geopolitical perspective by India, the United States and some other countries. As Russia–China bonhomie has grown, both are trying to integrate their infrastructure strategies. Similarly, the EU, Japan and the United States are trying to build connectivity partnerships with like-minded countries, either bilaterally or through the G7 grouping.

Within the Indo-Pacific, geopolitics of maritime connectivity is becoming a major concern, particularly for India. The importance of the Indian Ocean for China has increased significantly in recent years due to its expanding trade, energy transport and investments. Sea lanes of communication running through Malacca Strait, Persian Gulf, Arabian sea, Indian Ocean and South China Sea are important for China for its increasing energy and raw material needs. Indian Ocean littorals are also becoming important due to increasing investments by Chinese companies in the region as well as Chinese citizens living and working in these areas (US China Commission 2016). For China, maritime expansion is also part of its strategy of economic integration of different regions of the Indo-Pacific with the Chinese economy. As a result, China has started increasing its footprint in the Indian Ocean. Within South Asia, it has made investments in strategic ports viz. Chittagong (Bangladesh), Gwadar (Pakistan), Colombo and Hambantota (Sri Lanka). It is also investing in Kyaukpyu (Myanmar). Pakistani and Sri Lankan authorities have given permission to Chinese companies to manage Gwadar and Hambantota ports for 40 years and 99 years respectively. However, it is not just South Asia; "nearly two-thirds of the world's 50 major ports are either owned by China or have received some Chinese investment" (Malik 2018). China is also dispatching increasing numbers of surface warships and submarines to the Indian Ocean region (Stratfor 2018).

As commercial ports could be converted into military use, these Chinese "string of pearls" in South Asia has already troubled many Indian policy-makers and analysts (Suri 2017). India considers itself a leading player in the Indian Ocean and at present has a considerable advantage over China. Although a peaceful maritime environment in South Asia is important for China for its economic expansion, this area may see increasing competition from India. Many Indian analysts talk about "Chinese encirclement" (Prakash 2017), which has already caused anxiety among policy-makers. China, however, would like to project these investments as purely commercial ventures and perhaps would welcome further Indian investments in South Asian ports, which would improve its own connectivity with the region (Sachdeva 2021).

Chinese maritime connectivity challenges have pushed India to have its own strategy. It has started fortifying its

> defences in the Indian Ocean through acquiring some bases, conducting joint naval exercises and by signing logistics exchange agreements with countries like France, Singapore and the United States and launched naval expansion programmes.
>
> (Malik 2018)

In addition, it has upgraded its development co-operation programs with the littorals, and to revive old cultural trade routes in the Indian Ocean, New Delhi also announced its own doctrine called SAGAR (Security and Growth for All in the Region). Many in India argue that to a large extent, upgrading the Indian "Look East" policy initiated in the early 1990s to the more recent "Act East" policy has widened India's engagement with eastern neighbours mainly from economic to security realms. Furthermore, its focus has widened from Southeast and Northeast Asia to the broader Indo-Pacific. Even the acceptance of the concept of Indo-Pacific means the acceptance of the Indian Ocean and the Pacific Ocean as a single strategic space and the importance of the maritime dimension in emerging challenges (Jaishankar 2019).

It is not only the Chinese BRI that has increased geopolitical worries. Earlier, the US NSRS raised similar fears in China and Russia. The main objective of the project was to push Central Asia away from Russia and China. While linking Central Asia with South Asia via Afghanistan these countries could find alternative markets in South Asia, mainly India. Similarly, Indian development activities involving road construction and proposed railway infrastructure along with Chahbahar port in Iran were aimed at bypassing Pakistan. India's Chabahar project in Iran is also seen as a counter-project of the Chinese-built port in Gwadar in Pakistan.

Although the Indo-Pacific narrative may have many dimensions of power rivalry between the United States and China and their partners, the first major contestation that has clearly emerged is in the area of infrastructure projects and connectivity strategies. To a large extent, this is in response to the growing geopolitical and geoeconomic influence of the Chinese BRI in the region and beyond. Although many countries were always heavily involved in infrastructure projects financing, for example, Member States of the EU, the United States and Japan, the BRI has led to many geopolitical worries. Dual use possibility of infrastructure projects is always possible. Any port or airport can be used both for business as well as military purposes. These worries have also led to competing infrastructure strategies. The increasing profile of the BRI is pushing many promotors of these plans in the Indo-Pacific to work out convergence strategies based on transparent behaviour, sustainable financing and quality infrastructure. Japan has now established partnership with the EU for 'sustainable connectivity'. Jointly with India, it has also launched an Asia–Africa Growth Corridor. It has also agreed to work with the United States and Australia. India has established a connectivity partnership with the EU.

As a response to the BRI, many official statements and speeches from the Quad nations as well as from the EU refer to global norms, financial responsibility, transparency, debt burdens, environmental sustainability and respect for sovereignty and territorial integrity etc (MEA 2017). These are all indirect references to Chinese infrastructure projects in the region. These issues are now routinely mentioned at all bilateral and multilateral meetings including at the G7 and G20. The EU has also started raising some of these concerns during its global engagements and has also come out with its own connectivity and Indo-Pacific strategies.

Interestingly, while looking at the discussions within the BRI partners, including China, they have also started raising some of these issues prominently. The BRI-2 Forum in 2019 talked about better co-operation and coordination and referred to the "importance of economic, social, fiscal, financial and environmental sustainability of projects." It also emphasised that "high-quality infrastructure should be viable, affordable, accessible, inclusive and broadly beneficial over its entire life-cycle, contributing to sustainable development of participating countries and the industrialization of developing countries" (Belt and Road Forum 2019a). This was clearly a Chinese response to the growing criticism of some of the infrastructural projects financed under the BRI initiative.

Japan and the EU have a lot of experience in building infrastructure projects in their neighbouring regions. They both believed that building regional infrastructure will lead to more economic growth, goodwill and prosperity. As a result of growing geopolitics in the Indo-Pacific, they have also started looking at some of the Chinese initiatives with some suspicion. The United States and India have emphasised geopolitical aspects of Chinese infrastructure engagements with Asia, Africa and the Indian Ocean in most of their interactions with other partners. The growing China–Russia bonhomie and their understanding of bringing BRI and EAEU closer have also raised some geopolitical worries among western nations.

Although the Quad nations have been working together or separately to peruse their connectivity strategies, in September 2021 they formally launched a new "Quad infrastructure partnership." Under the partnership they have agreed to "cooperate to provide technical assistance, empowering regional partners with evaluative tools, and will promote sustainable infrastructure development." Under the new partnership, they emphasised the "importance of supporting open, fair, and transparent lending practices in line with international rules and standards for major creditor countries, including on debt sustainability and accountability, and call on all creditors to adhere to these rules and standards" (The White House 2021b).

From the earlier geopolitical and developmental aspects of the initiative, the focus is now shifting more towards a political economy analysis of participating countries.

Increasing difficulties faced by connectivity projects in terms of the debt trap, corruption, political controversies, negative environmental implications and overall sustainability of projects are also being analysed. A significant amount of literature is appearing concerning problems faced by BRI projects in Pakistan, Sri Lanka, Southeast Asia and Africa.

Conclusion

Although the Indo-Pacific narrative has been dominated by strategic arrangements, the real competition is emerging in connectivity strategies. In the emerging Indo-Pacific connectivity architecture, every important country has its own connectivity plans, either individually or as part of multilateral frameworks. Although the Chinese BRI has dominated discussions in the last few years, there are many other important initiatives which are at different stages of implementation. Apart from the ASEAN connectivity plan, Japan, India, South Korea and other countries have their own designs. The EU announced its own Europe–Asia connectivity and Global Gateway strategy. The Quad nations have formed their own infrastructure partnership. The G7 and G20 have also outlined their principles for sustainable connectivity. The frameworks of these plans differ in terms of their origin, priorities, resource commitments and partnerships. All have strong Indo-Pacific or BRI dimensions.

Considering the infrastructural deficit within the region, these are very useful developments. This will help in facilitating quality infrastructure in many nations. However, the trouble is that many of these designs have strong geopolitical connotations. The moment a big infrastructure strategy is announced by a country or a group of countries, it immediately raises geopolitical concerns. This is exactly what happened earlier with the US New Silk Road Strategy and the Russian Eurasian Economic Union. The same worries are articulated by Quad nations and the EU concerning the Chinese BRI. Now it is up to the Indo-Pacific nations to evaluate their cost-benefit analysis. The ASEAN nations have greatly benefitted from infrastructure finance from both Japan and China. It seems they are keen to use their centrality in the Indo-Pacific narrative to their benefit by participating in the BRI as well as Quad initiatives. Beyond geopolitical assertions, the provision of finances is going to be crucial. The relative success of the BRI is because of strong Chinese financial support. The earlier US New Silk Road Strategy failed to take off because of a lack of funding support from the United States. The rise of competing visions of connectivity may give the impression of serious geopolitical competition emerging in the Indo-Pacific in future. However, pressure for sustainable and quality infrastructure may lead to the merging of some of these plans and projects. Due to fast-growing and integrating Asian markets, some of these plans may eventually complement each other's infrastructure strategies. As shown by various studies, these plans do have great potential to expand trade and improve prosperity.

References

ASEAN Secretariat (2017) *Master Plan on ASEAN Connectivity 2025*, Jakarta, https://asean.org/wp-content/uploads/2018/01/47.-December-2017-MPAC2025-2nd-Reprint-.pdf
ASEAN Secretariat (2021) *ASEAN Outlook on the Indo-Pacific*, Jakarta, https://asean.org/asean2020/wp-content/uploads/2021/01/ASEAN-Outlook-on-the-Indo-Pacific_FINAL_22062019.pdf

Asia Europe Meeting [ASEM] (2017, 21 November) "Strengthening Partnership for Peace and Sustainable Development (Chair's Statement)," *13th ASEM Foreign Ministers' Meeting Nay Pyi Taw*, Myanmar, https://www.mofa.go.jp/files/000309716.pdf

Belt and Road Forum (2019a) *Joint Communique of the Leaders' Roundtable of the Second Belt and Road Forum for International Cooperation*, http://www.beltandroadforum.org/english/n100/2019/0427/c36-1311.html

Belt and Road Forum (2019b) *Joint Communique of the Leaders' Roundtable of the Second Belt and Road Forum for International Cooperation*, http://www.beltandroadforum.org/english/n100/2019/0427/c36-1311.html

Brattberg, Erik and Etienne Soula (2018) *Europe's Emerging Approach to China's Belt and Road Initiative*, Washington DC: Carnegie Endowment of International Peace, https://carnegieendowment.org/2018/10/19/europe-s-emerging-approach-to-china-s-belt-and-road-initiative-pub-77536

Centre for Strategic and International Studies [CSIS] (n.d.) *Reconnecting Asia: Competing Visions*, https://reconasia.csis.org/competing-visions/

Chellaney, Brahma (2021, 2 May) "China's Debt-Trap Diplomacy," *The Hills*, https://thehill.com/opinion/international/551337-chinas-debt-trap-diplomacy/

Chen, Shaofeng (2018) "Regional Responses to China's Maritime Silk Road Initiative in Southeast Asia," *Journal of Contemporary China* 27(111): 344–361.

China State Council Information Office [SCIO] (2019) *The Belt and Road Initiative: Progress, Contributions and Prospects 2019, by the Office of the Leading Group for Promoting the Belt and Road Initiative*, Beijing: Foreign Languages Press Co. Ltd., http://english.scio.gov.cn/beltandroad/2019-04/23/content_74708971.htm

China State Council Information Office [SCIO] (2021) *Full Text: China's International Development Cooperation in the New Era*, http://english.www.gov.cn/archive/whitepaper/202101/10/content_WS5ffa6bbbc6d0f72576943922.html

Clinton, Hillary Rodham (2011) *Remarks on India and the United States: A Vision for the 21st Century, Chennai, July 20*, https://2009-2017.state.gov/secretary/20092013clinton/rm/2011/07/168840.htm

European Commission (2016) *Shared Vision, Common Action: A Stronger Europe : A Global Strategy for the European Union's Foreign and Security Policy*, Brussels, https://eeas.europa.eu/archives/docs/top_stories/pdf/eugs_review_web.pdf

European Commission (2018a) *Connecting Europe and Asia - Building Blocks for an EU Strategy*, Brussels, https://www.eeas.europa.eu/sites/default/files/joint_communication_-_connecting_europe_and_asia_-_building_blocks_for_an_eu_strategy_2018-09-19.pdf

European Commission (2018b, 16 July) *Joint Statement of the 20th EU-China Summit*, Brussels, https://www.consilium.europa.eu/media/36165/final-eu-cn-joint-statement-consolidated-text-with-climate-change-clean-energy-annex.pdf

European Commission (2021a, 1 December) "Global Gateway: Up to €300 billion for the European Union's Strategy to Boost Sustainable Links around the World," *Press Release*, https://ec.europa.eu/commission/presscorner/detail/en/ip_21_6433

European Commission (2021b) *The EU Strategy for Cooperation in the Indo-Pacific: Joint Communication to the European Parliament and the Council*, Brussels, https://www.eeas.europa.eu/sites/default/files/jointcommunication_2021_24_1_en.pdf

European Commission (2021c) *The Global Gateway*. Joint Communication to the European Parliament, the Council, the European Economic and Social Committee, the Committee of the Regions and the European Investment Bank, Brussels, https://ec.europa.eu/info/sites/default/files/joint_communication_global_gateway.pdf

European Council (2015) *EU-China Summit Joint Statement: The Way Forward after Forty Years of China-EU Cooperation*, https://www.consilium.europa.eu/media/23732/150629-eu-china-summit-joint-statement-final.pdf

European Parliament (2021, April) "Prospects for EU-Asia Connectivity: The 'European Way to Connectivity'," Updated Briefing Report, Brussels: European Parliament, https://www.europarl.europa.eu/RegData/etudes/BRIE/2021/690534/EPRS_BRI(2021)690534_EN.pdf

Huynh, Tam-Sang (2021, 6 July) "South Korea's 'Free and Open Indo-Pacific' Dilemma: Testing Seoul's Embrace of the United States' Regional Strategy," *The Diplomat*, https://thediplomat .com/2021/07/south-koreas-free-and-open-indo-pacific-dilemma-2/

India EXIM Bank (2019) EXIM Bank Annual Report 2018-19, Mumbai: EXIM Bank.

Jaishankar, Dhruv (2019) *Acting East: India in the Indo-Pacific*, New Delhi: The Brooking Institution.

Jones, Lee and Shahar Hameiri (2020) *Debunking the Myth of 'Debt-trap Diplomacy': How Recipient Countries Shape China's Belt and Road Initiative*, London: The Chatham House, https://www.chathamhouse.org/sites/default/files/2020-08-25-debunking-myth-debt-trap -diplomacy-jones-hameiri.pdf

Malik, Mohan (2018, 16 March) "The China-India Nautical Games in the Indian Ocean," *Inside Policy*, Part-1, https://www.macdonaldlaurier.ca/china-india-nautical-games-indian -ocean-part-one-mohan-malik-inside-policy/

Ministry of External Affairs [MEA] of India (2013, 20 May) *Joint Statement on the State Visit of Chinese Premier Li Keqiang to India*, 20 May 2013, http://mea.gov.in/bilateraldocuments .htm?dtl/21723/Joint+Statement+on+the+State+Visit+of+Chinese++Li+Keqiang+to+India

Ministry of External Affairs (MEA) of India (2017) *Official Spokesperson's Response to a Query on Participation of India in OBOR/BRI Forum*, https://mea.gov.in/media-briefings .htm?dtl/28463/Official+Spokespersons+response+to+a+query+on+participation+of+India +in+OBORBRI+Forum

Muhibat, Shafiah F. and M. Waffaa Kharisma (2019) "Connecting the Indo-Pacific: ASEAN Amidst Competing Connectivity Strategies," in *Responding to the Geopolitics of Connectivity: Asian and European Perspectives*, Singapore: Konrad-Adenauer-Stiftung, https://www .kas.de/documents/288143/10822438/Panorama_2019_02_4c_v5d_ShafiahFMuhibat_ MWaffaaKharisma.pdf/92159378-ae1a-a5a7-5d18-2441f7f1d83d?t=1606102326577

Organisation for Economic Co-operation and Development [OECD] (n.d.) *OECD and the Blue Dot Network*, https://www.oecd.org/corporate/oecd-and-the-blue-dot-network.htm

Organisation for Economic Co-operation and Development [OECD] (2019) "China's Belt and Road Initiative in the Global Trade, Investment and Finance Landscape," Chapter two of *Business and Finance Outlook 2018*, Paris: OECD, https://www.oecd.org/finance/Chinas -Belt-and-Road-Initiative-in-the-global-trade-investment-and-finance-landscape.pdf

Organisation for Economic Co-operation and Development [OECD] (2021) *Towards a Global Certification Framework for Quality Infrastructure Investment: Private Sector and Civil Society Perspectives on the Blue Dot Network – Highlights*, https://www.oecd.org/daf/ Towards-a-global-certification-framework-for-quality-infrastructure-investment-Highlights .pdf

Prakash, Arun (2017, 25 April) "A Strategic Encirclement," *The Indian Express*, https:// indianexpress.com/article/opinion/columns/indias-political-and-security-establishment -needs-a-strategy-in-light-of-chinas-naval-expansion-4626796/

Qingdao Declaration (2018, 10 June) *Qingdao Declaration of the Council of Heads of State of Shanghai Cooperation Organisation*, http://eng.sectsco.org/load/454877/

Research and Information System for Developing Countries [RIS] (n.d.) *Asia Africa Growth Corridor*, https://aagc.ris.org.in/en/about-aagc

Sachdeva, Gulshan (2018) "Indian Perceptions of the Chinese Belt & Road Initiative," *International Studies* 55(4): 285–296.

Sachdeva, Gulshan (2019, 2 May) "The Expansion of China's Belt and Road Initiative Poses New Challenges for India," Moneycontrol.com, https://www.moneycontrol.com/news/india /policy-the-expansion-of-chinas-belt-and-road-initiative-poses-new-challenges-for-india -3920231.html

Sachdeva, Gulshan (2021) "China's Current South Asia Strategy," in David B.H. Denoon (ed.), *China's Grand Strategy: A Roadmap to Global Power*, New York: NYU Press, pp. 146–173.

Sachdeva, Gulshan and Karine Lisbonne de Vergeron (2019) *European and Indian Perceptions of the Belt and Road Initiative*, New Delhi: The EU India Thinktanks Twinning Initiative, https://euindiathinktanks.com/2019/publications/european-and-indian-perceptions-of-the-belt-and-road-initiative/

Samaranayake, Nilanthi (2019) *China's Engagement with Smaller South Asian Countries,* Special Report No 446, United States Institute of Peace, April, https://www.usip.org/sites/default/files/2019-04/sr_446-chinas_engagement_with_smaller_south_asian_countries.pdf

Stratfor (2018, November 23) "India Looks for a Strategic Edge in Its Indian Ocean Contest With China," https://worldview.stratfor.com/article/india-looks-strategic-edge-its-indian-ocean-contest-china

Suri, Gopal (2017) *China's Expanding Military Maritime Footprints in the Indian Ocean Region: India's Response,* New Delhi: Vivekanand International Foundation, Pentagon Press.

The G20 (n.d.) *G20 Principles for Quality Infrastructure Investment,* https://www.mof.go.jp/english/policy/international_policy/convention/g20/annex6_1.pdf

The G20 (2020) *G20 Guidelines on Quality Infrastructure for Regional Connectivity,* https://dwgg20.org/app/uploads/2021/09/G20-Guidelines-Quality-Infrastructure-Regional-Connectivity.pdf

The United States Department of State [DOS] (n.d.) *Blue Dot Network,* https://www.state.gov/blue-dot-network/

The White House (2021a, 12 June) *President Biden and G7 Leaders Launch Build Back Better World (B3W) Partnership,* https://www.whitehouse.gov/briefing-room/statements-releases/2021/06/12/fact-sheet-president-biden-and-g7-leaders-launch-build-back-better-world-b3w-partnership/

The White House (2021b, 24 September) *Joint Statement from Quad Leaders,* https://www.whitehouse.gov/briefing-room/statements-releases/2021/09/24/joint-statement-from-quad-leaders/

The White House (2021c, 21 May) *U.S.-ROK Leaders' Joint Statement,* https://www.whitehouse.gov/briefing-room/statements-releases/2021/05/21/u-s-rok-leaders-joint-statement/

The World Bank (2019) *Belt and Road Economics: Opportunities and Risks of Transport Corridors,* Washington DC: The World Bank, https://www.worldbank.org/en/topic/regional-integration/publication/belt-and-road-economics-opportunities-and-risks-of-transport-corridors

TRACECA Route Map (n.d.) http://www.traceca-org.org/fileadmin/fm-dam/Routes_Maps/MAP_TRACECA_ROUTES_10_09_2017_300DPI.png

Transport Corridor Europe-Caucasus-Asia (TRACECA) (n.d.) http://www.traceca-org.org/en/about-traceca/

Uberoi, Patricia (2016) "Problems and Prospects of the BCIM Economic Corridor," *China Report* 52(1): 19–44.

US China Commission (2016) *US-China Economic & Security Review Commission 2016 Report to the Congress,* Washington: US Government Publishing House, 2016, p. 320.

Xinhua (2017a May) *The Belt and Road Forum for International Cooperation,* http://www.xinhuanet.com/english/special/201705ydylforum/index.htm

Xinhua (2017b, May 15) *Full Text: Joint Communique of Leaders Roundtable of Belt and Road Forum,* http://www.xinhuanet.com/english/2017-05/15/c_136286378.htm

Xinhua (2017c, May 15) *Full Text: List of Deliverables of Belt and Road Forum,* http://www.xinhuanet.com/english/2017-05/15/c_136286376.htm

Yanagida, Kensuke (2020) "Japan's Connectivity Initiatives in the Free and Open Indo-Pacific: An Economic Assessment," in *Responding to the Geopolitics of Connectivity: Asian and European Perspectives,* Singapore: Konrad-Adenauer-Stiftung, https://www.kas.de/documents/288143/10822438/Panorama_2019_02_4c_v5d_KensukeYanagida.pdf/5d1949fa-0529-2fd9-3087-e720599cf7c5?t=1606102326284.

Part III

Political and security issues in the Indo-Pacific

9 Military power as an instrument of international politics in the Indo-Pacific

Rafał Wiśniewski

War and means to wage it have been at the centre of reflection on international politics since its very beginning. The discipline of international relations (IR) was born from the need to properly study the circumstances of armed conflict. When we say that the concept of power is one of the central ones in IR, we must remember that, for a long time, it was understood to represent mainly military power. This focus on military matters has stimulated the development of strategic studies and other subdisciplines in the broader field of International Security Studies (ISS) (Buzan & Hansen 2009). Although the scale and character of military power's influence on international politics has evolved (especially since the end of the Cold War), it is still regarded as a useful tool of foreign policy. This chapters aims to explain how military power can be used by states to conduct international politics and illustrate how this affects the Indo-Pacific region.

The chapter consists of three parts. It starts with an introduction of basic concepts necessary for the study of international politics' military aspects. They include the constituent elements of military power, functions performed by armed forces in contemporary states, as well as strategy and doctrine, which organise how military forces are developed and used. Next comes a short overview of the Indo-Pacific region as a geostrategic area of military competition. The main part of the chapter offers an analysis of military strategies employed by selected Indo-Pacific states. It is meant as an illustration of how we can apply theoretical concepts outlined in the first section to study and understand the real-life exercise of military forces. The cases are organised in a way that allows for presentation of how states with different levels of power resources (global military powers, regional powers, middle powers and small powers) are using their militaries to influence regional politics.

Military power as an instrument of foreign policy – theoretical background

What is military power?

When defining military power, it is imperative to keep in mind the wider concept of national power. Both are widely associated with various material attributes, which can often be presented and compared in quantitative terms. However, the predominant view in political science is to understand power as a relation, namely an ability of actor A to make actor B do what A wants (even if it is contrary to B's interest and/or will) (Baldwin 2016). So, in the same way, military power should be understood not simply

DOI: 10.4324/9781003336143-13

as a sum of warfighting instruments in state's possession, but as an ability to influence other actors for political ends through use of organised armed violence (or threat of it). This brings us to the concept of military capability as a measure of military force's usefulness. Military capability has been defined by US Department of Defense as "the ability to achieve a specified wartime objective – for example, win a battle or a war or destroy a target" (*Measuring Military Capability. Progress, Problems and Future Direction* 1986: 7). In order to assess the level of military capabilities possessed by a given state we must look closer at their constituent parts. A study conducted by a recognised think-tank specialised in analysis of military affairs – RAND Corporation – provides two categories of factors which need to be taken into account when approaching this issue. The first one includes all strategic resources provided to the military by its government. The second is comprised of given military establishment's "conversion capabilities" which allow it to transform the aforementioned resources into effective military forces, capable of achieving objectives given to them by the national leadership (Tellis, et al. 2000: 133–176).

Taking this approach as the basis, we will understand military capabilities as being composed of two elements: resources and abilities (for details see Table 9.1). Military resources are generally speaking, material inputs mobilised or created for military service. These provide ingredients, which become actual military capabilities thanks to armed forces' abilities.

Counting military resources is the most popular way of judging given state's military power. This is an important measure in its own right and must be taken into serious consideration. However, it must be stressed that by studying statistics describing these resources we will not be able to reliably assess how capable given state's military really is. Only when we take into consideration the abilities (which, as we have seen, are immaterial in nature, so by definition very difficult to measure precisely) we can assess (rather qualitatively than quantitatively) the level of true capabilities residing in the military force in question.

Armed forces as a tool of statecraft – military's roles in contemporary states

It is obvious that there is a huge number of options to choose from when national governments decide which military capabilities to develop. The actual choice is naturally heavily constrained by available resources (primarily the scale of the defence budget which a particular state can afford). However, in this chapter we analyse military power as a tool of state policy. So in order to understand why certain states acquire some specific military capabilities (and not others) we must answer the question: what the state needs the armed forces for?

When discussing the evolving roles of European militaries in the post-Cold War period, Timothy Edmunds highlights two sets of imperatives – functional and socio-political – which account for what states maintain and prepare their armed forces for (Edmunds 2006). Functional imperatives are connected to traditional understanding of military power's utility in an anarchic international system. Namely it is meant to: "defend the state against real or potential external threats and as a coercive tool to promote and protect nation interests abroad" (Edmunds 2006: 1059). At the same time, the specific socio-political context of the society and state they serve (and its evolution) accounts for a variety of roles performed by armed forces beyond the aforementioned primary function of external defence. These insights lead us to the first

Table 9.1 Constituent elements of military capabilities

Military resources	Military abilities
Manpower – the number of men and women serving in the nation's armed forces; often potential reserves which could be mobilised into service in times of emergency are also taken into account.	**Doctrine and force structure** – this can be understood as an officially adopted "vision" of how a given military force will fight to win and an organisational structure resulting from it.
Weapons and equipment – all technical tolls with which a military force is equipped for conducting operations. Numbers, types and technical parameters of these systems must be taken into account.	**Military training and its quality** – when assessing it, we ask the question of whether the military personnel has been properly trained and educated to use its equipment in accordance with the doctrine, as well as whether these skills have been maintained (or even improved) through regular training.
Logistical systems – the supplies needed for the forces to survive and perform their roles (food, water, fuel, munitions, spare parts, etc.), as well as systems and organisations tasked with distributing them to military units.	**Quality of command** – the quality (level of competence and abilities) of commanders tasked with leading the troops and the effectiveness of the entire military command system (ensuring the timely and reliable distribution of orders to be executed and effective flow of information relevant to the command process).
Military infrastructure – military bases and other installations necessary to house, train and maintain military forces as well as launch military operations if necessary.	**Readiness** – the ability of forces to quickly start operations when ordered.
Defence Technological and Industrial Base (DTIB) – the industry which designs, produces and services weapons and military equipment needed by military forces.	**Experience** in conducting actual military operations (combat or otherwise).
Defence expenditure – financial resources devoted by the state for creation, sustainment and further development off all the elements of military capabilities.	**Morale** – basically understood as a willingness of soldiers to fight (and in consequence risk injury or death) in actual conflict.

Source: Author's research, inspired by: Tellis, et al. 2000 and *Measuring Military Capability. Progress, Problems and Future Direction*, 1986.

important conclusion which informs this section. The exact roles of armed forces in a particular state are determined by two sets of factors – objective threats faced by the nation (and their assessment by the politico-military leadership) and the needs determined by domestic and international politics.

Taking the aforementioned determinants into account, we can construct a typology of roles performed by contemporary armed forces (presented in Table 9.2). These are divided into two main categories – external and domestic. The author is fully aware that in the globalised and interconnected world of the early 21st century the distinction between external and domestic security is to a large degree superficial, due to transnational character of many security threats and challenges. However, looking at how military forces "think about themselves" (and how political leaders "think about

Table 9.2 Armed Forces' functions in contemporary states

External functions	Domestic functions
Defence (warfighting) – waging war in the defence of the state and its interests.	**Internal security** – in most states, the military is meant to support the civilian authorities in emergencies of exceptional scale and/or character (e.g. assisting in rescue efforts following large-scale natural disasters, supporting the law-enforcement agencies during large-scale riots or assisting counterterrorist operations). Some states face particular domestic threats (sometimes far graver than possible external ones) in the form of insurgencies or large-scale organised crime/terrorist operations. In such situations armed forces are often being focused on domestic roles, aimed at countering these threats.
Coercion (deterrence and compellence) – imposing one's will on the adversary through threatening the use of force. Either stopping the other from taking an action (deterrence) or forcing him/her to take a desired action (compellence). Further explained in Box 9.1.	**Preserving the political regime** – for some political regimes (mainly autocratic ones) armed forces play key role in the preserving their rule. More in Box 9.2.
International prestige – As military power is widely considered to be one of the key attributes of powerful states, armed forces can be considered a symbol of international status and prestige. Another aspect of prestige building function is the acquisition of "prestigious" weapon systems. These are usually understood to be the most advanced, capable and costly weapons of the given time (Art 1980: 10; Angstrom & Widen 2015: 176).	**Nation building** – tasks and missions related to building and maintenance of state structures and their legitimacy. The military can be called upon to provide some public services. It can also be used to strengthen national identity and unity (for example through common experience of compulsory military service) (Edmunds 2006: 1073–1074). Within this role the armed forces often enter the field of public governance which is usually reserved for the civilian administration. Further explained in Box 9.2.
Providing international public goods – military operations not directed against, and threatening to, other states. They are rather meant to manage different aspects of the international security environment to the benefit of not only their initiator, but also the wider international community. They include such activities as: different forms of peacekeeping operations (PKO), enforcing decisions of international organisations (e.g. UN arms embargoes), combating transnational threats (transnational crime or terrorism), search and rescue operations or Humanitarian Assistance/Disaster Relief (HA/DR) operations.	

Source: Inspired by the works of (Edmunds 2006) and (Art 1980), as well as author's own research.

them") and the corresponding tasking and organisation, the author believes that this distinction is still empirically and analytically useful.

Box 9.1 Explaining coercion, deterrence and compellence

Coercion is based on a threat of using force and not its actual use on the battlefield. Thomas C. Shelling (one of strategic studies' founding fathers) has called it a "diplomacy of violence." His understanding of coercion (a concept encompassing two distinct categories – deterrence and compellence) proved to be very influential for academic and official reflection on the utility of armed force (Biddle 2020: 97–98). All three concepts – coercion, deterrence and compellence have been analysed and debated intensely in the academic literature. At this point we can stick with a basic understanding of them. Coercion is a threat of force directed at other actors of international relations meant to convince them to submit to initiator's will. Both deterrence and compellence are based on this idea with the difference being that deterrence is meant to stop the adversary from doing something that he/she could otherwise have done ("don't attack us, or else...") while compellence aims to make the opponent do something he/she wouldn't otherwise have been willing to do ("stop attacking our ally" or "give up your claim to waters X") (Art 1980: 6–10) (Biddle 2020).

It may seem that there is not much difference, from the perspective of how a military force is organised, between the roles of defence and coercion. A military force capable of effectively fighting a real war can also be successful in coercing the adversary. However, focusing on one of these two functions can lead to building quite different military forces. As observed by Art:

> Defense is possible without deterrence, and deterrence is possible without defense. A state can have the military wherewithall to repel an invasion without also being able to threaten devastation to the invader's population or territory. Similarly, a state can have the wherewithall credibly to threaten an adversary with such devastation and yet be unable to repel his invading force.
>
> (Art 1980: 7)

When analysing the external functions of armed forces, it is worth to note that their relative significance evolved together with the changing international security environment. For centuries military forces were focused almost exclusively on warfighting, which was a legitimate and often practised form of international interaction. The dawn of the nuclear era and corresponding advent of the Cold War led to a significant change in thinking on military missions (at least among nuclear powers). Now the primary role of armed forces was avoiding war, not fighting it (Art 1980: 16). Deterrence and compellence became important (or arguably crucial) roles for militaries of Cold War super and great powers. When bipolar confrontation ended, the new security environment forced another shift. For many states (like NATO powers) the security environment suddenly lacked a clear and present threat posed by an identified adversary. Instead, the more diffuse "turbulences" in the international security environment became more pronounced security challenges. As a consequence, providing international public goods emerged as an important (and sometimes central) role of many armed forces. It is important to note that in the Indo-Pacific this shift was present but not as far reaching as in Europe. The persistence of severe interstates conflicts ensured that for many regional militaries defence and coercion remained primary functions. We can name here the situation on the Korean Peninsula, in the Taiwan Strait or on the Indian subcontinent.

Box 9.2 Domestic functions of armed forces in autocratic regimes – examples from the Indo-Pacific

Because this chapter deals with the use of military force in international politics, foremost the external functions of armed forces have received attention. Nonetheless, it is also worth to mention some significant domestic roles performed (both historically and currently) by some regional military forces, in the context of autocratic regimes. This short characterisation can be treated as supplementary to chapter 6 on political regimes of the Indo-Pacific.

For some political regimes armed forces play key role in preserving their rule. This can stem from the fact that particular regime is unsure of its legitimacy and thus relies on coercion to maintain its grip on power. It may also be the case that the leadership perceives significant threats to its position (real or imagined) coming from within the country and takes extra precautions to secure itself. When looking at the Indo-Pacific's recent history, the role of the Chinese People's Liberation Army should be highlighted. From its very beginning it has been first and foremost the "party's army." Throughout the People's Republic's history (and until today) its primary mission has been to protect the CCP's rule (Blasko 2006: 6–7; Tanner 2009). The PLA has been called to fulfil this role in the later stages of the Cultural Revolution, to reassert party leadership's control over the revolutionary movement. The most visible manifestation came in 1989 when CCP leaders, feeling threatened by mass protests at the Tiananmen square sent PLA units to supress them. Another example can be provided by the Royal Thai Armed Forces. Throughout the 20th century they have acquired the so-called "Pretorian ethos," seeing itself as the guardian and guarantor of the monarchy. That led to deep involvement in politics, often in the form of coup d'état (Macdonald 2018).

As part of the nation-building function, armed forces sometimes enter the field of public governance, which is usually reserved for the civilian administration. In many developed democracies such actions are considered contrary to the notion of "military professionalism." However, especially in newly independent developing states, scholars have identified "new professionalism" which provides for a bigger involvement of the military in state affairs, aiding administration and development (Alagappa 2001). This trend can be seen in curricula of military academies in several Indo-Pacific states which included courses dealing with civilian governance. That was the case in Republic of Korea during the military rule (Lee 2001: 51) or in Sukharto's Indonesia (Kristiadi 2001: 100–101). When conducting cross-country comparisons of armed forces' nation-building roles it is important to remember Mutiah Alagappa's conclusion that "The military's political salience is greatest when the political legitimacy of the civilian government is weak and coercion plays a crucial role both in domestic governance and in safeguarding the country's international security" (Alagappa 2001: 16). One of the primary examples of a state in which both these factors contribute to military's long-term and in-depth involvement in politics is Pakistan. It has endured many military regimes and military exceptionalism is a constant feature of its politics (Lieven 2011).

Throughout this section we have mapped out all main roles which armed forces can play in the state. In most cases, armed forces of a particular state are meant to fulfil several (or all) of them in different order of priority, depending on national circumstances. However, particular roles require different force structures, organisation, training and equipment. A military force meant to coerce a state of comparable power differs in all aforementioned characteristics from one focused on domestic counterinsurgency. Great powers, commanding the largest defence budgets, can usually afford to maintain versatile armed forces with capabilities needed to fulfil several roles simultaneously. However, even they have to prioritise.

How to wield the sword – military strategy and doctrine

In the preceding section we have learned for what aims states use their armed forces. Earlier we have discussed the means at their disposal in the form of military capabilities. But how do policymakers know which capabilities should be developed to make these aims achievable? And how should available capabilities be actually used to achieve these aims effectively? Finding the answers to these questions is the realm of strategy. The concept itself has been theorised and operationalised extensively in the discipline (Angstrom & Widen 2015: 33–55; Heuser 2010: 3–35). For our purposes it is sufficient to assume that strategy is: "a plan for how an actor employs and concentrates limited resources. A strategy, therefore, is an expression of an actor's management of scarce resources and how these are directed and used to punch above its weight" (Angstrom & Widen 2015: 35). Thus, in this chapter, we will understand military strategy as a way of using available military capabilities to achieve specified political objectives through the use of organised armed force. This is closely related to the concept of military doctrine. For the purpose of this chapter we can content ourselves with the understanding of doctrine as a particular military strategy which has been chosen by a particular state (and its armed forces) and institutionalised in official guidance, force structure and training (Angstrom & Widen 2015: 5).

When analysing how particular states build their strategies and doctrines we must first take it into account that, as Clausewitz famously remarked, war (or in our case the broader category of use of military force) is a continuation of policy (Angstrom & Widen 2015: 15–16). Thus, the military strategy is only one part of a broader foreign and security policy. To account for this reality, the concept of grand strategy has been developed. Like most other concepts discussed in this chapter (or in the entire handbook for that matter) it has been fiercely debated in the scholarly community producing a multitude of definitions (Lissner 2018; Milevski 2019: 4–15). At this point, let us assume that grand strategy is an overarching concept of how to employ all resources of the state (military and non-military) to achieve long-term political aims (in peace, crisis and war) (Lissner 2018: 55). At this point we should consider what is the relation between military and non-military means in a particular grand strategy. As observed by Lukas Milevski:

> When combining military and non-military power in war, non-military power must be integrated into and benefit the main military effort. Non-military power must bow to the basic facts of war and warfare. Combining the two in peace requires military power to be integrated into non-military power and act along the lines required by diplomacy and statecraft, an altogether different task.
>
> (Milevski 2019: 7)

As in this handbook we are dealing with the post-Cold War Indo-Pacific, we will mostly deal with the second option mentioned by Milevski. As the region has not experienced a major inter-state war in the last four decades, the military force has mainly been used to support other forms of state power, without taking the centre stage. Naturally, this does not change the fact that regional militaries are devising and refining their doctrines in anticipation of actual warfare.

As already mentioned, the range of possible strategies available to decision-makers, when establishing a military doctrine is highly varied. So, how do decision-makers choose a particular strategy as a basis for their state's military doctrine? Angstrom and Widen identify six primary dimensions shaping the "strategic context": geography, history, ideology, economy, technology and political system (Angstrom & Widen 2015: 36–43). Naturally, there is another important (maybe even the most important) factor which must be taken into account during strategy making – opposing side's strategic choices. Military strategy (as war itself) revolves around interaction of two opposing actors (Heuser 2010: 15–17). That is why military doctrine is rarely (if ever) developed "in abstract." Rather it is directed against a possible adversary and must react to his/hers own strategy making. It is important to remember that, while the theory and accumulated experience of strategy making may produce a very coherent and logical strategic concept which might look as "deemed to succeed," it can only be conclusively verified in an actual conflict, tested against an actual opponent. It may seem a rather banal remark, but actual application of strategy is way more difficult than pre-conflict theoretical strategising (Gray 2014).

Military characteristic of the Indo-Pacific region

After introducing some theoretical background on military power and its utility for foreign policy, it is important to outline the kind of military competition taking place in the Indo-Pacific and how this dynamic is shaping the region. Previous chapters of this handbook have already explained and analysed in detail the political considerations leading to the emergence of Indo-Pacific as a geopolitical construct. It is worth to remind the reader at this point that one of the first authors to introduce the concept was an Indian naval officer (Khurana 2007) and it has been relatively quickly adopted by architects of security and defence policies of some regional states (like Australia and USA). In United States the defence community arguably led the government bureaucracy in adopting Indo-Pacific as geopolitical concept organising policy towards the region. It has been symbolised by renaming US military's Pacific Command as Indo-Pacific Command in 2018 (Ali 2018). All this suggest, that political shifts tying the

Western Pacific and Indian Ocean basins together are closely related to military developments and considerations. From the perspective of defence policy the rationale for adopting an Indo-Pacific outlook is based on two closely related trends: 1) the significance of Sea Lines of Communication (SLOCs) going through the Indian Ocean (IO) for the prosperity and security of East Asian states; 2) the widening of Sino-Indian military rivalry to the maritime space encompassing the Western Pacific and Indian Ocean basins and its linkage with the Sino-American rivalry.

The security significance of the Indian Ocean for the People's Republic of China has been spelled out by President Hu Jintao in the 2003 speech, which is credited with formulating the so-called "Malacca Dilemma" (Mohan 2012: 119–124). The Chinese leader has observed that a great proportion of his country's foreign trade passes through the Malacca Strait (which connects the Indian and Pacific Oceans flowing along the shores of Indonesia, Malaysia and Singapore). This includes both a great deal of manufacturing exports contributing to China's trade surplus and energy imports (primarily oil and liquified natural gas) from the Middle East and Africa fuelling the country's economic growth. The dilemma part stems from the fact that if any military power could effectively block this transit route, it could apply powerful economic pressure on Beijing. Naturally, Chinese strategists worry about US or Indian Navy making such a move (individually or in cooperation).[1] This strategic reality provided an additional impulse for the modernisation and expansion of the People's Liberation Army Navy (PLAN) with the purpose of protecting shipping in the Indian Ocean and countering any potential blockade. Although the "Malacca dilemma" is associated with China, other trade dependent East Asian states (like Japan or South Korea) face similar challenges. In consequence, building the capability to protect Indian Ocean SLOCs drove the modernisation of their respective navies as well. This dynamic has been reflected in regional powers' response to the threat of piracy in the waters around the Horn of Africa. Starting around 2007–2008 the activity of Somali pirates became a serious concern for seafarers navigating through this important shipping lane. In response various states from around the world deployed their warships for maritime security operations in the Indian Ocean. On this occasion the PLAN has executed the first transoceanic operational deployment in its history. Japan and ROK also dispatched their vessels to counter-piracy operations. Ostensibly, these states used their navies for the provision of the international public goods function. Besides that it was also a potent demonstration of the capability to operate in IO waters for prolonged periods of time (useful for deterring possible state based threats to their shipping) (Medcalf 2020: 85–88; Yung et al. 2010).

Considerations outlined above led to the growing Chinese naval presence in the Indian Ocean. That has led to the second military dynamic cementing the Indo-Pacific – the widening of Sino-Indian rivalry. As explained in more detail in other chapters, the military rivalry between Beijing and New Delhi is a product of their land border dispute. However, Chinese naval activity in the IO has been perceived by the Indian side as an encroachment on its traditional sphere of influence. This partially motivated more active Indian policy towards the Western Pacific Basin, including naval deployments and security cooperation with regional states. This overlapping military activity contributed to cementing the Indo-Pacific (Mohan 2012; Medcalf 2020). It has been further strengthened by US desire to gain Indian support for counterbalancing China. The US military easily adopted the Indo-Pacific concept as it viewed the potential conflict with China as taking place in both Basins (Bisley & Phillips 2013; Basu 2021).

All the aforementioned geopolitical trends contributed to the development of significant initiatives in the sphere of security cooperation, whose logic is clearly based on the Indo-Pacific geopolitical framework. The most prominent of these is the Quadrilateral Dialogue (or simply Quad), established by Australia, India, Japan and United States. Although its emergence as a stable and coherent form of cooperation has taken almost a decade, by the early 2020s it has become an important element of foreign policy and security strategies of participating states (Rai 2018). Despite protestations of Quad members' leaders that it is not aimed against any particular actor, it is quite clear that the main purpose of this initiative is to counterbalance the growing Chinese power through cooperation between four "democratic powers of the Indo-Pacific." It should be stressed that as of 2021 the Quad has not taken the form of a military alliance (there are no mutual support obligations tying all four participants), nor has it led to intense cooperation and interoperability of all four armed forces. So far, the concrete cooperation between members has been more focused on so-called "soft security issues," including countering transnational threats and challenges (Upadhyay 2021). This situation does not change the fact, that the very establishment and development of Quad is a sign that defence establishments of its participants view their potential operating environment as encompassing what we identify as Indo-Pacific.

As we have outlined the military considerations contributing to the emergence of the Indo-Pacific concept and the area's characteristics as a theatre of military operations, we should follow with a short analysis of military power's distribution in the region. We will start painting this picture with data on three important military resources: troop numbers, defence expenditure and nuclear weapons (which are presented in Tables 9.3,[2] 9.4 and 9.5).

When it comes to the defence expenditure across the region, it is important to note, not only the absolute numbers, but also their growth dynamic. During the 21st century's second decade the total defence expenditure in Asia increased by more than 50% (from US $275 billion in 2010 to US $423 bn in 2019 in real terms IISS, 2020). As noted by the Stockholm Peace Research Institute, just two states – China and India – together accounted for 62% of total military expenditure in the Asia and Oceania region in 2020 (Silva, et al. 2021). Such a dynamic growth in resources devoted to national defence, leads many to assume that Indo-Pacific is in the midst of an intense arms race.

Table 9.3 Indo-Pacific states with biggest total armed forces personnel number (year 2018)

No.	State	Total military manpower
1.	India	3026500
2.	PRC	2695000
3.	DPRK	1469000
4.	Russia	1454000
5.	USA	1379800
6.	Pakistan	944800
7.	Indonesia	675500
8.	ROK	608000
9.	Vietnam	522000
10.	Myanmar	513000

Source: ("Armed forces personnel data," n.d.)

Table 9.4 Indo-Pacific states with biggest defence expenditure in 2020

No.	State	Defence expenditure (bn$)
1.	USA	778
2.	PRC	252
3.	India	72.9
4.	Russia	61.7
5.	Japan	49.1
6.	ROK	45.7
7.	Australia	27.5
8.	Canada	22.8
9.	ROC	12.2
10.	Singapore	10.9

Source: (Silva, et al. 2021)

Table 9.5 Indo-Pacific's nuclear powers (2021)

No.	State	Number of nuclear warheads
1.	Russia	6257
2.	USA	5600
3.	China	350
4.	Pakistan	165
5.	India	160
6.	DPRK	45

Source: ("Status of World Nuclear Forces," n.d.)

Looking at the approximate distribution of military resources, outlined in the previous paragraphs, we can draw some conclusions on the balance of military power in the Indo-Pacific. We can clearly see that three states: China, Russia and United States are superior in military capabilities, which offer them practically global reach. Some regional powers (like India and Japan) make significant investments into their armed forces, which give them real capabilities to exercise military presence throughout the Indo-Pacific. Another group of states, often characterised as middle powers, makes a strategic calculation to develop some expeditionary capabilities, allowing them to undertake significant alliance obligations and provide some international security public goods. In this case Australia and ROK come into mind. Finally, the biggest group of small powers is making an effort to meet their most immediate defence needs through more locally focused military forces (although this group is also very varied).

Military strategies of selected Indo-Pacific states

In this chapters' final section we will apply the theoretical insights outlined in section one to describe how military power is being used to shape international politics of the Indo-Pacific. In the preceding section we divided regional actors into several categories based on the scale and character of their military power. We will use several states belonging to different military power categories as case studies of actual military strategies pursued by them and how they interact with one another.

Global military powers and their strategy towards the Indo-Pacific

We have established, that three states clearly belong to the global top league of military power: China, Russia and the United States. All three are active in the Indo-Pacific, and they are engaged in mutual rivalry. In this subsection we will explain how they use military instruments to shape the regional order.

Historically, the United States used military power to further and protect its interests in the Pacific and Indian Ocean Basins (Friedberg 2002). Military power, in the form of troops forward deployed in the bases provided by regional allies and constant naval presence, constituted one of the pillars of US-led regional order throughout the Cold War and also in later years. Primary functions of this military posture amounted to deterrence and provision of international public goods. In this context it is important to remember that armed coercion became one of the routine instruments of maintaining US-led regional order (Ayson & Pardesi 2017: 90–93). We can identify at least three major influences of US military power on post-WWII order of the Western Pacific Basin. First, American military might deterred armed expansion of the Communist bloc. Second, and less obviously, security guaranties Washington extended to its regional allies, had also been used to shape their foreign and defence policies in ways favourable to US interests. This was visible in US relations with both ROK and Japan. In the first instance, operational control of ROK armed forces by US-led UN Forces Command (and later also the bilateral Combined Forces Command), gave Washington greater control over the escalatory dynamic on the Korean Peninsula (like for example stopping ROK from reigniting hostilities) (Ehrhardt 2004). In the case of Japan, American protection allowed the country to maintain a minimal defence posture, unthreatening to regional states still beset by mistrust of their former aggressor (Hook et al. 2005: 144–146). Finally, the American protective umbrella, and stability it brought, created favourable conditions for economic development in non-communist Asia, creating ground work for the "Asian economic miracle." That was also aided by the fact that numerous Asian states could do away with significant defence expenditure, relying on US support to a greater degree (Overholt 2008: 11–31). In the post-Cold War period US strategic position in the region increased further and it served similar purposes as before. The 9/11 attacks led to greater US military engagement in the Indian Ocean basin, with troop deployments to Afghanistan accompanied by development of additional basing and naval presence throughout the region. In the 21st century's second decade, the People's Republic of China's (PRC) growing military power offered a growing challenge for further exercise of US might in such a way.

Turning to Chinese military developments we can start with the remainder that PLA was born as a "party's army" (see Box 9.2). It was oriented towards domestic security and fighting the "people's war" against foreign ground invasion of PRC territory. However, as Beijing's foreign policy changed, the party-state leadership tasked the PLA with being ready to fight "local wars under high-tech conditions" (the development of PLA's military capabilities is described in more detail in Box 9.3). Available analysis of Chinese strategic military guidance highlight two crucial roles which PLA is supposed to fulfil. The first would be to prevail in regional conflicts centred on Chinese territorial claims (Taiwan, South China Sea or Sino-Indian border). An important element of that is the ability to deter/defeat US military intervention (especially in the Taiwan scenario). Second, the PLA is supposed to protect expanding Chinese economic and political interests throughout the Indo-Pacific and beyond (Scobell et al. 2020: 73–99). The aforementioned expansion of Chinese naval presence in the Indian Ocean is an example of this.

Box 9.3 The development of the People's Liberation Army's military capabilities

As the "rise of China" became a trend of enormous importance in international politics, its military aspects have attracted significant attention. For a decade between 2010 and 2020 the defence expenditure of PRC rose by cumulative 86% in real terms (IISS 2020). This allowed a large-scale introduction of modern weapon systems, like multi-role combat aircraft, precision guided munitions, missiles, submarines, large surface vessels, etc. Many of these were not present in the Chinese arsenal at all, or only in limited numbers. Often the equipment of the PLA was older by a generation or two from that used in the world's leading militaries. The annual report on China's military power prepared by the US Department of Defense for 2020 admits that "China has already achieved parity with – or even exceeded – the United States in several military modernization areas" (*Military and Security Developments Involving the People's Republic of China 2020 Annual Report to Congress* 2020: VII). One of the examples provided concerns naval build-up. The report states that China possesses the biggest navy in the world – with 350 ships and submarines – overtaking US Navy which in 2020 possessed 296 ships (*Military and Security Developments Involving the People's Republic of China 2020 Annual Report to Congress* 2020: VII). Moreover, the military has been reformed in several important ways, to meet the new requirements. The ground forces have been reduced, and additional budgets allocated to air and naval forces (necessary for power projection). What is important, the changes went beyond troop numbers and equipment procurement. PLA has been freed from various domestic security and nation-building tasks in order to focus on preparations for classical military operations. The military command structure has been thoroughly reformed in order to make joint operations easier (Ng 2005; Blasko 2006; Wuthnow & Saunders 2017).

The situation described above begs the question: are PLA's abilities good enough to match US military capabilities? Looking for an answer it is useful to start from the observation that the Chinese military has introduced, in a relatively short time, a great number of weapons and systems which it previously either didn't have, had in small numbers and/or in the older and less capable form. As a consequence the PLA personnel (and the organisation as a whole) faces a challenging process of learning not only how to simply operate new types of equipment, but also how to incorporate them into its force structure and operations. Such a process needs to be backed by considerable practice and experience. Let's look at the much publicised example of carrier aviation. In 2010s the PLA Navy (PLAN) has launched, with much fanfare, its first two aircraft carriers. Building the ships and aircraft for their air wings is a big achievement in itself. However, by the opinion of majority of outside experts, PLAN is still many years away from full capability to deploy airpower from the sea.

Simply launching jet aircraft from a ship and recovering them after their mission's completion is one of the most challenging and dangerous undertakings in the entire aviation world. The US Navy is considered to be the most proficient in this regard, thanks both to the large size of its carrier force and its long history of operations. However, this capability has been built on a painful experience, including numerous fatal accidents at the beginning of the jet age (Erickson et al. 2012). Judging by this standard, the PLAN will most probably need years of intense training to develop capability for regular carrier aviation operations (which is a necessary first step towards ability to conduct complicated combat operations by carriers' airwings).

This is only one specific example of a bigger problem of PLA mastering the capabilities needed to successfully conduct joint operations (meaning military operations involving integrated use of units from various armed services – air force, ground forces, navy, etc.) during "local wars under high-tech/informatized conditions," as demanded by the party-state leadership (Ng 2005: 105–150). In 2019 Dennis J. Blasko observed, based on the analysis of numerous authoritative (but at the same time publicly available) Chinese publications on military matters, that PRC's central political and military leadership is still not satisfied with the progress in this regard (Blasko 2019). It was observed that the official Chinese discourse on military capabilities during Xi Jinping's tenure refers to "'Two Inabilities' (*liǎnggè nénglì bùgòu*, 两个能力不够), which says the PLA's ability to fight a modern war and the ability of its cadres (officers) at all levels to command modern war are not sufficient." There is also a specific mention of "'Five Incapables [Cannots]' (*wǔgè bùhuì*, 五个不会)" which mean that: "'some' officers cannot judge situations, understand higher authorities' intentions, make operational decisions, deploy troops, nor deal with unexpected situations" (Blasko 2019). If these assessments are accurate, then it would mean that the road the PLA needs to travel to translate increases in military resources into a corresponding rise in actual military capabilities is still quite long.

The short outline of US and Chinese military strategies presented above illustrates the fact that both states treat each other as potential adversaries. Thus, their military doctrines are developed in an interactive way, meant to counter each other. This dynamic is characterised in more detail in Box 9.4.

Box 9.4 Military strategies as part of Sino-American rivalry

Growing rivalry and adversity in relations between United States and People's Republic of China is a well described and analysed phenomenon. Many studies have been devoted to the issue of whether this can lead to an actual armed conflict.[3] As this debate is not within the scope of this chapter, we will focus on the fact that both state's armed forces are actually preparing themselves to fight one another. It is widely recognised that, after US military show of force in the Taiwan Strait crisis of 1996, countering possible American intervention in conflicts involving crucial Chinese national interests became a focal point of PLA's modernisation (Lai & Miller 2009: 7; Li 2011: 118). Correspondingly, as PRC's military build-up intensified, countering perceived Chinese aggression became a preeminent preoccupation of US military planning (Etzioni 2013). This created a feedback loop through which doctrinal and technical developments on both sides have been deliberately pursued to counter one another.

The geographical realities of the Indo-Pacific have a great influence on strategic choices in this contest. China is engaged in a range of disputes along its periphery while the United States relies on projecting military power from across the Pacific Ocean (with support of forward presence of forces in bases within the region). In the face of this reality, it is widely believed that PRC has adopted what is called the "counter-intervention" strategy through "anti-access/area denial" (A2/AD).[4] In short, this approach is meant to deter (or if that fails defeat) American military intervention in a conflict taking place in the Western Pacific by denying US forces the freedom of manoeuvre into and within the theatre of operations. Such capabilities as Integrated Air Defence networks, long-range precision attack against land and naval surface targets, anti-satellite weapons or cyber-attacks would be used in synergy to stop US military from executing its preferred option of deploying massive air and naval firepower which could threaten Chinese military objectives. To simplify, we can say that such strategy would not require China to build a large surface fleet which would defeat US Navy in an epic sea battle somewhere in the waters of the Western Pacific, but rather it would use a network of land based missiles, aircraft, submarines, space and cyber-attacks to create a virtual "no-go zone" in which American fleet would be unable to operate freely without taking heavy and painful losses.

The appropriate military strategy for a conflict with China is a matter of intense debate in the US strategic studies and policymaking communities. However, a particular approach, originally called the "Air-Sea Battle" (ASB) has been adopted as the basis for doctrine (van Tol et al. 2010; Greenert & Schwartz 2012). To put it shortly, ASB can be described as a strategy in which US air and naval forces would field new weapon systems and operational concepts in order to penetrate and destroy Chinese A2/AD networks and restore friendly forces' freedom of manoeuvre. It can be assumed that it would be achieved in rapid, decisive operations, aimed at stopping the PLA from achieving its wartime objectives. It can be remarked at this point that the choice of such a strategy might have been influenced by historical preference for quick, clear-cut military victory (as achieved in the Gulf War of 1990–1991) and fear of prolonged struggle for attrition (experienced in the Korean and Vietnam wars). It can also be remarked that US political leaders might be afraid that a long armed conflict, and inevitable casualties it would bring, could lose the support of domestic public opinion. The ASB concept is also based on the assumption that US industrial and technological base will be able to deliver required military capabilities, thanks to development of innovative technological solutions (again, this has historical precedent).

Although ASB seems to have been adopted as actual doctrine in early 2010s, an alternative solution has been proposed and intensely discussed. It has been referred to as "offshore control" and envisages long-term maritime economic blockade of China as an alternative to risky and costly challenge to Chinese A2/AD networks envisaged in ASB (Hammes 2012; Kline & Hughes 2012). In this scenario the cumulative costs of economic isolation would undermine Chinese government's willingness to continue the conflict. That approach could use advantages granted by Indo-Pacific's geography and US naval power to impose heavy economic (and in consequence political) costs on Chinese military challenge to US interests in the region. The debate surrounding the advantages and disadvantages of these two strategies highlights the ambivalent nature and challenges of strategy making. Strategy based on ASB concept seems to promise a quick and decisive military victory through thwarting enemy's plans. However, it also carries significant costs in terms of great financial investment in new military capabilities. It can also be very risky, especially if attacks on the Chinese mainland would lead to the conflict's further escalation. Also, its offensive character can exacerbate the bilateral security dilemma and increase crisis instability. On the other hand, the "offshore control" carries its own risks in terms of, for example, alienating allies (who might feel abandoned by lack of a direct response to Chinese military moves opening the conflict), practical difficulties of establishing an effective naval blockade or uncertain effects of economic isolation on opposing side's decisions (Beckley 2017; Sand 2020).

However, the role of military instruments in Sino-American rivalry is not limited to mutual deterrence, sought through development of duelling strategies and resources for a full-scale war (as detailed in Box 9.4). Both powers actively use their armed forces' peacetime deployments for signalling resolve and shaping the international environment to their liking. Throughout the 2010s, China used its naval and maritime paramilitary forces to assert control over disputed land features and waters in South and East China Seas, as well as ground forces' advances in territories disputed with India (Ayson & Pardesi 2017; Le Mière 2011a and 2011b; Mastro & Tarapore 2017; Panda 2020). Especially operations in the South China Sea (SCS), coupled with the construction of artificial islands, have allowed Beijing to quite effectively improve its political and military position *vis-à-vis* other claimant states (as well as against US opposition to these moves) (Ayson & Pardesi 2017; Dahm 2020). As these actions have mostly been planned and executed in such a way, as not to provoke a wider military crisis, they are often considered a part of a growing global trend towards what is often called "hybrid warfare" and "grey zone" conflicts. The concepts and their relevance for explaining Chinese actions are explained in Box 9.5. United States has been effectively caught by surprised by these Chinese actions and struggled to formulate an appropriate response (Ayson & Pardesi 2017; Brands & Cooper 2018). Eventually, the most visible military response amounted to the so-called Freedom Of Navigation Operations (FONOPs). This form of military demonstration was meant to signal American unwillingness to accept Chinese actions and shape both international perceptions and practice (Wiegand & Ryou-Ellison 2020).

Box 9.5 Hybrid strategies and Chinese coercion

As the potential costs of inter-state wars between great powers rose exponentially (due to introduction of nuclear and ever more effective conventional weapons), many actors of international relations searched for ways of forcefully securing their political objectives without initiating open armed conflict. Thus, what we are seeing and are likely to see in the future, is the major powers of the Indo-Pacific using military force in a limited (in scope and intensity) manner, alongside other non- and paramilitary instruments to achieve their political objectives, thus initiating political-military crisis. This approach is not necessarily new in historic perspective, but certainly has attracted a growing academic and policymaking interest, leading to popularisation of various associated concepts. The most popular ones (at least in Western academic and analytical communities) are "hybrid warfare" (Hoffman 2009; Rácz 2015) and "grey zone" conflicts (Kapusta 2015; Hughes 2020). In his study of the hybrid warfare concept the author has proposed his definition of a broader category of "hybrid strategies" – coordinated and coercive employment of a flexible combination of power tools (military, political, economic, social, informational, etc.), fluidly adjusted across time and space to exploit opponent's vulnerabilities in order to achieve strategic political objectives through the erosion of opponent's political will to resist (Wiśniewski 2018: 99).

Such an approach has been used on several occasions by the PRC. In the South China Sea dispute, in the last decade, China decided not to try to take land features occupied by other claimants, but rather strengthened its position by practically creating new ones or expanding those already under its control (Altman 2018: 87). Another interesting aspect of Chinese approach to maritime territorial disputes (which is also practised by other countries) is the use of maritime law-enforcement vessels instead of actual navy warships to assert claims in disputed waters. The reasoning here is that the engagement of ostensibly civilian vessels will not be as provocative and will make escalation less likely compared with the presence of heavily armed warships, manned by soldiers trained for war (Le Mière 2011a; Martinson 2016). PRC actually takes it even further by employing "maritime militia," civilian vessels mobilised for state service (Gady 2015). Mutually recognised constraint of not using firearms in border skirmishes between China and India can be another example of attempting to at least "stretch" the red lines concerning the use of force (although, the experience of 2020 clashes sadly shows that it does not rule out deadly combat).

Looking at Russia's role in the Indo-Pacific military balance of power, it can be noted that it cannot be neither ignored nor overestimated. The main point of focus for Russian military power lies in Europe and the Caucasus. However, Russian Federation's Eastern Military District (and the Pacific Fleet) does have significant military capabilities at its disposal. Russian military presence in the Pacific is instrumental in Moscow's rivalry with United States. It also provides military safeguards in the territorial dispute with Japan over the Kurile islands/Northern Territories.

In author's opinion, the most significant aspect in which Russian military power has affected the Indo-Pacific during the post-Cold War period is its military cooperation with regional states (primarily China, India and Vietnam). The first two decades of the 21st century witnessed growing military ties between Beijing and Moscow. They go beyond arms transfers and reach into joint exercise and military demonstrations (like joint bomber patrols or fleet movements throughout the region) (Wiśniewski 2019). Although (at the time of writing) it hardly amounts to a military alliance, both states clearly draw important political benefits from this increased military cooperation. The mere perception of building capability for joint military operations aids both states' deterrence towards the United States (Charap et al. 2017; Kaczmarski 2020). Russian arms sales and technical support played a very significant role in the development of Chinese military capabilities. It is also important to note, that Russia also sales arms to Beijing's competitors (India and Vietnam). Generally, the significance of wider military-technical cooperation with Asian states goes beyond generating export revenue. It serves wider overall objectives of maintaining major power status and influencing regional politics (Blank & Levitzky 2015).

Military strategies of regional powers

The second category we will consider consists of two major powers, whose military reach has historically being focused on their extended neighbourhoods – India and Japan. Quite obviously, geopolitical considerations led their armed forces to develop in distinct ways. India has consistently focused on land forces, while the island nation of Japan developed air and naval capabilities to a greater extent.

For most of the post-independence period Indian armed forces focused on two functions crucial for their state's security – territorial defence and domestic security. The two are naturally interlinked. As amply characterised in other chapters of this handbook, territorial conflict with Pakistan over Kashmir has been the defining feature of India's strategic thinking. The history of four major armed confrontation (1947–1948, 1965, 1971 and 1999) and numerous political-military crisis (Chari et al. 2007) reaffirmed the need for large land forces, able to conduct both offensive and defensive operations against the main regional opponent. At the same time, New Delhi has faced numerous insurgencies, including the Naxalite movement, secessionism in the northeastern states and (most prominently and connected to the external Pakistani threat) in Kashmir. For that reason Indian Army has been consistently called upon to perform the internal security role, supporting numerous police and paramilitary forces (Chadha 2005).

As observed by Arzan Tarapore Indian military doctrine has consistently put the premium on offensive operations (Tarapore 2020). It is worth observing that, although such an approach can be seen as reasonable from a purely military-operational point of view, it did contribute to persistence of an acute security dilemma in relations with Pakistan. India's quantitative superiority and history of success in combat against its Pakistani counterpart, led Islamabad to look for other options to effectively compete militarily with India. The most prominent one is the development of a nuclear arsenal. The declared (or implied) nuclear doctrines of India and Pakistan are starkly different. Relying on its superior conventional capabilities to deter Pakistan (and defeat it if the need arises), India declared a "no-first-use" nuclear posture. Thus, Indian nuclear forces are organised to be used only in retaliation for a nuclear attack on their home-land. Although official Pakistani stance on possible use of nuclear weapons is more opaque, it implies that these weapons could be used to stop a large-scale Indian conventional offensive. The consequence of all this is that every politico-military crisis between the two South Asian powers unfolds under the shadow of nuclear escalation (Chari et al. 2007; Sugden 2019; Kapur 2005). The nuclear aspect of Indo-Pakistani nuclear rivalry is connected to and exacerbated by another Pakistani strategy to indirectly challenge New Delhi – support for armed groups operating in Kashmir and sheltering terrorist organisations targeting India. Effective response to this threat proved to be challenging to Indian armed forces. In the early 2000s New Delhi tried to use its massive conventional forces to coerce Pakistan to cease support and prosecute terrorist groups attacking India. The results proved to be very limited at best. Pakistani nuclear arsenal proved to be an effective counter-deterrent and the prospect of a nuclear crisis led United States to mediate between both powers (Ladwig III 2008; Chari et al. 2007).

Preoccupation with threats to land borders didn't mean that Indian armed forces hadn't been used for regional power projection. In the 1980s New Delhi conducted small scale military interventions in the Indian Ocean basin to stabilise the international situation (Maldives, Sri Lanka). In the 21st century, naval power projection became a more important piece of Indian military strategy (Pant & Joshi 2016). As already explained earlier in the chapter, this has been mainly prompted by growing Chinese presence in the Indian Ocean basin. At the turn of 2010s and 2020s one of the main strategic dilemmas of Indian defence policy was the need for simultaneous naval rivalry with China and maintaining significant force posture on land borders (Lalwani 2020).

The military strategy of the second regional power under consideration – Japan, has been shaped by very different forces than India's. The evolution of Japanese Self Defence Forces (JSDF) took place in the context of very strict legal and political constraints imposed on the military after WWII. These limited the JSDF to strictly defensive external role. It was basically preparing for repelling direct attacks on Japan and securing the SLOCs. It should also be stressed that from the very beginning, JSDF has been not only a tool for securing Japan but also an important element of managing the alliance relationship with the United States. It is worth remembering that originally the JSDF has not been conceived as a force capable of effectively defending the home islands on its own. It was rather meant to complement US forces devoted to this task and assure a minimal level of military "burden sharing" within the alliance (Samuels 2007; Pyle 2007). However, starting in 1980s some Japanese leaders decided to initiate reforms which would make JSDF a more traditional instrument of major power foreign policy. This evolution has taken pace in the post-Cold War years. The reasons have been two-fold: new threats (like North Korean missile and nuclear program, or China's military rise) and expectations of the American ally for JSDF to take greater responsibility and support allied efforts. Japanese governments supporting the "normalisation" of Japanese foreign and security policy adopted international public goods function by sending JSDF on peacekeeping missions and "contingency operations" supporting US military operations (like Iraq or Afghanistan) (Samuels 2007; Hook Gilson et al. 2005: 163–166, 382–386). It also worth noting how participation in UN PKOs provided an opportunity to legitimise new roles of the JSDF and loosen the strict constitutional limitations on their use (Samuels 2007: 86–108;

Hook Gilson et al. 2005: 163–166, 382–386). The National Security Strategy adopted by the Japanese government in 2013 and following legislation, present new missions of the JSDF (beyond the direct defence of Japan) as "proactive contribution to peace" (National Security Strategy, Japan 2013; *Japan's Legislation for Peace and Security Seamless Responses for Peace and Security of Japan and the International Community* 2015). Today's JSDF is being prepared to undertake a broader set of external missions than originally envisioned. The current security environment, with more assertive Chinese conduct towards Japan led Tokyo to develop offensive capabilities for use in a potential conflict with China – such as amphibious forces (for retaking captured islands) or potential strike capabilities (Caverley et al. 2020). It must also be noted that there is a growing debate in Japan about potential military involvement in a Taiwan conflict (Ashley 2021).

Military aspects of middle powers' strategies

The concept of "middle power" is often used in IR scholarship and political debates. For the purpose of this chapter we will understand middle powers as states with limited power resources and standing in the regional hierarchy, which nevertheless aspire to actively influence the international environment (which is often characterised as "punching above their weight"). Middle powers pursue active foreign policies in order to increase their influence in the international order, usually by utilising coalitions, alliances and international institutions (Chapnick 1999; Ungerer 2007; Jordaan 2017). In military terms, we can identify them as states unable to sustain large-scale military operations far away from their borders (with their defence policies usually concerned with dealing with security challenges emerging in their immediate neighbourhood), but nevertheless purposefully developing limited capabilities for expeditionary operations. Such capabilities are nurtured for fulfilling the function of international public goods provision.

Two Indo-Pacific states – Australia and Republic of Korea – provide good case studies of this dynamic. What do the defence policies of these two countries of very different histories and geopolitical surroundings have in common? Both consistently sustain significant investments in their armed forces. At the same time, their military potential is widely considered insufficient to independently neutralise most probable threats to their security. For that reason, both states have made the alliance relationship with United States the cornerstone of their security policies. At the same time, thanks to aforementioned investments into defence capabilities, they are able to be a "net security producers" in these relationships, through shouldering a significant part of their own defence's burden, as well as contributing to other security commitments of the superpower ally.

As we identified important similarities between Australia's and ROK's positions in regional balance of military power, we can shortly characterise the evolution of their defence policies. From its very creation South Korean armed forces had one overarching function – to defend the country from further North Korean aggression. Almost 70 years after armistice was signed, this mission remains relevant. From the very beginning, the deterrence of Communist aggression (and actual defence if it failed) was to be undertaken in an alliance. Throughout the Cold War the Operational Control (OPCON) of ROK military forces (in both peace and wartime) lay in the hands of a multinational (in practice American) command. Peacetime OPCON has been transferred to ROK authorities in 1994. However the wartime control remains in Combined Forces Command at the time of the writing (Kim 2021a). In this context, it can be easily understood why the development of ROK armed forces has always unfolded in the context of alliance politics. In the 1960s South Korea sent a sizeable military contingent to fight in the Vietnam War. That was both a response to Washington's request and an investment in strengthening the alliance by proving Seoul's worth as a reliable ally (Ehrhardt 2004).

By the turn of the century, South Korea's growing economic and industrial potential combined with ambitions for defence self-sufficiency allowed the country to build a *de facto* ocean going navy, able to conduct expeditionary operations (which has been utilised in anti-piracy operations in the Indian Ocean) (Koda 2010; Bowers & Hiim 2021). This created the means for ROK armed forces to engage in the provision of international public goods more energetically. Moreover, in the early 2010s Seoul codified a new deterrence strategy aimed at countering the threat of nuclear-armed North (although it has been also described as "omni-directional," in terms of its targets). It is based on air and missile defences, as well as conventional strike capabilities targeting both Democratic People's Republic of Korea's (DPRK) missile arsenals (to pre-empt enemy's first strike) and its leadership (as a retaliation option) (Bowers & Hiim 2021). It is a hugely ambitious undertaking as "Few, if any, nonnuclear states have sought to rely on advanced conventional capabilities to deter a nuclear-armed adversary" (Bowers & Hiim 2021: 8). This led to an unprecedented (for non-nuclear weapon state) build-up of cruise and ballistic missile arsenal. Several rationales for this approach have been proposed, including this arsenal being an insurance in case of American abandonment (even building potential basis for an independent nuclear arsenal) (Bowers & Hiim 2021) or bolstering the case for the transfer of wartime OPCON to Seoul (Kim 2021a) (obviously these are not mutually exclusive). All these developments make ROK an important player in military affairs of the Indo-Pacific.

In the case of Australia, geopolitical circumstances also proved crucial drivers of defence policy. Although the basic mission of the Australian Defence Force (ADF) is, quite naturally, the defence of the continent from possible military attack, throughout post-WWII period defence policy envisioned actual military operations throughout what we today call the Indo-Pacific region. This stems from two long-term constants of Australian strategic thinking: key role of the alliance with the United States in ensuring national security and a desire to counter potential threats before they reach waters surrounding Australia (Evans 2005; McCraw 2011). For that reason, Australian military forces have consistently been put to use in expeditionary operations. In both World Wars they participated in "imperial defence," during the Cold War the Canberra government deployed troops to Vietnam. The latter move served to both stop Communist expansion in South-East Asia (which was perceived as an eventual threat to Australia itself), as well as to confirm and strengthen the strategic alliance with US (Dibb 2007). The 1980s saw Canberra's defence policy focus more on defending the homeland (and more specifically the air and sea approaches to it) and preparations for possible conflict with Indonesia (which Australian strategists thought possible to be provoked by Jakarta's designs on Papua-New Guinea). This led to emphasis on self-sufficiency in military matters. Nevertheless, military planning did tend to assume that eventual operations in defence of Australian interests would be conducted in cooperation with allies (Frühling 2014). In the post-Cold War period ADF has been deployed quite often in support of what we can call "activist middle-power" foreign policy. These operations can be divided into two categories. The first was connected with Canberra's role as (sub)regional power in the Southern Pacific. Military deployments in Timor-Leste or in the Solomon Islands were part of a wider strategy to ensure a stable and peaceful neighbourhood (White 2007; Bergin et al. 2008). The second category amounted to participation in US-led Global War on Terror with ADF operating in Afghanistan and Iraq. These can (again) be interpreted as including both provision of international public goods and cementing the security relationship with Washington (Dibb 2007),

At the turn of the 2010s and 2020s Australian defence policy has undergone further significant changes. They can be characterised as a response to a growing probability of large-scale regional conflict involving US and China. For that reason ADF is investing in resources and capabilities perceived as crucial in such high-intensity warfare (*Defence Strategic Update 2020* 2020). This includes long-range air launched weapons, heavy armoured vehicles and (most prominently) nuclear-powered submarines. As ably noted by Hugh White – some of these capabilities are not best suited for strictly understood defence of Australia's shores (White 2020). There are configured more for "sea control" which implies projecting power from the sea, rather than stopping the enemy from doing the same. Such moves can be interpreted as preparations for participation in US-led operations against China in maritime Indo-Pacific in an event of conflict. Such hypothesis is strengthened by Australian officials' suggestions that their country might support US military action in the case of Chinese attack on Taiwan (Sevastopulo 2021).

Small powers' defence policies

The most populous category of military powers in the Indo-Pacific (and globally) can be summarily (if imprecisely) called "small powers." For the purpose of this chapter, we can characterise them as states which lack effective means of power projection beyond their land and sea borders (apart from presence in multilateral PKOs) and which are quite widely recognised as possessing military capabilities insufficient to independently mount an effective defence against a determined major power opponent. Here we will consider two cases – DPRK and Republic of China (ROC) on Taiwan. Naturally, military forces these states have at their disposal are neither small nor irrelevant for regional stability. DPRK is the world's smallest nuclear power (in terms of probable size of its arsenal). Its conventional capabilities are also formidable for a state of its size and economic potential. However, it should be noted, that its ability to militarily influence its international environment is limited to being an effective "rogue state," threatening its neighbours either with invasion or missile attacks. We can safely assume that Pyongyang does not possess sufficient power resources to actively shape the international order in a way aforementioned middle powers do. In the other example, ROC's armed forces are organised to defend their nation from armed coercion or outright invasion by the PRC. They lack means for significant power projection farther afield.

North Korea and Taiwan have quite different military strategies. They are considered here as examples of small powers' defence policies due to some strategic similarities. Both states make significant investments in their armed forces (in the case of Pyongyang, harming its economy and social welfare in the process). This is an obvious consequence of them both being at the centre of crucial international conflicts in the region. What is important for strategy making, they share similar key security concern

– an existential threat of armed coercion or outright attack by a great power. It is not surprising then, that military thought in both states is exploring "asymmetric" options to deal with a way more powerful opponent.

The Korean People's Army (KPA) can be understood through three main and one supportive functions it performs. The absolutely critical mission of this forces is to ensure the survival and security of the Kim family's regime. This includes both a domestic regime security function (performed alongside internal security forces) and external defence of regime's crucial interests (McEachern 2008; Byman & Lind 2010). In the Cold War years the latter amounted to being prepared for a full-scale invasion and conquest of the rival state south of the 38th parallel. After DPRK experienced a deep economic crisis, starting after USSR's collapse, it can be argued that, more realistically, the strategic orientation (at least partially) shifted to defending the North from possible armed regime change at the hands of United States and its regional allies. Additionally to domestic regime security and external defence functions, the KPA has also often been used for compellence aimed at Seoul (and occasionally US forces in and around Korea). In the post-Cold War era Pyongyang has consistently used armed provocations to gain leverage in international negotiations and extract concessions. Actually, as aptly described by Michishita Narushige the North Korean regime has developed its own approach to "military-diplomatic actions" (Michishita 2010). As an addition to these crucial missions, it can be argued that the KPA, and especially its relentless development of high-end missile weaponry, is regularly used for prestige functions. Displays of military might and technical sophistication in the form of elaborate military parades serve to build regime's image in the eyes of both domestic and foreign audiences. This is even more important if we consider that weapon systems are practically only technologically sophisticated products North Korean industry can prove its worth with.

North Korean military strategy is centred on deterring an external challenge to the regime's survival. The main component is currently composed of nuclear weapons and a growing missile arsenal for their delivery. However, the vast conventional forces at Pyongyang's disposal can also be effective in this regards. They pose a credible threat of massive destruction in the South, and also make any attempt at military intervention in the North very risky (Bennett & Lind 2011). DPRK's deterrence strategy can be assessed as effective considering that that Pyongyang has been able to use limited force against the ROK (like to sinking of ROKN warship *Choenan* and shelling of the island of Yeonpyong in 2010) without provoking a large-scale retaliation from the South and its American allies (N. Kim 2011). Tracing the expert debate on the subject it can be inferred that Pyongyang's opponents are struggling at devising an effective counter-deterrence approach to its nuclear arsenal (J. Kim et al. 2020).

Republic of China's armed forces have also been developed in the context of a long-term conflict. After the conclusion of the Chinese civil war their primary function amounted to protecting ROC's diminished territorial possession from further PRC attack. The Kuomintang regime also envisioned a campaign to retake the mainland, although it is questionable whether this was ever a realistic proposition. Up until the beginning of the 21st century, strategy for defending Taiwan rested on two key assumptions – technological superiority of ROC air and naval forces over the PLA and assumed (if not legally guaranteed after 1978) American military support (Gitter & Sutter 2016; An 2018). This approach had to be re-evaluated in the light of changing cross-Strait balance of military power. By the beginning of the 2020s it is widely assumed that PLA has reached something close to qualitative parity with ROC armed forces. This led Taipei strategists to look for more asymmetric alternatives. One of the steps taken was the development of long-range cruise-missiles to hold targets on mainland at risk. That was meant to serve as a strengthening deterrence. Other options included operating lighter, more manoeuvrable air, land and sea forces, able to inflict significant loses on attackers and maintaining effective armed resistance for as long as possible (Beckley 2017; Hunzeker 2021; Timbie & Ellis 2021). At the time of the writing, the foundations of Taiwanese defence policy remained debated and perspectives for American military aid in case of conflict remained one of the crucial elements of this discussion (Hunzeker 2021; Timbie & Ellis 2021; Blackwill & Zelikow 2021).

Developments analysed in this chapter leave little doubt that military power remains an important tool of international politics in the early 21st century Indo-Pacific. Unresolved inter-state conflicts and escalating great power rivalries push many states in the region into significant increases in their military resources and corresponding development of new military capabilities. As presented throughout the chapter, actors of varying resources and ambitions are devising their military strategies to effectively counter perceived threats and shape their international environment. This creates a complex interactive dynamic, resulting in further military build-up. American military dominance led PRC to develop a counter-strategy which was supposed to allow Beijing to protect its vital interests from US interference. This increased insecurity not only in Washington (leading to counter developments) but also in several regional states (Japan, India, ROC, ROK, etc.). Their reactions naturally feed into Beijing's threat calculus. This dynamic is an important driver of the regional arms race. Moreover, regional powers' appetite for using armed forces below the threshold of open war (arguably) increased in 2000s and 2010s. This increases the likelihood of future politico-military crisis. Naturally, no outcome is inevitable, and decision-makers across the region not once exhibited significant self-restraint in military operations. Nevertheless, military aspects of regional politics will most probably remain a very important aspect of Indo-Pacific developments.

Notes

1 Whether such a naval blockade would be practical to undertake under contemporary conditions is a matter of debate among the experts – see Collins & Murray (2008); Biggs et al. (2021); Sand (2020).

2 The data presented in Table 3 are taken from the World Bank database, which itself relies on numbers compiled by the International Institute for Strategic Studies. They present the total number of armed forces personnel meaning: "active duty military personnel, including paramilitary forces if the training, organization, equipment, and control suggest they may be used to support or replace regular military forces" ("Armed forces personnel data," n.d.).

3 Examples of various arguments in this debate can be found (among others) in: Allison 2017; Chong & Hall 2014; Glaser 2015; Liff & Ikenberry 2014.

4 This strategic concept is cited and explained mainly by non-Chinese experts and observers. It has been widely popularized by US defence analysts (Krepinevich & Watts 2003; Cliff et al. 2007). However, a conclusive confirmation from authoritative Chinese sources of its adoption as an actual doctrine is (as of this writing) lacking. This leads some experts to pose the question of whether the "anti-access/area denial strategy" is not, in fact, an American projection instead of actual Chinese strategy (Fravel & Twomey 2014). The author decided

to adopt this concept (for the purpose of this chapter) as reflecting Chinese strategy due to its role in shaping US response. Thus, even if it does not fully reflect Chinese strategic posture, it serves the purpose of illustrating the interaction of Chinese and American strategies.

References

Alagappa, M. (2001). Military Professionalism: A Conceptual Perspective. In M. Alagappa (Ed.), *Military Professionalism in Asia: Conceptual and Emipirical Perspectives*. Honolulu: East-West Center.

Ali, I. (2018). In Symbolic Nod to India, U.S. Pacific Command Changes Name. Retrieved November 30, 2021, from Reuters website: https://www.reuters.com/article/us-usa-defense -india-idUSKCN1IV2Q2.

Allison, G. (2017). *Destined for War: Can America and China Escape Thucydides's Trap?* Boston: Houghton Mifflin Harcourt, 1–18.

Altman, D. (2018). Advancing Without Attacking: The Strategic Game Around the Use of Force. *Security Studies*, 27(1), 58–88. https://doi.org/10.1080/09636412.2017.1360074.

An, D. (2018). *Reconstructing Taiwan's Military Strategy Achieving Forward Defense through Multi-Domain Deterrence*. Retrieved from https://www.nbr.org/publication/reconstructing -taiwans-military-strategy-achieving-forward-defense-through-multi-domain-deterrence/.

Angstrom, J., & Widen, J. J. (2015). *Contemporary Military Theory The Dynamics of War*. Abingdon: Routledge.

Armed Forces Personnel Data. (n.d.). Retrieved from The World Bank website: https://data .worldbank.org/indicator/MS.MIL.TOTL.P1.

Art, R. J. (1980). To What Ends Military Power? *International Security*, 4(4), 3–35.

Ashley, R. (2021). Japan's Revolution on Taiwan Affairs. Retrieved December 13, 2021, from War On The Rocks website: https://warontherocks.com/2021/11/japans-revolution-on -taiwan-affairs/.

Ayson, R., & Pardesi, M. S. (2017). Asia's Diplomacy of Violence: China–US Coercion and Regional Order. *Survival*, 59(2), 85–124.

Baldwin, D. A. (2016). *Power and International Relations: A Conceptual Approach*. Princeton: Princeton University Press.

Basu, P. (2021). *Brass Tacks: Unpacking the Indo-Pacific Template*. Retrieved from https://www .orfonline.org/research/brass-tacks-unpacking-the-indo-pacific-template/.

Beckley, M. (2017). The Emerging Military Balance in East Asia How China's Neighbors Can Check Chinese Naval Expansion. *International Security*, 42(2), 78–119. https://doi.org/10 .1162/ISEC.

Bennett, B. W., & Lind, J. (2011). The Collapse of North Korea: Military Missions and Requirements. *International Security*, 36(2), 84–119. https://doi.org/10.1162/ISEC_a_00057.

Bergin, A., Dobell, G., Firth, S., Chand, S., Goldsmith, A., Lowry, B., … Herr, R. (2008). *Australia and the South Pacific: Rising to the Challenge*. Retrieved from https://www.aspi.org.au/report /special-report-issue-12-australia-and-south-pacific-rising-challenge.

Biddle, T. D. (2020). Coercion Theory: A Basic Introduction for Practitioners. *Texas National Security Review*, 3(2), 1–30. Retrieved from https://tnsr.org/2020/02/coercion-theory-a-basic -introduction-for-practitioners/.

Biggs, A., Xu, D., Roaf, J., & Olson, T. (2021). Theories of Naval Blockades and Their Application in the Twenty-First Century. *Naval War College Review*, 74(1), art.9.

Bisley, N., & Phillips, A. (2013). A Rebalance to Where?: US Strategic Geography in Asia. *Survival*, 55(5), 95–114.

Blackwill, R. D., & Zelikow, P. (2021). The United States, China, and Taiwan: A Strategy to Prevent War. In Council on Foreign Relations. Retrieved from https://www.cfr.org/report/ united-states-china-and-taiwan-strategy-prevent-war.

Blank, S., & Levitzky, E. (2015). Geostrategic Aims of the Russian Arms Trade in East Asia and the Middle East. *Defence Studies*, *15*(1), 63–80. https://doi.org/10.1080/14702436.2015 .1010287.

Blasko, D. J. (2006). *The Chinese Army Today Tradition and Transformation for the 21st Century*. New York: Routledge.

Blasko, D. J. (2019). The Chinese Military Speaks to Itself, Revealing Doubts. Retrieved from War On The Rocks website: https://warontherocks.com/2019/02/the-chinese-military-speaks -to-itself-revealing-doubts/.

Bowers, I., & Hiim, H. S. (2021). Conventional Counterforce Dilemmas: South Korea's Deterrence Strategy and Stability on the Korean Peninsula. *International Security*, *45*(3), 7–39. https://doi.org/10.1162/isec_a_00399.

Brands, H., & Cooper, Z. (2018). Getting Serious about Strategy in the South China Sea. *Naval War College Review*, *71*(1), art.3.

Buzan, B., & Hansen, L. (2009). *The Evolution of International Security Studies*. Cambridge: Cambridge University Press.

Byman, D., & Lind, J. (2010). Pyongyang's Survival Strategy Ools of Authoritarian Control in North Korea. *International Security*, *35*(1), 44–74.

Caverley, J. D., Dombrowski, P., Hinata-Yamaguchi, R., Schreer, B., Murano, M., & Pekkanen, S. M. (2020). Policy Roundtable: The Future of Japanese Security and Defense. Retrieved December 13, 2021, from Texas National Security Review website: https://tnsr.org/roundtable /policy-roundtable-the-future-of-japanese-security-and-defense/.

Chadha, V. (2005). *Low Intensity Conflicts in India: An Analysis*. New Delhi: Sage.

Chapnick, A. (1999). The Middle Power. *Canadian Foreign Policy Journal*, *7*(2), 73–82. https:// doi.org/10.1080/11926422.1999.9673212.

Charap, S., Drennan, J., & Noël, P. (2017). Russia and China: A New Model of Great-Power Relations. *Survival*, *59*(1), 25–42.

Chari, P. R., Cheema, P. I., & Cohen, S. P. (2007). *Four Crises and a Peace Process American Engagement in South Asia*. Washington, DC: The Brookings Institution.

Chong, J. I., & Hall, T. H. (2014). The Lessons of 1914 for East Asia Today Missing the Trees for the Forest. *International Security*, *39*(1), 7–43. https://doi.org/10.1162/ISEC.

Cliff, R., Burles, M., Chase, M. S., Eaton, D., & Pollpeter, K. L. (2007). *Entering the Dragon's Lair Chinese Antiaccess Strategies and Their Implications for the United States*. https://doi .org/10.4324/9781315665825-91.

Collins, G. B., & Murray, W. S. (2008). No Oil for the Lamps of China? *Naval War College Review*, *61*(2), 79–95.

Dahm, J. M. (2020). Beyond "Conventional Wisdom": Evaluating the PLA's South China Sea Bases in Operational Context. Retrieved from War On The Rocks website: https:// warontherocks.com/2020/03/beyond-conventional-wisdom-evaluating-the-plas-south-china -sea-bases-in-operational-context/.

Defence Strategic Update 2020. (2020). Retrieved from https://www.defence.gov.au/about/ publications/2020-defence-strategic-update.

Dibb, P. (2007). Australia–United States. In B. Taylor (Ed.), *Australia as an Asia Pacific Regional Power Friendships in Flux?* (pp. 33-49). Oxon: Routledge.

Edmunds, T. (2006). What are Armed Forces For? The Changing Nature of Military Roles in Europe. *International Affairs*, *82*(6), 1059–1075. https://doi.org/10.1111/j.1468-2346.2006 .00588.x.

Ehrhardt, G. (2004). The Evolution of US-ROK Security Consultation. *Pacific Affairs*, *4*, 665–682.

Erickson, A. S., Denmark, A. M., & Collins, G. (2012). Beijing's "Starter Carrier" and Future Steps Alternatives and Implications. *Naval War College Review*, *65*(1), 15–54.

Etzioni, A. (2013). Who Authorized Preparations for a War with China? *Yale Journal of International Affairs*, *37*. https://doi.org/10.4324/9781315133447-11.

Evans, M. (2005). *The Tyranny of Dissonance Australia's Strategic Culture and Way of War 1901–2005* (No. 306).

Fravel, M. T., & Twomey, C. P. (2014). Projecting Strategy: The Myth of Chinese Counter-intervention. *Washington Quarterly*, 37(4), 171–187. https://doi.org/10.1080/0163660X.2014.1002164.

Friedberg, A. L. (2002). United States. In R. J. Ellings, A. L. Friedberg, & M. Wills (Eds.), *Strategic Asia 2002–03 Asian Aftershocks* (pp. 17–48). Seattle: National Bureau of Asian Research.

Frühling, S. (2014). Australian Defence Policy and the Concept of Self-reliance. *Australian Journal of International Affairs*, 68(5), 531–547. https://doi.org/10.1080/10357718.2014.899310.

Gady, F.-S. (2015). 'Little Blue Men:' Doing China's Dirty Work in the South China Sea. Retrieved from The Diplomat website: https://thediplomat.com/2015/11/little-blue-men-doing-chinas-dirty-work-in-the-south-china-sea/.

Gitter, D., & Sutter, R. (2016). *Taiwan's Strong but Stifled Foundations of National Power* (No. 54). Retrieved from https://www.nbr.org/publication/taiwans-strong-but-stifled-foundations-of-national-power/.

Glaser, C. L. (2015). A U.S.-China Grand Bargain? The Hard Choice between Military Competition and Accommodation. *International Security*, 39(4), 49–90. https://doi.org/10.1162/ISEC.

Gray, C. S. (2014). Why Strategy is Difficult. In T. G. Mahnken & J. A. Maiolo (Eds.), *Strategic Studies A Reader* (pp. 40–46). Abingdon: Routledge.

Greenert, J. W., & Schwartz, N. A. (2012). Air-Sea Battle. *The Amrican Interest*. Retrieved from https://www.the-american-interest.com/2012/02/20/air-sea-battle/.

Hammes, T. X. (2012). *Offshore Control: A Proposed Strategy for an Unlikely Conflict*. National Defence University Strategic Forum No. 278.

Heuser, B. (2010). *The Evolution of Strategy Thinking War from Antiquity to the Present*. Cambridge: Cambridge University Press.

Hoffman, F. G. (2009). *Hybrid Threats: Reconceptualising the Evolving Character of Modern Conflict* (No. 220).

Hook, G. D., Gilson, J., Hughes, C. W., & Dobson, H. (2005). *Japan's International Relations: Politics, Economics, Security*. Abingdon: Routledge.

Hughes, G. (2020). War in the Grey Zone: Historical Reflections and Contemporary Implications. *Survival*, 62(3), 131–158.

Hunzeker, M. A. (2021). Taiwan's Defense Plans are Going Off the Rails. Retrieved December 20, 2021, from War On The Rocks website: https://warontherocks.com/2021/11/taiwans-defense-plans-are-going-off-the-rails/?utm_source=pocket_mylist.

IISS. (2020). The Military Balance 2020 Press Release. Retrieved from https://www.iiss.org/press/2020/military-balance-2020.

Japan's Legislation for Peace and Security Seamless Responses for Peace and Security of Japan and the International Community. (2015). Retrieved from http://www.mofa.go.jp/files/000143304.pdf.

Jordaan, E. (2017). The Emerging Middle Power Concept: Time to Say Goodbye? *South African Journal of International Affairs*, 24(3), 395–412. https://doi.org/10.1080/10220461.2017.1394218.

Kaczmarski, M. (2020). The Sino-Russian Relationship and the West. *Survival*, 62(6), 199–212.

Kapur, P. S. (2005). India and Pakistan's Unstable Peace: Why Nuclear South Asia Is Not Like Cold War Europe. *International Security*, 30(2), 127–152.

Kapusta, P. (2015). The Gray Zone. *Special Warfare*, 28(4), pp. 18–25.

Khurana, G. S. (2007). Security of Sea Lines: Prospects for India–Japan Cooperation. *Strategic Analysis*, 31, 139–153.

Kim, J., Warden, J. K., Mount, A., Rapp-Hooper, M., Narang, V., Panda, A., … Dodge, M. (2020). Colloquium: Deterring a Nuclear North Korea. *Survival*, 62, 29–59.

Kim, L. (2021). A Hawkish Dove? President Moon Jae-in and South Korea's Military Buildup. Retrieved December 16, 2021, from War On The Rocks website: https://warontherocks.com/2021/09/a-hawkish-dove-president-moon-jae-in-and-south-koreas-military-buildup.

Kim, N. (2011). Korea on the Brink: Reading the Yonp'yong Shelling and its Aftermath. *Journal of Asian Studies*, 70(2), 337–356. https://doi.org/10.1017/S0021911811000908.

Kline, J. E., & Hughes, W. P. (2012). Between Peace and the Air-sea Battle A War at Sea Strategy. *Naval War College Review*, 65(4), pp. 1–7.

Koda, Y. (2010). The Emerging Republic of Korea Navy A Japanese Perspective. *Naval War College Review*, 63–2(Spring 2010), 13–34. Retrieved from http://www.usnwc.edu/getattachment/c54ee0a4-987f-4a66-800e-ef88de9381d1/The-Emerging-Republic-of-Korea-Navy--A-Japanese-Pe.

Krepinevich, A. F., & Watts, B. (2003). *Meeting the Anti-Access and Area-Denial Challenge*. Retrieved from https://csbaonline.org/research/publications/a2ad-anti-access-area-denial.

Kristiadi, J. (2001). Indonesia: Redefining Military Professionalism. In M. Alagappa (Ed.), *Military Professionalism in Asia: Conceptual and Emipirical Perspectives* (pp. 93–110). Honolulu: East-West Center.

Ladwig III, W. C. (2008). A Cold Start for Hot Wars? The Indian Army's New Limited War Doctrine. *International Security*, 32(3), 158–190.

Lai, D., & Miller, M. (2009). Introduction. In R. Kamphausen, D. Lai, & A. Scobell (Eds.), *Beyond the Strait: Pla Missions Other than Taiwan* (pp. 1–27). Carlisle: US Army War College.

Lalwani, S. (2020). Revelations and Opportunities: What the United States Can Learn from the Sino-Indian Crisis. Retrieved December 13, 2021, from War On The Rocks website: https://warontherocks.com/2020/07/revelations-and-opportunities-what-the-united-states-can-learn-from-the-sino-indian-crisis/.

Le Mière, C. (2011a). Policing the Waves: Maritime Paramilitaries in the Asia-Pacific. *Survival*, 53(1), 133–146 .

Le Mière, C. (2011b). The Return of Gunboat Diplomacy. *Survival*, 53(5), 53–68. https://doi.org/10.1080/00396338.2011.621634.

Lee, M. Y. (2001). South Korea: From "New Professionalism" to "Old Professionalism". In M. Alagappa (Ed.), *Military Professionalism in Asia: Conceptual and Emipirical Perspectives* (pp. 47–59). Honolulu: East-West Center.

Li, N. (2011). The Evolution of China's Naval Strategy and Capabilities: From "Near Coast" and "Near Seas" to "Far Seas". In P. C. Saunders, C. Yung, M. Swaine, & A. N.-D. Yang (Eds.), *The Chinese Navy: Expanding Capabilities, Evolving Roles* (pp. 109–140). Washington, DC: National Defense University.

Lieven, A. (2011). Military Exceptionalism in Pakistan. *Survival*, 53(4), 53–68. https://doi.org/10.1080/00396338.2011.603562.

Liff, A. P., & Ikenberry, G. J. (2014). Racing toward Tragedy? China's Rise, Military Competition in the Asia Paciac, and the Security Dilemma. *International Security*, 39(2), 52–91. https://doi.org/10.1162/ISEC.

Lissner, R. F. (2018). What is Grand Strategy? Sweeping a Conceptual Minefield. *Texas National Security Review*, 2(1), 109–140.

Macdonald, A. (2018). Perpetual Transitions: The Institutionalization of Military Tutelage Systems in Myanmar and Thailand. *Asian Affairs(UK)*, 45(3–4), 139–164. https://doi.org/10.1080/00927678.2018.1538622.

Martinson, R. D. (2016). Shepherds of the South Seas. *Survival*, 58(3), 187–212.

Mastro, O. S., & Tarapore, A. (2017). Countering Chinese Coercion: The Case of Doklam. Retrieved from War On The Rocks website: https://warontherocks.com/2017/08/countering-chinese-coercion-the-case-of-doklam/.

McCraw, D. (2011). Change and Continuity in Strategic Culture: The Cases of Australia and New Zealand. *Australian Journal of International Affairs*, 65(2), 167–184. https://doi.org/10.1080/10357718.2011.550102.

McEachern, P. (2008). Interest Groups in North Korean Politics. *Journal of East Asian Studies*, 8(2), 235–258.

Measuring Military Capability: Progress, Problems and Future Direction. (1986). Retrieved from http://www.gao.gov/assets/210/208215.pdf.

Medcalf, R. (2020). *Indo-Pacific Empire: China, America and the Contest for the World's Pivotal Region.* Manchester: Manchester University Press.

Michishita, N. (2010). *North Korea's Military-Diplomatic Campaigns, 1966–2008.* Abingdon: Routledge.

Milevski, L. (2019). Grand Strategy is Attrition: The Logic of Integrating Various Forms of Power in Conflict. In *Strategic Studies Institute.* US Army War College.

Military and Security Developments Involving the People's Republic of China 2020 Annual Report to Congress. (2020). Retrieved from https://media.defense.gov/2020/Sep/01/2002488689/-1/-1/1/2020-DOD-CHINA-MILITARY-POWER-REPORT-FINAL.PDF.

Mohan, C. R. (2012). *Samundra Manthan Sino-Indian Rivalry in the Indo-Pacific.* Washington, DC: Carnegie Endowment for International Peace.

National Security Strategy, Japan. (2013). Retrieved from https://www.mofa.go.jp/fp/nsp/page1we_000081.html. Accessed 21 February 2020.

Ng, K. P. (2005). Interpreting China's Military Power: Doctrine Makes readiness. In *Interpreting China's Military Power: Doctrine Makes Readiness.* https://doi.org/10.4324/9780203325902.

Overholt, W. H. (2008). *Asia, America and the Transformation of Geopolitics.* Cambridge: Cambridge University Press.

Panda, A. (2020). Why the 'Old Normal' Along the Sino-Indian Border Can No Longer Stand. *The Diplomat.* Retrieved from https://thediplomat.com/2020/07/why-the-old-normal-along-the-sino-indian-border-can-no-longer-stand/.

Pant, H. V., & Joshi, Y. (2016). The American "Pivot" and the Indian Navy: It's Hedging All the Way. In G. Kennedy & V. Pant Harsh (Eds.), *Assessing Maritime Power in the Asia-Pacific the Impact of American Strategic Re-Balance* (pp. 185–205). Oxon: Routledge.

Pyle, K. B. (2007). *Japan Rising the Resurgence of Japanese Power and Purpose.* New York: Public Affairs.

Rácz, A. (2015). *Russia's Hybrid War in Ukraine Breaking the Enemy's Ability to Resist* (No. 43).

Rai, A. (2018). Quadrilateral Security Dialogue 2 (Quad 2.0)–A Credible Strategic Construct or Mere "Foam in the Ocean"? *Maritime Affairs, 14*(2), 138–148. https://doi.org/10.1080/09733159.2019.1572260.

Samuels, R. J. (2007). *Securing Japan: Tokyo's Grand Startgy and the Future of East Asia.* Ithaca: Cornell University Press.

Sand, E. (2020). Desperate Measures: The Effects of Economic Isolation on Warring Powers. *Texas National Security Review, 3*(2), 12–37.

Scobell, A., Burke, E. J., Cooper, C. A., Lilly, S., Ohlandt, C. J. R., Warner, E., & Williams, J. D. (2020). *China's Grand Strategy: Trends, Trajectories, and Long-Term Competition.* Retrieved from https://www.rand.org/pubs/research_reports/RR2798.html.

Sevastopulo, D. (2021, November 13). Australia Vows to Help US Defend Taiwan from Chinese Attacks. *Financial Times.* Retrieved from https://www.ft.com/content/231df882-6667-4145-bc92-d1a54bccf333.

Silva, diego lopes da, Tian, N., Marksteiner, A., & World. (2021). Trends in World Military Expenditure, 2020. In *SIPRI Fact Sheet.* Retrieved from https://reliefweb.int/report/world/sipri-fact-sheet-april-2021-trends-world-military-expenditure-2020.

Status of World Nuclear Forces. (n.d.). Retrieved November 25, 2021, from Federation of American Scientists website: https://fas.org/issues/nuclear-weapons/status-world-nuclear-forces/.

Sugden, Bruce M. (2019). A Primer on Analyzing Nuclear Competitions. *Texas National Security Review, 2*(3), 105–126. https://doi.org/10.17146/aij.2007.105.

Tanner, M. S. (2009). How China Manages Internal Security Challenges and Its Impact on Pla Missions. In R. Kamphausen, D. Lai, & A. Scobell (Eds.), *Beyond the Strait: Pla Missions Other Than Taiwan* (pp. 39–98). Carlisle: Strategic Studies Institute, U.S. Army War College.

Tarapore, A. (2020). *The Army in Indian Military Strategy: Rethink Doctrine or Risk Irrelevance.* Retrieved from https://carnegieindia.org/2020/08/10/army-in-indian-military-strategy-rethink-doctrine-or-risk-irrelevance-pub-82426.

Tellis, A. J., Bially, J., Layne, C., & McPherson, M. (2000). *Measuring National Power in the Postindustrial Age.* Retrieved from http://www.rand.org/pubs/monograph_reports/MR1110.html.

Timbie, J., & Ellis jr., J. O. (2021). A Large Number of Small Things: A Porcupine Strategy for Taiwan. *Texas National Security Review,* 5(1). Retrieved from https://tnsr.org/2021/12/a-large-number-of-small-things-a-porcupine-strategy-for-taiwan/.

Ungerer, C. (2007). The "Middle Power" Concept in Australian Foreign Policy. *Australian Journal of Politics and History,* 53(4), 538–551. https://doi.org/10.1111/j.1467-8497.2007.00473.x.

Upadhyay, S. (2021). Covid-19 and Quad's "Soft" Reorientation. *Research in Globalization,* 3, pp. 1–6.

van Tol, J., Gunzinger, M., Krepinevich, A. F., & Thomas, J. (2010). *AirSea Battle: A Point-of-Departure Operational Concept.* Retrieved from https://csbaonline.org/research/publications/airsea-battle-concept/publication/1.

White, H. (2007). Australia–South Pacific. In B. Taylor (Ed.), *Australia as an Asia Pacific Regional Power Friendships in Flux?* (pp. 117–128). Oxon: Routledge.

White, H. (2020). Facing an Uncertain Future. *New Zealand International Review,* 45(2), 2–5.

Wiegand, K. E., & Ryou-Ellison, H. J. (2020). U.S. and Chinese Strategies, International Law, and the South China Sea. *Journal of Peace and War Studies,* 2, 49–68.

Wisniewski, R. (2018). EU-NATO Cooperation in Countering Hybrid Threats: Comparing Capabilities and Defining Roles. In C. Morsut & D. Irrera (Eds.), *Security Beyond the State: The EU in an Age of Transformation* (pp. 93–114). Opladen: Barbara Budrich Publishers.

Wiśniewski, R. (2019). Military-Technical Cooperation between Russian Federation and People's Republic of China – Drivers and Perspectives of Future Evolution. *The Copernicus Journal of Political Studies,* 1, 5–19. https://doi.org/10.12775/cjps.2019.001.

Wuthnow, J., & Saunders, P. C. (2017). Chinese Military Reform in the Age of Xi Jinping: Drivers, Challenges, and Implications. In *China Strategic Perspective* (Vol. 10). Center for the Study of Chinese Military Affairs Institute for National Strategic Studies National Defense University.

Yung, C. D., Rustici, R., Kardon, I., & Wiseman, J. (2010). *China's Out of Area Naval Operations: Case Studies, Trajectories, Obstacles, and Potential Solutions* (No. 3). Retrieved from https://ndupress.ndu.edu/Publications/Article/717794/chinas-out-of-area-naval-operations-case-studies-trajectories-obstacles-and-pot/.

10 Energy security in the Indo-Pacific region

Case studies of China, India and Japan

Rafał Ulatowski

Economically, the Indo-Pacific region has been the most dynamic region of the world in the 21st century. The economic success of China, India and other emerging markets has created a commodity boom. Due to their limited local resource bases, the three largest economies of the region – China, Japan and India – are the leading commodity importers (like the United States) (Büyükşahin et al. 2016), and energy security has become a priority for their policy makers. Dependence on foreign oil supply is especially worrying for them due to the political and economic relevance of this resource. As global oil production spare capacity started to shrink in the 21st century, the danger of conflicts over limited resources began to be discussed (Calder 1996; Klare 2013).

At the end of the second decade of the 21st century, the rise of China and a resurgence of Russian power have altered the global balance of power – from unipolarity to multipolarity, with three great powers, the United States, China and Russia, dominating international relations (Mearsheimer 2019). As the United States and China have the biggest potential, the fiercest competition is between these two and takes place mainly in the Indo-Pacific region (Mearsheimer 2021). Also in the Indo-Pacific, regional powers are reshaping their foreign policies to cope with the deteriorating relations between the United States and China (Liu 2020; Koga 2020; Rajagopalan 2020; Taylor 2020). The region is now the focal point of great power competition (Beeson & Lee-Brown 2021), with energy-related issues playing a significant role in the strategies of regional powers (Scott 2019a, b)

The energy sector is enormously important for economic as well as political power. Since World War I, the dependence of many countries on foreign oil supplies has been used by their adversaries as a means of coercion (Kelanic 2016). Today, worries that such dependence may be used for political purposes are expressed mainly in China, though in other countries as well (Mirski 2013; Cunningham 2020). The purpose of this chapter is to compare the energy security policies of the three largest Indo-Pacific powers: China, Japan and India. Decisions taken by their authorities have a profound impact on the region and the world. I argue that they employ a diversified mix of instruments for enhancing their energy security, a mix that includes improving energy efficiency, investing in nuclear and renewable energy, and engaging in energy diplomacy to secure oil and gas supplies. All three governments are seeking to reduce the role of fossil fuels in their energy mix.

The chapter has the following structure. Firstly, the term "energy security" is discussed in the context of political realism and liberalism. Secondly, challenges to the energy security of China, India and Japan are discussed. Thirdly, their energy policies are analysed. Finally, I compare the energy diplomacy they are conducting.

DOI: 10.4324/9781003336143-14

Energy security in the context of political realism and liberalism

The issue of energy security emerged for the first time in the early 20th century in Great Britain, when the Royal Navy shifted away from coal to oil as the fuel of choice for its fleet. Sir Winston Churchill offered an early definition of energy security in 1913, arguing that "safety and certainty in oil lie in variety and variety alone" (*The Economist* 2005).

There is no universally accepted definition of energy security (Checchi et al. 2009: 1); 45 of them were identified in the literature (Sovacool 2011: 3–6). The concept is "abstract, elusive, vague, inherently difficult and blurred" (Löschel et al. 2010: 1665). Although some scholars reduce the issue of energy security to imperfect market competition and advocate support for the free market (Noël 2008), most scholars see energy security in a broader sense, as "encompassing technology, fuels, trade, behaviour, institutions, the environment, and education" (Sovacool & Vivoda 2012: 951). Definitions of energy security can be divided into three groups. The first group emphasises undisturbed access to energy resources, and arose under the impact of the oil crisis of the 1970s. From it sprang the two other groups of definitions. The second group highlights not only access to energy resources but also the cost of the energy supply, while the third group include further aspects such as the quality of energy services or environmental sustainability (Winzer 2012: 4–6). Despite their broad range, the most popular definition is still that proposed by the International Energy Agency (IEA). The IEA defines energy security as "the uninterrupted availability of energy sources at an affordable price" (IEA 2019).

Energy security became the focus of political debates in the 1970s, as a consequence of the first oil crisis. Realism and liberalism, two major theories of international relations, offer different perspectives on energy security. Realists concentrate on interstate relations. They point out that international relations are in a state of anarchy, states that are primary actors distrust each other, and there is a permanent danger of war between them. Their research on energy security is based on four assumptions. Firstly, the main component of a state's strength is access to and control over energy reserves, because access to energy is crucial for economic strength and military might. Secondly, reserves of raw materials are in decline, and accessing them is becoming increasingly difficult. Thirdly, competition between states over access to and control over reserves is increasing. Fourthly, the probability of conflicts, and even wars, over control of reserves is also increasing. Liberals criticise the realist approach. They claim that progress in international relations is possible and emphasise the role of the development of international institutions and regimes. They argue in favour of trade liberalisation. They see economic cooperation as an instrument for increasing prosperity, strengthening political cooperation and preventing wars. They also address the economic consequences of resource wealth, as well as to the importance of issues such as corruption and the links between oil companies and governments. Liberals argue in favour of improved transparency and better regulation, the development of corporate social responsibility programmes by oil companies, the promotion of good governance, international and regional cooperation in the energy sector, and the liberalisation of the energy sector (Dannreuther 2010; Van de Graaf et al. 2016 15).

In this chapter, I take a realist view on energy security. Although there are regional initiatives for depoliticising energy (Goldthau & Sitter 2015), energy is still an important foreign policy instrument in the hands of governments. In the energy sector, market forces constantly clash with actions taken by governments. Since realism concentrates on the great powers – the most important actors in international relations – another consequence is that the energy policies of minor powers are not considered.

Challenges for energy security in China, India and Japan

China, Japan and India face a number of challenges to their energy security.

Firstly, they are poor countries in terms of energy resources; China and India have significant coal reserves, but they are poor in oil and gas. China's share of global coal reserves is 13.2%, and India's 9.9%. China's share of global proven oil reserves is 1.5%, and India's only 0.3%. China's share of global proven natural gas reserves is 4.2%, and India's 0.7%. Japan has no significant reserves of fuels at all (BP 2020) as shown in Table 10.1.

Secondly, rising oil demand has caused an upsurge in resource nationalism in the 21st century. Access to energy resources has become difficult, and producing countries (such as Russia, but also Venezuela and Iran) see energy as a political instrument (Stegen 2011); consequently, oil importers cannot be sure that market mechanisms alone will ensure supply (Vivoda 2009; Dreyer & Stang 2014).

Thirdly, all three countries are dependent on foreign oil and gas, with Persian Gulf countries being their primary suppliers. This has an adverse effect on their energy security, especially since the stability of Persian Gulf supplies is regularly questioned (Qiang Ji et al. 2019)

Fourthly, dependence on the sea lines of communication is another challenge. Oil transported from the Persian Gulf to India goes through the Strait of Hormuz, and shipments to China and Japan also need to pass through the Strait of Malacca (EIA 2017). The security of sea lines of communication is increasingly questionable. The Persian Gulf and the Indian Ocean have been traditionally controlled by the United States. That worries Chinese politicians. In response, China has increased its naval presence in the region in the early 21st century – a matter of concern for India and Japan, and a challenge for United States (Frankel 2011; Upadhyaya 2017, 2019; Bhaskar 2010).

Energy policies of China, India and Japan

Japan was the first country in Asia to become an industrial power. In the two decades following WWII, it experienced an "economic miracle." The Japanese economy was modernised and transformed into one based on oil. That transformation proved to be

Table 10.1 Share of China, India and Japan in global reserves of coal, oil and natural gas at the end of 2019

Country	Coal	Oil	Natural gas
China	13.2	1.5	4.2
India	9.9	0.3	0.7
Japan	–	–	–

Source: BP 2020.

Table 10.2 Japan's Total primary Energy consumption (TPEC) in 2019

Source of energy	Share in %
Petroleum and other liquids	40
Coal	26
Natural gas	21
Nuclear energy	3
Hydroelectric power	4
Other renewables	6

Source: EIA 2020a.

problematic in 1973, when Arab oil exporters started an oil embargo and oil prices quadrupled (Duffield 2015: 196–198).

Although Japanese governments have been working for decades to improve the country's energy security, Japan still faces several challenges. Among industrialised countries, it has the lowest ratio of domestic energy production to total consumption, the highest share of oil in total energy consumption (along with Italy), and is the industrialised country most dependent on Middle East oil supplies (Calder 2008).

In 2019, Japan was still the world's fifth-largest energy consumer, although for years its total primary energy consumption (TPEC) has been gradually declining. Japan's TPEC was still dominated by fossil fuels, divided as follows: petroleum and other liquids 40%; coal 26%; natural gas 21% as shown in Table 10.2. The share of nuclear energy was 3%; hydroelectric 4%; other renewables 6%. In 2010, the share of nuclear energy was 13%, but after the accident at the Fukushima Daiichi power plant in 2011 all of the country's nuclear power plants were temporarily shut down. Nuclear energy was replaced by fossil fuels and renewables (EIA 2020a).

Japan is successfully reducing the energy intensity of its economy. Compared with 2005, its total primary energy supply (TPES) has gone down by 16% after peaking in the first decade of the 21st century. For decades, Japanese energy policy was centred on developing nuclear power to reduce the country's dependence on foreign fuel suppliers and to limit greenhouse emissions. In 2009, at the 15th Conference of the Parties (COP15) Japan pledged a 25% reduction of GHG emissions by 2020 against 1990. This plan assumed a growing share of nuclear energy in electricity production, from 30% to 50%. The shutting down of all nuclear powerplants in 2011 left a gap of around 30% in the electricity supply – the biggest challenge faced by the Japanese economy in decades. Since then, nuclear power plants have been replaced by power plants burning LNG, oil and coal. To manage the crisis, energy savings were stepped up, and since 2012 Japan's renewable electricity capacity has increased. Yet, despite these efforts, dependence on energy imports rose from 80% in 2010 to 94% in 2013. Annual CO_2 emissions in power generation increased by 110 million tonnes. Electricity prices increased by 16% for households and 25% for industry. In 2014, the Japanese government published its 4th Strategic Energy Plan (SEP), on the basis of which in 2015 the Ministry of Economy, Trade and Industry (METI) adopted a "Long-Term Energy Supply and Demand Outlook" to 2030. The key assumption was a reduction in the share of fossil fuels in electricity generation, a return to the use of nuclear power plants, and increased use of renewables. According to the Intended Nationally Determined Contributions (INDC) to COP21, Japan will reduce GHG emissions by 26% from 2013 to 2030, and the goals of energy security, economic efficiency, and environmental protection and safety should be balanced. To implement the INDC successfully, three issues are critical: energy efficiency, increasing the renewable energy supply and restarting nuclear power generation. The Fukushima Daichi accident prompted reforms of the electricity market in Japan that entailed a paradigm shift from regional monopolies towards a competition-friendly environment. Firstly, in April 2015 the Organization for Cross-Regional Coordination of Transmission Operators (OCCTO) began operating, with the goal of assessing generation adequacy and ensuring that adequate transmission capacity is available. Secondly, in February 2016 a full liberalisation of the retail market took place. Thirdly, in April 2020 the energy transmission and distribution companies were unbound from the generation and retail segments. The gas market has also been reformed, with the introduction of full retail market competition in 2017 and improved third-party access to pipelines and LNG terminals. Japan is also promoting renewables, which are seen as a strategic opportunity that will limit dependence on imported energy resources. In July 2012, Japan introduced feed-in tariffs to increase generation; this led to rapid growth in installed capacity. But since renewables require a more flexible energy infrastructure, additional investments are needed. Photovoltaic energy dominates renewables, but wind and geothermal energy are also expanding (IEA 2016).

The 5th Strategic Energy Plan published in 2019 declared a target of an 80% reduction in GHGs by 2050, focused on energy transformation and decarbonisation. But no clear plan on how to achieve these goals is found in the document. Different scenarios and priorities are discussed that the government can choose from after a scientific review. Renewables are now seen as a major source of power in the future, and nuclear energy as only one option for decarbonisation (*Strategic Energy Plan* 2018). The lack of precision in the 5th Strategic Energy Plan has been seen as a sign of weakness on the part of Japan's leaders (Takeuchi 2019). Nevertheless, in October 2020 there was a shift in Japan's energy policy. In his first speech to parliament, the then new prime minister Yoshihide Suga declared that Japan will achieve carbon dioxide neutrality by 2050 and will build a "green society." He declared a need for deep changes in the economy and society. The details of the new energy plan should be presented by the summer of 2021, though Suga has already declared that nuclear energy will continue to play an important role in Japan's energy mix (Welter 2020).

As in Japan, in China energy security is at the top of national priorities (Taylor 2014). Table 10.3 shows that TPEC of China in 2019 was dominated by coal, with a share of 58%. Petroleum and other liquids had a 20% share, hydro energy and

Table 10.3 China's Total primary Energy consumption (TPEC) in 2019

Source of energy	Share in %
Coal	58
Petroleum and other liquids	20
Hydroelectric power	8
Natural gas	8
Nuclear energy	2
Renewables	5

Source: EIA 2020c.

natural gas 8% each. The share of nuclear energy was 2%, that of renewables 5% (EIA 2020c).

This energy mix reflects the Chinese resource base. China is rich in coal, but poor in oil and gas. The country's energy policy has three main goals. Firstly, to ensure the security of supply. Secondly, to secure cheap energy resources to promote stability and rapid economic growth. Thirdly, to implement energy policies that are environmentally neutral. But, as David Robinson points out, there are tensions between these three goals. Natural gas is more environmentally friendly than locally-produced coal, but is more expensive, and there are concerns regarding the security of supply (Robinson 2013: 7). An important guideline for the situation in the Chinese energy sector is the 13th Five-Year Plan, which is seen as crucial for the Chinese energy sector on three levels. Firstly, there is the question of the transformation of the Chinese economy towards one that is consumer-driven. Secondly, the Chinese economy is in the process of rebalancing: demand for light petroleum products (jet fuel, gasoline) and petrochemicals is on the rise, while the prospects for diesel are pessimistic. Thirdly, environmental protection is a high priority for the Chinese government. 10 out of the 25 numerical targets in the 13th Five-Year Plan are related to the environment. The government plans to reduce the energy intensity of the economy by 15%; in 2010–2015, China managed to do so by 18.2%. The plan also reflects the country's desire to shift from oil-based fuels in the transport sector to alternative sources of energy (Meidan 2016). Researchers expect that the 14th Five-Year Plan will give priority to clean energy (Meidan 2020). Renewables are moving to the forefront of China's energy and economic transformation (Mathews 2019).

Although in the 1950s and 1960s rich oil fields were discovered (Daqing in 1959, Shengli in 1963, Dagang in 1964 and Liaohe in 1969), today these are described as legacy fields where production can only be sustained using expensive enhanced oil recovery techniques. To keep the production from these fields profitable, market prices have to be relatively high. Due to the oil price slump after 2014, production experienced downward pressure for three years (2016–2018), and only began to rise again in 2019. The role of natural gas in the energy mix is growing. The 13th Five-Year Plan foresees growth in local production from 134.1 billion m^3 in 2016 to 207 billion m^3 in 2020, and growth in imports from 73.3 billion m^3 in 2016 to 153 billion m^3 in 2020. The government is offering financial incentives to producers, especially for production of non-conventional gas, and projects growth in the share of natural gas in TPEC to 14% by 2030. Several factors contribute to the growing consumption of natural gas in China. Firstly, the Chinese government is enforcing a switch from coal to gas for power generation, industrial use, residential use and commercial heating in order to combat deteriorating air quality, especially in winter in north-eastern China. In 2017, the government set strict environmental targets. Secondly, global gas prices declined in the second half of the 2010s, improving gas competitiveness. Thirdly, gas is increasingly used in China's transport system. Fourthly, developing and improving gas transport infrastructure will result in a better supply to centres of demand. Yet at the end of 2018, China's government relaxed its coal-to-gas switch programme due to the natural gas shortage observed during the winter of 2017/2018 in the northern part of the country. Together with slower economic growth in 2019, there was less demand for gas than in 2017 or 2018. The future role of natural gas in the Chinese energy mix depends on three factors: firstly, the environmental policies of the government; secondly, the future of the coal-to-gas switch; and thirdly, infrastructure development

(Zhen Wang & Qing Xue 2017). With coal being China's most important energy resource, future coal policy will be crucial to achieving the country's goal of becoming "carbon neutral" by 2060. That goal was set by president Xi Jinping in a speech to the United Nations General Assembly (Shepherd et al. 2020). In 2018, nearly 60% of coal in China was consumed in the power sector, the rest in industry (mainly steel and cement production) and heating. The future of coal depends on climate policy, fuel switching and the move towards a less energy-intensive economy. Cleaner fuels and energy savings encourage a reduction in coal consumption, though the abundant local resource base and the government's promotion of clean coal technologies may help coal remain a pillar of China's energy system in the future. China is developing the infrastructure it needs to transport coal efficiently from production centres to places of high demand; the newly-opened Haoji Railway serves as an example of this. At the same time, China's government increasingly prefers renewables for electricity generation. China was the world largest wind energy producer in 2018, and in the same year solar power was its fastest growing source of electricity generation, with growth of 51% over 2017. This high rate has led to reductions in subsidies for solar power generation since 2016, due to overcapacity. Crucial to the future role of renewables in the Chinese energy mix will be the construction of transmission lines, including ultra-high-voltage (UHV) transmission lines. As with renewables, China is also intensively investing in nuclear energy. The Fukushima Daichi accident in Japan slowed down this process, but only temporarily. Currently, China has 46,000 MW of installed nuclear capacity, with more than half of that being added after 2015. An additional 11,000 MW of nuclear capacity is under construction, and several other nuclear power plants are at different stages of planning (EIA 2020c).

In India, even before independence in 1947 there was a clear need for a comprehensive energy policy, but none was formulated until the 1970s. Since then, however, energy has been a high priority (Kumar 2017). In India, the main threat to energy security is perceived as dependence on imported oil and natural gas (Sovacool & Vivoda, 2012: 960).

India has the lowest GDP per capita of the countries discussed here. Yet in 2018 it was the world's third-largest energy consumer (after China and the United States). As presented in Table 10.4, India's major sources of energy in 2018 were: coal, with a 45% share in total energy consumption; petroleum and other liquids at 26%; biomass and waste at 20%; and natural gas at 6%. The shares of nuclear power, hydroelectric power and other renewables were 1% each (EIA 2020b).

Table 10.4 India's Total primary Energy consumption (TPEC) in 2018

Source of energy	Share in %
Coal	45
Petroleum and other liquids	26
Biomass and waste	20
Natural gas	6
Nuclear energy	1
Hydroelectric power	1
Other renewables	1

Source: EIA 2020b.

Between 2007 and 2017, TPES increased by 55%. In 2017 it was 882 million tonnes of oil equivalent (Mtoe), of which 554 Mtoe were covered by local supply. India faces important energy challenges, including growing dependence on oil and gas imports, a low level of access to electricity, and wide use of traditional biomass in cooking, which causes indoor air pollution. Electricity generation has been dominated by coal, which is cheap and being increasingly produced in local mines, but is highly pollutive. Access to electricity has been improved thanks to active government policies. Between 2000 and 2019, around 750 million people obtained access to electricity. During the same period, liquefied petroleum gas replaced much traditional biomass in indoor cooking. India's government is also promoting solar photovoltaics as an alternative to off-grid electrification. India has made progress towards meeting UN Sustainable Development Goal 7 on delivering energy access, and has opened up its energy market to private investments. A single national power system has been created. The government is promoting a greater share of renewables. Yet a growing challenge is increasing demand for crude oil and natural gas, which can only be satisfied by imports. Local production, especially of oil, is stagnant. Oil consumption in India is continually growing and made India the world's third-largest consumer in 2017. Its total oil net imports were 3.4 million barrel per day (mb/d), up 54% from 2007. India's dependence on imported oil will increase. Local production peaked at 910 kb/d in 2011 and declined to 840kb/d by 2018. The IEA forecasts that India's oil consumption growth rate will surpass that of China in the mid-2020s. India's government prioritises reducing oil imports, increasing upstream investments and local production, diversifying its sources of oil imports, and supporting local companies in foreign investments. Driven by the desire for a more environmentally neutral energy system, the government plans to increase the share of natural gas from its current 6% up to 15% by 2030. Natural gas is being increasingly used in the residential and transport sectors. But in power generation its role is limited by cheap renewables and coal. As a consequence, between 2007 and 2017 the share of natural gas in TPES fell. Gas production in India has been stagnant since the early 2000s, at just above 30 billion cubic meter (bcm) a year; simultaneously, consumption rose, and India become an importer in 2003. India imports gas in the form of LNG. For years, Qatar was the main supplier, but since 2015 India has successfully diversified its suppliers, with Nigeria, Equatorial Guinea and Australia playing a growing role. In 2017, the share of Qatar in India's import fell to 49%. Although energy consumption in India is continuously growing, the energy intensity and emissions intensity of India's GDP have decreased by over 20% in the last decade (IEA 2020c).

The IEA forecasts a further increase in India's energy demand, which could double by 2040. Electricity demand is expected to triple. The structure of India's energy sector is changing. In a report, the IEA stated that in 2018 India's investments in solar PV were bigger than in all fossil fuel sources together. The importance of renewables in India's energy system is rising. At the end of November 2019, 84 GW out of 366 GW of total generating capacity were renewables. This 84 GW consisted of 32 GW from PV, about 37 GW from onshore wind, and the rest from small hydro power plants. The original target of 175 GW of grid connected renewables capacity by 2022 was raised in 2018 to 227 GW by 2022. In 2019, at the United Nation's Climate Summit, Prime Minister Narendra Modi declared that India will increase its renewable energy capacity up to 450 GW, although he did not specify a date. Nuclear power, which could limit the use and imports of fossil fuels, still plays a limited role in India's electricity generation. Only 2% of India's installed generation capacity is nuclear (IEA 2020). Japan has been seen as an important partner for the development of nuclear energy, but cooperation between the two countries, while frequently discussed, faces serious obstacles. The most important of these is the fact that India does not participate in the Nuclear Non-Proliferation Treaty, though this obstacle was eased somewhat by an India-USA agreement on nuclear energy cooperation. Also, the possibility of India becoming an important partner for Japan in diplomacy, security and the economy favoured cooperation on civil nuclear technology. The Fukushima Daichi accident, however, along with the pre-existing security concerns of Japan, weakened this prospect (Nakanishi 2014).

Energy diplomacy of China, India and Japan compared

Because of their limited local energy reserves Japan, China and India have all developed energy diplomacy (Lesbirel 2013; Lee 2019; Chaudhuri 2015). Although no universal definition exists (Uludag et al. 2013; Bovan et al. 2020), most authors follow the definition proposed by Andreas Goldthau: "the use of foreign policy to secure access to energy supplies abroad and to promote (mostly bilateral, that is, government to government) cooperation in the energy sector." This definition suggests that the primary units of analysis are states or states actors; that the primary driver behind the conclusion of oil and gas deals is not necessarily maximising business opportunities but national security goals; and that "the underlying cost-benefit calculations do not follow an economic logic but rather a political one" (Goldthau 2010: 28).

China's energy diplomacy has the biggest scope of the three analysed countries and has been successful in terms of diversifying sources of supply (Vivoda & Manicom 2011). There are two perspectives on Chinese energy diplomacy. The first is a "realist" perspective, according to which China's energy diplomacy seeks to balance resource-rich countries (such as Iran and Russia) against the United States, and is connected with China's increased global presence. The second is a liberal integrationist perspective that views China as increasingly recognising the role of market forces (Dannreuther 2011).

Although in the 1970s and the 1980s China was also able to export oil in substantial quantities, due to rising consumption and stagnant production by 1993 it had become an oil importer. In order to improve the efficiency of the industry, make it competitive on a global scale and separate government functions from the major industries, the Chinese government conducted six rounds of industry reforms beginning in early 1982 (Liao 2015). Three NOCs were established: China National Petroleum Corporation (CNPC), China Petroleum and Chemical Corporation (Sinopec), and China National Offshore Oil Corporation (CNOOC). These are vertically integrated companies and dominate the local market.

The history of China's energy diplomacy goes back to 1992, when CNPC acquired the rights to develop blocks in the aging Talala oil field in Peru. By the mid-1990s it was also investing in Sudan and Kazakhstan. But in the early 1990s, China's "top leaders did not envision overseas upstream investments as a sound strategy, and instead even emphasised continued domestic investments" (Xiaojie Xu 2007: 4). That situation changed as Chinese dependence on oil imports increased. The Chinese government became determined to transform CNPC, Sinopec and CNOOC into global players (Chih-shian Liou 2009: 671) and directed the country's energy diplomacy towards the Middle East, Africa, Latin America, Russia and Central Asia. Most Chinese investments were in Africa, with Angola, Sudan, the Democratic Republic of Congo and Gabon being the prime targets of oil companies. This development of Chinese-African relations in the energy sector was facilitated by the withdrawal of the United States and the EU from playing an active role in Africa. China has been frequently criticised for cooperating with non-democratic governments that violate human rights (Hongyi Harry Lai 2007: 522–529), and Chinese companies have been seen to prefer high-risk investments in countries with institutional deficiencies. This behaviour contradicts the conventional investment according to which international investors should look for countries with "good" institutional qualities that reduce political risk and promote a stable business environment (Buckley et al. 2007; Yuanfei Kang & Fuming Jiang 2012; Ramasamy et al. 2012; for the opposite view see Jiao-Hui Yang et al. 2018).

The global financial crisis in the autumn of 2008 caused commodity prices to fall, and many oil producing countries found themselves in financial difficulty. China used this opportunity to offer them loans guaranteed by oil supplies. In the years 2009 and 2010 alone, the "loans-for-oil" offered to nine countries were worth USD 77 billion. All of the borrower countries were outside the Middle East, which suggests that those contracts should help China diversify (Kennedy 2015: 29). China also achieved successes in diversifying its gas supply. The first milestone was the start of LNG imports in 2006, followed by natural gas pipeline imports from Central Asia in 2010, and then from Russia in 2019. Since 2017, China has been the second-largest LNG importer in the world after Japan. China has diversified its gas suppliers, with 38% of imports as pipeline natural gas, and 62% as LNG, the latter mainly from Australia (29% of imports), Turkmenistan (25%), and Qatar (9%) (EIA 2020c).

Despite the successful expansion of Chinese NOCs, the strategy does not enjoy universal support. There are four arguments against it. Firstly, NOCs mostly sell oil produced by their foreign subsidiaries in the global market and do not send it to China. Secondly, when they do sell oil produced by their foreign subsidiaries in China, they demand market prices, and there is no guarantee that in the event of a global shortage oil produced abroad by Chinese NOCs would be available for China. Thirdly, some analyses show that Chinese NOCs have overpaid for foreign assets, especially at the beginning of their global expansion. They suffer from *latecomer syndrome*. Fourthly, Chinese NOCs have invested in many countries that are in conflict with the United States and Western European countries, which may become a foreign policy liability for China (Kennedy 2015: 26–27).

Since 2017 China has been the biggest crude oil importer. In 2019, it imported an average of 10.1 million b/d, with Saudi Arabia and Russia as its biggest suppliers, accounting for 16% and 15% of imports, respectively (EIA 2020c).

India also exercises energy diplomacy. Its Ministry of Petroleum and Natural Gas (MOPNG) is responsible for the oil and gas sector in India, including regulation of the entire oil sector value chain. Several state companies are active in the oil business: Oil and Natural Gas Corporation (ONGC) (the biggest oil company in India); Oil India Limited (OIL), Indian Oil Corporation Ltd (IOCL), Bharat Petroleum Corporation Limited, and Gas Authority of India Ltd. (GAIL). Private companies such as Reliance Industries (RIL) and Essar Oil have also emerged as important players in India's oil industry although, unlike their state-owned competitors, they concentrate on the refinery business (IEA 2020b).

The history of Indian energy diplomacy goes back to the 1950s. In 1958, ONGC considered exploring for oil in Nepal, and in the 1950s and 1960s Kuwait, Saudi Arabia and Iran offered to cooperate with ONGC. These early initiatives failed, for international and domestic reasons. At that time there was a strong belief that oil would be found in India. Later, ONGC decided to invest together with AGIP, Philips and NIOC in an offshore field in Iran. In 1973, ONGC was also awarded service contracts in Iraq and Tanzania. But the first major international expansion started only in the 21st century (Madan 2007: 50). In 2000, the government of India commissioned Hydrocarbon Vision 2025, recommending that exploration efforts be intensified and access secured to reserves in energy-rich countries in order to ensure sustainable long-term supplies (*India Hydrocarbon Vision – 2025* 2000). In 2005, Prime Minister Manmohan Singh set out three goals of India's energy diplomacy. Firstly, to coordinate investments by Indian NOCs and private companies in overseas projects. Secondly, to coordinate the construction of pipelines to mitigate dependence on sea lines of communication. Thirdly, to support the conclusion of bilateral agreements between India and resource-rich countries (Madan 2010: 5). The list of potential partners deemed the most attractive in Hydrocarbon Vision 2025 included Russia, Iran, Iraq and the countries of North Africa (*India Hydrocarbon Vision – 2025* 2000). Together with Angola, Myanmar, Sudan, Syria, Venezuela and Vietnam, they are now investment targets of Indian companies (Madan 2007: 23). To expand its relations with resource-rich countries, India uses a variety of economic and non-economic incentives, such as preferential loans. They have been taken out by Angola, Brazil, Chad, Colombia, Côte d'Ivoire, Gabon, Iran, Kazakhstan, Myanmar, Nigeria, Russia, Sudan, Syria, Trinidad and Tobago, Vietnam and others. India is also developing military cooperation with energy-rich countries, for example, in the joint exercises run by the Indian and Nigerian armies in 2007 (Madan 2010: 11).

But the argument that the international expansion of Indian oil companies furthers India's energy security is controversial. Firstly, the oil produced by Indian companies abroad is mostly sold on the global market. Secondly, it is said that ONGC, the major NOC of India and a key instrument in its energy diplomacy, overpaid for foreign assets, and suffers from *latecomer syndrome*. Thirdly, ONGC's technological capability is inadequate for it to take full advantage of its foreign assets. Fourthly, there are worries that India's energy diplomacy may adversely affect its foreign policy. This is especially important in the face of a US-Indian rapprochement and a strengthening of bilateral relations between these two countries. Fifthly, supporters of market solutions argue that oil can be purchased on the market. Sixthly, foreign expansion may also reduce investments in the local industry (Dadwal 2012; Madan 2007: 51–53; 2010).

The Indian authorities are struggling not just to secure access to resource reserves overseas, but also to develop alternative, non-maritime oil transport routes. Several pipeline projects have been discussed in the 21st century, though there are many challenges, and for now India remains dependent on sea transport for deliveries of energy resources (Kulkarni 2013).

Although both China and India actively pursue energy diplomacy, Chinese companies are much more successful than their Indian competitors, for various reasons. Chinese companies have access to financing from Chinese banks, and diplomatic support. China is also developing military relations with oil-rich countries and offers diplomatic support as a permanent member of the UN Security Council, enticing such countries with economic assistance and offering strategic partnerships. While India's government offers a similar set of instruments, it is on a much smaller scale. The international expansion of Indian companies is mainly driven by commercial reasons, and interestingly, the Indian government also sometimes inhibits that expansion. In 2005, OVL was not allowed to bid for exploration blocks in Ecuador and Nigeria, and in 2007 it was again not allowed to bid for a block in Nigeria. Conversely, in 2012 OVL wanted to withdraw from a block in the South China Sea off the coast of Vietnam but was forbidden from doing so by the Indian government for the sake of maintaining strong relations with Vietnam. The implementation of effective energy diplomacy in India is also hampered by institutional fragmentation (Meckling et al. 2015).

Although India and China mainly compete on the energy market, there are also signs of cooperation between them. In 2006, they concluded a Memorandum of Understanding on cooperation in the production of energy resources, investments in pipelines and refineries, though the document was nothing more than an expression of goodwill (Hulbert 2010). Cooperation between India and China is hampered by political contradictions, a lack of trust (Heiduk & Paul 2015), and similarities between their companies. Both are rich in capital, but their technological capabilities are modest compared with those of European or US companies, which have the state-of-the-art technologies (Wysoczyńska 2011: 196).

Although the government of Japan supports the liberal order of the oil market, in the face of increased competition for energy resources it also decided to develop energy diplomacy. This shift was first felt in Japan's National Energy Strategy of 2006, and was confirmed by a number of politicians, as well. In 2014, a Strategic Energy Plan was approved. It indicates "diversification of supply sources" as one of the priorities. At the same time, international institutions such as the IEA are encouraging Japan to diversify its energy supply. But in fact, Japan's energy diplomacy is neither active nor successful. Japan still imports most of its oil from the Middle East (mainly Saudi Arabia and the United Arab Emirates), although that region's role as a source of supply has been declining. Russia's share in Japan's imports increased from negligible levels in 2005 to 8.3% in 2015 (IEA 2016). Japan is trying to reduce its dependence on Middle Eastern suppliers but at the same time develop mutually favourable relations with them. On the other hand, Japan has achieved diversified and well-balanced list of LNG suppliers; Australia and Malaysia are the largest, although LNG from the United States is on the rise. Since the role of LNG in Japan's energy mix is supposed to grow as that of oil falls, the country's energy security should improve (EIA 2020a). Rather than gaining direct access to energy sources outside the country, Japan is employing a multifaceted strategy that includes maintaining a close alliance with the United States, which protects sea lines of communication; maintaining friendly relations with resource-rich countries; and engaging in maritime cooperation with Asian countries (Lam 2009).

China, India and Japan all participate in developing global energy governance. India is trying to contribute to cooperation between suppliers and consumers, and also to cooperation among consumers, especially in Asia, and it is very much interested in taking part in transforming the global energy system to a clean energy system (Dubash 2011). China is an even more active global player. It participates in many existing energy organisations and is creating one of its own. Because of the weight it carries globally, China is transforming global energy governance (Christoffersen 2016; Xuantong Zhu Julia 2016). Yet, despite numerous voices and arguments supporting cooperation on energy between the countries of the Indo-Pacific (Fengying Chen & Jiejun Ni 2008; Li Zhidong 2007; Wishnick 2009; Itoh 2008) and numerous declarations on energy cooperation from the governments of those countries, things have not moved beyond non-binding obligations. One of the forums for such cooperation is ASEAN+3 (Yoshimatsu 2012).

Conclusion

The energy security policies of China, India and Japan have several features in common.

Firstly, these countries maximise the use of locally available resources. In China and in India these are mainly coal but also include oil and gas. The intensive use of coal in China and India shows how the security of supply and low prices take priority over environmental considerations. In contrast, in Japan, which is extremely resource-poor, almost all of the country's demand for fossil fuels must be satisfied with imports.

Secondly, the analysed countries are rich in technology and capital (Japan), or are becoming so (China and India), and this makes it possible for them to engage in developing alternative sources of energy supply. For decades, Japan successfully developed its nuclear energy sector, but this came to an abrupt halt after the accident at the Fukushima Daichi power plant. China is also successfully developing a nuclear energy sector, and India has nuclear power plants as well. At present, renewables are seen as the biggest opportunity for developing a cheap, indigenous energy supply. The countries of the Indo-Pacific are leaders in developing renewables, with the importance of climate protection gradually gaining in importance.

Thirdly, energy savings and energy efficiency play an important role. For decades, Japan has been seen as a leading nation in the creation of energy-efficient technologies, while the importance of the demand side is also recognised in China and India.

Fourthly, energy diplomacy has been developed in the three analysed countries. China has successfully used its NOCs to secure investments in oil and gas production. Close cooperation between oil companies, financial institutions and the government have made it possible for Chinese NOCs to achieve a prominent position in the industry in just two decades. The successes of India's energy diplomacy have been much more modest, mainly due to the more market-orientated calculations of Indian companies and fragmentation in decision-making. Both Chinese and Indian NOCs have invested in fossil fuel exploration around the world in the 21st century, while to secure its energy supply Japan mostly uses and supports market mechanisms. That support is rooted both in Japan's alliance with the United States and in the economic effectiveness of the energy market. Although energy diplomacy has been discussed in Japan, the country has not been very active in this area. One important success has been Japan's diversification of oil supplies away from the Middle East towards Russia.

References

Beeson, Mark & Lee-Brown, Troy, "Regionalism for Realists? The Evolution of the Indo-Pacific," *Chinese Political Science Review*, 6, no. 2 (2021): 167–86. https://doi.org/10.1007/s41111-020-00163-0.

Bhaskar, C. Uday, "China and India in the Indian Ocean Region: Neither Conflict Nor Cooperation Preordained," *China Report*, 46, no. 3 (2010): 311–18.

Bovan, Ana, Vučenović, Tamara, Peric, Nenad, "Negotiating Energy Diplomacy and Its Relationship with Foreign Policy and National Security," *International Journal of Energy Economics and Policy*, 10, no. 2 (2020): 1–6.

BP (2020), "Statistical Review of World Energy," *BP*.

Buckley, Peter J., Clegg, L. Jeremy, Cross, Adam R., Liu, Xin, Voss, Hinrich and Zheng, Ping, "The Determinants of Chinese Outward Foreign Direct Investment," *Journal of International Business Studies*, 38, no. 4: 499–518.

Büyükşahin, Bahattin. Mo, Kun and Zmitrowicz, Konrad, "Commodity Price Supercycles: What are they and What Lies Ahead?" *Bank of Canada Review* (Autumn 2016): 35–46.

Calder, Kent, "Asia's empty gas tank," *Foreign Affairs*, 75, no. 2 (March/April 1996): 55–69.

Calder, Kent, "Japan's Energy Angst: Asia's Changing Energy Prospects and the View from Tokyo," *Strategic Analysis*, 32, no. 1 (2008): 123–9.

Chaudhuri, Pramit Pal, "Fragmented and Fitful: India's Energy Diplomacy," *Oxford Energy Forum*, no. 99 (2015): 39–41.

Checchi, Arianna, Egenhofer, Christian and Behrens, Arno, "Long-Term Energy Security Risks for Europe: A Sector-Specific Approach," *CEPS Working Document*, no. 309 (2009). file:///C:/Users/Admin/AppData/Local/Temp/1785.pdf.

Christoffersen, Gaye, "The Role of China in Global Energy Governance," *China Perspectives*, no. 2 (2016): 15–24.

"Country Analysis Executive Summary: Japan," EIA (2020a). https://www.eia.gov/international/content/analysis/countries_long/Japan/japan.pdf.

"Country Analysis Executive Summary: India," EIA (2020b). https://www.eia.gov/international/content/analysis/countries_long/India/india.pdf.

"Country Analysis Executive Summary: China," EIA (2020c). https://www.eia.gov/international/content/analysis/countries_long/China/china.pdf.

Cunningham, Fiona S., "The Maritime Rung on the Escalation Ladder: Naval Blockades in a US-China Conflict," *Security Studies*, 29, no. 4 (2020): 730–68. https://doi.org/10.1080/09636412.2020.1811462.

Dadwal, Shebonti Ray, "India's Overseas Assets: Do They Contribute to Energy Security?" *Strategic Analysis*, 36, no. 1 (2012): 12–17.

Dannreuther, Roland, "China and Global Oil: Vulnerability and Opportunity," *International Affairs*, 87, no. 6 (2011): 1345–64.

Dannreuther, Roland, "International Relations Theories: Energy, Minerals and Conflict," *Polinares Working Paper*, no. 8 (2010).

Dreyer, Iana and Stang, Gerald, "Energy Moves and Power Shifts – EU Foreign Policy and Global Energy Security," *EU Institute for Security Studies*, no. 18 (2014), https://www.iss.europa.eu/sites/default/files/EUISSFiles/Report_18.pdf.

Dubash, Navroz K., "From Norm Taker to Norm Maker? Indian Energy Governance in Global Context: Indian Energy Governance in Global Context," *Global Policy*, 2, (2011): 66–79.

Duffield, John S., *Fuels Paradise: Seeking Energy Security in Europe, Japan, and the United States* (Baltimore, MD: Johns Hopkins University Press, 2015).

EIA, "World Oil Transit Chokepoints," 2017, https://www.eia.gov/international/content/analysis/special_topics/World_Oil_Transit_Chokepoints/wotc.pdf.

Fengying, Chen and Jiejun, Ni, "Asian Energy Security: The Role of China and India," *Strategic Analysis*, 32, no. 1 (2008): 41–55.

Frankel, Francine R., "The Breakout of China-India Strategic Rivalry in Asia and the Indian Ocean," *Journal of International Affairs*, 64, no. 2 (2011): 1–17.

Goldthau, Andreas and Sitter, Nick, *A Liberal Actor in A Realist World: The EU Regulatory State and the Global Political Economy of Energy* (Oxford: Oxford University Press, 2015).

Goldthau, Andreas, "Energy Diplomacy in Trade and Investment of Oil and Gas," in: Andreas Goldthau and Jan Martin Witte (eds.), *Global Energy Governance, the New Rules of the Game* (Berlin: Brooking Institution Press, 2010), 25–48.

Heiduk, Felix and Paul, Michael, "Seas of Trouble: Enduring Territorial Conflicts in East and Southeast Asia," *SWP Comment*, no. 10 (2015). https://www.swp-berlin.org/fileadmin/contents/products/comments/2015C10_hdk_pau.pdf.

Hulbert, Matthew, "Chindia: Asia's Energy Challenge," *Public Policy Review*, 17, no. 3 (2010): 152–6.

IEA (2016), "Energy Policies of IEA Countries. Japan 2016 Review," *International Energy Agency*.

IEA (2019), "What is energy security?," *International Energy Agency*. https://www.iea.org/topics/energy-security.

IEA (2020a), "Japan 2020. Energy Policy Review" *International Energy Agency*.

IEA (2020b), "India 2020. Energy Policy Review" *International Energy Agency*.

IEA (2020c), "China 2020. Energy Policy Review" *International Energy Agency*.

"India Hydrocarbon Vision – 2025," Government of India (2000). http://petroleum.nic.in/sites/default/files/vision.pdf.

Itoh, Shoichi, "China's Surging Energy Demand: Trigger for Conflict or Cooperation with Japan?" *East Asia*, 25, no. 1 (2008): 79–98.

Ji, Qiang, Zhang, Hai-Ying and Zhang, Dayong, "The Impact of OPEC on East Asian Oil Import Security: A Multidimensional Analysis," *Energy Policy*, 126 (2019): 99–107.

Kang, Yuanfei and Jiang, Fuming, "FDI Location Choice of Chinese Multinationals in East and Southeast Asia: Traditional Economic Factors and Institutional Perspective," *Journal of World Business*, 47, no. 1 (2012): 45–53.

Kelanic, Rosemary A., "The Petroleum Paradox: Oil, Coercive Vulnerability, and Great Power Behavior," *Security Studies*, 25, no. 2 (2016): 181–213. https://doi.org/10.1080/09636412.2016.1171966.

Kennedy, Andrew, "China's Search for Oil Security: A Critique," in: David Steven, Emily O'Brien and Bruce Jones (eds.), *The New Politics of Strategic Resources: Energy and Food Security Challenges in the 21st Century* (Washington, DC: Brookings Institution Press, 2015), 23–39.

Klare, Michael, *Resource Wars* (New York: Henry Holt and Company, 2013).

Koga, Kei, "Japan's 'Indo-Pacific' Question: Countering China or Shaping a New Regional Order?" *International Affairs*, 96, no. 1 (January 2020): 49–73. https://doi.org/10.1093/ia/iiz241.

Kulkarni, Sanket Sudhir, "India's Pipeline Diplomacy: Case of Lost Opportunities," *ISSSP Reflections*, no. 4 (2013). http://isssp.in/indias-pipeline-diplomacy-case-of-lost-opportunities/.

Kumar, G. Sathis, "Anatomy of Indian Energy Policy: A Critical Review," *Energy Sources Part B: Economics, Planning and Policy*, 12, no. 11 (2017): 976–85.

Lai, Hongyi Harry, "China's Oil Diplomacy: Is It a Global Security Threat?" *Third World Quarterly*, 28, no. 3 (2007): 519–37.

Lam, Peng Er, "Japan's Energy Diplomacy and Maritime Security in East Asia," in: Hongyi Lai (ed.), *Asian Energy Security* (New York: Palgrave Macmillan, 2009), 115–34.

Lee, Chia-Yi, "China's Energy Diplomacy: Does Chinese Foreign Policy Favor Oil-Producing Countries?" *Foreign Policy Analysis*, 15, no. 4 (2019): 570–88.

Lesbirel, S. Hayden, "The Insuring State: Japanese Oil Import Security and the Middle East," *Asian Journal of Political Science*, 21, no. 1 (2013): 41–61.

Liao, Janet Xuanli, "The Chinese Government and the National Oil Companies (NOCs): Who is the Principal?" *Asia Pacific Business Review*, 21, no. 1 (2015): 44–59.

Liou, Chih-Shian, "Bureaucratic Politics and Overseas Investment by Chinese State-Owned Oil Companies: Illusory Champions," *Asian Survey*, 49, no. 4 (2009): 670–90.

Liu, Feng, "The Recalibration of Chinese Assertiveness: China's Responses to the Indo-Pacific Challenge," *International Affairs*, 96, no. 1 (January 2020): 9–27. https://doi.org/10.1093/ia/iiz226.

Löschel, Andreas, Moslener, Ulf and Rübbelke, Dirk T.G., "Indicators of Energy Security in Industrialised Countries," *Energy Policy*, 38, no. 4 (2010): 1665–71.

Madan, Tanvi, "India's ONGC: Balancing Different Roles, Different Goals," *The James A. Becker III Institute for Public Policy, Rice University* (2007). https://www.bakerinstitute.org/media/files/page/9bd070e0/noc_ongc_madan.pdf.

Madan, Tanvi, "India's International Quest for Oil and Natural Gas: Fuelling Foreign Policy?" *India Review*, 9, no. 1 (2010): 2–37.

Mathews, John A., "The Green Growth Economy as an Engine of Development: The Case of China," in: R. Fouquet (ed.), *Handbook on Green Growth* (Cheltenham: Edward Elgar Publishing Limited, 2019), 325–42.

Mearsheimer, John J., "Bound to Fail: The Rise and Fall of the Liberal International Order," *International Security*, 43, no. 4 (2019): 7–50.

Mearsheimer, John J., "The Inevitable Rivalry: America, China, and the Tragedy of Great-Power Politics," *Foreign Affairs* (November/December 2021). https://www.foreignaffairs.com/articles/china/2021-10-19/inevitable-rivalry-cold-war.

Meckling, Jonas, Kong, Bo and Madan, Tanvi, "Oil & State Capitalism: Government-Firm Coopetition in China and India," *Review of International Political Economy*, 22, no. 6 (2015): 1159–87.

Meidan, Michael, "China's 13th Five-Year Plan: Implications for Oil Markets," *Oxford Energy Comment* (2016): 1–16.

Meidan, Michael, "Current Direction for Renewable Energy in China," *Oxford Energy Comment* (2020): 1–8.

Mirski, Sean, "Stranglehold: The Context, Conduct and Consequences of an American Naval Blockade of China," *Journal of Strategic Studies*, 36, no. 3 (2013): 385–421. https://doi.org/10.1080/01402390.2012.743885.

Nakanishi, Hiroaki, "Japan-India Civil Nuclear Energy Cooperation: Prospects and Concerns," *Journal of Risk Research*, 18, no. 8 (2015): 1083–98.

Noël, Pierre, "Challenging the myths of energy security," *Financial Times*, (10 January 2008), http://www.ft.com/intl/cms/s/0/40c2f8aa-bf93-11dc-8052-0000779fd2ac.html#axzz3TiHlW945.

Rajagopalan, Rajesh, "Evasive Balancing: India's Unviable Indo-Pacific Strategy," *International Affairs*, 96, no. 1 (January 2020): 75–93. https://doi.org/10.1093/ia/iiz224

Ramasamy, Bala, Yeung, Matthew and Laforet, Sylvie, "China's Outward Foreign Direct Investment: Location Choice and Firm Ownership," *Journal of World Business*, 47, no. 1 (2012): 17–25.

Robinson, David, "China's Growing Energy Demand: Some International Implications," *OIES* (2013). https://www.oxfordenergy.org/wpcms/wp-content/uploads/2013/12/Chinas-growing-energy-demand.pdf.

Scott, David, "The Geoeconomics and Geopolitics of Japan's 'Indo-Pacific' Strategy," *Journal of Asian Security and International Affairs*, 6, no. 2 (2019a): 136–61.

Scott, David, "China's Indo-Pacific Strategy: The Problems of Success," *The Journal of Territorial and Maritime Studies*, 6, no. 2 (2019b): 94–113.

Shepherd, Christian, Zhou, Emma and Manson, Katrina, "Climate Change: China's Coal Addiction Clashes with Xi's Bold Promise," *Financial Times* (2 November 2020), https://www.ft.com/content/9656e36c-ba59-43e9-bf1c-c0f105813436.

Sovacool, Benjamin, "Defining, Measuring, and Exploring Energy Security," in Benjamin Sovacool (ed.), *The Routledge Handbook of Energy Security* (New York: Routledge, 2010), 1–42.

Sovacool, Benjamin and Vivoda, Vlado, "A Comparison of Chinese, Indian, and Japanese Perceptions of Energy Security," *Asian Survey*, 52, no. 5 (2012): 949–69.

Stegen, Karen Smith, "Deconstructing the 'Energy Weapon': Russia's Threat to Europe as Case Study," *Energy Policy*, 39, no. 10 (October 2011): 6505–13.

"Strategic Energy Plan," Government of Japan (2018). https://www.enecho.meti.go.jp/en/category/others/basic_plan/5th/pdf/strategic_energy_plan.pdf.

Takeuchi, Sumiko, "Japan's Energy Policies at a Critical Juncture," *The Japan Times* (1 July 2019), https://www.japantimes.co.jp/news/2019/07/01/business/japans-energy-policies-critical-juncture/.

Taylor, Monique, *The Chinese State, Oil and Energy Security* (Basingstoke: Palgrave Macmillan, 2014).

Taylor, Brendan, "Is Australia's Indo-Pacific Strategy an Illusion?" *International Affairs*, 96, no. 1 (January 2020): 95–109. https://doi.org/10.1093/ia/iiz228.

The Economist, "The Real Trouble with Oil," *The Economist* (28 April 2005). http://www.economist.com/node/3910260.

Uludag, Mehmet Bulent, Karagul, Soner and Baba, Gurol, "Turkey's Role in Energy Diplomacy from Competition to Cooperation: Theoretical and Factual Projections," *International Journal of Energy Economics and Policy*, 3, no. 4 (2013): 102–114.

Upadhyaya, Shishir, "Expansion of Chinese Maritime Power in the Indian Ocean: Implications for India," *Defence Studies*, 17, no. 1 (2017): 63–83.

Upadhyaya, Shishir, "India's Maritime Security Relations with the Gulf Cooperation Council Countries – Prospects Amid Rising Chinese Influence," *Maritime Affairs: Journal of the National Maritime Foundation of India*, 15, no. 1 (2019): 27–40.

Van de Graaf, Thijs, Sovacool, Benjamin K., Ghosh, Arunabha, Kern, Florian and Klare, Michael T., "States, Markets, and Institutions: Integrating International Political Economy and Global Energy Politics," in Thijs Van de Graaf, Benjamin K. Sovacool, Arunabha Ghosh, Florian Kern, and Michael T. Klare (eds.), *The Palgrave Handbook of the International Political Economy of Energy* (London: Palgrave Macmillan, 2016), 3–44.

Vivoda, Vlado, "Resource Nationalism, Bargaining and International Oil Companies: Challenges and Change in the New Millennium," *New Political Economy*, 14, no. 4 (2009): 517–34.

Vivoda, Vlado and Manicom, James, "Oil Import Diversification in Northeast Asia: A Comparison between China and Japan," *Journal of East Asian Studies*, 11, no. 2 (2011): 223–54.

Wang, Zhen and Xue, Qing, "To Fully Exert the Important Role of Natural Gas in Building a Modern Energy Security System in China: An Understanding of China's National 13th Five-Year Plan for Natural Gas Development," *Natural Gas Industry B*, 4, no. 4 (2017): 270–77.

Welter, Patrick, "Atomkraft wird ausgebaut: Japan will bis 2050 klimaneutral werden," *Frankfurter Allgemeine Zeitung* (26 October 2020). https://www.faz.net/aktuell/wirtschaft/klima-energie-und-umwelt/atomkraft-wird-ausgebaut-japan-will-bis-2050-klimaneutral-werden-17020155.html.

Winzer, Christian, "Conceptualizing Energy Security," *Energy Policy*, 46 (2012): 36–48.

Wishnick, Elizabeth, "Competition and Cooperative Practices in Sino-Japanese Energy and Environmental Relations: Towards an Energy Security 'Risk Community'?" *The Pacific Review*, 22, no. 4 (2009): 401–28.

Wysoczańska, Karolina, "Sino-Indian Co-operation in Africa: Joint Efforts in the Oil Sector," *Journal of Contemporary African Studies*, 29, no. 2 (2011): 193–201.

Xu, Xiaojie, "Chinese NOCs' Overseas Strategies: Background, Comparison and Remarks," The James A. Baker III Institute For Public Policy Rice University (2007).

Yang, Jiao-Hui, Wang, Wei, Wang, Kai-Li and Yeh, Chung-Ying, "Capital Intensity, Natural Resources, and Institutional Risk Preferences in Chinese Outward Foreign Direct Investment," *International Review of Economics & Finance*, 55 (2018): 259–72.

Yoshimatsu, Hidetaka, "Sino-Japanese Energy Relations: Processes and Constraints," *Asian Journal of Political Science*, 20, no. 2 (2012): 180–202.

Zhidong, Li, "China's Long-Term Energy Outlook and the Implications for Global Governance," *Asia-Pacific Review*, 14, no. 1 (2007): 13–27.

Zhu, Julia Xuanatong, "China's Engagement in Global Energy Governance," *IEA* (2016): 1–8.

11 Dynamics of environmental security in the Indo-Pacific

Jayati Srivastava

Introduction

The Indo-Pacific region is becoming a fulcrum of growing environmental concerns with widespread political and security implications. The region is comprised of a diverse range of countries with varying levels of economic growth, a diverse range of socio-political systems and myriad environmental problems, making it difficult to make sweeping generalisations. However, one can discern some common concerns, especially as an ecological zone, it encompasses shared waters, maritime resources, oceanic currents, weather patterns and climatic conditions. At the same time, the wider political implications of environmental problems in the region such as water scarcity, hazardous waste, air pollution, sea-level rise, global warming, food security and climate change, etc. cannot be overstated. Temporarily speaking, environmental problems faced by countries in the Indo-Pacific region have political ramifications in both immediate, medium and long terms, while spatially such ramifications are likely to go beyond the region and impact the world as a whole.

Before we discuss these issues in detail, it is important to earmark the geographical area of the term Indo-Pacific which is both fluid and open to multiple interpretations.

The space called Indo-Pacific

The term Indo-Pacific is difficult to conceptualise spatially, given the different geographic imaginations associated with it, but it is a term of enormous geopolitical significance in view of the changing chessboard of world politics. As a strategic concept, it is seen as a response of the US-led initiative to counter the rise of China. The very idea of the Indo-Pacific as a geographical construct is imbued with strategic overtones in view of its increasing usage by the US strategic community and administration as a part of its pivot to East Asia strategy and adoption by Quad countries.[1]

Described as the "confluence of the two seas," (Abe 2007) the geographical spread of the Indo-Pacific extends from the East African coast, across the Indian Ocean, to the Western Pacific in an expansive sense, although different countries including Quad members have come up with their own geographical imagination associated with the concept (see Map 4).

As a socio-economic concept, on the other hand, it is seen as a space of long-distance exchange of goods, trade and services, maritime routes, sea lanes of communications, migration and cross-cultural exchanges.

DOI: 10.4324/9781003336143-15

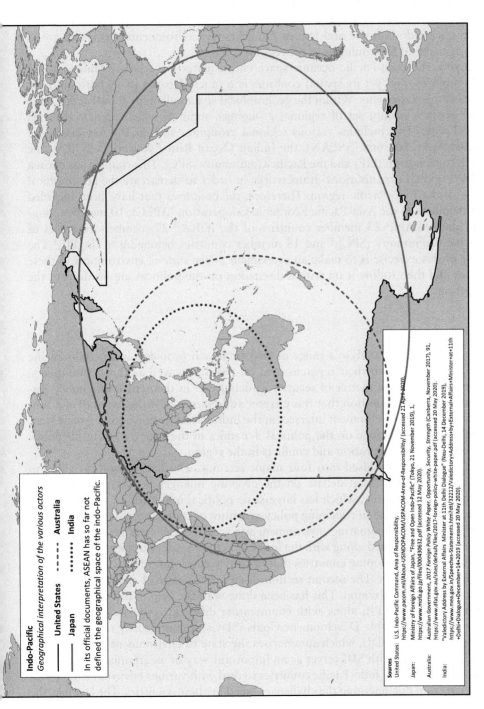

Indo-Pacific
Geographical interpretation of the various actors

— United States ---- Australia
⋯⋯ Japan ⋯⋯⋯ India

In its official documents, ASEAN has so far not
defined the geographical space of the indo-Pacific.

Sources
United States: U.S. Indo-Pacific Command, Area of Responsibility,
https://www.pacom.mil/About-USINDOPACOM/USPACOM-Area-of-Responsibility/ (accessed 21 April 2020).
Japan: Ministry of Foreign Affairs of Japan, "Free and Open Indo-Pacific" (Tokyo, 21 November 2019),
https://www.mofa.go.jp/files/000430632.pdf (accessed 12 May 2020).
Australia: Australian Government, *2017 Foreign Policy White Paper. Opportunity, Security, Strength* (Canberra, November 2017), 91,
https://www.dfat.gov.au/sites/default/files/2017-foreign-policy-white-paper.pdf (accessed 20 May 2020).
India: "Valedictory Address by External Affairs Minister at 11th Delhi Dialogue" (Neu-Delhi, 14 December 2019),
https://www.mea.gov.in/Speeches-Statements.htm?dtl/32212/Valedictory+Address+by+External+Affairs+Minister+at+11th
+Delhi+Dialogue+December+14+2019 (accessed 20 May 2020).

Map 4 Different geographical imaginations of the Indo-Pacific amongst the Quad countries.

Source: Felix Heiduk and Gudrun Wacker, 2020, *From Asia-Pacific to Indo-Pacific: Significance, Implementation and Challenges*, SWP Research Paper 9, Berlin: Stiftung Wissenschaft und Politik, German Institute for International and Security Affairs :10 https://www.swp-berlin.org/publications/products/research_papers/2020RP09 _IndoPacific.pdf [accessed on 27 October 2021]

As an ecological zone, it denotes shared waters, maritime resources, oceanic currents, weather patterns and climatic conditions. It encompasses countries from small island states who face existential threat due to climate change associated with sea-level rise to some of the largest economies of the world who contribute majorly to climate change in terms of their historic and continued emission of greenhouse gases – the major driver of climate change – to countries that are facing severe problems of air pollution, hazardous waste and loss of biodiversity; environmental problems are as diverse as many of the countries in the region.

Arguably, the Indo-Pacific oceanic space encapsulates a myriad of landmass and island countries, and yet its spatial contours is a much-debated issue, both amongst scholars and governments. Within the geographical space called the Indo-Pacific, there already exists a vibrant set of regional groupings, some of which predate the idea of Indo-Pacific. This includes various regional groupings such as the Association of Southeast Asian Nations (ASEAN), the Indian Ocean Rim Association (IORA), the Pacific Islands Forum (PIF) and the Pacific Community (SPC). This chapter has chosen to utilise regional organisations' frameworks in order to demarcate the geographical expanse of the Indo-Pacific region. Therefore, the countries that have been included are 21 members of the Asia-Pacific Economic Cooperation (APEC); 10 member countries of the ASEAN;[2] 23 member countries of the IORA;[3] 27 members countries of the Pacific Community (SPC);[4] and 18 member countries belonging to the PIF.[5] The purpose of this exercise is to make an assessment of the state of environment in these countries and then follow it up with a discussion on the political implications in the later sections.[6]

Outline of the chapter

This chapter seeks to analyse a range of environmental problems in the Indo-Pacific region in terms of both their repercussions on politics as well as threat multipliers, making environment a matter of security as delineated in theoretical and policy discourses. The central question that this chapter addresses is how the issues of environment, security and development intersect in the Indo-Pacific region and to what extent such intersections impinge on the political dynamics in the region in terms of policy prioritisation and cooperation and conflicts in the region.

This chapter is organised into four major sections. The first section provides an overview of the theoretical debate on the evolving linkages between environment, development and security, which has large-scale political implications, not just in setting the agenda but also in reshaping policy priorities of states and other stakeholders. The implications of designating environment as a security issue *inter se* – securitisation – have also been outlined along with the focus on economic development, as the region consists of many developing countries that prioritise development as a way to ameliorate environmental ills. The second section discusses the state of environment in different countries of the region. This has been done with the help of the Environmental Performance Index (EPI), along with enumerating different countries' performances based on the Sustainable Development Goals (SDGs), quantified by the Sustainable Development Index (SDI), which summarises the state of environment in these countries. The EPI along with SDI serves as an important way of ascertaining the progress and advances made by Indo-Pacific countries to deal with various environmental problems, apart from documenting the challenges faced by these countries. The lacunae, the challenges and the missed targets so enumerated offer direction for targeted political action to address and ameliorate environmental problems.

The third section discusses the political dynamics of environmental concerns in the Indo-Pacific, along with enumerating the larger geopolitical implications of the same as security aspects of environment are foregrounded more and more, especially because many countries in the region are facing existential threats. The World Risk Index (WRI) ranking of the Indo-Pacific countries that maps risks along the axis of exposure, vulnerability, adaptability and coping capacity of countries has been discussed to highlight huge risk variations amongst countries in the Indo-Pacific leading to competing political priorities. In this context, the section also elaborates on how the dynamics of conflict and cooperation play out in the North-South context, especially on whether to consider environment as a strategic or developmental issue at the discursive level which gets particularly highlighted in the move at securitisation of climate change and the thrust given to the blue economy. Myriad environmental partnerships in the region that involve many micro-regional groupings in addition to outside powers are also discussed to understand cooperation in the field of environment. The section also deals with the rise of China and its implications in the region to understand its strategic significance and its implications for environmental security. The fourth section provides a summary of the chapter.

Environment, security and development: Intersecting goals

For the longest time, security in an international context was seen only through a statist lens, reducing it to military dimensions and making the state its principal referent object, and individual security was considered as a derivative of state's security. However, the human security paradigm that emerged in the 1990s shifted the focus from the states to individuals to articulate a multi-dimensional approach to security that included economic security, human development, food security, employment security and environmental security, with individuals as its principal referent object.[7]

An important sub-set within the human security discourse is environmental security, which has emerged as an important issue given the enormity of environmental problems and their multi-scaler impact. It stems from making a case for broadening the definition of security to include non-military aspects as the focus shifted from anthropocentric to ecological-centric paradigms, marking a turning point in the debate about the meaning, definition and scope of security. Ullman while talking about the vulnerability of society to non-military harm underlined the need for "limiting population growth, enhancing environmental quality, eradicating world hunger, protecting human rights" (Ullman 1983). A strong case is made for the horizontal widening and vertical deepening of the concept of security to focus on non-military threats and environment is included as one important dimension of security, in addition to military, economic, societal and political security, thus expanding it horizontally. The vertical expansion meant adding more referent objects such as individuals, social groups, humanity, environment, in addition to the state (Buzan 1998). International organisations like UNDP likewise adopted a multi-dimensional approach to security that included a range of issues from people's security, economic security, human development, food security, employment security to environmental security (UNDP 1993).

The concept of environmental security is therefore based on "the fundamental recognition that environmental issues can no longer be thought of as ancillary, rather than integral components of industrial, social, and economic systems" and must be treated as an integral part of the strategic domain and national security discourse (Allenby 2000). A six-fold framework offers a useful and expansive conceptual framework to understand the linkages between environment and security. It includes taking into account, first, the impact of human activities on environment; second, the impact of military-industrial complex, war and conflict on environment; third, the effects of environmental change on the security concerns common to all states, e.g. climate change; fourth, the impact of environmental changes on national security such as resource depletion or energy crisis; fifth the linkages between environmental changes and violent conflict; and, sixth, the impact of environmental changes on human security (Barnett 2009).

Such an expanded framework of security-environment interface drew the attention of scholars and policy-makers towards the strategic aspects of environment by drawing connections between environmental changes and conflict/war, christening it "*the* national-security issue of the early twenty-first century" (Kaplan 2000) (emphasis in original). One of the most cited articulations on environmental change being the harbinger of conflict came from Thomas F. Homer-Dixon who offered an analytical framework to map the correlation between environmental/resource scarcity and conflicts ranging from war and terrorism to trade and diplomatic conflicts, either as a proximate or a distant cause. He underlined that environmental/resource scarcity leads to a myriad of social effects which in turn leads to conflicts (Homer-Dixon 1991). Homer-Dixon further went on to argue that "as the human population grows and environmental damage progresses, policymakers will have less and less capacity to intervene to keep this damage from producing serious social disruption, including conflict" (Homer-Dixon 1991: 79).

The causal correlation between the two, however, is not simplistic, and Homer-Dixon does underline a complex correlation by bringing in other intervening variables, of which economic development is considered an important factor. In other words, there is a correlation between the level of development of countries on the one hand and mitigation and adaptive capacities of countries to withstand environmental changes, on the other (Homer-Dixon 1991: 78). "Systems with high adaptive capacity are able to reconfigure themselves without significant declines in crucial functions" (Zurlini 2008). Here, developed countries are showing much greater preparedness as well as resilience compared to developing ones, partly on account of technological innovation and partly on account of better institutional architecture and adequate financial heft.

This means that developmental thrusters are essential for achieving environmental goals, including mitigation and adaptation which require huge economic costs, while the depletion of environmental resources casts a long shadow over meeting some of the basic requirements such as food security aggravated by climate change and population bulge in many developing parts of the region, making them prone to many environmental related risks and its attendant political consequences (see Table 11.1).

The state of environment in the Indo-Pacific

The environmental problems faced by these countries are as diverse as the countries themselves, although all are impacted by environmental problems to varying degrees.

Table 11.1 The World Risk Index and the ranking of Indo-Pacific countries

Name of country	Rank	WRI	Exposure	Vulnerability	Susceptibility	Lack of coping capacities	Lack of adaptive capacities
American Samoa	n.a.	n.a.	n.a.	n.a.	n.a.	n.a.	n.a.
Australia	123	4.54	18.07	25.12	15.66	43.67	16.02
Bangladesh	13	16.23	28.11	57.74	32.57	85.57	55.07
Brunei Darussalam	6	22.77	58.17	39.14	15.33	68.13	33.96
Cambodia	15	15.80	26.89	58.76	38.89	86.61	50.79
Canada	156	2.81	10.36	27.10	15.07	47.49	18.73
Chile	33	11.32	32.51	34.83	17.79	59.44	27.25
China	95	5.87	14.29	41.08	21.64	71.42	30.17
Chinese Taipei	n.a.	n.a.	n.a.	n.a.	n.a.	n.a.	n.a.
Comoros	20	14.91	23.62	63.13	45.93	85.39	58.06
Cook Island	n.a.	n.a.	n.a.	n.a.	n.a.	n.a.	n.a.
Fiji	14	16.06	34.51	46.55	22.06	76.63	40.95
France	166	2.51	9.63	26.06	16.68	45.10	16.41
French Polynesia	n.a.	n.a.	n.a.	n.a.	n.a.	n.a.	n.a.
Guam	n.a.	n.a.	n.a.	n.a.	n.a.	n.a.	n.a.
Hong Kong	n.a.	n.a.	n.a.	n.a.	n.a.	n.a.	n.a.
India	90	6.65	12.52	53.09	32.15	78.70	48.42
Indonesia	38	10.67	21.30	50.10	26.06	78.71	45.54
Iran	115	5.03	10.90	46.15	21.67	82.62	34.17
Japan	46	9.66	38.51	25.09	17.92	39.42	17.94
Kenya	41	10.33	16.63	62.13	50.80	85.50	50.10
Kiribati	19	15.14	26.41	57.34	39.67	82.82	49.52
Laos	126	4.46	8.01	55.64	32.86	82.91	51.14
Madagascar	39	10.44	14.97	69.71	65.83	86.32	56.97
Malaysia	71	7.73	19.09	40.49	17.05	71.19	33.22
Maldives	175	1.69	4.18	40.39	15.59	65.82	39.76
Marshal Islands	n.a.	n.a.	n.a.	n.a.	n.a.	n.a.	n.a.
Mauritius	51	9.04	23.85	37.92	17.39	58.21	38.17
Mexico	94	6.03	14.20	42.44	20.86	74.25	32.20
Micronesia	81	7.11	14.03	50.71	31.04	72.21	48.89
Mozambique	50	9.11	13.26	68.73	62.60	88.45	55.13
Myanmar	79	7.25	12.92	56.11	29.42	86.27	52.64
Nauru	n.a.	n.a.	n.a.	n.a.	n.a.	n.a.	n.a.
New Caledonia	n.a.	n.a.	n.a.	n.a.	n.a.	n.a.	n.a.
New Zealand	117	4.96	17.59	28.20	16.06	47.45	21.08
Niue	n.a.	n.a.	n.a.	n.a.	n.a.	n.a.	n.a.
Northern Mariana Islands	n.a.	n.a.	n.a.	n.a.	n.a.	n.a.	n.a.
Oman	164	2.54	6.04	42.02	23.68	66.65	35.73
Palau	n.a.	n.a.	n.a.	n.a.	n.a.	n.a.	n.a.
Papua New Guinea	9	20.90	30.62	68.27	55.28	86.16	63.37
Peru	86	6.75	14.92	45.26	26.29	76.22	33.27
Philippines, the	8	21.39	42.68	50.11	28.63	82.14	39.56
Pitcairn Islands	n.a.	n.a.	n.a.	n.a.	n.a.	n.a.	n.a.
Russia	137	3.53	9.50	37.21	18.64	65.83	27.15
Samoa	109	5.54	11.46	48.32	25.56	79.83	39.56
Seychelles	118	4.89	11.94	40.97	18.23	64.82	39.86
Singapore	167	2.50	8.88	28.10	10.34	54.01	19.94
Solomon Islands	2	31.16	51.13	60.95	46.07	81.14	55.63
Somalia	n.a.	n.a.	n.a.	n.a.	n.a.	n.a.	n.a.
South Korea	148	3.13	11.40	27.45	13.36	48.48	20.50

(*Continued*)

Table 11.1 (Continued)

Name of country	Rank	WRI	Exposure	Vulnerability	Susceptibility	Lack of coping capacities	Lack of adaptive capacities
South Africa	93	6.46	13.47	47.93	30.90	73.35	39.54
Sri Lanka	75	7.55	15.99	47.19	23.05	76.35	42.17
Tanzania	52	8.94	13.97	64.00	56.49	83.21	52.30
Thailand	92	6.52	14.79	44.06	17.62	78.65	35.91
Tokelau	n.a.	n.a.	n.a.	n.a.	n.a.	n.a.	n.a.
Tonga	3	30.51	63.63	47.95	28.42	79.81	35.62
Tuvalu	n.a.	n.a.	n.a.	n.a.	n.a.	n.a.	n.a.
United Arab Emirates	147	3.14	10.48	29.97	9.82	54.52	25.57
United Kingdom	140	3.51	12.58	27.92	16.18	48.71	18.87
United States of America	133	3.98	13.03	30.58	15.92	54.15	21.68
Vanuatu	1	47.73	82.55	57.82	39.66	81.21	52.59
Vietnam	43	10.27	22.04	46.60	23.73	76.73	39.34
Wallis and Futuna	n.a.	n.a.	n.a.	n.a.	n.a.	n.a.	n.a.
Yemen	106	5.72	8.27	69.12	44.85	93.17	69.34

Key:

Classification	WorldRiskIndex	Exposure	Vulnerability	Susceptibility	Lack of coping capacities	Lack of adaptive capacities
very low	0.30 – 3.25	0.85 – 9.57	22.68 – 34.21	9.03 – 16.68	38.35 – 58.92	14.22 – 24.78
low	3.26 – 5.54	9.58 – 12.04	34.22 – 42.02	16.69 – 21.56	58.93 – 71.19	24.79 – 34.10
medium	5.55 – 7.66	12.05 – 14.83	42.03 – 48.32	21.57 – 28.16	71.20 – 77.87	34.11 – 40.66
high	7.67 – 10.71	14.84 – 19.75	48.33 – 61.04	28.17 – 44.85	77.88 – 85.50	40.67 – 52.59
very high	10.72 – 47.73	19.76 – 82.55	61.05 – 75.83	44.86 – 70.52	85.51 – 93.17	52.60 – 70.13

Max. value = 100, classification according to the quintile method

Source: Aleksandrova, Mariya, Balasko, Sascha, Kaltenborn, Markus, et al., 2021, *World Risk Report 2021*, Berlin: Bündnis Entwicklung Hilft, pp. 54–57, https://weltrisikobericht.de/wp-content/uploads/2021/09/WorldRiskReport_2021_Online.pdf [accessed on 10 November 2021].

These include the problem of climate change, natural disasters, water scarcity, maritime pollution, resource scarcity and overfishing, to quote a few major ones.

Given the diversity of countries in the Indo-Pacific, the costs and gains are unevenly distributed with many countries overwhelmingly sharing the burden for the environmental ills brought upon by a completely different set of countries, both in historical and contemporary contexts. This also has a bearing on how the linkages between environment and security are conceptualised by countries, which in turn is determined by the different kinds of developmental trajectory, and countries who face existential crises on account of impending environmental catastrophe.

Within the Indo-Pacific region, the Indian Ocean region is considered the "world's hazard belt" as it is prone to both natural (earthquakes, tsunamis, floods and tidal surges) and man-made disasters (spills, fires, leakage of poisonous and destructive substances, and illegal dumping) (IORA 2017a).

Further, the smaller island states (SIS) in the Pacific Islands Forum, such as Cook Islands, Federated States of Micronesia, Kiribati, Nauru, Niue, Palau, Republic of the Marshall Islands, and Tuvalu are the most vulnerable on account of natural resource deficit as also developmental challenges due to their small size.[8] Countries in the

ASEAN region are faced with environmental problems on account of unsustainable economic growth patterns, which are compounded by regional inequities and population bulge (ASEAN 2021). South East Asian Countries are also faced with peatland fires (nearly 56% of global tropical peatlands are found in the ASEAN region), and Indonesia which is home to 70% of peatland in the region is worst affected by it, apart from Brunei Darussalam, Cambodia, Laos, Malaysia, Myanmar, the Philippines, Thailand and Vietnam, which together houses 30% of the peatlands in the region.

During 1997–1998, Brunei Darussalam, Indonesia, Malaysia, the Philippines, Singapore and Thailand faced the worst haze pollution in recorded history and released an estimated 1–2 billion tonnes of carbon haze pollution, while its economic cost was estimated to be USD 9 billion in economic, social and environmental losses. Peatland fires result in transboundary haze pollution in the region, damage to human health, and adverse impacts on food production and biodiversity. Peatland fires also contribute to global climate change as peatlands store 5% of carbon in the land surface, but draining and land clearing are destroying the fragile ecosystems, turning them turn into carbon emitters (ASEAN 2020).

The Pacific Community countries also face high vulnerability on account of climate change which could lead to widespread food and water insecurity, and health risks compounded by lack of access to social services and even forced displacements due to rise in sea level, as close to 55% of the Pacific's region's people (with the exception of Papua New Guinea) live less than 1 km from the sea. Rising temperatures would also have an adverse impact on tuna habitat and add pressure on food availability.[9]

The EPI[10] and SDI taken in tandem can be a good measure of the progress or the lack thereof for ascertaining the state of environment in these countries.

As can be discerned from Table 11.2, the state of environment in the Indo-Pacific countries varies as widely as the ecosystems they inhabit, with some countries performing much better as compared to others. Amongst the 180 countries ranked by EPI, the countries in the region, spanning the entire spectrum of this score from a very high-ranking UK at 4 to a low-ranking Myanmar at number 179, point to a diverse set of environmental problems faced by countries in the entire region. High-income countries such as Australia, Canada, France, the UK and the USA show better results on the Environment Performance Index compared to low-income or developing countries, many of which are at the bottom rungs of the EPI. These include, amongst others, the EPI laggards such as China, Comoros, India, Madagascar, Marshall Islands, Papua New Guinea, Solomon Islands and Tanzania. The data thus point to a positive correlation between developmental drivers to a better environment.

The Sustainable Development Index[11] likewise tells us a chequered story of compliance and non-compliance in meeting the Sustainable Development Goals which can also be used as a measure of a country's progress and political will towards a better environment, as also economic development amongst 193 member countries of the United Nations. A high score points to better compliance in contrast to the countries with lower scores, who are seen as laggards. A better EPI ranking and SDI, with a few exceptions, corresponds to a high rate of economic development in the country concerned, making development and environment complementary, rather than contradictory, variables. Therefore, more developed countries like Australia, Canada, France, New Zealand, South Korea, the UK and the United States show better progress with respect to achieving Sustainable Development Goals in contrast to Bangladesh, Cambodia, India, Kenya, Laos, Madagascar, Mozambique, Myanmar, Papua New

Table 11.2 State of environment of the Indo-Pacific countries

Country	Environment Performance Index (EPI) rank	EPI score	Sustainable Development Index (SDI) Rank	SDI score
American Samoa	n.a.	n.a.	n.a.	n.a.
Australia	13	74.9	35	75.58
Bangladesh	162	29	109	63.45
Brunei Darussalam	46	54.8	84	68.27
Cambodia	139	33.6	102	64.54
Canada	20	71	21	79.16
Chile	44	55.3	30	77.1
China	120	37.3	57	72.06
Chinese Taipei	n.a.	n.a.	n.a.	n.a.
Comoros	148	32.1	n.a.	n.a.
Cook Islands	n.a.	n.a.	n.a.	n.a.
Fiji	134	34.4	62	71.24
France	8	80	8	81.67
French Polynesia	n.a.	n.a.	n.a.	n.a.
Guam	n.a.	n.a.	n.a.	n.a.
Hong Kong, China	n.a.	n.a.	n.a.	n.a.
India	168	27.6	120	60.07
Indonesia	116	37.8	97	66.34
Iran	67	48	74	70.01
Japan	12	75.1	18	79.85
Kenya	132	34.7	118	60.60
Kiribati	118	37.7	n.a.	n.a.
Laos	130	34.8	110	63.01
Madagascar	174	26.5	159	49.01
Malaysia	68	47.9	65	70.88
Maldives	127	35.6	79	69.27
Marshall Islands	152	30.8	n.a.	n.a.
Mauritius	82	45.1	95	66.71
Mexico	51	52.6	80	69.1
Micronesia	143	33	n.a.	n.a.
Mozambique	136	33.9	152	51.05
Myanmar	179	25.1	101	64.95
Nauru	n.a.	n.a.	n.a.	n.a.
New Caledonia	n.a.	n.a.	n.a.	n.a.
New Zealand	19	71.3	23	79.13
Niue	n.a.	n.a.	n.a.	n.a.
Northern Mariana Islands	n.a.	n.a.	n.a.	n.a.
Oman	110	38.5	73	70.13
Palau	n.a	n.a.	n.a.	n.a.
Papua New Guinea	146	32.4	151	51.33
Peru	90	44	63	71.1
Philippines, the	111	38.4	103	64.51
Pitcairn Islands	n.a.	n.a.	n.a.	n.a.
Russia	58	50.5	46	73.75
Samoa	120	37.3	n.a.	n.a.
Seychelles	38	58.2	n.a.	n.a.
Singapore	39	58.1	76	69.89
Solomon Islands	172	26.7	n.a.	n.a.
Somalia	n.a.	n.a.	162	45.61
South Africa	95	43.1	107	63.74

(*Continued*)

Table 11.2 (Continued)

Country	Environment Performance Index (EPI) rank	EPI score	Sustainable Development Index (SDI) Rank	SDI score
South Korea	28	66.5	28	78.59
Sri Lanka	109	39	87	68.10
Tanzania	150	31.1	132	56.43
Thailand	78	45.4	43	74.19
Tokelau	n.d.	n.d.	n.a.	n.a.
Tonga	82	45.1	n.a.	n.a.
Tuvalu	n.a.	n.a.	n.a.	n.a.
United Arab Emirates	42	55.6	71	70.17
United Kingdom	4	81.3	17	79.97
United States of America	24	69.3	32	76.01
Vanuatu	163	28.9	119	60.52
Vietnam	141	33.4	51	72.85
Wallis and Futuna	n.a.	n.a.	n.a.	n.a.
Yemen	n.a.	n.a.	145	52.86

Source: Wendling, Z.A., Emerson, J.W., de Sherbinin, A., Esty, D.C., et al., 2020, *2020 Environmental Performance Index*. New Haven, CT: Yale Center for Environmental Law & Policy, https://epi.yale.edu /downloads/epipolicymakersummaryr11.pdf [accessed on 8 November 2021] & Sachs, Jeffrey, Traub-Schmidt, Guido, et al., 2021, *The Decade of Action for the Sustainable Development Goals: Sustainable Development Report 2021*, Cambridge: Cambridge University Press. https://s3.amazonaws.com/sustainable development.report/2021/2021-sustainable-development-report.pdf [accessed on 10 November 2021].

Guinea, the Philippines, Somalia, Vanuatu, Yemen, etc., which are at the lower end of the spectrum in achieving SDGs. The positive correlations between development and better environmental variables cannot be overstated.

This scale of variations and complexity of environmental problems are bound to have political repercussions in the Indo-Pacific region as countries have competing priorities, which have been discussed in the following section. This includes the vexed interlinkages between environment, development and security, dimensions of environmental risks faced by the countries in the region, climate change-security dynamics and environment vs developmental goals as a chief thrust area for developing countries in the region.

Environment-security-development conundrum in the region

Political dynamics can be both cooperative and conflictual, leading to different kinds of outcomes. This is shaped by different contexts and distributions of gains and costs involved for the actors concerned. The very recognition of environment as an important issue is a political decision which has widespread bearing on actors and actions taken to address the problem and varies significantly amongst countries. Overall,

> "the developed countries are more likely to think of environment and security in terms of global environmental changes and the potential for instability and conflict in geo-strategically important areas. Developing countries tend to be more concerned with the human security implications of local and regional problems"
>
> (Dabelko & Simmons 1997).

Dimensions of environmental risks

The wide divergence amongst countries in terms of EPI and SDGs in the Indo-Pacific region are apparent in the countries facing risks and vulnerability on account of natural disaster and sea-level rises because of climate change. The risk here is "understood as the interaction of hazard and vulnerability, it results from the interaction of exposure to extreme natural events and the vulnerability of societies" (Aleksandrova et al. 2021). According to WRI, amongst the 181 countries, Vanuatu faces the highest risk followed by the Solomon Islands and Tonga. Brunei Darussalam, Papua New Guinea and the Philippines also rank highly in terms of WRI. Vanuatu is also the most exposed, followed by Tonga, Brunei Darussalam, Solomon Islands, the Philippines, Japan, Fiji and Papua New Guinea, while the most vulnerable countries in the Indo-Pacific region are Kenya, Comoros, Tanzania Papua New Guinea, Mozambique, Yemen and Madagascar, with a score of more than 30 in the vulnerability matrix (see Table 11.1).

The resilience and adaptive capacity of countries to cope with environmental changes and risks may also depend on three major factors: the first is the lack of political will to address the environmental problem. The second is the lack of understanding of complex reality and a reductionist approach to look at the problem; and, the third is the lack of capacity of the system to deal with the problem that can range from either one or a combination of factors such as "inadequate institutions, lack of financial resources, unskilled human resources, weak infrastructure, plain poverty, and other limitations" that particularly, though not exclusively, affect developing countries (Zurlini & Muller 2008).

Many of these countries are facing existential threats due to the impact of climate change making it the primary security issue for them, something they highlight at various environmental fora, including those on climate change. The "we are sinking speech," delivered by the foreign minister of Tuvalu standing in knee-deep water in Funafuti, for the 26th Conference of Parties (COP-26) of the UN Framework Convention on Climate Change in 2021, was meant to underline the enormity of sea-level rise for this island country which is sinking 0.5 centimetres every year since 1993 (Philipose 2021). These states thus foreground their vulnerability to demand corrective measures as also developmental aid to cope with environmental catastrophe, rather than making it a geo-strategic concern, something that gets highlighted in the move to securitise climate change.

Climate change-securitisation debate

One of the biggest threats facing many countries in the region is that of climate change – an issue which has become an important vertical of the changing political dynamics in the region, having been pitched as an important security issue in recent years, especially by developed countries – a move that has found support amongst vulnerable small island states. The German Advisory Council, European Council and UNSC used the terminology of climate change as a threat multiplier "which exacerbates existing trends, tensions and instability" (CEU 2008). The reason why climate change is seen as a threat multiplier is because it causes extreme weather patterns, flash floods, severe storms, global warming, corresponding sea-level rise and adverse impact on agriculture. In addition, temperature rise can lead to a variety of health impacts including rises in zoonotic, water and vector-borne diseases with a spread to areas other than their traditional habitats. Climate change is likely to induce mass migration and create resource deficits, particularly food and energy deficits, leading to ethnic tensions, conflicts and, in extreme cases, war within and across societies. In the case of climate change, it has been termed as "climatisation" of the security field and thus is limited to only "securing global circulation from disruptions caused by climate change induced disasters" (Oels 2012).

Particular importance needs to be given to economically poorer regions within the region wherein climate change may contribute to exacerbating conflict already mired in poverty, inequality, resource deficits, mass migration, ethnic tensions and food insecurity. The US navy *Climate Change Roadmap 2010* underlined that "climate change is a national security challenge with strategic implications ... [wherein]economically unstable regions will be more vulnerable to the effects of climate change ... that may increase instability" (US Navy 2010).

However, there is no consensus among the Indo-Pacific countries about this issue, leading to wide political divisions among them. Many developed countries in the Indo-Pacific region have been highlighting the security dimension of the climate change discourse and have accordingly included that as a part of the strategic domain, thus pushing for its securitisation. The United States and New Zealand in particular have given adequate attention to climate-related threats as a part of their strategic planning while Japan and Australia have acknowledged the impact of climate threats in their defence policies. Japan has set up a Ministry of Defence Climate Diplomacy Task Force in 2018 to strengthen climate change diplomacy (Fetzek 2021) while the Indo-Pacific strategy adopted by France also underlines the interlinkages between environment, climate change and security policy in the region (SWP 2020).

The UK government designated climate change as one of the biggest threats back in 2004, thus paving the way for its inclusion in the security domain and foreign, security and defence policy. Amongst intergovernmental organisations, the European Union and NATO are integrating climate into defence policy and strategic planning (Fetzek 2021).

Within the UN, the issue of climate change as a security issue was piloted by the UK as the president of the UN Security Council in 2007 (Oels 2012). The discussion at a special session of the UN Security Council brought to the fore, the divergent political opinions between the developed and developing countries on the climate change-security nexus. While small island states, given their vulnerability to climate change, welcomed the interlinkages between climate change and international peace and security at the UNSC, they envisaged it within the framework of expanding the definition of security to include human and environmental security. The developed countries' focus on securitisation of climate change however was driven by geo-strategic considerations, making it a state of exception and hence, requiring extraordinary measures, including bringing it within the jurisdiction of the UN Security Council.

Many other developing countries on the other hand question the rationale of designating climate change as a security issue and the jurisdiction of the UN Security Council on climate issues (UN 2007). Thus, the move towards securitisation of climate change is not shared by many countries in the Indo-Pacific region, especially China and India along with G-77 countries, pointing to the huge differences in political positions.

A quote by the Chinese delegate, which was echoed by the G-77 representative and many developing countries, including India, summarises this position:

> The developing countries believe that the Security Council has neither the professional competence in handling climate change nor is it the right decision-making place for extensive participation leading up to widely acceptable proposals (UN 2007)

On the other hand, speaking on behalf of the Pacific Islands Forum, the representative from Papua New Guinea, while underlining the security dimensions of climate change, noted that "the impact of climate change on small islands was no less threatening than the dangers guns and bombs posed to large nations." He nevertheless underlined the interconnections between environmental and developmental goals to say that "climate change, climate variability and sea-level rise are, therefore, not just environmental concerns, but also economic, social and political issues for the Pacific Islands" (UN 2007). The focus on their part was thus on environmental security/human security, not securitisation which called for better developmental initiatives. Likewise, the Indian delegate, while underlining the need for resource flow, adaptation and technology as a way to tackle the problems that might lead to conflict, called for a greater thrust on poverty eradication as "a prerequisite for acceleration of growth in developing countries … mitigating the potential for conflict, poverty eradication had positive implications for global peace and security" (UN 2007). The Indian delegate reiterated the position that the Security Council is not the place to discuss climate action and climate justice. It argued that the attempt to do so appears to be motivated by a desire to evade responsibility in the appropriate fora. Underscoring the point that developed countries have fallen well short of their promises, the Indian delegate pointed out that any attempt to link climate with UN security architecture seeks to obfuscate a lack of progress on critical issues under the UNFCCC process underlining that developed countries must provide climate finance of $1 trillion, and climate funding must be tracked with the same diligence as climate mitigation (UN 2021b).

Since then, the matter of climate change has been repeatedly brought to the table of the UN Security Council, finding mention in many of its reports and also in its thematic meetings specially held on climate change and security.[12] In December 2021, a draft to integrate climate-related security risk into conflict-prevention strategies co-sponsored by Niger (Council President for December) and Ireland was again brought to the UNSC, but was rejected, though it got 12 votes in favour. China abstained while India and Russia (veto) voted against this draft.

The debate again drew a strong connection between climate change and conflict with more than 60 speakers underlining "that people and countries most vulnerable to climate change also are most vulnerable to terrorist recruitment and violence," thus reinforcing the connection between climate/environmental change and insecurity.

This brings us to another vertical of political dynamics which is related to cooperation in the field of environment led by many international organisations as also by developed countries in a bilateral, regional and multilateral framework for accelerated development as a way of mitigating environmental problems. What is central in this is the dynamic interplay between environment and economic development and the synergies and complementarities between the two. This underlines the need for adequate initiatives taken by various countries to spur development while simultaneously providing necessary funding and capacity-building mechanisms to ameliorate environmental problems in developing countries.

Partnering for environment

The overarching political dynamic in the region often takes the tangent of the traditional North-South divide wherein the winners and losers often find themselves at different ends of the spectrum, although countries facing greater risks and vulnerability such as small island developing nations do bandwagon with developed countries on the underlining the security aspects of climate change, albeit from different vantage points – environment/human security rather than national/strategic dimensions of security, respectively. The principles such as historical responsibility, burden sharing, "polluter pays" and differentiated responsibilities dominate the political landscape of negotiations between the developed and developing countries in the Indo-Pacific region, which gets reflected in different positions taken by them at various international fora, including at the UN.

Many countries, especially small developing island states (SIDS) and least developing countries (LDCs) in the Indo-Pacific region have made little contribution to the global emission load of greenhouse gases but have been facing existential crises as a result of sea-level rise, brought upon by climate change and concomitant global warming, and, therefore demand equitable voice and also adequate monetary assistance to deal with the problem faced by them. The equity issue has consistently been raised by developing countries, in addition to vulnerability through coalition building, such as by the Alliance of Small Island States (AOSIS) which since 1990 has brought to the fore the problems and issues faced by 39 small island states[13] (many of those who inhabit the Indo-Pacific region and are a part of the Pacific Island Forum) in international environmental negotiations particularly in climate change negotiations, consistently demanding emission reduction to meet the targets of global temperature rise below 1.5 degree Celsius.

Many low-income countries in the region demand accelerated economic development to better mitigate and adapt to changing climate threats, which incidentally are also the countries continue which are at the receiving end of the environment ills plaguing the region. Seen as a harbinger for a better environment, and also better mitigation and adaptative capacity to deal with environmental problems, demand for development has dominated the political landscape of the low-income developing countries in the Indo-Pacific region. These include demand for adequate funding, aid, capacity building, debt financing and alleviating debt burdens as many of these countries bear the enormous cost of indebtedness and poverty that impedes economic development, poverty reduction and meeting the targets outlined in the Sustainable Development Goals.[14]

The WRI also highlights the strong connection between disaster risk, geographic location and social aspects such as poverty, inequality and their consequences (Aleksandrova et al. 2021). The report thus makes a strong case for social protection measures to ensure the protection of vulnerable populations slipping back into the poverty trap. This overarching discourse of development as a way to cope with environmental threats also gets magnified in the policy initiatives on the blue economy.

The blue economy: Ocean as a resource

As the capacity of countries to deal with environmental problems is varied as their vulnerability and adaptability and very often linked to their economic heft or the lack of it, a crucial vertical of political dynamic in the Indo-Pacific region therefore revolves around advancing the concept of the blue economy, which is aimed at generating employment, food security, poverty alleviation and ensuring sustainability. Anchored in the principle of sustainable development,

> the blue economy captures the goals of sustaining economic development opportunities while maintaining ocean ecosystem health … The growing pressures on oceans, and the recognition of their central importance for human well-being have heightened policy attention and the development of local, national and international policies, roadmaps and benchmarks for sustainable ocean governance (Keem & Schwartz et al. 2017).

The blue economy has been accorded policy priority as it encompasses many activities including a focus on sustainable marine energy and sustainable fisheries, ameliorating rising sea-levels and coastal erosion, and waste management, particularly marine waste management and acidification, not least because oceans act as important carbon sinks and help in mitigating climate change. The geo-economic aspect of the blue economy also includes a focus on sustainable aquaculture,[15] maritime transport and maritime tourism, which can be a good source of revenue generation and economic development (World Bank 2017).

The key challenge again is to strike a balance between the goal of environmental conservation and protection and economic development. The blue economy "aims to balance sustainable economic benefits with long-term ocean health, in a manner which is consistent with sustainable development and its commitment to intra- and inter-generational equity" (Keem & Schwartz et al. 2017) and thus, aligns closely with ecological economics. In this context, it is important to underline SDG Target 14 on Life Below Water, which targets the conservation and sustainable use of the oceans, seas and marine resources.[16] According to the World Bank, these countries "often lack the technical, institutional, technological and financial capacities to benefit fully from the marine resources" and must be addressed in order for the blue economy to allow "economic diversification, job creation, poverty reduction, and economic development in SIDS and coastal LDCs" (World Bank 2017b).

Of particular relevance in the region are fisheries, which apart from providing for food security have a positive feedback loop to securing livelihoods, poverty alleviation and income generation. However, over the last few years, a decrease in fish stocks has been reported due to unsustainable fishing practices. According to one estimate, of the 441 fish stocks about which information is available, "47% of the stocks were fully exploited, 18% were overexploited, 9% were depleted and 1% was recovering." This requires urgent action in the Indo-Pacific region for the sustainable conservation, management and development of fisheries resources (IORA 2017a).

Challenges to blue economies remain formidable due to multiple jurisdictions and competing interests. In the South Pacific, for example, 22 island states and territories share ocean resources with exclusive economic zones (EEZs) that cover an area approximately the size of Africa. Ocean resource management is further complicated by overlapping and often competing institutions at the national and regional levels, not to mention the problems due to the lack of state capacity for successful management of the blue economy. This links up with the interconnections made between environment, security and development, seen as working in tandem as underlined by various regional partnerships.

Within the region, the debate on environmental security and development remains unresolved. Many regional groupings underline the development aspects in setting regional priorities while others foreground the security aspects even though the two are intertwined. For instance, IORA has come up with six priority pillars with a greater thrust on the blue economy and seeks to synergise environmental and developmental goals. It includes a focus on: (i) fisheries and aquaculture; (ii) renewable ocean energy; (iii) seaports and shipping; (iv) offshore hydrocarbons and seabed minerals; (v) marine biotechnology, research and development; and (vi) tourism (IORA 2017b). Similarly, five themes were prioritised in 2016 by small island states of the Pacific island states, viz., (i) climate change; (ii) labour (mobility); (iii) health; (iv) marine; and (v) air and sea transportation.[17] This is in consonance with the requirements of specific countries dealing with different dimensions of environmental threats.

On the blue economy specifically, two other regional agencies, the Pacific Islands Forum Fisheries Agency (FFA) and the Pacific Community (SPC) have come up with a Regional Roadmap for Sustainable Pacific Fisheries in the Pacific island countries, in addition to providing technical assistance, monitoring and surveillance for better fisheries management (Keem & Schwartz et al. 2017), further strengthening regional partnerships, which are also supported by Australia.

The Pacific Community gives thrust to development by underlining three interlocking goals: sustainable economic development (Goal 1), empowerment and resilience (Goal 2), full realisation of human potential and long and healthy lives (Goal 3) and a focus on cross-cutting themes such as climate change, disaster risk management, food security, gender equality, human rights, non-communicable diseases and youth employment. In addition, Small Island Developing States Accelerated Modalities of Action (SAMOA) Pathway, 2014, called for an ocean agenda within the sustainable development framework in order to sustain ecosystem services, livelihoods, economic development, food security and "institutional integration across national, subregional and regional scales." The SAMOA pathway is important because it continues to reinforce the developmental dimension which is central to securing a better environment by affirming the need for

> inclusive and equitable economic growth, creating greater opportunities for all, reducing inequalities, raising basic standards of living, fostering equitable social development and inclusion and promoting the integrated and sustainable management of natural resources and ecosystems that supports, inter alia, economic, social and human development while facilitating ecosystem conservation, regeneration, restoration and resilience in the face of new and emerging challenges.[18]

Echoing similar sustainable development priorities, the Indo-Pacific Ocean Initiative of the government of India rests on seven pillars focusing on (i) maritime security; (ii) maritime ecology; (iii) maritime resources; (iv) capacity-building and resource-sharing; (v) disaster risk reduction and management; (vi) science, technology and academic cooperation; and (vii) trade connectivity and maritime transport (GOI 2020).

Within the east Asian region in the Indo-Pacific, ASEAN has an elaborate strategic environmental plan with seven strategic priorities: (i) nature conservation and biodiversity; (ii) coastal and marine environment; (iii) water resources management; (iv) environmentally sustainable cities; (v) climate change; (vi) chemicals and waste; and (vii) environmental education and sustainable consumption and production(ASEAN 2021) ASEAN Member States also signed the ASEAN Agreement on Transboundary Haze Pollution (AATHP) on 10 June 2002 to deal with the problem of haze pollution due to land and/or forest fires.[19] It is also implementing various regional projects in partnership with other stakeholders for sustainable use of peatland and haze mitigation (ASEAN 2016).

The APEC, which accounts for nearly 60% of total world energy demands and is one of the most vulnerable regions in terms of climate change-induced natural disasters (nearly 70% of such disasters occur in this region), has also taken many collaborative initiatives to reduce energy consumption, shift to renewable energy sources, with an additional focus on conservation of oceans and forests, trade in environmental goods and provides assistance to fishing and farming communities to deal with the impact of global warming and changing weather patterns (APEC 2021). In addition, it remains one of the fastest growing economic regions and yet comprises of 50% of the world's poor population, faced with the twin challenges of environmental security and economic development and the ways to reconcile the two. This gets further complicated given the geo-strategic implications of great power games in the region.

The great power redux

The regional political dynamics of the region are getting buttressed by an expanding footprint of the bigger powers in the Indo-Pacific, something that is marked by both cooperation and contestation, especially when it comes to defining priorities within the broad framework of sustainable development. The European Union for instance combines environmental and development objectives in its Indo-Pacific strategy by looking at (i) sustainable and inclusive prosperity; (ii) green transition; (iii) ocean governance; (iv) digital governance and partnerships; connectivity; (v) security and defence; and (vi) human security as its priority areas in the Indo-Pacific region. It also aims to support Green Alliances and Partnerships with Indo-Pacific partners to fight against climate change, environmental degradation, marine pollution, plastic pollution, loss of biodiversity, etc, in addition to "increasing the EU's support for Indo-Pacific countries' fisheries management and control systems, the fight against Illegal, unreported and unregulated fishing and the implementation of Sustainable Fisheries Partnership Agreements" (EC 2021).

The Indo-Pacific strategy of the United States underlines the need for energy security and adapting to the energy transitions to renewables, in addition to focusing on infrastructure development and harnessing the benefits of economic transitions in the region with a particular focus on building critical-infrastructure resilience. It also calls upon the need to build and strengthen collective regional capabilities to prepare for environmental and natural disasters and underlines the need for innovation for the deployment of US military to deal with environmental threats. The US strategy is also focused on addressing the problem of natural disasters, resource scarcity, internal conflict and governance challenges in the region, which have the potential to destabilise the region (US 2022).

The Pacific Environmental Security Forum (PESF) which is a part of the US Indo-Pacific Command's (USINDOPACOM) programme, on the other hand, largely devotes itself to environmental security matters in the Indo-Pacific region with an exclusive focus on (i) maritime environmental security; (ii) countering wildlife trafficking; (iii) water security; (iv) oil spill response capabilities; (v) waste management, (vi) illegal, unlawful and unrelated (IUU) fishing; (vii) coastal zone management; and (viii) engineering solutions to environmental change (PESF 2021).

Australia, as one of the Quad members, has also invested heavily in the Indo-Pacific region both in the form of extending development assistance in the area of sustainable development and climate change. In 2019, Australia pledged $500 million for five years beginning in 2020 to help Pacific nations invest in renewable energy, climate change and disaster resilience, given the strategic and economic threat that they face on account of climate change (Government of Australia 2021).

Given the sheer diversity of interests amongst various countries, not to mention the socio-economic and political diversity amongst countries, Indo-Pacific regional cooperation, while it does build on existing micro-regionalism to make some progress on sustainable development and the environment front, it would be a while before a robust cooperative mechanism are put in place, not least because different countries in the region have different priorities and agenda, making them work at cross-purposes on environment-security and developmental issues. This gets compounded by the rise of China, which has widespread ramifications for environmental security and wider geopolitics.

The China factor

The rise of China and its attendant geopolitics has driven the very coinage of the term Indo-Pacific. It has made the region a theatre of emerging geo-strategic dynamics, particularly between the United States and China. All such alliance partnerships in the Indo-Pacific are driven by the impending threat from China and aim at ensuring that China does not undermine the principle of free and open seas, human rights and international law in the Indo-Pacific.

Most developing countries tend to underplay the geo-strategic dimension of environmental challenges. Instead, they keep underlining the development and poverty alleviation as a key to a better environment, a goal that is shared by small island developing countries, too. Many countries in the region, particularly island countries wish to steer clear of this impending power rivalry and underline environmental security and not strategic dimensions of security. These countries in particular, given their environmental vulnerability, underline non-traditional security with a particular focus on climate change, illegal and unregulated fishing, plastic pollution, and oil spills; issues that do not find prominence amongst major powers in the region who keep giving thrust to the geo-strategic implications of the same (Baruah 2022).

Notably, given the rapid economic growth in China, the environmental impact of its rise cannot be overstated. China stands at a lower rung on the Environment Performance Index (at 120) while its performance measured by SDI is also that of a laggard state, ranked at 57. This indicates that China is not paying adequate attention to environmental issues and is focused on meeting high economic growth targets, even when it comes at the cost of the environment. In terms of risk assessment, China is categorised as a country facing medium risk, as per the WRI with its rank of 95, which is comparatively much better than many low-income Indo-Pacific countries bulk of which fall under the category of high-risk countries. The trade-off between environment and economic development made by China to a large extent is contributing to environmental insecurity in the region, given its transnational impact.

A significant geopolitical imperative of the Chinese rise is also manifesting itself in the growing conflict in the South China Sea and the Chinese Belt and Road initiative (BRI), both with widespread environmental consequences too.

The South China Sea is a rich pool of marine life and biodiversity. It has however been faced with the devastating impact of human activity over a period of time, as countries assert their territorial claims and over the ocean's resources. China, Taiwan, the Philippines, Vietnam, Malaysia and Brunei are mired in conflict over claims on islands, namely the Paracel Islands and the Spratly Islands in the South China Sea. The militarisation of the region has also escalated air and water pollution made worse by activities such as hydrocarbon drilling and deep-sea mining and over-exploitation of marine resources. Countries such as China and Vietnam have started building artificial islands on the sea to claim territorial sovereignty, causing lasting damage to the fragile marine ecosystem. The over-exploitation of marine species has undermined cooperative mechanisms for the sustainable use of marine resources, further undermining the cause of the environment (Houdre 2018).

The South China Sea dispute also marks a turning point in the Chinese defiant position on international law, as China did not participate in the proceedings of the Permanent Court of Arbitration in the Philippines vs. China case and refused to accept its binding obligations. The arbitration ruled that China's fishing practices and island-building activities were in violation of Articles 192 and 194 of UNCLOS. China is also set to undermine the long-standing EEZ rule to 200 nm, as it is seen to restrict China's maritime space, a trend that also gets reflected in the case of the BRI project, underwritten by China.

The BRI promises to be this century's largest infrastructural investment project devoted to regional connectivity and economic development, linking nearly 115 countries but has raised environmental stakes in its wake. The United Nations Environment Programme (UNEP) warns of it leading to "unsustainable infrastructure, technology, and resource extraction, [that] will create long-lasting negative environmental consequences [and] seriously undermine the ability of many countries to meet their targets under the 2030 Agenda for Sustainable Development" (UNEP 2022). Some steps have been taken to ameliorate the environmental costs of BRI, one leading example of which is the Belt and Road Initiative International Green Development Coalition (BRIGC or The Coalition). Such environmental considerations are however largely trumped by the larger thrust accorded to economic development, thus short-changing the cause of the environment.

Conclusion

This chapter has provided an overview of the theoretical debate on the evolving linkages between environment and security, which has been in the making for many decades as a part of broadening the concept of security, both vertically and horizontally. A border definition of security, especially that which uses the discourse of security in environmental matters, has made its foray into the policy domain and has large-scale political implications, not just in setting the agenda but also in reshaping policy priorities of states and other stakeholders.

Within the Indo-Pacific region, a diverse set of opinions exists among countries in the region, particularly about designating the environment and climate change as security issues. This chapter has highlighted that the security dimension of environment/climate change has been given particular importance by developed countries, which is also echoed by small island developing states facing existential crises on account of sea-level rise and not necessarily of securitisation – a concern which is not shared by other countries in the region such as India and China although they continue to privilege and underline the need for developmental thrusters to ameliorate their environmental problems. This chapter also elaborates on different dimensions of risks and also the political implications of the securitisation of climate change in particular and environment in general, especially at the UN Security Council, much to the disquiet amongst many countries including India, China and Russia, on the one hand. On the other hand, small island states continue to use the discourse of vulnerability to underline the security dimensions of environment and climate change in a human security framework while at the same time pursuing a developmental agenda which they see as an imperative to boost not only environmental conservation and preservation but also mitigation and adaptive strategies to deal with environmental disasters, in particular, that loom large on them.

This chapter has also deployed EPI, SDI, and WRI to make an assessment of the state of the environment amongst countries in the Indo-Pacific region. For the purposes of this chapter, countries in the Indo-Pacific region have been demarcated along the lines of important regional groupings in the region spanning from APEC, ASEAN and IORA to PIF and SPC. Taken together, these indices point to a dizzying variation amongst countries in terms of their environment and sustainable development performance but also the risks that they face, which are multivariate along the axis of vulnerability, susceptibility and adaptive capabilities to deal with human-made and natural disasters. The particular environmental problems faced by countries in the region have also been documented to understand the political implications which often acquire North-South overtones at various international fora. Even though many small developing island states remain in the camp of developed countries on the issue of reiterating the connections between the environment and security, they do emphasise the importance of development in ameliorating their problems, like many developing countries. The chapter has also analysed how the environmental development and security paradox are featured in the blue economy debate, which has acquired an important place in the Indo-Pacific political lexicon, especially for its developmental promise without losing sight of sustainability. Last but not the least, the chapter has analysed Indo-Pacific regional political dynamics, especially on account of the rise of China, which has brought many players in the region into cooperative and conflictual relationships, leading to many environmental partnerships and bringing diverse countries to a common platform, yet leading to fissures given the geo-strategic imperatives and competing priorities on environment, development and security amongst various countries in the region.

Notes

1 Australia, India, Japan and the United States.
2 Brunei Darussalam, Cambodia, Indonesia, Laos, Malaysia, Myanmar, the Philippines, Singapore, Thailand and Vietnam.
3 Australia, Bangladesh, Comoros, France, India, Indonesia, Iran, Kenya, Madagascar, Malaysia, Maldives, Mauritius, Mozambique, Oman, Seychelles, Singapore, Somalia, South Africa, Sri Lanka, Tanzania, Thailand, United Arab Emirates, and Yemen.
4 Formerly known as South Pacific Commission (SPC) although the acronym continues to be used, despite legal name change to Pacific Community in 2015. It includes American

Samoa, Australia, Cook Islands, Micronesia, Fiji, France, French Polynesia, Guam, Kiribati, Marshal Islands, Nauru, New Caledonia, New Zealand, Niue, Northern Mariana Islands, Palau, Papua New Guinea, Pitcairn Islands, Samoa, Solomon Islands, Tokelau, Tonga, Tuvalu, UK, USA, Vanuatu, Wallis and Futuna.

5 Australia, Cook Islands, Micronesia, Fiji, French Polynesia, Kiribati, Nauru, New Caledonia, New Zealand, Niue, Palau, Papua New Guinea, Marshall Islands, Samoa, Solomon Islands, Tonga, Tuvalu, and Vanuatu.

6 Many of these groupings have overlapping memberships and hence the overall number of countries in the tables in this chapter may not be congruent with the aggregate group membership.

7 UNDP, 1993, *Human Development Report 1993*, New York: Oxford University Press. p. 2.

8 PIF, n.d. "Smaller Island States," Pacific Islands Forum, www.forumsec.org/smaller-island -states/ [accessed on 30 November 2021].

9 Pacific Community, n.d., "Climate Change and Environmental Sustainability," www.spc .int/cces, [accessed on 3 November 2021].

10 The EPI index uses 32 performance indicators across 11 issue categories and ranks countries as "leaders or laggards" based on their environmental health and ecosystem vitality. Wendling, Z.A., Emerson, J.W., de Sherbinin, A., Esty, D.C., et al., 2020, *Environmental Performance Index*, New Haven, CT: Yale Center for Environmental Law & Policy, https:// epi.yale.edu/downloads/epipolicymakersummaryr11.pdf [accessed on 8 November 2021].

11 Sustainable Development Goals (SDGs) are 17 goals adopted by the United Nations in 2015 to guide its programmes until 2030. These comprise: SDG 1: No Poverty; SDG 2: Zero Hunger; SDG 3: Good Health and well-being; SDG 4: Quality Education; SDG 5: Gender Equality; SDG 6: Clean Water and Sanitation; SDG 7: Affordable and Clean Energy; SDG 8: Decent Work and Economic Growth; SDG 9: Industry, Innovation and Infrastructure; SDG 10: Reduced Inequalities; SDG 11: Sustainable Cities and Communities; SDG 12: Responsible Consumption and Production; SDG 13: Climate Action; SDG 14: Life Below Water; SDG 15: Life on Land; SDG 16: Peace, Justice and Strong Institutions; and SDG 17: Partnerships for Goals. "The overall score measures a country's total progress towards achieving all 17 SDGs. The score can be interpreted as a percentage of SDG achievement. A score of 100 indicates that all SDGs have been achieved" while any lower score would mean lack of progress in meeting SDGs. Each of these goals have a subset of targets, making it a total of 169 targets. Source: https://dashboards.sdgindex.org/rankings [accessed on 9 November 2021].

12 For details see, UN, 2021, *The UN Security Council and Climate Change* www.securitycou ncilreport.org/atf/cf/%7B65BFCF9B-6D27-4E9C-8CD3-CF6E4FF96FF9%7D/climate _security_2021.pdf [accessed on 14 December 2021].

13 Antigua & Barbuda, Bahamas, Barbados, Belize, Cabo/Cape Verde, Comoros, Cook Islands, Cuba, Dominica, Dominican Republic, Fiji, Grenada, Guinea-Bissau, Guyana, Haiti, Jamaica, Kiribati, Maldives, Marshall Islands, Mauritius, Micronesia, Nauru, Niue, Palau, Papua New Guinea, Saint Kitts and Nevis, Saint Lucia, Saint Vincent and the Grenadines, Samoa, Sao Tome & Principe, Seychelles, Singapore, Solomon Islands, Suriname, Timor Leste, Tonga, Trinidad & Tobago, Tuvalu and Vanuatu.

14 For further details, see www.aosis.org.

15 E.g. include integrated multi-trophic aquaculture, seaweed aquaculture, shellfish aquaculture and sustainable fish rearing.

16 It has ten targets which comprise to: reduce marine pollution (14.1); protect and restore ecosystem (14.2); reduce ocean acidification (14.3); sustainable fishing (14.4); conserve costal and marine areas (14.5); end subsidies contributing to overfishing (14.6); increase the economic benefits from sustainable use of marine resources (14.7); increase scientific knowledge, research and technology for ocean health (14.8); support small scale fisheries (14.9); and implement and enforce international sea law (14.10). Of particular relevance in the Indo-pacific region is SDG 14.7 which by the year 2030 aims to "increase the economic benefits to Small Island developing States and least developed countries from the sustainable use of marine resources, including through sustainable management of fisheries, aquaculture and tourism." UN, 2015, *Sustainable Development Goal 14*, www.un.org/sustain abledevelopment/oceans/ [accessed on 11 December 2021].

17 PIF, n.d., "Smaller Island States" Pacific Island Forum, www.forumsec.org/smaller-island -states [accessed on 30 November 2021].
18 UN, *SIDS Accelerated Modalities of Action (SAMOA) Pathway*, Sustainable Development Knowledge Platform, A/RES/69/15 https://sustainabledevelopment.un.org/samoapathway .html / [accessed on 9 December, 2021].
19 The agreement entered into force on 2003 and has since been ratified by all member countries.

References

Abe, Shinzo, 2007, 'Confluence of the Two Seas Speech' by Prime Minister of Japan at the Parliament of the Republic of India, 22 August 2007, https://www.mofa.go.jp/region/asia -paci/pmv0708/speech-2.html [accessed on 27 October 2021].

Aleksandrova, M., Balask, S., Kaltenborn, M., et al., 'World Risk Report 2021,' https://www .preventionweb.net/publication/world-risk-report-2021-focus-social-protection [accessed on April 26 2022].

Allenby, Braden R., 2000, 'Environmental Security: Concept and Implementation,' *International Political Science Review*, 21: 1, pp. 5–21.

APEC Economic Policy Report 2021, APEC Secretariat, Singapore 2021.

ASEAN, 2016, 'Roadmap on ASEAN Cooperation towards Transboundary Haze Pollution Control with Means of Implementation,' https://asean.org/wp-content/uploads/2021/01/ Roadmap-ASEAN-Haze-Free_adoptedbyCOP12.pdf [accessed on 12 December 2021].

ASEAN, 2020, 'Haze,' https://asean.org/our-communities/asean-socio-cultural-community/haze -2/# [accessed on 7 December 2021].

ASEAN, 2021, 'About ASEAN Cooperation on Environment,' https://environment.asean.org/ about-asean-cooperation-on-environment/ [accessed on 11 December 2021].

Auslin, Michael R., ed., 2020, *Asia's New Geopolitics: Essays on Reshaping the Indo-Pacific*, Stanford, CA: Hoover Institution Press.

Balzacq, Thierry, 2010, 'Constructivism and Securitization Studies,' in Mauer, Victor and Dunn Cavelty, Myriam, eds., *The Routledge Handbook of Security Studies*, London: Routledge, pp. 56–72.

Barnett, J., 2009, 'Environmental Security,' in Kitchin, Rob and Thrift, Nigel, eds., *International Encyclopedia of Human Geography*, Elsevier Science, pp. 553–557, https://doi.org/10.1016/ B978-008044910-4.00774-4.

Baruah, Darshana M., 2022, 'What Island Nations Have to Say on Indo-Pacific Geopolitics,' Carnegie Endowment for International Peace and Sasakawa Foundation. https:// carnegieendowment.org/files/Baruah_IslandNations_final.pdf [accessed on 1 May 2022].

BBC, 2004, 'Global Warming "Biggest Threat",' *BBC*, 9 January, http://news.bbc.co.uk/2/hi/ science/nature/3381425.stm [accessed on 3 November 2021].

Bergsten, C. Fred, 2008, 'A Partnership of Equals: How Washington Should Respond to China's Economic Challenge,' *Foreign Affairs*, 87: 4, pp. 57–69.

Blair, Dennis and Hornung, Jeffrey W., 2016, 'China's Self-defeating Provocations in the South China Sea,' *The Washington Post*, 2 March.

Bush III, Richard C., 2009, 'Testimony before the Sub-Committee on Asia, the Pacific and Global Environment,' *Committee on Foreign Affairs*, US House of Representatives, 10 September.

Buzan, Barry, Wæver, Ole and Wilde, Jaap de, 1998, *Security: A New Framework for Analysis*, Boulder, CO: Lynne Rienner.

Campbell, John and Warrick, Olivia, 2014, *Climate Change and Migration Issues in the Pacific*, Fiji: United Nations Economic and Social Commission for Asia and the Pacific Office: UN.

CEU, 2008, *Report from the Commission and the Secretary-General/High Representative: Climate Change and International Security*, Brussels: Council of the European Union, 7249/08.

Chan, N., 2018, '"Large Ocean States": Sovereignty, Small Islands, and Marine Protected Areas in Global Oceans Governance,' *Global Governance*, 24: 4, pp. 537–555. https://doi.org/10 .1163/19426720-02404005.

Collins, Gabe and Erickson, Andrew S., 2011, 'Energy Nationalism Goes to Sea in Asia,' NBR Special Report No. 31, *National Bureau of Asian Research*, September, pp. 15–27.

Dabelko, Geoffrey D. and Simmons, P. J., 1997, 'Environment and Security: Core Ideas and US Governments Initiatives,' *SAIS Review* (1989–2003), 17: 1, pp. 127–146.

Denisov, I., Paramonov, O., Arapova, E. and Safranchuk, I., 2021, 'Russia, China, and the Concept of Indo-Pacific,' *Journal of Eurasian Studies*, 12: 1, pp. 72–85. https://doi.org/10 .1177/1879366521999899.

Deudney, Daniel, 1990, 'The Case Against Linking Environmental Degradation and National Security,' *Millennium*, 19: 3, pp. 461–476.

Dokken, Karin, 1997, 'Environmental Conflict and International Integration,' in Gleditsch, Nils Petter, ed., *Conflict and the Environment*, Dordrecht: Kluwer, pp. 523–539.

Doyle , Timothy and Rumley, Dennis, 2020, *The Rise and Return of the Indo-Pacific*, Oxford: Oxford Scholarship Online, https://doi.org/10.1093/oso/9780198739524.001.0001

EC, 2021, *Joint Communication to the European Parliament and the Council, The EU strategy for Cooperation in the Indo-Pacific*, Brussels: European Commission. https://eeas.europa.eu/ sites/default/files/jointcommunication_2021_24_1_en.pdf.

European Commission, Addamo, A., Calvo Santos, A., Carvalho, N., et al., 2021, *The EU Blue Economy Report 2021*, European Commission Directorate-General for Maritime Affairs and Fisheries, Publications Office. https://data.europa.eu/doi/10.2771/8217.

Fetzek, Shiloh, 2021, 'Building Partnerships for Climate Security: US Strategy in the Indo-Pacific,' August, London: The International Institute for Strategic Studies (IISS). https://www.iiss.org/blogs/analysis/2021/08/climate-security-us-indo-pacific?__cf_chl _captcha_tk__=b5fJMkiYoa_mwK0vcL5eRmJD6Xxb1ICkubJYg9N9pDE-1639380903-0 -gaNycGzNB6U.

Gleditsch, Nils Petter, 1998, 'Armed Conflict and Environment: A Critique of the Literature,' *Journal of Peace Research*, 35: 3, pp. 381–400.

GOI, 2020, 'Indo-Pacific Division Briefs,' New Delhi: Ministry of External Affairs, Government of India. https://mea.gov.in/Portal/ForeignRelation/Indo_Feb_07_2020.pdf [accessed on 18 November 2021].

Gopal, D. and Ahlawat, D., eds., 2016, *Indo-pacific: Emerging Powers, Evolving Regions and Global Governance*, New Delhi: Aakar Books.

Government of Australia, 2020, *Development Assistance in the Pacific: Pacific Regional: Climate Change and Resilience*, Department of Foreign Affairs and Trade. https://www.dfat.gov.au/geo/ pacific/development-assistance/climate-change-and-resilience [accessed on 29 November 2021].

Heiduk, Felix, and Gudrun Wacker, 2020, *From Asia-Pacific to Indo-Pacific: Significance, Implementation and Challenges*, Berlin: German Institute for International and Security Affairs. www.swp-berlin.org/fileadmin/contents/products/research_papers/2020RP09_ IndoPacific.pdf.

Herberg, Mikkal, 2014, *China's Energy Crossroads: Forging a New Energy and Environmental Balance*, Washington, DC: National Bureau for Asian Research.

Homer-Dixon, Thomas F., 1991, 'On the Threshold: Environmental Change as Causes of Acute Conflict,' *International Security*, 16: 2 Fall, pp. 76–116.

Hong, Nong and Shicun, Wu, 2014, *Recent Developments in the South China Sea Dispute: The Prospect of a Joint Development Regime*, New York: Routledge, 2014.

Hong, Nong, 2012, *UNCLOS and Ocean Dispute Settlement: Law and Politics in the South China Sea*, New York: Routledge.

Houdre, Chloe, 2018, 'Environmental Ramifications of the South China Sea Conflict: Vying for Regional Dominance at the Environment's Expense,' *Georgetown Environmental Law Review*, 12 July, https://www.law.georgetown.edu/environmental-law-review/blog/

environmental-ramifications-of-the-south-china-sea-conflict-vying-for-regional-dominance -at-the-environments-expense/#_ftnref11 [accessed on 3 May 2022].

Idris, I., 2020, *Trends in Conflict and Stability in the Indo-Pacific*, K4D Emerging Issues Report 42, Brighton: Institute of Development Studies. https://doi.org/10.19088/K4D.2021.009.

IORA, 2017a, 'Blue Economy,' Indian Ocean Rim Association, https://www.iora.int/en/priorities -focus-areas/blue-economy [accessed on 30 November 2021].

IORA, 2017b, 'Disaster Risk Management,' Indian Ocean Rim Association, https://www.iora .int/en/priorities-focus-areas/disaster-risk-management [accessed on 30 November 2021].

IORA, 2017c, 'Fisheries Management,' Indian Ocean Rim Association, https://www.iora.int/en/ priorities-focus-areas/fisheries-management [accessed on 30 November 2021].

Kaplan, Robert D., 2000, *Coming Anarchy: Shattering the dreams of the Post Cold War*, New York: Random House, pp. 19–20.

Keen, M. R. and Schwarz, Anne-Maree et al., 2017, 'Towards Defining the Blue Economy: Practical Lessons from Pacific Ocean Governance,' *Marine Policy*. http://doi.org/10.1016/j .marpol.2017.03.002.

Konar, M. and Ding, H., 2020, *A Sustainable Ocean Economy for 2050: Approximating its Benefits and Costs: Secretariat of the High Level Panel for a Sustainable Ocean Economy*, World Resources Institute. https://www.oceanpanel.org/Economicanalysis.

Kraska, James, 2011, *Arctic Security in the Age of Climate Change*, Cambridge: Cambridge University Press.

Kraska, James, 2011, *Maritime Power and Law of the Sea*, Oxford: Oxford University Press.

Levy, Marc A., 1995, 'Is the Environment a National Security Issue?,' *International Security*, 20: 2, pp. 35–62.

Medcalf, Rory, *Contest for the Indo-Pacific?: Why China Won't Map the Future*, Apple Books, Carlton: La Trobe University Press in conjunction with Black Inc.

OECD, 2018, *Making Development Co-operation Work for Small Island Developing States*. http://www.oecd.org/dac/financing-sustainable-development/development-finance-topics/ OECD-SIDS-2018-Highlights.pdf.

Oels, Angela, 2012, 'From "Securitization" of Climate Change to "Climatization" of the Security Field: Comparing Three Theoretical Perspectives,' in Scheffran, Jürgen, Michael Brzoska, et al., eds., *Climate Change, Human Security and Violent Conflict: Challenges for Societal Stability*, Heidelberg: Springer, pp. 185–206.

Pacific Community, n.d., 'Climate Change and Environmental Sustainability,' https://www.spc .int/cces, [accessed on 3 November 2021].

PESF, n.d., 'About Pacific Environmental Security Forum,' U.S. Indo-Pacific Command's (USINDOPACOM) Pacific Environmental Security Forum (PESF), https://pesforum.org/ about.html [accessed on 11 December 2021].

Tangney, Peter, Nettle, Claire, Clarke, Beverley, Newman, Joshua and Star, Cassandra, 2021, 'Climate Security in the Indo-Pacific: A Systematic Review of Governance Challenges for Enhancing Regional Climate Resilience,' *Climatic Change*, 167: 3 August, pp. 1–30.

Philipose, Rahel, 2021, 'Explained: Why Tuvalu's Foreign Minister Gave COP26 Speech Knee-deep in the Ocean,' Indian Express, 11 November, https://indianexpress.com/article /explained/explained-tuvalu-simon-kofe-cop26-speech-climate-change-7616857/ [accessed on 25 November].

PIF, n.d., 'Smaller Island States,' Pacific Island Forum. https://www.forumsec.org/smaller-island -states [accessed on 30 November 2021].

Sachdeva, Sam, 2019, *Where the Pacific Fits in the Security Debate, Newsroom*, 4 June. www .newsroom.co.nz/2019/06/04/619389/where-the-pacific-fits-in-the-security.

Sachs, J., Kroll, C., Lafortune, G., Fuller, G., and Woelm, F., 2021, *The Decade of Action for the Sustainable Development Goals: Sustainable Development Report 2021*, Cambridge: Cambridge University Press.

Simon, Julian L., 1996, *The Ultimate Resource 2*, Princeton, NJ: Princeton University Press.

Simon, Julian, 1989, 'Lebensraum: Paradoxically, Population Growth May Eventually End Wars,' *Journal of Conflict Resolution*, 33: 1, pp. 164–180.

Steiner, A., 2014, 'Help Small Island States Win their Battle against Climate Change,' *The Guardian*, 29 August. https://www.theguardian.com/environment/2014/aug/29/small-island -states-climate-change-sea-level.

SWP, 2020, *From Asia-Pacific to Indo-Pacific*, Berlin: Stiftung Wissenschaft und Politik (German Institute for International and Security Affairs) July., https://www.swp-berlin.org/fileadmin/ contents/products/research_papers/2020RP09_IndoPacific.pdf [accessed on 19 November 2021].

The Valdai Club, 'Toward the Great Ocean - 5: From the Turn to the East to Greater Eurasia,' September 2017. http://valdaiclub.com/files/15300/.

Trinder, B. R., 2019, 'Climate Change as a Security Issue in the Indo-Pacific Region: Borders, Environmental Phenomena and Preexisting Vulnerabilities,' *Inquiries Journal*, . 11. http:// www.inquiriesjournal.com/a?id=1759.

Ullman, Richard H., 1983, 'Redefining Security,' *International Security*, 8: 1 Summer, pp. 129–153.

UN, 2007, 'Security Council Holds First-Ever Debate on Impact of Climate Change on Peace, Security, Hearing over 50 Speakers,' 17 April, SC/9000. https://www.un.org/press/en/2007/ sc9000.doc.htm [accessed on 11 December 2021].

UN, 2015, *Sustainable Development Goal 14*. https://www.un.org/sustainabledevelopment/ oceans/ [accessed on 11 December 2021].

UN, 2021a, 'Security Council Fails to Adopt Resolution Integrating Climate-Related Security Risk into Conflict-Prevention Strategies,' *Meeting Coverage and Press Release*, 13 December, SC/14732. https://www.un.org/press/en/2021/sc14732.doc.htm [accessed on 14 December 2021].

UN, 2021b, *The UN Security Council and Climate Change*. https://www.securitycouncilreport .org/atf/cf/%7B65BFCF9B-6D27-4E9C-8CD3-CF6E4FF96FF9%7D/climate_security_2021 .pdf [accessed on 14 December 2021].

UN, 2015, *SIDS Accelerated Modalities of Action (SAMOA) Pathway*, Sustainable Development Knowledge Platform, A/RES/69/15, https://sustainabledevelopment.un.org/samoapathway .html/ [accessed on 9 December 2021].

UNDP, 1993, *Human Development Report 1993*, Oxford: Oxford University Press.

UNDP, 2017, *Small Island Nations at the Frontline of Climate Action, UNDP News*. https:// www.undp.org/content/undp/en/home/presscenter/pressreleases/2017/09/18/small-island -nations-at-the-frontline-of-climate-action-.html.

UNEP, n.d., 'The Belt and Road Initiative International Green Development Coalition (BRIGC),' https://www.unep.org/regions/asia-and-pacific/regional-initiatives/belt-and-road-initiative -international-green [accessed on 3 May 2022].

UNFCCC, 2005, *Climate Change, Small Island Developing States*, Bonn: Climate Change Secretariat.

UNGA, 2009, *Climate Change and its Possible Security Implications: Report of the Secretary-General*, A/64/350, New York: UN. https://digitallibrary.un.org/record/667264?ln=en.

US Navy, 2010, *Climate Change Roadmap: April 2010*, Washington, DC: US Department of Navy. https://www.hsdl.org/?view&did=8466 [accessed on 10 December 2021].

US President Office, 1996, 'A National Security Strategy of Engagement and Enlargement,' Washington, DC: White House. https://www.hsdl.org/?view&did=444939 [accessed on 15 November 2021].

US, 2022, *The Indo Pacific Strategy of the United States*, Washington, DC: White House. https:// www.whitehouse.gov/wp-content/uploads/2022/02/U.S.-Indo-Pacific-Strategy.pdf [accessed on 30 April 2022].

Wæver, Ole, 1995, 'Securitization and Desecuritization,' in Ronnie, D. L., eds., *On Security*, New York: Columbia University Press, pp. 46–86.

Watson, I. and Pandey, C. L., 2015, 'Introduction: Environmental Security in the Asia-Pacific,' in Watson, I. and Pandey, C. L., eds., *Environmental Security in the Asia-Pacific*, New York: Palgrave Macmillan. https://doi.org/10.1057/9781137494122_1.

WBGU, 2008, *World in Transition: Climate Change as a Security Risk*, London: Earthscan/German Advisory Council on Global Change. http://www.wbgu.de/wbgu_jg2007_engl.html/.

Wendling, Z. A., Emerson, J. W., de Sherbinin, A., Esty, D. C., et al., 2020, *Environmental Performance Index*, New Haven, CT: Yale Center for Environmental Law & Policy. https://epi.yale.edu/downloads/epipolicymakersummaryr11.pdf [accessed on 8 November 2021].

Wilner, Alexandre S., 2006/2007, 'The Environment-Conflict Nexus: Developing Consensus on Theory and Methodology,' *International Journal*, 62: 1 Winter, pp. 169–188.

Wolfers, Arnold, 1962, *Discord and Collaboration: Essays on International Politics*, Baltimore, MD: John Hopkins University Press, p. 150.

World Bank & UN Department of Economic and Social Affairs, 2017, *The Potential of the Blue Economy: Increasing Long-term Benefits of the Sustainable Use of Marine Resources for Small Island Developing States and Coastal Least Developed Countries*, https://openknowledge.worldbank.org/bitstream/handle/10986/26843/115545.pdf.

World Bank, 2017, 'What is the Blue Economy?,' 6 June. https://www.worldbank.org/en/news/infographic/2017/06/06/blue-economy/ [accessed on 12 December 2021].

World Bank, 2022, 'On the Frontlines of Climate Change, Small Island States Can Lead in Resilience,' *Feature Story*, 11 April.

World Bank, United Nations Department of Economic and Social Affairs, 2017, *The Potential of the Blue Economy: Increasing Long-term Benefits of the Sustainable Use of Marine Resources for Small Island Developing States and Coastal Least Developed Countries*, Washington, DC: World Bank, pp. 2–3. https://openknowledge.worldbank.org/bitstream/handle/10986/26843/115545.pdf?sequence=1&isAllowed=y [accessed on 30 November 2021].

Young, Oran R., 1994, *International Governance, Protecting the Environment in a Stateless Society*, Ithaca, NY: Cornell University Press.

Zheng, X. T., 2019, 'Indo-Pacific Climate Modes in Warming Climate: Consensus and Uncertainty Across Model Projections,' *Current Climate Change Report*, 5, pp. 308–321. https://doi.org/10.1007/s40641-019-00152-9.

Zurlini, G., and Muller, F., 2008, 'Environmental Security,' in Jørgensen Sven Erik and Brian D. Fath, eds., *Systems Ecology*, Vol. 2 of Encyclopedia of Ecology, 5 Vols., Oxford: Elsevier, pp. 1350–1356.

Zurlini, Giovanni and Müller, Felix, 2008, *Environmental Security*. https://doi.org/10.1016/B978-008045405-4.00707-2.

12 Strategic alliances and alignments in the Indo-Pacific

Barbara Kratiuk

The aim of this chapter is to discuss the different strategic alliances and partnerships in the Indo-Pacific region. Looking at the connections, overlapping interests and common enemies/rivals, this chapter will analyse the relationships between different states. Strategic alliances, alignments and partnerships are a way for states to strengthen their connections, without always formalising them. They are also a way to fulfil certain goals, be it security, deterrence or economic growth.

Some of these alliances have endured throughout the Cold War and beyond: US–Japan, US–Korea and US–Australia relations have all been building blocks for regional architecture in Asia, largely based around US presence and liberal values. On the other hand a new group of partnerships has emerged, driven by common interests and common security threats. These new partnerships also play a role in strengthening the role of each individual state in the region and power consolidation.

The many lines of partnerships and alliances make the Indo-Pacific a very tricky region to navigate, as even allies have sometimes opposing interests, while states without friendly relations find themselves siding together to fight off a common threat.

12.1 Concept and definitions of alignments and alliances

The dynamics of Asia-Pacific and later the Indo-Pacific have always been complicated. Nothing show this as much as the increasingly tangled web of alliances, alignments and strategic partnerships in the region. To understand the complexity of this web we first need to fully understand the meaning of alignments, alliances and strategic partnerships as these have often been used interchangeably to describe vastly different dynamics. Traditionally the term "alliances" has been used to denote any type of security based relationship between states, where there was reasonable expectation of help and cooperation in policies. However not only is it wrong to use that term so uniformly, but also new forms of alliances have emerged since the end of Cold War, as the standard moulds have ceased to fit the needs of the regional actors. As Woodman said, "there has been a shift away from formal alliances structures based on military force to more transient marriages of convenience on specific issues" (1997: 81).

Alignments is the term that should be considered the widest term for cooperation between states that assumes a convergence of interests, encompassing in its meaning both alliances and strategic partnerships as well as other types of "marriages of convenience." According to Glen Snyder (1997: 2) "any interaction between states, friendly or hostile, no matter how minor, may create expectations and feelings of alignment or opposition or both." The increased number and levels of interactions

DOI: 10.4324/9781003336143-16

between states since the end of the Cold War ensures that the old understanding of cooperation, even one based on convergent interests is no longer applicable. "Alignment is a crucial aspect of interstate relations in the international system" (Wilkins 2012: 55).

These interactions in the Indo-Pacific have been intensified by multiple conflicts, rivalries and old alliances, all of which impact the expectations. Alignments can therefore be defined as a broad term for both military and non-military cooperation of states with "the expectation of some degree of policy coordination" (Barnett et al. 1991). It is important to note that alignments are wider in scope that alliances and can simply denote common interests and a call for common policies (Morgenthau 2005: 194). According to Ward "Alignment is not signified by formal treaties, but is delineated by a variety of behavioural actions. It is a more extensive concept than alliance since it does not focus solely upon the military dimension of the international politics."

Alignments are born out of commonalities. Miller has identified five main ones:

1. similarity of cultural background;
2. economic equality (or the lack of economic inequality);
3. the habit of association in past international enterprises;
4. a sense of common danger;
5. pressure from a greater power (Miller 1968: 195).

However, increasingly the sense of common danger and pressure from great power seem to be the most important considerations. Vietnam, which until 1995 did not have formal diplomatic relations with the United States, is now considered by the government in Washington DC to be one of the most important actors in balancing against China. When the first three points Miller made are considered, US and Vietnam should not have any form of alignment at all due to differences in culture, economic inequality and lack of habit of past association.

Using the term "alignment" to describe the cooperation between states in areas of common interests allows for better understanding of the overall dynamic, especially since an increasing number of challenges are non-military or have a non-military component. Therefore the "old understanding" of alliances and limiting the analysis of regional cooperation to formal alliances would not adequately present reality (Wilkins 2011; Synder 1997).

Alignments have three main functions:

1. reassuring the small and middle powers of the possibility of help and safety net from a major power;
2. promoting predictability of interactions between states;
3. contribution to regional equilibrium (O'Neill 2020).

Different types of security arrangements have been built due to the need for increased capability to deter threats and potential adversaries. This is very often a result of a change in the balance of power in the region, where suddenly a new powerful actor emerges (Walt 1985). The new distribution of power forces the actors to react and protect their own international positions and interests. There are four main ways to mitigate relative power loss (Paul 2005), and most of them include some form of alignment:

1. balancing – willingness to use own resources to increase own capability and decrease the power gap, but also willingness to work with other actors in similar positions to decrease the power of the potential threat;
2. bandwagoning – joining the new/rising power or the existing hegemon in support of their position;
3. hedging – maintaining balance and relations with all major powers, not aligning with any;
4. enmeshing – trying to establish close relations with all the major powers to increase their investment in the existing distribution of power (Goh 2007).

Two of these are important for entering alliances, because that is when a state either places itself in the opposition to the source of threat (balancing) or when a state sides with their main source of threat to mitigate the danger by allying with it (Wolfers 1959). Therefore alignments and alliances both can be associated with the distribution of power and its regional balance.

It could be argued that alignments are the same as what Morgenthau called tacit alliances. Tacit alliance "occurs when their [state] interests so obviously call for policies and actions that an explicit formulation of these interests, policies and actions in the form of a treaty of alliance appears to be redundant" (Morgenthau 1976: 193). Alignments do not have to be openly declared either, at the very least not in their entirety. Such is the case with a subset of alignments: strategic partnerships, in which the actual cooperation can take any shape within an ambiguous and imprecise declaration (see the section in this chapter on alignment and partnerships).

12.2 Alliances

Stephen Walt defined alliance as "formal or informal relationship of security cooperation between two or more sovereign states" (Walt 1987). This definition however is very broad in its meaning, because it encompasses all security arrangements, including collective security and multilateral organisations. This definition also conflates various types of security cooperation, like war coalitions and alliances proper.

Another way to define alliances is as a

> sustained cooperation among governments in the face of severe external threats results from culmination of four factors: shared preference for existing state of affairs; consensus that no state wants to change the status quo; security cannot be archived through expansionism; recognition that warfare and arms are incredibly costly.
>
> (Jervis 1982)

That definition is a more detailed one that the one proposed by Walt and have basic conditions that an alliance must fulfil to be called such. An earlier definition by Osgood (1968: 7) might be an even better one. He defined alliances as

> a formal agreement that pledges states to cooperate in using their military resources against a specific state or states and usually obligates one or more signatories to use force or to consider (unilaterally or in consultation with allies the use of force in specified circumstances).

Alliances in Asia and in the Indo-Pacific are not the most popular solution for security cooperation (more on this in further sections in this chapter). The cause is, among other things, the alliance security dilemma (Snyder 1997). That dilemma assumes there is a tension between the allied states: the more powerful one fears being forced into a conflict started by a smaller state, which might not be in their own interest. Meanwhile the smaller state fears abandonment and, at the same time, overreliance on their partner. An example of such an alliance could be in the post-Korean War relations between the United States and South Korea: the US administration feared another Korean war and another confrontation with China, while the Korean president Syngman Rhee knew that US presence on the peninsula was the only deterrent from another invasion and dreamed of unifying the two Koreas himself.

This dilemma, which stems from the formalisation of most alliances, has been one of the causes of the lack of a wider multilateral alliance, similar to NATO (He & Feng 2011). Very often alliances were built around a major power, working closely with smaller states. Such alliances were also helpful in managing risks related to the unstable environment of post-war Asia. The asymmetry of an alliance relationship between a major power and a small power can further contribute to control over actions of the weaker state.

Building an alliance system can also bolster the legitimacy of actions undertaken by the major power. "building a hub-and-spokes network creates certain infrastructures, practices, norms and rules that continue to legitimize the superior position of the hub" (Cha 2009). It could be argued that bilateral alliances work best and are especially favourable to great/major powers for three reasons: 1. Maximal power gap facilitates control; 2. maximal power gap mutes counterbalancing strategies; and 3. Maximal power gap encourages bandwagoning (Cha 2009). This also implies that unipolarity is good for alliances. However, while during the period of US unipolarity after the Cold War NATO expanded its membership, the alliances in Asia actually went through periods of crises (especially in the case of US alliances and close military cooperation with the Philippines and Thailand).

Alliances have had to evolve in the post-Cold War period, since for many of them, and for many multilateral institutions, the main source of threat ceased to exist. NATO no longer had to guard against a possible invasion by the Warsaw Pact (and accepted some of the old Pact members), ASEAN admitted Vietnam into its fold in 1995. Even Non-Aligned Movement lost its previous identity. New alliances emerged and new alignments and they were "order-based" instead of "threat-based" (Tow 2008). These "order-based" alignments were focused on maintaining the status quo to ensure that individual states were able to grow and realise their individual interests.

Strategic partnerships

Strategic partnerships are defined as "structured collaboration between states (or other actors) to take advantage of economic opportunities or to respond to security challenges more effectively than could be archived in isolation" (Wilkins 2011: 67). It is worth noting that while, as Wilkins said, these collaborations are structured, the structure itself is usually lax. It's all the more important since strategic partnerships have no limit to time or scope of the operation (Le 2015) and allow the partners to shape the cooperation in a way that will suit their needs.

As Carl Thayer observed: for small and middle powers "the purpose of strategic partnerships is to promote comprehensive cooperation across a number of areas and to give each major power equity" (Thayer 2016). The idea then, behind the strategic partnerships is to ensure that the great powers have that stake also outside of multilateral arrangements.

There is a growing number of strategic partnerships being signed across the international system, which shows how inadequate the alliance system was and an easy rejection of the old solutions as well. China signed 15 different strategic partnership agreements just between 2014 and 2018.

It should be noted that even for one state not all of these partnerships would be equal. There are always levels of commitment and cooperation within the scope of strategic partnerships.

Strategic partnerships are usually: 1. organised around a general purpose; 2. goal-driven; 3. informal in nature with low commitment costs; and 4. economic relations are a key aspect (Wilkins 2011). So this type of alignment can be a common substitute for alliances especially for states, which do not want to formalise their relationships. It can also be a basis for developing closer relations, as due to the informal nature of the partnership, it can be shaped towards the desired outcome. Strategic partnerships have become increasingly popular as way for states to show their close cooperation. China, for example, has signed strategic partnerships with most of the states involved in Belt and Road Initiative.

12.3 Other forms of alignment

Other forms of alignment include security communities and coalitions. Both of these assume working closely with other states that have similar goals, but the end result is different by definition. Coalitions are groups that come together for a specific purpose, a specific action without expectations for a long commitment. The coalitions of the willing during both Iraq and Gulf War could serve as examples.

Coalitions often occur in wartime. They have no formal treaty and are usually a grouping of like-minded states that pursue a joint action on a specific case or problem. There is no expectation or commitment to a long term relationship. Coalition of the willing[1] that invaded Iraq could be considered to be an example. The Big Three (the United States, UK, USSR) during the Second World War is another.

Security communities are another form of alignment. Karl Deutsch (1968: 5) defined security community as "the attainment, within a territory, of a sense of community and of institutions and practices strong enough and widespread enough to assure, for a long time, dependable expectations of peaceful change among its population." Security communities are supposed to come together both when they have common interests and when they have a common threat. So even though the development of security communities was developed separately from alignments, it could be argued easily that the first are a form of the later (Wilkins 2011). Security communities have three distinct characteristics: 1. shared values, identities and meaning; and 2. many-sided, direct relations and reciprocity and long-term interests (Adler & Barnett 1998).

Security communities remain elusive to build, as they require much more focus and many more commonalities than a simple alignment or even an alliance. A security community requires compatibility of values; expectations of stronger economic ties or gains; marked increase om capabilities of at least some participating units; superior economic growth in some units; unspoken links of social communication; broadening of political elite; predictability of behaviour (Deutsch 1968). Security community then means focusing on both economic and political integration to a much larger degree than other forms of alignment would allow.

We can identify three stages of building such a community. The first, nascent stage is when mutual security is increased, the cost of transactions lowers and further interactions are encouraged. During the second stage (ascendant one), there is tighter military cooperation, deepening trust, transition towards more collective identity. Finally in the mature stage, greater institutionalisation, supranationalism and high degree of trust with low probability of conflict can be observed (Adler & Barnett 1998).

To briefly summarise, alignment can mean: policy cooperation with a general goal; an alliance; a strategic partnership; a security community or a coalition. All of these have or are part of the Indo-Pacific multilateral network, but the region's characteristics forced them to fit into a very specific mould.

12.4 Evolution of alignments and alliances in Asia

In the Indo-Pacific the most prevalent forms of alignment would be the general type of policy alignment, alliances and strategic partnerships. There is only one, the nascent security community and sometimes, ad hoc coalitions. The alliances, however, all predate the end of the Cold War. Currently the drive towards structured alliances is much lower, almost non-existent.

Alignments in the Indo-Pacific are important for understanding the dynamics of the region. They are one of the defining features of regional security. For the Indo-Pacific it is all the more important since the region can be considered a regional security complex. Barry Buzan (2003: 106) defined a regional security complex as "groups of states whose primary security concerns link together sufficiently closely that their national securities cannot realistically be considered apart from one another." That means that the potential for a conflict or a low-level existing conflict (see Chapter 14 on International conflicts) can impact the security of other states or even spread across the border to neighbouring states.

Multilateralism was never easy to build in the Indo-Pacific. One of the reasons is the vast differences between states in the Indo-Pacific: they differ in everything from the level of economic development, through political systems to the geographic placement (Cha 2009). Another is the inherent distrust of major powers and guarding against anything that might impinge on the state sovereignty.

12.4.1 Informality and self-reliance

On the other hand, despite the fact that all the different aspects of security in the region are so closely connected for the regional actors, most of them have been and remain very reluctant to commit to a formal alliance of any type. Even historically, there has been no multilateral security institution in the region that was successful. Southeast Asia Treaty Organization (SEATO) was mostly unsuccessful and the plans for PATO have never been realised. SEATO modelled on NATO, had a membership largely incompatible with the needs of the early Cold War period: Australia, United States, United Kingdom, France, New Zealand, Thailand, Pakistan and the Philippines. The lack of cohesion in terms of geographic placement, aims and security needs made this organisation incapable of fulfilling its goals of increasing peace in the region and fighting communism. It was dissolved in 1974. PATO, Pacific Treaty Organization was an idea presented to the US administration by South Korean President Syngman Rhee. It was also supposed to be modelled on European NATO and help increase security as well as fight against communism. However, at the time, due to the increasing security dilemma that Mr Rhee posed for the government in Washington, the idea was not supported.

There hasn't been any regional organisation that would encompass the whole of East Asia, not to mention the Indo-Pacific. The largest ones in scope are organisations centred on trade, such as CPTTP or RCEP (more in Chapters 3 and 4), but even these have very little in terms of membership in South Asia.[2] Most states in Asia, both South and East, prefer informal gathering and institutions, as informality allows for greater flexibility in terms of policy and adapting to the current needs of the member states. Walt (1995) has argued that states should not join in an alliance with those who can easily dominate it. For most of states in the Indo-Pacific all the major powers have capabilities to dominate and since this is an undesirable situation, they try to avoid it. However outright rejection is also not beneficial for weaker states.

That is why they reject the rigid form of formal alliances and instead propose more informal institutions such as treaties of peaceful co-existence[3] or strategic partnerships. This characteristic of rejecting alliances that were not rooted in Cold War has played an important role in the shaping of regional architecture in general and alignment system in particular. US allies have started to take more active roles in the shaping of the Indo-Pacific, trying to increase their own standing in the changing landscape and also increase expand cooperation and common goals across the region.

These alliances have long been characterised by distrust towards each other and other regional players (Cha 2010). They also do not want to risk the already mentioned, overdependence as that could lead to them having to change policy to better accommodate an ally. Since each ally, aligned partner would have at least somewhat different needs and priorities, the states would not want to engage in formal institutions.

That is why minilateral or informal structures work much better in the region and are much more successful. These minilateral alignments of states with similar goals or temporary challenges have experienced a lot of success: the cooperation after the 2004 Thailand tsunami is a very good example of the informal formation of states with a similar goal working in tandem. The minilaterals overlaid on the complex regional architecture, where the membership is already overlapping between similar structures (like East Asia Summit, ASEAN Regional Forum and Shangri La Dialogue) help maintain an institutional balance and absence of hierarchy, both of which are crucial to cooperation in the region.

Most Asian states will primarily look to themselves to defend their interests, then to states with similar aims and only then to regional institutions (Green et al. 2009). 45% of the regional leaders preferred to rely on their own military power, while only 25% on alliances. Alliances are more of a burden to regional cooperation in the Indo-Pacific than help. Most states prefer more loose forms of cooperation, which is clear with the success of strategic partnerships, which are very vague in their meaning and aims.

For the Indo-Pacific understanding the alignment dynamics is important because of the institutional security dilemma that has emerged together with the concept itself. States allied and aligned with the United States as well as their combined efforts can be seen as efforts to contain China and limit Chinese power and influence. On the other hand Chinese efforts to increase power and influence can be seen as limiting the power and influence of the United States and therefore potentially threatening the status quo.

Most states in the Indo-Pacific try not to choose between alignment with any of the major powers. They see it as limiting their options for political decisions. They attempt small scale bandwagoning as a form of appeasement (Walt 1995) to avoid direct attack and benefit from cooperation with that state.

12.4.2 *US hub-and-spoke system and its influence on the Indo-Pacific*

One of the defining systems of alliances and alignments for Asia and now for the Indo-Pacific is the network of American alliances and partnerships. Victor Cha (2010) called it a "complex patchwork" of bilateral, trilateral and other plurilateral configurations. This hub-and-spoke system war created at the end of the second world war to secure US presence and influence in the region. It included deeply asymmetric alliances with states such as Japan, South Korea, Republic of China (Taiwan), the Philippines, Thailand and Australia. All of these were supposed to ensure that the United States would have influence over the security decisions (or even complete control in the case of Japan and South Korea) and would be able to shape the security arrangements and political dynamics of Asia-Pacific. These alliances also strengthened the hegemonic position of the United States after the end of the Cold War (Green 2019). This notion carried over into the Indo-Pacific with the continued existence of all the alliances.

What is important for the hub-and-spoke system is the central role the United States played in it. There would be no network of alignments and partnerships without the core of US alliances. For example, the United States has long established alliances with both Japan and South Korea. However these two states, despite having cooperated together on security matters for decades, have not signed any type of official partnership beyond treaties about cooperation. There is no strategic partnership, very few declarations about cooperation.

These alliances that the United States has shaped during the Cold War remain some of the most crucial for the Indo-Pacific and for individual states. For Japan, South Korea and Australia the alliance with the United States outweighs any other commitments they might have (as exemplified by AUKUS – see Box 12.1). They remain the corner stone of any foreign policy considerations.

These alliances have long been characterised by distrust towards each other and other regional players (Cha 2009). They also do not want to risk the already mentioned, overdependence as that could lead to them having to change policy to better accommodate an ally. Since each ally, aligned partner would have at least somewhat different needs and priorities, the states would not want to engage in formal institutions.

The Cold War has provided stability in the overall balance and distribution of power. It was stabilised by a set of alliances, which have barely shifted over the course of 40 years. US allies, including NATO and the Asian hub-and-spoke system provided one pole, while the USSR and Warsaw Pact provided another. In Asia there was also a third pole: PRC with its allies, working on extending its own sphere of influence at the very least since 1972.[4]

The Cold War also stalled the growth of regional institutions. With the exception of ASEAN, most of them did not survive the change. It was only after the end of the Cold War that a proliferation of multilateral institutions could be observed and new alignments found. Ideological factors prevented them from emerging earlier.

Alignments and partnerships in the Indo-Pacific

The alignments in the Indo-Pacific present a very complex network, as most states in the region have formed some sort of alignment with many others, even while they might otherwise have conflicting interests. The Indo-Pacific contains a set of alliances in the United States hub-and-spoke system that, when established, had a lot of impact on the shape and dynamics of the Indo-Pacific since the end of the Second World War. That alliance is shaping the region even today with the coordinated policies and initiatives.

It is important to note that the driving forces of the current alignments and the restructuring/rebuilding of the regional security architecture is primarily due to the rivalry between USA and China. The introduction of the US Indo-Pacific strategy (more in Chapter 16), together with the revival of the Indo-Pacific strategies of India and Japan (Chapters 18 and 19) have led to a re-conceptualisation of both South Asia and Asia-Pacific. This in turn forced the other states, especially the smaller ones to seek out better solutions for their problems and to increase their cooperation with various great powers in a bit to increase their own capabilities and not be left behind. The introduction of the Indo-Pacific as a geostrategic zone linking two oceans forced a change in the perception of both short and long term interests. It also increased the pragmatic approach of many of the smaller states.

Box 12.1 AUKUS

AUKUS is the newest alliance that has been formed in the Indo-Pacific. It was formed on 15 September 2020 as an alliance based on the exchange of military technology between Australia, United States and United Kingdom. Close cooperation is to include fields such as artificial intelligence, IT, long and mid-range missile technology and quantum technologies.

The initial idea was to help Australia increase military capabilities, especially opposed the increasingly assertive China. This was also a clear signal that US was going to strengthen its alliances in the Indo-Pacific and rely on them and the increasing strength of its partners when it came to the growing rivalry between Beijing and Washington. This alliance is also supposed to increase capabilities and technological advances of the other two partners to maintain and possibly increase the technological edge that US and its allies have.

This alliance has been poorly received by most states in the region, which fear the further increase in rivalry between China and US and their allies. Even India, a Quad member, is not looking favourably at the increase of nuclear-powered submarines in the region, especially since Australia stands to gain at least ten submarines to only one in the Indian Navy (see more on military competition in Chapter 10). Chinese officials have called this alliance highly irresponsible and undermining the regional stability. It does definitely increase the security dilemma for China, which fears that there is a containment strategy in place and both AUKUS and Quad are part of the larger plan to limit China's influence on the region. It is however one of the most significant alliances in the region and the first truly significant one signed in the region after the end of Cold War.

There is only one strategic community in the Indo-Pacific and that is ASEAN. ASEAN as a security community is still in an early building stage, where the trust and expectations of benefits from cooperation are low and composed mostly of a non-war community, where the possibility of an armed conflict is non-existent. Political considerations also take priority for the institution over economic gains, even with the establishment of the ASEAN Economic Community in 2015. That security community is supposed to be a barrier to extreme behaviour for other states (Acharya 2001). It is also possible to observe how smaller states that belong to ASEAN have presented a much more restrained position towards these strategies than the United States and their allies would like (Quayle 2020).

Box 12.2 Quad

Quad (Quadrilateral Security Dialogue) remains one of the most important alignments in the Indo-Pacific to the point where it is often considered to be an informal alliance. It is more influential every year, which is important considering the inauspicious beginnings. Quad came to be in 2006 on the wave of success of the 2005 Tsunami Core Group (a group of states that coordinated their response and humanitarian relief to Thailand after the disastrous tsunami of 26 December 2004. It comprised of USA, Australia, India and Japan). In 2007 Shinzo Abe, then Prime Minister of Japan, made a speech at the Indian Parliament, when he talked about the "Confluence of the Two Seas" (Abe 2007). He said that "The Pacific and the Indian Oceans are now bringing about a dynamic coupling as seas of freedom and of prosperity. A "broader Asia" that broke away geographical boundaries is now beginning to take on a distinct form. Our two countries have the ability – and the responsibility – to ensure that it broadens yet further and to nurture and enrich these seas to become seas of clearest transparence." This was a clear signal that Japan and India were increasingly aligned with each other. Free and Open Indo-Pacific became the focal part for all involved, especially with their growing unease over the growth of China.

The cooperation within the Quad soon fizzled out, as China became vocal about its opposition, with South Korea and Australia hesitating about upsetting their relations with Beijing. Instead, for a time, Quad was reconstructed as two trilaterals: Japan, India and USA and Australia, India and Japan.

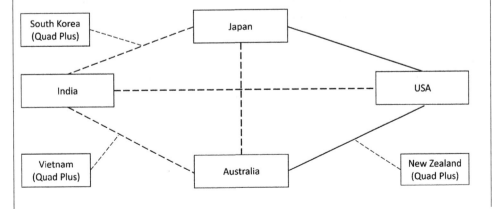

Figure 12B1.1. Graph shows the Quad alignment dynamics. The dotted line shows alignments, while the solid line presents the alliances with the Dialogue. It should be noted that South Korea, which is not officially part of the Quad, has an alliance with USA.

"Japan and Australia constitute two high-capability 'nodes' that should be central to any Indo-Pacific security network. Tokyo and Canberra have found incipient security networking appealing, given both its relative informality and its potential for substantive cooperation" (Fontaine 2020: 139). Australia and Japan, both being heavily reliant on trade with China, have had a similar outlook on the regional dynamics for years. Japan especially has been strengthening its ties with not only other Quad members, but also Quad Plus. The only exemption remains South Korea, where the Moon government was not open to Tokyo's security overtures. "But it is Australia and India's newfound bonhomie that sets the stage for a trilateral. In addition to the long-time Australia–Japan nexus in the Asia-Pacific, the increasing use and precedence of the Indo-Pacific over the erstwhile Asia-Pacific as part of the larger strategic vocabulary terminologically as well as territorially, by way of inclusion of the Indian Ocean eases India into that emerging trilateral strategic calculus" (Ranjan 2015: 2).

It is only in 2017 that the Quad returned to much scepticism about its longevity. It's basic objectives were to build up the Indo-Pacific as a region and area of cooperation; focus on economy and security; freedom of navigation and overflight and finally to establish a rule-based, free and open regional order. However the deciding factor was the rising assertiveness of China in the region. As Walt mentioned, states can ally "in response to threats from proximate power. Because the ability to project power declines with distance, states that are nearby pose a greater threat than those that are far away" (Walt 1995: 10). That is one of the reasons for Quad as an important alignment of interests of major Indo-Pacific powers. The rise of the Quad and the new alignments is therefore directly related to the rise of China and the US–China rivalry. Both states are trying to increase their spheres of influence by creating institutions and partnerships within the region. Belt and Road Initiative (previously One Belt One Road – see Chapter 17). Since 2017 Quad has held yearly meetings on ministerial and higher levels as well as military exercises, including Malabar military exercises, which have become some of the most complex in the world.

In 2020 Quad invited South Korea, Vietnam and New Zealand for talks during their week of meetings. This was a beginning of an informal expansion of Quad into what is called Quad Plus format (Vasudeva 2020). This illustrates the general support for this institution and growing unease with the shakiness of the status quo. Middle and small powers would much prefer to strengthen the existing balance of power than to disrupt it in any way. So they aligned themselves with great powers, which share their interests.

Alignments amidst rivalry in the region

"Throughout much of the post-Cold War period, the dynamics of the Sino–US relationship have been a critical factor of the Southeast Asian states' foreign policy" (Tow 2004). For a long time there was a division of influence between the two powers. Southeast Asia and the, larger, Indo-Pacific are still heavily influenced and divided by these two great powers. Ross (1999) assumed that small and middle powers would not have a large margin for decision-making and therefore would align with a close great power to ensure their security. However as Tow (2004) pointed out smaller states wanted to have greater manoeuvrability and independence. That is why during the Cold War so many of them chose Non-Aligned Movement instead of following either USA or USSR. So the rivalry between China and USA was good for them for a long period of time. It allowed the smaller powers to pick and choose siding with which state would serve their interests better on an almost case-by-case basis.

Table 12.1 lists all the strategic partnership agreements signed by some of the Indo-Pacific states. It clearly shows that most middle and small powers have multiple agreements, and usually these agreements include at least two great powers. It also shows how strategic partnerships have been used in the Indo-Pacific to build alignments and trust as well as closer cooperation without institutionalisation. These states are actually working actively to make a regional hegemony impossible due to overlapping networks of alignments, interests and interactions.

Table 12.1 List of strategic partnerships in the Indo-Pacific (compiled by the author)

State	The states with which it has strategic partnerships agreements (omitting alliances)
United States	**Australia**, **Bangladesh**, **India**, Indonesia, **Singapore**, **Vietnam**, Thailand
China	Brunei, Cambodia, **India**, Malaysia, Myanmar, Pakistan, the Philippines, South Korea, **Singapore**, Sri Lanka, Thailand, **Vietnam**,
India	Australia, **China**, Indonesia, **Japan**, Malaysia, **Singapore**, South Korea, **United States**, **Vietnam**
Japan	ASEAN, **Australia**, **India**, **the Philippines**, South Korea, **Vietnam**, New Zealand
Australia	ASEAN, **India**, Indonesia, **Japan**, Malaysia, Papua New Guinea, the Philippines, **Singapore**, South Korea, **Vietnam**
Indonesia	**Australia**, China, **Japan**, Vietnam, USA
Vietnam	**Australia**, **China**, **India**, Indonesia, **Japan**, Malaysia, the Philippines, **Singapore**, South Korea, Russia, **USA**, Thailand
Singapore	**Australia**, **China**, **India**, **Japan**, Vietnam, **USA**
Thailand	**Australia**, **China**, Vietnam, **USA**
Myanmar	**China**
Malaysia	**Australia**, **China**, **India**, **Japan**, Vietnam
Philippines	**Australia**, **China**, **Japan**, Vietnam,
Sri Lanka	**China**,
Pakistan	**China**, Russia

This table lists the strategic partnerships of the chosen major powers in the Indo-Pacific as well as chosen South and Southeast Asian states. In bold on the list are states that have signed multiple agreements with many of the major powers. ASEAN and individual member states have also separately signed strategic partnership agreements, which is why sometimes they appear in the same list.

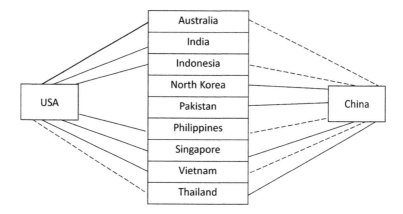

Figure 12.1 Dynamics between two main rivals in the Indo-Pacfic and chosen states. Solid line shows strong alignment, while dotted line shows alignment and indicates issues.

The result is that most of the middle and small powers have developed relations with both USA and China. These two great powers are now locked in a strategic rivalry over dominion in the Indo-Pacific (Scobell 2021) (see Chapters 16 and 17 of the handbook for US and Chinese strategies in the Indo-Pacific) and it has been increasing in its intensity. That increased intensity might lead to a disturbance of the status quo, which would be an undesirable outcome for most of these states. This is also one of the reasons why most of these states perceive the growing rivalry between US and China as undesirable since it can impact the status quo because the two great powers are trying to increase their influence over them. Figure 12.1 shows clearly how some states have strong ties to both US and China and they are unwilling or unable to commit themselves to one.

All of these connections between various actors in the Indo-Pacific make for a very complex network. Australia, while remaining one of the key allies of the United States in the region, has developed a heavy dependency on Chinese markets. South Korea is in a similar situation, as is Japan, another of US allies in the Indo-Pacific. For Vietnam, China is the most important economic partner and a neighbouring country. As such Vietnam cannot afford to damage its relationship with Beijing. The Philippines under the presidency of Mr Duterte has drawn closer to China, but still has to contend with the rival claim to parts of the South China Sea. Thailand, while a traditional US ally, has drawn closer to China in the last decade. None of these states however have declared their full support behind one or the other instead preferring to maintain an equidistant position and the existing balance of power. For that reason most of the Indo-Pacific states have been looking for other solutions, taking into consideration the pre-existing alliances, agreements and historical affinity.

This graph shows the mercenary approach of the states to strategic partnerships. As these are largely shaped by the individual needs in relation to their partners, many states have signed partnership agreements where they have conflicting interests or even conflicts. The Philippines, Vietnam and Thailand have all developed partnerships with both the United States and China despite the fact that these two great powers are regional rivals. Here the local, individual interests take precedent: the smaller states cannot afford not to have close relations with either of the bigger ones. As strategic partnerships are much less binding than other formalised forms of alignment, this is the path that is often chosen to illustrate close relations and secure own interests.

Trilateral alignments

As has been mentioned before, the regional architecture in the Indo-Pacific is largely comprised of bilateral and minilateral alignments as well as multilateral institutions. According to Green (2014; Lee-Brown 2018) these groups help secure and stabilise the region. Especially prevalent are "trilaterals," groups of three states that have aligned themselves together based around common interests or threats. The most important trilaterals are based around the United States and its allies: United States–Japan–South Korea is one such trilateral, Japan–India–Australia is another. There is also a trilateral alignment between China, India and Russia as well as between Japan, India and Vietnam. These are only some of the more prominent and influential trilaterals in the region. The fact that there is a need for many such trilateral groupings of states in the Indo-Pacific speaks to diversity of interests, regime types and threat assessments within the region.

We can identify four main drivers for such trilateral alignments in the Indo-Pacific:

1. deficiencies in regional institutions when it comes to effectiveness and consensus on rule-making;[5]
2. divergent views on how regional architecture and community should be like:
3. deficiencies of the hub-and-spoke system;
4. confidence-building (Green 2014).

What should be noted is that many states in the Indo-Pacific engage in trilaterals with both US and China to maintain a balance and avoid becoming part of a block. This need to maintain relations with both great powers in the region could be seen already in the way many of the Indo-Pacific states have signed strategic partnerships with the United States, China and other regional powers.

As can be easily observed based on Figure 12.2 there are multiple trilateral alignments within the Indo-Pacific with the participation of the same actors. Being part of one grouping does not preclude being part of another one. Some groupings might have divergent interests (like Vietnam, India and Russia vs Vietnam, Australia and Japan). This helps stabilise the region and increase cooperation within.

The trilateral relations between Japan, South Korea and the United States is, for example, focused on the issue of North Korea. It was heavily influenced by the North Korean nuclear programme. This trilateral plays an important role, as it functions instead of a trilateral alliance between these states. It remains, since the end of the Second World War, one of the defining features of security architecture in Asia. It is the primary grouping or alignment that is based around the insecurity drawn from North Korea and, increasingly, from China. This close cooperation (that sometimes is put on hold due to political tensions between Japan and South Korea) is also a source of insecurity for China, which has repeatedly called for the dissolution of Cold War-era alliances.

The trilateral relationship between Russia, Vietnam and India also dates back to the Cold War period. For India cultivating good relations with Vietnam is important in the

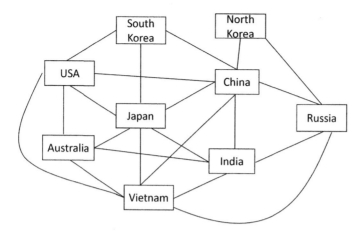

Figure 12.2 Selected trilateral dynamics presents in the Indo-Pacific (prepared by author).

context of maintaining the regional role and Act East Policy. For Vietnam both Russia and India have been traditional sources of arms and military support. Russia maintains relations with Vietnam to ensure a better reach into the Pacific, as the Russian navy is allowed to use the Cam Ranh Bay port facilities. The invasion of Ukraine in February 2022 and the very restrained response from the governments in both New Delhi and Hanoi has shown that those states still consider Russia an important partner, especially when it comes to arms sales and development.

Very often these trilaterals play an important role in the individual strategies of states. The need to maintain a regional balance and pragmatic approach to political and economic interests means that states are looking for alignments with different partners depending on their current needs. This fits very well with the overall dynamic of the regional architecture in the Indo-Pacific. Most smaller states also hope that maintaining engagement in some areas will deter the great powers from any too assertive policies. Great powers agree to this type of regional organisation because they also believe it to be beneficial to them. After all

> multilateral constrains, whether in the form of membership in an alliance or in international institutions, are necessary to bind the great power, discourage unilateralism and give the small powers a voice and voting opportunities that they would not otherwise have. Similarly, if control is sought by a great power over another great power that multilateral controls may be most useful.
>
> (Cha 2010: 165)

Japan is one of the states, beyond China and the United States, building multiple trilateral alignments. As Kei Koga noted

> All this diplomatic work supports Japan's coalition-building efforts to maintain existing international rules and norms and to prevent subregions from being dominated by a single major power, particularly China. To be sure, these

coalition-building efforts do not entail an expectation that every participant state will play the same role.

(Koga 2020)

What Koga called coalitions are in fact alignments designed to strengthen the Japanese FOIP strategy (see Chapter 19). Japan has built trilateral alignments with Australia and India, which is an important factor of the Quad (see Box 12.2). But the government in Tokyo also build closer relations with Vietnam and India, Vietnam and Australia and Vietnam and USA. All of these different configurations of trilateral alignments have been built to fulfil Japanese interests in the region.

Most Southeast Asian states involved in alignments in the Indo-Pacific, such as Vietnam, Singapore or Indonesia, have employed what is called an enmeshing or omni-directional strategy (Goh 2007). The goals of this strategy are to increase the stability of the region through increased institutionalisation of cooperation and to keep the existing balance of power in the region, as it allows these states the greatest range of decision-making capabilities and guarantees continued sovereignty and territorial integrity. They align themselves with great powers such as the United States and China, but also Japan and India, in hopes of maintaining a balance of power in the region and make sure that they do not fall too strongly under the sphere of influence of any individual great power. By aligning themselves in sectoral interests, like trade, freedom of navigation, infrastructure investment, military exercises, the middle and small powers ensure that the great powers remain engaged in the region and in their well-being.

This is a strategy often employed by states that have to deal with asymmetrical relations, as it allows them to alleviate threats and make the resistance against the larger state easier. A multitude of trilateral alignments and multiple strategic partnerships would stabilise the existing balance of power and, if executed properly, strengthen the institutionalisation of the region, hence constraining the possible behaviour of great powers. There are three ways in which such a strategy can function: legitimate inclusion; institutionalised interaction; cooperative security. "States fervently pursue the aim of bringing together the potential great power adversaries in the region in institutions to mediate their balancing tendencies" (Goh 2013: 130) That strategy depends on the political framework[6] ASEAN and its individual members were able to build in Southeast Asia. As one Vietnamese diplomats put it "For the first time we are relying on diplomacy to safeguard security. In the past, it was only used as a crown to military victory" (Vu 2011).

The minilateral alignments are therefore of utmost importance to smaller states that know they have little chance of fending off a great power in a direct conflict. Instead, the smaller states prefer to build many connections, including many minilateral cooperation networks to strengthen their capabilities indirectly. It should be noted that most of the smaller states have some sort of alignment with both great powers, which is reflected often in strategic partnerships.

This will naturally limit the alignments and possibility of alliances in the Indo-Pacific. While there is and will be considerable cooperation, the smaller states are not going to resign from their multidirectional policy willingly, as it would be counter to their interests. While they benefit from working closely with the United States and their allies, these states also benefit from working with China and Russia. These overlapping alignments will remain in place and probably strengthen the Indo-Pacific as a region, since many of them have formed over the two oceans. As India has grown to a great power status and built its own alignments, including with states in the Pacific

Ocean and China's involvement in South Asia has increased as well it is very much possible that the Indo-Pacific as a geostrategic space will increase in importance.

Conclusion

Alignments in the Indo-Pacific are an ever-more complex network. They include traditional alliances, like those of the United States with Japan, Australia and South Korea or the one between China and North Korea. There is a growing security community in ASEAN, which has been experiencing some growing pains these last couple of years due to the increasing rivalry between the United States and China in the region. Finally there are strategic partnerships, of which a multitude had been signed in the Indo-Pacific.

All of these are expressions of alignment, of policies and goals being coordinated by governments of all the states involved in the Indo-Pacific. Very often, depending on the alignment and its membership, some of the goals and policies will be complete opposites of each other. What is important for the alignments is that they provide stability and predictability to a very unstable and unpredictable region, fraught with rivalry, conflict and competition. The multitude of these alignments shows a significant shift in the way most states, especially medium-sized, think about politics and cooperation. Rarely do they constrain themselves to only one grouping, preferring to work towards greater cooperation in many directions for as long as they are able. The great powers on the other hand, cannot stop that for fear of turning away the smaller states, which are potential allies and places to increase their own influence. Hence the increased number of alignments.

It should also be considered that such alignment and alliance building can create instability among those excluded from such formations. Glen Snyder put it best when he analysed the security dilemma:

> even when no state has any desire to attack others, none can be sure that others' intentions are peaceful, or will remain so; hence each must accumulate power for defence. Since no state can know that the power accumulation of others is defensively motivated only, each must assume that it might be intended for attack.
>
> (Snyder 1984: 461)

This means that with the creation of alliances the sense of insecurity actually increases in the states not in the alliances. They assume all the more that they would be a target of attack, why else would alliances be formed after all? Fear of attack would further increase in case of already existing rivalry such as the one between China and the United States in Asia and the Indo-Pacific. Wang Yi, the Foreign Minister of the PRC has mentioned multiple times that the US Indo-Pacific strategy has caused increased security concerns for China and other states in Asia-Pacific. With such a perception the state that feels threatened will increase their arms and solidify their alliances and alignments thus causing an increased sense of insecurity in the main rival. This clearly illustrates how increasing or formalising alliances could lead to increased insecurity.

That security dilemma is one of the main reasons why states now very rarely formalise their alignments into something more formal than strategic partnerships. Most alignments either remain completely informal (like Quad) or have a very vague shape (like strategic partnerships). This is especially important since most states in the Indo-Pacific do not want to limit themselves to only one set of states or alignments, especially since that could limit their own foreign policy and prove to be inconvenient in realising their own interests.

The alignments and alliances in the Indo-Pacific cannot therefore be determined as simply a stabilising factor for the region. The alignments and alliances provide a sense of seciurty for the states in the region, but at the same time they provide a sense of insecurity for those states, which remain outside of those structres.

Notes

1 The coalition included USA and 31 other states: Afghanistan, Albania, Australia, Azerbaijan, Bulgaria, Colombia, Czech Republic, Denmark, El Salvador, Eritrea, Estonia, Ethiopia, Georgia, Hungary, Iceland, Italy, Japan, South Korea, Latvia, Lithuania, Macedonia, the Netherlands, Nicaragua, the Philippines, Poland, Romania, Slovakia, Spain, Turkey, United Kingdom and Uzbekistan.
2 India has been invited to participate in the RCEP negotiations but declined to participate.
3 The first treaty of peaceful coexistence, officially the Agreement on Trade and Intercourse Between Tibet Region of China and India, was signed by India and China in 1954. It introduced the Five Principles, which were later spread into Non-Aligned Movement and to ASEAN Treaty of Cooperation,
4 In 1972 China started rapprochement with USA. This ended the period of PRC policies which were targeting both USA and USSR. USSR became a more important rival for the government in Beijing, especially after the Shanghai Communique and further official normalisation of relations with USA in 1979.
5 Most states have low expectations of rule-making from ASEAN or ARF. While ASEAN remains central for regional architecture, due to the need for a lax format of the organization and lack of hierarchy, the effectiveness of the organisation remains low as well.
6 The argument of balance of power depending on political framework is mostly associated with the English School of international relations, most notably Hedley Bull and his "The Anarchical Society: A study of Order in World Politics."

Bibliography

Abe, S. 2007. "Conflucence of the Two Seas" Speech by H.E.Mr. Shinzo Abe, Prime Minister of Japan at the Parliament of the Republic of India. https://www.mofa.go.jp/region/asia-paci/pmv0708/speech-2.html.

Adler, E., & Barnett, M. (Eds.). 1998. *Security Communities* (Cambridge Studies in International Relations). Cambridge: Cambridge University Press.

Becker, J. 2021. Order, Counter-Order, Disorder. *Alliances, Orders, and International Security* (March 6, 2021).

Buzan, B., & Wæver, O. 2003. *Regions and Powers: The Structure of International Security*. Cambridge University Press.

Cha, V.D. 2009. Powerplay: Origins of the U.S. Alliance System in Asia. *International Security*, 34(3), 158–196.

Cha, V.D. 2010. *Powerplay: The Origins of the American Alliance System in Asia*. Princeton University Press.

Deutsch, K. 1968. *The Analysis of International Relations*. Englewood Cliffs, NJ: Prentice-Hall, Inc.

Fontaine, R. 2019. *Southeast Asian Alliances and Partnerships*. M.J. Green (ed.). Ironclad: Forging a New Future for America's Alliances CSIS. https://csis-website-prod.s3.amazonaws.com/s3fs-public/publication/Ironclad_web.pdf. Accessed: 10 February 2020.

Goh, E., 2007/2008. Great Powers and Hierarchical Order in Southeast Asia: Analyzing Regional Security Strategies. *International Security*, 32(3), 113–157.

Goh, E. 2013. *The Struggle for Order: Hegemony, Hierarchy and Transition in Post-Cold War East Asia*. Oxford: Oxford University Press.

Green, M.J., Gill, B., & Tsuji, K. 2009. *Strategic Views on Asian Regionalism*. CSIS. https://www.csis.org/analysis/strategic-views-asian-regionalism. Accessed: 22 February 2020.

Green, M.J. 2014. Strategic Triangles in Asia. In S. Pekkanen, J. Ravenhill, & R. Foot (eds.), *The Oxford Handbook of the International Relations of Asia*. London: Oxford University Press.

Green, M.J. 2019. Ironclad: Forging a New Future for America's Alliances CSIS. https://csis
-website-prod.s3.amazonaws.com/s3fs-public/publication/Ironclad_web.pdf. Accessed: 10
February 2020.

Jervis, R. 1982. Security Regimes. *International Organization, 36*, 357–378.

Koga, K. 2020. Japan's 'Indo-Pacific' Question: Countering China or Shaping a New Regional
Order? *International Affairs*, 96(1), 49–73. https://doi.org/10.1093/IA/IIZ241.

Le, H.H. 2015. *Vietnam's Alliance Politics in South China Sea*. Singapore: ISEAS Publishing.

Lee-Brown, T. 2018. Asia's Security Triangles: Maritime Minilateralism in the Indo-Pacific. *East
Asia, 35*(2), 163–176. https://doi.org/10.1007/S12140-018-9290-9.

Miller, J.D.B. 1968. The Conditions for Co-operation. In J.D.B. Miller (ed.), *India, Japan,
Australia: Partners in Asia*. Canberra: Australian National University Press.

Morgenthau, H.J. 1976. Alliances in Theory and Practice. In A. Wolfers (ed.), *Alliance Policy in
the Cold War*. Westport: Greenwood Press, pp. 184–212.

Morgenthau, H.J. 2005. *Politics among Nations: The Struggle for Power and Peace*. Boston:
McGraw-Hill.

O'Neill, A. 2020. The Future of Alliances in Asia. In S. Ganguly & J. Liow (ed.), *Handbook of
Asian Security Studies* (pp. 357–371). New York: Routledge.

Paul, T.V. 2005. Soft Balancing in the Age of US Primacy. *International Security, 30*(1), 46–71.

Quayle, L. 2020. Southeast Asian Perspectives on Regional Alliance Dynamics: The Philippines
and Thailand. *International Politics, 57*, pp. 225–241.

Ranjan, V. 2015. Australia, India and Japan Trilateral-Breaking the Mould ORF Occasional
Paper.

Ross, R.S. 1999. The Geography of the Peace: East Asia in the Twenty-first Century. *Quarterly
Journal: International Security, 23*(4 Spring), 81–118.

Scobell, A. 2021. Constructing a U.S.-China Rivalry in the Indo-Pacific and Beyond. *Journal of
Contemporary China, 30*(127), 69–84. 10.1080/10670564.2020.1766910.

Snyder, G. 1984. The Security Dilemma in Alliance Politics. *World Politics, 36*(4), 461–495.

Snyder, G. 1997. *Alliance Politics*. Ithaca: Cornell University Press.

Thayer, C. 2016. Vietnam's Proactive International Integration: Case Studies in Defense
Cooperation. *Vietnamese National University Journal of Science, 32*. https://js.vnu.edu.vn
/SSH/article/view/4396.

Thomas S. Wilkins, Japan's alliance diversification: a comparative analysis of the Indian and
Australian strategic partnerships, International Relations of the Asia-Pacific, Volume 11,
Issue 1, January 2011, Pages 115–155.

Tow, S. 2004. Southeast Asia in the Sino-U.S. Strategic Balance. *Contemporary Southeast Asia,
26*(3), 434–459.

Tow, W. T. 2008. Tangled Webs: Security Architecture in Asia. ASPI Strategy Paper.

Vasudeva, A. 2020. US–China Strategic Competition and Washington's Conception of Quad Plus.
Journal of Indo-Pacific Affairs, 3(5). https://media.defense.gov/2021/Mar/12/2002599860/
-1/-1/0/2-VASUDEVA.PDF/TOC.pdf.

Vu, T.N. 2011. Vietnam's Security Challenges: Hanoi's New Approach to national Security and
Implications to Defense and Foreign Policies. *National Institute for Defense Studies*. http://
www.nids.mod.go.jp/english/publication/joint_research/series5/pdf/5-8.pdf.

Walt, S. 1985. Alliance Formation and the Balance of World Power. *International Security, 9*(4),
3–43.

Walt, S. 1987. *The Origins of Alliances*. Ithaca: Cornell University Press.

Walt, S. 1995. Alliance Formation and the Balance of Power. In M. E. Brown, S. M. Lynn-Jones,
& S. E. Miller (eds.), *The Perils of Anarchy*. Cambridge: Cambridge University Press, pp.
208–248.

Wilkins, Thomas S. 2011. Japan's Alliance Diversification: A Comparative Analysis of the
Indian and Australian Strategic Partnerships. *International Relations of the Asia-Pacific,
11*(1), 115–155.

Woodman, S. 1997. Beyond Armageddon? The Shape of Conflict in the Twenty-First Century. In
D. Roy (ed.), *The New Security Agenda in the Asia-Pacific Region* (p. 81). London: Macmillan.

13 Strategic rivalries in the Indo-Pacific
Contest, claims and conflicts

Astha Chadha

Indo-Pacific's inter-state contentions: introduction

The Indo-Pacific, a region stretching from the West shores of Africa to the East shores of the United States, is witnessing a period of conflicts involving several states that are contesting over interests and influence, even as they engage with strategic rivals for trade and economic interdependence. The nature of rivalries in the Indo-Pacific is transforming into issue-based conflicts, made severe by an emerging multi-polar world order with several regional powers projecting influence in the Indo-Pacific, which the US and its like-minded partners and allies view as a free, open, and inclusive region.

The conceptualisation of the Indo-Pacific as a strategy entails the region being 'free, open and inclusive', which points to the freedom of navigation, free movement of goods and people across the key maritime lanes and access to the Sea Lines of Communication (SLOCs) for all Indo-Pacific states. However, due to the strategic importance of these choke points as well as the shipping routes, the navies of several conflicting powers in the Indo-Pacific currently maintain a presence in the region through bilateral, trilateral and multilateral naval exercises and FONOPs among countries like the US, India, Japan, Australia, Vietnam and the Philippines.

With rapid globalisation in the last decade of the twentieth century, the energy shipping routes in over 70 million square kilometres of the Indian Ocean became quintessential. The US established its naval presence in the Indian Ocean supported by its presence in the Middle East, and military bases in Oman and Qatar, amid an absence of Soviet presence in the region in 1991. In the 2000s, a Chinese military presence in the three regions of the Indian Ocean, East China Sea and South China Sea, reignited existing territorial disputes with India, ASEAN nations and Japan. Security tensions flared up in Asia with China, Pakistan and Russia spending larger portions of their GDP towards defence expenditures, threatening nations like the US, Japan and India (SIPRI 2020).

In the backdrop of China's claims in the East and South China Sea where it claims almost the entire maritime region, its policy towards the maritime zone close to the Indian peninsula in the Indian Ocean was very different. In 2015, while referring to an increased presence of Chinese submarines close to Sri Lanka and Pakistan, Beijing remarked that thinking of the Indian Ocean as India's backyard is a "mistake" which could lead to "clashes" (Dasgupta 2015). The region is not only important for trade but also strategically located at the hub of energy and commercial routes from the Middle East (Map 5).

DOI: 10.4324/9781003336143-17

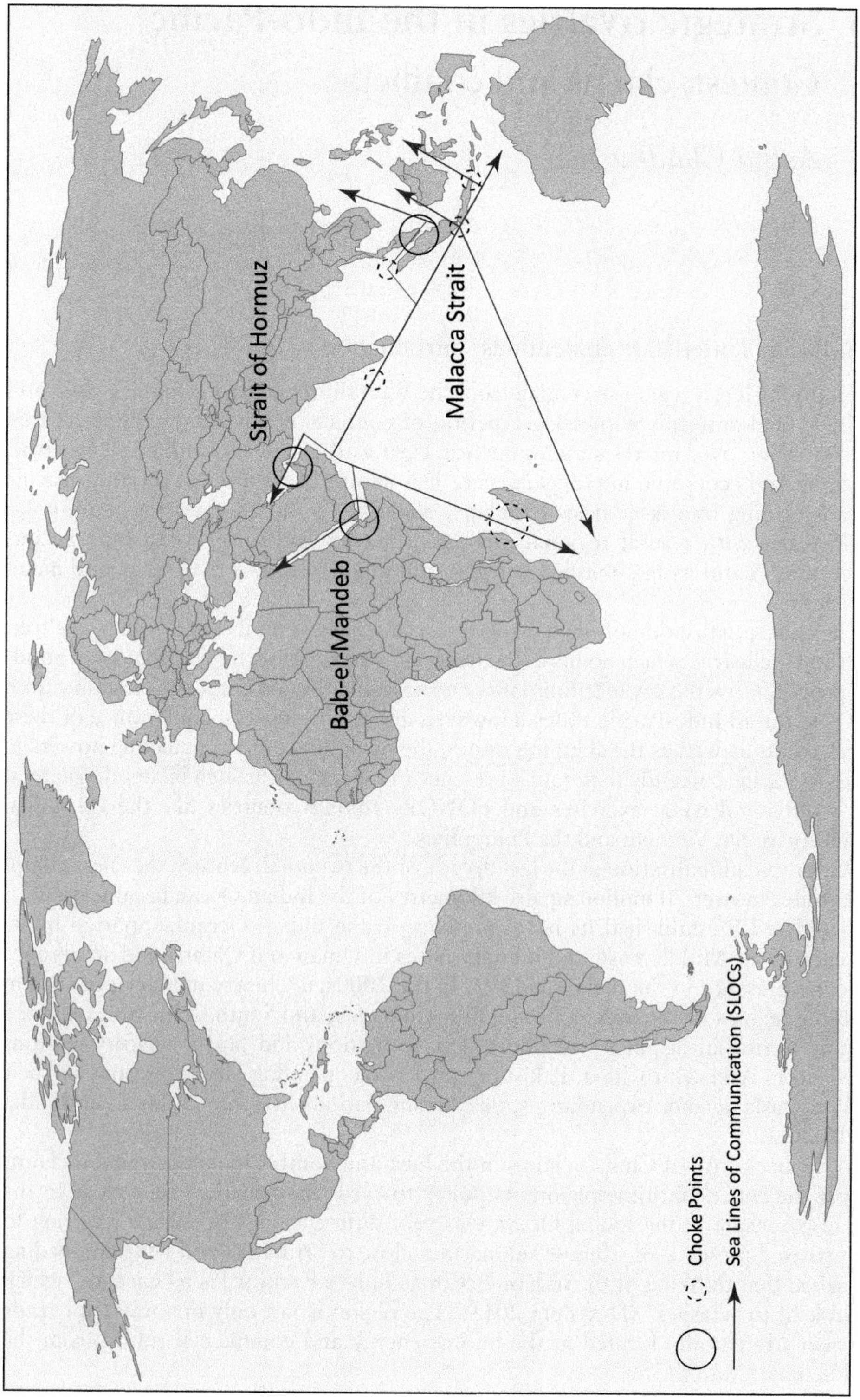

Map 5 Key sea lines of communication (SLOCs) and choke points in the Indo-Pacific maritime region. Source: Prepared by author with data from (Lauriat 2021: 9)

As of 2018, maritime trade accounted for up three-quarters of the total commodities shipped through seas. The Indo-Pacific maritime area is the hub of global trade supporting some of the world's largest economies such as the US, China, Japan, India, etc., utilising the sea routes in the region for international trade. The Indo-Pacific also accounts for over 50% of the world's population, seven of the world's ten largest armies, six nuclear powers and more than 60% of the global maritime trade (Department of Defense 2019: 9). The shipping lanes and SLOCs in the Indian Ocean region of the Indo-Pacific contain some of the key maritime choke points which are defined as narrow and congested shipping lanes along the shipping routes. These choke points pose the dual risks of ships blocking the narrow sea route due to the natural geography of the route and the security risk of the sea route being blocked during a pirate attack or amid geopolitical tension in the region (Liss 2014: 5).

This chapter explores the evolution of various strategic rivalries in the Indo-Pacific. These enmities are analysed from the dual lens: the engagement of existing power rivalries of the Indo-Pacific in other regional disputes; and small powers being dragged into the larger network of strategic rivalries in the Indo-Pacific. Key rivalries discussed are those of the US (with China and Russia), India (with China and Pakistan) and Japan (with China and North Korea). The chapter then traces how these rivalries have grown over time with the engagement of larger powers in the largely bilateral disputes, and/or engagement of these powers in disputes of other states, thereby forming a network/web of rivalries in the Indo-Pacific. The overall aims of the chapter are two-fold: first, to trace the (nature of) development of strategic rivalries since WWII in the Indo-Pacific region; and second, to provide a web of strategic rivalries in the Indo-Pacific explaining the engagement of several contesting and conflicting states in the Indo-Pacific.

Strategic rivalries: definition and concept

Rivalries have been discussed in the international relations' literature, both as a theoretical concept and as case studies of great powers such as the United States and the Soviet Union, or the current rivalry between the US and China. The significance of understanding the concept and evolution of rivalries is not only as a step towards conflict management or conflict resolution but also that it acts as a cautionary sign to the evolution of potentially severe rivalries escalating into wars. In the case of a dismal probability of resolution of conflicts, rivalry linkages may help identify potential flashpoints or clashes, thus allowing states to recalibrate their strategies based on informed perceptions (Diehl & Goertz 2000: 243). The underlying assumption here is that conflict can lead to a war or a militarised confrontation between states. Hence it is important to carefully distinguish between conflicts and rivalries, as discussed in some key works in the field.

Conflicts can be short and definite, or extended and persistent, embodying military action between conflicting states. While conflicts can sustain for longer periods of time and indicate rivalries, all rivalries need not be identified through a militarised conflict. The extended conflicts share some characteristics of rivalries, such as both could be based on a historical/territorial issue, contention over clashing national interests, their relative (power) position in global politics, etc., that might lead to observable consequences like an arms race, seeking allies and acts of coercion, further intensifying the conflict or rivalry. Colaresi and Thompson (2002: 263) have argued that "rivalry not only makes escalation more likely, but also significantly interacts with more traditional predictors of conflict, such as capability ratios, the number of actors in a crisis, democracy, and the issues under contention."

The existing scholarship has approached the concept of rivalry as a competitive relationship between states characterised by commonly observable factor(s) such as intensity and frequency of militarised conflict, period of inter-state hostility, relative capabilities to sustain conflicts or any issue with stakes involved on the part of both states (Ben & Maoz 1999; Diehl & Goertz 2000; Goertz & Diehl 1992; Vasquez 2009; Vasquez & Valeriano 2010). A sizeable proportion of the scholarship has focused on enduring international rivalries which define "a set of relationships between states characterized by repeated conflict" (Ben & Maoz 1999). These are illustrated by the existence of frequent militarised conflict in a specified time period between two states such as a minimum of three disputes in 15 recent years (Diehl 1985a, 1985b) or at least five disputes in 25 years (Waymann & Jones 1991, as cited in Vasquez 2009: 78–79).

In contrast, a strategic rivalry differs from an enduring rivalry in that the former can be formed even without a militarised conflict. Thompson (2001) has defined strategic rivalries as competitive relationships between two states that identify each other as a threat and as an enemy. For Colaresi and Thompson (2002: 275) a strategic rivalry is "a highly competitive relationship that is separable from more benign conflict by the criteria of mutual identification" where all identified threats from the rival do not carry equal weight. Since the definition clarifies that strategic rivals need not engage in militarised confrontation, a dispute density data set is unlikely to explain alone the cause or intensification of a strategic rivalry (Colaresi et al. 2008). While strategic rivals also compete over scarce resources, conflicting interests and overlapping objectives, the emphasis here is on "perceptions about threatening competitors who are categorized as enemies (strategic rivalries) and an empirical emphasis on satisfying a minimal number of militarized disputes within some time limit (enduring and interstate rivalries)" (Colaresi et al. 2008: 22).

For Thompson (2001: 560), strategic rivalries are mirror opposites of "cooperative special relationships" largely between states of similar capabilities, i.e., a small weak state and a strong threatening state cannot be strategic rivals due to asymmetry in capabilities. Therefore, strategic rivals are mutually identified and explicitly selected as competitors, possible threats capable of engaging in (armed) conflicts and enemy states. Unlike enduring rivals, strategic rivals can have conflicting issues of varying degrees of severity, need to have a history of war and can thus put each other on close surveillance after clearly identifying the other as a rival without actually engaging in violence (Colaresi & Thompson 2002: 265). Additionally, since resources are limited, (mild or extreme) conflicts between strategic rivals could be caused by perceived "incompatibilities in attaining material and nonmaterial goals" causing "inability to occupy the same space, share the same position, or accept the superiority of another's belief system" (Colaresi & Thompson 2002: 559).

Thus, based on above conceptualisations, this chapter defines a *strategic rivalry* as follows:

> Explicitly recognized enmity between two states engaged in conflict over limited availability of material/nonmaterial objectives and interests, where each conflict is characterized by a zero-sum game amid element of mutual threat perception

implying clear identification of the adversary and significant probability of militarized conflict of any scale.

Strategic rivalries too can take up different forms based on the reason for conflict. The existing literature identifies strategic pairs of rivalries as (Colaresi et al. 2008: 73–96; Lacey 2016: 6):

- spatial (rivals contesting for absolute territorial/regional hegemony);
- ideological (rivals seeking to establish a dominant economic, political, religious ideology and belief system);
- positional (rivals striving for greater influence and higher rank in an established power hierarchy/system).

Another type of strategic rivalry has been identified by Dreyer (2010: 783–784), who defines identity-issue conflict among strategic rivals arising from "objection to the perceived mistreatment of a group of individuals (with which one shares transnational similarities in identity) within another state." Adding this issue increases the explanatory power of the strategic rivalry typology by separating ideology from identity-based issues in regional and global politics.

In line with the concept, this chapter will adopt a SPIN framework denoting spatial, positional, ideological and identity-issue strategic rivalries, to examine the conflicting states of the Indo-Pacific and present a flexible and evolving web of strategic rivalries that are neither defined by any one reason for enmity nor limited to a certain number of wars in a specific time span. Embedded in the concept of strategic rivalries is the premise that no rivalry is permanent, and that rivalries can change over time rather than being fixed by structural conditions (Hensel 1999: 183). States identify their adversaries against the backdrop of their "strategic interests," which can lead to clashes and conflicts. Strategic rivalries thus also allow mutually peaceful states to turn into "issue-specific rivals" over strategic interests. This chapter hypothesises that while identity-issue and ideological rivalries could be sufficient to stoke a strategic rivalry, it is usually sustained long-term by the accumulation of other issues such as spatial or positional (in a global, regional or sub-regional context).

Adopting a qualitative analysis approach through the case study method, this chapter will consider the four types of strategic rivalries and discuss three key cases of evolving Indo-Pacific rivalries surrounding the US, India and Japan. While the US is a global power and influences the course of international politics, India and Japan are like-minded regional powers in the Indian and Pacific Oceans respectively, with enough capability to withhold or resist the Indo-Pacific order. Together, the three nations maintain high stakes in instating an Indo-Pacific vision of a free, open and prosperous region driven by economy, security and power concentration. As a point of departure from previous studies, the creation of a web of rivalries does not limit itself to pairs of rival states or dyads (Diehl & Goertz 2000; Goertz & Diehl 1992; Thompson 2001). Though this chapter analyses important strategic rivalries in the Indo-Pacific region since the end of WWII, the study seeks to provide a multi-layered rivalry linkage among more than two states, with the aim of more accurately highlighting the multiple interests of states in the Indo-Pacific region.

Evolution of strategic rivalries in the Indo-Pacific since WWII

The whole world was impacted by the consequences of the Second World War (WWII, 1939–45), which saw the alignment of powers in two major camps – axis powers comprising Germany, Japan and Italy opposing the Allied powers of the United States, France, Great Britain and the Soviet Union. A brief glance at rivalry-alliance structures at the end of WWII is important for understanding the development of Indo-Pacific strategic rivalries for three reasons. One, the strategic rivalries (and even some alliances) that emerged as a consequence of the WWII in Asia and the West laid the foundation for some persisting strategic rivalries that have survived till today. Second, being one of the rare events involving a large number of warring states and massive destruction, the event drastically changed the nature of rivalries among global and regional powers into one where war was no longer the defining characteristic of recognised enmity. Third, as Colaresi et al. (2008: 4) have argued, the adversaries may mistrust each other as issues accumulate but conflict can be "punctuated with periods of cooperation" while strategic rivalry continues to hold. Some WWII strategic rivalries fit into the third trend as well. In fact, it is these rivalries, and a bid to form counter-partnerships, that led to the evolution of the Indo-Pacific concept.

The end of WWII coincided with the victory of Allied forces as Germany, Italy and Japan lost the war. It also led to the eventual defeat of Japan in the Pacific after the Hiroshima and Nagasaki bombings, and the end of Japanese expansion in China (and parts of the British Indian colonies) in 1945 with the US support to China's local Nationalist government. Japan's acceptance of the terms of the Potsdam Declaration also marked the end of the US–Japan strategic rivalry in the Pacific, culminating into an Asia-Pacific alliance. After Japan's defeat, China slipped into civil war for two decades ending with the emergence of victory of the Communists in 1949, formation of People's Republic of China and the Nationalists' retreat to Taiwan. The US maintained support for Taiwan's Republic of China government, provoking the evolution of relations between once-allied China and the US into a mutually identified strategic rivalry. Meanwhile, independence movements against European imperialism culminated into the partition of British India into India and Pakistan that stood at geostrategically important locations in the Indian Ocean and marked the region's most daunting spatial, ideological and identity-issue strategic rivalry in the following decades.

The allies turned positional and ideological strategic rivals, the Soviet Union and the US slipped into the beginning of the Cold War. The threat of Communist expansion in a divided Europe pushed the US to form an alliance with 11 European states in 1949 called the North Atlantic Treaty Organization (NATO) to rival the Soviet Union and its influence in states captured from the Nazis during WWII (Kortunov 1996). A counter alliance, the Warsaw Pact was signed between the Soviet Union and East European territories. Other states led by India, Indonesia, Ghana, Yugoslavia and Egypt, that denied alliance with the Western or Communist blocs, formed the Non-Alignment Movement in 1960, stressing their independent foreign policy, anti-colonial stance and strategic autonomy (Suslov 2016).

The Cold War further spilled the ideological strategic rivalry into Asia with Western and Communist-backed forces clashing in Korea (1950–1953, which ended in the division of Communist North Korea and the US-ally South Korea) and Vietnam (1955–1975, which ended in the victory of the Communists and withdrawal of the US troops), as tabulated in Table 13.1. Similarly, once-allied China and the US clashed

Table 13.1 Key strategic rivalries of the Indo-Pacific until the end of the Cold War

Strategic rivals	Key conflicts during or after WWII	Wars since 2000
The US and Russia[1]	Korean War (1950–1953) Vietnam War (1955–1975)	0
The US and China	Korean War (1950–1953) First Taiwan Strait Crisis (1954–1955) Second Taiwan Strait Crisis (1958) Vietnam War (1965–1969) Third Taiwan Strait Crisis (1996)	0
Japan and China	Second Sino-Japanese War (1937–1945)	0
Japan and Russia	Soviet–Japanese War (1945) (WWII)	0
India and China	Sino-Indian War (1962) Nathu La and Cho La clashes (1967) China–India skirmishes (2020–2021)	1 (skirmish on disputed borders)
India and Pakistan	Indo-Pakistan War (1947–1948) Indo-Pakistan War (1965) Bangladesh Liberation War (1971) Siachen conflict (1984–2003) Kargil War (1999)	0 (excluding Kashmir insurgency)

[1]The pair, in part, reflects the US and Soviet Union rivalry during the Cold War (1945–1991)

Source: Created by the author from several sources.

during the Korean War, in Vietnam and in the Taiwan Strait. During this time, Soviet–China relations underwent strain and led to skirmishes at the Sino–Soviet border in 1969, pushing the Soviets as a bigger threat to China that the US. Soviet Union's 1979 invasion of Afghanistan to support Kabul's communist government against the US and Saudi Arabia-backed fighters and weapons supplied through Pakistan carved the fate of Pakistan as a non-NATO US ally for decades.

These five decades also saw several clashes between India and China on the Himalayan frontier, who had otherwise maintained cordial relations during India's independence struggle. India, a non-aligned nation friendly with the Soviet Union, and Pakistan, the US ally, also fought several wars over the administration of Kashmir and one war over the independence of East Pakistan in 1971 (now Bangladesh), which saw the US and European powers materially supporting West Pakistan while the Soviet Union pledged support to India. However, during this time the India–Pakistan rivalry had acquired dimensions of spatial and positional strategic enmity, rather than being a purely ideological identity-issue rivalry, even though the latter remains relevant. During this time China and Pakistan formed closer strategic ties, as India had identified each as a strategic rival with increased potential threat of militarised conflict in future.

As the world's nations embarked on the journey towards rapid industrialisation, economic growth and global integration, there were fewer direct wars fought between the traditional rivals. Asia became the hub of rapid economic growth and development. Japan, South Korea and South East Asia began expanding economically amid globalisation. China overtook several leading European economies to become the second-largest world economic power behind only the US. Despite an absence of direct wars between the pre-2000 enmity among nations, strategic rivalries thrived in the Indian and Pacific Oceans.

Between 2001 and 2010, existing maritime disputes between China and other nations intensified with the increased presence of Chinese forces guarding territories and maritime economic zones claimed by China. In March 2007, China declared an increase in defence spending to over US$45 billion (an 18% rise against a 15% rise between 1990 and 2005). Countries like the US and Japan expressed their suspicion over Beijing's challenge to the regional order and rapid militarisation (Chen & Feffer 2009; Lague 2008). Against the backdrop of the rising economic and military might of China, Japanese Prime Minister Abe addressed the Indian Parliament in his August 2007 speech about the "Confluence of the two Seas," i.e., the Indian Ocean and the Pacific Ocean, followed by a Quadrilateral meeting (Quad 1.0) in 2008 among India, Japan, the US and Australia. The move alarmed China but the Quad 1.0 bore no strategic fruit although it paved the way for strategic co-operation among Quad nations even as their economic dependence on China further increased (Chadha 2020b: 68–69). But the Indo-Pacific as a geostrategic and geoeconomics term used today, took the next decade to shape into a concept by the group of like-minded democracies (Japan, the US, India and Australia) in 2017 for a free, open and inclusive Indo-Pacific.

Thus, the emergence of the Indo-Pacific as a defining concept recognising the centrality of the Indian and Pacific Ocean powers is also characterised by these strategic rivalries of varying types. With greater economic development accompanying increased capabilities, medium and small powers are assertively recognising and identifying their issues, conflicts and contests with regional powers. But some of these strategic rivalries have the potential to impact or recalibrate existing power structures. The following sections discuss three of these strategic rivalries' cases in the Indo-Pacific to eventually present a web of rivalries in the region.

The US's strategic rivalries and emergence of the Indo-Pacific

US–China relations since 1971 have been divided into three phases marking their relationship, being an anti-Soviet alignment (1971–1989), evolving into an unsettled accommodation (1990–2007) as China emerged as a rising power and a great power rivalry (2008–) marking the launch of the Quad and eventual conception of the Indo-Pacific (Scobell 2020). These periods also denote a distinct trend in the US–China strategic rivalry that requires some examination. Despite tumultuous China–US relations during and after the Cold War, in 1979 the US diplomatically recognised the One China Policy, while maintaining economic and cultural relations with Taiwan. Despite the ideological rivalry between the two due to the Tiananmen Massacre of 1989, it was the US effort towards normalising relations with its strategic rival China, by integrating it into the global economy as opposed to the other rival Russia, that had been largely isolated. However, the stability of US–China relations, despite their ideological clashes, was not eternal.

China experienced a 10% growth rate on average during the period 1990–2000, slowly catching up to the US among major world economies (Table 13.2). After establishing normalised trade ties with Washington in 2000, China's bilateral trade with the US rose to US$231 billion in 2004, thereafter securing itself as America's second-largest trade partner in 2006. China's rapid rise was a threat to the US economic hegemony, and the nature of their strategic rivalry was to be defined largely in terms of geoeconomics conflicts and positional rivalry. China increased its world market share to 9% in 2010, attracted two-fifths of the total foreign direct investment to low- and

Table 13.2 Ten countries with the highest GDP (US$m) between 2000 and 2019 GDP (at constant 2010 US$)

2000		2010		2019	
Country	GDP US$m	Country	GDP US$m	Country	GDP US$m
United States	12,620	United States	14,992	United States	18,300
Japan	5,349	China	6,087	China	11,520
Germany	3,119	Japan	5,700	Japan	6,211
France	2,334	Germany	3,396	Germany	3,944
China	2,232	France	2,643	France	2,972
United Kingdom	2,101	United Kingdom	2,475	India	2,940
Italy	2,069	Brazil	2,209	United Kingdom	2,921
Brazil	1,539	Italy	2,134	Brazil	2,347
Canada	1,207	India	1,676	Italy	2,151
Spain	1,152	Canada	1,613	Canada	1,939

Source: Created by the author with data from World Bank.

Table 13.3 Nuclear weapons stockpiles (till 2019)

Country	Nuclear weapons stockpile
Russia	6,500
The United States	6,185
France	300
China	290
The United Kingdom	200
Pakistan	150–160
India	130–140
Israel	80–90
North Korea	20–30

Source: Stockholm International Peace Research Institute (SIPRI 2020).

middle-income countries and decreased its poverty ratio from 80% in the 1980s to 13% in the same period (Dorrucci et al. 2013: 5–9).

In the decade of the 2010s, China and India were catching up with the developing world among the world's ten largest economies (Table 13.3). The new imperative for the regional development and greater US influence in Asia were identified as infrastructure support and connectivity across Asia till Europe (Grossman 2013: 69). In 2011, the US Secretary of State Hillary Clinton announced the US aim to develop and connect the Afghanistan economy with South Asia and Central Asia, in a vision called New Silk Road (Clinton 2011a). Initiatives such as a pipeline passing through Turkmenistan, Afghanistan, Pakistan and India (TAPI) as well as the Afghanistan–Pakistan Transit Trade Agreement (APTTA) were announced in the backdrop of efforts to normalise trade relations between strategic rivals India and Pakistan (Kaplan 2011: 14–15).

The Russia-led Eurasian Economic Union had been a post-Cold War initiative since 1994 targeted at the economic integration of Russia with Central Asian countries, a region where Russia had been a traditional hegemon. However, the Chinese presence in the region to cater to its energy needs challenged both the US and Russia (Freeman 2018). Especially after the fall in oil prices in 2008–2009, Beijing extended infrastructure funding to Central Asia without raising domestic political issues, unlike the US loans that focused on development alongside promoting democratic values or Russian financial aid to the region that came seeking political influence or the need for domestic policy modifications (Olcott 2013). To counter the growing Chinese influence, the US outlined its "pivot to Asia" in 2011, underlining the need for strategic connectivity in the Asia-Pacific region, and President Obama's multilateral free trade agreement, the Trans-Pacific Partnership (Clinton 2011b).

The Global Financial Crisis of 2008 shrunk the double-digit growth rate of China to 7% but bared the US–China economic interdependence and imbalances as Beijing emerged as the largest holder of US treasuries worth US$600 billion. In 2010, China overtook Japan as the world's second-largest economy (Table 13.3). By 2011, China represented 75% of the total rise in the US trade deficit in which China accounted for US$295 billion. As the US began recognising the rising economic and strategic presence of Beijing, China's new leadership under President Xi Jinping announced his vision of great power relations between the US and China, marking the beginning of a maritime spatial rivalry in the contested seas of the East and South China Sea where China claimed regional hegemony.

In order to re-accelerate economic growth in China and curb the separatists in Xinjiang province, President Xi launched the Belt and Road Initiative (BRI) in 2013, connecting Asian economies on land through the Silk Road Economic Belt, and maritime routes through a series of ports in the Indian Ocean under the Maritime Silk Road. The launch of the BRI was mainly funded by the setting up of Beijing-headquartered Asian Infrastructure Investment Bank (AIIB) for land and maritime infrastructure development across Asia and beyond (Dollar 2015: 162). The US responded by accelerating negotiations over its Trans-Pacific Partnership (TPP) initiative in 2014 while asking nations to refrain from joining either the BRI or AIIB, with little success as over 60 nations joined the Beijing initiatives (Dollar 2015: 172).

Through the 2017 Executive Order by the President, the US imposed extremely severe sanctions on North Korea (Democratic People's Republic of Korea) after a series of Intercontinental Ballistic Missile (ICBM) tests by the latter threatening regional security (Bureau of East Asian and Pacific Affairs 2021). North Korea has continued

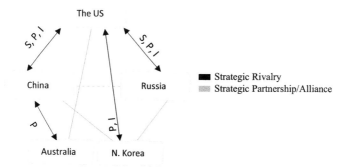

Figure 13.1 Key US rivalries in the Indo-Pacific.

Note: S-P-I-N denote spatial, positional, ideological and identity-issue strategic rivalries. Source: Prepared by author.

to pose a challenge for the US due to its nuclear ambitions, creating an asymmetric security dilemma in the region (Richey 2019). The nature of the North Korean strategic rivalry with the US is unique. Its ideological roots point towards the Cold War US–Soviet Union rivalry and DPRK's authoritarian government. On the other hand, its positional strategic rivalry with the US is indicative of the persistent level of threat it senses from the US and its allies and seeks to balance that through its nuclear proliferation, but also the threat it poses to states like Japan that could seek development of nuclear weapons as a countermeasure (Tan & Park 2020).

The US under President Trump, withdrew from the TPP in 2017, leaving Japan to lead the 11-nation negotiation and signing of the Comprehensive and Progressive Agreement for Trans-Pacific Partnership (CPTPP) in 2018. The 2017 US National Security Strategy explicitly recognised China and Russia as revisionist powers (Satake & Sahashi 2020). President Trump in 2018 announced tariffs on Chinese imports over Beijing's breach and theft of US technology and intellectual property, while China responded with counter-tariffs on American products beginning a trade war. As their bilateral relations worsened, both nations imposed additional tariffs on US$34 billion worth of goods, furthering the trade animosity, followed by US Vice-President Pence stating the prioritisation of contest over co-operation by imposing tariffs against Beijing's economic aggression (United States Trade Representative 2018; Hoyama & Suzuki 2018).

China's rise as a global economic power and emerging maritime competitor forced the US to mark it as a global strategic rival in the Indo-Pacific. While Chinese assertion in the seas and military buildup near contested territories in the South and East China Sea were a threat to the US, US naval presence in these seas was a concern for China. The US Indo-Pacific Strategy Report of 2019 clarified not only the significance of the Indo-Pacific as a geostrategic (maritime) territory but also highlighted the US concerns over Chinese actions in the region, which were threatening to the US security vision as well as the security of its Indo-Pacific like-minded allies namely Japan, Australia and the rising Indian Ocean power, India (Scobell 2020). The new grouping AUKUS (Australia–United Kingdom–US), formed in September 2021 (to be implemented by March 2023) to arm Australia with a minimum of eight nuclear-powered submarines, is another instance of the gravity with which the US seeks to align its security objectives with its allies in the region versus China (The White House 2021). This also implies greater militarisation of the region with the presence of European nuclear powers.

For the US, the Indo-Pacific is the consequence as well as the policy response to its strategic threats from China. On the spatial rivalry, it shows a renewed US commitment to the Indo-Pacific (maritime) region, where Chinese assertions in the South and East China Sea have created insecurity for ASEAN nations, Taiwan, Japan and South Korea. Identifying China as a rival enables the US to counter it through an increased naval presence in the region, while also inviting like-minded European and North American partners and allies to increase their presence in the Indo-Pacific. It also sends a deterrence signal to Russia about the increasing influence of the US and its allies in the region. For the positional rivalry with Beijing (and to some extent Russia), the Indo-Pacific is a platform to advocate for free, open and rule-based order where newer partners like India and Vietnam can join the US in its initiative to deter China. It will also enable regional powers like India (in the Indian Ocean) and Australia (in the Pacific Ocean) to take up a larger security role in the region. For the ideological rivalry that the US shares with Beijing and Moscow (partly as a relic of the Cold War era), the Indo-Pacific is the new geopolitical definition of a great power rivalry that seeks to promote democratic values in the region. The role of the Indo-Pacific here is more symbolic in that regard as the Quad only comprises democratic partners of the US. Overall, the Indo-Pacific as a concept and vision only increases in significance as more states from within the region and even beyond support, join and adopt the US vision.

India's territorial conflicts and power rivalries in the Indo-Pacific

New Delhi's foreign policy has been largely non-aligned in the Cold War era, and later took up a form characterised by strategic autonomy and issue-based parentships, where it neither seeks to abandon independent foreign policy and bandwagon with great power nor aims to create a unilateral order of its own on the global scale. That is the reason India has been able to reestablish ties with the US while maintaining its Cold War-era partner Russia. At the same time, New Delhi has been relatively less active in recognising its threats from China, when compared to the animosity it shares with its other western neighbour Pakistan.

India–US economic relations shadowed their ideological affinities versus China and Russia till the end of the 2010s. 1991 was a landmark year for India, which after decades of socialist economic policies based on the Soviet model, finally opened up the economy to liberalisation of trade rules, privatisation and globalisation, balancing its relations with the US, which had supported New Delhi's territorial claims in the 1962 Sino–India war. But US support drifted in the 1971 Bangladesh War of Independence to Pakistan owing to the latter's role in the resumption of Sino–US relations despite Pakistan's genocide in Bangladesh. Post-1998 nuclear tests by New Delhi, the US imposed economic sanctions on India. After India's victory in the Indo-Pakistan War in 1999, New Delhi signed a Special Strategic Partnership Agreement with its long-time development partner Moscow in 2000, and thereafter signed the Strategic Partnership Agreement in 2001 with the US, prompting Japan to resume its foreign aid to New Delhi as well. Meanwhile, Russia increased its engagement with China against the US sanctions, despite the risk of being reduced to Beijing's junior partner (Paikin et al. 2019).

Threat balancing and persistence of mistrust in South Asia became evident when, after the Sino–India war of 1962, India was compelled to recognise China as a spatial strategic rival. India emerged as the first nuclear nation apart from the existing five to conduct nuclear tests in 1974. But it took longer for New Delhi to identify China as a positional rival in the Indian Ocean, as the former focused on internal security and its immediate neighbourhood (Lobo 2021). In contrast, India and Pakistan had already identified each other as spatial rivals owing to the violent partition in 1947 followed by disputes over absolute control over Kashmir which was both a religious as well as an identity contention between the rivals. New Delhi's India's identity and religious ideology spurred strategic rivalry with Islamabad turned into an intense positional rivalry in South Asia as Pakistan conducted its successful nuclear test in 1998, adding the nuclear dimension to the Kashmir conflict with India.

India's relations with China, which had been good until the war of 1962, deteriorated with growing China–Pakistan affinity and only gained momentum after India and China signed the Strategic Partnership Agreement in 2005 for greater economic development. As the two economies began experiencing growth in the early 2000s,

India expanded its 1991 Look East Policy in 2003, shifting the focus to emerging economies of South East Asia and integrating economies with infrastructure connectivity projects (Haokip 2011). Meanwhile, as China increased its presence in the Indian Ocean, India's attention moved to countering the same in its own maritime domain, with a reciprocal naval presence in the Arabian Sea, Indian Ocean and Bay of Bengal. However, with China's rising initiatives towards maritime and territorial connectivity projects in several nations under the BRI, India's threats increased as did its perceptions of China as a strategic rival. China announced the infrastructure investment of the China–Pakistan Economic Corridor (CPEC) worth over US$40 billion connecting Xinjiang in China to Gwadar port in the Indian Ocean via Pakistan-administered and India-claimed Kashmir territory. India declined to attend or participate in the BRI Summit citing debt-trap issues and maritime and territorial sovereignty concerns related to the BRI, even as its bilateral trade with China continued to be high (Frankel 2011).

Even till as recently as 2014, India's China policy has been focused on maintaining good relations with its northern neighbour to avoid any escalated conflict. Some of the examples of this passive diplomacy were visible when Indian Prime Minister Narendra Modi initially supported deeper India–China ties and became the second-largest contributor to AIIB, despite territorial disputes with Beijing, People's Liberation Army's activities in Pakistan-administered Kashmir and near the Line of Actual Control (LAC). India, despite maintaining unofficial cultural relations with Taiwan, and giving refuge to Tibetan refugees since 1959, reiterated support for the "One China Policy" with a reciprocal "One India Policy" during China's Foreign Minister Wang Yi's India visit in 2014 (Samanta 2014).

But China's military expansion at the Indo–China border as well as in maritime zones was seen as an event that increased the likelihood of an India–China conflict. While several European powers had maintained naval bases in the strategic areas of the Indian Ocean since colonisation in the region, China established its first military base close to Bab-el-Mandeb in Djibouti, which owed 80% of its total debt to China in 2017 (where existing military bases belonged to France, Japan, Italy and the US). It set off a base race among regional powers of the Indo-Pacific as India, Australia and Japan eventually signed a military co-operation to allow access to each other's military bases in the region. As a result of huge amounts of loans extended to smaller nations under China-led BRI projects, several nations began losing strategic ports and national structures over non-repayment of debt (termed debt-trap policy by China's rivals). One instance was New Delhi's Indian Ocean neighbour Sri Lanka's Hambantota port that was leased to China for 99 years in 2017 apart from a 70% stake over its inability to service debt to the Chinese construction company China Merchants, whose US$93 billion revenue was more than Sri Lanka's GDP (Ondaatjie & Sirimanne 2019; Calinoff & Gordon 2020). With US$1.5 billion outstanding loans to the Maldives in 2018, the Chinese presence was further solidified around the Indian peninsula with the development and control of Pakistan's Gwadar port located close to the Strait of Hormuz.

In response to the Chinese "string of pearls" strategy to surround the Indian peninsula through a series of ports and Chinese naval presence, India began the development of Chabahar port (Iran) in 2016, Colombo port (Sri Lanka) in 2019 and Sabang port (Indonesia) in 2019. New Delhi also focused on increased engagement in Africa with Japan, to enable alternate development opportunity versus China (Chadha 2022a). Indian investment in other nations such as Seychelles, the Maldives and Bangladesh.

was intended to strengthen its own presence in its neighbourhood, and counter China's influence in the economies as well as security of the smaller Indian Ocean nations (Chadha 2020a). While India was supported by the US and Japan over increasing connectivity in the region, Washington's sanctions on Iran, as well as Russia, impeded Indian commitment to Chabahar. Meanwhile, Russia once again began showing aspirations to increase its presence in the Indian Ocean not just as a weapons supplier to India, but also as an emerging maritime power in 2015. While the Indian Indo-Pacific vision aligns with the US in terms of a "peaceful, and rule-based" regional order, New Delhi has remained grounded in its relationship with the US rival Russia, as its largest defence and military equipment partner in order to pursue a more independent foreign policy, grounded in multi-alignment and issue-based engagements. India has traditionally supported greater "inclusivity" of the Indo-Pacific, where it sees scope for a peaceful rise of several powers (Chadha 2021). However, increased skirmishes with China at the Indo–China border and their inability to resolve the issue through diplomacy have led India to revise its stance on its neighbourhood rivalries. Pakistan continues to hold the position of its long-term rival that shares territorial disputes over Kashmir, challenges India as an Islamic nuclear power and continues to maintain severe ideological and identity-based (religious) conflicts. China has emerged as a complex strategic rival which despite sharing a strategic partnership with New Delhi, does not have a "normal" relationship that India needs to ensure regional stability (Mint 2022).

Thus, the Indo-Pacific vision aligned well with New Delhi's revived interest in playing a larger regional role in the Indian Ocean. At the same time, it provided a new perspective for Indian foreign policy that strived to be autonomous and independent of great power politics. The Indo-Pacific vision facilitated India's national interest taking a visible centrality in New Delhi's alignment of its own neighbourhood security policies with the larger Indo-Pacific policy of the US and Japan (Chadha 2022b). Chinese investments and military buildup in the Indian Ocean cautioned New Delhi to prioritise relations in its South Asian neighbourhood, but propelled New Delhi to strengthen India which joined hands with Japan to build ports in Sri Lanka (Trincomalee port), Iran (Chabahar port) and Bangladesh (Matarbari port) to counter Chinese infrastructure projects in the Indian Ocean such as Sri Lanka (Hambantota port), Pakistan (Gwadar port) and Djibouti (Djibouti port and military base), besides roads, rails

Figure 13.2 Key India rivalries in the Indo-Pacific.

Note: S-P-I-N denote spatial, positional, ideological and identity-issue strategic rivalries. Source: Prepared by author.

and buildings in Cambodia, Myanmar, the Maldives, Seychelles, etc. (Chadha 2020a, 2020c). Overall, the Indo-Pacific might be a platform to push for converging India–US interests, but Indian foreign policy is not entirely aligned with the other Indo-Pacific partners. New Delhi, while recognising the threats from Beijing, continues to resist forming an alliance or even calling out its strategic rival China as a belligerent power, unlike the US, Australia or Japan. It seeks to maintain a multi-aligned foreign policy with enough flexibility to form partnerships for its national interest, while also allowing it to constantly work towards conflict resolution with its strategic rivals (China and Pakistan), despite a history of intermittent clashes with them.

Japan in the Indo-Pacific and its struggle for capabilities development

The bombings of Hiroshima and Nagasaki by the US in 1945 brought WWII to an end and led to surrender of Japan as US forces occupied Japanese islands (Ryukyu Islands including the Senkaku/Diaoyu Islands) but ushered in a new era of nuclear weapons proliferation. The Cold War set the tune for nuclear rivalry among several nations who deployed a huge amount of national resources towards a sizeable nuclear arsenal. After the Cold War, the nuclear arsenal for the US, Russia and nations in Europe became the source of power projection, enemy deterrence and influence (Waltz 1981). Meanwhile, Japan had settled with the San Francisco Peace Treaty and become an indispensable part of the US hub-and-spoke alliance network in the Asia-Pacific (Wilkins 2021). But the Japan–China dispute moved from its historical oppressor–oppressed relation into a new strategic rivalry based on spatial and positional factors. The discovery of energy deposits near Senkaku/Diaoyu Islands in 1969 began the Japan–China dispute over the islands as Japan initiated East China Sea energy explorations projects with South Korea and Taiwan (Sato & Chadha 2022).

In 2004, Pakistan's nuclear programme scientist Abdul Qadeer Khan was charged with the illegal sale of nuclear technology to Iran, North Korea and Libya. During the same time, the US accused North Korea and Iran of secret nuclear programmes and imposed sanctions on both, post which North Korea withdrew from the NPT to become an unstable nuclear threat to the US allies South Korea and Japan (Table 13.4). The risk of regional destabilisation pushed Japan to involve Russia as a mediator in its North Korea engagements, knowing the influence of China on Pyongyang's politics. The alliance with the US was Japan's greatest tool to deter any aggression by its rivals in the Korean Peninsula or close to the Taiwan Strait (Oren & Brummer 2020; Smith 2021). But the China–Japan Senkaku/Diaoyu Islands dispute necessitated a new Japan–US "Alliance Co-ordination Mechanism" in 2015 for crisis management in light of threats from China as well as North Korean missile launches (Japan Ministry of Foreign Affairs 2015).

Between 2001 and 2010, existing maritime disputes between China and other nations had intensified with an increased presence of Chinese forces guarding territories and maritime economic zones claimed by China. Countries like the US and Japan expressed their suspicion over Beijing's challenge to the regional order and rapid militarisation (Chen & Feffer 2009; Lague 2008). Against the backdrop of the rising economic and military might of China, Japanese Prime Minister Abe addressed the Indian Parliament in his August 2007 speech about the "Confluence of the two Seas", i.e., the Indian Ocean and the Pacific Ocean, followed by a Quadrilateral meeting (Quad 1.0) in 2008 among India, Japan, the US and Australia. The move alarmed China but the

Table 13.4 Mapping types of strategic rivalries in the Indo-Pacific

Indo-Pacific states	Identified strategic rivals									
	US	Japan	India	Russia	China	Pakistan	Iran	N.Korea	Taiwan	Australia
US		A	T	SPI	SPI	A	PI	PI	T	A
Japan			T	SP	SPN	–	–	SPI	T	T
India				T	SPT	SPIN	T	–	–	T
Russia					T	–	T	T	–	PI
China						T	T	A	SPIN	PT
Pakistan							–	T	–	T
Iran								T	–	–
North Korea									–	–
Taiwan										T
Australia										

Source: Prepared by author.

Note: S-P-I-N denote spatial, positional, ideological and identity-issue strategic rivalries. Likewise, A and T denote the existence of a formal alliance and strategic partnership or quasi-alliance respectively. The absence of a strongly categorisable rivalry or deep partnership does not indicate an absence of relations.

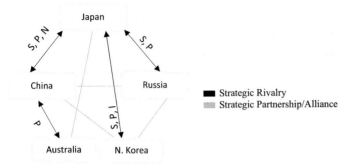

Figure 13.3 Japan's key strategic rivals in the Indo-Pacific.

Note: S-P-I-N denote spatial, positional, ideological and identity-issue strategic rivalries. Source: Prepared by author.

Quad 1.0 bore no strategic fruit although it paved the way for strategic cooperation among Quad nations even as their economic dependence on China further increased (Chadha 2020b: 68–69). But the Indo-Pacific, as a geostrategic and geoeconomics term used today, took the next decade to shape into a concept by the group of like-minded democracies (Japan, the US, India and Australia) in 2017 for a free, open and inclusive Indo-Pacific.

Japan and China had strained their relations over the Senkaku/Diaoyu islands in the East China Sea, but the dispute intensified after Beijing's 2013 declaration of an Air Defence Identification Zone (ADIZ) in the East China Sea, restricting not just maritime activities and exclusive economic zones (EEZs), but also overflight through the zone, also claimed in part by Taiwan and South Korea.[1] In fact, China had expressed its eventual aim of reintegration of Taiwan into China, a territory it has always claimed citing ancient history. Similarly, owing to the rapid development in these nations as well as increased trade activity, the South China Sea became a key waterway for energy and goods exports to countries like Japan and South Korea, besides accounting for over 50% of global merchant ships passing through in 2010. In 2009, China officially claimed almost the entire South China Sea including its resource-rich zones, reefs and islands by marking a U-shaped nine-dash line, before the United Nations.[2]

But China's military presence and influence is not restricted to the East and South China Sea and rather extends across the Info-Pacific. Chinese missiles aimed at Taiwan also threaten Japanese sovereignty and security (Calder 2006). Over the years, the pacifist Japan has sought to alter its constitutional constraints to enable greater power projection in the whole Indo-Pacific in military terms. Once such initiative was led by Japanese former PM Abe whose reinterpretation of the Japanese Constitution's Article 9 directly implied increased co-operation between Japanese Self-Defence Forces and American military (Hughes et al. 2021). Japan also raised its defence expenditure through successive years and has secured a place for its Self-Defence Forces in joint military exercises with US allies such as Australia, and European nations, as well as US partners such as India (Atanassova-Cornelis & Sato 2019; Sato 2020). In this regard, the Indo-Pacific has helped project better maritime stability in the region, where Japan can play a larger role as a regional power with better capabilities to counter any rival forces through collaboration with like-minded partners.

On the other hand, Tokyo's Indo-Pacific commitment, and its clear aim to curb the rise of any power challenging the status quo also means that Japan needs a stable economic relationship in the region, including with China, its largest trade partner. With its increasing strategic closeness to Australia, Japan is also wary of China's capability to negatively impact its strategic rivals after Chinese sanctions on Australia (Sarkar 2020; Smith 2021). Moreover, recent events such as the pandemic have bared Japan's incapability regarding effectively combating a serious health emergency through vaccines, despite its attempt towards active Indo-Pacific diplomacy. Rather than being able to pursue a more autonomous foreign policy, Japan has stayed right in the US orbit, as more European nations seek influence in the Indo-Pacific. While Tokyo can continue to play an active role in the region, the rise of frameworks such as the AUKUS does shed light on Japan's military and economic dependence on the Western powers, as well as its constraints in being able to respond in crisis independently.

Concluding remarks: overview of Indo-Pacific strategic rivalries

Within the Indo-Pacific, China's rise as an economic giant and global power has not been perceived as peaceful by democratic nations like the US, Japan, Australia or India, who view the Indo-Pacific as a geopolitically decisive region for shaping the next global order. European interests in the free, open and inclusive Indo-Pacific through French, British and German naval presence has only added to the contests and claims in the region as more powers clash over influence and presence, if not absolute power. Russian stakes in the Indo-Pacific by partnering with Iran and China have further complicated the existing strategic rivalries in the region, with alternate centres of power arising in the region. However, maritime and military power is only one of the many indicators of strategic rivalries. The emerging global order has been impacted by recent shocks such as the pandemic, which was a geopolitical opportunity for Indo-Pacific states to reaffirm their influence within the partnership/alliance networks, while also assertively countering the influence of their strategic rivals in terms of trade, maritime capabilities and medical diplomacy.

Figure 13.4 illustrates the web of rivalries as it stands today in the Indo-Pacific, with the alliances and strategic partnerships (grey) against the rivalry linkages (black). While the states are pursuing issue-based cooperation with their competitors, the nature of their rivalries has become strategic, with disputes ranging from territorial to maritime. As partnerships are fluid, so are strategic rivalries, with states pursuing national interests as a zero-sum game, identifying issue-based adversaries in their quest for regional dominance.

Table 13.1 shows the several categories of strategic rivalries in the Indo-Pacific and highlights that ideological rivalry cannot sustain as a standalone basis for enmity in the region; it needs to be augmented through spatial and positional strategic rivalries. Moreover, even if a state does not directly face a threat of military confrontation, it is likely to take up the characteristics of strategic rivalry shared by its strong allies in the Indo-Pacific. The case of Japan is specific, and there is the emerging case of Australia, owing to its alliance with the US. In that context, an increasing presence of the European powers will only likely make more complex the web of strategic

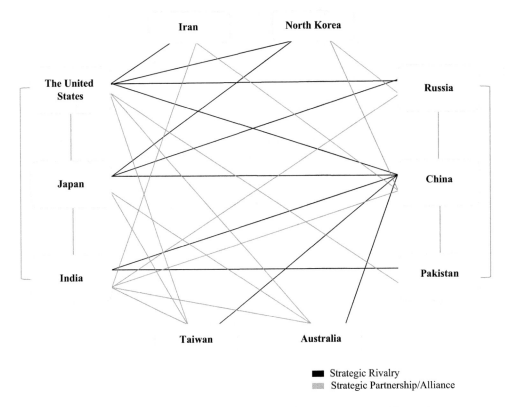

Figure 13.4 Web of strategic rivalries in the Indo-Pacific. Source: Prepared by author.

rivalries, as they approach the region not out of alliance commitments, but because of the potential of the emerging power rivalry and economic growth in the region with several developing nations, and seeking new partners.

Several trends are also revealed for the three cases discussed in the chapter. The US maintains mainly alliance commitments with its key historical partners, against its traditional Russian rivalry, and evolving rivalry with China. As a consequence, it is likely to continue to enforce the alliance mechanism by strengthening its core allies' capabilities (such as in AUKUS or through the US–Japan–Australia trilateral). Additionally, the US shares ideological rifts with all of its rivals, implying that these rivalries have the potential to escalate through different spatial and positional issues, as long as there is an ideological rift.

India aims to maintain its issue-based partnerships across the region, where it sees itself as a (net) security provider. Its key rivalries are with its bordering neighbours, whereas its partnerships are more diverse and flexible due to its aversion to restrictions following alliances. Consequently, its biggest challenge is to continue to hold and project influence in a region that is increasingly witnessing an accumulation of powerful states, conflicts/issues and contests for capabilities augmentation.

Japan continues to maintain good relations with India but its rivalries mirror those of the US, mainly owing to its alliance with the latter. But unlike the US, Japanese capabilities to counter Chinese threats are limited, and thus it also seeks strategic partnerships in the region with like-minded partners like India, Vietnam, Singapore and Indonesia, even as it has shown a proactive regional presence despite struggling to drastically move beyond its pacifism.

Overall, the Indo-Pacific vision entails the realisation that unlike the Western-centric Cold War bloc politics, the present geopolitical challenges, and opportunities, both lie in Asia. In the Indo-Pacific, a complex web of strategic rivalries implies that no power can entirely contain the other, creating some intermittent phases of possible areas of cooperation despite contests, besides alternate networks of rivalry–partnership relations with other states in the region. As there is an increase in the economic and military capabilities of more states in the Indo-Pacific, there is the emergence of a multi-polar order that could sustain longer in light of the complex and intertwined rivalry–partnership relations among Indo-Pacific states. This complex interconnectedness (whether by way of rivalry or partnership) also implies that in the case of complete non-cooperation and absolute mistrust and breakdown of relations, all states stand to lose.

Notes

1 United Nations Convention for the Law of the Sea (UNCLOS) defines EEZ as an exclusive maritime area for commercial use and resource exploration to coastal countries beginning from their coast till 200 nautical miles but neither implies militarisation of the EEZ nor applies to artificially created islands. It also assures right to passage for naval and military vessels (including aircraft).
2 Within the South China Sea some of the key disputes include Scarborough Shoal (claimed by the Philippines and China), Paracel Islands (claimed by China, Vietnam and Taiwan but controlled by China), Spratly Islands (claimed by Vietnam, China and Taiwan in entirety, but controlled in parts by Malaysia, the Philippines, Taiwan, Vietnam and China).

References

Atanassova-Cornelis, E., & Sato, Y. (2019). The US-Japan Alliance Dilemma in the Asia-Pacific: Changing Rationales and Scope. *International Spectator*, 54(4), 78–93. https://doi.org/10.1080/03932729.2019.1665272.
Ben, D. M., & Maoz, Z. (1999). Learning and the Evolution of Enduring International Rivalries: A Strategic Approach. *Conflict Management and Peace Science*, 17(1), 1–48. https://doi.org/10.1177/073889429901700101.
Bureau of East Asian and Pacific Affairs. (2021, February 23). *U.S. Relations With the Democratic People's Republic of Korea*. US Department of State.
Calder, K. E. (2006). China and Japan's Simmering Rivalry. *Foreign Affairs*, 85(2), 129–139.
Calinoff, J. & Gordon, D. (2020). Port investments in the belt and road initiative: Is Beijing grabbing strategic assets? *Survival*, 62(4), 59–80.
Chadha, A. (2020a). India's Foreign Policy towards Japan: Special Partnership amid Regional Transformation. *Ritsumeikan Journal of Asia-Pacific Studies*, 38(1), 2020. https://doi.org/10.34409/RJAPS.38.1_19.
Chadha, A. (2020b). *India's Strategy towards Japan & FOIP amid Regional Transformations: Analysis from the Realistand Constructivist Perspectives*. Ritsumeikan Asia Pacific University. https://doi.org/10.34382/00013844.
Chadha, A. (2020c). *India and the Seychelles: Economics First, Defense Later*. The Diplomat. https://thediplomat.com/2020/12/india-and-the-seychelles-economics-first-defense-later/.
Chadha, A. (2021). India's COVID-19 Strategy and Implications for Its Relations in the Indian Ocean. *Ritsumeikan Journal of Asia Pacific Studies*, 39(1), 81–104.

Chadha, A. (2022a). India's Relations with Africa: Evaluating Changes in India's Africa Policy during COVID-19. In N. M. Raman (Ed.), *Reimagining South Asia: Multilateralism in the Contemporary Times* (pp. 10–29). Pentagon Press LLP.

Chadha, A. (2022b). Walking a tightrope: India's security challenges in its neighborhood. Asian Studies, The Twelfth International Convention of Asia Scholars (ICAS 12), 1, 73–80. Amsterdam University Press. ISBN: 9789048557820. https://doi.org/10.5117/9789048557820/ICAS.2022.009

Chen, S., & Feffer, J. (2009). China's Military Spending: Soft Rise or Hard Threat? *Asian Perspective, 33*(4)(Special issue on Arms Race in Northeast Asia), 47–67.

Clinton, H. (2011a, July 20). *Remarks on India and the United States: A Vision for the 21st Century.* U.S. Department of State.

Clinton, H. (2011b, October 11). America's Pacific Century. *Foreign Policy, 189*, 56–63.

Colaresi, M. P., Rasler, K. & Thompson, W. R. (2008). *Strategic rivalries in world politics: Position, space and conflict escalation.* Cambridge: Cambridge University Press.

Colaresi, M., & Thompson, W. R. (2002). Strategic Rivalries, Protracted Conflict, and Crisis Escalation. *Journal of Peace Research, 39*(3), 263–287.

Dasgupta, S. (2015, July 1). China Says India Must Not Think of Indian Ocean as Its Backyard. *Times of India.* Retrieved June 21, 2022, from https://timesofindia.indiatimes.com/india/china-says-india-must-not-think-of-indian-ocean-as-its-backyard/articleshow/47899583.cms.

Department of Defense. (2019). *Indo-Pacific Strategy Report: Preparedness, Partnerships, and Promoting a Networked Region* (June 1, pp. 1–55). U.S. Department of Defense. Retrieved June 15, 2022, from https://www.defense.gov/News/Releases/Release/Article/1863396/dod-releases-indo-pacific-strategy-report/.

Diehl, P. (1985a). Arms Races to War: Testing Some Empirical Linkages. *Sociological Quarterly, 26*(3), 331–349.

Diehl, P. (1985b). Contiguity and Military Escalation in Major Power Rivalries, 1816–1980. *Journal of Politics, 47*(4), 1203–1211.

Diehl, P., & Goertz, G. (2000). *War and Peace in International Rivalry.* University of Michigan Press. https://doi.org/10.3998/mpub.16693.

Dollar, D. (2015). China's Rise as a Regional and Global Power: The AIIB and the 'One Belt, One Road'. *Horizons, Summer*(4), 162–172.

Dorrucci, E., Pula, G., & Santabárbara, D. (2013). China's Economic Growth and Rebalancing. *European Central Bank Eurosystem, Occasional*(142), 1–54.

Dreyer, D. R. (2010). Issue Conflict Accumulation and the Dynamics of Strategic Rivalry. *International Studies Quarterly, 54*(3), 779–795. https://doi.org/10.1111/j.1468-2478.2010.00609.x.

Frankel, F. R. (2011). The Breakout of China-India Strategic Rivalry in Asia and the Indian Ocean. *Journal of International Affairs, 64*(2), 1–17.

Freeman, C. P. (2018). New Strategies for an Old Rivalry? China–Russia Relations in Central Asia after the Energy Boom. *Pacific Review, 31*(5), 635–654. https://doi.org/10.1080/09512748.2017.1398775.

Goertz, G., & Diehl, P. (1992). The Empirical Importance of Enduring Rivalries. *International Interactions, 18*(2), 151–163. https://doi.org/10.1080/03050629208434799.

Grossman, M. (2013). Seven Cities and Two Years: The Diplomatic Campaign in Afghanistan and Pakistan. *Yale Journal of International Affairs, 8*(2), 65–75.

Haokip, T. (2011). India's Look East Policy. *South Asian Survey, 18*(2), 239–257. https://doi.org/10.1177/0971523113513368.

Hensel, P. R. (1999). An Evolutionary Approach to the Study of Interstate Rivalry. *Conflict Management and Peace Science, 17*(2), 175–206. https://doi.org/10.1177/073889429901700203.

Hoyama, T., & Suzuki, W. (2018, July 6). *China hits back against Trump's $34bn tariffs.* Nikkei Asia.

Hughes, C. W., Patalano, A. & Ward, R. (2021). Japan's Grand Strategy: The Abe Era and Its Aftermath, *Survival*, *63*(1), 125–160, DOI: 10.1080/00396338.2021.1881258

Japan Ministry of Foreign Affairs. (2015, April 27). The Guidelines for Japan-US Defense Co-Operation. *MOFA Japan*, 1–23. https://www.mofa.go.jp/files/000078188.pdf.

Kaplan, R. D. (2011). *Monsoon: The Indian Ocean and the Future of American Power*. Random House Trade Paperbacks.

Kortunov, A. (1996). The U.S. and Russia: A Virtual Partnership. *Comparative Strategy*, *15*(4), 335–352. https://doi.org/10.1080/01495939608403084.

Lacey, J. (2016). Introduction. In J. Lacey (Ed.). *Great Strategic Rivalries: From the Classical World to the Cold War* (pp. 1–52). Oxford University Press.

Lauriat, G. (2021). Global maritime choke points. *American Journal of Transportation*, *724*, 8–10. https://www.ajot.com/ajot_digital/724/?page=8

Lague, D. (2008, March 4). China Increases Military Spending. *The New York Times*. https://www.nytimes.com/2008/03/04/world/asia/04iht-military.2.10691808.html .

Liss, C. (2014). Assessing Contemporary Maritime Piracy in Southeast Asia. *Trends, Hotspots and Responses*, PRIF Report, 125, Frankfurt/M, 1-32.

Lobo, J. S. (2021). Balancing China: Indo-US Relations and Convergence of Their Interests in the Indo-Pacific. *Maritime Affairs*, *17*(1), 73–91. https://doi.org/10.1080/09733159.2021.1952618.

Mint, W. Y. (2022, March 25). *Relationship with China 'Not Normal': S Jaishankar after Meeting with Wang Yi*. Mint. https://www.livemint.com/news/india/relationship-with-china-not-normal-s-jaishankar-after-meeting-with-wang-yi-11648201121609.html.

Olcott, M. B. (2013, September 18). *China's Unmatched Influence in Central Asia*. Carnegie Endowment for International Peace.

Ondaatjie, A., & Sirimanne, A. (2019, November 29). *Sri Lanka leased Hambantota Port to China for 99 yrs. now it wants it back*. Business Standard News. https://www.business-standard.com/article/international/sri-lanka-leased-hambantota-port-to-china-for-99-yrs-now-it-wants-it-back-119112900206_1.html.

Oren, E. & Brummer, M. (2020). Threat perception, government centralization, and political instrumentality in Abe Shinzo's Japan. *Australian Journal of International Affairs*, *74*(6), 721–745. https://doi.org/10.1080/10357718.2020.1782345

Paikin, Z., Sangar, K., & Merlen, C. R. (2019). Russia's Eurasian Past, Present and Future: Rival International Societies and Moscow's Place in the Post-cold War World. *European Politics and Society*, *20*(2), 225–243. https://doi.org/10.1080/23745118.2018.1545186.

Richey, M. (2019). US-Led Alliances and Contemporary International Security Disorder: Comparative Responses of the Transatlantic and Asia-Pacific Alliance Systems. *Journal of Asian Security and International Affairs*, *6*(3), 275–298. https://doi.org/10.1177/2347797019886690.

Samanta, P. D. (2014, June 12). One China? What about One India Policy: Sushma Swaraj to Wang Yi. *The Indian Express*. http://indianexpress.com/article/india/india-others/one-china-what-about-one-india-policy-sushma-to-wang/.

Sarkar, M. G. (2020). China and Quad 2.0: Between Response and Regional Construct. *Maritime Affairs*, *16*(1), 110–130. https://doi.org/10.1080/09733159.2020.1794526.

Satake, T., & Sahashi, R. (2020). The Rise of China and Japan's 'Vision' for Free and Open Indo-Pacific. *Journal of Contemporary China*, *30*(127), 18–35. https://doi.org/10.1080/10670564.2020.1766907.

Sato, Y. (2020). *The Sino-Japanese Maritime Disputes in the East China Sea*. Center for International Maritime Security.

Sato, Y. & Chadha, A. (2022). *Understanding the Senkaku/ Diaoyu Islands Dispute: Diplomatic, Legal, and Strategic Contexts*. In M. de Souza, Karalekas, D. & Coutaz, G. (eds.), *Asian Territorial and Maritime Disputes: A Critical Introduction*. E-International Relations, 48–64. https://www.e-ir.info/publication/asian-territorial-and-maritime-disputes-a-critical-introduction/

Scobell, A. (2020). Constructing a U.S.-China Rivalry in the Indo-Pacific and Beyond. *Journal of Contemporary China*, 30(127), 69–84. https://doi.org/10.1080/10670564.2020.1766910.

SIPRI. (2020). *World Nuclear Forces*. Stockholm International Peace Research Institute. https://www.sipri.org/research/armament-and-disarmament/nuclear-disarmament-arms-control-and-non-proliferation/world-nuclear-forces.

Smith, S. A. (2021). The Growing Risk for Japan in the US-China Rivalry. *Global Asia*, 16(4), 30–34.

Suslov, D. (2016). US-Russia Confrontation and a New Global Balance. *Strategic Analysis*, 40(6), 547–560. https://doi.org/10.1080/09700161.2016.1224069.

Tan, E., & Park, J. J. (2020). The US-North Korean Asymmetrical Security Dilemma: Past the Point of Nuclear No Return? *International Area Studies Review*, 23(2), 194–209. https://doi.org/10.1177/2233865920918508.

The White House. (2021). *Joint Leaders Statement on AUKUS*. The White House. https://www.whitehouse.gov/briefing-room/statements-releases/2021/09/15/joint-leaders-statement-on-aukus/.

Thompson, W. R. (2001). Identifying Rivals and Rivalries in World Politics. *International Studies Quarterly*, 45(4), 557–586. https://doi.org/10.1111/0020-8833.00214.

Vasquez, J. A. (2009). *The War Puzzle Revisited*. Cambridge University Press.

Vasquez, J. A., & Valeriano, B. (2010). Classification of Interstate Wars. *The Journal of Politics*, 72(2), 292–309. https://doi.org/10.1017/S0022381609990740.

Waltz, K. (1981). The Spread of Nuclear Weapons: More May Be Better. *Adelphi Papers*, 21171, 1–10. https://doi.org/10.1080/05679328108457394.

Wilkins, T. (2021, September 22). *Japan as a Contributor to the Rules-Based Order in the Indo-Pacific*. The Sasakawa Peace The Spread of Nuclear Weapons: More May Be BetterFoundation.

14 International conflicts in the Indo-Pacific region

Przemysław Osiewicz

Introduction

The history of mankind is an intertwining of periods of peace and war. Yet conflicts draw the attention of the international community far more than examples of successful co-operation. The achievement of the goal by the state or other entity through an armed conflict is more spectacular. At the same time, it is always the most expensive solution, the consequences of which often extend beyond the foreseeable future. Armed conflict is a universal phenomenon that is not conditioned or assigned to specific cultural or ethnic groups. For this reason, the history of the world, but also of each region, is filled with records of past and current conflicts. The Indo-Pacific region is no exception.

The inhabitants of the Indo-Pacific region experienced many armed conflicts both during and after the Cold War. Solutions proposed by some leaders served to strengthen security and peace in the region. Unfortunately, at the same time, there were also many leaders who exposed their countries or communities to great losses or confrontation with their neighbours. They also used force many times even against their compatriots, just to be able to maintain their power and possession.

The main objective of this chapter is to analyse trends in the development and nature of conflicts in the Indo-Pacific region. The main hypothesis is as follows: conflicts in the Indo-Pacific region do not stand out from those in other regions in terms of both their types and course, but this is likely to change due to an increasing rivalry between China and the US. In order to verify the abovementioned hypothesis, the following research questions were formulated:

1 What are the most common conflict types in the Indo-Pacific?
2 How important are those conflicts for the Indo-Pacific?
3 How does the Indo-Pacific qualify as a region, regarding its conflicts?

An important issue is the selection of an appropriate definition of the Indo-Pacific, which will allow for the selection of the analysed cases. The choice of definitions is very wide. There is no agreement among researchers of international relations as to the subjective or territorial scope. However, two definitions can be identified that are representative of most of them. According to Felix Heiduk and Gudrun Wacker (2020: 7), although each country has its own understanding of the concept, in terms of both the geographical extent of the Indo-Pacific region and its strategic orientation and essential attributes, there is a common denominator: the two oceans, the Indian Ocean and the Pacific, are imagined as one contiguous area. This understanding is based on

DOI: 10.4324/9781003336143-18

the fact that the vast majority of the world's flows of goods, but also energy supplies, are transported via sea routes that traverse these two oceans.

In addition, the Indo-Pacific basin has become an arena of rivalry between the only superpower, the United States, and the People's Republic of China, aspiring to the role of a global hegemon. The second selected definition of the region was proposed by Robert Kaplan. He presented his concept of an interconnected region in what he calls the Greater Indian Ocean, which links the Horn of Africa, past the Arabian Peninsula to the Indian subcontinent, past the Indonesian archipelago and beyond to the Pacific. This reference accounts for the geographic extent of what is referred to as the Indo-Pacific (Kaplan 2010: xi). This area includes three big maritime realms, namely Central Indo-Pacific, Eastern Indo-Pacific, and Western Indo-Pacific.

This analysis will primarily focus on cases connected with such countries as Australia, Bangladesh, Bhutan, Brunei, the People's Republic of China, Cambodia, Fiji, India, Indonesia, Iran, Japan, Kenya, Laos, Madagascar, Malaysia, Maldives, Myanmar, Nepal, New Zealand, Oman, Pakistan, Papua New Guinea, Philippines, Saudi Arabia, Singapore, Somalia, Sri Lanka, Taiwan, Tanzania, Thailand, Timor-Leste (East Timor), United States, Vietnam and Yemen.

There are many typologies of international conflicts. However, one should choose those that allow you to analyse trends to the greatest extent, both in terms of quantity and quality. Such an arrangement allows for a better understanding of the specifics and characteristics of conflicts in a given region of the world. There are quite a few publications dedicated to case studies of international conflicts in the Indo-Pacific, yet there is a clear lack of publications on the categorisation of these conflicts. This chapter is an attempt to divide and organise the knowledge about international conflicts in the Indo-Pacific region. The analysis is qualitative, not quantitative, in order to understand the specificity, diversity and complexity of conflicts in the Indo-Pacific region.

The chapter is divided into three main parts. The first is dedicated to definitions of international conflicts. The second part of the text is devoted to typologies of international conflicts. The third part of the chapter, in turn, attempts to categorise regional conflicts according to a selected typology of international conflicts. While the first two parts are theoretical, the third is empirical and examines selected conflict cases in the Indo-Pacific region.

The adopted division of content enables the subject of research to be analysed from general to particular. It also makes it possible to notice convergent and divergent aspects of given armed conflicts, especially in terms of their causes and course.

What is an international armed conflict?

There are many definitions of international conflicts. Their proper selection is essential as it defines which events of an international nature should be taken into account and which should be ignored. It is also the first step that must be made in any attempt to categorise conflicts.

The four 1949 Geneva conventions apply to "all cases of declared war or of any other armed conflict which may arise between two or more of the High Contracting Parties, even if the state of war is not recognized by one of them" (The Geneva Conventions 1949). The 1949 conventions refer only to conflicts between states. However, due to the dynamic development of the international situation, their content was later supplemented in 1977 by the Protocol Additional to the Geneva Conventions of 12 August 1949 and relating to the Protection of Victims of International Armed Conflicts. Changes were forced especially by the experiences of postcolonial conflicts. For this reason, the definition of armed conflict was expanded to include henceforth as well "armed conflicts in which peoples are fighting against colonial domination and alien occupation and against racist regimes in the exercise of their right of self-determination" (Protocol I 1977).

According to Joyce P. Kaufman, one should distinguish between conflicts, armed conflicts and wars. A conflict arises from a difference of interests or positions, but it does not always turn into an armed conflict. Most international conflicts are resolved by peaceful means. Only some of conflicts turn into armed conflicts and the use of force becomes a means to an end. Not every armed conflict, in turn, can be classified as war. In Kaufman's opinion, "war is an organised armed conflict between or among states – *inter-state war* – or within a given state – *civil war*" (Kaufman 2013: 97).

James M. Scott, Ralph G. Carter and A. Cooper Drury define wars as "organized, violent conflict between two or more political actors – occurs when the participants engage in armed struggles to gain or defend territory, resources, influence, authority, and other things of high value" (Scott et al. 2019: 125).

Joyce Kaufman's definition meets the basic requirements. It also corresponds most closely to the actual situation in contemporary international relations. The dynamic development of the international situation requires taking into account both conflicts between states as well as civil wars. This is particularly important as a series of civil wars are internationalised through the involvement of external forces, for example, of global or regional powers. The specificity of the Indo-Pacific region should also be taken into account. Due to the great diversity in terms of culture, religion and ethnicity, especially within individual countries, researchers cannot focus solely on inter-state conflicts. Various internal conflicts of varying intensity should also be taken into account. Not all have the potential to turn into armed conflicts, but most may turn into armed conflicts in the near future if local authorities and the international community do not take appropriate preventive action.

However, adopting one of the many definitions available is only the first step in the process of studying regional conflicts. The next step is to present the available typologies of international conflicts. This action will allow for the selection of a few of them, which will be used to divide the conflicts that have arisen in the region according to the appropriate patterns and thus allow for the discovery of certain regularities and trends. As part of the study of international relations in the Indo-Pacific region, it is worth presenting and applying typologies that would take into account subjective, objective and depending on the purpose.

Typologies of international conflicts

What is typology? According to David Collier, Jody LaPorte and Jason Seawright, "typologies – defined as organized systems of types – are a well-established analytic tool in the social sciences. They make crucial contributions to diverse analytic tasks: forming and refining concepts, drawing out underlying dimensions, creating categories for classification and measurement, and sorting cases" (Collier et al. 2012: 217). A typology approach attempts to classify conflicts into predictable groups or patterns. There are many typologies of international conflicts depending on the adopted division criterion. The available approaches include legal, subject, subjective, range and scale approaches.

For the purposes of this chapter, three typologies have been selected, which allow for the analysis and comparison of conflicts in the Indo-Pacific region on the basis of subjective and objective criteria as well as depending on their purpose.

Adopting the subjective criterion as a starting point for classifying individual conflicts creates a chance to avoid potential simplifications. According to Sven Chojnacki, one can distinguish four types of conflicts on the basis of entities involved in conflicts. These are:

- Inter-state violent conflicts. These are conflicts between two or more states.
- Intra-state violent conflicts, namely conflicts between state and non-state actors within existing borders.
- Extra-state violent conflicts. These are conflicts fought by state and non-state actors beyond existing borders.
- Sub-state violent conflicts, namely conflicts involving non-state actors independent of existing borders (Chojnacki 2006: 34).

In the opinion Christopher Moore, conflicts can also be categorised based on the object of the conflict. The objective approach allows for the best identification of the causes of conflicts between the parties, and in particular for determining which of them occur most frequently. Moore divided conflicts into five main groups:

- Structural conflicts – their main sources are inequalities and discriminations, namely an unequal distribution of resources.
- Ideological conflicts – they are caused by ideological differences and differences in the sphere of dominant values.
- Relational conflicts – caused by misunderstandings, communication problems or deliberate misinformation.
- Data conflict – different interpretations of facts or data are sources of misunderstanding, e.g., these may be differences of views on the interpretation of the border between countries.
- Interest conflict – caused by differences of interest or divergent goals of the parties (Moore 2006).

Each of these groups will be considered and analysed separately. Such a division will allow us to define the specificity of conflicts in the Indo-Pacific region, and in particular to identify their main causes.

Some researchers distinguish between conflicts according to their purpose. In the opinion of Bruce Pilbeam, wars can be divided into two groups, namely wars of conquest and wars of liberation. The main purpose of conflicts of conquest is to conquer a territory or acquire certain resources, for example, raw materials. The goal of the liberation wars, in turn, is to gain independence and liberate from domination by another national or ethnic group. In addition, conflicts can be divided depending on the methods of combat used. In this case, two main groups can be identified – conventional wars and guerrilla wars (Pilbeam 2015: 89–90).

The division of conflicts according to their purpose also allows us to indicate the main premises of the parties involved in conflicts, especially those that initiate them. All categories of conflicts will be briefly described and supplemented with selected examples. Of course, their list will not be exhausted here. Nevertheless, such an approach allows for a subsequent self-completion of lists of conflicts and their appropriate assignment to the relevant groups.

Conflicts in the Indo-Pacific: a subjective approach

Inter-state violent conflicts

These are conflicts between two or more states. During the Cold War, the region was the site of many inter-state conflicts. The conflicts of greatest importance were the armed clashes between China and India, between Pakistan and India, the Vietnam war, the Korean War, the Iran–Iraq war, the second Persian Gulf war, the Sino-Vietnamese war, and the Cambodian-Vietnamese war from 1979 to 1989.

After the end of the Cold War, the former Soviet-American rivalry was replaced by rivalry between the People's Republic of China and the United States. This time, the decisive factor is not so much the ideological factor as the struggle for economic primacy and control over the most important shipping routes, especially in the Indian Ocean and the waters surrounding Southeast Asian countries. In the opinion of Rory Medcalf and C. Raja Mohan (2014: 3), after decades of stability under unchallenged US dominance, the Asian strategic order is changing and uncertain. This has been driven by the rise of China as a great power, perceptions of US relative decline, and the ways in which other Asian nations are responding to both. China's economic growth, its increases in military spending, and the extension of China's interests and reach across the wider region have been key features of this changing strategic landscape.

Thus, the risk of major conflict between states in the Indo-Pacific region is greatest in any direct or indirect confrontation between China and the United States. Such a confrontation could take the form of a proxy war (Ali 2017). The greatest probability of a new inter-state conflict in a region in which the United States may also be involved is connected with sovereignty claims in the South China Sea. Taiwan's status may be an important flash point. Both the PRC and the US perceive the situation in Taiwan as a direct threat to their vital interests in the region (Chen 2017; Cheng-Yi & Roy 2011).

The international situation in this part of the region is extremely complex and complicated. At stake are not so much territorial claims as, above all, exceptionally rich deposits of fossil fuels. According to reports of the Council of Foreign Relations,

> China's sweeping claims of sovereignty over the sea—and the sea's estimated 11 billion barrels of untapped oil and 190 trillion cubic feet of natural gas—have antagonised competing claimants Brunei, Indonesia, Malaysia, the Philippines, Taiwan, and Vietnam. As early as the 1970s, countries began to claim islands and various zones in the South China Sea, such as the Spratly Islands, which possess rich natural resources and fishing areas.
>
> (*Territorial disputes* 2020)

Box 14.1 Territorial disputes in the South China Sea

Territorial disputes in the South China Sea have the potential to turn into a conflict of regional or even global scope. Their importance is primarily due to the growing importance of this sea area in global trade flows. For this reason, not only littoral states are involved in them, but also the United States, which treats the South China Sea as an area of global competition with the People's Republic of China. If there were to be an outbreak of an open conflict between the US and China, it is very likely that it will begin with incidents in this part of the world.

The disputes involve both islands and maritime boundaries. In the 1970s, regional actors began to claim islands and various zones in the South China Sea, such as the Spratly Islands, which possess rich natural resources and fishing areas. The parties to the disputes are the People's Republic of China, the Republic of China on Taiwan, Vietnam, the Philippines, Malaysia, Indonesia and Brunei. Yet the main states involved in the disputes are primarily the Philippines, Vietnam and the People's Republic of China. In addition, the United States challenges China's assertive territorial claims and land reclamation efforts by conducting freedom of navigation operations and increasing support for Southeast Asian allies. Although in 2016, the Permanent Court of Arbitration at the Hague issued its ruling on a claim brought against China by the Philippines under the UN Convention of the Law of the Sea, ruling in favour of the Philippines on almost every count, the People's Republic of China still refuses to accept the court's authority.

On the one hand, the People's Republic of China constructed various military installations on the Spratly and Paracel Islands. Another factor complicating the situation in the region is the constant expansion of artificial islands by China, especially their gradual militarisation, which negatively affects regional security. Due to the growing volume of trade flows through the South China Sea, disputes may only intensify over time. China's confrontational stance prevents the achievement of a constructive resolution and poses a threat to regional security. On the other hand, the continued US military presence in the region can be seen as a challenge to China and an excuse for Chinese actions.

(Buszynski & Do Thanh Hai 2020; Kipgen 2021; Raditio 2018; Roy 2016; Strangio 2020.)

Intra-state violent conflicts

These are conflicts between state and non-state actors within existing borders. They are mainly conflicts of liberation. The parties to such conflicts are, on the one hand, government forces, seeking to maintain the status quo, and, on the other, separatist forces, seeking to change this state of affairs. Examples of such conflicts may include but are not limited to the Nepal civil war 1996–2006, the war in Waziristan, the Baluchistan conflict, the Sri Lankan Civil 1983–2009, the Indonesian invasion of East Timor 1975–1999, the insurgency in Aceh 1976-2005, the Islamic insurgency in the Philippines 1969–2019, the Naxalite-Maoist insurgency since 1967, the Khmer Rouge insurgency 1979–1998 and the Solomon Islands civil war 1998–2003. Some of these examples will be described in more detail later in this chapter.

Extra-state violent conflicts

These are conflicts fought by state and non-state actors beyond existing borders. In such a situation, two or more states or two or more non-state actors clash on the territory of a third country. The Korean War was an example of the Soviet-American and Sino-American confrontation in Korean territory. The clashes between Iraqi troops and the troops of the international coalition, led by the United States, in Kuwait were of a similar nature. The same phenomenon appeared when the French and North Vietnamese forces clashed in Laos between 1953 and 1954. Another example is the later fighting in Laos by Thailand, the United States and South Vietnam against North Vietnamese forces.

Sub-state violent conflicts

Such conflicts involve non-state actors independent of existing borders. They may include, for example, clashes between rival terrorist organisations or other non-state actors across national territories. This is the case in Afghanistan, where various jihadist organisations such as the so-called Islamic State and al-Qaeda compete with each other. For now, the situation is controlled by the Taliban, who are reluctant to engage the Islamic State, but this does not exclude the possibility of fighting between these groups in the future.

Box 14.2 Typologies of conflicts: the subjective criterion

- Inter-state violent conflicts.
- Intra-state violent conflicts.
- Extra-state violent conflicts.
- Sub-state violent conflicts.

Conflicts in the Indo-Pacific: an objective approach

Structural conflicts

The main sources of structural conflicts in international relations are inequalities and discriminations, namely an unequal distribution of resources. Analysts of the Peace Research Institute in Oslo (PRIO) indicate the fact that "both shortages and abundance of resources have increasingly been linked to conflict activity. Natural resources such as oil and diamonds can affect the likelihood of conflict, but also contribute to its prevention" (*Conflict trends* 2020). Conflicts of this type most often take the form of confrontation between government forces and a military organisation representing the interests of an ethnic or religious minority whose members are convinced of discrimination by the central authorities. It happens that members of a given community are not only discriminated against, but also even persecuted by the authorities of the country where they live. An example of this is the persecution of the Rohingya minority in Myanmar (Holt 2019). The Rohingya people, a stateless Indo-Aryan group which is mainly Muslim, became victims of the crime of genocide.

Ideological conflicts

Ideological conflicts are caused by ideological differences and differences in the sphere of dominant values. The Chinese civil war was the first major conflict of this kind in the region and lasted intermittently between 1927 and 1949. The war was fought between the forces loyal to the Kuomintang-led government and the Communist Party of China (Lynch 2010). It was an extremely devastating and bloody conflict. In addition, it was a clash of two great personalities in Chinese politics, namely the KMT's leader Chiang Kai-shek and the CPC leader Mao Zedong. One of the most important consequences of this conflict, still of great importance for the regional balance of power, is the actual existence of two Chinese states – the People's Republic of China and the Republic of China on Taiwan. In the Taiwan Strait, tensions and disputes occur regularly between the administrations of both entities. Many researchers and analysts believe that unregulated issues pose the greatest real threat to international security and peace in East Asia. There are also opinions that if a major armed conflict was to arise in the Indo-Pacific region, it would be because of the tensions in the Taiwan Strait, and more precisely because of the PRC authorities' desire to take administrative control over Taiwan. However, regardless of the differences of opinion among analysts, one thing is certain. This conflict is worth in-depth study and constant monitoring as it affects and will continue to affect the balance of power in the region. At this point, there are no indications that the United States would cease to cover the Republic of China in Taiwan with security guarantees, sell its weapons, let alone allow the authorities of the People's Republic of China to take any offensive action (Chen 2017: 141).

A historical example of an ideological conflict is the war in Vietnam. This conflict spread to the territories of two other states in Southeast Asia – Laos and Cambodia. Although hostilities officially ended in 1975 and communist forces seized power in all three countries, the situation was far from peaceful and stable (Evans & Rowley 2010). One of the consequences of the international conflict was internal fighting and mass persecution and executions of members of armed groups or civilians accused of supporting American forces during the war. The situation was particularly dramatic in Cambodia. The communist authorities, led by the Khmer Rouge leader Pol Pot, committed the crime of genocide. Mass cruelty and internal violence, in turn, led to another inter-state conflict, which occurred as a result of the intervention of the armed forces of Vietnam in 1978. The Red Khmer were removed from power but continued their guerrilla warfare in the Cambodian jungle. Some of them found refuge in Thailand thus indirectly involving another state in the region in the conflict. The Cambodian civil war lasted until 1991 (Nhem 2017).

Both during and after the Cold War, many of the conflicts in the region were ideological. The only significant difference is that there are few strictly ideological conflicts, especially those between the parties supporting either the communist ideology or those supported by the West.

Box 14.3 Case study: the Vietnam war as an ideological conflict

The Vietnam war, often referred to as the Second Indochina War, lasted for 20 years and claimed over 1.5 million victims, according to low estimates. It was one of the most devastating and bloody conflicts in the world in the twentieth century. The main parties to the conflict were South Vietnam, supported mainly by the United States, and North Vietnam, supported by the People's Republic of China and the Soviet Union. The main underlying cause of the conflict was

ideological, although in reality both superpowers aimed at gaining an advantage in Southeast Asia. Thus, Vietnam became the theatre of the Cold War confrontation. The conflict also spilled over into other countries in the region, such as Laos and Cambodia. The war ended with the withdrawal of American forces and the victory of the communist regime in 1975. The lost war campaign was an image failure of the United States, especially as a country promoting democratic values and civil liberties in other parts of the world. However, despite the end of hostilities, Vietnamese and American societies and the societies of Vietnam's neighbours struggled with the consequences of this conflict for many years.
(Hastings 2019; Logevall 2013)

One of the ongoing conflicts with such characteristics is the inter-Korean conflict. It constitutes an example of an ideological conflict between two sovereign states, namely the Democratic People's Republic of Korea and the Republic of Korea. The Korean War of 1950–1953 permanently divided the Korean peninsula. Since the end of military operations, both sides have not concluded a peace treaty. Such a state of affairs poses a real risk of a re-emergence of the armed conflict, the more so in that in the past decades there have been many misunderstandings, provocations and sharp tensions between Seoul and Pyongyang. A characteristic feature of this conflict is the fact that it has been involving world powers continuously since the 1950s. During the Cold War, Korea was an area of rivalry between the Soviet Union and the United States. After the end of the Cold War, the People's Republic of China became North Korea's main ally. At that time, the Russians had neither the resources nor any special interests in Korea. Chinese authorities have replaced the Russian Federation, and North Korea continues to function largely thanks to Beijing's economic aid. The international sanctions imposed on North Korea under the United Nations system, as well as by the United States, are very severe and, in practice, condemn the authorities of that country to co-operate with China, regardless of circumstances and real interests. The easing of tensions in relations between the US and North Korea during the presidency of Donald Trump has resulted in summit meetings between the leaders of both countries but has not yet contributed to a lasting solution to the conflict.

Among the internal conflicts of an ideological nature, one can point to the activity of the Maoist Naxalite movement in India. Naxalites promote a radical interpretation of communism, as well as carry out activities that really threaten security and public order in India.

Currently, almost all regional conflicts of an ideological basis result from religious differences. The most visible dividing lines, especially in some countries of the region, are between Christians and Muslims, or Hindus and Muslims. Sectarian rivalry is most pronounced in India and Indonesia. Its manifestations can also be seen in the Philippines.

Relational conflicts

Relational conflicts are caused by misunderstandings, communication problems or deliberate misinformation. Such conflicts may arise from an intentional or unintentional communication problem, especially a misinterpretation of the intentions and actions of the other party. A conflict characterised by a high level of mistrust and an exceptionally low level of communication is the inter-Korean conflict. Communication can also be confrontational. The Indo-Pakistani conflict can serve as an example of such verbal skirmishes. The "confrontational communication addresses a conflict issue that as a rule is expressed in explicit demands as a clearly delineated interest-based conflict item. Communication in a cultural conflict centres on one or several not overtly formulated identity-related themes" (Croissant & Trinn 2009: 6–7). Linguistic, cultural, ethnic, religious and philosophical differences may lead to the aforementioned misunderstandings and tensions.

Data conflict

These conflicts are caused by different interpretations of facts or data are sources of misunderstanding; e.g., these may be differences of views on the interpretation of the border between countries. Disagreements about the boundary line were the basis, officially at least, of the Iraq–Iran war of 1980–1988 (Razoux 2015). Numerous crises and tensions in inter-Korean relations also resulted from a lack of communication or misinterpretation of facts. The best way to avoid conflicts of this type is dialogue, seeking a compromise and adopting a flexible negotiating position. Unfortunately, many disputes and conflicts in the Indo-Pacific region resulted from a lack of good will and a lack of effective communication.

As mentioned before, disputes in the South China Sea have the greatest conflict-generating potential in the region, both due to the number of countries directly or indirectly involved in them, but also due to the great geostrategic importance of this basin for international security and trade (Kaplan 2015; Winston & Sachdeva 2020). The disputes in this sea mainly concern territorial claims and the division of waters and the continental shelf. Seven countries are involved in them, namely the People's Republic of China, the Republic of China on Taiwan, Brunei, Malaysia, the Philippines, Indonesia and Vietnam. The situation is particularly important given the geostrategic importance of this sea basin from the point of view of energy supply and maritime transport.

Interest conflict

Interest conflicts are caused by differences of interest or divergent goals of the parties. In practice, almost any international conflict can be classified as an interest conflict. Conflicts are caused by differences in positions or goals. The catalogue of divergent interests may be smaller or larger depending on the specifics of a given case, but in almost every situation the parties first try to resolve the disputed situation through armed struggle rather than dialogue. There are also many relationships between the various actors in the region that can be considered potential hot spots. For example, the United States has different goals and interests in the region from the People's Republic of China. The goals and interests of countries such as India and Pakistan or Japan and China are likewise different. The greatest challenge is therefore to bring about a situation in which it is possible to make the positions of the parties more flexible and to work out compromise solutions.

Box 14.4 Typologies of conflicts: the objective criterion

- Structural conflicts.
- Ideological conflicts.
- Relational conflicts.
- Data conflicts.
- Interest conflicts.

Conflicts in the Indo-Pacific: the purpose of the conflict

Conflicts of conquest

The main goal of this type of conflict is to gain control over specific areas, most often due to their strategic importance and/or resources, for example, raw materials. In many cases, the goal is also to change the border line due to local historical, ethnic or religious determinants. One of the many historical examples of this type of conflict is the Sino-Indian war of 1962.

The underlying cause of this conflict was a border dispute related to the control over the border regions of Aksai Chin and Arunachal Pradesh, which was then referred to as the North Eastern Frontier Agency (NEFA). The Chinese authorities, dissatisfied with the status quo, decided to attack India (Raghavan 2010). Their main goal was the annexation of the Aksai Chin region, although the war was fought simultaneously on two fronts, also in the NEFA region. The conflict ended in a military victory for China, but India's territorial losses were relatively small. Beijing has extended administrative control to the Aksai Chin region, but it is still under dispute between China and India (Singh 2013). At the same time, it is also a potential flashpoint (Lintner 2018).

The attack and annexation of Kuwait by Iraq in August 1990 could serve as another example of a conflict of this nature. The Iraqi invasion resulted in the annexation and transformation of Kuwait into the 19th province of Iraq. However, Iraqi aggression was met with strong condemnation and a strong reaction from most of the international community, especially the UN Security Council. The United States led an international coalition of 35 countries. What was extremely important, for the first time this coalition included countries that until recently competed with each other during the Cold War. Although the Soviet Union did not engage its armed forces during the liberation of Kuwait, it gave unequivocal support to the coalition forces' operation under the UN Security Council. The support, however, included only the displacement of the Iraqi armed forces from Kuwait, not the removal from power of the Iraqi leader Saddam Hussein. On the one hand, more than 36,000 people lost their lives during the conflict; economic losses were also very high, especially given that the Iraqis set 600 oil wells on fire during the withdrawal of their forces from Kuwait. This unprecedented action also led to a great ecological disaster (Finlan 2003; Khadduri & Ghareeb 1997). On the other hand, the liberation operation involved the largest coalition of states since the end of WWII.

Conflicts of liberation

The initial stages of the Cold War were marked by the gaining of independence by the nations of Asia and the dynamic process of decolonisation. After WWII, local conflicts and armed struggle led to the victories of independence movements in many countries of the region, including Vietnam, East Timor and Bangladesh.

India's independence was the most important event in the first decade after the end of WWII. The Pakistani state was also created at the same time. It consisted of West Pakistan and East Pakistan. Both parts of the new state, however, were thousands of kilometres apart. Thus, there was no territorial continuity. The Bengali nationalists, dominant in eastern Pakistan, demanded independence from the authorities in Islamabad, and sought to create their own sovereign state. The lack of will to compromise, the relentless attitude of the authorities in Islamabad and the determination of the local population eventually led to the outbreak of a bloody armed conflict. The 1971 Bangladesh Liberation War resulted in transforming of East Pakistan into a new independent state – Bangladesh (Dowlah 2016). The conflict was of an internal nature and fulfilled all the criteria to be classified as a conflict of liberation. Yet the engagement of the Indian authorities to help Bangladesh, including military aid, should be emphasised (Azad 2006).

In turn, in some countries there were or are still independence movements seeking to secede part of the territory and establish their own states. The list is quite long. Among those ethnic groups which fought for independence were Bengali Hindus in Bangladesh, the Acehnese in Indonesia and Sri Lankan Tamils. On the other hand, those still trying to achieve their political goals through armed struggle include, for example, the Kuki people in Myanmar and India, Uyghurs and the People's Republic of China, Kashmiris in India, the Baloch in Iran and Pakistan, Kurds in Iran, the Moro people in the Philippines, the Qatif conflict in Saudi Arabia and the South Thailand insurgency. The aforementioned ethnic groups founded their own political and military organisations and often refused to obey the central authorities. The forms of combat they choose range from occasional social unrest to regular warfare.

Some separatist movements were involved in many years of very bloody fights with government troops. This was the case in Sri Lanka. The Sri Lankan Civil lasted over 25 years. Tamils in Sri Lanka attempted to create their own state in the north and east of the island, namely Tamil Eelam. They formed their own armed organisation and started regular military operations against government forces and the civilian population, especially representatives of the state administration. The Sri Lankan authorities fought against the Liberation Tigers of Tamil Eelam and nearly 100,000 people lost their lives in these clashes. The conflict ended with the victory of the governmental forces. The Sri Lankan government re-established control over the entire island and managed to preserve the territorial integrity of the state (Bandarage 2008; Subramanian 2015). However, it should be remembered that, both in the case of this and other long-term armed conflicts, ending hostilities does not solve all problems. The social and economic consequences are most often felt for many years to come and divide societies permanently.

Box 14.5 Typologies of conflicts: the purpose of the conflict

- Conflicts of conquest.
- Conflicts of liberation.

The nature of conflicts in the Indo-Pacific region

What sets the Indo-Pacific region apart from other international regions is the increasing rivalry between the United States and the People's Republic of China. Should there ever be a military confrontation between the world's two greatest powers, it will be in the Indo-Pacific region. In the opinion of Yoichi Kato, there are four possible scenarios related to the regional order in the Indo-Pacific. These are:

- Continued American primacy.
- Power-sharing between the People's Republic of China and the United States.
- Parallel world.
- China primacy (Kato 2020: 27).

At present, the advantage of the United States is noticeable, especially in the context of control over strategic points and routes in the Pacific. Nevertheless, the growing importance of the People's Republic of China and the superpower ambitions of its leader Xi Jinping have increasingly led to tensions in relations with the American side. China is already challenging US supremacy and it should be assumed that over time such actions will only get stronger.

Trade and investment flows are making the Indo-Pacific communication routes ever more important. A state that will control the main communication routes and will be able to set the rules of the game in the Indo-Pacific region will in practice control the majority of world trade flows and impose its point of view on other international actors. The Euro-Atlantic zone is losing its importance, and at the same time the significance of the Pacific basin and the Indian Ocean is growing dynamically. Yet an increase in political and economic interactions will translate into a greater risk of disputes and confrontations. Future disputes and conflicts in the region may define the new regional order.

At the same time, as major states in the region such as China and India regain their power lost in the nineteenth century, the threat posed by the ambitions of their leaders and divergent regional interests will increase. The process of growing economic importance and population is accompanied by the process of significant expansion and modernisation of the armed forces. China's 2022 defence budget was over thrice the size of India's spending and reached $229.7 billion (Singh 2020). However, even with India's lower investment outlays, its growing military importance should not be underestimated. Moreover, it should be emphasised that four countries in the region possess nuclear weapons. These are the United States, China, India and Pakistan. Given the highly probable possession of warheads and their means of delivery by North Korea, the Indo-Pacific region can be considered the most vulnerable to conflict with the potential use of weapons of mass destruction.

Conclusion

The above analysis proves that in the Indo-Pacific region various international conflicts have often erupted and still are. In the opinion of Ash Rossiter and Brendon J. Cannon, "the world is entering a period of intense major power rivalry, and that the epicentre of this heightened competition will be the maritime region spanning the Indian and Pacific Oceans – i.e., the Indo Pacific" (Rossiter & Cannon 2020: 1).

Fortunately, such a pessimistic vision is not yet confirmed by the facts, but the potential for conflict in the region should be assessed as high. Also in the perspective of a real military clash between the United States and the People's Republic of China in the Pacific in the twenty-first century.

The analysis of conflicts in the region on the basis of selected typologies allowed us to show both the degree of their diversity and the complexity of international relations in this part of the world. The acceptance of both the subjective and objective criteria allows us to notice that within each distinguished category, historical or current examples of such conflicts can be indicated. The same is true of the typology of dividing conflicts according to the criterion of the purpose of the conflict.

International conflicts continue to pose a significant threat to international security in the Indo-Pacific region. Moreover, many of the regional disputes may turn into conflicts over time if the parties directly involved and the international community fail to take appropriate preventive measures. Many years of unresolved conflicts continue to divide and antagonise the nations in the region, even after hostilities ended several decades ago. The inter-Korean conflict is a prime example of this. Since the ceasefire in 1953, both Korean states have regularly stood on the brink of an open armed conflict that would certainly involve external powers such as the United States and China.

Both the number of potential conflicts and their possible scale may destabilise the situation in the region. Not only current but also historical examples of international disputes and conflicts in this part of the world prove how complex and complicated the international situation is. In many cases, the threat is posed not only by tensions in inter-state relations, but also by complicated internal relations within individual states of the region, especially in those with significant ethnic and religious differences. Such a situation requires constant commitment on the part of the international community as well as consistent and continuous support for civil society. Only an increase in the awareness of interdependence and the belief in the advantage of peaceful solutions over armed ones can contribute to the gradual reduction of mutual antagonisms and prejudices. Such an approach to the issue proves at the same time how great is and will be in the future the importance of education. On the inter-state level, the increasing institutionalisation of international relations in the Indo-Pacific region would be an effective means of counteracting local and regional conflicts. Perhaps in the future, an international organisation will be created, bringing together all the countries of the region, which will be more effective and influential than the existing sub-regional organisations such as the Association of Southeast Asian Nations.

Of course, the chapter does not exhaust the topic of the Indo-Pacific conflicts. As has been shown, other definitions and other typologies of conflicts are available. Nevertheless, the ones discussed above are representative and can be a good starting point for your own in-depth study. Check the future reading list below to find publications that will enable a deepening knowledge of the conflicts in this region of the world.

References

Ali, Mahmud S., *US-Chinese Strategic Triangles: Examining Indo-Pacific Insecurity*, (Cham: Springer International Publishing, 2017).

Azad, Salam, *Contribution of India in the War of Liberation of Bangladesh*, (New Delhi: Bookwell Publications, 2006).

Bandarage, Asoka, *The Separatist Conflict in Sri Lanka: Terrorism, Ethnicity, Political Economy*, (New York and Abingdon: Routledge, 2008).

Buszynski, Leszek & Do Thanh Hai, *The South China Sea: From a Regional Maritime Dispute to Geo-strategic Competition*, (Basingstoke: Routledge, 2020).

Chen, Dean P., *US-China Rivalry and Taiwan's Mainland Policy*, (Cham: Palgrave Macmillan, 2017).

Chojnacki, Sven, 'Anything New or More of the Same? Wars and Military Interventions in the International System,1946–2003'. *Global Society*, 1(20), 2006: 25–46.

Collier, David; Jody LaPorte & Jason Seawright, 'Putting Typologies to Work: Concept Formation, Measurement, and Analytic Rigor'. *Political Research Quarterly*, 1(65), 2012: 217–232.

Conflict Trends, (Peace Research Institute in Oslo, 2020), https://www.prio.org/Projects/Project/?x=1631.

Croissant, Aurel & Cristoph Trinn, *Culture, Identity and Conflict in Asia and Southeast Asia*, (Gutersloh, Bertelsmann Stiftung, 2009).

Dowlah, Caf, *The Bangladesh Liberation War, the Sheikh Mujib Regime, and Contemporary Controversies*, (Lanham: Lexington Books, 2016).

Evans, Grant & Kelvin Rowley, *Red Brotherhood at War: Vietnam, Cambodia and Laos Since 1975*, (London: Verso, 1990).

Finlan, Alastair, *The Gulf War 1991*, (Oxford: Osprey Publishing, 2003).

The Geneva Conventions of 12 August 1949, (International Committee of the Red Cross, 1949), https://www.icrc.org/en/doc/assets/files/publications/icrc-002-0173.pdf (2.11.2020).

Hastings, Max, *Vietnam: An Epic Tragedy, 1945–1975*, (New York: Harper Collins Publishers, 2019).

Heiduk, Felix & Gudrun Wacker, *From Asia-Pacific to Indo-Pacific: Significance, Implementation and Challenges*. SWP Research Paper No. 9 (Berlin: German Institute for International and Security Affairs, 2020).

Holt, John Clifford, *Myanmar's Buddhist-Muslim Crisis: Rohingya, Arakanese, and Burmese Narratives of Siege and Fear*, (Honolulu: University of Hawaii Press, 2019).

Kaplan, Robert D., *Monsoon: The Indian Ocean and the Future of American Power*, (New York: Random House, 2010).

Kaplan, Robert D., *Asia's Cauldron: The South China Sea and the End of a Stable Pacific*, (New York: Random House, 2015).

Kato, Yoichi, 'Shift of US-China Relations and Its Impact on the Regional Order'. In Masashi Nishihara; Céline Pajon (eds.), *East Asia Security in Flux: What Regional Order Ahead?* (Paris: French Institute of International Relations/the Research Institute for Peace and Security in Tokio, 2020), 21–28.

Kaufman, Joyce P., *Introduction to International Relations: Theory and Practice*, (Lanham: Rowman & Littlefield, 2013).

Khadduri, Majid & Edmund Ghareeb, *War in the Gulf, 1990–91: The Iraq-Kuwait Conflict and Its Implications*, (New York: Oxford University Press, 1997).

Kipgen, Nehginpao, *The Politics of South China Sea Disputes*, (Basingstoke: Routledge, 2021).

Lin, Cheng-Yi & Denny Roy, *The Future of United States, China, and Taiwan Relations*, (New York: Palgrave Macmillan, 2011).

Lintner, Bertil, *China's India War: Collision Course on the Roof of the World*, (New Delhi: Oxford University Press, 2018).

Logevall, Fredrik, *The Origins of the Vietnam War*, (New York and Abingdon: Routledge, 2013).

Lynch, Michael, *The Chinese Civil War 1945–49*, (Oxford: Osprey Publishing, 2010).

Medcalf, Rory & Raja C. Mohan, *Responding to Indo-Pacific Rivalry: Australia, India and Middle Power Coalitions*, (Lowy Institute, 2014), https://www.files.ethz.ch/isn/182718/responding_to_indo-pacific_rivalry_0.pdf.

Moore, Christopher, *The Mediation Process*, (San Francisco: Jossey-Bass, 2006).

Nhem, Boraden, *The Chronicle of a People's War: The Military and Strategic History of the Cambodian Civil War 1979–1991*, (Abingdon: Routledge, 2017).

Pilbeam, Bruce, 'Reflecting on War and Peace'. In Peter Hough; Shahin Malik; Andrew Malik; Bruce Pilbeam (eds.), *International Security Studies: Theory and Practice*, (London and New York: Routledge, 2015), 103–119.

Protocol Additional to the Geneva Conventions of 12 August 1949 and Relating to the Protection of Victims of International Armed Conflicts (Protocol I), 8 June 1977, (International Committee of the Red Cross), https://ihl-databases.icrc.org/applic/ihl/ihl.nsf/Article.xsp?action=openDocument&documentId=6C86520D7EFAD527C12563CD0051D63C (2.11.2020).

Raditio, Klaus Heinrich, *Understanding China's Behaviour in the South China Sea: A Defensive Realist Perspective*, (Singapore: Palgrave Macmillan).

Raghavan, Srinath, 'The Disputed India-China Boundary 1948–1960'. In Srinath Raghavan (ed.), *War and Peace in Modern India*, (London: Palgrave Macmillan, 2010), 227–266.

Razoux, Pierre, *The Iran-Iraq War*, (Cambridge and London: The Belknap Press of Harvard University Press, 2015).

Rossiter, Ash & Brendon J. Cannon, 'Conflict and Cooperation in the Indo-Pacific: New Geopolitical Realities'. In Ash Rossiter; Brendon J. Cannon (eds.), *Conflict and Cooperation in the Indo-Pacific: New Geopolitical Realities*, (New York and Abingdon: Routledge, 2020).

Roy, Nalanda, *The South China Sea Disputes: Past, Present, and Future*, (Lanham: Lexington Books, 2016).

Scott, James M.; Ralph G. Carter & A. Cooper Drury, *International, Economic, and Human Security in a Changing World*, (London: Sage Publications, 2019).

Singh, Jasjit, *China's India War, 1962: Looking Back to See the Future*, (New Delhi: KW Publishers, 2013).

Singh, Suchet Vir, *China Raises Defence Spending by 7.1% despite Lowest GDP Growth Forecast in 3 Decades*, (The Print, 2022), https://theprint.in/world/china-raises-defence-spending-by-7-1-despite-lowest-gdp-forecast-in-3-decades/859889/.

Strangio, Sebastian, *In: The Dragon's Shadow, Southeast Asia in the Chinese Century*, (New Haven and London: Yale University Press, 2020).

Subramanian, Samanth, *The Divided Island: Life, Death, and the Sri Lankan War*, (New York: Thomas Dunne Books, 2015).

Territorial Disputes in the South China SEA, COUNCIL on Foreign Relations, 2020, https://www.cfr.org/global-conflict-tracker/conflict/territorial-disputes-south-china-sea.

Winston, Rachel & Ishika Sachdeva, *Raging Waters in the South China Sea: What the Battle for Supremacy Means for Southeast Asia*, (Irvine: Lizard Publishing, 2020).

15 Maritime governance in the Indo-Pacific

The European conceptualisation

Tomasz Łukaszuk

The twenty-first century brought the shift of global political and economic gravity towards the Indo-Pacific. The primary beneficiaries of the process of globalisation in the world economy became Indo-Pacific littorals. They transformed their economies, gaining significance on a global scale, aspiring to the role of regional or global powers. As a consequence of that process, the Indo-Pacific became the busiest and most significant communication corridor with the most extensive world container traffic and world petroleum transit, providing vital resources for all the region's countries. Furthermore, the task of ensuring the security of sea lines of communication (SLOCs) has been included in the maritime strategies of states, turning them from coastal to oceanic beyond their national jurisdiction. Growing asymmetric threats of piracy and terrorism, as well as the rise of China's naval blue-water capabilities and its assertiveness in the South China Sea, elevated the importance of the Indo-Pacific as not only an area of significant international commercial transportation but also the area of the competition of the regional and extra-regional actors. The geopolitical significance of Indian Ocean Region (IOR) is also marked by China's quest to access the Indian Ocean and the Western Pacific as areas of fundamental strategic meaning through the SLOCs, and the theatre of maritime military operations. The ocean is increasingly subject to asymmetric threats. The diversified character of threats and complexity of the challenges influenced the maritime strategies of countries published at the beginning of the twenty-first century.

The maritime domain also became the most significant part of Indo-Pacific states' sustainable development concepts. They developed their ways of economic exploitation of seas and oceans, turning them into blue economies. The related areas of maritime governance, like protection of the marine environment and legal management also found their place in the Indo-Pacific littorals maritime strategies.

The main aim of the chapter is to explain how the littorals of the Indo-Pacific region apprehend maritime governance in the twenty-first century and how that apprehension influences their maritime policies. The Indo-Pacific region is understood in the chapter as defined in the introduction to the Handbook as the greater Indian Ocean, which links the Horn of Africa, past the Arabian Peninsula to the Indian subcontinent, past the Indonesian archipelago and beyond to the Pacific. Maritime governance implicates the co-operation of the states, which are interdependent. In contrast to the land surface, it is impossible to set physical borders on

DOI: 10.4324/9781003336143-19

seas, to limit positive or negative phenomena in the environment (rise of sea level) or security (piracy and terrorism). Various activities focused on the use of living and non-living resources of oceans and seas; ways of securing their maritime transportation and protecting the marine environment from the adverse effects of these activities constitute the best example of the growing interlinkage among different activities at sea. Understanding the significance of those phenomena, the countries of Indo-Pacific created a network of organisations and multi-lateral agreements to tackle challenges in a holistic way. Some areas like military security have limited space for convergence of interests in the context of the rise of China and its strategy in the South China Sea. The chapter also highlights the existing and potential co-operation mechanisms between regional and extra-regional partners, including the European Union members like France, Germany and the Netherlands, which also created their concepts apart from the European Union Indo-Pacific strategy.

The chapter is structured first to explain the definition of maritime governance, then to show the most important players, furthermore to explore the dependencies among them and how that impacts the region. In the following part, the chapter addresses the origins of the architecture of co-operation in maritime governance at different levels – from local up to regional, trying to ask questions about a long-term forecast of how maritime governance will develop in the Indo-Pacific region. Finally, it discusses the perspectives of the cooperation between the European Union and Indo-Pacific countries to utilise in the region the best practices of the EU Integrated Maritime Policy in the region.

What is maritime governance

> While the world below the ocean's surface is more than twice the size of the world above it and contains an estimated 94 percent of the space where life can exist on Earth, only 5 percent of the world's oceans have been fully explored.
>
> (Dalio & Benioff 2018)

As NASA claimed, we have better maps of the surface of Mars and the moon than oceans (Stillman 2009). The situation is similar with regard to the terminology and the coherent naming system for maritime governance. There is a lack of its precise definition in fundamental United Nations conventions, including the 1982 UN Convention on the Law of the Sea (UNCLOS), concentrating on selected aspects of maritime governance. There are diverse research approaches towards maritime governance depending on whether we are dealing with a realist or neoliberal vision of international relations and the scope of analysis from security to environmental protection. Its interdisciplinary character and fragmentation of the maritime institutions created within the United Nations Convention of Law of the Sea system also contributed to that variety.

Realists have always seen the oceans as battlefields instrumental to the military and commercial domination of vast maritime spaces and littorals. That domination helped the Britain to govern the Indian Ocean and the whole of its basin in the nineteenth century and the United States to take over the dominion in the second half of the twentieth century. The terms like sea power (Kemp 1981; Till 2018), and maritime power (Kemp 1981; Kraska 2011), describe maritime governance as a competition among global super or middle powers, based on which of them has the more developed navy, merchant navy and maritime infrastructure.

Sea power	Maritime power
A state with naval strength – ships and shipping capabilities that permit the extensive use of military force for certain missions (Kemp 1981). A state with military and civil capabilities used in its naval and commercial operations in order to influence other states and people at sea and from the sea (Till 2018).	A state that makes extensive use of access to the sea resources to pursue economic activities with other groups, which, in turn, influences its power relations with them; these economic activities can include the transportation of land-based goods and services by sea or the exploitation of sea-based resources (Kemp 1981).

The neoliberals have always seen the necessity to cooperate in maritime affairs due to the vastness of the oceans. Keohane and Nye (2012) chose oceans as one of the case studies of their theory of interdependence within the framework of the institutional neoliberal theory of international relations. The maritime governance implicates the co-operation of the interdependent states. In contrast to the land surface, it is impossible to set physical borders on seas, to limit positive or negative phenomena in the environment (rise of sea level) or security (piracy and terrorism). Transnational activities in fishing, offshore drilling, transportation and the security of sea lines of communication (SLOCs) are functionally interlinked and exemplify growing interdependence among different activities at sea. The maritime domain space, and its complexity, covering all kinds of activities within and beyond national jurisdiction, made the institutions created by the states necessary. Without them, due to the vastness of the oceans and interdependence of all actors involved, it would be impossible to reach the goals within the national and common interests of littorals. The scope of the definitions and descriptions has constantly been expanding due to the emergence of new phenomena and non-state actors at seas and oceans. As highlighted by Suarez de Vivero and Rodriguez Mateos (2010), the transition to the twenty-first century marks the beginning of a phase in which a significant number of new marine policies and strategies have sprung up to respond to the new maritime paradigm that involves a new strategic vision of the seas and oceans: the old paradigm, associated with discoveries, the creation of colonial empires and trade, which is giving way to a model that is deeply rooted in competitiveness, innovation and knowledge. This new vision means a loss of strategic interest in traditional activities and the shifting of the maritime centre of gravity towards the new technologies, energy security and global leadership. The growing number of actors in maritime affairs, the development of the law of the sea (1958 and 1982 UN Conventions on the Law of the Sea) and the increasing intensity of maritime transport drew the attention of neoliberal scientists to the legal dimension of maritime governance. The public order of the oceans (McDougal & Burke 1962) and the order at sea (Bekkevold & Till 2016) focused on the international law of the sea. The scope of ocean governance (Mann Borghese, Haward & Vince, Tanaka, Kundis Craig, Pyc, Kimball), and oceans governance (Lowry 2007; Rothwell & Stephens 2016; Pretlove & Blasiak 2018), is mainly limited to environmental issues. In the twenty-first century, the terms of integrated oceans management (Scott), integrated maritime policy (Adamczak-Retecka 2014), maritime governance (McLaughlin 2010; Roe 2016) were introduced in order to describe the holistic and sustainable approach towards maritime management covering all the areas of activities at sea and showing their interdependence. In the context of the Indian Ocean region study and based on the general definition of the governance (Thakur & Van Langenhove 2006), maritime governance was described as "the complex of formal and informal institutions, mechanisms, relationships, and processes between and among states, markets, citizens and organizations, both inter and non-governmental, through which collective interests on the maritime plane are articulated, rights and obligations are established, and differences are mediated" (Schöttli 2015).

Nowadays, maritime governance with its complexity and dynamic character is more a process than a static description of policies at global, regional and national levels, regulating and monitoring all spheres of state and non-state actors' activity at seas and oceans (Lukaszuk 2018). It went through different phases of development of the conceptual framework and terminology due to its dynamism under the conditions of constant changes in maritime affairs in terms of technological progress in shipping and mining, legal regulations and growing interdependence in the economy as a part of globalisation. The majority of the researchers use the neoliberal way of description and definition of maritime governance as the adequate way to capture its main features like dynamism, imperative of coordinating international and national institutions, interrelation of main areas like legal framework, security, marine safety (the protection of the environment) and blue economy. Keohane's and Nye's model of complex interdependence and Roe's meta-governance reflect the modern shape of maritime governance.

The integrated maritime policy of the European Union focuses on

- issues that do not fall under a single sector-based policy e.g., "blue growth" (economic growth based on different maritime sectors);
- issues that require the coordination of different sectors and actors e.g., marine knowledge.

Specifically, it covers these cross-cutting policies

- Blue growth;
- Marine data and knowledge;
- Maritime spatial planning;

- Integrated maritime surveillance;
- Sea basin strategies.

It seeks to coordinate, not to replace policies on specific maritime sectors (European Commission 2007).

The most distinctive features of maritime governance in the twenty-first century

- the necessity of neoliberal institutional rather than realist approach while dealing with global issues regarding oceans – to attain their interests and achieve the stable co-operation of states voluntarily creating intergovernmental institutions, which can mitigate the negative effects of the dynamic interrelated phenomena at sea;
- dynamism – maritime governance is more a process than a static set of rules and regulations organised under an institutional framework of cooperation;
- wide scope of stakeholders, including states, international organisations, international corporations, local communities, media, non-governmental organisations;
- horizontal and vertical multi-layered interdependency between all actors at national and international level, and areas of activities – legal regulations, security, blue economy and environmental issues;
- urgency of coordinated international approach with multinational consideration of interests of particular countries, regions and global community.

Who are the most important players

The role of the states in shaping maritime affairs directly or through international institutions remains central, despite the diffusion of competencies and power, transferred to international institutions, global enterprises in shipping and seabed oil and gas exploitation, as part of the process of globalisation through the networks of interdependence. States are responsible for the effectiveness of the mechanisms of maritime governance (Roe 2013, 2016). They create strategies and roadmaps within the organisations, then introduce regulations, coordinate its execution at the national level, and monitor others' performance at the international level. Ensuring the security of strategic ocean routes (the Sea Lines of Communication) through own naval forces or international co-operation with other countries, providing necessary technical and legal infrastructure, taking care of Large Marine Ecosystems – those elements are still within the competence of governments and their institutions as well.

The selection of the most critical players in shaping maritime governance in the Indo-Pacific was based on analysis of both quantitative parameters such as the length of the coastline, the size of the Exclusive Economic Zone (EEZ) and Large Marine Ecosystems (LME), the size of the population living in coastal areas, and qualitative as the scale and the degree of implementation of maritime governance at the domestic level, and participation in international co-operation.

Table 15.1 Critical players in the maritime governance in Indo-Pacific

Country	Coastline (km)	EEZ (million km2)	LME (million km2)	Population in coastal areas (million)	Maritime governance domestic institutions	Participation in international maritime organisations, fora and conventions
India	7516,6	2,37	Arabian Sea (3,95), Bay of Bengal (3,65)	560[1]	Ministry of Fisheries, Animal Husbandry & Dairying, National Centre for Polar and Ocean Research (NCPOR), Indian National Centre for Ocean Services (INCOIS), Indian Tsunami Early Warning Centre (ITEWC), National Maritime Security Coordinator (NMSC) IONS	IORA, BIMSTEC, IMO, IONS, IOGOOS[2], UNCLOS (ratified 1995), Heads of Asian Coast Guard Agencies Meeting (HACGAM), QUAD
Indonesia	54720	6,2	Indonesian Sea (2,29), Sulu-Celebes Sea (1,01,)	180[3]	Ministry of Maritime Affairs and Fisheries, Indonesian Maritime Information Centre (IMIC), Maritime Security Agency (Bakamla)	IORA, IONS, Heads of Asian Coast Guard Agencies Meeting (HACGAM), IOGOOS, IMO, UNCLOS (ratified 1986), Partnerships in Environmental Management for the Seas of East Asia (PEMSEA)
Australia	25780	8,2	North Australian Shelf (0,77), Northeast Australian Shelf (1,3), East-Central Australian Shelf (0,66), Southeast Australian Shelf (1,2), Southwest Australian Shelf (1,05), West-Central Australian Shelf (0,54), Northwest Australian Shelf (0,91)	21,76	Department of Agriculture, Water and the Environment, Department of Infrastructure, Transport, Regional Development and Communications, National Oceans Advisory Group, Ocean Policy Science Advisory Group (OPSAG), National Oceans Office (NOO), Regional Marine Plan Steering Committees and the National Oceans Advisory Group (NOAG)	IORA, IONS, IOGOOS, IMO, UNCLOS (ratified 1994), The Pacific Islands Forum, SPREP (Secretariat of the Pacific Regional Programme) (metropolitan member), QUAD

(*Continued*)

Table 15.1 (Continued)

Country	Coastline (km)	EEZ (million km2)	LME (million km2)	Population in coastal areas (million)	Maritime governance domestic institutions	Participation in international maritime organisations, fora and conventions
Japan	29751	4,48	Sea of Japan/East Sea (1,05), Kuroshio Current (1,33), Oyashio Current (0,66)	126	Japan Agency for Marine-Earth Science and Technology (JAMSTEC), Headquarters for Ocean Policy	UNCLOS (ratified 1996), IMO, IORA (dialogue partner), Partnerships in Environmental Management for the Seas of East Asia (PEMSEA), Heads of Asian Coast Guard Agencies Meeting (HACGAM), QUAD
United States	68911		East Bering Sea (1,2), Gulf of Alaska (1,5), California Current (2,22), Insular Pacific-Hawaiian (0,97)	53	National Marine Fisheries Service (NMFS), National Ocean Service	IMO, IORA (dialogue partner), UNCLOS (signed not ratified), SPREP (metropolitan member), QUAD

1. Centre for Coastal Zone Management and Coastal Shelter Belt, Anna University, Chennai, iomenvis.nic.in/index2.aspx?slid=758&sublinkid=119&langid=1&mid=1.
2. The Indian Ocean Global Ocean Observing System (IOGOOS) is comprised of 24 marine institutes from 16 countries in the Indian Ocean region.
3. (Jprhj-Guldberg & Jompa 2016).
4. The states taken into account: Alaska, California, Hawaii, Oregon, Washington. https://www.worldatlas.com/articles/us-states-by-length-of-coastline.html, https://www.lmehub.net/.

The indicators in the table show how significant players in not only regional but also global dimensions are the key Indo-Pacific countries. They are among the top ten countries with the longest coastline and the top ten with the most extensive Exclusive Economic Zone. The coastal areas are densely populated, with all the biggest cities of India, Indonesia, Australia and Japan being located on the sea-shore. 85% of Australia's Australian Government 2016), 80% of Japan's (Statistics Bureau of Japan 2020), 40% of the United States (National Ocean Service 2020), 43% of India's (Center for Coastal Management 2017) and 70% of Indonesia's (Hoegh-Guldberg & Jompa 2016) population lives and works in coastal areas. Such a location made the blue economy and maritime infrastructure a key factor of their economic and social development. 34% of Japan's shoreline was transformed for ports, harbours and other industrial facilities (Terashima & Hayashi 2015). The biggest Large Marine Ecosystem in the world – the Great Barrier Reef – is located off the coast of Australia (United Nations 2016). Indonesia is the largest by territory (Indonesian Ministry of Trade 2013), and Japan is the fourth among the archipelagos in the world (Anwar 2018). With such potential and, at the same time, being aware of the responsibility for such huge sea basins and adjacent land territories, these countries have created an extensive network of national institutions responsible for managing individual sectors of maritime governance and the coordination of co-operation between them.

The decisive moments and starting points of their institutional architecture were preparations before the Third Conference of the Law of the Sea (1973–1982), the debate during its deliberations and the UN Convention on the Law Sea (1982) as a result and the road map for future endeavours. The United States, Australia, India, Japan and Indonesia were among the most active participants of the Conference, feeling responsible for the success of the talks and breaking the long-term deadlock in negotiations on territorial sea, continental shelf and archipelago waters. They started to incorporate the draft provisions agreed during the Conference and the regulations included in the Convention into their national law, even before the document's ratification in 1994. The US National Ocean Service and Japan Agency for Marine-Earth Science and Technology (JAMSTEC) were pioneers as they were established in 1970 and 1971, respectively, just after the resolution of the UN General Assembly to convene the Conference. All those domestic institutions underwent modernisation and transformation in the twenty-first century, striving to decentralise their competencies in major areas and adjust them to changing and growing multi-sectoral international interdependence. As presented in the table, the major players are among the International Maritime Organisation active members being constantly elected to the organisation's council. As all of them belong to the signatories of UNCLOS, they participated in the process of establishment of international, regional institutions covering different parts of the Indo-Pacific region following the provisions of the Convention and subsequent documents like the Rio Declaration on Environment and Development and Agenda 21 of the United Nations Conference on Environment and Development (1992). Japan and Indonesia have been founding members of the Partnerships in Environmental Management for the Seas of East Asia (PEMSEA), the project, which started in 1993, aimed at the prevention and management of marine pollution in the East Asian Seas, involving the United Nations Development Programme (UNDP) in implementation and the International Maritime Organization (IMO) in execution (PEMSEA 2021). PEMSEA focused on sustainable management of coastal and marine areas through a regional mechanism to augment national and regional commitment. Since its inception in 1997, the Indian Ocean Rim Association (IORA), involving all key actors as members or dialogue partners, has expanded the span of its activities related to maritime governance from year to year, starting from the sustained growth and balanced development, through maritime safety and security, trade and investment facilitation, fisheries management, disaster risk management, academic, science and technology co-operation, tourism and cultural exchanges, up to the blue economy and women's economic empowerment (IORA 2017). The Bay of Bengal Initiative for Multi-sectoral Technical and Economic Cooperation (BIMSTEC), established in 1997, has similar goals with an additional emphasis on port and transport infrastructure development on seashores of countries located on the largest and the most strategic bay of the world. Organisations with a similar profile have been created in the South Western Pacific, a vast part of the Indo-Pacific Region, uniting small island countries of Oceania and their bigger neighbours (Japan, Australia, Indonesia and the United States) as strategic partners. The Pacific Islands Forum has gone through slow evolution since its emergence in 1971, increasing the number of members and dialogue partners from seven to 18 members, striving in the twenty-first century towards sustainable and inclusive development. The Secretariat of the Pacific Regional Programme (SPREP) has less than general goals and focuses on areas of maritime governance vital to islands' existence, related to climate change resistance and waste management and pollution control. Both IOGOOS and IONS started their activities in the twenty-first century, dealing with two different areas. The first one, established in 2001, focused on enhancing oceanography, exchanging and utilising data related to the Indian Ocean Observing System between 25 marine operational and research agencies from 17 countries. The second one, inaugurated in 2008, serves as a biennial forum of dialogue of navies of Indian Ocean littorals, including Australia, India, Indonesia and their partners from Europe and East Asia like Japan, working in the fields of humanitarian assistance and disaster relief, maritime security and information sharing and inter-operability. "The Tsunami Core Group," created by Australia, India, Japan and the United States, after the tsunami in December 2004 (International Tsunami Information Center 2014), the biggest recorded in modern history (it killed 227,898 people in 14 countries across the Indian Ocean), has been considered as incipient of the Quadrilateral Security Cooperation (QUAD) of those four countries. The second attempt was made in 2007 on the sidelines of the ASEAN Regional Forum meeting when the representatives of four countries met, but the final restart of QUAD took place in 2017. The coordination of the regional security strategy has been set so far as the goal of that informal forum of security dialogue and naval co-operation.

The key actors attached great importance not only to the institutional and legal framework of maritime governance but also to the conceptual one in the form of white/blue papers or strategies. The United States published documents prepared and focused on the naval and legal dimension of maritime governance (US Department of Defense 2007). Japan (Government of Japan 2007), India (Ministry of Defence 2015), Australia (Royal Australian Navy 2010) and Indonesia (Coordinating Ministry For Maritime Affairs 2017) also published their strategies in the twenty-first century. In Japan's case, it was the long-term consequence of the limitations of Japan's activities in the new constitution 1947 as a result of WWII defeat and negative connotations associated with Japanese pan-Asian concepts of the early twentieth century. Three other countries reactivated and extended maritime policies from coastal to oceanic, rooted in a dichotomous semiotic approach (Lukaszuk 2020). The partition to the maritime South and land-concentrated Subcontinental North influenced the Indian approach towards maritime governance for centuries and put limitations on it, narrowing to the closest neighbourhood up to recent times. Impacted by the Hindu sacred attitude to the sea as a place meant for gods, Indonesian states located on the islands of Sumatra and Java did not explore the Indian and Pacific oceans beyond coastal waters. At the same time, Bugis sailors from Sulawesi were famous across the Indian Ocean with their pinisi boats (Liebner 2005). Modern Indonesia, the biggest archipelago in the world, with the dominant population of Java, was limited in its maritime apprehension to interisland transportation until the twenty-first century. Australia was for a long time divided between the desire to tame the unfavourable climatic conditions and to develop the largest possible territory of the smallest continent and the legacy of British power in the seas in the nineteenth century.

How main players impact the region through the mechanisms of bilateral and multi-lateral co-operation

Using their institutional capacities, the leading players influence the maritime governance of the region as a whole, including its sub-regions and countries and non-state actors. They are aware that maritime governance is a complex and dynamic process and attach great significance to the holistic approach at all levels of subjectivity in the maritime domain and all areas of maritime governance from legal, naval and economic, up to the marine environment. Only such an approach guarantees the successful implementation of the integrated maritime policy as the executive framework of maritime governance. Another critical factor is that they made responsibility for particular regions and countries a part of their maritime policy: Australia – Western Pacific and Southeast Asia, Japan – all less developed countries in Indo-Pacific, Indonesia – Southeast Asia, India – South Asia and small islands in the Indian Ocean. Small and medium countries of the Indo-Pacific expect them to be not only providers of security, in the context of China's growing assertiveness in the South China Sea, but also contributors to sustainable maritime development related to the blue economy and protection of the marine environment. They use their development assistance programs to boost cooperation in maritime infrastructure development, environmental protection and management of exclusive economic zones and other maritime zones under their jurisdiction to meet those expectations.

In his vision of the "Free and Open Indo-Pacific Strategy," Japanese prime minister Shinzo Abe presented the holistic perspective of modern maritime governance in the Indo-Pacific (Abe 2007, 2016). The Japanese concept assumes that a key for stability and prosperity of the Indo-Pacific is the combination of "Two Continents" – Asia and Africa and "Two Oceans" – free and open Pacific Ocean and the Indian Ocean. Following the structure of maritime governance, the Strategy consists of critical features like promotion and establishment of the rule of law, freedom of navigation and free trade; pursuit of blue economy serving economic prosperity; development of connectivity through the synergy of land and maritime infrastructure; capacity building on maritime law enforcement (Embassy of Japan to ASEAN 2021). Carrying the burden of its deeds during WWII in bilateral relations with Northeast and Southeast Asia,

Japan initiated security cooperation programs in the twenty-first century only. The Regional Cooperation Agreement on Combating Piracy and Armed Robbery against Ships in Asia (ReCAAP) was announced in 2006 as the first regional government-to-government agreement to promote and enhance cooperation against piracy and armed robbery against ships in Asia (ReCAAP ISC 2021). Executing its Strategy and striving for a rules-based maritime order, Japan cooperates with not only the main actors in the Indo-Pacific but also with other littorals from ASEAN and the Middle East. Complementary to the Strategy, there are also Japanese activities in another area of maritime governance – climate change mitigation and struggle with its immediate and current consequences. Since 2007 the Japan-initiated Dialogue on Environmental Cooperation with ASEAN, focusses in the maritime area on the Biodiversity Capacity Building Programme and the Marine Plastics Debris Knowledge Centre. In 2019, JICA (Japan International Cooperation Agency) funded and extended grant aid for the Pacific Climate Change Centre – a partnership between the governments of Japan and Samoa (Pacific Climate Change Centre 2020), beneficial for all Western Pacific islands, facing a critical threat to their existence caused by rising ocean levels. The Pacific Climate Change Centre delivers capacity development programs in adaptation, mitigation, climate services and project development. It also promotes and fosters applied research, drive innovation and build capacity in these areas. Another significant task is to improve the flow of practical information between met services, climate practitioners, policymakers, researchers, scientists and those implementing policies, programs and projects. Providing the space for visiting researchers and experts to work from the PCCC and directly, the support is extended to benefit of Pacific Island countries and territories. A crucial aim is bringing together partners to find innovative solutions to the challenges that climate change presents. Search and rescue capacity building activities constitute another significant element of the Japanese impact on the Indo-Pacific region in the context of climate change and natural disasters related to the complex of challenges in the maritime domain. The foundation of Japan's active co-operation in that area was the extensive assistance to all littorals affected by the 2004 tsunami. Japanese Maritime Self Defence Forces carried out operations off the coasts of Southeast Asian countries like Thailand, Indonesia and Malaysia, which suffered tremendous losses. Japan initiated and co-founded the establishment of a tsunami early-warning mechanism under the auspices of the United Nations Office for Disaster Risk Reduction, additionally facilitating several countries of Indo-Pacific with buoys and sensors located at the deep sea.

Australia's vision of the region as "A Stable and Prosperous Indo-Pacific" (Australian Government 2017) also covers all the layers of maritime governance. It assumes the support for dialogue and co-operation, the peaceful settlement of disputes in accordance with the international law of the sea, open markets facilitating the flow of goods, services, capital and ideas, an inclusive and open economic integration and freedom of navigation with the rights of small states protected. As a part of the program, Australia established the Pacific Climate Partnership, linking its climate change actions and coordinating with other countries and regional initiatives also related to geohazards. For small archipelagic states like Nauru, Fiji or Vanuatu, climate change is a matter of survival as they are most vulnerable to rising sea levels. The Western Pacific, together with the Eastern Indian Ocean, is a part of the Ring of Fire characterised by high seismic activity, which has a significant impact on all activities in the region as earthquakes of varying severity occur there every day. Australia facilitated littorals of those two oceans basins in prevention, alert system and disaster relief. In the area of the blue economy, the tuna fishery in the waters under the jurisdiction of the Western Pacific Islands is considered the largest and most productive in the world (Haward & Vince 2008). Australia is a member and donor to the Pacific Islands Forum Fisheries Agency and the Pacific Community. Australia is implementing additional programs to tackle illegal, unreported and unregulated fishing (IUU), including coordinated engagement under Australia's Pacific Maritime Security Program. The Program supports Pacific islands in their endeavours to attain sustainable development goals in managing coastal fisheries (Australian Government 2021). Piracy, terrorism and people smuggling constituting asymmetric phenomena are part of the regional Indo-Pacific security concern where Australia is active with its programs. It started its co-operation in 2002 when the "Bali Process" (Conference on People Smuggling, Trafficking in Persons and Related Transnational Crime) was initiated within the bilateral program with Indonesia and became the platform of dialogue and cooperation of 45 countries and four UN institutions (the Office of the United Nations High Commissioner for Refugees – UNHCR; the International Organization for Migration – IOM; the United Nations Office on Drugs and Crime – UNODC and the International Labour Organization – ILO) (the Bali Process). As the result of the regional discourse on irregular migration in the 1990s and the increased flow of refugees from the Middle East and Afghanistan to Australia in 2001–2002, the Bali Process was the manifestation of the multilateral, regional process (Kneebone 2014). In 2016, Australia signed a legally binding agreement with regional partners to combat irregular migration, people smuggling and human trafficking.

As the biggest in terms of population and territory, Indonesia is a leading member of the Association of Southeast Asian Nations (ASEAN), playing the role of *primus inter pares*, and has been striving to focus on its maritime governance activities through that organisation, mainly in the area of security. Jakarta argued that those activities of ASEAN with its "special way," in the absence of the coherent system of collective security in the region, have played a critical role in building confidence measures between main actors. "The ASEAN way" model, utilised since the 1970s, has focused on promoting dialogue and co-operation, and the importance of the maritime domain in the regional architecture. ASEAN leaders assumed that institutional ties and dialogue mechanisms created like ASEAN Regional Forum (ARF), ARF Inter-sessional Meeting on Maritime Security (ISM-MS), ASEAN Defence Ministers Meeting +8 (ADMM), Expanded ASEAN Maritime Forum (EAMF), have prevented conflicts at sea and engaged both intra- and extra-regional players in co-operation to secure the maritime domain, including SLOCs. In order to maintain the pivotal role of ASEAN, Indonesia initiated and led to the adoption in 2019 of the "ASEAN Outlook on Indo-Pacific" (AIOP) with four priority areas: maritime cooperation, connectivity, sustainable development and economic co-operation. The document emphasised the ASEAN-centred Indo-Pacific region concept with the limited role of extra-regional powers following the ASEAN+ model of regional co-operation shaped successfully in the last four decades. Using its potential as the largest archipelago globally, Indonesia started to present initiatives outside the ASEAN framework in 2013. Indonesian Foreign Minister Marty Natalegawa proposed the Indo-Pacific Treaty of Friendship and Cooperation based on the "Bali Principles," the Principles for Mutually Beneficial Relations agreed at the East Asia Summit (EAS) 2011 (East Asia Summit 2011). He stressed that the Indo-Pacific should be "pacific" (peaceful) with "the commitment to solve disputes by peaceful means" (Natalegawa 2013). A year later, at EAS 2014, Indonesian President Joko Widodo proposed the concept of "Global Maritime Fulcrum" (GMF), considered as a response to China's Belt and Road Initiative. Among his main postulates were maintaining and managing marine resources, with a focus on building marine food sovereignty through the development of the fishing industry, developing maritime infrastructure and connectivity, establishing deep seaports and logistical networks, developing the shipping industry and maritime tourism, eliminating the source of conflicts at sea, such as illegal fishing, violations of sovereignty, territorial disputes, piracy and marine pollution (Witular 2014). As for 2021, GMF is still awaiting implementation.

The Indian concept of Security and Growth for All (SAGAR) presented by Prime Minister Narendra Modi in 2015 (Modi 2015) epitomised the most characteristic futures of Indian maritime policy throughout the development of civilisation in the Indian subcontinent. It consists of an amalgam of the wisdom of the ancient books of Hinduism (Vedas), the experience of old Indian kingdoms (Chola), Gandhi and Nehru non-violence and peaceful coexistence, and twenty-first-century Indian maritime doctrine of 2005 (updated in 2009 and 2015) (Ministry of Defence 2009) and strategy of 2007 (updated in 2015) (Ministry of Defence 2015). SAGAR focused on confidence and trust, shared commitment to peace and prosperity, lasting stability and prosperity in the region and developing co-operation in the blue economy. The idea was supported by the number of development assistance grants and loans for island nations of the Indian Ocean, accompanied by naval equipment. Another concept presented Modi proposed in 2019 – the Indo-Pacific Oceans Initiative (IPOI) (Ministry of External Affairs 2020). From the elements of maritime governance, he pointed first at legal aspects, especially the sovereignty and territorial integrity and the application of international law (UNCLOS) to all states equally. In that context, he argued that the equal utilisation of the principle of the freedom of navigation would be beneficial to all. Modi also mentioned other features like sustainable development, protection of the marine environment and an open, free, fair and mutually-beneficial trade and investment system guaranteed to all actors. Goal 14 of the Sustainable Development Goals (life below the water) was place among the priorities of IPOI. It called for sustainable use of the maritime domain and visible efforts to create a safe, secure and stable maritime domain. The co-operation among states in the region, working to safeguard the oceans, including from plastic litter, should be imperative for all, similarly in terms of building capacity and fairly sharing resources to reduce the disaster risk. The academic co-operation, enhancement of science and technology, as well as the promotion of mutually beneficial trade and maritime transport were also included in the program. Australia is co-leading with New Delhi in the marine ecology pillar of the initiative. Vietnam and the Philippines also agreed to co-operate under the auspices of IPOI as it recognised the centrality of ASEAN in the Indo-Pacific region. Indian officials stressed that IPOI is in line with ASEAN Outlook on Indo-Pacific. They emphasised that the Indian Ocean region is primarily a political concept based on the values constituting the region. There is a need to maintain maritime governance in the Indo-Pacific that refers to liberal values and alliances. Maintaining the respect for those values and following the rules-based maritime governance, making it inclusive is considered an alternative to China's proposal of the Maritime New Silk Road (Maritime Belt and Road Initiative), announced in 2013.

Among the main players in the Indo-Pacific Region, the United States has the most challenging task to fulfil, has been expected to continue and extend its role as a net security provider and the maritime policy leader for many countries of the region. The US Indo-Pacific Command, renamed in 2018 from Pacific Command, with its 375 thousand personnel, 200 vessels and 1,100 aircraft (Indo-Pacific Command 2021), still remains the critical instrument in the region's security area of maritime governance. The United States has also been active in other areas of security related to search and rescue. In the aftermath of the 2004 tsunami, the Pacific Tsunami Warning Centre (PTWC), established in 1967 in Hawaii (the United States), extended its operations to the Indian Ocean and the South China Sea, taking responsibility for informing and warning all Indo-Pacific countries about earthquakes and tsunamis (Pacific Tsunami Warning Center 2021). The Indo-Pacific Command has provided humanitarian assistance for all regional littorals affected by maritime natural disasters. Understanding the growing role of other areas of maritime governance, and increased expectations of the countries of the region in the context of China's assertive economic diplomacy, US President Donald Trump announced in 2017 the American concept of "Free and Open Indo-Pacific" (Department of State 2019), based on Japanese Prime Minister Shinzo Abe's proposal. The US vision also aligned closely with India's Act East Policy and Australia's Indo-Pacific concept. In its comprehensive approach, the United States emphasised that the main goal is to build a flexible, resilient network of like-minded security partners to address common challenges. One of the significant features is the capacity building of security sector forces to respond to traditional and non-traditional, asymmetric threats like transnational crime, protect the maritime domain, address environmental challenges and respond collectively to emerging threats. The blue economy with maritime infrastructure projects also occupies an important place in the US program for the Indo-Pacific. Executing its vision, the United States strived to consolidate and coordinate security systems at the sub-regional levels. In 2018, it expanded the Southeast Asia Maritime Law Enforcement Initiative and a year later co-organised the first naval exercise with all ASEAN countries. In order to improve interoperability US convinced India to reengage Australia in Malabar naval exercises. The Washington administration provided US$1.1 billion for South and Southeast Asia maritime security programs, including the Southeast Asia Maritime Security Initiative (SAMSI), created by the United States in 2016 and the Bay of Bengal Initiative for Multisectoral Technical and Economic Cooperation (BIMSTEC). Within the framework of capacity building programs in maritime governance law reinforcement area, the US Coast Guard transferred patrol boats to Bangladesh, Sri Lanka, the Philippines and Vietnam. With the aim to enhance information sharing, interoperability and multi-national maritime co-operation among the sub-regions of the Indo-Pacific, the US extended know-how assistance by sending advisors to enhance maritime security and defence reforms in the Pacific Islands. In other areas of maritime governance, using the United States Agency for International Development (USAID) and its Oceans and Fisheries Partnership, the United States helps to strengthen regional co-operation to combat illegal, unreported and unregulated (IUU) fishing and conserve marine biodiversity in the region. USAID cooperates with the Southeast Asia Fisheries Development Center (SEAFDEC) and the ASEAN Sectoral Working Group on Fisheries (US Mission to ASEAN 2021). In the area of the marine environment, USAID utilises its experience and resources from the Adapt Asia-Pacific programme (2011–2017), with primary goals aiming at integrated knowledge transfer, capacity building and technical assistance to link climate funding organisations with eligible Asia-Pacific countries and help prepare projects that increased resilience to the negative impacts of climate change (USAID 2021).

Apart from the individual initiatives of main players, there have also been a number of trilateral and quadrilateral co-operation mechanisms involving them. The Australia–India–Indonesia (AII) trilateral (Panda 2021), conceived formally in 2017, the Japan–US–India established in 2015 (Berkshire Miller 2017) and Australia–India–Japan (AJI) (West 2020) created in 2017. They enhance the interconnectedness among the key players in the Indo-Pacific region, especially if it concerns the biggest littorals and the leaders of the subregions – Australia, India and Indonesia. The dialogue at the level of foreign and defence ministers and joint naval exercises helped them build up trust, coordination and apprehension of the convergence of strategic goals while facing China's growing assertiveness and aggressiveness. The trilateral format of co-operation of the principal actors successfully complements the existing fragmented institutional security framework and elevates their effective utilisation.

What are the mechanisms of Indo-Pacific countries' co-operation with the European Union and its member countries?

The European Union published its Indo-Pacific Strategy in 2021 only (EEAS 2021) with maritime governance placed among top priorities. However, the EU has been involved in developing maritime governance in the region for the last three decades through bilateral and multi-lateral channels. The EU has been active for example through participation in the Contact Group on Piracy off the Coast of Somalia (CGPCS) established in 2009. During its chairmanship in CGPCS in 2014 the EU focused on analytical reporting aimed at improvement of methodological and strategic approach towards the piracy (Tardy 2014).

The main aim of the 2021 document was to reinforce the EU's strategic focus, existing presence and future actions in the Indo-Pacific in the context of the dynamics in all areas of maritime governance in the region. The increased emphasis on maritime security co-operation was the most significant feature of the strategy, responding to the expectations of the main players in the region related to their security concerns. Apart from the existing protection of critical maritime routes through the EU Naval Force (EU NAVFOR) Operation Atalanta since 2008, the co-operation with Indo-Pacific countries would be extended to joint exercises and port calls of naval units. The European Union Critical Maritime Routes in the Indian Ocean program (CRIMARIO), launched in 2015, would also cover the Southern Pacific (Council of the European Union 2021). Despite meaningful successes in the twenty-first century in joint endeavours against piracy and terrorism, illicit acts at sea threatening 90% of trade between the regions remain the challenge. The situation in the South China Sea has been getting worse, and the matter of freedom of navigation has become even more pressing. The EU Council pointed in the Indo-Pacific Strategy at the necessity to establish comprehensive monitoring of compliance of all actors with the United Nations Convention on the Law of the Sea (UNCLOS).

As the biggest global donor of the development assistance, the EU would continue its support for Indo-Pacific countries in achieving the UN's Sustainable Development Goals (SDGs) in the blue economy. Being the largest market for fishery and aquaculture products in the world (Scholaert 2020) and a member of all Regional Fishery Management Organisations (RFMOs), the EU focused its activities on those sectors of the maritime economy. It utilises the existing multi-lateral channels of co-operation like the Pacific-European Union Marine Partnership Programme (PEUMP).

PEUMP is a multilateral fund financed by the European Union (EU) and the Swedish International Development Cooperation Agency (SIDA), aimed at building sustainable fisheries in the Pacific region (Institute of Marine Resources 2019). The PEUMP programme would be implemented by the Forum Fisheries Agency (FFA), the Pacific Community (SPC), the Secretariat of the Pacific Regional Environment Programme (SPREP) and the University of the South Pacific (USP), with SPC being the lead agency. In the case of the Indian Ocean, the EU constitutes one of the driving forces of the Southern Indian Ocean Fisheries Agreement (SIOFA) and the Indian Ocean Tuna Commission (IOTC), whose main goals embody Agenda 21 (UN Comprehensive Sustainable Development Plan) – the conservation and optimum utilisation of stocks and encouraging sustainable development of fisheries based on such stocks. EU-ASEAN Strategic Partnership is utilised as a platform of co-operation in the fishery by building ASEAN Common Fishery Policy on EU experience in implementation of the Policy. The EU is still not a member of two currently (2020) concluded regional agreements – the Comprehensive and Progressive Agreement for Trans-Pacific Partnership (CPTPP) and the Regional Comprehensive Economic Partnership (RCEP), in contrast to ASEAN members. Both agreements have critical importance for the prospects of blue economy co-operation in the Indo-Pacific. The EU would be forced to utilise the framework of its bilateral co-operation agreements (types of agreements: Partnership and Cooperation Agreements – PCA, Economic Partnership Agreements – EPA, Free Trade Agreements – FTA) and strive to finalise negotiations with the more considerable number of Indo-Pacific countries like India, Indonesia, Thailand, Malaysia and the Maldives to elevate maritime co-operation to a higher level. In its bilateral co-operation with Indo-Pacific countries, the EU also utilises Sustainable Fisheries Partnership Agreements (SFPAs).

The climate change policy plays a vital role in EU co-operation with the Indo-Pacific, of which many island and coastal states are particularly vulnerable to the consequences of climate change in the form of sea-level rise. ASEAN and Asia–Europe Meetings (ASEM) have been utilised as platforms of dialogue and climate policy implementation. EU–ASEAN High-Level Dialogue on Environment and Climate Change, established in 2019, focused on not only sea-level issues but also exchanges of experiences on environmental and climate goals and promoting regional solutions for a green transition. ASEM's Asia-Europe Environment Forum

(ENV Forum) serves as a forum to intensify Asia–Europe co-operation in technology transfer, capacity building and information sharing based on best practices. The EU is the largest development assistance provider in Indo-Pacific, committing millions of euros to various programs related to marine environmental issues and climate change (European Commission 2021). The objective of the programs is to promote renewable energy and energy efficiency, helping to reduce dependency on fossil fuels and improve climate change resilience. The growing intensity of cyclones or tropical storms, which recurrently hit countries in the region, creates conditions when some islands and even entire countries (the Maldives, Tuvalu, Kiribati) could see their physical existence at risk (EEAS 2012).

France is the only country acknowledged as an Indo-Pacific country among EU members since its overseas territories and 93% of its Exclusive Economic Zone (EEZ) are located in the region. One-and-a-half million French people live there (Ministry of Europe and Foreign Affairs 2021). France shares borders with five countries in the Indian Ocean and 12 in the Pacific Ocean (Morcos 2021). Considering itself as

"Indo-Pacific power," France has joined regional international organisations like the Indian Ocean Rim Association (2020), with the aim, presented in the Indo-Pacific Strategy in 2018, to act as "inclusive and stabilizing mediating power" (Macron 2018). In the field of maritime governance, France is involved in security activities, participating in the EU Atalanta program, bilateral cooperation with ASEAN through regular deployments and stopovers of vessels in the region in addition to its five naval bases (Djibouti, Port des Galets and Dzaoudzi in the Indian Ocean; Nouméa and Papeete in the Pacific) (EEAS). There are 8,000 French soldiers stationed in the region. In the area of the marine environment and climate change mitigation France has contributed to the creation of the International Solar Alliance, launched with India in 2018, the Pacific Initiative for Adaptation and Biodiversity (2018) and the Climate Risk and Early Warning Systems (CREWS), initiated at COP21 in Paris in 2015 (Embassy of France in Singapore 2021). France is also involved in trilateral cooperation with Australia and India (2020), striving to implement projects in the maritime sector to promote global commons awareness in climate, environment and biodiversity (Ministry of Europe and Foreign Affairs 2020).

Following the example of France, in 2020 the German government published in 2020 "Policy Guidelines for the Indo-Pacific region. Germany – Europe – Asia. Shaping the 21st Century Together" (the Government of Germany 2020). Maritime issues occupy a significant part of the document. It emphasised the necessity of securing maritime trade routes critical for the supply chains to and from Europe. Germany pledged to promote the enforcement of rules and norms of UNCLOS in the region, participating more in strategic dialogues and other institutional activities, including naval exercises and other forms of maritime presence to strengthen stability and law enforcement. Germany joined the Information Fusion Centre (IFC) in Singapore, which focuses on exchanging information in the fields of proliferation, drug smuggling and maritime terrorism. In the part dedicated to multi-lateral activities the document stressed the necessity to intensify and institutionalise Germany's dialogue with the Bay of Bengal Initiative for Multi-Sectoral Technical and Economic Cooperation, building on existing projects like one to strengthen maritime governance in Sri Lanka. The task to expand co-operation with the Indian Ocean Rim Association (IORA) in maritime safety was also placed among priorities. Understanding the importance of the climate change issue for the Indo-Pacific countries, Germany pledged to double its commitment which in 2020 amounted to €4 billion. In 2018, Germany launched the multi-lateral Group of Friends on Climate and Security, an organisation bringing together all the countries of the Indo-Pacific region. Germany also extends the support to the Regional Pacific Nationally Determined Contributions (NDCs) Hub, helping 15 Pacific countries develop and implement their climate pledges.

The Netherlands published its Indo-Pacific policy note "Indo-Pacific: Guidelines for Strengthening Dutch and EU cooperation with partners in Asia" in 2020, declaring that it would promote safe passage and maritime security by helping with capacity building in the area of the international law of the sea. The security of sea routes, initiatives and activities in the region related to that issue are of utmost interest to the Netherlands. It pledged to continue to support Indo-Pacific countries in the area of the law of the sea, offering them annual courses on the law of the sea through the Clingendael Institute and the Netherlands Institute for the Law of the Sea (NILOS). Six months after the strategy's publication, the Dutch government sent one of its vessels to accompany a United Kingdom Carrier Strike Group on its mission to Japan (Okano-Heimans 2021).

The Netherlands was hesitant to return militarily to the waters of the Eastern Indian Ocean and the Western Pacific, although it was actively involved in EU Naval Force Operation Atalanta off the coast of the Horn of Africa since 2008 (Schmidt 2015). It was conditioned by a shared colonial history and a desire to avoid confrontation with China. The Dutch government decided to expand its maritime co-operation beyond traditional areas such as the blue economy and the marine environment through bilateral agreements with countries like Indonesia, Vietnam and Bangladesh (The Dutch Fund for Climate and Development 2020). It assumed that in the situation of growing expectations of its trade and development assistance partners in the region, it should participate on similar terms to France, emphasising the necessity to build confidence measures and rules-based maritime order.

Conclusion

The Indo-Pacific region has become in the twenty-first century the most crucial ocean basin in the world, gaining its weight as a result of the dynamic economic development of its littorals followed by the traffic intensity on strategic sea lines of communication. The leading players presented in the chapter occupy the most significant places among maritime governance powers of the modern world. Their capacity in domestic maritime governance in all areas of security, marine environment protection, legal order and blue economy serve as examples of successful implementation of UNCLOS and the concept of integrated maritime policy placed among sustainable development goals. Their international activities and influence in maritime governance in the Indo-Pacific region proved the urgency of further expanding the institutional framework of cooperation in all areas. The visions presented by the United States, Australia, Japan, Indonesia and India showed the challenge of the lack of one coherent vision. All of them proposed their strategies of the development of maritime governance in the twenty-first century, assuming the advantage of their concept over others. It stemmed from the sense of the exceptionalism of their organisational systems, as well as the uniqueness of historical and contemporary civilisational experiences. They also came with different burdens and ambitions to attain their particular goals. However, it is essential to note the common elements of their visions with awareness of the convergence of the interests as a consequence of increasing interdependence and growth of the economic factor. At their core, these strategies are all centred on economic, environmental, legal rules-based and security order in the Indo-Pacific. Therefore, it would be possible for them to find synergy with each other. The rise of China also influenced changes in the United States, India, Indonesia, Japan and Australia approach towards the urgency of developing co-operation in maritime governance at the regional level. It impacted the concept of leadership, making them comprehend the necessity of elevating efforts to assist middle and smaller countries of the region to attain sustainable development goals in the maritime domain as an alternative to the Chinese concept. The extra-regional partners like the European Union and its members have come to similar conclusions. All actors in Indo-Pacific and their extra-regional strategic partners have to move out of their traditional areas of activities as extraordinary endeavours are needed to develop all spheres of maritime governance. Compared to China's New Maritime Silk Road, their efforts to date are too limited and too modest. The security and marine environment areas are still fragmented, organised on a sub-regional scale. There is a need for a coherent attitude and deeper engagement of both state and non-state actors at national and international levels. By definition, maritime governance requires cooperation at multi-layer vertical and horizontal levels and an executive program that would cover all those levels from regional to local, taking into account the dynamics of processes in the maritime domain. All the main actors and the EU introduced integrated maritime policies as executive programs for maritime governance. The regional program of integrated maritime policy for the Indo-Pacific requires an inclusive approach as suggested by India and the EU, and France. An inclusive approach does mean not only the implementation of integrated maritime policies in small and middle-size countries. In the conditions of interdependence, almost all prominent actors in the East Indian Ocean and the Western Pacific apprehend the necessity to include China and finding spheres of co-operation. The irrelevance of war at sea and the consequences of the disruption of strategic lanes of communication for economies are understandable by both sides. The example of a free trade block in the Indo-Pacific – Regional Comprehensive Economic Partnership (RCEP) – constitutes the evidence that such co-operation is possible. RCEP, established in 2020, also illustrated that pan-regional coordination and co-operation over the differences is possible. Maritime governance in the Indo-Pacific would develop in the direction of meta-structures covering all countries. All those determinants would influence maritime governance in the further decades of the twenty-first century.

References

Adamczak-Retecka, Monika, "'Błękitna' polityka Unii Europejskiej", *Gdańskie Studia Prawnicze*, Gdańsk, Vol. 32 (2014): 17–24.

Anwar, Shakeel, "Top 10 largest Archipelagos in the World", *Jagran Josh*, 1 February 2018. https://www.jagranjosh.com/general-knowledge/top-10-largest-archipelagos-in-the-world-1517481912-1

Australian Government, "Australia State of Environment Report 2016: Coasts", Canberra 2016. https://soe.environment.gov.au/theme/coasts

Australian Government, "2017 Foreign Policy White Paper, Chapter Three – A Stable and Prosperous Indo-Pacific". 37–47. https://www.dfat.gov.au/sites/default/files/minisite/static/4ca0813c-585e-4fe1-86eb-de665e65001a/fpwhitepaper/foreign-policy-white-paper/chapter-three-stable-and-prosperous-indo-pacific.html

Australian Government, "Development Assistance in the Pacific", Department of Foreign Affairs and Trade, Canberra 2021. https://www.dfat.gov.au/geo/pacific/development-assistance/fisheries-assistance

Australian Parliament, "Australia's Maritime Strategy", Canberra June 2004, https://www.aph.gov.au/Parliamentary_Business/Committees/Joint/Completed_Inquiries/jfadt/maritime/report

Bali Process. https://www.baliprocess.net/

Bekkevold, Jo Inge, Till, Geoffrey (Eds.), *International Order at Sea. How It Is Challenged. How It Is Maintained*, (London: Palgrave Macmillan, 2016).

Berkshire Miller, Jonathan, "The US-Japan-India Relationship: Trilateral Cooperation in the Indo-Pacific", Foreign Expert Perspective, National Institute of Defense Studies, Tokyo 2017. http://www.nids.mod.go.jp/english/publication/backnumber/pdf/20171108.pdf

Borghese, Elisabeth Mann, *Ocean Governance and the United Nations*, (Halifax: Centre for Foreign Policy Studies, Dalhousie University, 1995).

Center for Coastal Management, "Database on Coastal States of India, Center for Coastal Zone Management and Coastal Shelter Belt, Anna University Chennai", Chennai 17 February 2017. http://iomenvis.nic.in/index2.aspx?slid=758&sublinkid=119&langid=1&mid=1

Coordinating Ministry for Maritime Affairs, "Indonesian Ocean Policy", Jakarta 2017. https://maritim.go.id/konten/unggahan/2017/07/offset_lengkap_KKI_eng-vers.pdf

Council of the European Union, "EU Strategy for Cooperation in the Indo-Pacific - Council Conclusions", document number 7914/21, Brussels, 16 April 2021, p. 8, https://data.consilium.europa.eu/doc/document/ST-7914-2021-INIT/en/pdf

Craig, Robin Kundis, *Comparative Ocean Governance. Place-Based Protections and in an Era of Climate Change*, (Cheltenham: Edward Elgar, 2012).

Dalio, Ray, Benioff, Marc, "It's Time for the Next Wave of Ocean Exploration and Protection", *Wired*, 8 June 2018. https://www.wired.com/story/forget-space-oceans-need-exploring/

Department of State, "A Free and Open Indo-Pacific. Advancing a Shared Vision", Department of State, United States of America, Washington, DC 2019. https://www.state.gov/wp-content/uploads/2019/11/Free-and-Open-Indo-Pacific-4Nov2019.pdf

East Asia Summit, "The Principles for Mutually Beneficial Relations", Bali 19 November 2011. https://eastasiasummit.asean.org/storage/eas_statements_file/WMtc5OsrOpkdwjNGAI2tb5Pv51whqJuDQIwmfWLf.pdf

Embassy of France in Singapore, "The Indo-Pacific Region: A Priority for France". https://sg.ambafrance.org/The-Indo-Pacific-region-a-priority-for-France

Embassy of Japan to ASEAN, "A New Foreign Policy Strategy: Free and Open Indo-Pacific Strategy". https://www.asean.emb-japan.go.jp/files/000352880.pdf

European Commission, "Integrated Maritime Policy", Brussels 2007. https://ec.europa.eu/info/research-and-innovation/research-area/environment/oceans-and-seas/integrated-maritime-policy_en

European Commission, "International Climate Finance". https://ec.europa.eu/clima/policies/international/finance_en

European Union External Action Service and ASEAN Secretariat, "EU-ASEAN Strategic Partners. Maritime Cooperation", Jakarta, Brussels 2020.

European Union External Action Service, "EU Strategy for Cooperation in the Indo-Pacific", Brussels 2021. https://eeas.europa.eu/headquarters/headquarters-homepage/96741/eu-strategy-cooperation-indo-pacific_en

European Union External Action Service, "Pacific Islands – EU Relations: Focus on Climate Change". ttps://eeas.europa.eu/archives/delegations/new_zealand/documents/press_corner/news/20120613_mediarelease_pacificislands.pdf

Government of Japan, Basic Act on Ocean Policy (Act No. 33 of 2007), https://leap.unep.org/countries/jp/national-legislation/basic-act-ocean-policy-act-no-33-2007

Haward, Marcus and Vince, Joanna, *Oceans Governance in the Twenty-first Century. Managing the Blue Planet*, (Cheltenham, Northampton: Edward Elgar, 2008).

Headquarters, United States Indo-Pacific Command, https://www.pacom.mil/About-USINDOPACOM/#:~:text=Of%20note%2C%20component%20command%20personnel%20numbers%20include%20more,the%20United%20States%2C%20its%20people%2C%20and%20its%20interests

Hoegh-Guldberg, Ove and Jompa, Jamaluddin, "Indonesia and Australia are Sleeping Ocean Superpowers", *The Conversation*, 15 December 2016. https://theconversation.com/indonesia-and-australia-are-sleeping-ocean-superpowers-69886

https://euinasean.eu/maritime-cooperation/

https://www.usaid.gov/indo-pacific-vision

https://www.weadapt.org/knowledge-base/climate-finance/usaid-adapt-asia-pacific#:~:text=The%20USAID%20Adapt%20Asia-Pacific%20programme%20%282011-2017%29%20integrated%20knowledge,resilience%20to%20the%20negative%20impacts%20of%20climate%20change

Indian Ocean Rim Association. https://www.iora.int/en/about/about-iora

Indonesian Ministry of Trade, Embassy of Indonesia in Washington, "Facts and Figures about Indonesia", 2013. https://www.embassyofindonesia.org/basic-facts/

Institute of Marine Resources, "Pacific-European Union Marine Partnership Programme", The University of the South Pacific, Suva 2019. https://www.usp.ac.fj/index.php?id=peump

International Tsunami Information Center, "10 Years Since Dec 26, 2004 Indian Ocean Tsunami, Honolulu 2014". http://itic.ioc-unesco.org/index.php?option=com_content&view =article&id=1940:10-years-since-dec-26-2004-indian-ocean-tsunami&catid=1136&Itemid =1373

Japan's Government, "Japan's Basic Act on Ocean Policy (Act No. 33 of April 27, 2007)", Tokyo 2007. https://www8.cao.go.jp/ocean/english/act/pdf/law_e.pdf

Kemp, Geoffrey, "Maritime Access and Maritime Power: The Past, the Persian Gulf, and the Future", in Alvin J. Cottrell and Associates (Eds.), *Sea Power and Strategy in the Indian Ocean,* (London: Sage Publications, 1981): 15–72.

Keohane, Robert O., Nye Jr., Joseph S., *Power and Interdependence.* Fourth Edition, (London: Longman, 2012).

Kimball, Lee, *International Ocean Governance. Using International Law and Organizations to Manage Marine Resources Sustainably,* (Cambridge: IUCN, Gland, 2001).

Kneebone, Susan Y., "The Bali Process and Global Refugee Policy in the Asia–Pacific Region", Oxford University Press, *Journal of Refugee Studies,* Vol. 27, No. 4 (2014): 599.

Kraska, James, *Maritime Power and the Law of the Sea: Expeditionary Operations in World Politics,* (New York: Oxford University Press, 2011).

Lehr, Peter, "Piracy and Maritime Governance in the Indian Ocean", in Jivanta Schöttli (ed.), *Power, Politics and Maritime Governance in the Indian Ocean,* (Abingdon: Routledge, 2015): 105.

Liebner, Horst Hubertus, "Indigenous Concepts of Orientation of South Sulawesian Sailors", *Bijdragen tot de Taal-, Land-en Volkenkunde (Journal of the Humanities and Social Sciences of Southeast Asia),* Brill, Vol. 161, No. 2/3 (2005): 269–317.

Lowry, Kem, Thia-Eng, Chua, "Building Vision, Awareness and Commitment: The PEMSEA Strategy for Strengthening Regional Cooperation", in Chua Thia-Eng, Gunnar Kullenberg, and Danilo Bonga (eds.), *Coastal and Ocean Governance. Securing the Oceans: Essays on Oceans Governance-Global and Regional Perspectives. Partnerships for Environmental Management of the Seas of East Asia (PEMSEA),* (Quezon City, Philippines, 2008): 343–370.

Lukaszuk, Tomasz, "Maritime Governance in International Relations", *Stosunki Międzynarodowe – International Relations,* Vol. 54, No. 4 (2018): 143.

Lukaszuk, Tomasz, "Indian and Australian Maritime Security Doctrines in the Indian Ocean Region in the 21st Century. Christian Bueger's Matrix of Maritime Security Approach", *Polish Political Science Yearbook,* Vol. 49, No. 4 (2020): 105–127.

McDougal, Myres S. and Burke, William T., *The Public Order of the Oceans. A Contemporary International Law of the Sea,* (New Haven and London: Yale University Press, 1962).

McLaughlin, Heather, "SKEMA Consolidation Study: Maritime Governance", SKEMA Coordination Action 'Sustainable Knowledge Platform for the European Maritime and Logistics Industry', European Commission, 2010.

Ministry of Defence (Navy) of India, "Freedom to Use the Seas: Indian Maritime Security Strategy", New Delhi 2007.

Ministry of Defence (Navy) of India, "Indian Maritime Doctrine", Indian Navy, Naval Strategic Publication 1.1. New Delhi 2009. https://www.indiannavy.nic.in/sites/default/files/Indian -Maritime-Doctrine-2009-Updated-12Feb16.pdf

Ministry of Defence (Navy) of India, "Ensuring Secure Seas: Indian Maritime Security Strategy", New Delhi 2015. https://www.indiannavy.nic.in/sites/default/files/Indian_Maritime_Security _Strategy_Document_25Jan16.pdf

Ministry of Europe and Foreign Affairs of France, "The Indo-Pacific region: a priority for France". https://www.diplomatie.gouv.fr/en/country-files/asia-and-oceania/the-indo-pacific -region-a-priority-for-france/

Ministry of Europe and Foreign Affairs of France, "The Indo-Pacific: 1st Trilateral Dialogue between France, India and Australia (9 September 2020)", France Diplomacy. https://www .diplomatie.gouv.fr/en/country-files/australia/news/article/the-indo-pacific-1st-trilateral -dialogue-between-france-india-and-australia-9

Ministry of External Affairs, Indo-Pacific Division Briefs, February 7, 2020, https://www.mea
.gov.in/Portal/ForeignRelation/Indo_Feb_07_2020.pdf

Modi, Narendra, "Address to the National Assembly of Mauritius", 12 March 2015. https://
www.narendramodi.in/text-of-pms-address-to-the-national-assembly-of-mauritius-2953

Morcos, Pierre, "France: A Bridge between Europe and the Indo-Pacific?", Centre for Strategic
and International Studies, Washington, DC 1 April 2021. https://www.csis.org/analysis/
france-bridge-between-europe-and-indo-pacific

Natalegawa, Marty, "An Indonesian Perspective on the Indo-Pacific, Center for Strategic
and International Studies", Washington, DC, 16 May 2013. https://csis-website-prod.s3
.amazonaws.com/s3fspublic/legacy_files/files/attachments/130516_MartyNatalegawa_
Speech.pdf

National Ocean Service, "What Percentage of the American Population Lives Near the Coast?"
U.S. Department of Commerce, Washington, DC 2020. https://oceanservice.noaa.gov/facts/
population.html

Okano-Heimans, Maaike, "Towards Meaningful Action: The Netherlands and the EU turn to
the Indo-Pacific", ISAS Insights, Institute for South Asian Studies, National University of
Singapore, 10 July 2021, https://www.isas.nus.edu.sg/papers/towards-meaningful-action-the
-netherlands-and-the-eu-turn-to-the-indo-pacific/

Pacific Climate Change Centre. https://www.sprep.org/pacific-climate-change-centre/

Pacific Tsunami Warning Center, U.S. Tsunami Warning System, United States Department of
Commerce, https://www.tsunami.gov/?page=history

Panda, Jagannath, "The Australia-India-Indonesia Trilateral. Fostering Maritime Cooperation
between Middle Powers", The National Bureau of Asian Research, Seattle, Washington,
DC, 23 April 2021. https://www.nbr.org/publication/the-australia-india-indonesia-trilateral
-fostering-maritime-cooperation-between-middle-powers/

"Partnerships in Environmental Management for the Seas of East Asia (PEMSEA)", Quezon
City 2021. http://www.pemsea.org

President Emmanuel Macron, "Discours à Garden Island", Base navale de Sydney, Elysee,
Sydney 3 May 2018. https://www.elysee.fr/emmanuel-macron/2018/05/03/discours-a-garden
-island-base-navale-de-sydney

Pretlove, Bente, Blasiak, Robert, "Mapping Ocean Governance and Regulation, Working
Paper for Consultation for UN Global Compact Action Platform for Sustainable Ocean
Business", United Nations Global Compact 2018, https://www.unglobalcompact.org/library/
5710

"Prime Minister Shinzo Abe address at the Opening Session of the Sixth Tokyo International
Conference on African Development (TICAD VI)", 27 August 2016. https://www.mofa.go.jp
/afr/af2/page4e_000496.html

Pyc, Dorota, Puszkarski, Jakub (Eds.), *Global Ocean Governance: From Vision to Action*,
(Poznań: Ars Boni et Aequi, 2014).

ReCAAP-ISC, https://www.recaap.org/about_ReCAAP-ISC

Roe, Michael, *Maritime Governance and Policy-Making*, (Heidelberg: Springer, 2013).

Roe, Michael, *Maritime Governance: Speed, Flow, Form, Process*, (Heidelberg: Springer, 2016).

Rothwell, Donald R., Stephens, T., *The International Law of the Sea*, (London: Hart Publishing,
2016).

Royal Australian Navy, *Australian Maritime Doctrine (RAN Doctrine 1)*, (Sydney: Sea Power
Center, 2010). https://www.navy.gov.au/sites/default/files/documents/Amd2010.pdf

Schmidt, Catherine Stella, "Royal Netherlands Navy in Operation Atalanta-1", *US-Europe
World Affairs*, 27 November 2015. https://useuworldaffairs.com/2015/11/27/royal
-netherlands-navy-in-operation-atalanta-1-catherine-stella-schmidt/

Scholaert, Frederik, Marketing of and trade in fishery and aquaculture products in the EU,
July 2020:2, https://www.europarl.europa.eu/RegData/etudes/BRIE/2020/652012/EPRS
_BRI(2020)652012_EN.pdf

Scott, Karen N., "Integrated Oceans Management: A New Frontier in Marine Environmental Protection", in Donald R. Rothwell , Alex G. Oude Elferink, Karen N. Scott, & Tem Stephens (eds.), *The Oxford Handbook of the Law of the Sea*, (Oxford: Oxford University Press, 2017): 463–490.

Statistics Bureau of Japan, "Statistical Handbook of Japan 2020", Tokyo 2020. https://www .stat.go.jp/english/data/handbook/c0117.html

Stillman, Dan, "Oceans: The Great Unknown", NASA, 10 August 2009, https://www.nasa.gov/ audience/foreducators/oceans-the-great-unknown.html

Suarez de Vivero, Juan Louis, Mateos, Juan Carlos Rodrıguez, "Ocean Governance in a Competitive World: The BRIC Countries as Emerging Maritime Powers – Building New Geopolitical Scenarios", *Marine Policy*, Vol. 34, No. 5(2010): 967–978.

Tanaka, Yoshifumi, *A Dual Approach to Ocean Governance: The Case of Zonal and Integrated Management in International Law of the Sea*, (Farnham: Ashgate, 2008).

Tardy, Thierry, "Fighting Piracy off the Coast of Somalia: Lessons Learned from the Contact Group", The European Union Institute for Security Studies, Brussels 2014. https://www.iss .europa.eu/content/fighting-piracy-coast-somalia-lessons-learned-contact-group

Terashima, Hiroshi, Hayashi, Moritaka, "Development of National Ocean Policy of Japan", in Biliana Cicin-Sain, David L. VanderZwaag, Miriam C. Balgos (eds.), *Routledge Handbook of National and Regional Ocean Policies*, (Abingdon: Routledge, 2015): 283–293

Thakur, Ramesh, Van Langenhove, Luk, "Enhancing Global Governance Through Regional Integration", *Global Governance*, Vol. 12, No. 3 (July–September 2006): 233.

The Dutch Fund for Climate and Development (DFCD), The Hague 2020. https://thedfcd.com/

The Government of Germany, "Policy Guidelines for the Indo-Pacific region. Germany – Europe – Asia. Shaping the 21st Century Together", Federal Foreign Office, Berlin 2020. https:// www.auswaertiges-amt.de/blob/2380514/f9784f7e3b3fa1bd7c5446d274a4169e/200901 -indo-pazifik-leitlinien--1--data.pdf

Till, Geoffrey, *Seapower. A Guide for the Twenty-first Century*. Fourth Edition, (London and New York: Routledge, 2018).

"UN Atlas of the Oceans", The United Nations 2016. http://www.oceansatlas.org/subtopic/en /c/773/

United States Agency for International Development (USAID)." USAID's 2021 Climate Readiness Plan. U.S. Agency for International Development, October 7 2021, https://www.usaid.gov/ climate/readiness-plan

US Department of Defence, "A Cooperative Strategy for 21st Century Seapower", US Marine Corps, US Navy, US Coast Guard, Washington, DC October 2007. https://www.hsdl.org/ ?view&did=479900

US Mission to ASEAN, "Maritime Cooperation", Jakarta 2021. https://asean.usmission.gov/ education-culture/maritime/

West, Lucy (Ed.), *Australia-Japan-India Trilateral Dialogue 2019. Leadership, partnership and ASEAN centrality in the emerging Indo-Pacific*, (Queensland: Griffith University, 2020): 1. https://www.griffith.edu.au/__data/assets/pdf_file/0025/1007728/AJI-trilateral-dialogue .pdf#:~:text=The%202019%20Australia-Japan-India%20Trilateral%20Dialogue%2C %20themed%20Leadership%2C%20Partnership,Affairs%20and%20the%20Consulate %20-General%20of%20Japan%20%28Brisbane%29

Witular, Rendi A., "Presenting Maritime Doctrine", *The Jakarta Post*, 14 November 2014. https://www.thejakartapost.com/news/2014/11/14/presenting-maritime-doctrine.html

Part IV
Indo-Pacific strategies

16 The United States in the Indo-Pacific

An overstretched hegemon?

Yoichiro Sato

Introduction

In August 2007, Japanese Prime Minister Shinzo Abe visited India to meet Indian Prime Minister Manmohan Singh. The speech Abe gave, known as the "Confluence of the Two Seas" speech, (Ministry of Foreign Affairs of Japan 2007) reiterated the idea that was not-so-new to the US Pacific Command in Honolulu, which had defined its area of responsibility across the Pacific and Indian Oceans. Japan, whose dependence on the sea lanes in the Indian Ocean Region (IOR) for resource imports from Middle East and Africa, depended on the US Navy for the secure maritime passage of its cargo ships, and the US presence in this region faced criticism in Washington for allegedly allowing Japan to enjoy a free ride. The post-Cold War realignment of the triangular relationship among the United States, India and Pakistan and their respective relationship with China created a momentum for Japan and India to jointly seek anchoring of the US engagement in the IOR.

The US attention to the IOR at the turn of the new century was ambivalent. The initial application of the nuclear nonproliferation framework in the late-1990s in response to the nuclear explosion tests by Pakistan and India was quickly compromised, first by the War on Terrorism in general and Pakistan's resurrected importance in this new framing. The IOR was not yet a main theatre of strategic competition between China and the United States in 2000–2010, but China's announcement of the Belt-and-Road Initiative (BRI) in 2013 that promised to invest billions of dollars into maritime infrastructure throughout the IOR rang alarm in Delhi, Washington, Tokyo and Canberra.

A shifting of economic gravity from the Asia Pacific westward with the rise of India is anticipated based on demographic trends (India's high birth rate, as opposed to the low birth rate in China), but India's inward-looking economy has not fully embraced integration with the broader region and the United States remains a limited player in the Indian economy unlike in China, not yet carrying sufficient weight. The security-driven rationale for active US presence in the IOR in the context of the rising perceptions about the Chinese threats to regional and global security led to resumption of the Quadrilateral Security Dialogue among the United States, Japan, Australia and India in 2017. US Secretary of State Michael Pompeo under President Donald Trump's aggressive anti-China framing of US foreign policy amid the COVID-19 pandemic set tones for the US Indo-Pacific strategy and is carried over into the Biden administration. However, as the strategic concept is being translated into more comprehensive policies by the Biden administration, the prevailing overall framing has shed the simplistic

DOI: 10.4324/9781003336143-21

anti-China rhetoric Trump preferred on one hand and cleverly sugarcoated the mercantilist and the off-shore balancing intents Trump did not hide.

This chapter will review the (in)significance of the IOR in the US strategy historically, the region's renewed treatment under the Trump and Biden administrations and implications of the crisis in Ukraine on the broad Indo-Pacific strategy.

The Indian Ocean Region (IOR) in the US Strategy

The US global Cold War strategy had two main fronts, but the Indian Ocean region remained of a lesser priority in comparison to them. The European front was most vividly represented by the East-West German border as well as the Berlin Wall that protected the Western enclave inside East Germany. The Asian front, which initially appeared to be a maritime line (known as the Acheson Line after the US Secretary of State Dean Acheson), which ran through the Sea of Japan, Tsushima Strait and the Taiwan Strait to separate Japan and Taiwan from the Eurasian Continent. The breaking out of the Korean War and the UN intervention, which resulted in a ceasefire at the 38th parallel, placed South Korea under US protection through a bilateral military alliance and the UN mandate that endorsed the US troops' presence in South Korea. The United States viewed the Soviet Union and its satellite states in Eastern and Central Europe as the threat against Western Europe. In Asia, the United States viewed the Soviet Union and the People's Republic of China as a combined (if not fully unified) threat against US allies. The United States held neutrality when Chinese troops invaded the India-controlled (but disputed) Himalaya in 1962, as India's non-aligned policy neither granted itself US protection nor spared it from the US suspicion that it was acting on behalf of the Soviet Union. The Middle East constituted the "half" part (a secondary priority) of the US "Two-and-a-half front" war strategy, which emphasised the force readiness to concurrently fight two major wars (in Europe and in Northeast Asia) and one minor war elsewhere. The unmatched US naval dominance in the IOR allowed the country access into the Persian Gulf region. The US dominance in the IOR did not require much help from its allies, with a notable exception of the United Kingdom whose colonial island possession in the IOR was offered to the United States for usage as a military base.

The relative absence of maritime threats in the IOR and the US naval dominance meant that the common goods aspect of the IOR security was provided by the United States. Significant criticism against this US commitment to the Persian Gulf-IOR sea lane security persisted in the United States. (Kattenburg 1989) The major users of the sea lanes in the IOR, such as Japanese, Korean and increasingly Chinese oil and gas tankers, enjoyed a free ride on this common goods, as even the most advanced navy of Japan stopped short of playing major security roles beyond the East China Sea through the 1980s.

Post-Cold War Changes in the IOR

The simultaneous terror attack against the US targets on 11 September 2001 by Al Qaeda operatives and the expansion of the War on Terrorism into the Middle East raised the importance of the IOR as a theatre of US military operations. The need for overflight through the Pakistani airspace for military operations against the Taliban and Al Qaeda forces inside Afghanistan temporarily and forcefully re-raised the profile of Pakistan in the US security diplomacy. While the Pakistani nuclear weapons did not make the country an addition to US President George W. Bush's list of the Axis of Evil, Pakistan faced the new US administration, which had more sympathetic ears to the lobbying by India. The United States quickly eased economic sanctions it earlier imposed on India and Pakistan in response to their testing of nuclear weapons in 1998. The terror attack on Mumbai by a Pakistani group in 2008 was quicky denounced by the United States, which did not tolerate Pakistan playing two sides: a covert backer of the Taliban and a host of terrorism against India on the one hand, and a co-operative member of the War against Terrorism on the other hand.

The signing of the agreement on civilian nuclear technological co-operation between India and the United States in 2005 effectively sealed the US effort to approach India with the international nuclear nonproliferation framework under the nonproliferation treaty (NPT), which permitted civilian use of nuclear energy to non-nuclear weapons states. Neither India nor Pakistan has joined the treaty, and they have pursued indigenous nuclear programs. The US decision in 2005 not to link the transfer of civilian nuclear technology to India to its abolition of nuclear weapons was a pragmatic one based both on commercial prospects of selling US-built reactors and the fear that the aging Soviet-built reactors in India might cause Chernobyl-like accidents.

The US equidistance approach toward India and Pakistan in effect only brought Pakistan half way back into the US embrace. The tripartite cooperation among the United States, China and Pakistan to keep the Soviet influence out of the region and roll back in Afghanistan during the 1980s (Crabb 1988: 465-467) was a thing of the past, and Pakistan tilted towards China in the post-Cold War era for obtaining military and economic assistance that the United States drastically cut down. Feeling once abandoned and now feeling coerced to cooperate by the United States, Pakistan keeps its China ties tight amid the growing Sino–US rivalry and the growing US–India ties.

The United States does not wish to commit itself single-handedly (like it did during the days of the Cold War) to the region that is dominated by the never-ending India–Pakistan dispute. The "de-hyphenation" of the US policy in the region post-Cold War intended to free its hands from the bilateral India–Pakistan context and redefine its bilateral relations with India and Pakistan respectively in the broader context of regional security. While the United States maintains neutrality in India's border disputes with China and Pakistan, Pakistan does not enjoy the equal level of tacit US acknowledgment of its nuclearised status. What keeps the United States from more actively going after Pakistan's nuclear weapons has less to do with an inclination to be equal between India and Pakistan than with a grimmer prospect that an unstable Pakistan might lose control of its nuclear weapons to terrorists.

The projection of the Cold War US–Soviet rivalry onto the rivalry between the two former British colonies – Pakistan and India – no longer defines the strategic framework for the US approach to the IOR. The evolution of the new framework, known today in the form of the QUAD – quadrilateral security dialogue among the United States, Japan, Australia and India – has been path dependent and did not necessarily start as an anti-China containment coalition. The first active four-party co-operation took place in the humanitarian and disaster relief operations after the Indian Ocean tsunami event of 2004. China's absence was due to its sheer lack of naval projection capability at a long distance.

Despite the rocky start in the bilateral relationship with China for President Bush, in which he had to negotiate an amicable return of a US electronics signal intelligence plane and its crews after a mid-air collision of this plane and a Chinese fighter plane over the South China Sea in 2001, US efforts to seek engagement of China into bilateral and multi-lateral security dialogues continued under Bush. In Northeast Asia, the US negotiation strategy *vis-à-vis* North Korea shifted from its previous bilateral approach to a multi-lateral "Six-Party Talk" framework, passing the honour of chairing the meetings to China along with US expectations that China grows into a "responsible stakeholder." (Sato 2006: 78-79) The US Global War on Terrorism (GWOT) framework accepted China's request to label the separatist movement in the Xinjiang province (the East Turkestan Islamic Movement) a terror organisation (Roberts 2020) – a designation which withered away as the Obama administration started criticising China of its handling of human rights issues. Another effort at engaging China was the 1,000-ship navy concept, which Admiral Dennis C. Blair of the US Pacific Command first promoted, availing navies of the entire Asia Pacific including China's for coalition operations to deal with a broad range of post-Cold War nontraditional security threats. Technological advances to utilise shale oil and gas have freed the United States from its dependence on Middle Eastern resources, aiding the voices to transfer the defence burden in the IOR onto the user states. (Leoni 2021: 82) China was invited to the Rim of the Pacific (RIMPAC) biennial multi-national naval exercise in 2014 and 2016 under Obama, but was eventually disinvited amid the growing tension with the Trump administration.

While the Bush administration's GWOT framing oversimplified the reality of the security situations throughout Southeast Asia and distorted the US responses, regional states took advantage of the US attention in order to enhance the state capabilities to deal with their domestic and transnational issues. However, much greater US attention was paid to Afghanistan and Iraq, (Leoni 2021: 80) resulting in a sense of neglect among the Southeast Asian countries. The Obama administration faced growing Chinese assertiveness in the South China Sea (Bader 2012: 105) and approached Southeast Asia with a more comprehensive strategic vision to bundle security and economic policies into a coherent framework. The United States appointed its first ambassador to ASEAN – the position Trump left vacant. Obama also brought the United States into the Trans-Pacific Partnership (TPP) negotiation, aiming to anchor US economic presence in the Asia Pacific. Trump pulled the United States out of the TPP negotiation in its final stage and returned to a bilateral approach to renegotiate free trade on a term that is more preferrable to various domestic interests. Trump also brought more bilateralism into US security policy toward Southeast Asia, proactively trying to seal a closer defence co-operation with Vietnam, and reactively trying to repair the damaged alliances with the Philippines. The US approach towards Southeast Asia has increasingly been framed in the former's strategic competition against China. The Biden administration largely continues on these bilateral initiatives, while attempting to resurrect the US diplomacy towards ASEAN.

Economic power shift

The relative insignificance of the IOR in the US global strategy was not only due to the relative absence of threats to the country's security interests, but also the underdeveloped state of the region's economy.

Moreover, the IOR remained outside the growing dynamism toward a greater economic integration, first attempted by the Asia Pacific Economic Cooperation (APEC). To be sure, even the APEC was more of a creation of Asian countries than a US initiative. The US drive for the North American Free Trade Area (NAFTA) alerted Asian exporters to the US market, resulting in a push for inter-regional (trans-Pacific) trade liberalisation.

Similar US reluctance was observable during the negotiations for a Trans-Pacific Partnership (TPP), which aimed at creating the largest free trade area of the world. The United States did not join the negotiation until 2008, three years after an initial agreement was signed by Brunei, Chile, New Zealand and Singapore in 2005. The Obama administration saw TPP as both an economic opportunity for US exporters and a price for smoother strategic partnerships with Asian countries. This economic engagement of the United States to Asia Pacific was a major component of the US Rebalance to Asia strategy. (Leoni 2021: 80) The Trump administration's decision to withdraw the United States from the TPP negotiation in 2017 did not intend to disengage the country from all its commitment to the region, but was a reflection of its preference for bilaterally approaching trade partners in order to better leverage its power of the huge domestic market and the security it could offer.

While the APEC failed to evolve into a binding region-wide free trade agreement that included China, the TPP without the United States (renamed the Comprehensive and Progressive Trans-Pacific Partnership, CPTPP) now faces politically charged entry applications from Taiwan and China. While the Democratic Party regained control of the presidency under President Biden, there appears to be no realistic attempt to bring the United States back into the TPP, as the Republican-controlled Senate is likely to block any such attempt. Instead, the Biden administration is preparing its trade policy under the Indo-Pacific Economic Framework.

The free and open Indo-Pacific

The US Defense Department under the Trump administration in 2017 announced its Indo-Pacific strategy. A symbolic renaming of the US Pacific Command as the Indo-Pacific Command, however, was accompanied by redrawing of its area of responsibility (AOR), which had more to do with bureaucratic politics among the regional military command headquarters than well-reasoned geostrategic rationale. The lead role of the Defense Department reflected a dysfunctional State Department during the first year of the Trump administration. The departure of numerous senior diplomats who disagreed with Trump's unilateralist "America First" approach to foreign policy left the State Department behind in policy making, while Trump-appointed Rex Tillerson remained an ineffective Secretary of State and resigned after barely one year in the office. The new US Secretary of State Michael Pompeo brought the State Department in line with the defense-led Indo-Pacific strategy, but economic strategy to de-link China under the name of supply chain revision was not yet well articulated. Overall coordination within the US government was absent, as the Treasury Department worried about the Chinese selling off of the US Treasury bonds and the Trade Representative's Office (Bolton 2020: 293-305) and the Commerce Department hitting both China and US allies and friends alike with investigation of unfair trade practices, and the Treasury Department bulging into trade issues with a threat of currency manipulator investigations against strategic friends and foes alike.

The COVID-19 pandemic severely damaged the bilateral relationship with China. Pompeo led a charge against China's lack of co-operation and initiated a diplomatic offensive in all fronts from vaccine diplomacy in Southeast Asia, human rights abuses in Xinjiang, defence partnerships with the littoral states of the South

China Sea, the status of Taiwan and the second QUAD foreign ministers meeting in October 2020:

> I'm confident that we can build on the good work of former Prime Minister Abe, a deeply valued friend of each of our three countries.
>
> The strength of our collaboration is a proud testament to his vision and legacy and a testament to the enduring power of democracy to bring free peoples together. Our partnership isn't multilateralism for the sake of it. All of us seek a free and open Indo-Pacific and our conversations aim to achieve that good outcome.
>
> When we met, now last year, the landscape was very different. We couldn't have imagined the pandemic that came from Wuhan. That crisis was made infinitely worse by the Chinese Communist Party's coverup. The regime's authoritarian nature led its leaders to lock up and silence the very brave Chinese citizens who were raising the alarm. America stands with each of you as we work to achieve victory over this horrible pandemic and rebuild our economies together, and I'm looking forward to that part of our conversation today.
>
> I also look forward to resolving – to renewing our resolve to protect our precious freedoms and the sovereignty of the diverse nations of the region. As partners in this Quad, it is more critical now than ever that we collaborate to protect our people and partners from the CCP's exploitation, corruption, and coercion. We've seen it in the south, in the East China Sea, the Mekong, the Himalayas, the Taiwan Straits. These are just a few examples. (Pompeo 2020)

Pompeo's strong anti-China rhetoric, however, could not be shared by other QUAD members, and this meeting did not produce a joint statement.

The crisis in Ukraine and Asian implications

The Russian invasion of Ukraine brought to the fore the dilemma the United States has faced since the Cold War period between prioritising the Atlantic and the Indo-Pacific. The Obama administration's Asian pivot, followed by the Trump administration's pressuring of the NATO allies to increase defence spending (thereby reducing the relative weight of the US presence in Europe), faced incremental Russian incursions into Ukraine, first with the annexation of Crimea in 2014 and insertions of irregular armed elements into the eastern provinces and then a full-scale invasion from multiple fronts in 2022. The US announcement that Ukraine is not a NATO member and the United States will not directly intervene with troops immediately raised a question about the US role in a hypothetical scenario of the Chinese invasion of Taiwan.

The parallel in the two distant regions shared concerns of the regional allies of the United States about the latter's commitment. It is not clear that China was intent on exploiting the turmoil in Europe to invade Taiwan, or rather was frustrated by Putin's act, which seemingly dragged Beijing together into a tight corner diplomatically. A precaution prevailed in the US policy. The United States immediately conducted a naval transit operation through the Taiwan Strait upon the start of the Russian invasion in 2022, backing its declared commitment to Taiwan's defence under the Taiwan Relations Act with a visible action. Moreover, the United States was bent on fully utilising the QUAD framework as the core of an expanded coalition in the Indo-Pacific.

The resurrection of the QUAD concept under Trump left three important gaps. First, South Korea was absent in the framework. This was equally due to the Moon administration's ambiguous attitude towards the US alliance and Trump's misguided summitry with the North Korean leader Kim Jong-un. Second, the ASEAN did not subscribe to the US "Free and Open Indo-Pacific" strategy, proposing instead its own "ASEAN Outlook for the Indo-Pacific (AOIP)." (ASEAN 2020) Although the United States managed to promote its bilateral defence co-operation with Vietnam and avoided termination of the bilateral alliance with the Philippines (which President Rodrigo Duterte of the latter threatened), it awkwardly neglected ASEAN as a collective diplomatic entity, symbolically leaving the US ambassador to ASEAN seat (which Obama created) vacant.

The QUAD Summit in Tokyo, May 2022

With the COVID-19 pandemic still inflicting human and economic pain around the world, tendencies for unilateral actions among states and a tragic conflict raging in Ukraine, we are steadfast. We strongly support the principles of freedom, rule of law, democratic values, sovereignty and territorial integrity, peaceful settlement of disputes without resorting to threat or use of force, any unilateral attempt to change the status quo, and freedom of navigation and overflight, all of which are essential to the peace, stability and prosperity of the Indo-Pacific region and to the world. We will continue to act decisively together to advance these principles in the region and beyond. We reaffirm our resolve to uphold the international rules-based order where countries are free from all forms of military, economic and political coercion. (MOFA 2022)

US President Joe Biden's participation in the QUAD summit in Tokyo in May 2022 became the test of his administration's restructured Indo-Pacific strategy. While returning to a softer China policy under the new Democratic administration as feared by defence hawks in and out of the United States did not happen, the gap between the tough rhetoric and the lack of coherent policy initiatives, which characterised the US approach to the Indo-Pacific during the Trump administration, has been narrowed.

The most significant development was that the United States seems to have finally acknowledged the advantage of reaching out to Asia through Japan. The much spoken primacy of the US–Japan alliance under the successions of US administrations (CSIS 2018) has met contradicting US behaviour of insufficient consultation with Japan and going over Japan to directly attempt to bargain with Asian countries. Prior to the Biden trip to Asia, Japanese Prime Minister Fumio Kishida made a trip to Indonesia, Vietnam and India to do the groundwork in preparation for the upcoming QUAD summit, which aimed at both showing the group's solidarity in the face of Russian and Chinese challenges to international security and expanding co-operative frameworks on certain issues beyond the four dialogue partners.

The primacy of the US–Japan alliance was differently expressed in their dealings with South Korea. Biden visited Seoul first before coming to Tokyo for the QUAD summit and met the newly elected South Korean President Yoon Seok-youl. South Korea, which has been under a diplomatic feud with Japan over the wartime claims and the war memory issues, attempted to drag the United States into negotiating a bilateral currency swap agreement. The Korean intent was to neutralise the negative effect of Japan's decision not to renew the similar agreement with South Korea in

2015. The United States did not discuss this issue with Korea. Meanwhile, the United States successfully brought South Korea into the Indo-Pacific Economic Framework, which was officially launched in Tokyo during the QUAD meeting. Korea's participation in the framework, which included a scheme of controlled trade of high-tech components with China, was symbolically praised by Biden's visit to a semiconductor factory of Samsung Electronics, which agreed to set up a new 17-billion dollar semiconductor factory in the United States. The pressure on Korea to cut trade with China was preceded by Japan's ban in 2019 on the export of chemical products, which were essential for chip production, to Korea. The Biden administration's approach to Korea made a clear departure from the Obama administration's failed policy of fostering trilateral cooperation via even-handed US brokership between Japan and South Korea.

South Korean entry into the IPEF, however, is not the only success against the country's growing inclination to hedge between China and the United States. In the face of the repeated provocations by North Korea, the United States has requested South Korea to join military drills with the United States and Japan. South Korea has been reluctant to do so, but it joined a four-party joint naval exercise (adding Australia) in 2019. The Biden administration has made a complete break from Trump's highly personalised diplo-entertainment over North Korea, yet has not come up with a new strategy of its own to deal with the latter's nuclear and missile development. Nonetheless, intelligence sharing among the United States, South Korea and Japan over the North's tests and their preparations have continued under the General Security of Military Information Agreement (GSOMIA) between South Korea and Japan, which Korea has *de facto* maintained by freezing its previous announcement in 2019 to discontinue. (KEIA 2020) The United States cautiously calibrates its approaches to the two Northeast Asian allies in the recurring historical animosity between them, in the context of the South Korean hedging. The growing missile improvement by North Korea is providing an overt rationale for both South Korea and Japan to improve their ground-attacking capabilities, which are also more subtly driven by their common fear of China and their mutual distrust. The United States is trying to manage the complex layers of security dilemma in Northeast Asia.

The US commitment to Taiwan has yet again become a key focus of the media, as the QUAD members attempted to downplay the group's relevance to the ongoing crisis over Ukraine. Asked by a journalist whether the United States would militarily intervene if Taiwan is attacked by China, Biden gave an explicit "Yes," only to be followed by usual modifier comments by State Department officials. The episode arguably shows continuity of the US policy of ambiguity, as never verbalising such a possibility would over time form a clarity in Chinese leaders' perception that the United States would not intervene. Biden was under criticism that his clarity that the United States would not send US troops in defence of the non-NATO Ukraine emboldened Russian President Vladimir Putin. Biden also discussed the Taiwan issue in a bilateral meeting with Kishida one day before the QUAD summit. The US preference for an increased Japanese defence spending was met with willing voices within the ruling Liberal Democratic Party and Kishida's commitment to a "substantial increase," but without new clarity about Japan's tactical roles in a Taiwan contingency

Although Taiwan was not among the foundational members of the IPEF due to avoiding further negative reactions from China, the United States soon after the QUAD summit entered a consultation with Taiwan over a bilateral framework of economic cooperation. Taiwan also has a pending application to the Comprehensive and Progressive Trans-Pacific Partnership (CPTPP), competing with China's application. The US attempt not to leave Taiwan in isolation, however, is handcuffed by US Congress, which would not allow Biden to return to the TPP framework but would bilaterally support Taiwan. Whether Japan will admit Taiwan and reject China's application to the CPTPP, thereby restoring Obama's strategic vision behind the original TPP, is unclear. Here again, the loss of US leadership is evident.

Conclusion

The "old order" in East Asia, founded upon the US-centered hub-and-spokes of alliances for security and liberal capitalism that fostered growth and integration of the world economies, was underwritten by a liberal hegemony of the United States. (Ikenberry et all 2013) The balance between coercion and consent in such an order has shifted in the perspectives of the participating states as much as it was altered by succeeding US administrations. At two historical turning points, both inclusion of Japan at the end of WWII and expulsion of China at present were imposed upon them. The order allowed rules-based competition, but the rules were subjected to constant but ideologically often inconsistent revisions. The effort to keep the seas open and international trade and investment free, as manifested in the "Free and Open Indo-Pacific" mantra, is retrenchment of the liberal hegemonic order in rhetoric but has not been faithfully pursued by the United States as it shows increasing tilts towards bilateralism and mercantilism whenever its leading status is under a serious challenge. Japan's ascent to an economic superpower in the 1980–90s resulted in a major trade war with the United States, as the latter made accusations about the former's "unfair" economic practices, which were rarely brought to multilateral dispute resolutions. The United States threatened Japan with abandonment (termination of the security alliance), which may have been a policy of choice for the off-shore balancers. The Japanese economic challenge was short-lived and the alliance endured, but a similar pattern has prevailed in the US–China relations where China's growing economic clout led to security concerns of the United States and efforts at containing China. Institutions that implement rules-based order rise and fall due to the hegemonic leadership commitment or lack thereof, and the US leadership is being tested. (Rothman et all 2017) The effort to rebuild a liberal coalition through Asian buy-ins must be made while Asian willingness to engage the United States (as opposed to China) is still sufficiently strong. (Inoguchi et all 2013)

> [T]he history of American grand strategy has shown that the United States was never a truly isolationist country, that is, a country that did not engage with geopolitical matters outside of its immediate region. Rather, American grand strategy has always swung between a 'realist internationalism rooted in alliances' – off-shore balancing – and 'commitment to a rules-based international order that favors democracy' – the more idealist but often more aggressive Wilsonian version of grand strategy. (Leoni 2021: 81)

Because the US strategy "that seeks to sponsor a post-imperial, globalized order while maintaining national geopolitical supremacy" is:

> based on getting other countries to join the model of technologically-driven, competitive global capitalism, some states have learned to compete in the global

economic arena very successfully to the point that they could undermine US strategy. This is especially the case of China, which poses a tremendous dilemma to the United States because Washington, D.C. policymakers struggle to find a balance between engagement and coercion. (Leoni 2012: 82)

A prominent realist strategic thinker, Zbigniew Brzezinski, admits a reduced US capability to shape order in the "new East" (Indo-Pacific) and calls for a coalition effort to do so that is grounded in US alliances, forward presence and economic engagement, and aimed at engaging China bilaterally and multi-laterally from a position of strength. (Brzezinski 2012) The US need for strategic partners is echoed by Posen, but for a different reasoning. Citing various limitations to China's power projection capabilities and more optimistically assuming a feasibility of the off-shore balancing strategy, Posen argues that reassurance of the allies by the United States is "not an unalloyed benefit, as there is little evidence that they are inspired to do more in their own defense." (Posen 2014) China may eventually prove itself to be too powerful to be singlehandedly contained by the United States, but the latter's:

> [r]estraint advises that the United States take advantage of the present moment to encourage its allies to assume more responsibility for their own defense. Moreover, should China prove very strong, the United States should not wish to replicate the extended nuclear deterrence commitments of the Cold War in any case. (Posen 2014)

The US Indo-Pacific strategy has evolved beyond its earlier military focus under the Trump administration, but its mode of regional economic engagement has lost both multi-lateralism (as manifested in TPP) and willingness to include China – key attributes under Obama's pivot/rebalance to Asia. The path-dependent trajectory of the US strategy, however, reveals a remarkable continuity in terms of its geopolitical priorities and the connectivity between the Pacific and the IOR, as well as an inherent off-shore balancing temptation. The strategy, however, has been cast into a new context in the twenty-first century, during which the relative decline of US power appears a certainty, but the concurrent ascent of China may not lead to a hegemonic transition but to a multi-polar world. With the rise of India and a seemingly growing authoritarian alliance between China and Russia, multi-polarity is also an uncertain prospect, however.

The oscillation between a "realist internationalism rooted in alliances" – off-shore balancing – and "commitment to a rules-based international order that favors democracy" has historically explained American foreign policy during its ascent. The clear display of the off-shore balancing orientation and economic protectionism of the Trump administration, however, should not be mistaken for a partisan position. The rhetoric of "rules-based order" in the US Indo-Pacific strategy represents support for the international maritime laws, which underwrite the naval dominance of the United States. At the same time, the US economic engagement in the region is less compliant with multi-lateralism and is more consistent with bilateralism and mercantilism. Biden, who inherits a strong anti-China framing of the US foreign policy from Trump, is nonetheless not equipped with economic inducements to line up allies and friends in the region. This strategic incoherence at the time of US relative decline may turn out to be a futile self-inflicted blow to its liberal global hegemony.

It is no coincidence that India remains the weakest link of the QUAD cooperation. Although the United States has valued India's democratic tradition since its independence in 1947, (Brzezinski 2012) complete de-hyphenation (India–Pakistan) of the former's South Asia policy is unlikely. Nor does India hold high hopes that the United States will side with it on the territorial disputes with China at the time the significance of the IOR in the overall US strategy, which was never the top priority, remains more ambivalent due to the US withdrawal from the wars in Central Asia and Middle East. In hindsight, it was Abe's speech in India that gave birth to the QUAD concept. The United States may join maritime security cooperation in the IOR, but its catalyst role awaits greater burden sharing by others.

References

Ambrose, Stephen E., & Brinkley, Douglas G. (2011). *Rise to Globalism: American Foreign Policy since 1938*, 9th revised edition. Penguin Books.

Association of the Southeast Asian Nations. ASEAN Outlook on the Indo-Pacific. https://asean.org/asean2020/wp-content/uploads/2021/01/ASEAN-Outlook-on-the-Indo-Pacific_FINAL_22062019.pdf.

Bader, Jeffrey A. (2012). *Obama and China's Rise: An Insider's Account of America's Asia Strategy*. Brookings, p. 105.

Bolton, John. (2020). *The Room Where It Happened: A White House Memoir*. Simon & Schuster, pp. 293–305.

Bremmer, Ian. (2015). *Superpower: Three Choices for America's Role in the World*. Portfolio/Penguin.

Brzezinski, Zbigniew. (2012). *Strategic Vision: America and the Crisis of Global Power*. Basic Books, pp. 155–181.

Clinton, Hillary R. (2014). *Decisiones Difíciles*. Simon & Schuster.

Crabb, Jr. Cecil V. (1988). *American Foreign Policy in the Nuclear Age* (5th ed.). Harper & Row, pp. 465–467.

Daalder, Ivo H., & Destler, I. M. (2009). *In the Shadow of the Oval Office: Profiles of the National Security Advisors and the Presidents They Served from JFK to George W. Bush*. Simon & Schuster.

Friedberg, Aaron L. (2011). *A Contest for Supremacy: China, America, and the Struggle for Mastery in Asia*. W. W. Norton.

Gaddis, John L. (2011). *George F. Kennan: An American Life*. Penguin Books.

Garrison, Jean A. (2005). *Making China Policy: From Nixon to G. W. Bush*. Lynne Rienner.

Hansen, Birthe, Toft, Peter, & Wivel, Anders (2009). *Security Strategies and American World Order*. Routledge.

Heer, Paul J. (2018). *Mr. X and the Pacific: George F. Kennan and American Policy in East Asia*. Cornell.

Hill, Christopher R. (2014). *Outpost: A Diplomat at Work*. Simon & Schuster.

Inoguchi, Takashi, Ikenberry, G. John, & Sato, Yoichiro. (2013). Conclusion: Active SDF, Coming End of Regional Ambiguity, and Comprehensive Political Alliance. In Inoguchi, Ikenberry and Sato, eds., *The US-Japan Security Alliance: Regional Multilateralism*. Palgrave, pp. 277–281.

John Ikenberry, G. (2013). East Asia and Liberal International Order: Hegemony, Balance, and Consent in the Shaping of East Asian Regional Order. In Takashi Inoguchi and G. John Ikenberry, eds., *The Troubled Triangle: Economic and Security Concerns for the United States, Japan, and China*. Palgrave, p. 16.

Kattenburg, Paul M. (1989). New Strategies for U.S. Security Interests in Southeast Asia, the Indian Ocean, and the South Pacific Region. In Ted Galen Carpenter, ed., *Collective Defense or Strategic Independence? Alternative Strategies for the Future*. CATO Institute and Lexington Books, pp. 141–143.

Korea-Japan GSOMIA Survives Amid Disputes over Historical, Trade Issues. *The Peninsula*. Korea Economic Institute. August 25, 2020. https://keia.org/the-peninsula/korea-japan-gsomia-survives-amid-disputes-over-historical-trade-issues/.

Leoni, Zeno. (2021). *American Grand Strategy from Obama to Trump: Imperialism after Bush and China's Hegemonic Challenge*. Palgrave, p. 82.

Luttwak, Edward L. (2012). *The Rise of China vs. the Logic of Strategy*. Harvard Belknap.

Mann, James. (2012). *The Obamians: The Struggle inside the White House to Redefine American Power*. Penguin Books.

Ministry of Foreign Affairs of Japan. Confluence of the Two Seas, Speech by H. E. Mr. Shinzo Abe, Prime Minister of Japan at the Parliament of the Republic of India, August 22, 2007. https://www.mofa.go.jp/region/asia-paci/pmv0708/speech-2.html.

Ministry of Foreign Affairs of Japan. Quad Joint Leaders' Statement, May 24, 2022. https://www.mofa.go.jp/fp/nsp/page1e_000401.html.

More Important Than Ever: Renewing the U.S.-Japan Alliance for the 21st Century. Center for Strategic and International Studies, October 2018. https://csis-website-prod.s3.amazonaws.com/s3fs-public/publication/181011_MorethanEver.pdf.

Pompeo, Michael R. (2020). Opening Remarks at Quad Ministerial, Iikura Guest House, Tokyo, Japan, October 6. https://2017-2021.state.gov/secretary-michael-r-pompeo-opening-remarks-at-quad-ministerial/index.html.

Posen, Barry R. (2014). *Restraint: A New Foundation for US Grand Strategy*. Cornell, p. 96.

Roberts, Sean R. (2020). Why Did the United States Take China's Word on Supposed Uighur Terrorists? *Foreign Policy*, November 10. https://foreignpolicy.com/2020/11/10/why-did-the-united-states-take-chinas-word-on-supposed-uighur-terrorists/.

Rothman, Steven B., Vyas, Utpal & Sato, Yoichiro, editors. (2017). *Regional Institutions, Geopolitics and Economics in the Asia-Pacific: Evolving Interests and Strategies*. Routledge.

Sato, Yoichiro. (2006). US North Korea Policy; the 'Japan Factor'. In Linus Hagström and Marie Söderberg, eds., *North Korea Policy: Japan and the Great Powers*. Routledge and the European Institute of Japanese Studies, pp. 78–79.

Tow, William T., & Stuart, Douglas, editors. (2015). *The New US Strategy towards Asia: Adapting to the American Pivot*. Routledge.

17 Chinese conceptions of the Indo-Pacific

The impact of identity and history

Chris Ogden and Catherine Jones

This chapter explores Chinese conceptions of the Indo-Pacific. It specifically explores whether China has a different conceptualisation of this region and whether that conceptualisation links back to Chinese history. The concept of the Indo-Pacific spans numerous types of activity that engage the partners in the Indo-Pacific, including geopolitics, security, economic engagement, safety (especially maritime safety), legal frameworks and socio-cultural connections. At a more abstract level, the Indo-Pacific concept is a vision and an overarching strategic framework that members can use to position their relations with one another, and with non-member states. However, this vision and strategic implications (alongside the practical means for implementing the concept) are contested (Taylor 2020; Wilson 2018). This contest exists between the region's partners but also between the region and external states. In other chapters in this handbook this contested nature *vis-à-vis* other states is dealt with more extensively, but the focus of this chapter is to look at China's perception of the Indo-Pacific and how it connects to wider narratives in China concerning its identity and regional narrative.

Since the collapse of the Soviet Union, the gradual expansion of the Association of Southeast Asian Nations (ASEAN) and the waning of the relevance and role of the Asia-Pacific Economic Cooperation (APEC), China and the United States have continually provided different visions of what/where the region is and which states it comprises (Jones & Breslin 2015). From Beijing's perspective, this contest is about more than lines on a map, it is also a contest about what leadership is and how states can (and should) maintain regional primacy. Notably, Xi Jinping in 2018 made the claim that China will not seek hegemony over either the world or the region (Loke 2019). At the same time, however, in his other speeches Xi Jinping has also consistently highlighted the importance of the Century of Humiliation (the period from the mid-nineteenth to the mid-twentieth centuries, during which China's regional stature was debased) and the historical differences between China's regional leadership and the type of leadership demonstrated by Western powers. Such an emphasis thus focuses upon the ongoing importance of status and influence for Beijing concerning how China conceptualises and interacts with the Indo-Pacific region. In 2019, Xi Jinping formalised this claim (and thus a competing vision of the Indo-Pacific) by formally inserting the concept of "Xi Jinping Thought" into the Chinese Constitution.

This Chinese alternative vision of the region draws upon the history of the Chinese world order, which is juxtaposed with the concept of the Indo-Pacific presented in the other chapters of this Handbook. By reading this chapter and engaging with the learning exercises at the end you will be able to describe the main features and periods of

DOI: 10.4324/9781003336143-22

China's regional history, and present or compare these different approaches concerning the understanding of these features and their relative importance in the different periods. This will then enable you to evaluate these alternative approaches and identify the different actors within China who are important concerning the management of China's current regional relations. Finally, this chapter will enable you to contextualise the varying importance of these actors in relation to a range of tensions and disputes across the Indo-Pacific and assess the extent to which understanding China's historical relations are important in its current regional relationships and definitions of the region.

The chapter is structured as follows: the first section considers conceptions of a traditional Chinese world order. The second section then connects these conceptions to Beijing's contemporary understandings of the Indo-Pacific, before the third section looks at China's peripheral relations policy. The chapter's two case studies on the South China Sea and the East China Sea then pull these elements together and serve as critical exemplars of how China's identity impacts upon its most crucial dispute in the region, and which thus reveal the core concerns and tensions in its vision of the Indo-Pacific. The chapter ends by summing up these perspectives and underlines the role of history in modern China.

Conceptions of the traditional Chinese world order

Due to the dominance of the Western world imposed throughout the world through colonialism, and the spread of liberal democracy since the end of the Cold War, as well as the European-centric nature of International Relations, history tends to be taught in schools through the lens of the experience of Western Europe. As a result, we frequently simplify the histories of other regions and try to compare them to the histories that we have been taught. Such a process is however extremely difficult when comparing the 2,000-year-old "Chinese world order" to European history over a similar timespan. Whilst China displayed a relative level of stability and continuity during such a period, the European landmass transitioned through the influences of the Roman Empire and the Vikings to the discovery of the new world and the emergence of colonialism, followed by the emergence of the sovereign state system, the subsequent emergence of liberal thought in the enlightenment, and then two World Wars, the Cold War and the Decolonisation Period. As such, studying the nature and basis of the "Chinese world order" is of utmost importance, especially when it comes to understanding the Indo-Pacific.

The concept of the traditional Chinese world order synthesises the history of China spanning more than 2,000 years (for longer analyses see: Fairbank, 1968; Callahan, 2008; Stuart-Fox 2003; Li 2002; Lind, 2018; Zhang 2009; Jones & Zhang 2021). Within this time period there were thirteen dynasties: Xia, Shang, Zhou, Qin, Han, the six dynasties period, Sui, Tang, the ten dynasties period, Song, Yuan, Ming and Qing. Although this period is identified and summarised by a single phrase "the Traditional Chinese Order," across these dynasties the Chinese empire covered different geographic spaces, had a range of internal political ordering systems and had a range of relations with its neighbouring societies. A single section of a chapter cannot fill in all of the detail of this 2,000-year history (although the further reading provided at the end of this chapter will allow you to investigate it further if you wish). Instead, this section will set out the main features associated with the traditional Chinese world order and identify how different features were important in different dynasties (Kang 2010). It will then set out three approaches to understanding the different approaches China has had towards its region. The following section will then identify how these different features and approaches connect to China's current international identity concerning the Indo-Pacific.

The central concept of the traditional Chinese world order is *Tian Xia* (天下) which can be literally translated as "all-under-heaven." This gives a geographical location for the Chinese world order and this area was ruled by the "Son of Heaven" or *Tianzi* (天子) – the Chinese Emperor. Land areas beyond the rule of the son of heaven were the inner vassals, outer vassals and then the land of the barbarians. In the texts concerning this order, it is normally presented as a series of concentric circles. One such example can be seen in Figure 17.1. In this figure we have excluded hard-line distinctions between the distinct circles to represent there were degrees of control exerted by the Tianzi. Over the different periods of the empires the strength of control and the geographical distance from the emperor also changed.

The evidence for this organisation of the region can be found in a number of sources. One of them is in the philosophical texts from the period. Another is through visual representations from the period, for example, we can see a depiction of these areas on a map of the voyage of Zheng He, whereby the closer the land areas are to the middle of the map, the greater detail they have, and the further away they are from China, the less detail they have, as is shown in Figure 17.2.

This map depicted in Figure 17.2 is both famous and infamous. On the one hand it reports to be a clear indication of the advances of the Chinese civilisation: Zheng He's voyage set sail in 1405 and if the map in Figure 17.2 is from this time it would indicate that China was able to build a ship and navigate the world long before the European explorers (Christopher Columbus's first voyage departed from Spain in 1492). The map in Figure 17.2 has been identified as a later reconstruction but it was still intended to accurately map out the voyage of Admiral He, although we cannot know for certain whether any detail was added by later map makers. However, one concept is consistently represented within these maps and images of the time, wherein China is at the centre of the map. Indeed, the characters of *Zhongguo*, literally translates to meaning "middle country," which is another important concept in understanding the

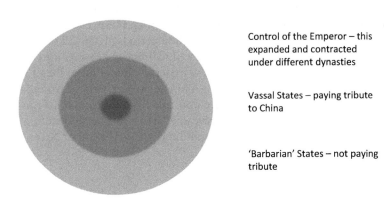

Control of the Emperor – this expanded and contracted under different dynasties

Vassal States – paying tribute to China

'Barbarian' States – not paying tribute

Figure 17.1 Depiction of the structure of the traditional Chinese world order Note that there is no hard line between the groups of states but a fading in the picture signifying the different approach to boundaries and borders to the Westphalian State system. (Created by authors).

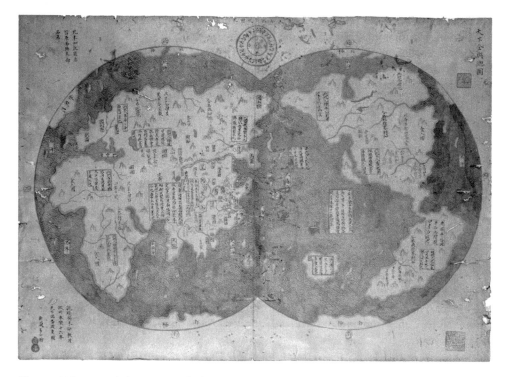

Figure 17.2 Map of the voyage of Zheng He – reproduced after his death.

Source: Wikimedia Commons

traditional world order. Sino-centrism is a vital element of the maintenance of this polity but also in determining how other countries or rather political communities related to the Chinese empire. We can learn more about this concept from historical texts and other sources that discuss this period.

A second source we can use for tracing the concept of "all-under-heaven" is through philosophical texts. From these we can identify that the concept and term can be traced back at least as far as the Shang (1600–1046 BCE) and Zhou periods (1026–221 BCE). However, it should be noted that the claims of authority of "all-under-heaven" differed between dynasties (Wang 2012: 342). As a result, these materials reveal more than the geographical knowledge and scope of the area of the Chinese empire – they also indicate how such an expansive area was held together and ruled by the emperor. From these texts some additional important concepts are revealed: Sino-centrism and cultural superiority, social order and Confucianism, hierarchy and the role of the son of heaven.

Sino-centrism and cultural superiority

From the maps discussed above and the image of the Chinese world order as a series of concentric circles, it is clear that within the traditional Chinese order, China was culturally at the centre of the region. The inner and outer vassals (also known as tributary states) had to act accordingly. This included paying deference to the superiority of

China and paying a "tribute" to the emperor. The Chinese demonstrated their cultural superiority through the creation of goods including fine pottery, bronzes figures, the creation of writing and through other intellectual and power related pursuits including the voyages of Zheng He.

Why did these vassal states pay a tribute to the Chinese empire? There are some debates within the academic texts and evaluations here and it is important to note that the reason could vary over the different dynastic periods of the empire. One reason for paying tribute was that it was a low-cost way of preventing conflict and ensuring political and social autonomy from the Chinese empire. Another argument is that because China was culturally superior it had no need of these gifts and thus tributes were a socially acceptable exchange based upon relative status and influence. Notably in this regard, the goods China provided to these states in return, through enhanced trade and regional peace, were much higher than the tributes that it received. In looking at the debates within International Relations and Chinese history we have at least three versions of why this system of tribute was maintained: (1) to maintain trade; (2) to provide a system of foreign affairs bureaucracy; and (3) to maintain social norms (Zhang 2009).

Social order and Confucianism

Social order was certainly important for the maintenance of social cohesion between all peoples "under heaven" and potentially among some of the vassal states. According to Confucianism, every individual within a community had to respect their position within the social order, and fulfil the roles associated with it, as failure to do so would lead to disorder and disarray. These societal roles encompassed the whole of society and included a specific role for the emperor as the "son of heaven." Within society it was also important for every individual to fulfil their role in order to maintain order. These roles included outlining how people should behave towards each other in society and was reinforced through the observance of rituals and through normal conventions. This also included a moral code for society, for individuals and for the emperor. According to Confucius, this morality or the qualities that needed to be demonstrated by a moral person included "human-heartedness" and "humaneness" (*ren*); filial piety (*xiao*); loyalty (*Zhong*); courage (*yong*); righteousness (*yi*); reciprocity (*shu*); intellect and integrity (*xian*) (Mutschler 2019: 14).

These qualities identify how people should relate to each other and also provide a pattern for how to live in a community. These community expectations were then applied to the vassal states who were given a position and roles to fulfil within this social order and were also expected to exhibit these same principles and those internal to the Chinese empire. These included participating in ceremonies and rituals (including tribute giving). One consequence of this system of values and norms was that China's external order was closely related to its internal order and one could not survive without the other. In the next section of this chapter we will explore the current norms and values pursued by China and how they relate to the Indo-Pacific.

Son of heaven

According to Confucian principles the son of heaven was the emperor of the polity because he enjoyed the mandate of heaven (Glanville 2010). He had to rule in accordance with that mandate, and if the Sino-centric order was challenged or disintegrated or territory was lost it was evidence that the emperor had lost the mandate of heaven. For modern China, the territorial disputes in the East and South China Seas illustrate how these disputes can be linked to this norm of the mandate of heaven, whereby losing these territories would result in delegitimising China's leaders. Frequently, losing the mandate of heaven had the potential to lead to the transfer of the leadership of the empire to a different dynasty. This could be a relatively peaceful transfer of power or could be hallmarked by violence and conflict. Leadership was not only about maintaining the territory of China, but it also had to be moral so that it could be imposed through social conventions. When individuals felt they have been socially wronged, they always had recourse to appeal to the morality of the emperor as a last resort for redress. This morality in leadership was intended to relate to how the emperor dealt with vassal states, and in some of the ideas emanating from a Chinese School of International relations the concept is called "moral realism" (Yan 2014).

Hierarchy

From the above information, it is clear that throughout these different elements of the traditional order, hierarchy is vitally important. But there were a number of interlocking hierarchies. Within the Chinese polity there was a social hierarchy, and a political hierarchy. Externally there was a hierarchy of states that was based on both the distance from the Middle Kingdom but also the degree of conformity to the social and political norms of the kingdom. In this logic, hierarchy leads to stability (Qin 2006: 33; quoted in Jones & Zhang 2021). However, this hierarchical order is more concerned with seeking and maintaining Chinese centrality rather than dominance (Jones & Zhang 2021), and is achieved though morality and deference.

What was the traditional Chinese world order?

For Fairbank (1968) and Teng the Chinese world order was a description of the conduct of Chinese foreign relations and diplomacy. In this understanding, the distinguishing feature of Chinese leaders is to lead through a moral code, whereas foreign or "barbarian" leaders are seen to lead through the acquisition of material goods and power. For historians of China's tribute system and traditional order, it is a description of the bureaucracy of the conduct of China's foreign relations and thus focuses on the constitutional elements of that order (Zhang & Buzan 2012). Tributes and the rituals associated with them were thus the equivalent of a modern day "summit meeting," with the exchange of gifts being the prerequisite for the discussion of terms of trade, state borders and mutual support. For Feng Zhang (2009), the Chinese world order is an early example of the institution of a normative regional order or international society, which is held together by the sharing of common customs, practices and values.

It is also important to highlight that "until the Western powers invasion of East Asia in the mid-nineteenth century, the conduct of China's foreign affairs had been primarily directed under the traditional Chinese world outlook based upon a political philosophy that had been in effect since time immemorial" (Li 2002: 25). How we understand what the traditional order was will therefore affect how we analyse China's contemporary attempts to recreate it. It is also important to reiterate that the previous Chinese world order was brought to an end by the arrival of the British in

1839 with the start of the Opium Wars and loss of the territory of Hong Kong to the British until 1997. This started the Century of Humiliation (Callahan 2004), as China lost its position as the central state in Asia. From this basis, it is important to consider how China engages with Western powers and whether in seeking to develop a regional order it also seeks to share moral leadership with the former "barbarians."

How does this description of the traditional Chinese world order connect to Chinese perceptions of the Indo-Pacific?

The Indo-Pacific concept

As mentioned in the introduction of this chapter, the Indo-Pacific is a contested concept. It also has a long history that contributes to its current iteration. According to some analysts, the concept of the Indo-Pacific has antecedents in the Japanese empire. In 1895, Japan colonised Taiwan (also known as Formosa) and then gradually extended its dominance of the region of East Asia, including the annexation of Korea in 1910. In imposing its rule, Japan adopted different strategies within local populations, including providing education (that foregrounded the teaching of Japanese) and investing in infrastructure and manufacturing. As the empire further expanded through aggressions during WWII, Japan also adjusted its strategies for control to include the idea of "pan-Asianism," which was promulgated through the concept of the "co-prosperity sphere" (Draft Plan n.). According to this plan, Japan sought to provide a rationale for a new regional order, that was based on the commonalities between Asian societies and put in place both visions of hierarchy and equality between different Asian communities. In effect, this ensured the Japanese empire could divide and rule in Asia.

It could be argued that in some ways this part of Japanese history has nothing to do with the concept of the Indo-Pacific. As such, within the contemporary Indo-Pacific concept, Japan does not seek to dominate the region, nor does it seek to create a collective Asian identity. However, the legacies of the Japanese Imperial period and the co-prosperity sphere still inform how regional states view Japan, and therefore affect the type of role Japan can assume and claim in the region. These perceptions include those emanating from China which was occupied for much of the twentieth century prior to WWII. We argue that this history helps to explain some of the differences between the parties in the Indo-Pacific and their different visions and strategies (as well has how the concept has developed over time). It also sets the grounds for contested visions of what the Indo-Pacific is and is not.

The Japanese Prime Minister – Shinzo Abe – is often seen as the initiator of the concept that has now become known as the Indo-Pacific. In 2007 (during his first period as Prime Minister), Abe made a speech to the Indian Parliament, where he discussed the concept of the "Confluence of the Seas" and the importance of the "arc of freedom and prosperity" (MOFA 2007). In this speech, Abe highlighted that India and Japan should form a "strategic global partnership," whereby closer ties would be developed on the basis that "we share fundamental values such as freedom, democracy, and the respect for basic human rights as well as strategic interests" (MOFA 2007). At the time, these comments generated concerns from Japan's neighbours that Japan was seeking to revert to some of the behaviours associated with the colonial period. It was also important that the concerned states – particularly those within Southeast Asia that had been previously occupied by Japan – were more concerned with the threat from Japan than the rise of China. However, shortly after the speech, Abe resigned as Prime Minister and the concept languished for the next five years.

In 2012, when Abe ran for office again, he advocated a reformed version of the concept through the notion of "the security diamond" (Hughes 2016: 139). At this time, Abe faced a different geopolitical reality in that after the global financial crisis of 2008, China's position in the region and globally had increased. States in Southeast Asia were also becoming more concerned about China's regional ambitions. As a result, after taking office Abe visited all ten member states of ASEAN within his first year. Through these visits, Abe's newly crafted concept took on a new focus concerning security that was informed by shared values and goals. It was also backed up by increased investment in infrastructure to counter the Chinese investment through the Asian Investment Infrastructure Bank (Hughes 2016: 140). As a result, for Japan the concept of the Indo-Pacific came to encompass at least three elements: common values, security and economic development.

From an Indian perspective, the Indo-Pacific came about as a result of its strategic re-orientation within the region in the early twenty-first century that resulted in much closer strategic ties with Japan, as well as towards the United States (Ogden 2014). This greater proximity was accompanied by a redefinition of its "geo-strategic frontiers" whereby India's dominant position in the Indian Ocean Region to the West fused with Japan's crucial location in the Pacific in the East to result in the newly emergent "Indo-Pacific" region (Panda 2019). Importantly, this understanding differs from what China regards as its regional positioning concerning the term "Indo-Pacific" and is emblematic of how conceptions of the Indo-Pacific vary between states as each of their geo-strategic frontiers (and associated perceptions of them) also necessarily vary (Khurana 2019). For New Delhi, embracing the Indo-Pacific concept was also illustrative of a deepening and extending strategic reach eastwards over the last few decades. This process had begun with the "Look East" policy of the early 1990s, taken further by the "Act East" policy from 2014 under Narendra Modi and then bolstered by ever-closer ties with ASEAN (especially through the East Asia summit from 2005 onwards).

India's growing global relevance as a major trading and diplomatic partner, and as a potential balancer against a rapidly rising China, further underscored its importance to regional partners. Moreover, because a number of key Asian states relied upon the Indian Ocean Region's sea lines of communication (SLOC) for the vast majority of their gas and oil supplies, and also used it as a key trade route, helped to accentuate India's contemporary importance. This sense of inter-reliance was the major driver for closer India–Japan, as well as India–US relations, and effectively created a strategic triad between them. In recent years, this troika has been extended further to become the "Quad" that includes Australia, resulting in as a democratic strategic quadrangle that seeks to counter China in the region, evoke a "rules-based" international order primarily emanating from extra-regional (mainly western) perspectives and to re-conceptualise it as the Indo-Pacific (Mohan 2021).

That stated, New Delhi does not entirely embrace the United States and Japanese vision of the Indo-Pacific. In part this is reflective of a continued desire by India to maintain as much strategic flexibility as possible in its foreign relations (Ogden 2018). It is also because China and India share many interests, ranging from continued economic development and prosperity, maintaining a stable region and – most importantly – reasserting their past status as great powers in the region and in global politics (Ogden 2017). Any sense of being exploited by external actors also triggers memories of (British) imperialism and colonialism for New Delhi, and – in a striking similarity to Chinese memories of the Century of Humiliation – results in a counter-sentiment to avoid being exploited again at any cost. This is a crucial influence in informing the complex and multi-faceted Indian outlook on the Indo-Pacific (Scott 2012).

In contrast, US engagement and advocacy for the Indo-Pacific has been strongly associated with President Trump. Under his presidency, the US administration moved from its previous vision of the region as the "Asia Pacific" towards that of the "Indo-Pacific." This shift has subsequently been reflected in the changed terminology within US policy-making circles. However, this is not only a change in words, but it has also been seen as being a significant shift to an explicitly maritime focus that incorporated India into the region, and through the focus upon the terms "free" and "open" seeks to exclude and counter balance China's regional advances (Pascal 2021). For the United States under President Trump the Free and Open Indo-Pacific was therefore clearly a tool to challenge China's rise and its increasing assertiveness.

China's perceptions of the Indo-Pacific

Against this backdrop China's perspective is distinctive and informs China's own regional strategy. This regional strategy has changed over time, particularly since the Asian Financial Crisis in 1997, but China's approach is also linked to its own identity and history in the region. It was clear that the speech made by Abe in 2007 had annoyed China, as at the time Chinese scholars indicated that they viewed this approach as divisive and potentially a return to a Cold War mentality that would promote conflict not peace (Rediff 2007). However, as Abe withdrew from office and the Liberal Democratic Party (LDP) lost the next election in 2007 to the Democratic Party of Japan (DPJ) (Hemmings 2021), concerns were initially frozen as the plan seemed to lack popularity and depth. However, China again became more concerned in 2011 when President Obama made a speech in Canberra that focused on the United States's "pivot to Asia." Such a move was widely seen in China as being motivated by wanting to encircle and entrap China, thus preventing it from regaining the status it had lost in the Century of Humiliation. The re-election of Abe in 2012 only deepened this concern within China. However, the greatest concern was felt through President Trump's 2017 speech whereby the new "Free and Open Indo-Pacific" concept was viewed by Beijing as being explicitly anti-Chinese. From this basis, according to Liu, "Chinese scholars generally take the view that the Indo-Pacific strategy will have negative implications for China's security environment" (Liu 2020: 17).

Within this broad frame of understanding, however, there have been at least three different views within China of how to respond to the Indo-Pacific concept. The first of these was to try and develop an approach that highlighted the common values of Asian civilisations. This was articulated by Xi Jinping in 2014 in Shanghai where he highlighted the idea of "Asian collective security" (He 2018: 121). Within this concept he claimed that security needed to be inclusive (as opposed to the exclusive security framework of the Indo-Pacific) and that this should be based on "Asian values" which offered a counter-argument to the values of Western-orientated democracy and human rights. This articulation seems to directly draw on the experience of the Chinese world order, as outlined above. It also makes a claim that Asian states should act collectively, for their common good, and at the centre of this organisation should be China acting as a beneficent leader. However, this concept excludes the United States as well as potentially Russia. As a result, the framing of Xi Jinping's ambitions later changed from being based on Asianism towards a "respect for diversity" (He 2018: 121).

The second view of China's regional concept and approach to the Indo-Pacific is geopolitical. As noted above, a key element of the Indo-Pacific is its maritime focus. However, China has sought to instead focus on its land connections. This can be seen in how the Belt and Road Initiative (BRI) has developed in developing ties between Western China and towards South Asia and the Middle East. Such a land focus also echo's China's traditional world order, and as Baogang He notes "Chinese perceptions of its region are largely continental. Chinese civilisation has evolved around plateaus, rivers, lakes and, generally speaking, stopped at sea, even though the Ming dynasty had a strong naval force" (He 2018: 120). From this understanding of China's self-perception and response to the Indo-Pacific concept, there are thus also clear links back to China's continental identity and its view of history. Interestingly, it takes the view that if China's perception is that it is being contained to the East and the South, then it can re-enforce its position to the North and West. If needed this strategy can also be linked to Beijing's viewpoint concerning "respect for diversity." However, as noted in the case studies below, this creates some difficulties for understanding China's territorial claims in the East and South China Seas.

The third view of China's perception of the Indo-Pacific concept is perhaps the most radical. It suggests that China should almost co-opt the Indo-Pacific concept to further advance the BRI (He 2018: 125). This perception identifies that there are significant overlaps in terms of the objectives of the Indo-Pacific, whereby both the BRI and the Indo-Pacific concept seek to achieve development in the region and also to produce a more stable and predictable security environment. As a result, by engaging with the Indo-Pacific in a positive win-win frame would avoid confrontation and have greater potential benefit for China's continued economic growth. This view of the potential to usurp the concept also connects to an underpinning assumption in China that although the concept could be a threat, the US cannot commit the costs to fully implement it, because the US has fallen into a "decline trap" (Liu 2020: 17). They also highlight that the commitment of regional partners to the Indo-Pacific may not be values-driven but is instead seen as an economic opportunity, and again they question the ability of the United States to outweigh the contributions of China to these states (Liu 2020: 18). Hence, in a very different way this perception of the Indo-Pacific has a link back to the Chinese world order, when Admiral He was voyaging and exploring the globe with the hope of finding new peoples and trading opportunities. However, as history reveals, in the longer term this engagement view did not endure under the traditional world order. Nonetheless, such a perception of the region and the Indo-Pacific does also highlight the aspects of the Chinese traditional world order that are based upon trade links and economic success rather than direct control over regional governance.

This section has highlighted that – just as there are different views of the Indo-Pacific – there are also different Chinese conceptions of the concept and how China should respond to it. In the next section we explore China's current behaviour in its peripheral relations to see if any one of these conceptions seems to dominate China's current behaviour.

China's contemporary peripheral relations policy

It is claimed by some scholars that the major dimensions and attributes of a "Chinese world order" can be seen to be evident in China's contemporary foreign policy towards its neighbours in the East Asian region and beyond, as crafted by the Chinese Communist Party (CCP). Incorporating a contemporary reading of *Tian Xia*, paramount within this policy has been asserting the centrality of China to the region's fortunes, most clearly through greater trade links that have resulted in the creation of deep-seated economic dependencies between China's neighbours and Beijing. This view can also be seen in the different perceptions China has towards the concept of the Indo-Pacific, as detailed above.

Such relations have implicitly implied – and hence effectively reassert – a prevailing regional hierarchy with China at the top, which in turn has bolstered its desired self-image and status as an important – if not dominant – regional actor. From this basis, we can see how the past connects to the present and indeed the future, whereby "civilizational constructs, cultural factors and state identities" (Ruggie 1998: 867) all act as crucial factors that shape policy, behaviour and outcomes within international relations. Thus, although the tribute system of old is no longer explicitly in place, such a Sino-centric perspective "persists in the mentality" (Jacques 2012: 375) of China's leaders and thus affects its conduct of international relations.

Many of these broad contemporary aims also relate to the desire by China's elites to overturn the perceived injustices associated with the Century of Humiliation. This was the period from the Opium Wars (1839-42 / 1856-60) to the establishment of the People's Republic of China (PRC) in 1949 when China's wealth and status were debased by external imperial powers (Ogden 2019). This period is seen as having reduced China's international and regional stature, and the CCP now actively seeks to reaffirm China's leading regional status, and in a general sense for China to "stand up" as proclaimed by the first leader of the PRC Mao Zedong. Making China rich again and into a modern and developed state, as well as restoring lost territory taken by other countries during the Century of Humiliation (including in the East and South China Seas as detailed below) are central tenets of such a restoration, and are clarion calls for China's nationalists. The principle of "great national unity" (*da yi tong*) also seeks to achieve peace and stability in China via its cultural, territorial and political consolidation and unison, and includes the positive resolution of all disputes across its land and maritime borders.

In the last decade, other core ideas have informed and permeated the way in which China approaches its international relations, and which in turn inform its attitude towards its relations with states in the Indo-Pacific as part of its peripheral diplomacy. These include the notion of a "China Cultural Revival" (*zhonghua wenhua fuxing*), a political slogan which "seeks to restore China to its former status of being a great power in world affairs based upon using the country's increasing economic and military power to boost its international standing, leadership, and stability, as well as reasserting its cultural heritage" (Ogden 2019). An accompanying motto is that of the "Chinese Dream" (also called China Dream) (*zhongguo meng*), which is a call to arms for China's population to work together to collectively help achieve this renaissance. Together, such mantras connect China's glorious past to the country's ambitions for a glorious future and underscore how "historical memory is the prime raw material that has constituted and shaped China's national identity" (Zheng 2012: XX). Going further, Jacques notes how cultural factors "shape the way people think, behave and perceive others" (Jacques 2012: 269), which has a particular resonance when we consider the longstanding, civilisational basis of China and its conception of "world order" than spans two millennia.

The principles underpinning China's "zhoubian" (peripheral) diplomacy

Building upon these themes and encapsulated within the term "*zhoubian*" (peripheral) diplomacy, China's approach to its region encompasses several different elements. Broadly, Lanteigne has demarcated China's peripheral diplomacy as various "attempts to improve international ties with bordering states in the Asia-Pacific region" (Lanteigne 2016: 156). At the very heart of this policy is the realisation that "preserving regional stability also aids China's continued economic growth and modernization, as do its undergirding principles of being 'amicable, tranquil, and prosperous' (*mulin, anlin, fulin*)" (Ogden 2019). These inter-connected elements can be further disaggregated to encompass: (1) the importance of basing bilateral/regional relations upon cooperation rather than conflict, so as to ensure regional stability; (2) using trade as the central pillar upon which successful bilateral/regional relations can be built; and (3) aiming to positively resolve all outstanding territorial disputes.

Summing up these perspectives, Chinese Premier Wen Jiabao remarked that this "*zhoubian*" diplomacy aimed to present China as "a good neighbour and a good partner, to strengthen good neighbourly ties, to intensify regional cooperation, and to push China's exchanges and cooperation with its neighbours to a new high" (quoted in Beeson & Li 2012: 37). From its inception in the mid-1990s, "*zhoubian*" diplomacy has also broadly stressed "a restrained, non-confrontational mode of competition" (Deng & Wang 2005: viii) as the primary *modus operandi* of China's regional diplomacy. Importantly, overarching such an approach was also "the desire for 'international status' (*guoji diwei*) – so as to achieve power, security and respect" (Ogden 2017: 104), which entered Chinese foreign policy discourses in the 1990s.

Such diplomatic approaches have also been reflected in other official doctrines, such as the "new security concept" (*xin anquan guandian*), which materialised in the mid-1990s after the end of the Cold War and set out a peaceful approach to China's foreign policy. As a policy essential to the handling of China's international affairs, it proclaims that "force cannot fundamentally resolve disputes and conflicts … (whereby) the use of force and the threat to use force can hardly bring about lasting peace" (FMPRC 1996). Such an attitudinal and doctrinal basis endeavours to seek solutions to regional relations not through war but via soft power means that rest upon finding common ground and mutual "win-win" solutions, so as to prevent regional conflict through the avoidance of creating any negative perceptions.

This importance – at least in the 1990s when China's rapid economic rise became significantly pronounced – was further shown by how the policy of "peaceful rise" was scrapped in favour of "peaceful development," due to concerns that the word "rise" could inadvertently imply "violence" or a "challenge" (Glaser & Medieros 2007: 304). Such concerns also relate back to the Confucian tradition of seeking "*datong*" or harmony, which has a continuing and substantial impact upon the nature of Chinese peripheral relations policy (Lampton 2004: 110). Such an adaptation further feeds into the wider notion of charm offensive (*meili gongshi*), "a term and strategy used in Chinese diplomacy to proactively project an image abroad of China as a trustworthy, benevolent, and benign partner" (Ogden 2019). Such a term is deployed to assure countries concerned about China's swift economic and military ascent that China does not threaten their stability or that of the wider Indo-Pacific region.

These perspectives also have the tacit aim of presenting an alternative image to its neighbours that contrasts with the United States, whose foreign policy – including in East Asia – has rested upon the use of force, explicit alliances and arms racing. Much of this effort rests upon how, from the late 1970s onwards, China renounced its prior Cold War policy under Mao Zedong of supporting revolutionary movements across South East Asia. During that period, China "attempted to export the communist revolution across the region, most notably in Cambodia, Indonesia, and Vietnam, and used China's military power to attempt to control regional affairs via the invasion of Vietnam in 1979 [under Deng Xiaoping]" (Ogden 2019). Mao's successor Deng Xiaoping's transformation of foreign and domestic policy came to rest upon economic modernisation and development, which could be significantly maximised through having a stable periphery. Furthermore, after the events in Tiananmen Square in 1989 when protestors were brutally dealt with by the CCP, China actively sought to proactively present itself as a co-operative and non-ideological partner rather than a would-be regional hegemon. This strategy also based itself upon a desire to counteract Beijing's mounting international isolation after 1989 and to neutralise wider regional efforts to restrain its ambitions to become a great power (as led by the United States and its allies Japan and South Korea).

Frictions and challenges

Notably, China's contemporary re-assertion of its great power status is a phenomenon whose wider parameters are having an impact upon Beijing's regional policy. A central part of these dynamics – and something that features within the discourses associated with the "China Renaissance" and "China Dream" – is the modernisation and development of China's military capabilities. Through a "revolution in military affairs," Beijing is upgrading the country's military capabilities, including the development of asymmetric capabilities such as anti-satellite weapons and anti-ship ballistic missiles, as well as other stealth and hypersonic technologies. From the point of view of its regional relations, such advancements play into a central prong of its military approach towards the Indo-Pacific concerning the mantra of "area denial," which "seeks to fashion a protective buffer around a country's continental and maritime periphery, so as to deter military attacks against its mainland" (Ogden 2019). They also inform the aim of enabling a "blue-water strategy" (*lanshui zhanlue*) for China's naval capabilities, which would give Beijing the ability to operate in all of the world's oceans, and to protect the country's interests, including trade routes and energy supplies (Tseng 2017).

This modernisation and incremental expansion in terms of the scope and scale of China's strategic footprint both within the region and beyond is *producing frictions and challenges within Chinese foreign policy*. Crucially, military force informs China's ability to protect vital sea routes, so as to enable the import and export of raw commodities and manufactured goods but also to safeguard the vital oil supplies that are essential for sustaining the Chinese economy. China's fear of these trade and energy routes being blocked, perhaps by its regional competitors, additionally informs the strategic logic underpinning this approach. Furthermore, enhanced military capabilities can also be deployed to assert particular territorial claims either through pressurising competitors or actively controlling portions of disputed land or water. When viewed together – protecting trade and energy routes in conjunction with backing up attempts to reclaim lost territories (which can take place concurrently) – China's peripheral relations can be seen to be much more complex than simply a benign, win-win engagement with the region. They also result in tensions between China's modernisation and development goals, which other countries can mutually gain from, and China's territorial and status ambitions, which – if achieved – other countries will only lose from. Such a contrast results in frictions and challenges for both China and the region.

These tensions have manifested themselves in several disputes across China's periphery, and which encapsulate the various dimensions crucial to Beijing's *"zhoubian"* diplomacy in terms of trade, energy, territory and status. These factors are mutually inter-dependent, in the sense that gains made in one domain can lead to gains in the others, and which makes China's disputes in the South China Sea and the East China Sea of such strategic significance. Moreover, because of this intertwining the importance of prevailing in such contestations is effectively amplified – and arguably then amplified again by domestic nationalism – particularly concerning the issue of status and image, and China's overall restoration to international prominence. For these reasons, as much as assertively – and as we will see, at times aggressively – pursuing claims for small islands in the South China Sea and the East China Sea (as shown by the two boxed case studies) goes against the central pillars of China's *"zhoubian"* diplomacy, they are regarded as essential and are deeply emblematic of its national identity, as shaped by its long culture and history. Finally, observers also note Beijing's growing "need to assert the natural order of things and, if necessary, punish those who step out of line" (Jacques 2012: 381) in the region.

Case study 1: the South China Sea

The South China Sea dispute has been a longstanding issue within Chinese foreign policy and its wider peripheral policy. The extensive area of around 3,500,000 km^2 – including the assorted islands that dot the area – is variously claimed by China and Vietnam, while Brunei, Indonesia, Malaysia and the Philippines all have overlapping claims to its adjoining areas and their associated Exclusive Economic Zones (ICG 2012: 6–7). Such declarations have featured on Chinese maps for many centuries, and fall within the "nine-dash line" (*jiuduan xian*) declared in 1947 that demarcates China's territorial claims in the South China Sea (amounting to about 80% of its total area), and also encompasses Taiwan (another "lost territory" yet to be reclaimed after the Chinese Civil War of 1945–49). After WWII, China formally claiming sovereignty over the Paracel and Spratly Islands in 1951 during Allied peace treaty negotiations with Japan (Fravel 2011: 293). Other prominent territorial claims include Scarborough Shoal, which extend China's strategic reach deep into the south of the region, and all of which can be seen in Map 6.

At the beginning of the twenty-first century, China signed various agreements with the Association of South East Asian Nations (ASEAN), whose members include all the other countries who have claims in the South China Sea. These agreements – the "Declaration of the Code of Conduct in the South China Sea" signed in 2002, and the "Treaty of Amity and Cooperation" signed in 2003 – "formally commit(ted) China to enforcing the principles of non-aggression and non-interference" (Shambaugh 2005: 75). Such principles were central to the "Five Principles of Peaceful Coexistence," which have played a central part within Chinese foreign policy since the 1950s, and are part of China's wider stated peripheral relations policy. Notably, ASEAN and China signed an additional agreement in 2011 that stated China's re-adherence to the "Declaration

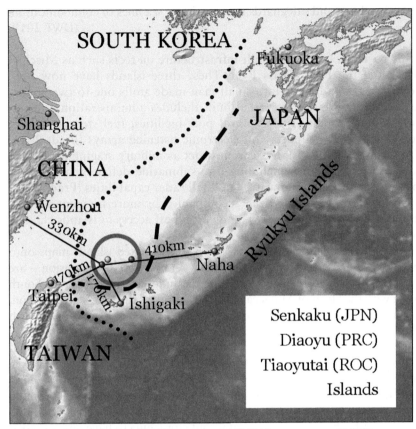

EXCLUSIVE ECONOMIC ZONES: ▬ ▬ CHINA   •••• JAPAN

Map 6 Territorial claims in the East China Sea

of the Code of Conduct in the South China Sea," which indicated to observers that this Declaration was not a binding agreement and could not be expected to fully constrain Chinese behaviour concerning the dispute (Fravel 2011: 311).

In 2016, the United Nations Permanent Court of Arbitration in the Hague ruled that China (and indeed the other countries with competing assertions) had no legal claim to the South China Sea (The Hague 2016: 1–2), which was a judgment that Beijing subsequently refused to recognise. China's claims were argued to violate the "United Nations Convention on the Laws of the Sea (UNCLOS)," as they fall within the 200 nautical mile Exclusive Economic Zones of five South East Asian countries. Regardless of this decision, and reflective of the trade, energy, territorial and status elements intrinsic to China's "*zhoubian*" diplomacy, in conjunction with a growing assertiveness and confidence in its regional diplomacy, China's 2019 "Defense White Paper" explicitly declared that:

> the South China Sea islands … (are an) inalienable part of the Chinese territory. China exercises its national sovereignty to build infrastructure and deploy necessary defensive capabilities on the islands and reefs in the South China Sea, … it

firmly upholds freedom of navigation and overflight by all countries in accordance
with international law and safeguards the security of sea lines of communication.

(DWF 2019)

In line with this position, China has built infrastructure on reefs such as Mischief
Reef, Subi Reef and the Fiery Cross Reef. These three islands have now been
reclaimed from the seas and made into small man-made atolls one-to-two square
miles in size. Infrastructure that has been built includes administration and service buildings, military landing strips, naval port facilities, fuel storage depots,
missile launch capabilities, heliports and electronic listening arrays (Pradt 2016:
137–139). From this basis, the islands can now act as military staging areas, and
encompass defensive capabilities including anti-submarine defences, air-defence
guns, antennas for satellite communication and full radar capabilities (Pradt 2016:
137–139). Such developments have been accompanied by more frequent sea and
air patrols in the region (Schuman 2016), and cutting off access to islands claimed
by other countries (Vuving 2017).

The importance of the disputed maritime area and associated islands maps onto
the central pillars of China's "*zhoubian*" diplomacy, and hence – by extension – are
thus indicative of its wider worldview concerning the Indo-Pacific. Firstly, the South
China Sea, along with the Strait of Malacca is at the fulcrum of the Indo-Pacific region,
interlinking Asia to India, Africa, the Middle East and Europe to the east and North
America to the west. The United Nations Conference on Trade and Development has
estimated that 70% of the total value of world trade, as well as one-third of all world
trade by volume passes through the South China Sea. This trade is valued to be worth
about \$3 trillion annually (The Guardian 2020). Underlying its centrally to China's
economy, and hence its modernisation and development goals *en route* to rebecoming
a great power, more than 60% of all China's trade transits the South China Sea (China
Power 2017). The South China Sea is also a vital route for China to have much-needed
oil and gas supplies transported to it from the Middle East.

Secondly, the South China Sea and in particular its myriad small islands are argued
to house vast energy resources. Although the precise amount of hydrocarbons is disputed, the potential benefits to Beijing in terms of meeting its ever-growing energy
needs – as well as the lower costs that such deposits would provide in terms of transport and protection, as well as reducing its dependence upon unstable regions such as
the Middle East – are clear. Securing such resources are seen as crucial to securing its
long-term prosperity and stability.

Thirdly, China's actions in the South China Sea contain a symbolic dimension which
relates to the dispute having a significant status element from the perspective of Beijing.
As such, many observers note how China uses territorial disputes in the South China
Sea (and elsewhere along its borders) as "diplomatic instruments to send signals to
other states and to test their commitments and responses" (Akos & Peragovics 2018:
372–376). Underlying such a strategy is the deeper aim of asserting China's pre-eminent
regional position, whilst limiting the presence of the United States in the Indo-Pacific.
In this way, the building of critical military infrastructure aims to deter the presence of
US naval vessels in the area (ICG 2012: 11–13). Overarching all of these elements is
the further motivation of using the dispute to evidence China's growing power projection capabilities as part of the modernisation of the country's military proficiency. Such
shows of strength also ably play to the domestic nationalist audience as evidence of

China "standing up" and asserting her historical civilisational rights, whereby China's true "natural position lies at the epicentre of East Asia" (Jacques 2012: 347).

Case study 2: the East China Sea

The dispute between China and Japan in the East China Sea centres on the Diaoyu (Chinese name)/Senkaku (Japanese name) islands. These islands are positioned between the Southern tip of Japan and Taiwan (see Map 7). The dispute over them also involves the government of the Republic of China (in Taipei) where these islands are known as Diaoyutai. The disputed island group is composed of five islands that are about 170 kilometres from both the nearest Japanese island and Taiwan but further from the mainland of the People's Republic of China (Sato 2019). As we will show, the strongest claim that the PRC makes in relation to sovereignty over these islands is through the claim of Taiwan. In short, if Taiwan is part of the People's Republic of China, then there is a strong (albeit disputed) historical claim, however if Taiwan is itself a separate and potentially sovereign entity, then the dispute over the islands is between Taiwan and Japan.

The history of the islands

The dispute over these islands came to global attention in the 1970s, since when it has variously punctuated relations between China and Japan. As noted at the outset of this

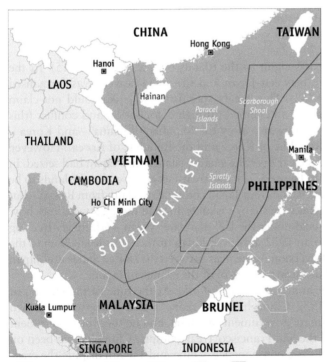

China and Taiwan   Malaysia   Vietnam   Brunei   Philippines

Map 7 Diaoyu/Senkaku disputed islands (Wikimedia Commons, David Vasquez)

chapter, under the traditional Chinese world order, China was an empire in which its borders and the level of direct political control of its landmass and population varied across different dynasties. However, unlike the clearly demarcated lines of boundaries between states that began to emerge in Europe after the Peace of Westphalia in 1648, the boundaries between states or cultures in East Asia were more fluid and permeable.

The Japanese claim to these islands is two-fold. First, Japan makes a claim based on historical ownership. In 1884, a Japanese businessman (called Koga) explored the islands and surrounding waters and found them to be excellent fishing grounds. The Japanese government subsequently investigated the ownership of the islands and declared them *terra nullius* or no-one's land. As a result, the islands became incorporated into the province of Okinawa, which subsequently leased the islands to Koga and houses were built on them (99 houses by 1909) (Sato 2019). According to the Japanese government this demonstrates ownership and occupation of the islands since 1884 and that they had been incorporated into the Japanese state since 1895 (MOFA 2015). During this period, the final dynasty in China was in power – the Qing. They made no opposition to the declaration of ownership, presence of buildings, or the use of the islands during this period, all of which further seemed to support the Japanese historical claim. However, China's argument is a little more nuanced. As China's approach to statehood was not based upon having direct control of land or a population, the legal understanding of the presence of the Japanese on these islands had different implications in China. In the Taiwanese records, these islands are "fishing posts" and from a Chinese perspective this is what the Japanese were using them for, whereby fishing outposts are distinct from owned lands. From this basis, until the advent of Western legal claims over the land in the inter wars years, there was no internal need for the Qing dynasty to claim "ownership."

The second premise for Japan's claim to the islands is legal (MOFA 2015). At the conclusion of WWII, the peace between Japan and the allied powers was formalised in the San Francisco Treaty (1952). This Treaty specified that Japan could not claim sovereignty over territories that it had claimed through colonisation and conflict (this included large territories such as Taiwan – now the Republic of China – and Korea – now the Democratic People's Republic of Korea and the Republic of Korea). However, unfortunately, the treaty was less clear over the smaller islands that Japan had seized. In Chapter 2, Article 2 (as shown in Figure 17.3), the Treaty sets out details of islands to be surrendered – including the Kuril Islands that Japan continues to claim from Russia – but it makes no mention of the Senkaku or Diaoyu islands. Instead the Treaty outlines how the "Pacific Islands" would be held under the UN mandate system – effectively freezing the determination of ownership. In 1972, however, Japan furthered its legal claim to the islands through the Okinawa Reversion Agreement between the United States and Japan that specified the return of administrative control of the islands to Japan.

China's challenge to this legal argument is two-fold. At the time of the signing of the San Francisco Treaty in 1952 China had undergone a civil war, producing two rival claims to being the legitimate government of China, and neither the government in Beijing nor in Taipei signed the San Francisco Treaty, despite China having been on the side of the victors in WWII. As a consequence, China and Taiwan dispute the credibility of the legal argument based on the Treaty put forward by Japan. The challenge placed against the 1972 reversion is importance because this was during the Cold War, just at the time when relations between the United States and China were warming.

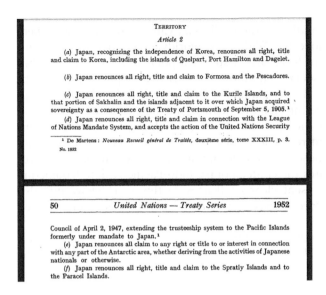

TERRITORY

Article 2

(a) Japan, recognizing the independence of Korea, renounces all right, title and claim to Korea, including the islands of Quelpart, Port Hamilton and Dagelet.

(b) Japan renounces all right, title and claim to Formosa and the Pescadores.

(c) Japan renounces all right, title and claim to the Kurile Islands, and to that portion of Sakhalin and the islands adjacent to it over which Japan acquired sovereignty as a consequence of the Treaty of Portsmouth of September 5, 1905.[1]

(d) Japan renounces all right, title and claim in connection with the League of Nations Mandate System, and accepts the action of the United Nations Security

[1] De Martens : *Nouveau Recueil général de Traités,* deuxième série, tome XXXIII, p. 3.
No. 1832

50   *United Nations — Treaty Series*   1952

Council of April 2, 1947, extending the trusteeship system to the Pacific Islands formerly under mandate to Japan.[1]

(e) Japan renounces all claim to any right or title to or interest in connection with any part of the Antarctic area, whether deriving from the activities of Japanese nationals or otherwise.

(f) Japan renounces all right, title and claim to the Spratly Islands and to the Paracel Islands.

Figure 17.3 UN Treatise, 1952 San Francisco Treaty, Chapter 2, Article 2.

There is one further complicating factor to China's claim to the islands. According to the San Francisco Treaty the land that has to be surrendered included "Formosa" an alternative name for what is now Taiwan. The disputed islands in the East China Sea have historically been a part of the territory of Formosa. As a result, the People's Republic of China's claim to the islands is premised on the ownership of Taiwan as well, which makes it a difficult legal argument to present internationally. In turn, as Taiwan could be argued to be the legal owner, but as Taiwan does not enjoy international legal status as a sovereign state, it cannot present its argument.

Current island relations

The dispute between China, Taiwan and Japan continues over the ownership of these islands. It became an issue of international significance in 2012 when the Japanese government agreed a deal to "buy" the islands from a Japanese businessman. This sparked months of tensions between the governments, with Chinese sailing patrol vessels close to the islands, and the Chinese people attacking Japanese businesses on mainland China. Tensions culminated in a crisis phone line agreement being set up between the two governments in order to avoid the eruption of conflict through a "mistake" by either the navies or the coastguards from either side. Since 2012, tensions between the PRC and Japan have oscillated over the islands, but neither side has revised its claim over the islands. As a result, it remains a point of potential conflict between both countries. This risk was increased after then US Secretary of State Clinton announced the inclusion of the Senkakus in the security protections covered under the US–Japan alliance. This coverage creates the potential that an issue between China and Japan over the Senkakus could ultimately produce conflict between China and the United States.

Conclusion

This chapter has presented an outline of the traditional Chinese world order, where borders were permeable and moveable. Within this worldview, control was less concerned with the legitimate use of force over a specified population or landmass but was instead imposed through social and cultural norms that required the consent of the governed to the emperor. The communities that were peripheral to this kingdom had a relationship governed through the payment of tributes but were rewarded with enhanced economic access and opportunities along with great assurance of non-interference. China's status, and recognition of this status, were central to such an order and, as this chapter has shown, is an understanding of the world that influences how Beijing conceives and relates the contemporary Indo-Pacific region. Competing accounts of the Indo-Pacific present clear challenges to this worldview, and also threaten Beijing's desire to restore its past civilisational position as a unrestrained regional power.

Through the chapter's case studies concerning China's current peripheral relations in the South China Sea and East China Sea, we have underscored the importance of the centrality and identity of the PRC. These case studies are emblematic of the Chinese conception of the Indo-Pacific and, more specifically, of the key points of contestation that this conception has with alternative views emanating from Japan, India and the United States, among others. We have also highlighted that, from Beijing's perspective, if other states acknowledge and defer to the power and centrality of China it will result in economic rewards for the region whether through bilateral win-win relations or through formal regional multilateral platforms including the Asian Infrastructure Bank or the Belt and Road Initiative. Such a perspective is not shared by other major regional powers – notably Japan, India and the United States – and is the basis for contestation and potential future confrontation between them.

Furthermore, the chapter showed that the legal frameworks and international law that form the basis of Japan's claim over the East China Sea islands, and in regard of the South China Sea dispute, presents a clear contrast to how China has traditionally governed the region, in particular highlighting the non-Western history of China's approach to peripheral relations. Again, such differences accentuate the deeper differences in how the Indo-Pacific region is regarded, and act as critical reference points for better understanding how notions of a Chinese world order – and thus the underlying identity and associated values/norms informing this identity – clearly affect and inform the nature and relevance of the Indo-Pacific and the relations between its constituent states.

References

Akos, Kopper and Tamas Peragovics (2018) 'Overcoming the Poverty of Western Historical Imagination: Alternative Analogies for Making Sense of the South China Sea Conflict', *European Journal of International Relations*, 25 (2): 360–382.

Beeson, Mark and Fujian Li (2012) 'Charmed or Alarmed? Reading China's Regional Relations', *Journal of Contemporary China*, 21 (73): 35–51.

Callahan, William (2004) 'National Insecurities: Humiliation, Salvation, and Chinese Nationalism', *Alternatives: Global, Local, Political*, 29: 199–218.

Callahan, William (2008) 'Chinese Visions of World Order: Post-Hegemonic or a New Hegemony?' *International Studies Review*, 10 (4): 749–761.

China Power (2017) 'How Much Trade Transits the South China Sea?' *China Power*, 2 August. Accessed at https://chinapower.csis.org/much-trade-transits-south-china-sea/.

Deng, Y. and F. Wang (2005) *China Rising: Power and Motivation in Chinese Foreign Policy* (Lanham, MD: Rowman and Littlefield).

DWF (2019) 'Full Text of 2019 Defense White Paper: "China's National Defense in the New Era" (English & Chinese Versions)', July 24. Accessed at https://www.andrewerickson.com /2019/07/full-text-of-defense-white-paper-chinas-national-defense-in-the-new-era-english -chinese-versions/

Fairbank, John King (1968) 'A Preliminary Framework', in John King Fairbank (ed.), *The Chinese World Order: Traditional China's Foreign Relations* (Cambridge, MA: Harvard University Press), 1–20.

FMPRC (1996) 'China's Position Paper on the New Security Concept', *Permanent Mission of the PRC to the UN*. Accessed at http://www.fmprc.gov.cn/ce/ceun/eng/xw/t27742.htm

Fravel, M. Taylor. (2011) 'China's Strategy in the South China Sea.' *Contemporary Southeast Asia*. 33(3): 292–319. JSTOR, http://www.jstor.org/stable/41446232. Accessed 27 Nov. 2022.

Glanville, Luke (2010) 'Retaining the Mandate of Heaven: Sovereign Accountability in Ancient China', *Millennium - Journal of International Studies*, 39 (2): 323–43.

Glaser, Bonnie S. and Evan S Medeiros (2007) 'The Changing Ecology of Foreign Policy-Making in China: The Ascension and Demise of the Theory of "Peaceful Rise"', *The China Quarterly*, 190: 291–310.

He, Baogang (2018) 'Chinese Expanded Perceptions of the Region and its Changing Attitudes towards the Indo-Pacific: A Hybrid Vision of the Institutionalization of the Indo-Pacific', *East Asia*, 35: 117–132.

Hemmings, John (2021) 'Measuring Shinzo Abe's Impact on the Indo-Pacific', East-West Centre. Accessed at 25 October 2021. https://www.eastwestcenter.org/publications/measuring-shinzo -abe%E2%80%99s-impact-the-indo-pacific.

Hughes, Christopher W. (2016) 'Japan's "Resentful Realism" and Balancing China's Rise', *The Chinese Journal of International Politics*, 9 (2): 109–150. https://doi.org/10.1093/cjip /pow004.

ICG (2012) 'Stirring Up the South China Sea', *International Crisis Group*, Asia Report, 223, April 23. Accessed at https://d2071andvip0wj.cloudfront.net/223-stirring-up-the-south -china-sea-i.pdf.

Jacques, M. (2012) *When China Rules the World*, Second Edition. (London: Penguin).

Jones, Catherine and Chi Zhang (2021) 'Chinese World Order, Sovereignty, and International Practice', in Christopher Smith (ed.), *Sovereignty in Global Perspective, Proceedings of the British Academy* (Oxford University Press, forthcoming).

Jones, Catherine and Shaun Breslin (2015) 'China in East Asia: Confusion on the Horizon', in Jamie Gaskarth (ed.), *Rising Powers, Global Governance and Global Ethics* (Abingdon: Routledge), 115–132.

Kang, David (2010) *East Asia before the West: Five Centuries of Trade and Tribute* (New York: Columbia University Press).

Khurana, Gurpreet M. (2019) 'What is the Indo-Pacific? The New Geo-Politics of the Asia-Centred Rimland', in Axel Berkofsky and Sergio Miracola (eds.), *Geopolitics by Other Means: The Indo-Pacific Reality* (Milan: Ledizioni LediPublishing), 13–32.

Lampton, David M. (2004) *Following The Leader: Ruling China, From Deng Xiaoping To Xi Jinping* (Berkeley, CA: University Of California Press).

Lanteigne, M. (2016) *Chinese Foreign Policy: An Introduction* (London: Routledge).

Li, Zhaojie (2002) 'Traditional Chinese World Order', *Chinese Journal of International Law*, 1 (1): 20–58.

Lind, J. (2018) 'Life in China's Asia: What Regional Hegemony Would Look Like', *Foreign Affairs*, 97 (2): 71–82.

Liu, Feng (2020) 'The Recalibration of Chinese Assertiveness: China's Responses to the Indo-Pacific Challenge', *International Affairs*, 96 (1): 9–27.

Loke, B. (2019) 'China's Rise and U.S. Hegemony: Navigating Great-Power Management in East Asia', *Asia Policy*, 26: 41–60.

Mutschler, Fritz-Heiner (2019) 'Comparing Confucius and Cicero: Problems and Possibilities', in Andrea Balbo and Jaewon Ahn (eds.), *Confucius and Cicero: Old Ideas for a New World, New Ideas for an Old World* (Dresden: De Gruyter), 7–28.

MOFA (2007) '"Confluence of the Two Seas" Speech by H.E.Mr. Shinzo Abe, Prime Minister of Japan at the Parliament of the Republic of India'. Accessed at 25 October 2021. https://www.mofa.go.jp/region/asia-paci/pmv0708/speech-2.html.

MOFA (2015) 'Japanese Territory: Senkaku Islands Information'. Accessed at 11 December 2020. https://www.mofa.go.jp/a_o/c_m1/senkaku/page1we_000009.html.

Mohan, Raja C. (2021) 'AUKUS, the Quad, and India's Strategic Pivot', *Foreign Policy*, September 23.

Ogden, Chris (2014) *Indian Foreign Policy: Ambition & Transition* (Cambridge: Polity).

Ogden, Chris (2017) *China and India: Asia's Emergent Great Powers* (Cambridge: Polity).

Ogden, Chris (2018) 'Tone Shift: India's Dominant Foreign Policy Aims Under Modi', *Indian Politics and Policy*, 1 (1): 3–23.

Ogden, Chris (2019) *A Dictionary of Politics and International Relations in China* (Oxford: Oxford University Press).

Panda, Jagannath P. (2019) 'India and the Pacific Ocean: The "Act East" between Trade, Infrastructure and Security', in Axel Berkofsky and Sergio Miracola (eds.), *Geopolitics By Other Means: The Indo-Pacific Reality* (Milan: Ledizioni LediPublishing), 71–97.

Pascal, Cleo (2021) 'Indo-Pacific Strategies, Perceptions Partnerships', Chatham House. Accessed at 25 October 2021. https://www.chathamhouse.org/2021/03/indo-pacific-strategies-perceptions-and-partnerships/02-us-and-indo-pacific.

Pradt, Tilman (2016) *China's New Foreign Policy: Military Modernisation, Multilateralism and the China Threat* (Basingstoke: Palgrave Macmillan).

Qin, Y. (2006) 'The Chinese School of International Relations Theory: Possibility and Necessity', [国际关系理论中国学派的可能与必然]. *Global Review*, 534: 32–33.

Rediff News (2007) 'Abe's Broader Asia Plan Irks China', Accessed at 25 October 2021. https://www.rediff.com/news/2007/aug/23japan.htm.

Ruggie, J.G. (1998) 'What Makes the World Hang Together? Neo-Utilitarianism and the Social Constructivist Challenge', *International Organisation*, 52 (4): 855–885.

San Francisco Treaty (1952) Accessed at 11 December 2020. https://treaties.un.org/doc/publication/unts/volume%20136/volume-136-i-1832-english.pdf.

Sato, Koichi (2019) 'The Senkaku Islands Dispute: Four Reasons of the Chinese Offensive - A Japanese View', *Journal of Contemporary East Asia Studies*, 8 (1): 50–82.

Schuman, Michael (2016) 'A South China Sea of Uncertainty: Anxieties are Growing Over Beijing's Activities in the Waterways Across East Asia', *US. News & World Report*, 10 June. Accessed at http://www.usnews.com/news/best-countries/articles/2016-06-10/why-you-need-to-care-about-the-south-china-sea.

Scott, David (2012) 'India and the Allure of the "Indo-Pacific"', *International Studies*, 49 (3–4): 165–188.

Shambaugh, David (2005) 'China Engages Asia: Reshaping the Regional Order', *International Security*, 29 (3): 64–99.

Stuart-Fox, Martin (2003) *Short History of China and Southeast Asia: Tribute, Trade and Influence* (Crows Nest: Allen and Unwin).

Taylor, Brendan (2020) 'Is Australia's Indo-Pacific Strategy an Illusion?' *International Affairs*, 96 (1): 95–109.

The Guardian (2020) 'South China Sea: US Unveils First Sanctions Linked to Militarisation', *The Guardian*, August 27. Accessed at https://www.theguardian.com/world/2020/aug/27/south-china-sea-us-unveils-first-sanctions-linked-to-militarisation.

The Hague (2016) *The South China Sea Arbitration*. Permanent Court of Arbitration. Accessed at https://pca-cpa.org/wp-content/uploads/sites/175/2016/07/PH-CN-20160712-Press-Release-No-11-English.pdf.

Tseng, Katherine Hui-Yi (2017) *Rethinking South China Sea Disputes: The Untold Dimensions And Great Expectations* (London: Routledge).

Vuving, Alexander L. (2017) 'How America Can Take Control in the South China Sea', *Foreign Policy*, February. Accessed at https://foreignpolicy.com/2017/02/13/how-the-u-s-can-take-control-in-the-south-china-sea/.

Wang, Mingming (2012) 'All Under Heaven (*tianxia*): Cosmological Perspectives and Political Ontologies in Pre-modern China', *HAU: Journal of Ethnographic Theory*, 2 (1): 337–383.

Zheng Wang. (2012) *Never Forget National Humiliation: Historical Memory in Chinese Politics and Foreign Relations*. New York: Columbia University Press.

Wilson, J.D. (2018) 'Rescaling to the Indo-Pacific: From Economic to Security-Driven Regionalism in Asia', *East Asia*, 35: 177–196.

Yan, Xuetong (2014) 'From Keeping a Low Profile to Striving for Achievement', *Chinese Journal of International Politics*, 7 (2): 153–184.

Zhang, Feng (2009) 'Rethinking the Tribute System: Broadening the Conceptual Horizon of Historical East Asian Politics', *Chinese Journal of International Politics*, 2: 545–574.

Zhang, Yongjin and Barry Buzan (2012) 'The Tributary System as International Society in Theory and Practice', *The Chinese Journal of International Politics*, 5 (1) Spring: 3–36.

18 India's tryst with the Indo-Pacific

Jitendra Uttam

India's tryst with the "Indo-Pacific"

India's discernible pivot to the evolving "Indo-Pacific" order has roots in its twin structural imbalances – one in the strategic sphere and the other in the economic domain.[1] The first imbalance, deeply embedded in India's security architecture, has been overtly focused on mitigating threats crossing continental borders but somewhat insufficient to build appropriate defences in the maritime domain. This over-emphasis on protecting continental borders has been shaped by India's traumatic history of numerous foreign invasions carried out through land routes. However, age-old pre-occupation with continental security in India has failed to take note of security breaches from the maritime domain that paved the way for the country's eventual colonisation. A highly imbalanced strategic approach has produced yawning gaps in India's security strategy. As a result, strategic discourse centred on continental vs. maritime threats has been raging on since independence (Gill 2016).

Adding further intricacy to this strategic imbalance, a remarkable economic rise of East Asia has contributed in the sudden spike of naval activities in the Indian and Pacific Oceans. In a more specific terms, China's rise and its naval build-up has made it almost impossible for India to continue with its traditional neglect of maritime security. In recent times, China's ascent in the global power hierarchy coupled with its aggressive posturing from the South China Sea to the Himalayan border with India has made it all the more important to seek early resolution of the accumulated strategic imbalance. Even at the time of independence, some scholars believed that India's fragmented strategic vision has effectively hindered the evolution of a balanced approach to address the country's pressing security needs (Panikkar 1945; Vaidya 1949). It is true that Mahanian "principles of sea power" attracted Indian strategic thinkers early on but in reality government has been unable to live with its own pronouncements to fund credible maritime defences.[2]

On top of this fragmented strategic approach, India's other imbalance emerges from its inward-looking developmental journey that has produced a stark developmental divide between India and the major economies of East Asia. A distinct unevenness in the process of economic development has transformed one part of Asia to nearly become a developed region but leaving the other part to remain embroiled in chronic poverty and acute joblessness. India could not become party to East Asia's unprecedented economic dynamism. Unfortunately, India with other South Asian peers remained very much part of this underdeveloped Asia. Mostly governed by the logic of "flying geese," the export-oriented East Asian production network could not accommodate

DOI: 10.4324/9781003336143-23

import-substitution dependent economies like India (Akamatsu 1962). A persistent "structure-strategy disconnect," defined by a mismatch between nationally available resources and the focus of developmental strategy, made India a reluctant partner of East Asia's significantly high economic convergence. The relative economic weakness of India diminished its chances to become part of Asia's geoeconomic regionalisation process spear-headed by an "Asia-Pacific" identity and aptly represented by organisations like APEC, ASEAN and ASEAN+3.

Clearly out of sync with East Asia's export-oriented bandwagon, Indian leadership started to concentrate on the politics of development, rather than sticking to the economics of development. In an attempt to counter East Asia's dominant geoeconomic rationale, India developed a degree of comfort with the Western geopolitical narrative on Asia, which saw the "future of Asia in the past of Europe (Yoon 2014). India's outright rejection to China's ambitious Belt and Road Initiative (BRI) and sudden U-turn from joining the Regional Comprehensive Economic Partnership (RCEP) hints at the country's growing apprehension towards the region's emergent geoeconomic arrangements. It can be said that India's persistent weakness in the economic front compelled its leadership to stand with "other likeminded countries" and "willing powers" to embrace a conflict-ridden geopolitical vision for Asia.

The abovementioned twin imbalances that India accumulated over the period became much sharper due to the rise of China as a great power. In the midst of a general disequilibrium marked by the Sino–US discord at the global level and a growing power asymmetry between India and China at the regional level, there seems to be urgency in New Delhi to address these imbalances. A growing presence of China in the Indian Ocean made India's ongoing strategic shift from continental to maritime all the more desirable. Similarly, India's spiralling trade deficits with a number of East Asian countries necessitated a better economic balance between its mass-manufacturing and knowledge-intensive services, including growing calls to restructure global supply chains overtly centred in China.

The mounting pressure to resolve ever-hardening structural imbalances came as a wake-up call to New Delhi. In its search to rebalance the twin imbalances, India stresses maintaining mutually beneficial symbiotic relations between the crucial spheres of security and economy. By highlighting complementarity between security and economy, India has been articulating a mutually reinforcing strategic and economic vision under the acronym "SAGAR," which means 'Sea" in the Hindi language but in English it stands for "security and prosperity to all." SAGAR highlights the fact that India is not convinced to see "security" in an isolated context but envisions it as complementary to prosperity and vice versa.

India's search for an appropriate venue to voice the legitimate concerns regarding its pronounced goals to simultaneously achieve security and prosperity ends with a much more inclusive "Indo-Pacific" order. "Confluence of the two Seas" – a famous speech delivered by Japanese Premier Shinzo Abe in the Indian Parliament provided further fillip to India's search for a broad-based multi-lateral platform. Though still at the level of a vision, the idea of "Indo-Pacific" offers a holistic security paradigm involving not only military affairs but also reaching out to trade, investment and maritime connectivity across the Indo-Pacific region. Aiming to undercut Chinese influence in the region, the Indian leadership has envisioned that a broad-based multi-lateral platform like the "Indo-Pacific" with the potential and necessary means to adequately address disjunctions arising from its accumulated imbalances is the need of hour.

A wider consensus to associate with a multilateral initiative in the Indo-Pacific framework has the potential to provide India with a chance to achieve greater strategic and economic rebalance (Khurana 2017; Gill 2016; Singh 2017; Trofimov 2020). Against this backdrop, India's political leadership and its diverse strategic community have visibly moved to embrace the US-led and its allies-supported "Indo-Pacific" initiative. This new found policy consensus made India's tryst with the "Indo-Pacific" destiny a rare reality.[3] "Geopolitically the adoption of the term Indo-Pacific reflects a shift of focus by India from land (the Indian subcontinent) to maritime concerns (Scott 2018). India's attraction to the Indo-Pacific is such that "Gradually, Act 'East' is getting transformed into Act 'Indo-Pacific'" (De 2020). Indeed, India's much talked about shift towards the Indo-Pacific strives to balance its twin imbalances that have existed due to its neglect of maritime security and persistent avoidance of economic imbalance with East Asian economies (Pant 2017).

Nonetheless, rebalancing the strategic and economic priorities of a large country like India are easier said than done. Historical legacies and contemporary interests often squabble against such priorities and preferences needed for wider adjustments. While attempting to achieve a difficult transition from an earlier era of "autonomy" to current needs of "coordination," India has come a long way to reset its foreign policy thinking based on accommodating its national interest with others' pursuit of power. Though, considering India's history of battling super power imposed bipolarity during the Cold War period and its long association with the non-aligned movement, there is still a space for an alternative narrative to India's over-hyped tilt towards the Indo-Pacific. Aptly representing this view, a report titled "NAM 2.0" argues that, "India can reap similar benefits, if it follows 'neutrality' with both, the US and China" (Khilnani et. al. 2012).

The ideas and arguments in this chapter are organised in the following manner. The next section locates how and why India's strategic and economic imbalances require lasting solutions. The following section discusses logics and rationales to resolve India's twin imbalances by tracing Mahanian logic to resolve its strategic imbalance as well as learning from East Asia's "structure-strategy connect" to effectively contain the imbalance in the economic sphere. The fourth section constructs an empirical foundation to gauge the momentum of India's evolving ideas, institutions and policies aimed at engaging with the "Indo-Pacific" vision. The fifth section highlights policy lessons requiring simultaneous management of opposing paradigms across polity, economy and security to make India an integral part of "Indo-Pacific" strategy. And the final section concludes that the "Indo-Pacific," not the earlier era of the "Asia-Pacific" order, has the potential to help India sort out its twin imbalances deeply embedded in its strategic and economic structures.

India's twin structural imbalances

A sub-continental sized geographic spread, a complex history of invasions and relative economic decline in comparison to East Asian countries – all of these factors contributed in the making of India's structural imbalances. However, for our discussion, we concentrate on the twin imbalances that have firmed-up in the strategic and economic spheres. The first "strategic imbalance" originates from India's persistent gap between continental and maritime security and the second "economic imbalance" is embedded in the country's relative underperformance as compared to economically dynamic East Asia, particularly China.

Strategic imbalance: continental vs. maritime focus

Historically, India has witnessed a series of invasions grossly undermining its security in the areas adjoining the North-Western frontier. The Archaemenians (549 BCE–331 BCE) the Huns (fourth and fifth century CE), the Kushans (second century BC–third century AD), and the Mughals (1526–1761), all came from the continental routes to establish their control over large swaths of Indian Territory. Numerous threats travelling through land routes continued even after independence. The War with Pakistan in 1965, 1971, border clashes with China in 1962 and the Kargil War in 1999 with Pakistan had continental dimensions. These security breaches made successive Indian rulers pay adequate attention to the continental dimension of national defence. In reality, safeguarding India's land frontiers became the top priority to its security establishment.

An obvious strategic polarisation favouring continental security and ignoring maritime challenges left a dangerous gap in India's strategic planning. A persistent weakness in maintaining India's credible maritime security did provide ample space for Portuguese, Dutch, British and French trading firms to establish their outposts in India's coastal areas. These Western trading outposts eventually became precursors to the nation's colonial subjugation. India paid dearly for its historical mistake of concentrating its energy on securing continental routes and allowing indifference to prevail over its maritime security.

Yet, India's reality of "a maritime ring around the continental interior" has always reminded its strategic planners to pursue a vigorous security strategy with the ability to simultaneously fight-off continental and maritime threats. Considering the complex nature of pressures and threats, it has been argued that India's security challenges have largely been continental in nature, though maritime security has not been outside its strategic purview (Gill 2016). Some even argue, "Indian maritime capabilities ... will have to be balanced by securing and strengthening the Indian heartland itself where India's core interests lie" (Singh 2014).

Responding to the complexities in managing the security of a large country, it has been argued that "India's geopolitical location requires a corresponding multi vector geo-strategy – where no one region or location must overwhelm or negate India's priorities, interests and projection of influence in other directions" (Singh 2014).This multi-faceted strategic situation in India has been termed as "territorially vexatious and aspirationally maritime" (Raghavendra 2014). Nonetheless, strategic understanding aimed at stressing both continental and maritime threats remains was limited to an abstract level, ignoring practical aspects involving economic means to adequately fund a balanced approach to national security.

In a noteworthy development, India's age-old strategic dilemma of whether to focus on continental or maritime defences is increasingly getting resolved in favour of upgrading maritime forces. A renewed push towards safeguarding maritime borders in India comes with the continuation of Asian prosperity. Decades of exponential growth in the Chinese economy have given significant rise to maritime activities in India's "extended neighbourhood." The rise of China, even aside from its aggressive behaviour exhibited in the South China Sea and in the Sino-Indian border in the high Himalayas, has become a complex strategic challenge for India. Significantly expanded Chinese activities in the vast oceanic expanse have culminated into enduring strategic rivalries. Some even fear that an extraordinary growth in the Chinese power has opened up the possibility of an emerging Sino-sphere indicating the relapse of the "Chinese World Order," which once brought many Asian countries under its "tributary system" – a distinct form of Chinese imperialism based on the symbolic conformity to Confucian values and norms (Fairbank 1941).

In the face of a dramatic rise in Chinese influence in the region, India has been confronting a fundamental strategic challenge – how to secure and promote its national interests in a grossly unbalanced strategic environment in Asia. Not only India but also, in view of the rapid expansion of East Asia's export-oriented mass-producing industries, governments in the region are increasingly worried about the security of sea-lanes carrying large amounts of industrial goods, raw materials and energy resources. This constant worry about economic security has translated into increased budgets for developing blue water naval power by a number of countries in Asia. An ever increasing presence of Chinese naval bases from Gwadar, a seaport located in Pakistan's Baluchistan province, to Djibouti, a strategic port on the mouth of the Red Sea, has caused alarm bells to ring in the capitals of the Indo-Pacific region, including New Delhi. Adding to the pressure, "The People's Liberation Army (PLA) is already making serious headway securing new bases in Cambodia, Tanzania, and the United Arab Emirates, among other locales" (Singleton 2021).

A marked rise in the strategic value of maritime security has compelled many strategic thinkers to see beyond India's traditional focus towards continental threats (Srinivasan 2011; Prakash 2012; Sakhuja 2011; Trofimov 2020; Singh 2021). "India now plans to fast-track its ongoing rebalance of military forces and firepower to the northern borders with China and the critical Indian Ocean Region (IOR), in a decisive shift away from the decades-long focus on the western front with Pakistan and combating militancy" (Pandit 2020).

Though consensus about India's security concerns seems to be moving firmly beyond the continental threats, India's strategic community has yet to develop an adequate maritime consciousness. Having almost 7,500 kilometres (km) of coastline and about 14,500 km of navigable waterways, India is blessed with a geography that touches major sea routes. Giving due consideration to its maritime potential, the first ever maritime India Summit was held on 14 April 2016 in Mumbai articulating "Sagar Mala National Perspective Plan" that aims at expediting the country's economic development by harnessing the potential of its coastline and river network. "It envisages about 572 projects at an investment of over Rs 8.4 lakh crore ($120 billion) over 20 years from 2015 – for port modernisation, port connectivity enhancement, port-linked industrialisation and coastal community development" (Press Information Bureau 2016). The importance of oceans to India's strategic interests is confirmed by the fact that the country's five among its top-ten destinations and seven top import origins, in value terms, are located in the Indo-Pacific rim. "The leading import destinations of India on the Indo-Pacific include China, UAE, Saudi Arabia, Iraq, Kuwait, Australia and Indonesia. The export destinations are UAE, China, Singapore, Hong Kong and Indonesia" (Raghavendra 2014).

"In military security terms, the budget share of the Indian Navy has increased from 14.9 percent to 19.3 percent during the period 2000–2013, but it continues to be the least funded among the three services" (Raghavendra 2014). "The Navy's share of the Defence Budget has declined from 18 per cent of India's defence budget in 2012 to approximately 13 per cent in 2019-20" (Bhalla 2019). However, the seriousness of the government's task to realise strategic rebalance has resulted in the enhanced focus on the Indian Ocean Region (IOR) and an overall willingness to upgrade maritime security. This is reflected in the defence budget of 2022–23, where a massive jump of around 43% has been marked for the modernisation of the Indian navy (Dutta 2022). Though late but at last, it seems that the Indian navy is getting attention back to fulfil its role as a balancer in a traditionally dominant continental focus.

India's willingness to strike a better balance between its continental and maritime security strategy is still not adequate to face mounting pressure from intensifying Chinese naval activities. There is growing awareness in New Delhi that a multi-lateral understanding is needed to counter strategic pressures coming from belligerent Chinese behaviour. A serious commitment to find a realistic resolution to India's strategic imbalance sees a highly inclusive Indo-Pacific order as an appropriate strategy to face growing security vulnerabilities in the region. To this end, India has shown strategic flexibility by moving out from its time-tested policy of "autonomy" based on "neutrality" and entering into the unchartered territory of "coordination" with "like minded countries."

Perspectives on India's approach to the Indo-Pacific

India's ever-tighter embrace of the Indo-Pacific strategy lies in the very process by which it intends to resolve long-standing imbalances adversely impacting its strategic and economic priorities. The ongoing efforts to resolve the strategic imbalance are been accomplished by re-invigorating India's traditionally neglected maritime defences. In order to institute a credible maritime strategy, India has taken inference from Mahanian realist principles favouring substantial enhancement in the country's naval preparedness (Mahan 1987) To this end, India's growing maritime centrality finds the "Indo-Pacific" as an appropriate framework to counter Beijing's growing encroachment in the Indian Ocean under the "string of pearls" strategy designed to encircle India (Ashraf 2017).

Mahanian perspective influencing India's maritime strategy

In a bid to resolve its long-standing strategic imbalance between over-emphasised continental threats and under-recognised maritime safety, India has shown flexibility in accommodating diverse perspectives and unorthodox views. Admittedly, striking a re-balance between India's continental and maritime security has never been easy but increasingly strategic thinking has been gravitating towards a convergence that a vigorous maritime strategy is key to resolve its strategic imbalance. An obvious tilt towards securing maritime frontiers in India derives its conceptual and operational logics from an American strategic thinker Alfred Thayer Mahan who propagated realism in diplomacy and identified the dominating role that sea power played in the shaping of the world history (Mahan 1987).

In recent times, due to the phenomenal rise of China as a new super power, maritime threats have become all the more vital for India. Unlike the Soviet Union, China is an export-oriented mass-producing economy that relies heavily on international trade conducted through oceanic routes. Hence, securing sea-lanes has become the utmost priority for the Chinese navy. The pressing need to secure the vast oceanic expanse has compelled China to establish a chain of naval bases. In this context, the strategic presence of China in Gwadar, a port in the Arabian Sea to Djibouti, a port located on the mouth of Red Sea has made New Delhi become extra vigilant.

Impact of Mahanian ideas on India's strategic thinking

In a bid to rebalance its strategic posturing, India after independence has increasingly come under the influence of a strategic doctrine put forward by Alfred Thayer Mahan. The mainstays of contemporary realist international thought, Mahanian ideas played a key role in shaping the US naval expansion that quickly filled the strategic void created by a retreating British naval presence in the oceans. India is witnessing the same impact the Mahanian ideas had on the shaping of the US maritime strategy at the turn of nineteenth century, while going through its naval expansion in the twenty-first century. Early on, some strategic thinkers in India echoed Mahanian ideas. In his book *India and the Indian Ocean* (1945), Indian historian and diplomat, Kavalam Panikkar invokes Mahanian argument by stressing the strategic value of the Indian Ocean. In a similar vein, Keshav Vaidya (1949) argued for a credible maritime strategy and advocated a whole ring of Indian naval bases, outside India, spanning the Ocean (Vaidya 1949). Mahanian ideas advocating naval expansion did help contemporary Indian strategic thinking to explore national power via the maritime route (Pugh 1996; Mohan 2012; Scott 2006). Unfortunately, the Mahanian strategic value attached to sea power could not be translated into Indian strategic planning and budgetary allocations.

It is believed that India's pivotal position in the Indian Ocean was suitable to deploy credible naval power (Tellis 1985). Indeed, "very few nations in the world geography dominate an ocean area as India dominates the Indian Ocean" (Misra 1986). India is a littoral state, but at the same time, it is the only country that geographically projects "into" the Ocean; its long triangular wedge-shaped landmass extends some 2413.5 km into the Indian Ocean (Scott 2006). Besides India's geographical pre-imminence in the vast oceanic expanse, its growth momentum post-1991 reforms facilitated a marked increase in international trade resulting in a growing dependence on the transport of energy and raw materials passing through a vast network of sea lanes. Moreover, China's expanding influence in the Indian Ocean through the launch of the BRI (Belt and Road Initiative), particularly its flagship US$62 billion China–Pakistan Economic Corridor (CPEC), are major drivers behind India realising its "Mahanian moment" with a decisive seaward turn.[4]

Mahanian impact on Indian Government

The forward-looking ideas of Indian strategic thinkers like Panikkar (1945) and Vaidya (1949) stressing Mahan's "principle of sea power" could not be fully comprehended by the leadership in New Delhi. India's first Prime Minister Jawaharlal Nehru, with ancestry in the Himalayan region of Kashmir, understood national security from the traditionally recognised continental prism, not in the Mahanian style of naval power projection. "In theory, Nehru gave weight to India's potential role in the Indian Ocean … but in reality his vision never became a reality" (Scott 2006). During his early years in the administration (1948–1951), the Indian navy's allocation in the total defence budget was a meagre 4.7 to 4.8%, which reached 10.1% in 1955–1957, but again slipped back to the single digit 9.7% in 1957–1958 (Scott 2006).

Even after Nehru, the Indian navy remained the least funded branch of the armed forces. Due to persistent economic constraints and other military contingencies, India's maritime sphere remained relegated to the margins in its strategic priorities and spending plans. India's naval weakness continued with minor adjustments. Following the 1962 border War with China, India's naval budget further received a jolt as it touched an all-time low of 3.4% in 1963–1964 (Scott 2006). Though allocation to the navy moved slightly higher touching 8.8% in 1979–1980, India's strategic focus persistently favoured the continental approach. India was "still a relatively weak naval power," only a "localized one" operating in its immediate coastal waters (Palmer 1972).

The Rajiv Gandhi administration demonstrated much more willingness to expand the country's naval power. India obtained a Charlie-class nuclear submarine from the Soviet Union, and re-commissioned it as *INS Chakra* during the period 1988–1991. However, disintegration of the Soviet Union and the resultant balance of payments crisis in India disrupted supply from the most significant source of weapons. India's economic downturn at the turn of the 1990s rendered "a major setback to the modernization and expansion plans of the Navy" (Singh 1999). Given India's limited capacity to allocate a budget for the navy, scholars even started to argue that "it may not be feasible for developing states to sustain a Mahanist momentum" (Pugh 1996; Dasgupta 1994).

Though Indian strategic thinking at the government level took a decisive turn after Hindu nationalist Bharatiya Janata Party (BJP) came into power in 1998. After a long time, India witnessed a strong political will to increase its overall defence spending. In its first budget for 1989–1999, the BJP-led Vajpayee administration allocated 14.5% of the budget to the navy in the total defence budget (Scott 2006). Echoing the new political thinking towards national security, the Ministry of Defence (2001) announced, "India's security environment extends from the Persian Gulf in the west to the Straits of Malacca in the east … to the Equator in the south."[5] For the first time, India provided a pan-Indian Ocean perspective to its maritime strategy (Singh 2003). India's tryst with its oceanic destiny, as envisioned by Panikkar (1945) and Vaidya (1949), took more than half a century to come into play

Acting earnestly to catch up with its own "Mahanian pronouncements," India has witnessed a substantial increase of around 43% allocated for the modernisation of the Indian navy in the defence budget of 2022–2023. Still, some are quite sceptical about India's ability to transform itself from continental to maritime power. According to Varun Sahni, the failed Soviet attempt to become a naval power in the 1970s to 1980s should act as "a cautionary tale for India's Mahanian navalists … [and] a grim warning of what happens to a continental state that harbours overly grandiose maritime ambitions" (Sahni 2010).

Economic context impacting India's outreach to the Indo-Pacific

East Asia's turn from geoeconomics to geopolitics has origins in its paradoxical process of economic development. On one side, East Asia's outward-oriented mass-production strategy led to the formation of a virtuous cycle based on mass-employment, mass-consumption facilitated via fulfilling overseas demand and eventually fuelling mass-prosperity. East Asia's extraordinary transformation from agrarian to industrial era accelerated intra-Asian trade, investment and technology flows. Surprisingly, within one generation, many of the paddy-growing poor agrarian economies were converted into highly industrialised clusters.

However, on the other side, a resounding success of East Asian economies could not impact anaemic growth that India and other South Asian countries experienced. India's failing developmental saga, marked by inward-looking, capital-intensive heavy industry, earnestly helped in perpetuating an age-old vicious cycle of mass-unemployment, low consumption and mass-poverty. India's persistent weakness in the mass-manufacturing industries and below average performance in the export sector resulted in the ever-growing trade deficits from economically dynamic East Asian economies. According to the Ministry of Commerce and Industry, "India's trade deficit with NEA countries in 2015-16 stood at USD 63.28 billion which is 53.3% of India's total trade deficit (USD 118.72 billion). China accounts for 56.6% of NEA's total trade, while Hong Kong, Japan and Korea contribute 14.5%, 11.6 % and 13.3 % respectively" (Pandit 2020). As a result, contrasting intra-regional development became the hallmark of the post-WWII Asian developmental landscape.

Being at the losing end, South Asia's biggest economy India increasingly became marginalised in the geoeconomically inclined East Asian regionalism. India could not gain entry into "Asia-Pacific" institutions in charge of promoting regional co-operation and integration. Institutions like APEC, ASEAN and ASEAN+3 kept their doors shut for India. Not only India but countries in the West also felt neglected in East Asia, which was fully engrossed in reaping the benefits of export-oriented growth momentum. In a short span of time, East Asia transformed itself into a "supply-side pole" and reduced India and other Western countries into a "demand-side pole." This glaring demand-supply mismatch helped economies in the region to corner large trade surpluses. Accumulated economic losses invoked political bickering. Soon, political churning provided a fertile ground for India and other like-minded countries to look for a way out from the loss-making geo-economic push that exclusively promoted the interests of the region's highly successful export-oriented economies, particularly China, that rapidly evolved as the new core of global mass-manufacturing.

A well thought out solution to contain growing economic imbalance, both at intra-regional and inter-regional levels, came in the form of geopolitical assertion organised in the multi-lateral framework. This shift ensured growing irrelevance of geo-economics which in turn led to the withering away of the Asia-Pacific identity construct that promoted trade and investment through institutions like APEC and ASEAN. Instead, deeply embedded in the region's geopolitical reality, the Indo-Pacific strategic re-imagination attracted the attention of many countries in the region and beyond. After seriously contemplating its various policy options, the leadership in New Delhi decided to embrace the Indo-Pacific vision. It makes sense to argue that India's demonstrated commitment to the Indo-Pacific lies on a highly visible intra-regional developmental divide. Caught in the middle of poverty and underdevelopment, India confronts two stark choices – either bridge the economic gap by removing the accumulated economic imbalance or bypass the economic imbalance by changing the policy track from geo-economics to geopolitics. India is in the process of choosing the second option. It aims to ignore the economic imbalance by articulating a geopolitical agenda in partnership with other countries increasingly wary of China's growing stature. It can be said that India's open-arm embrace of the Indo-Pacific vision is not exclusively linked to its strategic imbalance but it has a lot to do with the country's lagging behind in the Asian developmental race.

Considering Mahanian ideas emphasising a credible maritime strategy and economic ideas supporting changes in the regional strategy from geoeconomics to geopolitics,

India is up to a delicate balancing and bargaining to fulfil its dual objectives – security with prosperity. In other words, India's seemingly open-ended acceptance of the Indo-Pacific is conditional. India wishes to achieve a holistic security that encompasses prosperity, not a segmented and partial military security devoid of economic gains. Though India's engagement with the Indo-Pacific is seemingly tilted towards strategic ends the leadership in New Delhi is really concerned about capturing economic opportunities as well.

Evolution and development of India's "Indo-Pacific" strategy

India's concerted bid to resolve its long-standing imbalances has provided greater impetus to mend fences with the Indo-Pacific strategy. The ideas of leaders, policy makers and a strategic community in New Delhi started to converge into a coherent "Indo-Pacific" vision (Panikkar 1945). The pull of promises made by the "Indo-Pacific" is such that India decided to depart from its time-tested policy of "neutrality" promoted in the framework of "strategic autonomy." Instead, India has shown a clear inclination to follow the path of "strategic co-ordination" with like-minded countries in the Indo-Pacific region.

India's new-found interest in convergence with the Indo-Pacific vision reflects a fundamental change in its foreign policy thinking. "The Indo-Pacific therefore is a new domain in India's foreign policy engagements, representing a shift in New Delhi's strategic environment – expanding its threats solely from its continental borders to its maritime space." India's pivot to the "Indo-Pacific" hints towards a fusion of its *Look South* and *Look East* policies gradually widened since the 2000s (Pant 2017). Some even consider that the Indo-Pacific became a "new template of analysis" to examine the latest trends in Indian security and foreign policy (Pant 2018).

India's outreach to the "Indo-Pacific": from a reluctant observer to a close partner

India's engagement with the Indo-Pacific has witnessed two distinct phases – initially as a reluctant observer and then as a close partner. Considering its extensive trade relations and long land border with the northern neighbour China, India in the beginning adopted a cautious approach to any idea that Beijing saw in a negative light, including the Indo-Pacific (Pant 2019). Sensing India's foreign policy shift towards geopolitical considerations, China from the very beginning did develop resistance to any effort undermining its successful geoeconomic strategy. "When the Quad was originally proposed in 2007, diplomatic protest from China had caused India and Australia to roll back their commitments" (Park 2017).

However, India's perception and attitude towards China began to change with Beijing's turn to aggressiveness demonstrated during the Doklan (2017) and Galvan (2020) incidences. The military stand-off in the border region made India openly oppose China's assertive agenda. Beijing's unilateral attempts to rewrite the rule-based liberal democratic order persuaded New Delhi to fully embrace the Indo-Pacific order. India even joined seemingly anti-China groupings like QUAD and explicitly opposed China's ambitious infrastructural projects under BRI, particularly its flagship projects like CPEC and MSRI.

Indo-Pacific vision and Indian strategic community

The term Indo-Pacific is not as new as it has been projected. The first use of the term goes as far back as 1920 when Karl Haushofer, a German scholar of geopolitics, used "Indo-Pacific Space" to highlight the resurgence of Asia (Parthasarathy 2017). However, in its current understanding, Peter Cozens, a noted strategic analyst from New Zealand, used the term in 2005 (Parameswaran 2018). A significant rise in China's power projection provided greater impetus to India and Japan to initiate conversations discussing the Indo-Pacific in 2005. Though, in its contemporary context, "Indo-Pacific" acquires real meaning only after Japanese Prime Minister Shinzo Abe talked about "Arc of Freedom and Prosperity" (Pasinetti 1983). This was the first attempt to politically conceptualise the vision of the "Indo-Pacific" into a real foreign policy discourse.

Among the Indian strategic community, the first usage of the term "Indo-Pacific" took place in Indian naval circles. It was formally mentioned in India's 2004 Naval Doctrine which noted "the shift in global maritime focus from the Atlantic-Pacific combine to the Pacific-Indian Ocean region." Premvir Das, former Chief of Eastern Naval Command, made the first reference to the "Indo-Pacific" in 2006. Again, Gurpreet Khurana, former Commander in the Indian Navy, used the term "Indo-Pacific" in connection with maritime co-operation with Japan in 2007, and in 2008 in connection with competition with China (Prakash 2012). Shyam Saran, the former Foreign Secretary (2004–2006), provided further impetus to the idea of the "Indo-Pacific" by underlining it as "a logical corollary to India's Look East policy" (Saran 2011).

Discourse on the "Indo-Pacific" within the government

The Indian government's discourse on the Indo-Pacific moves from "geoeconomics" during the Congress-led Manmohan Singh administration to "geopolitics" under the BJP-led Narendra Modi administration (Press Trust of India 2018b). The reasons behind this directional shift in the foreign policy are deeply rooted in the process of how India tries to resolve its twin imbalances deeply embedded in the country's strategic and economic structures.

Box 18.1 Timeline: key statements and documents on the Indo-Pacific

Date	Country	Publication
May 3, 2013	Australia	Australia releases its Defence White Paper identifying the Indo-Pacific as the new theatre and highlights the strategic shift to the Asia-Pacific and the Indian Ocean Rim.
7 September 2013	China	Chinese president Xi Jinping announces the One Belt One Road project (now the Belt and Road Initiative [BRI]).
12 December 2015	India and Japan	India and Japan issue the first joint statement on the Indo-Pacific and the world.

(Continued)

Date	Country	Publication
10 October 2015	India	The Indian Navy releases the Indian maritime security strategy, identifying the shift to the Indo-Pacific.
27 August 2016	Japan	Japanese Prime Minister Shinzo Abe presents the Indo-Pacific vision at the Sixth Tokyo International Conference on African Development.
April 2017	Japan	Japan launches its report on free and open Indo-Pacific strategy.
December 2017	United States	The United States identifies the Indo-Pacific as the new theatre in its national security strategy.
30 May 2018	United States	The United States renames the US Pacific Command as the Indo-Pacific Command.
1 June 2018	India	Prime Minister Modi presents India's Indo-Pacific vision at the Shangri-La Dialogue.
22 June 2019	ASEAN	ASEAN releases a document on its outlook on the Indo-Pacific.
June 2019	France	France releases its strategy on the Indo-Pacific.
June 2020	India-Australia	Joint Declaration on a Shared Vision for Maritime Cooperation in the Indo-Pacific Between the Republic of India and the Government of Australia
October 2021	ASEAN-India	ASEAN-India Joint Statement on Cooperation on the ASEAN Outlook on the Indo-Pacific for Peace, Stability, and Prosperity in the Region.
February 2022	United States	Joint Statement on Quad Cooperation in the Indo-Pacific.

Note: Australia, Japan and the United States have continued to update their Indo-Pacific visions and strategies.
Source: Darshana M. Baruah (2020), and author's own compilation

MANMOHAN SINGH ADMINISTRATION'S APPROACH TO THE INDO-PACIFIC, 2011–2014

The arguments regarding the Indo-Pacific began to appear in India's mainstream foreign policy debates during the second term of the Manmohan Singh administration. Due to the accelerated pace of capital flows, investment linkages and the emergence of regional production networks, an added emphasis on building Asian regional architecture became a common practice. Converging geoeconomic interests became the prime mover to any dialogue focusing on regional co-ordination and integration. India's Ambassador to the United States, Nirupama Rao, officially used the term Indo-Pacific for the first time when she argued that "continuance of economic growth and prosperity ... is in many ways linked to the Indo-Pacific region" (Rao 2011). By July 2012, Salman Khurshid, Indian Minister of External Affairs, reaffirmed that "beyond ASEAN we are actually looking at the Indo Pacific now" (Press Information Bureau 2016). India initially viewed the Indo-Pacific from the geoeconomic lens though protecting geopolitical interests was not outside of its purview.

Prime Minister Manmohan Singh used the term "Indo-Pacific" for the first time at the India-ASEAN Commemorative Summit by asserting that "our future is inter-linked and a stable, secure and prosperous Indo-Pacific region is crucial for our own pro-gress and prosperity" (Press Trust of India 2018a). Indian foreign Minister Salman Khurshid also reiterated "the need for India to build partnerships across the Indo-Pacific" (Press Trust of India 2018b). He further added that "Indo-Pacific" could be looked upon as a natural corollary of the country's modern version of a "Look East Policy" (Pugh 1996).

MODI ADMINISTRATION'S APPROACH TO THE INDO-PACIFIC (2014–PRESENT)

The installation of a new BJP-led coalition headed by Narendra Modi brought a renewed push into the Indian Ocean under its "Act East" policy. With China in mind, India further enhanced its presence in the South Pacific and Indo-Pacific regions through strengthening bilateral and trilateral security co-operation with France, Indonesia, Vietnam, Japan, Australia and the United States (Rajagopalan 2021). During the inaugural edition of "The Gateway of India Dialogue" held on 13–14 June 2016, Dr. Subrahmanyam Jaishankar, then India's Foreign Secretary, indicated that "Underlying the endeavour to align business and strategic goals is our shifting understanding of the world itself ... end of the Cold War and the eco-nomic rise of Asia ... offer enormous leapfrogging possibilities to a country like India" (Rajagopalan 2021a).

Highlighting India's changing understanding of the world, Prime Minister Modi himself spoke about an "interdependent world" and emphasised that "With a 7,500-kilometer long coast line, India has a natural and immediate interest in the developments in the Indo-Pacific region" (Rajagopalan 2021b). Furthermore, the idea of the Indo-Pacific achieved profound importance when Prime Minister Modi decided to attend the Shangri-la Dialogue in June 2018 and stressed how "common prosperity and security require us to evolve, through dialogue, a common rules-based order for the region" (Ranjana 2019).

Following the mandate from the top leadership, other ministers, officials and pol-icy makers in the Modi administration started to speak in the Indo-Pacific context. India's Defence Ministry adopted the Indo-Pacific terminology when Defence Minister Manohar Parrikar talked about "the geopolitical and geoeconomic significance of the Indo-Pacific region" (Rao 2011). Nirmala Sitharaman, then the Minister of Commerce and Industry, signed an "Action Agenda for the India and the Indo-Pacific" with Japanese counterpart Yoichi Miyazawa in April 2015 to involve India with the Free and Open Indo-Pacific Strategy (FOIPS), a Japanese initiative aimed at strengthening infrastructure links across the Indo-Pacific.

India's continuous non-participation in China's MSRI, a route going across the South China Sea and the Indian Ocean and then refusing to send any representa-tive to the Belt and Road Forum held in Beijing in early May 2017 signalled a fundamental shift in India's China policy. "This sudden shift in India's position from non-endorsement to outright opposition has stoked much speculation over Delhi's calculations behind the move." This change at India's instance signals that a great game of the twenty-first century is about to get even more complicated and unpredictable (Sahil 2013). With the anti-China chorus getting louder by the day, institutions like QUAD and AUKUS have provided further impetus to the region's geopolitical manoeuvring.

Institutional context of India's outreach to the "Indo-Pacific"

Box 18.2 Non-aligned Movement 2.0

The Non-aligned Movement 2.0 (NAM 2.0) borrows heavily from the earlier era Non-aligned Movement (NAM), which was relatively successful in carving out an autonomous space for smaller powers in the international system. The pressing need to revisit the time-tested NAM framework comes from the growing fear that the international system is once again sliding back to the renewed Cold War conditions. Though, with only one difference – a rising China has largely occupied the great power space vacated by the erstwhile Soviet Union. In order to face a new round of bitterly contested great power rivalry, a section in the Indian foreign policy establishment argues for deriving a few policy lessons from its own tradition of "neutrality" under the NAM.

In an attempt to look back towards India's own experiment with neutrality, Prime Minister Modi made a serious overture by participating in the virtual NAM Contact Group Summit held on 4 May 2020. After missing three consecutive NAM Summit Meetings, India's decision to participate in the NAM Summit reveals its lingering ambiguity while dealing with great powers. A re-thinking about NAM finds appropriate reflection in a government Think Tank report, titled "*Non-Alignment 2.0*" that emphasises the country's historical connect with "neutrality" in "a revivalist endeavour." The much talked about report hints at a delicate diplomatic balancing between alignment and non-alignment. As a developing economy bordering a rising super power China, India is keen to safeguard its strategic interests but not at the cost of economic benefits. Hence, India has yet to resolve its own dilemma – how to protect security and enhance prosperity. Time will tell whether India's twin aspirations – safeguarding economic interests and protecting strategic concerns – would be satisfied by the promise of the Indo-Pacific or if its unfulfilled aspirations drive a country of 1.4 billion people to once again lean on the ideas of time-tested NAM.

Bilateral, trilateral and quadrilateral dialogues

As an "Indo-Pacific power," India has been very much part of various engagements that are behind the emergence of a new order in the region. The Indian government has worked to upgrade bilateral partnerships with countries around the South China Sea and Pacific Rim, including Japan, Australia, Indonesia, Vietnam, Singapore, France, Germany and the United States. Often these bilateral engagements evolved into useful trilateral arrangements (Singleton 2021). India has worked out prominent trilateral dialogues with the United States, Japan, Australia and Indonesia.

Behind the formation of these trilateral arrangements lies China's growing assertiveness in the East China Sea, South China Sea, Western Pacific and Indian Ocean as well as a dangerous stand-off in the long-Himalayan border facing India. "Initially, the Track-2 India-Japan-US trilateral meetings in 2011 and 2012 used Asia-Pacific terminology.

However, by the 2013 Track-2 trilateral meetings dropped 'Asia-Pacific' as a common point of reference and the use of 'Indo-Pacific' gained acceptance and popularity" (Singh 2021). Similarly, the India–Indonesia–Australia troika announced in 2012 has been seen as a "new grouping in the Indo-Pacific." Aiming to shape "a free, open, prosperous and inclusive Indo-Pacific region" India actively got involved in November 2017 to revive the quadrilateral mechanism or QUAD with Australia, Japan and the United States (Singh 2022). There has been wide range of activities under QUAD, including meeting with the heads of state and meetings at foreign minister level.

Outreach through regional and sub-regional institutions

India's involvement has not been limited to bilateral, trilateral and quadrilateral dialogues but it has made concerted efforts to partner with number of *de facto* Indo-Pacific institutions, including East Asia Summit (EAS), the ASEAN Regional Forum (ARF) and the ASEAN Defence Ministers' Meeting-Plus (ADMM-Plus) and Asia-Pacific Fishery Commission (APFC). India has become an observer of the West Pacific Naval Symposium (WPNS) and a leading member of the Indian Ocean Naval Symposium (IONS). Additionally, India is involved in the Indo-Pacific sub-regional mechanisms such as Mekong-Ganga Cooperation (MGC) established in 2000, which brings India and Myanmar together with Thailand, Cambodia and Vietnam and Forum for India Pacific Island Countries (FIPIC), set up in 2014, bringing India along with 14 island countries (Singh 1999).

In an ongoing rebalance favouring the maritime sphere, India has been busy to enhance maritime security by becoming partner in the various Indo-Pacific settings. A modest meeting between India, Indonesia, Singapore and Thailand in 1995 evolved into the MILAN naval exercises in the waters around India's Andaman and Nicobar Islands. By 2018, MILAN exercises involved navies from both wings of the Indo-Pacific, though China and Pakistan remained absent (Singh 2003). Not only did India organise but it also joined the ADMM-Plus naval Exercise on Maritime Security and Counter Terrorism (EMSCT) held in the South China Sea in May 2016. Crossing the set limits of its traditional maritime sphere, India in 2014, 2016 and 2018 took part in the RIMPAC-16, the world's largest multi-lateral naval exercise off the Hawaiian Coast. New Delhi's participation in the RIMPAC-16 has become "a demonstration of India's commitment to peace and prosperity of the Indo-Pacific region and Indian Navy's increasing footprint and operational reach" (Singh 2016).

India continued bilateral exercises with an explicit focus on the Indo-Pacific region. In this regard, India conducts SIMBEX exercises with Singapore in an alternate venue since 2005. In the Indian Ocean and the Western Pacific, India conducted INDRA exercises with Russia. JIMEX naval exercises between India and Japan took place in the Western Pacific in 2011 and the Eastern Indian Ocean in 2013. Since 2007, MALABAR naval exercises, which began bilaterally between India and the United States, have alternated between the Indian Ocean and the Western Pacific.

India's meaningful and open-ended engagement with the Indo-Pacific marks a directional shift in its strategic thinking. At the macro-level, this change highlights a structural shift from geoeconomics to geopolitics, but at the micro-level, it is directed by the needs of resolving India's twin imbalances. In order to mitigate the strategic imbalance, India has activated a creditable maritime strategy in co-operation with other Indo-Pacific powers. In addition, India has shown genuine interest in resolving the economic imbalance by embracing export-orientation with mass-manufacturing at the core.

In short, the Indo-Pacific construct has helped India to better manage strategic challenges thrown open by China's increasingly belligerent behaviour and mitigate developmental challenges imposed by the accumulated economic imbalance between India and countries of East Asia.

BOX 18.3 Concept of "SAGAR"

India's crucial foreign policy concept "SAGAR" was coined by the Indian Prime Minister Modi during his speech at Port Louis, Mauritius on 12 March 2015. The acronym SAGAR is a Hindi word that means "sea" but when expanded in English; it stands for – Security and Growth for All in the Region. SAGAR is not a formal project but a set of underlying objectives and rules guiding India's policy on maritime co-operation. The ideas behind SAGAR invoke mutually reinforcing symbiotic relations that bind together India's strategic and economic spheres. In a way, SAGAR echoes India's complex balancing between its geopolitical and geoeconomic interests.

In order to articulate the inclusivity embedded in the idea of SAGAR, India is trying to remove the dichotomy that exists between Asia's converging geoeconomic interests and diverging geopolitical concerns. Taking a clue from China's ambitious Belt and Road Initiative (BRI) and Maritime Silk Road Initiative (MSRI) project, India desires to see not only strategic cooperation but is also keen on having a clear focus on maritime connectivity across the oceanic terrain of the vast Indo-Pacific region.

Given the existing gap between economic and political interests in Asia, it is indeed a tall order to fuse twin interests into a coherent workable foreign policy instrument. India believes that the "balancing" of China can not only be confined to strategic domain but it should also undercut China's growing economic clout. In this context, India wishes to see the restructuring of global supply-chains overtly centred on China and supports greater movement of goods, capital and technology across the Indo-Pacific region. India's strategy in the framework of SAGAR has clearly articulated its conditional approach to the Indo-Pacific – that without a simultaneous focus on strategic and economic spheres, its commitment towards the Indo-Pacific may diminish over the period.

Policy implications

India's increasing engagement with the "Indo-Pacific" not only presents unforeseen opportunities to resolve its accumulated imbalances, but also opens up a set of complex challenges. On the one hand, the multi-lateral context of the "Indo-Pacific" vision has catapulted India from the backwaters of Asian leadership and placed the country at the helm of affairs. But on the other, anti-China grumbling from the leaders of the "Indo-Pacific" has substantially increased the threat to India's long-Himalayan border, escalating the risk of India further sliding to anti-China groupings and producing fears of over-stretching security commitments beyond the country's economic means. In addition, past experiences remind India how limited economic resources during the Cold War phase hindered its own vision of "neutrality" in the face of intense super-power rivalry. Once again, India is facing a similar challenge to simultaneously manage opposing paradigms with limited economic means.

In the midst of the abovementioned opportunities and challenges, New Delhi has developed its own set of ideas and institutions to effectively balance its pressing strategic and economic needs. At the micro policy level, India is trying to learn the logic behind the export-oriented rapid industrialisation exhibited by East Asian economies. In this context, India wishes to gain from active diversification of global supply-chains away from China. India not only sees itself as part of the wider Indo-Pacific production network but is also looking to gain from the large pool of Western capital, technology and increased maritime connectivity.

At the macro level, tackling the challenges that emerged out of India's ever-tighter embrace of Indo-Pacific strategy requires the creation of a manageable harmony among and between the opposing paradigms. There is a diversity of views suggesting how India's strategic interests can be better served. It has been suggested that by advancing a "functional-transactional approach," instead of pursuing a traditional grand strategy based either on "neutrality" of the non-alignment variety or alignment to great powers, India can adopt a much more pragmatic approach. Scholars have also cautioned India regarding the downside risks involved in the country becoming part of an alliance system that smaller countries like Korea, Japan and Taiwan followed since the beginning of the Cold War.

An increasingly popular view countering India's new found policy pragmatism argues that a transactional-functional approach could lead the country to strategic isolation. This view, supported by scholars like C. Raja Mohan (2012), Rajgopalan (2017) and Harsh V. Pant (2019), sees that the evolving strategic architecture in the Indo-Pacific offers India a rare opportunity to reasonably address its security concerns. They believe that the policy of "self-help" based on the nationalist concept of "strategic autonomy" and the non-aligned variety of "neutrality" is no longer a viable option. Responding to the fundamentally altered region's strategic reality, it has also been suggested that India should follow a regional balancing strategy in the wider Indo-Pacific framework. This strategy can offer India a policy choice to maintain close strategic cooperation with the United States rather than simply hedging or going back to the earlier era non-alignment with an elusive promise of strategic autonomy.

Considering the "grand strategy" and "functional-transactional strategy" as two extreme policy positions, we argue that a maritime inclined Indo-Pacific strategy strikes a better coordination between India's security concerns and pressing economic needs. The "Indo-Pacific" offers India a multi-lateral platform to voice its security concerns regarding Beijing's unilateral designs aimed at altering the basic tenets of its rule-based order. At the same time, Indo-Pacific mechanisms on connectivity and freedom of navigation provide India with better chances to realise its aspiration to develop economically.

Conclusion

The findings of this chapter confirm that India urgently requires effective resolution of its long-standing imbalances that have clouded its policies aimed at promoting its national interests. In order to resolve the lingering strategic imbalance, India needs to devote much more attention to maritime security than continuin with the perennially over-emphasised safety of its continental borders. At the same time, India is cautious that over-blown security concerns must not override the country's economic needs to battle with the equally crucial economic imbalance that has led to chronic poverty and massive unemployment. With the rise of China as a great military and economic power, India is in a greater hurry to find a workable resolution to its twin imbalances. Study confirms that India's tilt towards the Indo-Pacific is very much part of its bid to rebalance strategic and economic concerns aimed at fulfilling the existing security void and bridging ballooning trade deficits that New Delhi is experiencing with East Asia's powerful exporting economies.

China's astronomical rise and India's geographical pre-imminence in the Indian Ocean has not only threatened the regional strategic calculus but has also impacted the core of the global security order. These developments have paved the way for a twenty-first century "great game" where the Sino-Indian contest at the regional level has become part of the unfolding Sino-US contestation at the global level. The simultaneous rise of imbalances at the regional and global levels has added dangerous unpredictability in the security environment with long-term consequences for regional peace and prosperity. Caught in the vortex of strategic uncertainty and economic unpredictability, India has taken a U-turn from its long cherished idea of "strategic autonomy" with "non-alignment" as the main policy flank. It is trying to embrace "strategic coordination" with the "willing powers" in the vast Indo-Pacific region. Analysis confirms how efforts to manage a fluid strategic and economic environment surrounding India finds a multi-lateral platform, the "Indo-Pacific," as an appropriate instrument to effectively resolve its structural imbalances.

In order to fine tune its accommodation of the needs of a multi-lateral strategy under the Indo-Pacific order, India has developed a diversified approach involving bilateral, trilateral and multi-lateral strategies to actively engage a number of countries in the vast oceanic expanse. India is not only a member of regional institutions like East Asia Summit and dialogue partner in ASEAN but it is also involved in sub-regional groupings and various regional bodies such as the Mekong-Ganga Cooperation (MGC) and FIPIC (Forum for Indo-Pacific Island Countries). India's open-ended acceptance of the Indo-Pacific is such that its much publicised "Act East" policy is getting transformed into an "Act Indo-Pacific" policy.

India's ever-deeper engagement with the "Indo-Pacific" was also reflected in the newly formed partnerships with government bodies, various administrative branches and a number of other institutions. Acknowledging the growing interaction with the Indo-Pacific, India's foreign ministry has opened a new desk fully dedicated to handle Indo-Pacific affairs.[6] Utilising bilateral, trilateral and multi-lateral forums and initiatives, India has been participating in a number of naval exercises, including SIMBEX, INDRA, JIMEX and Malabar. India's profound commitment to the Indo-Pacific became known to the world when it joined QUAD. It highlights factors and forces contributing to a paradigm shift in India's foreign policy thinking from Cold War era "non-alignment" to post-Cold war era 'alignment" in the multi-lateral framework.

The most noticeable Indian assertion towards the Indo-Pacific strategy has come from none other than Prime Minister Modi himself who clearly laid out the country's changing approach to the region. During the Shangri-La Dialogue (1 June 2018) in

Singapore, Modi rearticulated his concept of "SAGAR," which stands for "Security and Growth for All in the Region." Being a developing economy, India wishes to strike a balance between peace and prosperity. Not only the government but also the Indian strategic community, including C. Rajamohan, Rajesh Rajgopalan and Brahma Chellaney, have hailed the country's turn towards the Indo-Pacific in the hope of resolving its strategic and economic concerns.

In its decisive turn toward the Indo-Pacific order, India has rekindled the idea of nineteenth century strategist Alfred Thayer Mahan who provided in-depth analysis of sea power and its influence upon history. Taking cues from the Mahanian vision, India is trying to make the Indian Ocean India's ocean, though a century later. Many strategic thinkers in the post-independent India such as Kavalam Panikkar (1945), Keshav Vaidya (1949), Sourendra Kohli (1978) and R. Roy-Chaudhury (1995) remembered Alfred Thayer Mahan, who advocated the dominating role that sea power has played in shaping the course of world history and advised the government to institute a credible maritime strategy.

With the Chinese navy spreading its sway over the vast Indian Ocean, there seems to be an urgency in India to see itself as a Mahanian-style sea power. It has been argued that geographically India's position has been literally "pivotal" in the Indian Ocean but now it is becoming the centre of its political economic activities as well. Indeed, the promise of maritime connectivity, the assurance of restructuring China-centred supply chains and the hope of gaining unfettered access to capital, technology and market in the vast Indo-Pacific area provides a fillip to India's legitimate economic aspirations.

Notes

1 Geographically, the Indo-Pacific refers to a large maritime region of warm water connecting the Indian and Pacific oceans but strategically thinking, it has profound geopolitical connotations.
2 American naval officer and historian Alfred Thayer Mahan, in his legendary work, *The influence of sea power upon history*, (1890) 'has articulated "principle of sea power" and provides in-depth analysis of sea power and its influence upon history. Mahanian views advocate significant expansion of naval forces.
3 India's open-ended embrace to the idea of "Indo-Pacific" reminds Nehru's famous speech on the eve of India's Independence, India's tryst with destiny'.
4 China–Pakistan Economic Corridor (CPEC) directly links China to the Indian Ocean through Pakistan's Gwadar port and Maritime Silk Road connecting key strategic nodes across the Indian Ocean.
5 Ministry of Defence (Indian Government), Ministry of Defence Annual Report 2000–2001.
6 Eshwar Ranjana, "India Sets Up New Indo-Pacific Desk, Experts Laud 'Strategic Move'", *The Quint*, April 15, 2019. Available at: https://www.thequint.com/news/india/india-sets-up-new-indo-pacific-desk-experts-laud-strategic-move (Retrieved on March 21, 2022).

References

Akamatsu, Kaname, "A Historical Pattern of Economic Growth in Developing Countries," *The Developing Economies*, 1(1), 1962: 3–25.
Amsden, Alice H., *Asia's Next Giant: South Korea and Late Industrialization*, (New York: Oxford University Press, 1989).
Ashraf, Junaid, "String of Pearls and China's Emerging Strategic Culture," *Strategic Studies*, 37(4), Winter 2017: 166–181.

Bajpaee, Chietigi, "Embedding India in Asia: Reaffirming the Indo-Pacific Concept," *Journal of Defence Studies*, 8(4), 2014: 83–110.

Baruah, Darshana M., "India in the Indo-Pacific: New Delhi's Theater of Opportunity," *Carnegie India*, 30 June 2020.

Basu, Titli, "India's Approach towards Indo-Pacific Triangularity," *IDSA News*, 27 May 2016.

Bhalla, Abhishek, "Navy's Modernisation Plans Take a Blow with Massive Fund Crunch," *India Today (Magazine)*, 3 December 2019.

Chacko, Priya, "The Rise of the Indo-Pacific: Understanding Ideational Change and Continuity in India's Foreign Policy," *Australian Journal of International Affairs*, 68(4), 2014: 433–452.

Chacko, Priya, "India and the Indo-Pacific from Singh to Modi: Geopolitical and Geoeconomic Entanglements," in P. Chacko (ed.), *New Regional Geopolitics in the Indo-Pacific: Drivers, Dynamics and Consequences*, 43–59 (London: Routledge, 2016).

Chang, Ha-Joon, *Kicking Away the Ladder: Development Strategy in Historical Perspective*, (London: Anthem Press, 2002).

Chaturvedi, Sachin, "India-Asean Ties Hold the Key to Indo-Pacific Stability," *Hindustan Times*, 25 January 2018.

Cook, Malcolm, "US-Southeast Asia Trade is Increasing, But So Are Deficits," *Asia Pacific Bulletin*, No. 493, 16 October 2019.

Constantine, Collin, "Economic Structures, Institutions and Economic Performance," *Journal of Economic Structures*, 6(2), 2017: 1–18.

"Confluence of the Two Seas," Speech by H.E. Mr. Shinzo Abe, Prime Minister of Japan at the Parliament of the Republic of India, Ministry of Foreign Affairs of Japan, 22 August 2007.

Dasgupta, S., "The Navy: In Troubled Waters," *India Today*, 30 April 1994, pp. 70–71.

De, Prabir, *Act East to Act Indo-Pacific: India's Expanding Neighbourhood*, (New Delhi: K. W. Publisher, 2020).

Desai, Bal, "Quadrilateral Security Dialogue (Quad) and India," *FINS Journal of Diplomacy & Strategy*, 2(4), January–March 2021.

Dutta, Amrita Nayak, "Defence Budget: With IOR Focus, Navy Gets 43% Capital Outlay Hike, Army Modernisation Funds Dip 12.2%," *News 18*, 1 February 2022.

Fairbank, John K. and Ssu-yu Teng, "On the Ch'ing Tributary System," *Harvard Journal of Asiatic Studies*, 6(2), June 1941: 135–246.

Ghosh, Deepshikha, "'Have Actually Taken Up Maximum Reforms' PM Modi To Wall Street Journal," *NDTV India*, 26 May 2016.

Gill, Danish Inder Singh, "India's Dilemma: A Maritime or a Continental Power?" *Indian Defence Review*, 12 February 2016.

Gokhale, Nitin, *From Look East to Engage East: How India's Own Pivot Will Change Discourse in Indo-Pacific Region*, Vivekananda International Foundation, 12 March 2013.

Government of India, *Indian Maritime Doctrine*, 65–67 (New Delhi: Integrated Headquarters, Ministry of Defence, 2004).

Grupe, Claudia and Axel Rose, "China, India, and the Socioeconomic Determinants of Their Competitiveness," *Economics Research International*, 2010, 2010: 1–14.

Gupta, Sourabh, Abe and Modi attempt to bridge the Indo-Pacific, *East Asia Forum*, January 5, 2016.

Hemmings, John and Genevieve Hull, "The New Great Game in the Indo-Pacific," *E-International Relations*, 20 April 2018: 1–3.

Hundt, David and Jitendra Uttam, *Varieties of Capitalism in Asia: Beyond 'Developmental State'*, (London: Palgrave Macmillan, 2017).

"Indian Navvy, Visit of Indian Warship to Port Majuro, Marshall Islands," 13–15 August 2016.

"Indo-Pacific is the New Geopolitical Reality," Press Release (Institute for Defence Studies and Analyses), 1 November 2012.

Institute for Defence Studies and Analyses (IDSA), *Speech of the Defence Minister Shri Manohar Parrikar at the Shangri-La Dialogue*, 4 June 2016.

Islam, TM Tonmoy, David Newhouse, and Monica Yanez-Pagan, "International Comparisons of Poverty in South Asia," *Asian Development Review*, 38(1), 2021: 142–175.

John, Jojin, "India Looks Beyond its Near Seas to Enhance its Interests in the Indo-Pacific," *Strategic Vision*, 4(22), 2015: 4–7.

Jha, Pankaj K. and Vo Xuan Vinh, *India, Vietnam and the Indo-Pacific: Expanding Horizons*, (Abingdon, Oxon, and New York: Routledge India, 2020).

Kapila, Subhash, "India's Strategic Pivot to the Indo Pacific," South Asia Analysis Group, (Paper), No. 5831, 27 November 2014.

Kaura, Vinay, "Securing India's Economic and Security Interests in the Indo-Pacific," *Indian Journal of Asian Affairs*, 31(1/2), June–December 2018: 37–52.

Khurana,Gurpreet S., "India's Maritime Strategy: Context and Subtext," *Maritime Affairs: Journal of the National Maritime Foundation of India*, 13(1), 2017: 14–26.

Khurana, Gurpreet S., "The Indo-Pacific Idea: Origins, Conceptualizations and the Way Ahead," *Journal of Indian Ocean Rim Studies*, 2(2), (Special Issue on Indo-Pacific), 2019: 58–76.

Khurana, Gurpreet, "The Indo-Pacific Concept: Retrospective and Prospect," *Issue Brief* (National Maritime Foundation), 2 February 2017.

Khurshid, Salman, "Keynote Address," in Rajiv Bhatia and Vijay Sakhuja (eds.), *Indo-Pacific Region: Political and Strategic Prospects*, (New Delhi: Indian Council of World Affairs, 2014), pp. 4–6.

Khurshid, Salman, "Interview ('India Eyes Stronger Ties with S-E Asia')," *Straits Times*, 5 July 2013.

Khilnani, Sunil, Rajiv Kumar, Pratap Bhanu Mehta, Prakash Menon, Nandan Nilekani, Srinath Raghavan, Shyam Saran, and Siddharth Varadarajan, "Non Alignment 2.0: A Foreign and Strategic Policy for India in the Twenty First Century," Centre for Policy Research, New Delhi, India, 2012.

Kohli, Surendra, *Sea Power and the Indian Ocean: With Special Reference to India*, (New Delhi: Tata-McGraw, 1978).

Lindner, Walter J., "Setting Sail for a Powerful India-German Partnership," *The Hindu*, 22 January 2022.

Mahan, Alfred Thayer, *The Influence of Sea Power Upon History, 1660–1783*, (1890; reprint) New York: Dover, 1987).

Mishra, Raghavendra, "India and 'Indo-Pacific': Involvement rather than Entanglement," *Indian Foreign Affairs Journal*, 9(2), April–June 2014: 93–137.

Misra, Raj Narain, *Indian Ocean and India's Security*, (New Delhi: Mittal Publications, 1986).

Mohan, C. Raja, *Samudra Manthan: Sino-Indian Rivalry in the Indo-Pacific*, (Washington, DC: Brookings Institution Press, 2012).

Ministry of Defence (Indian Government), "Ministry of Defence Annual Report 2000-2001." https://commerce.gov.in/about-us/divisions/foreign-trade-territorial-division/foreign-trade-north-east-asia/access: 17 November 2021.

Ministry of Commerce and Industry, Foreign Trade (North East Asia), Trade Statistics of the Territory (NEA Region).

Ministry of Defence, "Indian Navy to Host Exercise SIMBEX-20 in Andaman Sea," Press Information Bureau, 22 November 2020.

Ministry of External Affairs, "Prime Minister's Keynote Address at Shangri La Dialogue," 1 June 2018.

Ministry of Defence, "EXERCISE INDRA-21," Press Information Bureau, 27 July 2021.

Ministry of External Affairs, "Opening Statement by Prime Minister at Plenary Session of India-ASEAN Commemorative Summit," 20 December 2012.

Ministry of External Affairs, "External Affairs Minister's speech at the launch of ASEAN-India Centre in New Delhi," 21 June, 2013.

"Modi, Macron to Shape India-France Cooperation in Indo-Pacific," *Deccan Herald*, 6 March 2018.

Mukherjee, Rohan, "Looking West, Acting East," *Southeast Asian Affairs*, 2019: 43–52.

Mukhopadhaya, Gautam, "The Indo-Pacific Potential," *The Hindu*, 13 December 2016.

Naidu, G. Vijayachandra, "'Indo-Pacific' as a New Template of Analysis," *Indian Foreign Affairs Journal*, 9(2), 2014: 102–107.

Ollapally, Deepa, "Understanding Indian Policy Dilemmas in the Indo-Pacific," *Maritime Affairs*, 12(1), 2016: 1–12.

Palmer, N. "South Asia and the Indian Ocean," in A. Cottrell and R. Burrell (eds.), *The Indian Ocean: Its Political, Economic, and Military Importance*, (New York: Praeger, 1972).

Pandit, Rajat, "India to Rebalance Forces, Firepower to LAC and IOR," *Times of India*, 1 November, 2020.

Panikkar, K.M., *India and the Indian Ocean*, (London: G. Allen & Unwin, 1945).

Pandey, Pragya, "India-Australia: Strategic Partners in the Indo-Pacific," *Diplomatist*, 22 June 2020.

Pant, Harsh V., "Pivot to the Indo-Pacific," *The Hindu*, 12 April, 2017.

Pant, Harsh V., "India and Indonesia in the Indo-Pacific," *Observer Research Foundation (ORF)*, 24 May, 2018.

Pant, Harsh V., *New Directions in India's Foreign Policy: Theory and Praxis*, (New Delhi: Cambridge University Press, 2019).

Park, Soyen, "Why 'India Boycotted the Belt and Road Forum'," *East Asia Forum*, 13 June 2017.

Parthasarathy, G., "Revisiting Strategy in the Indo-Pacific," *The Hindu*, 20 September 2017.

Parameswaran, Prashanth, "India-Singapore Relations and the Indo-Pacific: The Security Dimension," *The Diplomat*, November 27, 2018.

Pasinetti, Luigi L., *Structural Change and Economic Growth: A Theoretical Essay on the Dynamics of the Wealth of Nations*, (Cambridge: Cambridge University Press, 1983).

Prabir De, *Act East to Act Indo-Pacific: India's Expanding Neighbourhood* (New Delhi: K. W. Publisher, 2020).

Prakash, Arun, "Maritime Security: An Indo-Pacific Perspective," *Defence Watch*, 9–14 March, 2012.

Prashanth, Parameswaran, "The Real Significance of India's MILAN Navy Exercise," *The Diplomat*, 28 February 2018.

Press Trust of India, "PLI Scheme to Unlock India's Manufacturing Capacity: Icra," *The New Indian Express*, 17 February 2022.

Press Information Bureau, Government of India, "Sagarmala National Perspective Plan Released," 14 April 2016.

Press Trust of India, "Donald Trump Says US Has Taken Toughest-Ever Action on China's Unfair Trade Practices," *Economic Times*, 13 October, 2018.

Press Trust of India, "India Has Trade Deficit with 10 Regional Comprehensive Economic Partnership (RCEP) Members," *Economic Times*, 17 June, 2018.

Pugh, Michael, "Is Mahan Still Alive? State Naval Power in the International System," *Journal of Conflict Studies*, 16(2), 1996: 109–123.

Rajagopal, Krishnadas, "The Divide between Haves and Have-nots Is Still a Reality: CJI (Chief Justice of India) Ramana," *The Hindu*, 14 November 2021.

Rajagopalan, Rajeswari Pillai, "JIMEX-21: India-Japan Maritime Exercise," *The Diplomat*, 12 October 2021.

Rajagopalan, Rajeswari Pillai, "The Quad Conducts Malabar Naval Exercise," *The Diplomat*, 27 August, 2021.

Ranjana, Eshwar, "India Sets Up New Indo-Pacific Desk, Experts Laud 'Strategic Move'," *The Quint*, 15 April 2019.

Rao, Nirupama, "Address by Ambassador Nirupama Rao at UC-Berkeley," India and the Asia-Pacific: Expanding Engagement, 5 December 2011.

Rodrik, Dani, "Getting Interventions Right: How South Korea and Taiwan Grew Rich," *Economic Policy*, 10(20), April 1995: 53–107.

Robert, Wade, "Selective Industrial Policies in East Asia: Is the East Asian Miracle Right?," in A. Fishlow, C. Gwin, S. Haggard, D. Rodrik and R. Wade (eds.), *Miracle or Design:*

Lessons from the East Asian Experience, (Washington, DC: Overseas Development Council, 1994).

Sahil, Saloni, "India and the Emerging Indo-Pacific Strategic Space," *Strategic Analysis Paper* (Future Directions), March 2013.

Sahni, Varun, "India's Security Challenges out to 2000," paper presented at the Australia-India Security Roundtable, Canberra, 11–12 April 2005.

Sakhuja, Vijay, *Asian Maritime Power in the 21st Century*, (Singapore: Institute of Southeast Asian Studies, 2011).

Saran, Shyam, "Mapping the Indo-Pacific," *Indian Express*, 29 October 2011.

Scott, David, "India and the Indo-Pacific Discourse," in Harsh V. Pant (ed.), *New Directions in India's Foreign Policy: Theory and Praxis*, 195–214 (Cambridge: Cambridge University Press, 2018).

Scott, David, "India's 'Grand Strategy' for the Indian Ocean: Mahanian Visions," *Asia-Pacific Review*, 13(2), 2006: 97–129.

Scott, David, "India and the Allure of the 'Indo-Pacific'", *International Studies*, 49(3&4), 2012: 165–188.

Setser, Brad W., *East Asia's (Goods) Trade Surplus*, (New York: Council on Foreign Relations, 22 July 2016).

Shaunik, Nyantara, "Conceptions of Security in the Regional Economic Cooperation Paradigm: The Curious Case of the Indo-Pacific," *Jindal Journal of International Affairs*, 4(1), 2016: 85–101.

Singleton, Craig, "Beijing Eyes New Military Bases Across the Indo-Pacific," *Foreign Policy*, 7 July 2021.

Singh, Abhijit, "Boosting India with Maritime Domain Awareness," *The Hindu*, 7 January 2021.

Singh, Bawa, Aslam Khan, Parvaiz Ahmad Thoker, Mansoor Ahmad Lone, *New Great Game in the Indo-Pacific: Rediscovering India's Pragmatism and Paradoxes*, (London: Routledge, 2022).

Singh, Jaswant, *Defending India*, (London: Macmillan, 1999).

Singh, K.R., "The Changing Paradigm of India's Maritime Security," *International Studies*, 40(3), August 2003: 229–245.

Singh, Zorawar Daulet, "Should India 'Be East' or Be Eurasian?" *Strategic Analysis*, 36(1), January 2012: 1–5.

Singh, Udai Bhanu, "The Significance of the ADMM-Plus: A Perspective from India," *Asia Policy*, 22, July 2016: 96–101.

Singh, Zorawar Daulet, "Foreign Policy and Sea Power: India's Maritime Role Flux," *Journal of Defence Studies*, 11(4), (2017): 21–49.

Srinivasan, Rajeev, "Putting China in Its Place: Towards an Indo-Pacific Century," *Firstpost*, 26 December 2011.

Subrahmanyam, Jaishankar, "Inaugural Keynote Speech (Gateway of India Dialogue)," June 13, 2016.

Surendra Kohli Sea Power and the Indian Ocean: With Special Reference to India Tata-McGraw 1978 New Delhi.

Suri, Gopal, "Case for a Regional Maritime Security Construct for the Indo-Pacific," *Occasional Paper* (Vivekananda International Foundation), January 2016.

Syrquin, M., Taylor, L., Westphal, L. (eds.), *Economic structure and performance: essays in Honour of Hollis B. Chenery*, (Orlando, FL: Academic Press, 1984).

Takenori, Horimoto, "The Free and Open Indo-Pacific Strategy: India's Wary Response," *Nippon.com*, 9 October 2018.

Tellis, Ashley, "Demanding Tasks for the Indian Navy," *Asian Survey*, 25(12), December 1985: 1186–1213.

Thankachan, Shahana, "India and the Free and Open Indo-Pacific: Present," *Global Affairs Journal*, 2, March 2020: 13–16.

Thomas, Roby, "Leveraging India's Maritime Diplomacy," *Journal of Defence Studies*, 14(3), 2020: 5–27.

Trofimov, Yaroslav, "India Seeks Naval Edge as China Penetrates Indian Ocean," *The Wall Street Journal*, 24 September 2020.

Upadhyay, Shreya, "The Indo-Pacific and the Indo-US Relations: Geopolitics of Cooperation," *Issue Brief (IPCS)*, 562, November 2014.

Vaidya, K., *The Naval Defence of India* (Bombay: Thacker, 1949).

Wade, R., *Governing the Market: Economic Theory and the Role of Government in East Asian Industrialization*, (Princeton, NJ: Princeton University Press, 1990).

Westphal, L.E., "Industrial Policy in an Export-Propelled Economy: Lessons from South Korea's Experience," *Journal of Economic Perspectives*, 4(3), 1990: 41–59.

World Bank, *The East Asian Miracle: Economic Growth and Public Policy*, A World Bank Policy Research Report, (London: Oxford University Press, 1993).

Yarmolinsky, Yuri M., "The Great Game 2.0 in Asia, Raisina Debates," 3 April 2021.

Yoon, Young-kwan, "Will Europe's Past be East Asia's Future?" *Politique étrangère*, 1, Spring 2014: 173–185.

19 Japan's Indo-Pacific strategy

Free and open Indo-Pacific as international public goods

Hidetaka Yoshimatsu

Introduction

After the formation of the second Abe Shinzo administration in December 2012, Japan intensified external engagements under the slogan of "proactive contribution to peace." In particular, the Indo-Pacific strategy assumed the core of Japanese diplomacy after Abe presented the Free and Open Indo-Pacific (FOIP) policy vision in 2016. The Japanese government has formulated and implemented tangible policies and measures to achieve the FOIP and strengthened external partnerships under the banner of this vision. The importance of the Indo-Pacific strategy in Japanese diplomacy is illustrated in a special website, "Free and Open Indo-Pacific," within the category of "Foreign Policy" at the homepage of the Ministry of Foreign Affairs (MOFA).[1] Moreover, various policy plans including the Basic Plan on Ocean Policy and the Basic Plan on Space Policy refer to the FOIP as a guiding principle.

Japan's Indo-Pacific strategy has a character of continuity from the past diplomacy, particularly that of the first Abe administration in 2006–2007. The administration promoted the value-oriented diplomacy that underscored universal values such as democracy, freedom, human rights and the rule of law in Japan's foreign policy. As a concrete strategy to promote these liberal values, the administration's foreign minister Taro Aso advocated the necessity of building an "arc of freedom and prosperity" around the outer rim of the Eurasian continent through diplomacy that underlined these liberal values. The second Abe administration's regional strategy turned over this universal-value orientation. At the same time, the Indo-Pacific strategy contains a feature of a rational response to both geopolitical and geoeconomic evolutions in the extended geographical scope. The strategy incorporates political, economic and security perspectives, and its tangible policies are related to bilateral, mini-lateral and multi-lateral dimensions. Moreover, key policy directions under the strategy have exhibited nuanced changes amid Sino–US strategic confrontation and the development of partnerships with like-minded states such as Australia, India and key members of the Association of Southeast Asian Nations (ASEAN).

This study aims at offering the overall picture of Japan's Indo-Pacific strategy. It elucidates the major contents of the strategy, explaining the development of the strategy and key external policies under the strategy. It also locates the Indo-Pacific strategy in broader frameworks and examines strategic objectives in great power politics. Moreover, this research explores the diplomatic implications of the Indo-Pacific strategy in the regional and global landscapes. Before undertaking these works, the

DOI: 10.4324/9781003336143-24

following section confirms Japan's special position in the development of the Indo-Pacific concept.

Japan's special status regarding the Indo-Pacific

Japan has maintained a special position in the development of the Indo-Pacific concept. First, Japan was a key player that advocated the importance of the concept. In the 2010s, political leaders in the Asia-Pacific began to use the term, Indo-Pacific, in specific diplomatic contexts. For instance, the US Secretary of State Hilary Clinton used the Indo-Pacific in a speech in Hawaii in October 2010. She referred to the Indo-Pacific basin as important for global trade and commerce in the context of the United States expanding its naval co-operation with India (Clinton 2010). Australian Minister for Defence Stephen Smith also underscored the Indo-Pacific concept at the 11th Shangri-La Dialogue in June 2012, contending that "the Indo-Pacific has risen as a region of global strategic significance including the growth of military power projection capabilities of countries in the Indo-Pacific" (Smith 2012). Ahead of the use of the Indo-Pacific by American and Australian political leaders in the 2010s, Prime Minister Abe exhibited a direction of grasping the Pacific and Indian Oceans integratively. During the first administration, Abe made a formal visit to New Delhi in August 2007. An epoch-making event during the visit was a 25-minute speech at the Indian Parliament entitled the "Confluence of the Two Seas." Abe mentioned that "The Pacific and the Indian Oceans are now bringing about a dynamic coupling as seas of freedom and of prosperity. A 'broader Asia' that broke away geographical boundaries is now beginning to take on a distinct form" (Abe 2007). The speech implied a harbinger to comprehend the Pacific and Indian Oceans as a united geographical zone.

Second, Japan was the original advocate of the FOIP. It is often argued that the FOIP is the US strategic vision after President Donald Trump launched this vision at the Asia-Pacific Economic Cooperation (APEC) Economic Leaders' Meeting in Vietnam in November 2017. Abe originally presented the FOIP strategy at the 6th Tokyo International Conference on African Development (TICAD VI) held in Kenya in August 2016. The FOIP presented there aimed at fostering the confluence of the Pacific and Indian Oceans and of Asia and Africa into a place that values freedom, the rule of law and the market economy, free from force or coercion. The FOIP was based on an assumption that the peace and prosperity of the international society depended on a free and open maritime order, and such a maritime order should be fostered from the Pacific to the Indian Ocean.

Third, Japan is the initiator of the Quadrilateral Security Dialogue or the Quad, a key mini-lateral framework that has developed an Indo-Pacific idea. The Quad has two versions (Hosoya 2019). The idea of the Quad 1.0 was first shown in Abe's book published just before becoming prime minister. Abe advocated the holding of ministerial- or summit-level consultation among the United States, Japan, Australia and India from a strategic standpoint to contribute to the sharing of universal values in Asia (Abe 2006). The Quad 1.0 was partially realised in the Exercise Malabar 07-2 where naval ships from the four states plus Singapore gathered at the Bay of Bengal in September 2007. When the Quad 1.0 move surfaced, China exhibited a strong negative response, regarding it as a framework aimed at containing it (Garver & Wang 2010). After the formation of the Kevin Rudd administration in Australia in December 2007, which put more emphasis on stable relations with China than the previous administration, the Quad 1.0 collapsed (Allen-Ebrahimian 2017; Horimoto 2018).

The Quad 2.0 was initiated by the "Asia's Democratic Security Diamond," a strategic idea that Abe exhibited in an article on the website of the non-profit Project Syndicate in late December 2012 (Abe 2012). In this short article, Abe recommended a strategy whereby Japan, Australia, India and the US state of Hawaii formed a diamond to safeguard maritime commons stretching from the Indian Ocean region to the western Pacific. Abe regarded this diamond partnership as a counterforce to China's growing influence in Asia as he warned that the South China Sea is on the verge of becoming a "Lake Beijing."

Abe and his entourage did not hope to flush out the diamond partnership because they feared that the concept might serve to create a hawkish image of the second Abe administration and narrow its diplomatic latitude (Suzuki 2017). It took several years before Japan moved to realising this partnership. Taro Kono, Foreign Minister of the administration, proposed holding a gathering among Japan, the United States, Australia and India at the August 2017 meeting of foreign ministers for the 7th Australia–Japan–US trilateral strategic dialogue, and again on the occasion of the 2nd India–Japan–US trilateral foreign ministers' meeting the following month (Horimoto 2019). Kono's proposal was realised through the holding of the first Australia–India–Japan–US Consultations on the Indo-Pacific on the margins of the East Asia Summit (EAS) in November 2017. After holding the consultation meeting at the director-general level an additional three times, the first quadrilateral foreign ministerial meeting took place in New York in September 2019. The four ministers held the second meeting in Tokyo in October 2020 where they agreed to institutionalise the gathering as an annual event. The Quadrilateral Security Dialogue became a high-level gathering quickly as the leaders of the four states held the first televised meeting in March 2021 following a proposal from US President Joe Biden.

Thus, Japan has maintained a prominent position in the development of the Indo-Pacific idea. Prime Minister Abe was deeply involved in the initiation of the Indo-Pacific concept, and the Quad – the major strategic framework for advancing the Indo-Pacific idea – was initiated by Japan. The Quadrilateral Security Dialogue where the four democratic nations discuss maritime security, a rules-based regional order and quality infrastructure and connectivity developed from a consultation at the director-general to the summit level.

The development of Japan's Indo-Pacific strategy and tangible policies

After returning to power in December 2012, Prime Minister Abe quickly developed the Indo-Pacific idea. During his planned visit to Southeast Asia in January 2013, Abe prepared for a speech entitled "The Bounty of the Open Seas: Five New Principles for Japanese Diplomacy."[2] In this speech, Abe planned to present five principles to underpin a new determination to expand the horizons of Japanese diplomacy. The first three principles were "protecting freedom of thought, expression, and speech in this region where two oceans meet," "ensuring that the seas, which are the most vital commons to us all, are governed by laws and rules, not by might" and "pursuing free, open, interconnected economies as part of Japan's diplomacy." The key ideas for the FOIP such as the confluence of the two oceans, free and open, and rules-based order were included in the five principles.

At the Centre for Strategic and International Studies (CSIS) in February 2013, Abe spelled out Japan's three tasks that he had considered during five years out of his prime ministership: to remain a leading promoter of rules "when the Asia-Pacific, or the Indo-Pacific region gets more and more prosperous"; to continue to be a guardian of global commons, like maritime commons, open enough to benefit everyone; and to work even more closely with the United States, South Korea, Australia and other like-minded democracies throughout the region. Abe used the term, the Indo-Pacific, for the first time in this speech as prime minister. Afterwards, Abe and the foreign ministers of his cabinet advocated the Indo-Pacific idea on various diplomatic occasions. During a Japan–India summit in November 2014, for instance, Abe showed his aspiration to add to Japan–India relations a standpoint of contributing to the stability and development of the Indo-Pacific. Abe also presented the Indo-Pacific concept during summit meetings with leaders of ASEAN members.

Japan has shaped and fulfilled practical policies and measures to flesh out the Indo-Pacific strategy. Such policies and measures are classified into three pillars: the promotion and establishment of fundamental values (rule of law, freedom of navigation, etc.), pursuit of economic prosperity through connectivity strength and capacity-building assistance to coastal countries and measures for securing peace and stability (MOFA 2017).

Japan has striven to promote and establish fundamental values such as the rule of law, freedom of navigation and overflight rights. Its efforts to diffuse and strengthen a rules-based order are seen in miscellaneous policy fields such as commerce, ocean, outer space and so on. In the trade field, for instance, Japan took the lead in finalising negotiations on the Comprehensive and Progressive Agreement for Trans-Pacific Partnership (CPTPP, or the TPP 11) after the US Trump administration withdrew from negotiations in January 2017. The CPTPP implied a significant achievement in international rule-making as it includes high-standard rules in intellectual property, state-owned enterprises, electronic commerce and so on (Yoshimatsu 2020a).

A particularly important element in establishing the rule of law is the creation of a rules-based maritime order. At the 13th Shangri-La Dialogue in May 2014, Abe presented the Three Principles of the Rule of Law at Sea: states shall make and clarify their claims based on international law, states shall not use force or coercion in trying to drive their claims and states shall seek to settle disputes by peaceful means. The Japanese government presented the three principles as crucial means to resolve maritime disputes typically seen in the South China Sea. During the 10th EAS meeting in November 2015, Abe stressed the importance of the three principles, stating that coastal states are required, under international law, whether for military use or civilian use, to refrain from unilateral actions that would cause permanent physical changes to the marine environment in maritime areas pending final delimitation. Moreover, the government strove to disseminate the three principles to the international community through multi-lateral forums such as the Japan-Caribbean Community (CARICOM) summit and the Pacific Islands Leaders Meeting (PALM).

As for economic prosperity through connectivity strength, Japan pushed forward support for infrastructure development under the banner of "quality infrastructure." In May 2015, Prime Minister Abe launched the Partnership for Quality Infrastructure (PQI), under which the Japanese government would provide US$110 billion for quality infrastructure investment in Asia from 2016 to 2020. On the sidelines of the Group of Seven (G7) Ise-Shima Summit in May 2016, the government announced the Expanded

Partnership for Quality Infrastructure. In this initiative, the government swore to provide US$200 billion from 2017 to 2021 to be allocated to infrastructure projects in
wider fields such as natural resources and hospitals. A distinctive feature of Japan's
connectivity support is the provision of quality infrastructure that is characterised as
economic efficiency in view of life-cycle cost, safety, resilience against natural disaster and addressing social and environmental impacts. The content and examples of
quality infrastructure are explained in detail in the "Quality Infrastructure Investment
Casebook" issued by five ministries and the Japan International Cooperation Agency
(JICA) in September 2015.

Japan has engaged in the development of infrastructure facilities in various parts
of the world. Typical cases are seen in the development of transport connectivity in
Southeast Asia such as the East-West Corridor that connects Da Nang in Vietnam
to Myanmar through Lao and Thailand, and the Southern Economic Corridor that
links Ho Chi Minh City in Vietnam and Dawei in Myanmar through Phnom Penh
and Bangkok. Besides, Japan has engaged in the development of ports and related
facilities in major countries in the Indian Ocean region: Matarbari Port in Bangladesh,
Trincomalee and Colombo Ports in Sri Lanka and Mombasa Port in Kenya. What is
important in these commitments is the combination of physical connectivity – ports,
railways, energy, information and communications technology (ICT) – with people to
people connectivity – education, training – and institutional connectivity and harmonisation and common rules including through economic partnership agreement (EPA)/
free trade agreement (FTA) (MOFA n.d.).

The capacity-building assistance, the third pillar of Japan's Indo-Pacific strategy,
has been implemented since the early 2010s. The Ministry of Defence (MOD) and
Self-Defence Force (SDF) have strengthened capacity-building assistance activities for
Southeast Asia since the Capacity Building Assistance Office was established within
the Bureau of Defence Policy in the MOD in 2011 (Satake 2020). In 2012–2019,
for instance, Japan organised seven seminars on underwater medicines for Vietnam
where experts shared knowledge and lessons about the basics of underwater medicine,
education systems for underwater medicine and real-life examples of underwater ill-
ness. Four out of the seven seminars were conducted as joint seminars with the US
and Australia.[3] The seminars contributed to strengthening the submarine operations
of Vietnam, which holds six Kilo-class submarines. Furthermore, during the Japan–
US Security Consultative Committee – the so-called 2+2 meeting – in August 2017,
Foreign Minister Kono Taro proclaimed that Japan would implement assistance total-
ling US$500 million in 2017–2019 to support capacity-building programs of maritime
security for coastal states in the Indo-Pacific region. The announcement at the 2+2
meeting indicates the importance of the programs through policy harmonisation with
the United States.

In order to offer capacity-building assistance flexibly, the Japanese government
revised the official development assistance (ODA) charter to allow support for
military groups engaging in peaceful purposes. The Development Cooperation
Charter adopted in February 2015 enables the government to provide aid funds
for foreign armed forces that engage in non-combat activities such as disaster relief
and those related to people's lives. After this revision, Japan could use ODA funds
flexibly such as the offering of patrol boats to the coast guard administration
under a military agency and an acceptance of former military soldiers for university education in Japan.

Diplomatic objectives in the Indo-Pacific strategy

As concrete policies and measures under the FOIP illustrate, Japan's Indo-Pacific strategy has been directed at pursuing specific diplomatic objectives under evolving regional climates. The objectives have geopolitical and geoeconomic natures, both of which are spurred by China's growing presence in the Indo-Pacific region.

The geopolitical objective has much to do with China's maritime behaviour in the East and South China Seas and the Indian Ocean. China has committed to frequent activities in Japan's controlled waters and airspace around the Senkaku/Diaoyu Islands in the East China Sea: the number of Chinese vessels identified within the Japanese territorial area in the sea decreased from 108 in 2017 to 70 in 2018 but increased to 126 in 2019 (MOFA 2021). The conflict over the islands became complicated with an associated dispute over claims of the Exclusive Economic Zone/Continental Shelf boundary in the East China Sea between Japan and China (Sato 2020). China has also raised tensions with claimants in the South China Sea by building artificial islands and facilities at an unprecedented speed. Beijing challenged the international rules-based maritime order, dismissing overwhelming support by an international tribunal in The Hague for claims by the Philippines in 2016. Moreover, China can enhance its naval presence through the expansion of the export of submarines to countries in the Indian Ocean region. China agreed to sell eight submarines to Pakistan in 2016, and Bangladesh gained two Chinese submarines in March 2017. The exports tend to urge the countries to develop dedicated repair and replenishment equipment for submarines and promote collaboration on data collection for submarine operations (Takeishi 2018).

China's growing presence in the South China Sea and the Indian Ocean raises Japan's concern about sea-line security. Japan's most important sea lines of communication (SLOCs) pass from the Indian Ocean to the East China Sea through the Malacca Strait and the South China Sea. The SLOCs are vital to Japan's trade and energy supplies as Japan has continuously relied on external sources for 96% of its energy resources, and the Middle East has provided most of Japan's oil demands. The growing number of port facilities under China's influence in the IOR makes Japan's SLOCs more vulnerable to a possible attack from Chinese submarines (Nagao 2019). This concern is reasonable as the People's Liberation Army Navy (PLAN) maintains a large number of submarines, between 65 and 70 through the 2020s, replacing older units with more capable units on a near one-to-one basis (Office of the Secretary of Defence 2020).

Japan has striven to maintain a rules-based international order through the FOIP as international public goods. The international public goods are goods whose benefits are extended to all countries, peoples and generations and are characterised as non-exclusiveness and non-competitiveness: whereas non-exclusiveness means no one will be excluded from sharing in the benefits of public goods once such goods are provided, non-competitiveness means consumption by one member will not cause a reduction in consumption by another member (Tao & Xi 2021). The FOIP's position for developing international public goods is confirmed in government documents. The "basic concept to realize free and open Indo-Pacific," issued by MOFA, states its aim to "develop a free and open Indo-Pacific region as 'international public goods', through ensuring the rule-based international order, in a comprehensive, inclusive and transparent manner" (MOFA n.d.). Michael Green, a famous Japan specialist and the Asia Desk chief of the National Security Council in the G. W. Bush administration, also contends that the FOIP flows from Japan's strategic goal to benefit "from a regional order that is based on rule-of-law; transparency; openness; high-quality rules for trade, investment and infrastructure; and the prevention of coercive actions against smaller states" (Green 2018). This contention also indicates Japan's pursuit of the rule of law to develop international public goods.

As explained in the previous section, the Japanese government has implemented the three sets of policies and measures under the banner of the FOIP. The capacity-building assistance to coastal countries could be regarded as a part of the strength of the rule of law, and the rule of law constitutes the main pillar of the measures under the FOIP (Aizawa 2018). This interpretation fits into policy programs such as the "Vientiane Vision," which Japan launched as a guiding principle for its defence co-operation with ASEAN in November 2016. The vision aimed at "ASEAN-wide" co-operation to facilitate a rules-based international order, maritime security and capacity-building (Koga 2020). Japan incorporated the learning of the principles of international law that governs peaceful conduct among states in capacity-building programs.

The geoeconomic aspect relates to China's attempt to enhance its economic and political presence through the Belt and Road Initiative (BRI). The BRI, which was launched in autumn 2013, raised its presence in broad areas from Asia to Europe and Africa. The BRI has gained a higher international presence by increasing the number of countries that concluded a memorandum of cooperation from 25 in 2015 to 137 in 2019 (Sano 2021). China's support for infrastructure development contributed to boosting the economic fundamentals of countries covered by the BRI. According to the estimate of the World Bank, BRI transport projects could increase trade between 2.8 and 9.7% for the corridor economies, producing real income gains of between 1.2 and 3.4% (World Bank 2019).

China has implemented the BRI as economic statecraft. Its investment in developing ports such as Gwadar in Pakistan, Hambantota in Sri Lanka, Chittagong in Bangladesh and Kyaukphyu in Myanmar contribute to undermining India's regional influence (Brewster 2017). China's engagements in major ports in the Indian Ocean region also serve to sustain its naval operations. A People's Liberation Army Navy (PLAN) Song-class conventional submarine and a submarine support ship made a stopover at Colombo Port in Sri Lanka in September and November 2014 (Sakhuja 2015). China built its first overseas military support facility in Djibouti in 2017, and it was reported in January 2018 that Beijing was planning to build an offshore naval base near the Pakistani Gwadar Port on the Arabian Sea (Berkofsky 2019b).

Japan's strategic objectives regarding the Indo-Pacific policy can be evaluated through two conceptual frameworks. First, Japan has formulated and implemented the FOIP as an inter-institutional balancing in which states can use one institution to challenge the relevance and the role of another institution. Under the inter-institutional balancing, a state does not target an individual state *per se* but another existing institution (He 2015). Japan has developed the FOIP as a key institution to counter against the BRI. This is particularly the case in connectivity development. As mentioned, connectivity development is one of the three policy pillars under the FOIP. Japan consolidated partnerships with the United States and its allies for connectivity development. In November 2018, Japan, the United States, Australia plus New Zealand agreed with Papua New Guinea to elevate the ratio of electricity connection from 13% to 70% of its population by 2030. The three governments then sent a joint mission to the country in April 2019 to discuss details of co-operation on infrastructure development.

The three countries considered other Pacific nations including the Solomon Islands and Palau as candidates for joint infrastructure financing (Kodachi 2019). These engagements aimed to counter the BRI's extended reach to Pacific Island nations. In November 2019, the United States launched a multi-stakeholder initiative called the Blue Dot Network (BDN) in collaboration with Japan and Australia. The Organisation for Economic Co-operation and Development (OECD) and the three governments began consultations on the development of this certification system in June 2021, and the BDN was envisioned as a part of the Build Back Better World (B3W) Partnership, the G7's initiative to sustain infrastructure development in the developing world. The BDN is designed to certify infrastructure projects that maintain international principles and promote high quality, trusted standards. This initiative is confrontational as it endorses infrastructure projects of the United States and its allies as "Blue Dot" against the Chinese as "Red Dot."

Second, Japan's FOIP can be evaluated as a part of "norm entrepreneurship." The norm entrepreneurship seeks to achieve diplomatic goals not through coercion or unilateral actions but the gaining of support from other states in pursuit of their perceived interests and to take advantage of norms, rules and principles as means to achieve the goals (Envall & Wilkins 2022; Ravenhill 2018). The FOIP is the key vehicle for Japan's norm entrepreneurship because it functions as a linchpin to forge multi-lateral partnerships to develop and diffuse international norms, rules and principles. Japan and its partners have underscored the free and open maritime order through the rule of law and freedom of navigation. Japan also sought to diffuse high-standard trade rules through the CPTPP and the RCEP. Furthermore, Japan took the initiative in disseminating liberal principles in infrastructure investment such as openness, transparency, economic efficiency and financial sustainability by using multi-lateral fora including the G7, G20 and APEC (Yoshimatsu 2022).

Regional perspectives on the Indo-Pacific strategy

After Japan first presented the FOIP in 2016, this diplomatic idea evolved in two dimensions. The first puts more emphasis on the inclusive posture under the FOIP "vision." The Japanese government sought to downplay the containment nature in the FOIP but the term, strategy, still indicates a confrontational nature. The government began to use the FOIP "vision" instead of the FOIP "strategy" in official use after 2018. Besides, Prime Minister Abe confirmed that the FOIP vision does not exclude any countries in his speeches at the EAS in November 2018 and at the Diet in January 2019 (Kamiya 2018). Foreign Minister Taro Kono directly confirmed the importance of co-operation with China and South Korea in realising the FOIP in the trilateral foreign ministers' meeting in August 2019 (Koga 2020).

The second is a subtler change in terminology used for explaining the three pillar policies under the FOIP. Previously, the Japanese government raised "the promotion and establishment of fundamental values (rule of law, freedom of navigation, etc.)" as the first pillar. In June 2019, this first pillar changed to "promotion and establishment of the rule of law, freedom of navigation, free trade, etc." The government intentionally deleted "fundamental values" (Koga 2020). This change in terminology was seen in Abe's policy speech to the Diet. Abe used the phrase that "Japan will work together with countries with which we share fundamental values such as freedom, democracy, human rights, and the rule of law" at his speech in January 2018.

Abe used a phrase "Japan will create a 'free and open Indo-Pacific,' working together with all the countries that share this vision" in his policy speech one year later. The drop of universal values dilutes the FOIP's confrontation against China, and at the same time expands the possibility of realising the "Quad plus" by inviting other countries such as Vietnam.

The above new orientations are derived from two factors. The first is a shift in strategic orientation in relation to China from confrontation to adaptation. Since the second Abe administration began in December 2012 under frozen relations with Beijing especially in Senkaku/Diaoyu Islands disputes, the administration did not undertake proactive diplomacy towards China. After behind-the-scene diplomatic engagements to reconstruct diplomatic relations through 2014 to 201616 (Cheung 2017), Abe exhibited a new policy stance by dispatching Toshihiro Nikai, Secretary-General of the Liberal Democratic Party (LDP), and Takaya Imai, chief executive secretary to the prime minister, to the first Belt and Road Forum for International Cooperation in May 2017. One month after this dispatch, Abe announced Japan's participation in the BRI under several conditions. Afterwards, policy talks on Sino–Japanese collaboration went on rapidly. Abe and Chinese leaders confirmed, at their summit meetings in November, the need to discuss how to contribute to the stability and prosperity of the region and the world including co-operation on BRI projects. In September 2018, the first meeting of the Committee for the Promotion of Japan-China Business Cooperation in Third Countries took place in Beijing. During Abe's visit to Beijing in October 2018 that accompanied more than 500 business executives, the first Japan–China Forum on Third Country Business Cooperation took place and 52 memorandums of co-operation were confirmed there.

The Abe administration did not wish to continue frozen relations with China and explored an opportunity to re-introduce stability in relations with this important neighbour. Moreover, the Japanese business community hoped for stable Sino–Japanese relations and participation in BRI projects. The growing Chinese market re-emerged as an important destination for overseas operations for Japanese business, and Japanese-affiliated companies in China raised their interests in expanding business operations in the market. The Japanese business community desired to expand business opportunities by consolidating bases in the Chinese market and strengthening partnerships with Chinese enterprises in overseas businesses through BRI projects. Given the worsening economic-security frictions with the United States, the Chinese government recognised the need to loosen the Japan–US political partnership and an economic engagement was regarded as a useful means to re-establish political connections with Japan. Under these complex domestic and international climates, Japan reformulated a diplomatic strategy towards China, which also influenced the fundamental principle of its Indo-Pacific strategy.

The second relates to diplomatic relations with ASEAN. ASEAN is strategically import for Japan's Indo-Pacific strategy both because Southeast Asia is the key link between the Indian and Pacific Oceans and because the association has led the building multi-lateral architectures for regional cooperation (Envall & Wilkins 2022). When Abe advocated the Quad 1.0 during the first administration in 2007, this diplomatic idea received a cool response from Southeast Asian countries both because this minilateral partnership included none of the ASEAN members and because it created the perception that Abe was seeking to supersede ASEAN centrality in multi-lateral discussions of regional strategic affairs (Lee 2016). Partly learning from the experiences during the first administration, Abe underlined the ASEAN-centred multi-lateralism of the EAS after returning to the prime ministership in 2012.

ASEAN members were generally passive about the FOIP because they were worried about its strong orientation to maintain a free and open maritime order on the premise of China's aggressive diplomacy and offensive actions. Singapore encouraged Japan to revise the FOIP's exclusive nature, and Tokyo changed its formal title from the FOIP strategy to the FOIP vision.[4] In the meeting with the Malaysian Prime Minister in November 2018, Abe formally used the term, "vision," instead of strategy. Thus, the change to the vision was partially an accommodation policy to respond to ASEAN's concerns.

Japan's positive perception of ASEAN in its Indo-Pacific strategy is reflected in additional two aspects. The first is the Quad members' sensitivity to ASEAN's position on multi-lateralism in Asia. The four members did not refer to ASEAN in their statement of the first consultation in November 2017. However, they have used a phrase to "pay respect to ASEAN centrality" since the 2nd consultation in November 2018. Several ASEAN members had raised concerns about the closed Quad framework and weak consideration of ASEAN's regional position. For instance, Singapore's foreign minister, Vivian Balakrishnan, exhibited reluctance to join the Quad in May 2018 because the concept does not adequately address whether ASEAN would continue to be central to the region's architecture (Yong 2018). Japan is a key member that realised the change because it has encouraged the United States to attach weight to relations with Southeast Asia (Y.A. 2020). The second is Japan's positive assessment of the association's Indo-Pacific vision. ASEAN adopted its own vision for the Indo-Pacific – the ASEAN Outlook on Indo-Pacific (AOIP) – at the 34th ASEAN Summit in June 2019. The AOIP includes terms such as respect for international law and freedom of navigation and overflight. Abe raised the AOIP as an epoch-making achievement, demonstrating its unity and centrality, even mentioning that "this year is the inaugural year of free and open Indo-Pacific of ASEAN, by ASEAN, and for ASEAN" (MOFA 2019).

Kuik (2016, 2020) has explained ASEAN members' diplomatic strategy as "hedging," which is characterised by insistence on not taking sides, attempts to pursue opposing measures to offset different risks and diversification to cultivate a fall-back position. ASEAN's overall posture towards the Indo-Pacific can be characterised as hedging. Whereas the AOIP contains norms and principles that have been emphasised by the United States and Japan for managing maritime affairs, it also includes the phrase "building strategic trust and win-win cooperation," which have been advocated by Chinese political leaders as crucial vehicles for advancing a regional partnership. Even under continuous Chinese pressure in the South China Sea, ASEAN as a whole remains reluctant to take sides with the United States, not giving support to its apparently confrontational approach. Japan is encouraged to lure ASEAN members to the US side by pursuing a prudent approach to accommodate their preferences and requirements, and the Indo-Pacific strategy is embraced in such a policy need.

Global perspectives on the Indo-Pacific strategy

Japan has promoted positive engagements in diffusing the FOIP concept and measures under its Indo-Pacific strategy on the global scale. At the 8th Pacific Islands Leaders Meeting (PALM8) in May 2018, Japan declared its intention to commit deeply to the stability and prosperity of the region based on the FOIP, and the Pacific island countries shared the importance of the basic principles of the strategy. The Yokohama

Declaration 2019 of the TICAD VII in August 2019 refers to taking good note of the initiative of the FOIP and a rules-based maritime order in accordance with the principles of international law. Japan's global efforts aimed to enhance the sense of ownership for maintaining free, open and sustainable oceans under the rule of law and make the international community recognise that the free and open Indo-Pacific should be developed as international public goods.

A key challenge for Japan in developing the FOIP is that major states have different perceptions of the Indo-Pacific and its associated strategies. Japan considers the Indo-Pacific that extends from the Pacific to eastern Africa but the American perception does not cover Africa. India has strengthened its engagement in the Quad under the banner of the FOIP. Yet, New Delhi remains less willing to develop the US-centred alliance, pursuing multilateral systems under its basic diplomatic tenet of "strategic autonomy."

Given these uncertainties in the Indo-Pacific, a stronger partnership with European nations has crucial implications for Japan's Indo-Pacific strategy. During the Abe administration, Japan tightened political and economic connections to the European Union (EU) by concluding the Japan-EU Economic Partnership Agreement (JEEPA) and the Strategic Partnership Agreement (SPA) in July 2018 (Berkofsky 2019a; Yoshimatsu 2020b). Whereas the former underpinned the preservation of a free trade system against protectionist movements, the latter confirmed common universal values between the two parties. Japan has also stiffened economic and strategic partnerships with major European nations such as the United Kingdom, France, Germany and Italy (Simón & Speck 2018). Furthermore, Japan toughened relations with the North Atlantic Treaty Organization (NATO) as Abe concluded the Individual Partnership and Cooperation Programme (IPCP) with NATO in May 2014. The Japanese government also established a representative office to NATO in Brussels in July 2018.

In advancing the Indo-Pacific strategy, Japan attaches great importance to a partnership with European nations. The inclusion of European nations into Asian security frameworks was Abe's long-term desire as he proposed that the United Kingdom and France join a coalition to safeguard the maritime commons in the Pacific and Indian Oceans in his security diamond article in 2012 (Koga 2020). These two states are direct parties for the Indian Ocean affairs because they hold external territories in the Indian Ocean: Réunion for France and British Indian Ocean Territory for the United Kingdom. In this point, France-organised Le Pérouse naval exercise in April 2021 where the four Quad members joined had significant strategic implications. Moreover, European nations become key partners for Japan in advancing a rules-based order in the Indo-Pacific. Not only do the nations share common values with Japan but they are global leaders that have developed rules-based governance in the international community.

Under such conditions, Japan has sought to gain support for its Indo-Pacific idea from European nations. When the Prime Minister and Foreign Minister have met with their counterparts of European nations, they raised achievement of the free and open Indo-Pacific as one of the key agendas. For instance, during a summit meeting in June 2019, Abe and French President Emmanuel Macron shared the recognition that one of the top priority issues for the two countries is to make the Indo-Pacific inclusive, free, open, peaceful and prosperous for all partners.

The EU members have a particular interest in advancing connectivity in partnership with Japan. In September 2018, the EU formulated the policy document entitled

"Connecting Europe and Asia: Building Blocks for an EU Strategy," in which the union underlined "sustainable, comprehensive and rules-based connectivity." When the EU organised the Europa Connectivity Forum in September 2019, Abe was invited as a key presenter. During the session, Abe and Jean-Claude Juncker, President of the European Commission, signed the document, the Partnership on Sustainable Connectivity and Quality Infrastructure between Japan and the EU. Their partnership for connectivity development covers various regions of the world, and the Indo-Pacific is identified as one of the five regions. The main value of the document lies in the confirmation of key principles – openness, transparency, inclusiveness, the ensuring of debt sustainability and so on – in undertaking infrastructure investment. These are principles that Japan incorporated into the Group of Twenty (G20) Principles under the G20 Osaka summit it hosted in June 2019. The EU hoped to share with Japan key principles in infrastructure investment and check China's diplomatic undertaking through BRI projects.

Conclusion

The main policy goal of Japan's Indo-Pacific strategy is to maintain and enhance the existing rules-based international order in the Indo-Pacific. In achieving this policy goal, Japan needed to meet two challenges: to dissuade China from strengthening a propensity to challenge the existing rules-based liberal order in the region, and to coordinate the relationship between unilateral, hard-edged US strategies and the multilateral, inclusive policy preferences of Asia-Pacific countries. In order to meet the challenges, Japan has presented and implemented various ideas and policies to advance the collective interests of the Indo-Pacific region in political, economic and security domains, and has sought to coordinate interests of major states in the region.

As confirmed in the regional and global perspectives, Japan's attempt has so far produced positive outcomes by diffusing the new geographical concept of the Indo-Pacific and the importance of rules and norms for managing geopolitics and geoeconomics in the Indo-Pacific region. However, Japan's Indo-Pacific strategy is facing new challenges especially under growing uncertainty in Sino–US rivalry. The Biden administration's diplomatic stance to consolidate partnerships with its allies in managing international affairs will have a positive impact for attaining the policy goal of Japan's Indo-Pacific strategy. However, the US diplomacy with a strong human rights orientation will invite China's strategic relations, which will destabilise international relations of the Indo-Pacific. The new global landscape after the COVID-19 pandemic is an additional risk for maintaining a rules-based liberal order in the Indo-Pacific region.

Notes

1 The webpage (https://www.mofa.go.jp/policy/page25e_000278.html) introduces the meaning of the FOIP and its references in speeches and meetings.
2 Abe was unable to deliver this policy speech because he was forced to go back to Tokyo due to a hostage incident involving the Japanese in Algeria.
3 Noryoku Kochiku Shien Jigyo, Betonamu [Project for Supporting Capacity Building, Vietnam]. Retrieved from: https://www.mod.go.jp/j/approach/exchange/cap_build/vietnam/index.html.
4 PM Abe Shuns Word 'Strategy' When Touting Free, Open Indo-Pacific. *Nippon. Com* (November 14, 2018). Retrieved from: https://www.nippon.com/ja/news/yjj2018111401238/.

References

Abe, S. (2006). *Utsukushii Kuni e [Towards a Beautiful Nation]*. Tokyo: Bungei Shunju.

Abe, S. (2007). Confluence of the two seas, speech at the parliament of the Republic of India, August 22. Retrieved from: http://www.mofa.go.jp/region/asia-paci/pmv0708/speech-2.html.

Abe, S. (2012). Asia's democratic security diamond. *Project Syndicate*, December 27. Retrieved from: https://www.project-syndicate.org/onpoint/a-strategic-alliance-for-japan-and-india-by -shinzo-abe?barrier=accesspaylog [accessed May 15, 2019].

Aizawa, T. (2018). Gaimushō HP kara yomitoku 'Jiyū de Hirakareta Indo-taiheiyō Senryaku (FOIP)' no rinen to jissen [Philosophy and practice of 'Free and Open Indo-Pacific Strategy (FOIP)' Red from the Foreign Ministry HP]. *Kaiyō Anzen Hoshō Jyōhō Kihō* 21, 69–85.

Allen-Ebrahimian, B. (2017). It's not China, It's you, India seems to tell spurned aussies. Foreignpolicy.com. Retrieved from: https://foreignpolicy.com/2017/06/05/its-not-china-its -you-india-seems-to-tell-spurned-aussies-malabar-australia-navy/.

Berkofsky, A. (2019a). The strategic partnership agreement: New and better or more of the same EU-Japan security cooperation? In A. Berkofsky et al. (eds.), *The EU-Japan Partnership in the Shadow of China: The Crisis of Liberalism*. London and New York: Routledge, 17–39.

Berkofsky, A. (2019b). Tokyo's 'free and open Indo-Pacific': Quality infrastructure and defence to the fore. ARI 34/2019, Elcano Royal Institute. Retrieved from: http://www .realinstitutoelcano.org/wps/portal/rielcano_en/contenido?WCM_GLOBAL_CONTEXT= /elcano/elcano_es/zonas_es/asia-pacifico/ari34-2019-berkofsky-tokyos-free-and-open-indo -pacific-quality-infrastructure-defence-fore.

Brewster, D. (2017). Silk roads and strings of pearls: The strategic geography of China's new pathways in the Indian Ocean. *Geopolitics* 22(2), 269–91.

Cheung, M. (2017). Japan's China policy on Yasukuni under Abe (2012–2015): A political survival interpretation. *Journal of Contemporary East Asia Studies* 6(1), 62–78.

Clinton, H. R. (2010). America's engagement in the Asia-Pacific, Honolulu, October 28. Retrieved from: https://2009-2017.state.gov/secretary/20092013clinton/rm/2010/10/150141.htm.

Envall, H. D. P. and Wilkins, T. S. (2022). Japan and the new Indo-Pacific order: The rise of an entrepreneurial power. *The Pacific Review*. http://doi.org/10.1080/09512748.2022.2033820.

Garver, J. W. and Wang, F. L. (2010). China's anti-encirclement struggle. *Asian Security* 6(3), 238–261.

Green, M. (2018). Japan's free and open Indo-Pacific Strategy as grand strategy. *We Are Tomodachi*. Retrieved from: https://www.japan.go.jp/tomodachi/2018/spring2018/ contributed_article.html.

He, K. (2015). Contested regional orders and institutional balancing in the Asia Pacific. *International Politics* 52(2), 208–222.

Horimoto, T. (2018). Indo taihei jidai no nichiin kankei [Japan-India relations in the Indo-Pacific era]. *Kokusai Mondai* 669, 36–48.

Horimoto, T. (2019). Relations between Japan and India in the Indo-Pacific Age — Transcending the quad framework. *Japan Review* 3(2), 54–70.

Hosoya, Y. (2019). FOIP 2.0: The evolution of Japan's free and open Indo-Pacific strategy. *Asia-Pacific Review* 26(1), 18–28.

Kamiya, M. (2018). Kyōsō senryaku no tame no kyōryoku senryaku [Cooperation strategy for competitive strategy]. Society of Security and Diplomatic Policy Studies. Retrieved from: http://ssdpaki.la.coocan.jp/proposals/26.html.

Kodachi, H. (2019). Japan, US and Australia Begin own 'Belt and Road' in South Pacific. *Nikkei Asian Review*, 25 June. Retrieved from: https://asia.nikkei.com/Politics/International -relations/Japan-US-and-Australia-begin-own-Belt-and-Road-in-South-Pacific.

Koga, K. (2020). Japan's 'Indo-Pacific' question: Countering China or shaping a new regional order? *International Affairs* 96(1), 49–73.

Kuik, C.-C. (2016). How do weaker states hedge? Unpacking ASEAN states' alignment behavior towards China. *Journal of Contemporary China* 25(100), 500–514.

Kuik, C.-C. (2020). Hedging in post-pandemic Asia: What, how, and why? *The ASAN Special Forum*, June 6. Retrieved from:http://www.theasanforum.org/hedging-in-post-pandemic -asia-what-how-and-why/.

Lee, J. (2016). In defense of the East Asian regional order: Explaining Japan's newfound interest in Southeast Asia. *Geopolitics, History, and International Relations* 8(1), 30–53.

MOFA (Ministry of Foreign Affairs). (2017). *2017-nenban Kaihatsu Kyōryoku Hakusho: Nihon no Kokusai Kyōryoku [2017 White Paper on Development Cooperation: Japan's International Cooperation]*. Tokyo: MOFA.

MOFA (Ministry of Foreign Affairs). (2019). The 14th East Asia summit, November 4. Retrieved from: https://www.mofa.go.jp/a_o/rp/page3e_001123.html.

MOFA (Ministry of Foreign Affairs). (2021). Trends in Chinese government and other vessels in the waters surrounding the Senkaku Islands, and Japan's response, March 3. Retrieved from: https://www.mofa.go.jp/region/page23e_000021.html.

MOFA (Ministry of Foreign Affairs). (n.d.). Free and open Indo-Pacific. Retrieved from: https:// www.mofa.go.jp/mofaj/files/000430632.pdf.

Nagao, S. (2019). What is Japan's Indian Ocean strategy? RIPS' Eye, February 28. Retrieved from: https://www.rips.or.jp/en/rips_eye/1575/.

Office of the Secretary of Defense (2020). *Military and Security Developments Involving the People's Republic of China 2020*. Washington, DC: Office of the Secretary of Defense. Retrieved from: https://media.defense.gov/2020/Sep/01/2002488689/-1/-1/1/2020-DOD -CHINA-MILITARY-POWER-REPORT-FINAL.PDF.

Ravenhill, J. (2018). Entrepreneurial states: A conceptual overview. *International Journal: Canada's Journal of Global Policy Analysis* 73(4), 501–517.

Sakhuja, V. (2015). Chinese submarines in Sri Lanka unnerve India: Next stop Pakistan? *China Brief* 15(11), 29 May. Retrieved from: https://jamestown.org/program/chinese-submarines-in -sri-lanka-unnerve-india-next-stop-pakistan/.

Sano, J. (2021) Sūchi kara mita Chūgoku no Ittai Ichiro Koso no jitsuzō [The real image of China's Belt and Road Initiative seen from numerical values]. *Kan-Taiheiyo Bijinesu Joho RIM* 21(80), 66–86.

Satake, T. (2020). Nihon: 'Jiyu de Hirakareta Indo-taiheiyo ni muketa torikumi' [Japan: Initiatives for a Free and Open Indo-Pacific]. In National Institute for Defense Studies (ed.), *Higashi Ajia Senryaku Gaikan [East Asian Strategic Review]*. Tokyo: Aban Konekushonzu, 189–212.

Sato, Y. (2020). The Sino-Japanese maritime disputes in the East China Sea. CIMSEC, September 16. Retrieved from: https://cimsec.org/the-sino-japanese-maritime-disputes-in-the-east-china -sea/.

Simón, L. and Speck, U. (eds.) (2018). Natural partners? Europe, Japan and security in the Indo-Pacific. Royal Elcano Institute Policy Paper. Retrieved from: http://www.realinstitutoelcano .org/wps/wcm/connect/e1b07fbdac5f-4d8d-874c-1fe1b7ff1892/Policy-Paper-2018-Natural -Partners-Europe-Japan-security-Indo-Pacific.pdf?MOD=AJPERES&CACHEID=e1b07fbd -ac5f-4d8d-874c-1fe1b7ff1892.

Smith, S. (2012). Deterrence and regional security, June 2. Retrieved from: http://www.minister .defence.gov.au/2012/06/02/minister-for-defencedeterrence-and-regional-security-at-the -11th-international-institutefor- strategic-studies-singapore/.

Suzuki, Y. (2017). *Nihon no Senryaku Gaiko [Japan's Strategic Diplomacy]*. Tokyo: Chikuma Shobo.

Takeishi, E. (2018). Chugoku, Indoyo engan koku ni sensuikan yushutsu [China exports submarines to coastal countries in the Indian Ocean] *Asahi Shimbun*, 14 January.

Tao, M. and Xi, C. (2021). Creating inclusive global value chains under the BRI from the perspective of public goods supply and demand. *China Economist* 16(4), 60–69.

World Bank. (2019). *Belt and Road Economics: Opportunities and Risks of Transport Corridors*. Washington, DC: World Bank.

Y. A. (2020). The virtues of a confrontational China strategy. *The American Interest*. Retrieved from: https://www.the-american-interest.com/2020/04/10/the-virtues-of-a-confrontational-china-strategy/.

Yong, C. (2018). Singapore not joining US, Japan-led free and open Indo-Pacific for now: Vivian Balakrishnan. *Straits Times*, May 14. Retrieved from: https://www.straitstimes.com/singapore/singapore-not-joining-us-japan-led-free-and-open-indo-pacific-for-now-vivian-balakrishnan.

Yoshimatsu, H. (2020a). High-standard rules and leadership capacity in Japan's mega-FTA strategy. *Asian Survey* 60(4), 733–54.

Yoshimatsu, H. (2020b). The EU-Japan free trade agreement in evolving global trade politics. *Asia Europe Journal* 18(4), 429–43.

Yoshimatsu, H. (2022). Japan's strategic response to China's geo-economic presence: Quality infrastructure as a diplomatic tool. *The Pacific Review*. http://doi.org/10.1080/09512748.2021.1947356.

Further reading

Envall, H. D. P. and Wilkins, T. S. (2022). Japan and the new Indo-Pacific order: the rise of an entrepreneurial power. *The Pacific Review*. http://doi.org/10.1080/09512748.2022.2033820.

Hosoya, Y. (2019). FOIP 2.0: The evolution of Japan's free and open Indo-Pacific strategy. *Asia-Pacific Review* 26(1), 18–28.

Koga, K. (2020). Japan's 'Indo-Pacific' question: Countering China or shaping a new regional order? *International Affairs* 96(1), 49–73.

Satake, T. and Sahashi, R. (2021). The rise of China and Japan's 'vision' for free and open Indo-Pacific. *Journal of Contemporary China* 30(127), 18–35.

20 The EU and the Indo-Pacific

The path towards a comprehensive strategy

Andrea Carteny and Elena Tosti Di Stefano

In the mid-1990s, the European Union (EU) identified the Asia-Pacific as one of its key strategic targets. At that time, the Union was driven by the ambition to expand the focus of its external action beyond its immediate neighbourhoods, building on the still embryonic, yet high-profile, EU Common Foreign and Security Policy (CFSP). The ensuing decades have seen a profound reconfiguration of the international order, marked, *inter alia*, by a shift in the balance of power towards Asia, that has been gradually replacing the trans-Atlantic area as the centre of gravity of global economics and politics. It is in this context that the idea of an Indo-Pacific (IP) region has progressively gained traction in the global strategic narrative, most notably in Japan, the United States, India and Australia, coming to supplant, at least partially, the Asia-Pacific frame of reference. As exhaustively detailed in Chapter 1 and 2 of the present volume, the IP construct – in its different domestic conceptualisations – reflects an increasingly polycentric regional scenario where China's ascent constitutes the major driver of competition.

The EU has progressively recognised the need to redefine its interests, role and policies in the area in light of an ever-evolving multipolar scenario. The 2016 foreign policy shift, encapsulated in the Global Strategy for the European Union's Foreign and Security Policy, heralded the formulation of a more active and comprehensive approach towards the IP. Yet, the Union has long been hesitant to internalise the "Indo-Pacific" construct, instead preferring to retain the term "Asia-Pacific" in official statements, policy documents and bilateral agreements. The unveiling of the EU Strategy for Cooperation in the Indo-Pacific in September 2021 introduced a significant novelty in the EU's approach. Such evolution was triggered, *inter alia*, by the release of IP national strategies in France, Germany and the Netherlands between 2018 and 2020.

The chapter will examine the evolution of the European Union's policies in the Asia-Pacific/Indo-Pacific from the mid-1990s to the present time, with the aim to assess both the achievements and shortcomings of its approach. Although the Union has only recently espoused the "Indo-Pacific" concept, for the sake of clarity only this designation will be used throughout the text. From this standpoint, terminological elucidations are needed. For the past two decades, the EU has employed the expression "Asia-Pacific" with reference to the area going "from Afghanistan in the west to Japan in the east, and from China in the north to New Zealand in the south, plus all points between" (European Commission 2001: 6). With the launch of the new strategy in 2021, the EU has provided its own understanding of the term "Indo-Pacific," i.e., "a vast region spanning from the east coast of

DOI: 10.4324/9781003336143-25

Africa to the Pacific Island States" (European Commission and High Representative of the Union for Foreign Affairs and Security Policy 2021: 1). The comparison between the two definitions shows that the latter is broader than the former, for it also comprises those countries that fall under the scope of the EU partnership with the African, Caribbean and Pacific (ACP) group of states.[1]

As previously said, the IP construct is not merely descriptive nor value-neutral, but intrinsically laden with geopolitical references. The strategic ingredient is particularly relevant for the European Union, which holds relevant interests in the region. Four of its top-ten trading partners are located in the Indo-Pacific (China, Japan, South Korea, India); the EU's 27 member states direct over 35% of their exports to this area, and about 90% of those transit through the two Oceans (Mohan 2020). Moreover, as economic prosperity is closely intertwined with the security environment, the European Union has to deal with Beijing's growing assertiveness in the region, as well as to navigate the trouble waters of China–US rivalry – the latter being its traditional transatlantic ally.

First, this chapter will present the EU's overarching policy frameworks and initiatives in the Indo-Pacific from the inception of the CFSP to the release of the EU Indo-Pacific Strategy, placing due emphasis on the changes in the geopolitical landscape. Starting from this background, the following section will focus on the Union's relations with four selected countries/group of countries, namely China, Japan, India and the Association of Southeast Asian Nations (ASEAN).

The EU's approach towards the IP in an evolving geostrategic context

Before delving into the EU's policies in the Indo-Pacific area, it is worthwhile introducing some background information related to its historical development and institutional architecture.

The Cold War provided a momentum for the newly created European Union – formerly European Communities (EC) – to enhance its credibility as an international actor within a Western-led liberal order. In fact, the collapse of the Soviet Union, German reunification, along with the prospective EU membership of the ex-communist states of Central and Eastern Europe, reinforced the Union's ambitions to use its political influence to foster stability and prosperity both around its borders and further afield. Linked to this is the EU's self-representation as a "normative power," with reference to its inner predisposition to promote the core Western values ("norms") of liberal democracy in world politics (Manners 2002). The 1992 Maastricht Treaty, which officially established the European Union, laid the foundations for the Common Foreign and Security Policy. Since 1999, the European Security and Defence Policy (ESDP) – then renamed Common Security and Defence Policy (CSDP) – was developed in this same framework. Yet, while the Union was attributed supranational competences in the economic and monetary domains, the CFSP was conceived as an intergovernmental field of action, meaning that the member states decide unanimously on foreign policy issues at the EU level. With the Lisbon Treaty, entered into force in 2009, the EU sought to enhance its international actorness by creating the position of the High Representative of the Union for Foreign Affairs and Security Policy (hereinafter High Representative), as well as the European External Action Service (EEAS).

From the New Asia Strategy ...

Soon after the launch of the CFSP, the EU endeavoured to deepen its relations with Indo-Pacific countries. Since 1994, it has participated in the ASEAN Regional Forum (ARF), founded in the same year, hence contributing to fostering dialogue on political and security themes of common interest in the region. In 1996, the then 15 member states of the EU and the European Commission, together with China, Japan, Southern Korea and the then seven ASEAN countries, set up the region-to-region dialogue ASEM (Asia-Europe Meeting) (Box 20.1). At the policy level, in 1994 the Union unveiled a first strategy paper entitled Toward a New Asia Strategy, in an early attempt to formulate a balanced and comprehensive framework *vis-à-vis* its Asian counterparts. The document was seemingly driven by a self-interested rationale, i.e., to strengthen the EU's economic presence across one of the most dynamic regions in the world in terms of economic growth (Wacker 2015). Indeed, a major focus was on helping integrate Asian partners into the open, market-based international trading system. Among the other objectives were poverty alleviation in concerned countries, as well as the promotion of stability through political dialogue in both bilateral and multilateral settings (European Commission 1994). In 2001, the Commission published the communication Europe and Asia: A Strategic Framework for Enhanced Partnership, through which it reviewed and updated its approach. Comparing the 1994 and the 2001 policy papers, it can be observed that the Union broadened the scope of engagement with the region. First, while the former targeted 26 countries in Northeast Asia, Southeast Asia and South Asia,[2] in 2001 the outreach was expanded to cover Australasia, so as to properly consider the intensified political, economic and cultural ties between Oceania – particularly Australia and New Zealand – and East Asia. Second, the latter *communiqué* takes more account of the political, economic, social and cultural heterogeneity of IP countries by distinguishing between "action points for the region as a whole" and "for each of the four key sub-regions" (European Commission 2001: 3). Third, the Union included a mention to "joint efforts" on global security and environmental issues. The strategic review thus seemed to signal an increased understanding of the IP due to the ongoing development of the EU's foreign policy competences along with policy reflections on past experiences (Song & Wang 2019). The core goal of the revised policy was defined as "strengthening the EU's political and economic presence across the region, and raising this to a level commensurate with the growing global weight of an enlarged EU" (European Commission 2001: 3). More in detail, six objectives were singled out: bolster peace and security; boost mutual trade and investment flows; enhance development cooperation; contribute to the protection of human rights and to the spreading of democracy, good governance and the rule of law; build global partnerships and alliances in appropriate international fora; promote mutual awareness. The approach was later complemented by the 2003 European Security Strategy, in which the Union underlined its interest in the Indo-Pacific, notably with regard to the challenges posed by nuclear proliferation and terrorism. In this context, Japan, China and India were identified as the Asian countries with which the EU planned to develop Strategic Partnerships,[3] which were *de facto* established between 2003 and 2004. Besides these three states, the Union has started negotiating partnership and cooperation agreements (PCAs)[4] and Free Trade Agreements (FTAs)[5] with other regional partners, such as Indonesia, Thailand, Malaysia, the Philippines, Singapore, and Vietnam.

**Box 20.1 The Asia-Europe Meeting (ASEM): A model
of effective inter-regionalism?**

Launched in 1996 on the initiative of the Singaporean and French governments, ASEM is an intergovernmental process to promote dialogue and co-operation between Asia and Europe. It initially consisted of 15 EU countries and seven ASEAN member states plus China, Japan, Korea and the European Commission. After five rounds of enlargement, the partnership today includes 51 countries: 27 EU member states plus Norway, Switzerland and the United Kingdom on the European side, the ten ASEAN states plus Australia, Bangladesh, China, India, Japan, Kazakhstan, the Republic of Korea, New Zealand, Pakistan and Russia on the Asian side. It further comprises two institutional partners, the European Union and the ASEAN Secretariat. Collectively, ASEM members represent around 60% of the worldwide population, 65% of global GDP, and 60% of global trade. Since its inception, the Asia-Europe Meeting has focused on three pillars – political, economic and socio-cultural and educational – whose contents have been continuously adjusted according to the growth of the partnership and the evolution of the international landscape. The first pillar deals with international crises, security, multi-lateralism, environment and human rights, while ASEM economic co-operation aims to increase trade and investment flows by reducing trade barriers and encouraging links between the governmental and private business sectors of the two regions; the third pillar is aimed at enhancing people-to-people links through joint cultural, social and educational activities involving in particular the younger generation. Another major issue of common interest is connectivity, which cuts across all three of ASEM's pillars (ASEM InfoBoard). From an organisational point of view, the multi-lateral platform has no permanent secretariat and works through meetings and activities organised at different levels, i.e., summits between the 51 heads of state or government and the president of the two participating institutions (held every other year), as well as ministerial and senior official gatherings.

   At the time of its creation, the Asia-Europe Meeting was hailed as the first real attempt to consolidate and strengthen relations between two increasingly significant and interdependent regions of a globalising world (Gilson 2002). As such, the partnership was described as an "implicit" inter-regional arrangement "in which loose coalitions of states come together as 'notional' regions" (Gilson 2020: 4) in response to international trends and challenges. The overall assessment of the first decade of ASEM was fairly positive, especially in the economic domain (e.g., the institution of the Asia-Europe Business Forum). However, starting from the mid-2000s, inter-regionalism between Europe and Asia has been called into question by a series of factors, ranging from the global recession to institutional weakness to the rise of China. Indeed, the Eurozone crisis, in conjunction with other pressing issues such as the migratory emergency and, most recently, Brexit, have challenged the EU's "normative" model, which had been considered for a long time as the gold standard for region-building. At the same time, ASEM has significantly increased its membership, to the point that a region-to-region structure has become difficult to discern. This has brought a complex range of other relations into the partnership, notably the EU–Russia relationship. Moreover, the level of institutionalisation remains low due to the absence of a formal ASEM secretariat. Lastly, the ascent of China has been profoundly reshaping Asian regional architecture. In this context, the growing competition between Washington and Beijing has a considerable impact on Asia–Europe relations (Gaens 2018; Gilson 2019). Despite the attempts to reinvigorate the forum, ASEM is largely seen as "lacking concrete outcomes, remaining at the level of a talking shop" (Gaens & Khandekar 2018: 1).

Suggested reading:

- ASEM InfoBoard, "ASEM Pillars," https://www.aseminfoboard.org/about/pillars-of-asem.
- Bart Gaens & Gauri Khandekar, 'Introduction,' *in:* Bart Gaens, Gauri Khandekar (eds.), *Inter-Regional Relations and the Asia-Europe Meeting (ASEM)*, (London: Palgrave Macmillan, 2018): 9–32.
- Julie Gilson, *Asia Meets Europe: Inter-Regionalism and the Asia–Europe Meeting* (Cheltenham: Edward Elgar Publishing, 2002).
- Julie Gilson, 'A European Pivot towards Asia? Inter-regionalism in a New Era,' *in:* Weiqing Song, Jianwei Wang (eds.), *The European Union in the Asia-Pacific. Rethinking Europe's strategies and policies*, (Manchester: Manchester University Press, 2019): 39–56.
- Julie Gilson, "EU-ASEAN Relations in the 2020s: Pragmatic Inter-regionalism?," *International Economics and Economic Policy* 17, 2020: 727–745.

Notwithstanding this proactive stance towards the IP, in the two following decades most attention and resources have been absorbed by the EU's internal challenges and the turmoil in its immediate neighbourhoods. Indeed, as the unipolar moment began to gradually give way to a "new multipolarity" (Geeraerts 2011), the European Union found itself caught in numerous crises. Internally, the difficult ratification of the Lisbon Treaty, the Eurozone sovereign debt crisis, the rise of populism and Euroscepticism, the Grexit and Brexit debates, put into question the very foundations of the European integration project. Externally, the Union saw the emergence of an "arc of instability" around its southern and eastern borders – from the 2011 Arab uprisings to Russia's annexation of Crimea in 2014 – and had to cope with the resulting spill-over effects, such as the massive influx of refugees from across the Southern Mediterranean and Southeast Europe. Against this backdrop, the EU's role in the Indo-Pacific has been plagued by a "capability-expectations gap" (Chen & Gao 2020). It is widely accepted that economic interactions have dominated European interests and relations, despite the stated efforts to diversify the areas of cooperation (Wacker 2015; Wu 2018; Song and Wang 2019). However, as the IP grew to become one of the most dynamic parts of the global economy, the EU's economic power has been significantly challenged. At first, the Union has not been able to respond to these transformations and revise its strategy accordingly, but rather continued to rely mostly on bilateral FTAs that, in turn, were jeopardised by competing plurilateral initiatives. In particular, the project of a Trans-Pacific Partnership (TTP) among 12 Pacific Rim countries has been a central plank in Obama Administration's "pivot" to Asia, although President Trump then withdrew the United States from the agreement in 2017. Furthermore, the Union has faced difficulties in pursuing its political and security engagement with the region, whose strategic horizon has undergone dramatic changes. The Indo-Pacific has become home to two of the five leading emerging powers, i.e., China and India. Besides, the area presents several tense flashpoints, notably the territorial disputes over the South China Sea and the Sino-Indian border, as well as the North Korean nuclear issue. Security uncertainty is further exacerbated by the Sino-Japanese geopolitical rivalry and growing strategic suspicion and competition between Beijing and New Delhi. In this context, the European Union has not been able to adopt a unified stance regarding the US rebalancing strategy towards the IP, particularly because of EU member states' divergent positions on the China issue (Casarini 2013). Linked to this are the institutional limitations inherent in the CFSP – and, consequently, the CSDP – which continued to rely on intergovernmental solutions, despite the innovations introduced by the Lisbon Treaty. In fact, the EU countries have traditionally been reluctant to hand sovereignty to supranational EU bodies in this policy field. As the idea of a European army was never realised, the European Union – as a unified entity – has no permanent troop deployment in the IP area. Among individual EU countries (United Kingdom excluded), only France has maintained a modest naval presence[6] in the Indian Ocean and the South Pacific, where are located its overseas territories, remains of the French colonial empire.[7]

To the EU Strategy for Cooperation in the Indo-Pacific

In light of the above, in the mid-2010s the EU embarked on a thorough rethink of its foreign policy approach, taking the European Security Strategy as a point of departure. This culminated in the 2016 Global Strategy for the European Union's Foreign and Security Policy, aimed to rise the ambitions of the Union's external action and enhance its position as a global player while reckoning with the global-scale transformations occurred since 2003 (EEAS 2016b) (Box 20.2). What have been implications of the new policy approach in the Indo-Pacific? First, the Global Strategy raised the nexus between European prosperity and Asia security, calling for an increased economic diplomacy and security engagement in the area. Additionally, it stressed the importance of a "connected" Asia. The EU institutions pinpointed a number of challenges for the Union in the IP, including managing the relationship with a growingly assertive China; deepening the relations with strategic partners, particularly India, Japan, ASEAN and South Korea; continuing "critical engagement" with North Korea; becoming an effective security actor in the region; and creating a more sustainable connectivity between Europe and Asia, and within Asia (EEAS 2016a). In 2018, two overarching documents have come to form the cornerstone of the reviewed Asia strategy: the Council Conclusions on Enhanced EU Security Cooperation in and with Asia and Connecting Europe and Asia – Building Blocks for an EU Strategy. The former *communiqué* exemplifies the willingness to prioritise tailor-made engagement with IP actors, primarily China, India, Japan and Republic of Korea, along with ASEAN and its members. Among the key areas for deeper security engagement are maritime security, cyber security, counter-terrorism, hybrid threats, conflict prevention and the proliferation of chemical biological radiological and nuclear weapons (Council of the European Union 2018). In the second policy paper, the Union put forward a "European way" to pursue sustainable, rule-based and comprehensive connectivity between the two regions, based on mutual interests, transparency, high environmental and social standards, a level playing field for businesses and fiscal and financial sustainability.

More in-depth, the EU proposed to co-operate with its diverse partners along three strands: the creation of transport links, energy and digital networks, and people-to-people contacts; the establishment of connectivity partnerships with Asian countries and organisations; and the promotion of sustainable finance in infrastructure projects (European Commission 2018). In view of this, the "European way to connectivity" has been widely perceived as an attempt to counterpoise China's Belt and Road Initiative (BRI) (Brattberg & Soula 2018; Geeraerts 2019). Such a posture was seemingly confirmed by the announcement in September 2021 of the upcoming EU grand strategy on connectivity, named Global Gateway – although it is still unclear how concretely this initiative will compete with the BRI (Sacks 2021).[8]

Box 20.2 Bridging the gap between idealism and pragmatism: the EU Global Strategy

In June 2016, then High Representative of the Union for Foreign Affairs and Security Policy, Federica Mogherini, unveiled the EU Global Strategy, which replaced the European Security Strategy of 2003. Adopted in a moment of deep internal crisis – the Brexit referendum – the policy document portrayed a "more connected, contested and complex world" where "[w]e live in times of existential crisis, within and beyond the European Union" (EEAS 2016: 13). As such, the strategy acknowledged the declining leverage of the EU within and outside its borders, marking a shift from the "normative power" approach to a more pragmatic stance. The new *modus operandi* was encapsulated in the notion of "principled pragmatism" (EEAS 2016: 8), in other words, a "Realpolitik with European characteristics" (Biscop 2016). On the one hand, this means that the EU and its member states should clearly identify and firmly advance their interests in an age of multi-polarity; on the other hand, in doing so, it is crucial for them to preserve some consistency between utilitarian conduct and the liberal principles defining Europe. Moreover, the Union set the goal to develop an appropriate level of "strategic autonomy," i.e., "the ability to act, preferably with others, beginning with NATO and the United States, but when necessary also alone" (Tocci 2019: 2). This latter aspect appeared all the more salient given the reawakening of isolationist tendencies and the strains in transatlantic relations under the Trump administration.

The *Global Strategy* laid out five priorities for the EU's external action: (1) ensuring the security of the Union by stepping up efforts on defence, cyber, counterterrorism, energy and strategic communications; (2) investing in the resilience of states and societies to the East stretching into Central Asia, and to the South down to Central Africa; (3) adopting an integrated approach to conflicts; (4) promoting co-operative regional orders worldwide; (5) striving for a multi-lateral rules-based order with a strong UN as the bedrock (EEAS 2016: 9–10).

Suggested readings:

- Sven Biscop, "The EU Global Strategy: Realpolitik with European Characteristics," *Egmont Security Policy Brief*, 75, 2016: 1–6.
- European External Action Service, "Shared Vision, Common Action: A Stronger Europe. A Global Strategy for the European Union's Foreign and

Security Policy," 2016, https://eeas.europa.eu/archives/docs/top_stories/pdf/
eugs_review_web.pdf.

- Nathalie Tocci, "Navigating Complexity: The EU's Rationale in the 21st
Century," *IAI Commentaries*, 19(6), 2019: 1–5.

In her 2021 State of the Union Address, the President of the European Commission,
Ursula von der Leyen, presented – concomitantly with the Global Gateway – the EU
Strategy for Cooperation in the Indo-Pacific, qualified as a "milestone" (von der Leyen
2021). Coherently with its previous strategies towards Asia, the Union puts forward a
sustainable, comprehensive and rules-based approach, which focuses on seven priority
areas (European Commission and High Representative 2021):

- *Sustainable and inclusive prosperity*: To ensure an effective recovery after COVID-
19, the EU stresses the need of resilient value chains to be developed through
enhancing and diversifying trade relations with IP partners, implementing existing
trade agreements, finalising ongoing trade negotiations and improving cooperation in strategic sectors.
- *Green transition*: The Union endeavours to conclude Green Alliances and
Partnerships[9] to tackle climate change and environmental degradation. In the
energy domain, the EU is committed to mobilising energy partnerships and financial instruments for sustainable and affordable energy, as well as develop R&D
initiatives on clean energy technology. Major attention is also paid to smart mobility to address the issues of decarbonisation and digitalisation.
- *Ocean governance*: As the largest export market for seafood products from the
Indo-Pacific, the Union seeks to further dialogue and joint initiatives with IP states
and organisations to ensure the sustainable management of the ocean's resources
and the safeguard of biodiversity.
- *Digital governance and partnerships*: The strategy sets out the goal to strengthen
and – in the most advanced cases – formalise digital partnerships with the objective to support values-based innovation, build more resilient technology supply
chains and provide business opportunities for start-ups and SMEs.
- *Connectivity*: Based on the goals set out in the 2018 EU-Asia Connectivity Strategy,
the Union reiterates its determination to expand Connectivity Partnerships and
joint projects with regional actors, while boosting cooperation with international
players such as the United States and Canada.
- *Security and defence*: Key priorities in this domain comprise: capacity-building
and enhanced naval presence by EU member states in the Indo-Pacific; increased
joint exercises with regional partners to fight piracy and protect freedom of navigation; and the strengthening of dialogue on other relevant issues including counterterrorism and cybersecurity.
- *Human security*: To cope with the impact of the pandemic, the Union is willing
to work with all IP partners to secure access to the COVID-19 vaccine and ensure
safe pharmaceutical industrial supply chains.

Even though the new strategy does not take a confrontational attitude towards China,
it is nevertheless "symptomatic of a change in perceptions of international power

relations and their potential impact on Europe" (Grare & Reuter 2021: 4). As such, the introduction of the "Indo-Pacific" concept shows not only that the EU and its member states are increasingly worried about Beijing's rise, but also their uncertainty about Washington's commitment to European security and its readiness to protect the EU's interests from the potentially negative repercussions of the US–China rivalry[10]. As said, France, Germany and the Netherlands have been the driving force behind the elaboration of the EU approach towards the IP (Box 20.3). Yet, a country survey conducted by the European Council on Foreign Relations in 2021 has clearly highlighted the lack of debate around the Indo-Pacific in several EU countries, as well as different understandings of both the region's geographic boundaries and strategic significance. Although the China question is unanimously regarded as a central component of a EU's long-term approach, diverging member states' interests in the region – and towards Beijing itself – risk to undermine the effective implementation of the EU-wide strategic framework (Grare & Reuter 2021).

Box 20.3 The French, German and Dutch Indo-Pacific strategies in a comparative perspective

Between 2018 and 2020, three EU member states – France, Germany and the Netherlands adopted a national strategy towards the Indo-Pacific region.

In May 2018, during a speech at the Garden Island naval base in Sidney, President Emmanuel Macron launched the French IP strategy, subsequently updated in 2021. In the strategic document, Paris highlights its position as a resident power in the Indo-Pacific, where are located its overseas territories and about two-thirds of its Exclusive Economic Zone (EEZ). The region is home to 1.65m French people and over 7,000 soldiers are stationed there. The strategy identifies four main areas of action. In the security and defence domain, France commits to ensuring and defending national integrity and sovereignty, as well as deepening military and security co-operation to settle regional crises and counter criminal and terrorist phenomena. To this end, Paris is developing a network of strategic partnership with Indo-Pacific states such as India, Australia, Japan, Malaysia, Singapore, New Zealand, Indonesia and Vietnam. For what concerns economy, connectivity and R&I, France's goals are to ensure diversification of the supply of strategic goods, promote existing international standards, meet needs in term of connectivity and infrastructure, support French companies in the area and strengthen research and innovation partnerships, particularly in the health domain. Under the third pillar, Paris puts emphasis on promoting multi-lateralism and the rule of law by fostering EU involvement in the IP and boosting ties with ASEAN and other regional organisations. The fourth priority area relates to climate change, biodiversity and sustainable management of the oceans (Government of the French Republic 2021).

In September 2020, the German government published a policy document entitled *Policy Guidelines for the Indo-Pacific Region. Germany – Europe – Asia: Shaping the 21st Century Together*, in which the country endorsed for the first time officially the "Indo-Pacific" concept. According to the guidelines, the IP architecture should be neither unipolar nor bipolar, as this would endanger an approach of enhanced and diversified partnerships in the region. Among the main priorities identified by

Germany is the strengthening of multi-lateralism, especially through increased engagement with ASEAN, but also other regional institutions such as the Pacific Islands Forum (PIF). At the security level, Berlin expressed its commitment to expand cooperation in the military, maritime and cybersecurity fields through working closely with IP countries among which Australia, Japan, New Zealand, Singapore and South Korea, as well as through enhancing the EU's security role. The document also points to the importance of ensuring a rules-based, fair and sustainable free trade by diversifying and intensifying relations with regional partners, assisting German companies and supporting the EU's trade policy in the Indo-Pacific. Major emphasis is also placed on rules-based networking and digital transformation, mainly through the enhancement of Germany's competitiveness in key technology and the implementation of the EU-Asia Connectivity Strategy. Other important domains of collaboration are climate and environment, as well as culture, education and science (Federal Government of Germany 2020).

Last but not least, in November 2020, the Ministry of Foreign Affairs of the Netherlands released the policy document Indo-Pacific: Guidelines for strengthening Dutch and EU cooperation with partners in Asia. As the title suggests, the guidelines put major emphasis on the need to develop a more coherent and engaged EU approach to the IP. At the domestic level, the Netherlands has relevant economic interest in the area; for instance, around 22.5% of total Dutch imports come from Asian countries, and in 2019 the Netherlands was the largest importer of goods from the ASEAN countries in the EU. As such, The Hague expressed willingness to step up action particularly in the domains of security co-operation and digital connectivity (Government of the Netherlands 2020).

The three strategies present both differences and similarities. First, France sets itself apart from the two other member states by reason of its status as a sovereign nation in the IP, while German and Dutch interests are those of major trading nations. Second, Paris seems to display an assertive attitude towards China, while Berlin seeks to build consensus by formulating a policy that antagonizes neither China nor the United States. Amsterdam, for its part, shows deep concerns regarding Chinese role in the region and pushes for a joined-up response at the EU level. Besides, by encouraging a more cohesive EU's posture, all three countries contributed to the development of the European Union's Indo-Pacific strategy.

Suggested reading:

- Federal Government of Germany, "Policy Guidelines for the Indo-Pacific Region. Germany –
- Europe – Asia. Shaping the 21st Century Together," 2020, https://rangun .diplo.de/blob/2380824/a27b62057f2d2675ce2bbfc5be01099a/policy -guidelines-summary-data.pdf.
- Government of the French Republic, "France's Indo-Pacific Strategy," 2021, https://www.diplomatie.gouv.fr/IMG/pdf/en_a4_indopacifique_v2_rvb _cle432726.pdf.
- Government of the Netherlands, "Indo-Pacific: Guidelines for strengthening Dutch and EU cooperation with partners in Asia," 2020, file:///C:/Users/ele na/Downloads/Indo-Pacific+Guidelines+EN%20(1).pdf.

The evolution of the EU's policies in China, Japan, India and ASEAN

Based on the above analysis, this section will examine the implementation of the EU's approach in the IP with respect to China, Japan, India and ASEAN. The choice of these case studies is twofold. In the first place, since the early days of the CFSP, these countries/association of states have been considered by the European Union as "strategic" or "key" partners in the region. In the second place, all of them play a significant role in the shaping of the Indo-Pacific architecture. As previously outlined, China has been advancing a geoeconomic strategy of centrality in every quadrant of the region and, by the way, its assertive behaviour is the main factor behind the rise of the IP construct itself, which has been adopted by all the other regional actors dealt with hereinafter. Japan, for its part, is taking on a greater role in the region's trade and technology landscape, while simultaneously undergoing a transformation of its foreign policy posture by steadily shifting away from its traditional non-military attitude. Along with the expansion of its geopolitical position, India is also bolstering its economic and military engagement in its immediate neighbourhood and looking for enhanced partnerships beyond the region. Other middle powers like Singapore and Indonesia – members of ASEAN – are emerging as critical players in framing the economic and security geography of the IP.

China

Building on the 1994 New Asia Strategy, the EU and the People's Republic of China (PRC) established a Cooperative Partnership in 1998, which was upgraded to a Comprehensive Partnership in 2001. The latter agreement was reached in the frame of the revised strategy Europe and Asia: A Strategic Framework for Enhanced Partnership, which set precise goals for the Union's relations with Beijing, i.e., ensure that China develops in a sustainable way so as to play a cooperative role in the international community; promote dialogue in the fields of human rights, good governance and sustainable development; and support China's integration in the world economy (European Commission 2001). In fact, Beijing's accession to the World Trade Organization (WTO) that same year was met with enthusiasm by the Union as a win-win scenario for both EU and Chinese exporters and investors. In 2003, the two parties jointly announced the creation of the China-EU Comprehensive Strategic Partnership, which should have heralded a period of "all-dimensional, wide-ranging and multi-layered" co-operation (Wen 2004). The agreement covered multiple areas of engagement, ranging from economy, to politics, to culture. With the rise of the Euro currency and the EU's large-scale enlargement to Central and Eastern Europe countries (2004–2007), the European Union grew into the PRC's biggest trade partner, while the latter became the EU's second largest external trade partner, only after the United States. As such, the first three years of the Comprehensive Strategic Partnership have been considered as a "honeymoon" of the relationship (Zhou 2017: 8). Nevertheless, diplomatic frictions and bilateral disputes over the understanding of the partnership soon started to emerge. Most notably, Beijing criticised the Union's delays in removing the ongoing arms embargo[11] and its condemnation against China's human rights record.[12] Besides, the EU's negative assessment of China's intellectual property standards, trade deficit and limits to market access led it to launch anti-dumping and anti-subsidy investigations against Beijing. Thus, during the first decade of co-operation, a real strategic partnership failed to materialise because of clashing political values and different conceptions of the world order (Maher 2016). Yet, although relations have at times been severely strained, they did not slide into stagnation, mainly because after 2003 ties became highly institutionalised (Christiansen 2016). Between 2008 and 2012, the percentage of China–EU trade declined due to both the impact of the global financial crisis and the long-pending problems that the PRC and the Union had failed to settle in the economic and trade domain. Still, as of 2012, the European Union had remained China's number one trade partner and origin of imports.

In the following years, the shift in balance of economic and political power had a clear impact on the EU's position *vis-à-vis* Beijing, contributing to putting the relationship on a more realist footing. As already mentioned, the Union found itself entangled in the US–China struggle, which rapidly expanded from issues of technological innovation to finance, health and security. Even if the Union did not take a resolute stance in this respect, apprehension over the PRC's growing assertiveness and ongoing initiatives – notably the BRI – started to dominate the EU–China debate. Only a month after the unveiling of the Global Strategy, the Union published a new strategy paper on China. On the one hand, the document identified major economic opportunities, including a comprehensive agreement on investment, a Chinese contribution to the investment plan for Europe, joint research and innovation activities and the development of connectivity networks. On the other hand, the *communiqué* expresses concerns about unfair competition and the human rights situation, with reference to the detention of lawyers, journalists and labour rights defenders (Council of the European Union 2016). As anticipated in the above section, several commentators saw in the Union's strategy a response to the BRI due to the emphasis on environmental and social standards, improved market access and fiscal and financial sustainability. This approach would entail, among other things, an implicit accusation against Beijing's debt-trap diplomacy through stringent loan-repayment conditions (Brattberg & Soula 2018; Di Donato 2020). Such a response would be consistent with long-standing scepticism at the EU level towards the Chinese global infrastructure strategy.[13] In March 2019, the strategic paper EU-China – A Strategic Outlook posited that the PRC may simultaneously act as a "cooperation partner" a "negotiating partner," an "economic competitor" and a "systemic rival promoting alternative forms of governance" (European Commission and High Representative 2019: 1) depending on the issue or policy area involved. The conclusion of the EU-China Comprehensive Agreement on Investment (CAI) in January 2021 appeared to be consistent with this posture. Yet, as detailed in the previous section, heightened concerns about Beijing's behaviour – fostered, *inter alia*, by the pandemic crisis – led to the adoption of a firmer EU stance, encapsulated in the 2021 Global Gateway initiative and the EU Strategy towards the IP. Moreover, the European Parliament has so far refused to ratify the CAI on the grounds of China's poor human rights record (European Parliament 2021).[14] However, coherently with the Strategic Outlook, the EU Indo-Pacific Strategy does not resort to "finger-pointing," but rather stress the need of pursuing a "multifaceted" engagement with Beijing,[15] thus leaving the door open for co-operation. Still, the recurring use of concepts such as "rules-based order" and "like-minded countries" indicates that the EU's approach is not value-neutral. Anyhow, the Strategy makes reference to necessary progress in ratifying the CAI and provide for closer collaboration with the PRC in a number of domains, notably environment and ocean affairs.

Japan

During the 1990s, the EC/EU's efforts to increase its actorness and presence in Asia was closely linked, *inter alia*, to its positive assessment of Tokyo's evolving foreign policy. In 1991, the European Communities and Japan signed the "Hague Joint Declaration," in which the two parties outlined their ambition to intensify dialogue and cooperation at the political, economic, social and sector-specific level. In 1995, the European Commission released the policy paper Europe and Japan: The Next Steps in the framework of the New Asia Strategy. In both documents, the European Union praised Japan's contribution to the development and stability of East Asia by means of its soft power, i.e., through trade and investment, development assistance and engagement in confidence-building initiatives (European Commission 1994, 1995). The country was then recognised as a strategic part-ner in 2003, along with China and India. During the first decade of co-operation, the two sides developed solid ties in the economic and trade fields, although China remained the main EU partner in the region (Berkofsky 2007). In around 2010, the Brussels and Tokyo opened informal talks on a Free Trade Agreement for which official negotiations were launched three years later with poor results.[16] Between the mid-1990s and the mid-2010s, security cooperation was mostly focused on non-traditional security sectors. In this respect, it should be stressed that the EU's conceptualisation of security as expressed in the 2003 European Security Strategy was in line with the approach embraced by Japan since the post-war years, that significantly relied on soft power (Atanassova-Cornelis 2010). In fact, both parties underscored the comprehensive nature of security threats, which goes beyond the solely traditional (military) dimension and requires the use of a variety of political, economic and civilian means. As a result, the Union and Japan have co-operated in non-military crisis and post-conflict reconstruction. Relevant initiatives include the joint promotion of the peace process in Sri Lanka in the early 2000s and post-war reconstruc-tion initiatives in Iraq, Afghanistan and Bosnia Herzegovina. In addition, Tokyo provided financial and technical assistance to the EU-led capacity-building missions in Niger and Mali, which started, respectively, in 2012 and 2014. In the late 2000s, the changes in the Indo-Pacific strategic landscape prompted a re-think of Shinzo Abe Administration's foreign policy approach, which began to be dominated by geopolitical concerns, notably linked to China's security behaviour and ambitions for a future domination of maritime East Asia, as well as the sustainability of the US military presence in the area. In the Guidelines on the EU's Foreign and Security Policy in East Asia, published in 2012, the Union recognised the numerous security challenges in the IP, with particular focus on the Korean peninsula and the South China Sea (Council of the European Union 2012). However, the EU's limited hard power capabilities came to represent a constraint in the Strategic Partnership and negatively affected Tokyo's willingness to engage in meaningful initiatives in the security domain. What is more, in the Guidelines the European Union adopted a "principled neu-trality" position on regional maritime and territorial disputes, encouraging the parties to settle disagreements in accordance with international law (Council of the European Union 2012: 19). The reluctance to be more outspoken on China's issues was frowned upon by Japan. These factors together explain Tokyo's preference to deal bilaterally with individual EU countries on these matters, notably France and the United Kingdom[17] (Atanassova-Cornelis 2015).

Following the launch of the Free and Open Indo-Pacific Strategy (FOIP) in 2016, Japan deepened its ties with other IP partners, such as India and ASEAN members, and intensified its relations with non-regional actors – the United States above all, but also the European Union. In 2018, the EU and Japan concluded a binding Strategic Partnership Agreement (SPA), which constitutes a framework to strengthen the overall partnership through co-operation in more than 40 areas of common interest, notably in the security sphere. Concomitantly with the SPA, the two parties signed an Economic and Partnership Agreement (EPA) after five years of intermittent negotiations, during which Japan had kept its position as the EU's second-biggest trading partner in Asia. The deal provides for the removal of export duties and regulatory barriers in different areas, ranging from agriculture to service markets. It further includes a chapter on trade and sustainable development, along with relevant clauses on labour standards, safety and consumer protection. Moreover, Tokyo was the first Indo-Pacific country to enter a connectivity partnership with the EU in 2019. As of now, it is the only IP country, together with New Delhi, to have signed such an agreement with the Union (Box 20.4). In mid-2021, Japan was again the earliest IP country to enter a Green Alliance with the European Union. The importance of the EU–Japan relationship was confirmed by the EU Indo-Pacific Strategy, which envisions enhanced cooperation in several fields. In the economic domain, the Union manifested its commitment to fully implement the EPA, focusing in particular on the need to address strategic dependencies in supply chains, as is the case with semiconductors. Concerning climate and environment, collaboration under the Green Alliance is set to go hand in hand with engagement at the multilateral level. What is more, Japan is – together with the Republic of Korea and Singapore – one of the three IP countries with which the Union is eager to launch negotiations for a Digital Partnership Agreement.[18] Finally, Tokyo is considered one of the core EU partners for maritime security activities.[19] It is also among the pilot partners of the EU project "Enhancing Security Cooperation in and with Asia" (ESIWA), started in 2020, which covers counter-terrorism, cybersecurity, maritime security and crisis management.

Box 20.4 The EU–Japan and EU–India Connectivity Partnership in context

Building on the strategic document Connecting Europe and Asia – Building Blocks for an EU Strategy, released in October 2018, the EU has so far concluded connectivity agreements with two Indo-Pacific countries, Japan and India.

In September 2019, Brussels and Tokyo adopted the EU-Japan Partnership on Sustainable Connectivity and Quality Infrastructure, as part of their commitment "to promoting rules-based connectivity globally" (European External Action Service, EEAS 2019: 1) across several, cross-cutting areas of co-operation including digital, transport, energy and people-to-people exchanges. Emphasising the importance of an accessible, reliable and secure cyberspace, the two sides agreed on developing digital and data infrastructure as well as policy and regulatory frameworks. In the domain of transportation, the partnership focuses on the interconnection of transport corridors and the enhancement of transport safety and security. As far as energy is concerned, the EU and Japan expressed their willingness to deepen already ongoing cooperation in areas such as electricity market regulation, hydrogen and fuel cells and liquefied natural gas (LNG), as well as to support sustainable energy connectivity through infrastructure investments. Finally, the agreement envisions the expansion of international people-to-people exchanges through cultural, education and sport initiatives. The geographical areas where the two parties would carry out joint infrastructure projects are the Indo-Pacific, the Western Balkans, Eastern Europe, Central Asia and Africa (EEAS 2019: 2–3). The EU–Japan Connectivity Partnership was backed by a €60 billion EU guarantee fund, which would serve to attract further investments from private investors and development banks. Furthermore, in parallel to the agreement, the European Investment Bank (EIB) and the Japan International Cooperation Agency (JICA) signed additional deals aimed at deepening collaboration on quality infrastructure investment, microfinance and renewable energy sources.

Brussels and New Delhi entered a connectivity partnership on the occasion of the EU-India Leaders' Meeting held in May 2021. The agreement puts forward a comprehensive approach to connectivity, in line with the EU–Asia Connectivity Strategy and the partnership between the European Union and Japan. The digital dimension is given major importance in light of the fact that India's digital economy is predicted to grow of over 250% between 2019 and 2025 (European Commission 2021). Activities under the agreement include co-operation on satellite networks, submarine cables and 5G. Among the priorities in the transport sectors are dialogue on smart and sustainable mobility, new investment in metros and air routes and projects in maritime industry. In the energy field, emphasis is placed on the implementation of the EU–India Clean Energy and Climate Partnership. Last but not least, people-to-people connectivity initiatives comprise, *inter alia*, enhanced opportunities under the Erasmus+ programme and joint work under the research and innovation program Horizon Europe (Council of the European Union 2021: 2–4). The conclusion of the Connectivity Partnership was accompanied by the signature of a new EIB financing of €300 million for the construction of the metros of Pune and Kanpur.

The two agreements are consistent with the narrative of the "European way to connectivity," based on transparency, high environmental and social standards, a level playing field for businesses and fiscal and financial sustainability. The EU–Japan and EU–India Connectivity Partnerships have come to form an integral part of the EU Indo-Pacific Strategy and the EU Global Gateway initiative, both unveiled in 2021. As detailed in this chapter, the latter initiative constitutes an explicit response to China's Belt and Road Initiative.

Suggested reading:

- Council of the European Union, "EU-India Connectivity Partnership," 2021, https://www.consilium.europa.eu/media/49508/eu-india-connectivity-partnership-8-may-2.pdf.
- European External Action Service, EEAS, "The Partnership on Sustainable Connectivity and Quality Infrastructure between the European Union and Japan," 2019, https://eeas.europa.eu/regions/africa/68018/partnership-sustainable-connectivity-and-quality-infrastructure-between-european-union-and_en.
- European Commission, "Principles, Partnership, Prosperity: EU and India Launch Collaboration on Sustainable Connectivity," 2021, https://ec.europa.eu/commission/presscorner/detail/en/IP_21_2327.

India

In 1994, the European Union and India concluded a Cooperation Agreement on Partnership and Development, which was mostly centred on "creating favourable conditions for a substantial development and diversification of trade and industry" (*Official Journal of the European Communities* 1994). These objectives were reiterated in the policy document EU-India Enhanced Partnership, which widened the scope of the previous deal to cover co-operation on regional stability and security, support to social and sustainable development and the strengthening of democracy (European Commission 1996). In 2004, the relationship was upgraded to a Strategic Partnership with the goal to: increase international co-operation based on multilateralism by promoting peace, non-proliferation of weapons of mass destruction and countering terrorism; deepen commercial and economic interaction; improve mutual understanding and contacts between European and Indian civil society (European Commission 2004). During the first decades of the twenty-first century, the progressive institutionalisation of ties was accompanied by a remarkable growth in the value of EU-India trade, that rose from €28.6 billion in 2003 to €79.9 billion in 2012. However, while the European Union – as a bloc of countries – affirmed itself as New Delhi's largest trading partner, India oscillated between the eighth and the ninth position in the EU's ranking. For example, India made up only 2.4% of the Union's overall trade volume in 2010, while the latter represented around 15% of India's foreign trade (Khorana & Narayanan 2017). Furthermore, the negotiations for an ambitious FTA, launched in 2007, were soon undermined by a lack of progress, mainly because of sectoral disagreements (Nataraj 2013). As far as security co-operation is concerned, it appeared clear from the very beginning that the two sides held different conceptions of security. As already examined, the European Union has traditionally been more of a "normative" and economic power than a military one. Instead, back to 1999, the Kargil war with Pakistan reasserted in India the centrality of hard power in world affairs. Therefore, the EU's soft power approach had scant traction in a nation that viewed itself as being engulfed in the "reality of war in South Asia" (Wülbers 2011: 14). From this perspective, New Delhi has negatively perceived the Union's unwillingness to discriminate between India and Pakistan and its attempts to balance between the two conflicting neighbours. In this context, the United States was seen an increasingly receptive partner that – unlike the European Union – seemed to share New Delhi's security concerns about the threats posed by Pakistan as well as by China, which is also involved in a longstanding border dispute with India. Against this background, there is widespread scholarly consensus that the first 20 years of co-operation under the Common Foreign and Security Policy resulted in a "rather paradoxical strategic partnership," i.e., "one that is neither very strategic nor really a partnership" (Kavalski 2016: 193).

Starting from the mid-2010s, India and the EU initiated a process of reassessing their bilateral relationship, at a time when the former was growing more and more alarmed at Beijing's rising economic and military capabilities and expanding footprints in the Indian Ocean. In this period, both sides acknowledged that the Strategic Partnership had become overfocused on the troubled negotiations of the FTA and declared their interest in furthering the relationship in other fields of co-operation. In the meanwhile, New Delhi embarked on efforts to re-calibrate its engagement with the Union in view of Brexit. Indeed, India had tended to see the United Kingdom – its former colonial ruler and leading partner in the Commonwealth – as its "gateway to

Europe and even its window on the EU" (Pal Chaudhuri 2020: 18). At the CFSP level, the desire to reinvigorate the partnership was translated into the policy document *Elements for an EU Strategy on India*, issued in 2018, which has replaced the 2004 strategy. India is here identified as "a heavyweight on the Asian continent," "an emerging global power" and a key pillar "for a balanced EU policy towards Asia as a whole" (European Commission and High Representative 2018: 1). Among the main priorities of the revised policy are formulating common responses to global and regional issues based on effective multi-lateralism; and supporting India's prosperity through sustainable modernisation, with particular reference to sustainable infrastructure and connectivity, circular economy, environmental protection and digitalisation. The timing and content of the strategic document seemingly reflected the EU's eagerness to encourage "middle power co-operation" with the aim to compensate for the unilateral action of Beijing and Washington under the Trump Administration (Pal Chaudhuri 2020: 18). The 15th EU-India Summit of July 2020 paid greater attention to security issues compared to earlier meetings, where trade and investment used to be the most debated issues (Klossek et al. 2020). On this occasion, the parties endorsed the *EU-India Strategic Partnership: A Roadmap to 2025*, whose stated goals are recalled in the EU Indo-Pacific Strategy. First, the document underlines the EU's eagerness to resume FTA negotiations and launch investment negotiations with India. The country is further hailed as one of the two EU "Connectivity Partners" as a result of the agreement concluded in May 2021 (Box 20.4). Another objective highlighted in the strategy is the enhancement of the EU–India digital partnership, as a follow-up of a co-operation agreement on emerging technologies signed in mid-2021. Just as Tokyo, New Delhi is presented as an important IP partner in maritime security, as well as one of the pilot countries of the project ESIWA. Finally, the strategic paper identifies India as a focus country for support in the health sector, i.e., access to the COVID-19 vaccine, provision of medical equipment and medicines, health expertise.

ASEAN

Back to the 1970s, the European Economic Community (ECC) was among the first to start informal and formal dialogue with the recently founded ASEAN organisation. In 2003, the European Commission adopted the communication *A New Partnership with South East Asia*, which singled out the co-operation priorities, namely, supporting regional stability, promoting democratic principles and good governance, bolstering regional trade and investment relations, assisting the development of less prosperous countries and intensifying dialogue and joint action in specific sectors (European Commission 2003). Interestingly, the strategic document includes a section labelled "Common features and values of the two regions," whereby the Union arguably sought to advance inter-regionalism (or bi-regionalism), i.e., a process characterised by the "widening and deepening [of] political, economic, societal [and ideational] interactions between international regions" (Rüland 2010: 1271).[20] In the wake of both the EU's and ASEAN's enlargement, the 2007 Nuremberg Declaration set out a longer-term vision of the partnership, pledging increased bilateral co-operation in fields as diverse as arms control, climate change and money laundering, as well as in relevant multi-lateral frameworks, such as ASEM. Notwithstanding the enhanced relations, the success of EU-ASEAN inter-regionalism was called into question, particularly in the trade domain. Indeed, the negotiations for a region-to-region FTA, launched in 2007, were suspended a year later due to limited progress. The stalemate was mainly caused by the EU's concerns over Myanmar's poor human rights record (Gilson 2019: 47), as well as by two interconnected factors, namely, the heterogeneity of ASEAN members and the EU's lack of understanding thereof (Wu 2019). The Union decided afterwards to engage with individual ASEAN countries, concluding FTAs with Singapore and Vietnam in 2013 and 2015, and launching formal talks with Malaysia, Thailand and the Philippines in the first half of the 2010s. In the area of security and defense, interactions intensified at the turn of the century. In 2005, the European Union deployed the Aceh Monitoring Mission in Indonesia and supported the peace processes in Mindanao and Myanmar. Furthermore, the EU actively participated to the ASEAN Regional Forum (ARF), a platform designed to foster security dialogue in the Indo-Pacific through confidence building and preventive diplomacy. The 2007–2012 Action Plan to implement the Nuremberg Declaration – then renewed for the period 2013–2017 – lists a wide range of non-traditional areas in which co-operation should have been expanded, such as counter-terrorism, maritime security, disaster management and crisis response. Yet, also in this domain, concrete progress was difficult to achieve, as initiatives remained mostly confined to dialogue facilitation and exchange of best practices (Heiduk 2016). As already seen in the case of China, Japan and India, the European Union was not regarded as a strategic actor able to answer ASEAN's security challenges. Not even the Aceh Monitoring Mission had great resonance in many of the ASEAN countries and, from this point forward, the Union came to be seen as a crisis manager and peacebuilder, rather than a security actor *per se* (Wong 2019). This perception was reinforced by the lack of the EU's on-site presence as a unified actor, ascribable to its inability/unwillingness to deploy hard security instruments in Southeast Asia and, more in general, in the IP region.

Between the mid-1990s and the mid-2010s, the image of a benevolent China and the preeminence of the United States contributed to lessen ASEAN's interest in the European Union. Over the past years, however, Beijing's behavior has generated concern among ASEAN members – although it is rarely openly declared – and uncertainties about Washington's commitment to the region's security have increased. Already prior to the Union's foreign policy shift in 2016, the joint-communication EU and ASEAN: A Partnership with a Strategic Purpose (2015) represented a first step to re-energise the relationship in a fast-changing regional and international scenario. Apart from the goal of enhancing trade and investment and foster intra- and inter-regional connectivity, the document spelled out ways in which post-Lisbon Treaty EU could contribute to regional initiatives both sponsored and attended by ASEAN members, including the ARF, the South Asian Association for Regional Cooperation (SAARC) and the East Asia Summit (EAS). A new Action Plan covering 2018–2022 was agreed in 2017 at the ASEAN-EU Post-Ministerial Conference in Manila, with the purpose of framing a clearer strategic future for collaborative activities. In 2020, the two sides opened a new chapter in their 44-year-long formal relationship by entering in a Strategic Partnership. The agreement aims to consolidate and further broaden existing co-operative arrangements and shared objectives, which comprise, *inter alia*, economic co-operation, support to ASEAN integration, sustainable development, climate change, connectivity and maritime security, but also crisis management in the COVID-19 context. Although the prospect of a region-to-region FTA still appears far away, changing strategic dynamics in the IP and the EU's policy proactivity is likely to pave the way for strengthened co-operation on common ground. ASEAN's conception of the EU seems to be evolving positively, even if, from the security point of view, the perception of the Union as a weak strategic player is still the dominant one (Grare 2019). Such a dynamic trend seems to be confirmed by the EU IP Strategy, which acknowledges the "principle of ASEAN centrality, its efforts to build a rules-based regional architecture, and the multilateral anchor that it provides" (European Commission and High Representative 2021: 5). Among the main priorities in the economic field are the conclusion of PCAs with Malaysia and Thailand, the conclusion of a trade deal with Indonesia, as well as the resumption of trade negotiations with Malaysia, the Philippines and Thailand. The ultimate objective remains that of reopening talks on an EU-ASEAN FTA. Although ASEAN has not yet entered a Connectivity Partnership with the Union, it is qualified by the strategy as a privileged partner in this area of co-operation, as shown by the recent conclusion of the negotiations on the ASEAN-EU Comprehensive Air Transport Agreement (CATA), the first such region-to-region agreement. At the security level, the EU Indo-Pacific strategy indicates a general commitment to play a stronger role in the ASEAN security architecture, mainly by participating in regional fora a such as the ASEAN Defence Ministers Meeting Plus (ADMM+) and the East Asia Summit.

Conclusion

This chapter has examined the development of the European Union's policies in the IP, with the aim of assessing whether the EU has managed to assert itself as a relevant player and develop a comprehensive approach towards the region. During the first 20 years of co-operation under the CFSP, the evidence suggests a mixed balance sheet, with the Union failing to punch its weight in the area. Internal crises, external turmoil, institutional limitations and foreign policy divisions have undermined the EU's image as a cohesive actor and hindered its attempts to engage in an effective way with its key IP partners. Since the mid-2010s, the European Union has sought to re-calibrate its external action framework to address an increasing multi-polar environment. As illustrated by the case studies of China, Japan, India and ASEAN, this has resulted in a more pragmatic policy posture towards the region, culminating with the release of the EU Indo-Pacific Strategy. It is too early to provide an overall assessment of the EU's foreign policy shift, which is undoubtedly of strategic significance. Yet, it has already become clear that its actual implementation is not exempt from challenges, ranging from the structural weakness of the CFSP to divergent EU member states' approaches towards the region.

Notes

1 The EU-ACP partnership, governed by the Cotonou Agreement (2000), unites over 100 partner countries among which the 15 Pacific Independent Island Countries (PICs), which are now included into the EU Indo-Pacific strategy.
2 China, Japan, North Korea, South Korea, Mongolia, Taiwan, Hong Kong and Macao in East Asia; India, Pakistan, Bangladesh, Sri Lanka, Nepal, Bhutan, the Maldives and Afghanistan in South Asia; and the ASEAN states in Southeast Asia. In this latter respect, it should be specified that, at the time when the New Asia Strategy was released in 1994, ASEAN was composed of six countries (Indonesia, Malaysia, the Philippines, Singapore, Thailand, Brunei), and then enlarged to comprise Vietnam (1995), Laos and Myanmar (1997), Cambodia (1999).

3 Strategic Partnerships are an essential tool of the EU's foreign policy, although vaguely conceptualised. Yet, implicit in this notion is an element of joint decision-making and long-term mutuality of interests in the diplomatic, economic and security domains.

4 The PCA is a legally binding agreement between the EU and its member states, on the one hand, and a third country, on the other hand. It sets the objectives of cooperation in different fields.

5 FTAs deal with preferential duty rates on the shipment of goods between the EU and its member states, on the one side, and partner countries, on the other. Over time, this kind of agreements has evolved to cover a wider range of areas, such as government procurement opportunities, the certification of products, intellectual property rights as well as the cross-border trade in services.

6 Currently, around 7,000 soldiers are stationed throughout the whole area: 4,100 in the Indian Ocean and 2,900 in the Pacific Ocean.

7 La Réunion, Mayotte, French Southern and Antarctic Territories, New Caledonia, Wallis-and-Futuna, French Polynesia.

8 In spelling out the Global Gateway's *raison d'être*, the President of the European Commission, Ursula von der Leyen, affirmed: "We are good at financing roads. But it does not make sense for Europe to build a perfect road between a Chinese-owned copper mine and a Chinese-owned harbour. We have to get smarter when it comes to these kinds of investments" (von der Leyen 2021).

9 Green Alliances and Partnerships form an integral part of the European Green Deal, a set of policy initiatives with the overarching objective of making the EU climate neutral by 2050. These are concluded with like-minded partners that have signed up to the goal of climate neutrality and other ambitious climate and environmental objectives (European Commission 2021).

10 In this respect, it is interesting to note that the publication of the EU Indo-Pacific Strategy coincided with the announcement of a new US-led IP alliance which does not include any EU country. The trilateral security pact, called AUKUS, was indeed established with the United Kingdom and Australia.

11 The European Union stopped exporting arms to the PRC in 1989 after the Chinese government's violent suppression of demonstrations in Tiananmen Square. In 2004–2005, there was a debate at the EU level over whether to lift the embargo.

12 For instance, in spring 2005, the European Union reacted with harsh criticism when the Chinese National People's Congress passed an anti-secession law which mandated the use of military force if Taiwan were to declare formal independence.

13 It should be nonetheless noted that, over time, individual EU member states have adopted different positions towards the BRI – and, more broadly, China – producing specific dynamics of engagement – or non-engagement. For instance, Italy signed a Memorandum of Understanding (MoU) with the PRC in March 2019 in support of the Belt and Road Initiative. The MoU was accompanied by a series of commercial agreements. Another example is the 17+ Cooperation framework which currently includes China, sixteen Central and Eastern European countries, as well as Greece. A number of countries belonging in this framework have signed BRI MoU.

14 More in detail, the controversy concerns the sanctions imposed by Beijing on several European individuals and entities in response to the EU's decision to enact restrictive measures against Chinese officials over human rights abuses against the Uyghur Muslim minority in the Xinjiang region as well as the crackdown on opposition in Hong Kong.

15 "The EU will also pursue its multifaceted engagement with China, engaging bilaterally to promote solutions to common challenges, cooperating on issues of common interest and encouraging China to play its part in a peaceful and thriving Indo-Pacific region. At the same time, and working with international partners who share similar concerns, the EU will continue to protect its essential interests and promote its values while pushing back where fundamental disagreements exist with China, such as on human rights" (European Commission and High Representative 2021: 4).

16 Particularly, the process stalled because EU-ASEAN informal FTA talks were undertaken in parallel with negotiations on other mega-FTAs, i.e., the Trans-Pacific Partnership (TTP) and the Transatlantic Trade and Investment Partnership (TTIP) (Yoshimatsu 2020).

17 Following the 2016 Brexit referendum, the United Kingdom remained full member of the European Union until its official departure on 31 January 2020.

18 At the EU-Japan Summit held in May 2021, the two sides had agreed on strengthening their Digital Partnership with the aim to expand cooperation on Artificial Intelligence (AI), 6G, standardisation, block chain, quantum technology and cybersecurity, as well as innovation and resilient supply chains for semiconductors.

19 Throughout 2020 and 2021, Japan participated, together with Pakistan, India and Djibouti, to joint naval activities in the framework of EU Naval Force Somalia (EU NAVFOR) – Operation Atlanta, a counter-piracy military operation at sea off the Horn of Africa and in the Western Indian Ocean conducted by the Union.

20 According to the *communiqué*, "diversity is an intrinsic reality" for both the EU and ASEAN, and "one of the political and cultural cornerstones of the relations between their countries." Moreover, the two regions predilect "a peaceful and rule-based multipolar world" regulated under the auspices of effective multilateral organisations, and they are both committed to regional integration, for they have realised that "creating a regional identity is the best way to sustain economic development, to reinforce their security, (...) and to have a strong voice in world affairs" (European Commission 2003: 11). On this latter point, it is worth mentioning that ASEAN has regularly referred to the European Union as an inspiration with regard to its own institutional development (Allison 2015).

References

Allison, Laura, *The EU, ASEAN and Interregionalism*, (New York: Palgrave Macmillan, 2015).

Asia, European External Action Service, 2016a, https://eeas.europa.eu/regions/asia/334/asia_en.

Atanassova-Cornelis, Elena, "Constraining or Encouraging? US and EU Responses to China's Rise in East Asia," *Central European Journal of International and Security Studies*, 9(4), 2015: 6–27.

Atanassova-Cornelis, Elena, "The EU-Japan Strategic Partnership in the 21st Century: Motivations, Constraints and Practice," *Journal of Contemporary European Research*, 6(4), 2010: 478–495.

Berkofsky, Axel, "The EU and Japan: A Partnership in the Making," *European Policy Centre Issue Paper*, 52, 2007: 1–29.

Brattberg, Erik & Etienne Soula, "Europe's Emerging Approach to China's Belt and Road Initiative," 2018. Carnegie Endowment for International Peace, https://carnegieendowment.org/2018/10/19/europe-s-emerging-approach-to-china-s-belt-and-road-initiative-pub-77536.

Casarini, Nicola, "The Securitisation of EU-Asia Relations in the Post-Cold War Era," in Thomas Christiansen, Emil J. Kirchner and Philomena B. Murray (eds.), *The Palgrave Handbook of EU-Asia Relations*, (London: Palgrave Macmillan, 2013): 181–97.

Chen, Xuechen & Xinchuchu Gao, "Bridging the Capability-Expectations Gap? An Analysis of the New Dynamics in the EU's Security Strategy Towards Asia," *Asia-Pacific Journal of EU Studies*, 18(3), 2020: 9–36.

Christiansen, Thomas, "A Liberal Institutionalist Perspective on China-EU Relations," in Jianwei Wang and Weiqing Song (eds.), *China, the European Union, and the International Politics of Global Governance* (Houndmills: Palgrave Macmillan, 2016): 233–251.

"Cooperation Agreement between the European Community and the Republic of India on Partnership and Development," *Official Journal of the European Communities*, 1994, https://eur-lex.europa.eu/legal-content/EN/TXT/PDF/?uri=CELEX:21994A0827(01)&from=EN.

Council of the European Union, *Council Conclusions on EU Strategy on China*, 2016, https://data.consilium.europa.eu/doc/document/ST-11252-2016-INIT/en/pdf.

Council of the European Union, *Enhanced EU Security Cooperation in and with Asia*, 2018, https://data.consilium.europa.eu/doc/document/ST-9265-2018-REV-1/en/pdf.

Council of the European Union, *Guidelines on the EU's Foreign and Security Policy in East Asia*, 2012, https://eeas.europa.eu/archives/docs/asia/docs/guidelines_eu_foreign_sec_pol_east_asia_en.pdf.

Di Donato, Giulia, "China's Approach to the Belt and Road Initiative and Europe's Response," 2020. Istituto per gli studi di politica internazionale (ISPI), https://www.ispionline.it/it/pubblicazione/chinas-approach-belt-and-road-initiative-and-europes-response-25980.

EEAS*Shared Vision, Common Action: A Stronger Europe. A Global Strategy for the European Union's Foreign and Security Policy*, European External Action Service, 2016b, https://eeas.europa.eu/archives/docs/top_stories/pdf/eugs_review_web.pdf.

EEAS, *The Partnership on Sustainable Connectivity and Quality Infrastructure between the European Union and Japan*, European External Action Service, 2019, https://eeas.europa.eu/headquarters/headquarters-homepage/68018/partnership-sustainable-connectivity-and-quality-infrastructure-between-european-union-and_en.

European Commission, *A New Partnership with South East Asia*, 2003, file:///C:/Users/elena/Downloads/com2003_0399en01.pdf.en.pdf.

European Commission, *An EU-India Strategic Partnership*, 2004, https://eur-lex.europa.eu/LexUriServ/LexUriServ.do?uri=COM:2004:0430:FIN:EN:PDF.

European Commission, *Connecting Europe and Asia. Building Blocks for an EU Strategy : Joint Communication to the European Parliament, the Council, the European Economic and Social Committee*, The Committee of the Regions and The European Investment Bank, 2018, https://apcss.org/wp-content/uploads/2020/02/European-Union_Connecting_Europe_and_Asia_Building_Blocks_for_an_EU_Strategy.pdf.

European Commission, *EU-India Enhanced Partnership*, 1996, http://aei.pitt.edu/3974/1/3974.pdf.

European Commission, *Europe and Asia: A Strategic Framework for Enhanced Partnerships*, 2001, https://eur-lex.europa.eu/LexUriServ/LexUriServ.do?uri=COM:2001:0469:FIN:EN:PDF.

European Commission, *Europe and Japan: The Next Steps. Communication from the Commission to the Council*, 1995, http://aei.pitt.edu/4316/1/4316.pdf.

European Commission, "Green Alliances and Partnerships," 2021, https://ec.europa.eu/international-partnerships/topics/green-deal_en.

European Commission, *Towards a New Asia Strategy*, 1994, https://eur-lex.europa.eu/legal-content/EN/TXT/PDF/?uri=CELEX:51994DC0314&from=EN.

"European Commission and High Representative of the Union for Foreign Affairs and Security Policy," *Elements for an EU Strategy on India*, 2018, https://eeas.europa.eu/sites/default/files/jc_elements_for_an_eu_strategy_on_india_-_final_adopted.pdf.

"European Commission and High Representative of the Union for Foreign Affairs and Security Policy," *EU-China – A Strategic Outlook*, 2019, https://ec.europa.eu/info/sites/info/files/communication-eu-china-a-strategic-outlook.pdf.

"European Commission and High Representative of the Union for Foreign Affairs and Security Policy," *The EU Strategy for Cooperation in the Indo-Pacific*, 2021, https://ec.europa.eu/info/sites/default/files/jointcommunication_indo_pacific_en.pdf.

European Parliament, "MEPs Refuse any Agreement with China Whilst Sanctions are in Place," 2021, https://www.europarl.europa.eu/news/en/press-room/20210517IPR04123/meps-refuse-any-agreement-with-china-whilst-sanctions-are-in-place.

Geeraerts, Gustaaf, "China, the EU, and the New Multipolarity," *European Review*, 19(1), 2011: 57–67.

Geeraerts, Gustaaf, "Europe and China's Belt and Road Initiative: Growing Concerns, More Strategy," *Egmont Security Policy Brief*, 118, 2019: 1–6.

Gilson, Julie, "A European Pivot towards Asia? Inter-regionalism in a New Era," in Weiqing Song, Jianwei Wang (eds.), *The European Union in the Asia-Pacific. Rethinking Europe's strategies and policies*, (Manchester: Manchester University Press, 2019): 39–56.

Grare, Frédéric, "Defining New Grounds for Cooperation Between the EU and ASEAN," 2019. Carnegie Endowment for International Peace, https://carnegieendowment.org/2019/06/03/defining-new-grounds-for-cooperation-between-eu-and-asean-pub-80147.

Grare, Frédéric & Manisha Reuter, "Moving Closer: European Views of the Indo-Pacific," 2021. European Council on Foreign Relations (ECFR), https://ecfr.eu/special/moving-closer-european-views-of-the-indo-pacific/.

Heiduk, Felix, "Externalizing the EU's Justice and Home Affairs to Southeast Asia: Prospects and Limitations," *Journal of Contemporary European Research*, 12(3), 2016: 717–733.

Kavalski, Emilian, "The EU–India Strategic Partnership: Neither Very Strategic, nor Much of a Partnership," *Cambridge Review of International Affairs*, 29(1), 2016: 192–208.

Khorana, Sangeeta & Badri G. Narayanan, "Modelling Effects of Tariff Liberalisation on India's Key Export Sectors: Analysis of the EU–India Free Trade Agreement," *Margin: The Journal of Applied Economic Research*, 11(1), 2017: 1–22.

Klossek, Lara, Shounak Set & Tomasz Łukaszuk, "Breaking Glass Ceiling? Mapping EU-India Security Cooperation," *ORF Issue Brief*, 410, 2020: 1–20.

Maher, Richard, "The Elusive EU–China Strategic Partnership," *International Affairs*, 92(4), 2016: 959–976.

Manners, Ian, "Normative Power Europe: A Contradiction in Terms?" *Journal of Common Market Studies*, 40(2), 2002: 235–258.

Mohan, Garima, "A European Strategy for the Indo-Pacific," *The Washington Quarterly*, 43(4), 2020: 171–185.

Nataraj, Geethanjali, "Why can't India and the EU sign an FTA?" 2013. East Asia Forum, https://www.eastasiaforum.org/2013/06/14/why-cant-india-and-the-eu-sign-an-fta/.

Pal Chaudhuri, Pramit, "India, the European Union and the World Order," in Rajendra K. Jain (ed.), *India and the European Union in a Turbulent World*, (Singapore: Palgrave Macmillan, 2020): 1–26.

Rüland, Jürgen, "Balancers, Multilateral Utilities or Regional Identity Builders? International Relations and the Study of Interregionalism," *Journal of European Public Policy*, 17(8), 2010: 1271–1283.

Sacks, David, "Europe's Global Gateway Plans to Counter China, but Questions Remain," 2021. Council on Foreign Relations (CFR), https://www.cfr.org/blog/europes-global-gateway-plans-counter-china-questions-remain.

Song, Weiqing & Jianwei Wang, "Introduction: The European Union's Asia-Pacific Strategies and Policies at the Crossroads," in Weiqing Song and Jianwei Wang (eds.), *The European Union in the Asia-Pacific: Rethinking Europe's Strategies and Policies*, (Manchester: Manchester University Press, 2019): 1–14.

Wen, Jiabao, "Speech at the China-EU Investment and Trade Forum ," (12 May 2004). https://www.mfa.gov.cn/ce/cebe//eng/zt/t101949.htm.

von der Leyen, Ursula, "2021 State of the Union Address," 2021. European Commission, https://ec.europa.eu/commission/presscorner/detail/en/SPEECH_21_4701.

Wacker, Gudrun, 'The EU in the Asia-Pacific Region Strategic Approach or Self-Marginalization?' in Pascaline Winand, Andrea Benvenuti and Max Guderzo (eds.), *The External Relations of the European Union. Historical and Contemporary Perspectives*, (Bruxelles, Bern, Berlin, Frankfurt am Main, New York, Oxford, Wien: Peter Lang International Academic Publishers, 2015): 167–188.

Wong, Reuben, "The European Union's Security Strategy in the ASEAN Region," in Weiqing Song and Jianwei Wang (eds.), *The European Union in the Asia-Pacific: Rethinking Europe's Strategies and Policies*, (Manchester: Manchester University Press, 2019): 184–199.

Wülbers, Shazia Aziz *The Paradox of EU-India Relations: Missed Opportunities in Politics, Economics, Development Cooperation, and Culture*, (Lanham, MD: Lexington Books, 2011).

Wu, Chien-Huei, "The EU's Engagements with the Asia Pacific," in Ramses A. Wessel and Jed Odermatt (eds.), *Research Handbook on the European Union's Engagement with*

International Organisations, (Cheltenham, Northampton: Edward Elgar Publishing, 2019): 1–16.

Yoshimatsu, Hidetaka, "The EU-Japan Free Trade Agreement in Evolving Global Trade Politics," *Asia Europe Journal*, 18(1), 2020:429–443.

Zhou, Hong, "An Overview of the China-EU Strategic Partnership (2003–2013)," in Hong Zou (ed.), *China-EU Relations: Reassessing the China-EU Comprehensive Strategic Partnership*, (Singapore: Springer, 2017): 3–31.

21 Middle powers in the Indo-Pacific

Tran Phuong Thao

Introduction

It is not possible to fully examine a region without discussing the regional middle powers. Standing at the middle position of the power spectrum, middle powers are expected to have more responsibilities than small powers, but only to the extent that they do not exceed and threaten great powers. After the Cold War, middle powers all over the world have been expected to be more relevant and involved in the international community. They are deemed to be mediators among the great powers, to support multi-polarity by hindering great powers' dominance and to help up the smaller powers. When it comes to the regional level, the roles of middle powers become even more vivid, as they have gradually become important actors in the way a region functions. The Indo-Pacific is not an exception. Due to the region's diversity and dynamic, it is necessary to emphasise the traits of Indo-Pacific middle powers that differ from those of the whole world, along with the unique criteria that apply only to the definition of middle powers in the Indo-Pacific. Despite the differences, Indo-Pacific middle powers have the stance and ability to fulfill the roles of middle powers.

As the result, the purpose of this chapter is to bring out a general definition of Indo-Pacific middle powers, based on different approaches and theories, and examine how middle powers function in such a diverse region like the Indo-Pacific. The approaches and theories used in the chapter are hierarchal, functional, behavioural and rhetorical approaches; each is analysed under the theory of realism, functionalism, behaviourism and constructivism respectively. To do so, it is necessary to answer several important sets of questions. The first set of questions is on the definition of the Indo-Pacific, precisely (1a) What are the criteria for a power to be considered as a middle power in the Indo-Pacific? (1b) To what extent are these criteria unique to the Indo-Pacific region? and (1c) What are the countries that match these criteria? The answers to these questions will be illustrated by a policy study of three countries, namely Vietnam, Indonesia and Australia. Indo-Pacific middle powers are not limited to these countries, and the number of powers that are qualified as middle powers in the region may grow over time thanks to the region's rapid dynamic. These countries are chosen as their size, foreign policies, behaviours and relevance to the region serve as the most remarkable examples for each of the middle powers' definitions based on the approaches above.

The second set of questions is on the functions of Indo-Pacific middle powers, including (2a) What are the roles of Indo-Pacific middle powers in the region? and (2b) What are the challenges they face while playing the roles? The purpose of this part is to examine the characteristics of Indo-Pacific middle powers that distinguish them from

DOI: 10.4324/9781003336143-26

middle powers in other regions. As the Indo-Pacific region has its unique dynamic, it is important to emphasise what makes its middle powers unique.

The concept of middle powers

Jordaan (2003) coined the concept of middle power as "states that are neither great nor small in terms of international power, capacity and influence," with a specific highlight on states' ability to support cohesion in the world system. This definition emphasises the contribution of middle powers to the international community, shedding light on their responsibilities and sphere of influence. Aside from it, different approaches can also result in different defining criteria of middle powers. These are the hierarchical approach (which looks at the quantitative indicator of middle powers), rhetorical approach (which defines middle powers by their national identity), functional approach (which, as its name indicates, emphasises middle powers' function and relevance) and behavioural approach (which uses the qualitative indicator to define middle powers). The hierarchical approach looks at middle powers through the same lenses as realism, which uses a combination of economic, military, social and developmental indicators to define the rank of a state in the international system. While this approach can bring out an objective measurement for the powers and facilitate the process of comparing the powers, it focuses too much on the material indicators and the sizes of powers themselves and overlooks the small powers' roles and relevance (Theiss & Sari 2018). The rhetorical approach looks at middle powers through the lens of constructivism and uses a power's national identity as the indicator of their middle power status. The way a country's policy makers and leaders perceive the world can reflect the country's policy and interaction with the international community (Carr 2014). As a result, a state can be considered a middle power if its leaders assert an identity or role that resembles that of a middle power. There are two problems with this approach. First, due to an absence of the general definition of the term middle power in official speeches or documents, it is difficult to map out the criteria that a country's leader's vision should have to reflect the "middle power" identity (Chapnick 2013). Second, as this definition is based wholly on the vision of a country's leaders and/ or policy makers, it tends to dismiss the objectivity and the approval of significant actors (international or regional) and the audience of states.

The behaviour and functional approaches do not exist mutually exclusively from each other, but they rather adopt orientation, arguments and theories simultaneously or alternately between each other (Theiss & Sari 2018). Due to this characteristic, the author will use them interchangeably in this chapter. The functional approach characterises middle powers based on their function and sphere of influence. Scholars using this approach argue that middle powers tend to use "niche diplomacy," meaning these powers' foreign policies aim at specific areas that they can be most beneficial in return for their efforts and investments (Emmers 2015). Evans defines this as "concentrating resources in specific areas best able to generate returns worth having, rather than trying to cover the field" (Evans 2011: 29). Cooper, Higgot and Nossal have the same observation that middle powers simply have less power than great powers, and as a consequence, their resources are used only in the areas where they can have a comparative advantage to establish a leadership (Cooper et al. 1993). The behaviour approach discusses middle powers by their interaction with other powers in the international community, such as being good international citizens, hindering power dominance and supporting multi-lateralism, encouraging international order and serving as intermediaries in disputes (Efstathopoulos 2018). While these two approaches focus closely on the roles and values of middle powers, they do not give clear and objective criteria to define these roles and values. How to measure a "good international citizen," how to measure middle powers' efficiency in promoting multi-lateralism and how to tell if a power's contributions are enough to give them a middle power status are the questions left unanswered.

Each of the three approaches does not work separately, as each of them leaves behind questions that need further consideration. However, if we employ them together, they can make up for each other's shortcomings, hence bringing out a comprehensive definition of middle powers. The hierarchical approach gives the indicators and measurements for the size of the power, and the rhetorical approach examines the vision of such powers, while the functional and behavioural approaches discuss what roles a power of that size and vision can play and what values they can achieve. Precisely, a power is qualified as a middle power when it has the vision and power sufficiency strong enough to hedge and negotiate among great powers and the sphere of influence is limited. In addition, the middle powers' vision should include their willingness to form relationships with other powers in the region and contribute to the order of the international community, promote multi-lateralism and serve as mediators when disputes occur.

Middle powers in the Indo-Pacific

Indo-Pacific middle powers definition

The Indo-Pacific is a diverse region even in terms of power. Given that the new Indo-Pacific concept also highlights the importance of ASEAN, the number of emerging middle powers in the region is higher than what matches for traditional definition. While the traditional middle powers like Australia can be an example of how a developed democratic society acts in such a diverse region, emerging powers like Vietnam and Indonesia demonstrate the importance of regional geostrategic position and the effects of geopolitics on the countries' relevance. As the result, the definition of "middle power" in the Indo-Pacific will focus on emerging middle powers, rather than traditional middle powers. As the definition may vary based on the most remarkable traits that the states show acting in the region, it is necessary to adopt the indicators and arguments from all three approaches above to bring out a comprehensive definition of Indo-Pacific middle powers.

Following the same the three approaches model proposed in the previous section, the definition of Indo-Pacific in this chapter focuses on the states' (1) power measurement, (2) visions in the region, (3) relationships with other states in the region and (4) contribution to the shaping and dynamic of the region. The three states chosen, as examples of "middle powers" in the Indo-Pacific, are Australia, Vietnam and Indonesia. While the number of middle powers in the Indo-Pacific is not precisely limited to these three countries, each of them is chosen because they serve as the most remarkable example for each of the three criteria listed above. Precisely, Australia represents the hierarchical approach of examining middle power, due to its development size and indicator. Vietnam represents the rhetorical approach of Indo-Pacific middle powers because of its vision in the region. Indonesia represents the functional approach of Indo-Pacific middle powers because of its regional roles and contributions.

Examples of Indo-Pacific middle powers

Australia

Australia represents the hierarchical aspect of the middle power definition. Cha assesses Australia's power as sufficient to enable its choices of promoting multi-lateralism, norm-rule setting behaviour or regional exertions to have a greater impact than would be the case for smaller powers. (Cha 2009) In addition, it is necessary to mention some relevant rankings and measurements. In terms of hard power measurements, Scott provided the ranking which shows that Australia comes behind the great powers in the region, (Scott 2008) like China, Japan and India, but it also surpasses other small powers, including New Zealand, Nepal, Cambodia and Singapore. In terms of economy, it can be measured by the size of Australia's GDP, which is ranked 12th out of 184 economies all over the world.[1] When measuring the economy against the population, Australia's GDP per capita PPP-adjusted figure placed it higher up at tenth. The IMF designated the Australian economy as an Advanced Economy, but not a Major Advanced Economy, making the country a member of the G20, but not among the elites in G8.

Vietnam

In her research that employed Organski's theory of world order, Kratiuk argues that Vietnam should be considered a middle power (Kratiuk 2014). Emmers and Teo selected Vietnam as one of the three case studies of middle powers in the Asia-Pacific, based on Vietnam's functional adoption of regional security strategy depending on its resource availability and strategic environment (Emmers & Teo 2015). Vietnam reflects the rhetorical approach to the definition of the middle power, emphasising the country's vision of using its position and resources to act as a middle power in the region. In ASEAN, in particular, Vietnam shows its vision to take the role of a regional leader (Emmers & Le Thu 2021). What gives Vietnam such a vision is its relationship with the United States and China. To the United States, Vietnam gains its importance by its geostrategic position and political relevance, making it a key factor in the US Asia plan, hence a target worth investing in (Bourdeau et al. 2019). To China, Vietnam is a communist ally highlighted as a potential human resource and market, leading to the huge investment and financial aids Vietnam receives from China annually (Kang et al. 2019).

Indonesia

In the article about Indonesia's role as a middle power, Karim assesses that "the impetus for Indonesia to play a greater role at the global level is a logical implication of its material capability and its recent political and economic development." Furthermore, Karim noted that Indonesia is remarkable for its Muslim population which co-exists in terms of the state's stable democracy. This makes Indonesia a model for functioning democracy in the Islamic world and developing countries, and, as the result, increases international expectations for Indonesia to be a more significant player at the global level (Karim 2018).

Indonesia is evaluated as one of the oldest contributors to UN Peace Keeping Organizations (UNPKOs) Starting in 1956, when Indonesia first sent its peacekeepers to Sinai, Egypt, the effort went on in 1961, 1963, 1973–1975, and the 1980s and 1990s. This attempt to be a good international citizen has been recognised and encouraged by significant powers, such as Japan and the United States. Indonesia also contributes to the promotion of regional multi-lateralism by its efforts to initiate or endorse diplomatic proposals and back up ASEAN centrality with actions for conflict resolution.

The roles and challenges of Indo-Pacific middle powers

Middle powers are believed to be the ideal candidates to contribute to the region's multi-lateralism. Unlike great powers – whose actions can pose threats to smaller powers, and small powers – whose power efficiency is not enough to promote multi-lateralism, middle powers are the most benefited from multi-lateralism and they have the skills to do it. Chapnick, Behringer and Murray call these qualities "middlepower-manship" (Behringger 2013; Murray 2013; Chapnick 2013). Cox evaluates that middle powers' process of achieving multi-lateralism and their willingness to maintain a degree of autonomy from the major powers reflect their commitment to provide security and support orderly changes in the international system (Cox 1989). In addition, Cooper notes three ways that multi-lateralism can help middle powers gain their leadership in niche issues: middle power can initiate diplomatic proposals, facilitate a program of action and create and manage international institutions that regulate issue areas (Theiss & Sari 2018).

Thies and Sari reconceive that middle power is a status constituted by auxiliary roles that are seen as necessary and sufficient conditions (Theiss 2010). Thies defines auxiliary roles as "'positions' in an organized group and any socially recognized category of actors, i.e., the kinds of people it is possible to be in a society" (Walker 1992). Paired with Walker's definition of roles as "repertoires of behavior, inferred from others' expectations and one's conceptions, selected at least partly in response to cues and demands" (Theiss & Sari 2018). Theis and Sari concluded that the auxiliary roles reflect (1) positions in a hierarchy, (2) the vision of the role-taker, (3) functions in a social group and (4) repertoires of behaviour (Theiss & Sari 2018), which go hand in hand with the three-approach model to define middle powers. For middle powers, the process of fulfilling their "roles" is equal to the process of strengthening their middle power status. For middle powers in a diverse region like the Indo-Pacific, playing their roles also means gaining the recognition and engagement of great powers in the region (Poonkham 2020).

Unlike small powers whose power and influence are limited, the action of middle powers in the Indo-Pacific region is not restricted to staying neutral and bandwagoning. In a region like the Indo-Pacific, middle powers have the chance to hedge and even employ the strategy of leading-from-the-middle, which is defined by Poonkham as "a strategic vision that a small-to-middle state use to hedge with and bind great powers within a rule-based or norm-based order, while simultaneously initiating region-wide politico-diplomatic innovations and advocacy" (Poonkham 2020). This strategy aims to reduce strategic uncertainty for small and middle states amid great power rivalries.

With China and the United States looming large as the great powers of the region, the Indo-Pacific middle powers are often found staying at the centre of the Sino–US dynamic. They must avoid a regional security dilemma outcome, which could eventually force the regional players to choose one of the great powers. Hedging alone and by itself, according to Poonkham, increases the risks of the so-called Thucydides' Trap – where middle powers emerge and challenge the hegemonic role of great powers and in turn increase hegemonic warfare. A leading-from-the-middle strategy, on the other hand, reinforces hedging's more positive attributes, including the reduction in clashes of power, the even distribution of influence among middle powers on smaller powers and more opportunities to work together with other middle powers instead of the great ones. Indo-Pacific middle powers would prefer to strengthen the bargaining leverage to compel the United States and China to respect their interests and, in the long term, to avoid succumbing to the temptation of bandwagoning like small powers. Otherwise, hanging on to the attempt to balance between the United States and China could lead to an increasingly tense regional security environment for middle powers (Itakura 2020). This strategy gives the Indo-Pacific middle powers the role to act as both a conflict mediator and a hindrance to great powers' dominance.

Initiatives in conflict mediation

Unlike great powers, middle power countries cannot afford wars. Trade wars and other similar types of conflict can also be harmful to traditional middle powers like Australia. Take the Australia–China trade war as an example. In the last few years, Australia has blocked several Chinese investments on national security grounds. In addition, Australia is also the third most prolific user of anti-dumping measures against China over the last six years, according to the World Trade Organization with the claim from Beijing that Canberra has initiated 106 anti-dumping and anti-subsidy investigations against Chinese products. This has caused several instances of visible damage to Australia's economy, such as the country's hardship in economic recovery after COVID-19's ravages, a long list of Australian export products targeted to be curbed by China including iron – Australia's largest source of export revenue and a potential of a GDP reduction by 6% (Lien & Xu 2020).

To emerging middle powers, wars are even more devastating. Most of the emerging middle powers used to be colonies of bigger powers and fought their way to freedom and independence, hence they know the devastation a war may cause to their economy, political situation and human resources. Also, emerging middle powers gain their status by participating in regional and international organisations where they get their share in co-operation with bigger powers. An example of such co-operation are the middle powers that stay between the US and China trade war. Jeong and Lee have examined the position and stance of these middle powers under the circumstance that there is a risk of a military war breaking out as the result of the Sino–US trade war. They have brought up three reasons why war is not a preferable outcome for middle powers (Jeong & Lee 2021). First, a war can increase uncertainty in the market, as the Federal Reserve Bank reports in 2019 that the uncertainty related to the trade war could decrease the global GDP by one percentage point. Particularly, this causes a slowing in both the China and the US economy, thus bringing out negative impacts on middle powers whose exports depend deeply on their relationship with China. Second, a conflict between great powers, in this case, the United States and China, would put middle powers in a difficult position where they are pressed to take sides with either of the two great powers and risk losing the benefit from the other. To avoid the bad outcomes, middle powers need to focus on ways to prevent the tension from escalating.

However, the difficulties caused by wars are not the only factor that makes middle powers the most appealing when it comes to conflict mediators, because small powers have the same reasons, and great powers can act like small ones and take the role. What puts middle powers before small powers as suitable conflict mediators is their position at the "middle" spot on the power spectrum – their sphere of influence. Unlike small powers, middle powers have a certain weight in their voice that makes the big powers consider before making any move. Unlike great powers, middle powers can get involved without downplaying their role as smaller powers. This can be due to either their existing power (in the case of traditional middle powers), their growing relevance to the international community, their increasing influence and their ability to get other big powers involved (in the case of both traditional and emerging middle powers).

Addressing the conflicts among smaller powers is also another way for Indo-Pacific middle powers to work as conflict mediators and strengthen their middle power stance. The case of Indonesia and the continuous cases of conflict resolution in the ASEA area can serve as a telling examples of these. In the light of the 1978–1989 Vietnam–Cambodia war, Indonesia organised informal discussions to call for a reduction in the interference from China and the Soviet Union in South-East Asia. Although the Jakarta Informal Meetings failed to resolve the conflict, Indonesia's effort facilitated negotiations between Vietnam and Cambodia, serving as co-chair of the International Conference on Cambodia in Paris in 1991, which ultimately led to the settlement of the dispute, and confirmed Indonesia's support for the maintenance of the international order. Emmers evaluated this was an effort of Indonesia to gain a leadership role in regional conflict management. The roles continue with the Workshops on Managing Potential Conflicts in the South China Sea, which was initiated by Indonesia in 1990. Emmers assesses that this provided the groundwork for the ASEAN–China Declaration on the Conduct of Parties in the South China Sea (DoC) in November 2002. Weatherbee assesses that the DoC helps to commit ASEAN and China to the peaceful settlement of disputes, non-use of force or threat to use force and self-restraint in the conduct of activities that could complicate or escalate disputes. Currently, Indonesia has been getting involved in helping with Myanmar's domestic unrest by holding press conferences outlining their position on the situation, which highlighted their opposition to the war.[2]

Restraining great powers' expansion and promoting multi-lateralism

China, with its power and ambition, looms large as a big shadow in the Indo-Pacific. Not only does it possess enough power-efficiency to enhance influence all over the Indo-Pacific region, economically and militarily, China also continuously shows its ability and relevance to tackle regional matters, create regional platforms, promote regional integrity and aid smaller powers' development (Emmers 2014). With such powers, China can take the role of a regional hegemon (Weatherbee 2016). It is necessary to keep an eye on the leader's movement to restrain their ambition because the ambition can drive the leader to act ruthlessly. In the past decades, China's growing sphere of influence and expansionism has brought about both advantages and consequences to the region. Advantages include the increase in regional co-operative organisations, investment in smaller powers, facilitating improvement and the enlargement of human resources. Consequences include China's sense of hegemony, an unbalance in regional power distribution and territorial disputes due to China's expansionism. As the result, middle powers are expected to grow to maintain the advantages and restrain China's abuse of power to avoid the consequences.

Aside from China, the United States is another big power that has a strong influence on the Indo-Pacific. With its alliance with several middle powers, it is important to acknowledge the roles of the United States in the region as a whale having a strong and deep influence and a guaranteed supporter for smaller powers to rise against China's expansion. Like China, this involvement gives the Indo-Pacific reason to be aware. While the presence of the United States in ASEAN and its ties with Australia, Japan and Korea can be a hindrance to China's ambition to expand, the interference of a great power can also affect the function of regional powers. Several powers, such as Indonesia and Vietnam, have exchanged a part of their territory for US military bases, in exchange for military co-operation, protection against the rise of China and also economic development. In the case of Indonesia, the cost of economic development also includes environmental damage, the reduction of biodiversity – which is one of the traits that makes Indonesia a remarkable country in terms of resources – and the high rate of pollution. Unlike China, whose threats lie mostly in expansionism, the US's threats to the Indo-Pacific are shown in the case of Thailand and Indonesia. Therefore, Indo-Pacific middle powers are also expected to have a stance against the United States as much as China. Powers like Vietnam, which has a history of disobeying the United States and fighting against China in terms of politics, economy and even military, are looking forward to uniting as potential opponents to the US intervention, balance against the great power and protecting the Indo-Pacific from the hegemony of one great power.

In this context, ASEAN countries are highlighted as important factors to balance the Sino–US dynamics in the Indo-Pacific. The first reason is their geostrategic position, which causes both China and the United States to want to take over, hence, agree to sit down to a negotiation with them. Middle powers, technically, can raise their requirements to great powers in exchange for co-operation or influence and have the ability to turn down great power' orders if they feel threatened or deeply dependent. While it is true that in the past, emerging middle powers were not familiar with that and tended to give away their geostrategic benefits to big powers in exchange for aid, investment and co-operation opportunities, the situation has changed. Indonesia used to be heavily influenced by the United States, and Vietnam used to have a certain dependence on China as communist allies despite their rivalry; nonetheless, ASEAN is now developing more and more awareness about the consequences of great powers' involvement. That urges them to gain independence, shrug away the heavy influence of great powers and also create a platform on which middle powers can work together for the good of an integrated region that brings about benefits to middle powers themselves without a lot of control from great powers.

Australia is another example of a middle power balancing against the shadows of great powers. Australia has a tradition of close security ties with the United States, but it also has a long-term economic relationship with China. The balance between the United States and China is ideal for Australia's development; therefore, it has to be careful not to disrupt the balance. For example, during the G20 meetings where Australia was the host country, Downie noted that Australia had made a decision not to make any announcements about its security relationship with the United States, which could alarm China, or any statement that would strengthen its economic ties with China. In addition, under the rising tension between the United States and China, Australia used its position as the chair of the G20 to strengthen co-operation between the great powers. Downie points out that Australia's strategy in this situation is to combine "a careful bilateral approach towards both countries that was sensitive to their strategic interests with a multilateral approach that identified issues that the United States and China could cooperate on in the G20" (Downie 2017).

Conclusion

Middle power in the Indo-Pacific is not a novel topic, but rather a concept that does not have a definition that is universally agreed upon. As the region is diverse and developing rapidly, the traditional definition of middle powers in other regions should not be applied to them. To come up with a definition for the concept, it is necessary to borrow the indicators and arguments from different approaches. In this chapter, the method to define the concept of Indo-Pacific middle powers is to combine three approaches, namely hierarchical, rhetorical and behaviour/functional, to point out the indicator of middle powers' size, vision, roles and relevance, respectively. Each of the three categories is examined with three examples that serve as the most remarkable of the category: Australia, Vietnam and Indonesia.

Indo-Pacific middle powers' roles are important, as the roles help them secure the "middle power" status and define their position in the region. Given that the preferable strategy for Indo-Pacific middle powers is leading-from-the-middle, the two most significant roles for them in the region are to work as conflict mediators to facilitate conflict resolution in the region and avoid wars and restrain the expansion of great powers to prevent hegemony and promote multi-lateralism. To fulfill these roles, Indo-Pacific middle powers are posed with challenges coming to their position in between the great powers, which requires them to take a side in the case of serious conflicts or to play carefully to maintain their balanced position.

Notes

1 The International Monetary Fund Gross Domestic Produce (GDP) figures for 2012 from its World Economic Outlook Database (WEOD)
2 According to Drajat, in The Indonesian factor in ASEAN response to Myanmar. Retrieved from https://www.eastasiaforum.org/2021/05/21/the-indonesia-factor-in-aseans-response-to-myanmar/

References

Behringer, R. M. (2013). The dynamics of middlepowermanship. *Seton Hall Journals of Diplomacy & International Relation, 14*, 9–22.
Boudreau, J., Chau, M. N., & Energy, J. S. C. (2019). Vietnam goes from trade war winner to Trump target. *Bloomberg News*. Retrieved from https://www.bloomberg.com/news/articles/2019-07-11/from-trade-war-winner-to-trump-target-vietnam-braces-for-shocks
Capannelli, G. (2014). The ASEAN economy in the regional context: Opportunities, challenges, and policy options. In *ADB working paper series on regional economic integration*, 16–21.

Carr, A. (2014). Is Australia a middle power? A systemic impact approach. *Australian Journal of International Affairs, 68*(1), 70–84.

Cha, V. D. (2009). Powerplay: Origins of the U.S. alliance system in Asia. *International Security, 34*(3), 158–196. http://www.jstor.org/stable/40389236.

Chapnick, A. (2013). Middle power no more-Canada in world affairs since 2006. *Seton Hall Journals of Diplomacy & International Relation, 14*, 101–111.

Cooper, A. F. (Ed.). (2016). *Niche diplomacy: Middle powers after the Cold War.* Springer.

Cooper, A. F., Higgott, R. A., & Nossal, K. R. (1993). *Relocating middle powers: Australia and Canada in a changing world order* (Vol. 6). Ubc Press.

Cox, R. W. (1989). Middlepowermanship, Japan, and future world order. *International Journal, 44*(4), 823–862.

Downie, C. (2017). One in 20: The G20, middle powers and global governance reform. *Third World Quarterly, 38*(7), 1493–1510.

Drajat, in the Indonesian factor in ASEAN response to Myanmar. Retrieved from https://www.eastasiaforum.org/2021/05/21/the-indonesia-factor-in-aseans-response-to-myanmar/.

Efstathopoulos, C. (2018). Middle powers and the behavioural model. *Global Society, 32*(1), 47–69.

Emmers, R. (2014). Indonesia's role in ASEAN: A case of incomplete and sectorial leadership. *The Pacific Review, 27*(4), 543–562.

Emmers, Ralf, & Teo, Sarah. (May 2015). Regional security strategies of middle powers in the Asia-Pacific. *International Relations of the Asia-Pacific, 15*(2), 185–216.

Emmers, R., & Le Thu, H. (2021). Vietnam and the search for security leadership in ASEAN. *Asian Security, 17*(1), 64–78.

Emmers, R., & Teo, S. (2015). Regional security strategies of middle powers in the Asia-Pacific. *International Relations of the Asia-Pacific, 15*(2), 185–216.

Evans, G. (2011). Middle power diplomacy. *Inaugural Edgardo Boeninger Memorial Lecture, Chile Pacific Foundation, Santiago, 29.* June 2011. Retrieved from https://www.gevans.org/speeches/speech441.html

Flemes, D. (2007). Emerging middle powers' soft balancing strategy: State and perspectives of the IBSA dialogue forum. GIGA Working Paper No. 57, Available at SSRN: https://ssrn.com/abstract=1007692 or http://doi.org/10.2139/ssrn.1007692.

Gilley, B., & O'Neil, A. (Eds.). (2014). *Middle powers and the rise of China.* Georgetown University Press.

Godwin, P. H. (2004). China as regional Hegemon? In Jim Rolfe (Ed.), *The Asia-Pacific: A Region in Transition* (pp. 81–101). Asia-Pacific Center for Security Studies.

Itakura, K. (2020). Evaluating the impact of the US–China trade war. *Asian Economic Policy Review, 15*(1), 77–93.

Jeong, B., & Lee, H. (2021). US–China commercial rivalry, great war and middle powers. *International Area Studies Review, 24*(2), 135–148.

Jordaan, E. (2003). The concept of a middle power in international relations: distinguishing between emerging and traditional middle powers. *Politikon, 30*(1), 165–181. http://doi.org/10.1080/0258934032000147282.

Jordaan, E. (2017). The emerging middle power concept: Time to say goodbye? *South African Journal of International Affairs, 24*(3), 395–412.

Jordaan, E. (2018). Faith no more: Reflections on the distinction between traditional and emerging middle powers. In D. Walton & T. S. Wilkins (Eds.), *Rethinking middle powers in the Asian century* (pp. 111–121). Routledge.

Kang, D. C., Nguyen, D. X., Fu, R. T. M., & Shaw, M. (2019). War, rebellion, and intervention under hierarchy: Vietnam–China relations, 1365 to 1841. *Journal of Conflict Resolution, 63*(4), 896–922.

Karim, M. F. (2018). Middle power, status-seeking and role conceptions: The cases of Indonesia and South Korea. *Australian Journal of International Affairs, 72*(4), 343–363.

Keating, P., & Wiharta, S. (2012). Synthesis report of the baseline study on civilian capacity. Norwegian Institute of International Affairs.

Kratiuk, B. (2014). Vietnam as a middle power in Southeast Asia. In *Second international conference on Asian studies: ICAS*, Sri Lanka.

Lakitan, B. (2013). Connecting all the dots: Identifying the "actor level" challenges in establishing effective innovation system in Indonesia. *Technology in Society, 35*(1), 41–54.

Mackay, R. A. (2017). The Canadian doctrine of the middle powers. In M. Beloff (Ed.), *Empire and nations* (pp. 133–143). University of Toronto Press.

Mahbubani, K. (2022). Is China expansionist? In K. Mahbubani (Ed.), *The Asian 21st century* (pp. 131–140). Springer.

Ministry of Foreign Affairs of Japan. (2015). Joint statement first Japan–Indonesia foreign and defense ministerial meeting 2015 Retrieved from https://www.mofa.go.jp/s_sa/sea2/id/page3e_000437.html.

Murray, R. W. (2013). Middlepowermanship and Canadian grand strategy in the 21st century. *Seton Hall Journals of Diplomacy & International Relation, 14*, 89.

Poonkham, J. (2020). Thailand-Australia Relations and Regional Geopolitics: A Thai View. In A. Carr(Ed.), *The Centre of Gravity Series* (pp. 6–9). Australian National University.

Ralf Emmers, Sarah Teo, Regional security strategies of middle powers in the Asia-Pacific, International Relations of the Asia-Pacific, Volume 15, Issue 2, May 2015, Pages 185–216.

Scott, D. (2008). The great power 'great game' between India and China: 'The logic of geography'. *Geopolitics, 13*(1), 1–26.

Scott, D. (2013). Australia as a middle power: Ambiguities of role and identity. *Seton Hall Journals of Diplomacy & International Relation, 14*, 111–123.

Scott, D. (2018). The Indo-Pacific in US strategy: Responding to power shifts. *Rising powers quarterly, 2*(2), 19–43.

The International Monetary Fund Gross Domestic Produce (GDP) figures for 2012 from its World Economic Outlook Database (WEOD). Retrieved from https://www.imf.org/en/Publications/WEO/weo-database/2012/October/download-entire-database

Thies, C. (2010). Role theory and foreign policy. In N. Sandal et al. (Eds.), *Oxford Research Encyclopedia of International Studies*. International Studies Association.

Thies, C. G., & Sari, A. C. (2018). A role theory approach to middle powers: Making sense of Indonesia's place in the international system. *Contemporary Southeast Asia: A Journal of International and Strategic Affairs, 40*(3), 397–421.

Walker, S. G. (1992). Symbolic interactionism and international politics: Role theory's contribution to international organization. In M. L. Cottam, C. Shih (Eds.), *Contending Dramas: A Cognitive Approach to International Organizations* (pp. 19–38). Praeger.

Weatherbee, D. E. (2016). *Re-Assessing Indonesia's Role in the South China Sea*. ISEAS-Yusof Ishak Institute.

Xu, Y., & Lien, D. (2020). Dynamic exchange rate dependences: The effect of the US-China trade war. *Journal of International Financial Markets, Institutions and Money, 68*, 101238.

22 Small powers in the Indo-Pacific

Strategies, opportunities and challenges

Paolo Pizzolo and Stefano Pelaggi

In the last two hundred years, the number of states has steadily increased: while there were less than 20 states in 1815 and only 50 on the eve of WWII (Vandenbosch 1964), now there are about 190. Since 1945, the surge of new sovereign states often translated into the spread of countries that – due to economic, military, demographic or geographic factors – have been labelled as small powers in the international system. The large increase in the number of small states since the 1950s has been the result of two main historical events: the breakup of the colonial empires and the demise of the socialist bloc. Another crucial factor that boosted the importance of small states was the post-war proliferation of international organisations (IOs), especially the United Nations (UN). Since the birth of the Westphalian modern state in 1648, small sovereign states have found a formal recognition and enjoyed an official status in the international system. However, major events like the Congress of Vienna (1814–1815), the Concert of Europe and the Paris Peace Conference (1919–1920) seemed to have confirmed the prominent role of greater powers *vis-à-vis* smaller ones. Despite the optimistic but unlucky experiment of the interwar League of Nations, when great powers believed that the birth of a universalistic international organisation could avert the outbreak of new major wars, after 1945 the creation of the UN led to a new era of hopes for medium and small powers. Due to the official juridical equality among members, the UN became a forum that promoted the prominence and power of small states against the logic of great powers' supremacy (Keohane 1969).

Despite the formal juridical parity enshrined in the UN Charter and the UN ban on wars of aggression, today small powers face similar challenges that were faced before 1945, including the need to counter the geopolitical, economic and strategic might of neighbouring greater powers. This is true also in relation to the current Indo-Pacific (IP), where power interactions comprise a multi-faceted blend of competition, rivalry, co-operation and opportunism. As a rising pivotal region for worldwide influence, the IP presents a precious scenario for the understanding of how small powers adapt their strategies and policies in a volatile environment where the risks of relegation, oblivion, dependence or neocolonial vassalisation are significantly high. While relegation and oblivion would imply a complete marginalisation of these actors in the international community, dependence and neocolonial vassalisation would impede the adoption of independent political strategies. Due to its geographic expanse and diversity radius, the IP is poly-centric and a-peripheral. Because of the large number and spectrum of stakeholders and players, unilateral pursuit of hegemony by great powers is costly and perhaps unachievable. Thus, exceptionalism and unilateralism, so often associated

DOI: 10.4324/9781003336143-27

with great powers' strategy, need to confront with multi-lateralism and realities that follow a logic of multi-polarity.

While embodying a contested strategic large space affected by geopolitical and geo-economic competition, today the IP entails a vast spectrum of challenges and opportunities both for major and small powers. Specifically, in relation to small powers, the prospective that the IP region offers ranges from security and defence policy to economic and trade policy, cultural policy and climate policy, as well as infrastructure- and connectivity-related policy. In this frame, while greater powers tend to prioritise bilateral approaches and hub-and-spoke-like arrangements, smaller powers tend to privilege multi-lateral approaches and arrangements based on shared norms and rules of engagement (Köllner 2021).

In this sense, this chapter wishes to investigate the role of small powers in the contemporary frame of IP great power rivalry by addressing the following guiding questions:

1) What is the current strategic importance of small powers in the IP?
2) Can they play a role of protagonists, exploiting greater powers' rivalry for their own benefit, or do they exemplify mere buffers that great powers use to mitigate their rivalry?
3) Are they active or passive agents?
4) Can they act as gamechangers in international interactions in the IP?

The chapter's attempt is to offer an answer to these questions and to assess the contribution of small state IR theory to the understanding of small powers' strategies in the IP in relation to different variables – economic, cultural, military.

The chapter is divided as follows. The first section will introduce an overview of the scholarly debate around small powers, emphasising how small states have been treated in IR theory. Specifically, the section highlights the core themes that emerged from the literature and the way they contribute to the understanding of small states' agency in world politics. Also, the most recent literature on power asymmetries and small states strategies is brought in, while discussing the different options available to small states in their interaction with more powerful countries – including the chances of bandwagoning, balancing, nonalignment, hedging, back-passing and engagement. The second section will emphasise in the context of the IP the institutional, economic and diplomatic leverage that small powers have at their disposal to navigate the international system and advance their interests even under the conditions of severe asymmetries. Finally, the third section will present five case studies, namely Laos, the Maldives, Brunei, Papua New Guinea (PNG) and the Pacific Island Countries (PICs), as empirical evidence of small states' behaviour *vis-à-vis* the current geopolitical, geoeconomic and geostrategic developments in the IP. In particular, the section describes how these five actors conceived their presence and interests within the region and which strategies they have followed to manage the interactions with the major powers involved in the area. The summary at the end of the chapter will condense the key findings and results of the research.

Does size really matter? The scholarly debate around small powers and how small states are viewed in IR theory

The scholarly debate on small states

The literature on small states branched out in three directions. A first branch specialised in the investigation of the foreign policy of small states, focusing on the political-diplomatic strategies that these actors could adopt, from neutrality or isolation to alliance (Ørvik 1953; Fox 1959; Rothstein 1968). A second stream developed through the comparative analysis on politics and policy formation in small states (Katzenstein 1984; Alapuro 1985). Finally, a third strand was concerned with issues of recognition, self-determination, minorities, secession and irredentism, and with justifying small states' existence and their rights vis-à-vis great powers (Chazan 1991; Heraclides 1991).

Classic IR literature on small states and powers began to develop in the 1960s. At that time, the main task and aim was to offer a description and definition of what being "small" meant in the international system. After the ruthless clash of great powers during WWII, the competition between political-ideological blocs in the Cold War and the scenario of decolonisation, scholars attempted to understand what the role of small powers could be in the post-1945 environment (Knudsen 2002).

In the 1960s and 1970s, during the initial days of small state studies, the scholarly debate focused on the concepts of vulnerability and capacity (Neumann & Gstöhl 2004), especially in the process of decolonisation (Vital 1967). At that time, the literature questioned the capacity of small states to function independently in the international system due to their alleged exposure to political and economic pressure (Archer & Nugent 2002). Often, small states were accused of not being able to exercise relevant diplomatic power (Väyrynen 1971) and of lacking military strength, thus being highly vulnerable *vis-à-vis* their larger neighbours (Handel 1981). While larger states were viewed as proactive international actors, small states were perceived as reactive (Keohane 1969; Papadakis & Starr 1987). Back then, the literature (Vandenbosch 1964) considered the military aspect the most important variable to determine whether a state could be considered "small". In this sense, a small state would be unable to contend in war with great powers on equal terms. Also, its military weakness would make it diplomatically feeble and, consequently, insignificant in world politics, so that great powers generally viewed it as a vassal rather than as a peer. This alleged condition of inferiority had been already highlighted by the famous geopolitician Nicholas Spykman, who claimed that small states represented "a vacuum in a high-pressure area that do not live because of their strength but either because nobody claim their territory or because their preservation as a buffer is convenient for great powers" (Spykman 1942: 20).

Some classic studies (Väyrynen 1971) underlined how states can be described as small powers in relation to a specific variable: economic small powers are measured by their gross domestic power (GDP), political small powers by their low involvement in IOs and global diplomatic networks, and military small powers by their military expenditure. Clearly, while some states can be small in relation to one or more variables, they can be greater in relation to others. Also, a state may be defined as "small" in relation to the ranks and performances of other countries, to its behaviour, to its interests as contrasted with those of great powers and to its specific role. Thus, small powers have been defined as states which have a low objective and/or a low perceived rank in the context where they are acting, as actors whose role prescriptions differ from those of middle and great powers and whose global influence is negligible and countries with interests that are somewhat different from – and sometimes conflicting with – the interests of great powers (Väyrynen 1971). Other studies (Keohane 1969) focused their attention on the capacity of small states to influence the decision-making process in the international system, arguing that a small power or a group of small powers is characterised by a weak leadership that remains unnoticed by greater powers. Moreover, some (Rothstein 1968) considered the issue of security the topmost important variable and thus defined as "small" a state which recognises that it cannot obtain security through its own capabilities and that it must rely fundamentally on the aid of other states or institutions to do so. Also, others (Rosenau 1966) conceived smallness in terms of resource availability, arguing that the size of a state affected its dependence on external resources that it could not produce or did not possess domestically. Instead, some (Vital 1967) insisted in the importance of the demographic and economic factors as tools for interpreting the size of states, describing as "small" both the economically developed countries with a population of 10–20 million and the economically underdeveloped countries with a population of 20–30 million.

Despite the boundless nuances, the literature tends to agree that a small state is a country that rests on a relationship of marked inferiority of power *vis-à-vis* some other states, and whose inferiority is given essentially by four weaknesses, which clearly may not all occur at the same time: a modest population, a negligible territory, low economic performances and mediocre military capacity. Today, the relevance of these four variables in defining the size of states is questioned, since it is rooted in nineteenth-century European statehood when the success of states was primarily conceived in terms of defence capacity, territorial foreign expansion and military might. Foreign territorial acquisitions continued to be of importance until the mid-twentieth century but ceased to be relevant after 1945. The importance of the population variable was determined by its capacity in providing manpower for military force and workforce; however, the evolution of armies to small professional bodies and the development of military technology on one hand and the advances in industrial production on the other have downsized the importance of the demographic factor. At the same time, it is debatable whether the economic performances of states still reflect necessarily a correlation with population and army size. Also, arguably territory cannot be considered a decisive variable in describing the size of a state, since geographic extension does not always coincide with power.

Today, scholars acknowledge that no widely accepted definition of small states has yet emerged and thus many recent studies have referred to previous literature to justify the choice of criteria applied to define small states in IR (Crowards 2002; Plagemann 2021). The literature still strives to understand how to define the concept of small state and how to differentiate it from, for instance, those of "micro-state" and "middle power," which are often used in a blurry and arbitrary way (Thorhallsson & Wivel 2006). Given that the traditional concepts used to define the size of states, i.e., population, territory, GDP and military capacity may be at odds when relating theoretical perspectives to empirical evidence, part of the recent literature (Thorallson 2006) suggested six categories regarding the size of states, adding new explanatory variables: a fixed size (population and territory); sovereignty size (i.e., the state capacity to maintain effective sovereignty on its territory and its ability to keep a minimum state presence at an international level); political size (military, administrative and diplomatic capabilities); economic size (GDP, market size and development success); perceptual size (the perception that domestic and external actors have of the state); and preference size (ambitions and prioritisations of the governing elite). An innovative study (Crowards 2002) has investigated the issue through quantitative analysis, categorising the size of 190 states according to population, land area and total income and labelling 79 among them as "small". Also, some recent definitions (Thorhallsson

& Steinsson 2017) have considered once again the demographic factor as paramount, considering "small" that country with a population of 15-10 million or less. Also, the recent literature (Thorhallsson & Steinsson 2017) confirms that small states' structural disadvantages, including the great reliance on international trade, determine their needs and behaviours in international politics. Nonetheless, state smallness has also been described as not necessarily bad (Fiori & Passeri 2015), especially if combined with some specific asymmetric capabilities. For instance, small states would enjoy a natural inclination for supporting existing international institutions and multilateral organisations, where they can exercise global influence despite their structural weaknesses (Theys & Rietig 2020).

Gradually, the relatively abundant literature on small powers has promoted IR small state theory, which developed as a corollary to state theory in general (Knudsen 2002). The main questions referred to three main issues: state formation, i.e., the origin and conception of the state, its emergence, its survival over time and its disappearance due to exogenous (annexation, integration, fusion) or endogenous factors (dissolution, secession); security, both from within and without; and legitimacy, an issue closely connected to the quality of the leadership. From an IR theory perspective, the analysis of small states followed the different interpretations offered by the key conceptual paradigms (Thorhallsson & Wivel 2006). Realist approaches tended to underscore the importance of power, which has been quantified by variables like geographic location, degree of tension between leading powers, phase of power cycle for nearest great power, historical record of relations between small state and nearest great power, the policies of other great powers and the existence of multi-lateral frameworks of security co-operation (Knudsen 1996). On the other hand, liberal approaches stressed the importance of domestic interest groups and the small states' willingness to foster regional institutions in order to marginalise the costs of negative externalities of interdependence (Hansen 1997). Finally, constructivist interpretations suggested the importance of discourse, arguing that smaller states' narrative based on self-perception of littleness could explain mostly their dilemmas and problems but also their strategies and policies (Wæver 2002).

Small states' foreign policy strategies

Small states tend to remit their security on strategies like bandwagoning and balancing, which have been analysed in-depth by the IR realist paradigm. According to realism, especially structural realism, small states are generally expected to balance powerful actors by joining countervailing coalitions or bandwagoning with the most powerful one (Walt 1987; Waltz 1979). Specifically, bandwagoning and balancing are concepts that were developed during the Cold War to describe the alternative strategies of accommodating or resisting, respectively, a powerful or intimidating great power.

Bandwagoning is a strategy of a small or weak state to ally with a stronger power. Usually, it occurs when weaker states realise that the costs of opposing a stronger power exceed the benefits. Moreover, bandwagoning creates a dual asymmetric relationship in which the stronger party may offer incentives, such as the possibility of territorial gain, trade agreements or protection, to persuade the weaker party to join an alliance. According to neorealism, bandwagoning is a response to changes in the distribution of power. In this sense, it involves unequal exchanges that witness the vulnerable state making asymmetrical concessions to the dominant power and accepting a subordinate role (Walt 1988). Since the goal of bandwagoning is essentially to avoid attack, it can be defined as a typical defensive strategy, though, as noted, some view it as an approach driven by the prospects for gain. In fact, it has been argued that states bandwagon both for security and defence (Walt 1985), out of interest or "profit" (Schweller 1994) and to curry favour through military alliances or economic and diplomatic co-operation (Kang 2009). Since the small states' awareness of their lack of resources and capacity to influence the international system would compel them to adopt bandwagoning strategies, bandwagoning would be typical of small powers (Walt 1987). Moreover, bandwagoning can be divided into defensive when aimed at averting an external attack or aggressive when meant to share the booty of the powerful (Chun 2000). In addition, the availability of strategic support from the great powers, in particular defence and military capability, assures the propensity of small states to bandwagon with them. Since military build-ups are costly and often unpopular, through bandwagoning small states can benefit from external protection and security without paying the costs of military expenditures.

As for balancing, its conception derives from the realist balance of power theory and pivots on arms build-up and alliances. Balancing entails actions that a state takes to equalise the odds against more powerful states, for instance making it more difficult and hence less likely for powerful states to exert their military advantage over the weaker ones (Pape 2005). According to the balance of power theory, being motivated primarily by their desire for survival and security, a state will develop and implement military capabilities and hard power mechanisms to restrain the most powerful state that can substantiate a potential threat (Waltz 2008). In the case of external balancing, states come together and form an alliance to balance and gain more leverage over a dominant or rising power; in the case of internal balancing, a state tries to accrue its power by boosting economic resources and military strength in order to be able to rely on independent capabilities in response to a potential hegemon and be able to compete more autonomously in the international system. Balancing can be viewed as the opposite behaviour of bandwagoning: whereas balancing refers to the choice of joining the weaker side, bandwagoning is the choice of allying with the stronger side (Waltz 1979).

Scholarly debate has also stressed that oftentimes small states prefer non-alignment to balancing or bandwagoning (Labs 1992) or to adopt strategies like hedging, buck-passing and engagement (Murphy 2010). While non-alignment represents the condition or policy of being non-aligned or, in a stricter sense, neutral, hedging normally refers to an alignment strategy undertaken by one state toward another that comprises a mix of co-operative and confrontational elements. As such, hedging could embody a specific, albeit ambiguous, response to the vulnerabilities and structural uncertainties of small states (Korolev 2019). Hedging could be interpreted as a mixed strategy between engagement and containment, entailing a swinging behaviour that a state adopts *vis-à-vis* major powers. Instead, buck-passing refers to the act of attributing to a state that tries to get another state to deter or fight an aggressor state while remaining on the side-lines. Generally, when "passing the buck" a state refuses to confront a growing threat in the hopes that another state will instead. Finally, engagement is a diplomatic strategy that entails a multi-faceted contact between an international actor and a foreign audience, including public diplomacy, communication, the participation in international missions and the deployment of international aid.

Box 22.1 The trilateral security pact between Australia, the United Kingdom and the United States (AUKUS)

AUKUS – an acronym for the three signatory nations of Australia, the United Kingdom and the United States – is a trilateral security pact announced on 15 September 2021. Under it, the United States and the UK agree to help Australia to develop and deploy nuclear-powered submarines, in support of Western military presence in the IP. Although the joint announcement by Australian Prime Minister Scott Morrison, British Prime Minister Boris Johnson and US President Joe Biden did not explicitly mention any other country, the agreement is implicitly conceived to counter the influence of China in the region. The agreement would be aimed specifically to protect Taiwan from Beijing's revisionism and irredentism.

The deal covers key areas such as artificial intelligence, cyber warfare, underwater capabilities and long-range attack capabilities. It also includes a nuclear component, possibly limited to the United States and the UK, on nuclear defence infrastructures. The deal will focus primarily on military capability, unlike the so-called "Five Eyes" intelligence-sharing alliance that also includes New Zealand and Canada.

Suggested readings:

- Alexander Ward and Paul McLeary, "Biden announces joint deal with U.K. and Australia to counter China," *Politico*, 27 September 2021. https://www.politico.com/news/2021/09/15/biden-deal-uk-australia-defense-tech-sharing-511877.
- BBC News, "Aukus: China denounces US-UK-Australia pact as irresponsible," 16 September 2021. https://www.bbc.com/news/world-58582573.
- Matthew Cranston, "AUKUS causing Xi 'heartburn', says White House", *Australian Financial Review*, 21 November 2021. https://www.afr.com/world/north-america/aukus-causing-xi-heartburn-says-white-house-20211120-p59ajk.
- Lara Marlowe, "France recalls ambassadors from US, Australia over submarine deal," *The Irish Times*, 17 September 2021. https://www.irishtimes.com/news/world/europe/france-recalls-ambassadors-from-us-australia-over-submarine-deal-1.4677256.

Box 22.2 The 2050 Strategy for the Blue Pacific Continent

The 2050 Strategy for the Blue Pacific Continent is a long-term regional strategy aimed at protecting and securing the nations and environment of the Pacific. The Strategy entails close social, cultural, environmental and economic co-operation among regional actors. The initiative's imperatives include facing critical challenges like climate change, sustainable development and security. The promoters of the initiative share the idea that joint actions may prevent the occurrence of problematic issues related to human and environmental security. The priorities that the strategy considers paramount are climate change action, protection of the Pacific Ocean's health and integrity, sustainable management of the Pacific resources, connection of the oceanic continent via air, sea and ICT and higher standards of living for the people living in the region. Formally, the 2050 Strategy is led by the Forum Officials Sub-Committee on the 2050 Strategy for the Blue Pacific Continent with the inclusion of Council of Regional Organizations in the Pacific (CROP) agencies as observers.

Suggested reading:

- Pacific Island Forum, "The 2050 Strategy for the Blue Pacific Continent." https://www.forumsec.org/2050strategy/.
- Council Pacific Affairs, "The 2050 Strategy for the Blue Pacific Continent," https://www.councilpacificaffairs.org/ressources/the-2050-strategy-for-the -blue-pacific-continent/.

David against Goliath: small powers' dilemmas and great powers' competition in a rising Indo-Pacific

As seen in the previous chapters, currently the IP represents a strategic region in which key international powers like China and the United States, as well as other regional and extra-regional actors, compete for power and influence. As previously noted, although strategic priorities concerning the IP vary among state actors, they all highlight important and growing economic and security-related connections between the Pacific and Indian Oceans. Still, all powers involved in the region – with the obvious exception of China – believe in the need to counter the scenario of a China-dominated IP and to create a multipolar space that would respect the interests of all (Köllner 2021). In particular, as part of its pivot to Asia, the United States has recently shown a clear intention to counter the Chinese rise in the IP through initiatives like the trilateral security pact signed with close strategic partners – Great Britain and Australia – known as AUKUS (see Box 22.1).

Currently, small powers in the IP are facing the same questions that regional middle and great powers must challenge, namely the escalation of US–China geo-strategic competition. Indeed, this rivalry augmented after China's announcement to implement the ambitious Belt and Road Initiative (BRI), whose maritime branch deeply affects the IP region. While China is aiming to strengthen and expand its economic and political influences in the region under the umbrella of the BRI, major powers like the United States, Japan, Australia and India – the members of the Quadrilateral Security Dialogue (QUAD) – as well as small powers have been obliged to face the dilemma of Beijing's rise and to adopt strategies aimed at either countering China or cooperating with it. In this sense, middle and small powers have decided to pursue different policies, some adhering to the US-led anti-Chinese front, some aligning with China, and some opting for less engaging and more neutral strategies. Also, it has been argued that some regional powers are currently reluctant to join the US strategy for the IP and are attempting in various ways to tame rather than to contain China (Jung et al. 2021).

Among the small powers of the IP, small insular states are perhaps the most exposed to the risk of being pawns in the game of international interests and territorial powers. IP islands have been the source of interstate competition in the Indian Ocean between China and India and in the Pacific between China and the United States and between China and Japan (Scott 2021). The strategic importance of small IP islands rests upon their role as potential naval bases, refuelling stations and potential depots of commerce routes. The insular position enables sea power projection, which is complemented by airpower that makes such islands "unsinkable" aircraft carriers. Also, in terms of missile technology, high-mobility artillery rocket systems (HIMAR) placed on islands, for example in the first island chain or in the South China Sea (SCS), may serve as antiship missiles. Finally, from a geoeconomic perspective, the significance of IP small islands rests on the frame of their Exclusive Economic Zones (EEZ) prescribed by the UN Convention on the Laws of the Sea (UNCLOS) (Scott 2021).

Still, China's rise did not always manifest with negative outcomes. Small states in the IP have largely benefitted from the trade volumes between China and India and China and other Asian states (Paul 2019). Moreover, despite the huge power asymmetry with many of their neighbours, both China and India are not able to fully translate it in to influencing radically the behaviour of regional small states. While both China and India have made some efforts to induce regional small states to become partners, Sino-Indian rivalry has been exploited by smaller states to achieve maximum economic benefits. In other words, China's role as status quo challenger in the IP is fostering a spectrum of opportunities for small states, which – if smart strategies are adopted – can now utilise great power competition for their own benefits and goals.

Currently, the IP typifies an exceptional ground for fostering an intensified co-operation with influential regional actors. First, given their geopolitical and geoeconomic size, small states have more opportunities to gain when acting at a multi-lateral level and in a coordinated manner within the frame of regional fora and initiatives. In this sense, an active participation in IOs and fora like the Association of Southeast Asian Nations (ASEAN), the World Trade Organization (WTO), the Asia-Pacific Economic Cooperation (APEC), the East Asia Summit (EAS), the South Asian Association for Regional Cooperation (SAARC), Asia-Pacific Trade Agreement (APTA) or the Pacific Islands Forum (PIF) may represent a concrete tool to boost small states' visibility and relevance. Second, IP small states can achieve a lot from IP great power rivalry – especially from US–China competition, which they can utilise as a bargaining tool to promote their interests. Small states can engage in active negotiations with Washington and Beijing and decide which side may represent the most interesting partner.

Small states and their IP strategy: a comparative analysis

Based on the previous conceptual frame and broad scheme introduced earlier in the chapter, the present section will compare five case studies that typify empirical examples of small states in the IP. Case study selection is often an arbitrary and ambiguous procedure; however, in selecting the five samples, we included countries – or, in the case of the Pacific islands, a group of countries – that can reasonably be added in the list of small states. Still, the list does not claim to be exhaustive, since small states in the vast IP region are admittedly not limited to the ones mentioned below.

Laos

Laos is a country of about 7 million people that lies in the Indochinese Peninsula and borders with Myanmar and China to the northwest, Vietnam to the east, Cambodia to the southeast, and Thailand to the west and southwest. Historically part of French Indochina along with Vietnam and Cambodia, Laos is still the least developed and the most segregated of the three. Having suffered colonial rule, wars, and dictatorships, after years of isolation from the outside world this landlocked and sparsely populated nation is finally enjoying an epoch of stability thanks to the creation of more modern political and economic structures and to the opening of its borders to international tourism.

As a landlocked state, Laos faces the challenges that stem from the denied access to the seas and the dependence on foreign trade. Also, the country is surrounded by dynamic neighbours like Vietnam and China who exert a substantial political and economic influence on it. As a small state without access to international maritime trade routes, Laos is well exposed to the risk of becoming a vassal of major regional powers, especially China. Fully aware of its land-locked condition and smaller size, Laos has tended to be accommodating towards Beijing for patronage or leverage (Pang 2017).

Since 2010, Laos benefited from Foreign Direct Investment (FDI), particularly in the natural resource and industry sectors. The construction of several large hydropower dams and the expansion of mining activities have significantly boosted its economy. While retaining its official commitment to Marxism-Leninism, Laos upkeeps close ties with China (Heiduk & Wacker 2020). In the economic sphere, China provided 70% of the funding for a $5.9 billion 400-km railway line between the Chinese border and the capital Vientiane, which became fully operational in December 2021. Also, Laos financed the remaining 30% with loans from China (The World Factbook 2022).

Along with Cambodia, Laos is viewed by China as its most trusted political ally in Southeast Asia. In the coming years, China's footprint in Laos is expected to expand. The significance of the current Chinese influence in Laos is a phenomenon that began in the 1990s, since until then communist Laos was largely under Vietnam's sphere of influence and previously under French rule. Today, Laos have been sympathetic to all forms of Chinese overtures, showing a manifest interest in supporting Chinese initiatives. Not only has Vientiane welcomed Chinese capital, investment and people, but it has also actively advocated the BRI, which positions Laos as a key node of the framework's "Indochina Peninsular Corridor" into Southeast Asia (Pang 2017). In the frame of a fast-rising China, Laos has little or no choice but to acknowledge Beijing as the unmatched regional hegemon. Also, since its capacities to compete with the more advanced neighbours of Thailand and Vietnam are scarce, Laos is inevitably compelled to lean towards China's foreign policy.

Still, as the country becomes increasingly reliant on China, the real challenge for Vientiane will be that of benefit from the Chinese partnership without being fully absorbed by it. A clear risk exists that Laos may become, along with Cambodia, a "vassal" or "client state" of China (Pang 2017). In this sense, recently Laos has expanded its economic reliance on the West and other Asian countries like Japan, Malaysia, Singapore and Taiwan to counterbalance at least partially Beijing's influence.

Finally, as a full-fledged member of the APTA, the ASEAN, the EAS and the WTO, in accordance with its small state status, Laos is active in pursuing international strategies that rely on multilateralism. For instance, Laos has managed to strike a compromise between claimants, including China and Vietnam, to issue a communique of the

ASEAN Ministers' Meeting under its chairmanship in 2014 addressing tensions in the SCS. This showed how Laos utilised the ASEAN frame to pursue a balancing strategy and make its voice heard.

Considering the abovementioned theoretical frame, given its structural weaknesses, Laos is a country that relies on bandwagoning strategies aimed at allying with the stronger power, i.e., China. In this sense, a dual asymmetric relationship exists between Laos and China in which the former actor sides with the latter in the hope of achieving some gains in a win-win perspective.

Maldives

As a small South Asian archipelagic state of the Indian Ocean with a population of 500,000, the Maldives is affected by a strong pressure exercised by both China and India. In this context, Malé decided to maintain somewhat equidistance while attracting significant financial windfall. Stuck in-between the hammer and the anvil, the Maldives has attempted to gain the maximum benefits from its co-operation with India and China, despite their two antithetic and rival IP strategies. While India remains the Maldives' key security provider, China is viewed as an increasingly important commercial and economic partner.

Regarding China, the Maldives has become a pivotal point of Chinese efforts to gain access in the Indian Ocean, especially in the frame of the BRI. For instance, Beijing has offered key infrastructure projects, including expansion of the international airport under a 50-year lease by a Chinese firm signed in December 2016, a bridge linking the capital and the island where the airport is located and numerous other projects including the construction of a new harbour (Paul 2019).

As for India, the Maldives views the gigantic neighbour as the key provider of its security, defence and independence. For instance, the Maldives has a standing naval presence of India for its protection and has expressed willingness not to allow China any military facilities in the archipelago. In this respect, while the 2017 free trade deal gave China a major economic edge over India in Maldives, immediately afterwards Malé reassured India of no security concessions to China and expressed the state's "India-first policy" (Ramachandran 2018).

Significantly, the Maldives is a member of the SAARC, the official progress monitor of the Indian Ocean Commission, and a member of the Commonwealth of Nations, of the Organisation of Islamic Cooperation (OIC) and of the Non-Aligned Movement (NAM). The membership in IOs and international initiatives offers the Maldives visibility and prestige.

From a theoretical point of view, the Maldives' strategy *vis-à-vis* its gigantic neighbours of India and China is a typical example of hedging, since it implies a swinging behaviour that sees Malé attempting to gain the maximum benefits from its co-operation with India and China, despite their two antithetic and rival IP strategies, through keeping India as the key security provider and China as a more and more important commercial and economic partner.

Brunei

Brunei, also known as Brunei Darussalam, is a sultanate of 400,000 people located on the north coast of the island of Borneo in Southeast Asia, which, apart from its SCS coast, is completely surrounded by the Malaysian state of Sarawak. Like many other small and middle powers of the IP, today Brunei is challenged by the fast growth of Chinese influence in the region.

Brunei's strategy in the IP reflects the will to counter some of China's initiatives that are viewed as presumptuous. One of the major issues that thwart the improvement of relations between Brunei and China are the unsolved disputes in the SCS (Putra 2021). Continuous developments conducted by China in the Scarborough Shoal, Spratly Island and Paracel Islands have been the focus of attention for claimant states to the SCS, including Brunei. Also, the incessant Chinese construction of artificial islands in the SCS being transformed and filled with port facilities, military buildings and even airstrips have raised concerns among regional actors. Though less pressing than those of other Southeast Asian countries, Brunei's claims in the South China focus on a certain maritime boundary in the North of Borneo, which is currently being contested by China.

However, Brunei appeared reluctant to take a strict stance in the SCS disputes, prioritising economic opportunities in shaping and reorienting its foreign policy choices. While other claimant states to the SCS like Indonesia, Malaysia, Vietnam and the Philippines have consistently expressed their unwillingness to renounce to claims over their maritime boundaries *vis-à-vis* China, Brunei responded to China's assertiveness in the SCS by focusing on the possible benefits that the country may gain through a closer cooperation with Beijing. Despite being a party of the UNCLOS, Brunei has underestimated its claims on its EEZ though colliding with the so-called Nine-Dash line, i.e., the line segments that accompany China's claims in the SCS.

Currently, Brunei utilises the ASEAN as one of the main tools to implement its foreign policy, thus contributing to booster Southeast Asian regionalism and multilateralism. Through its active participation in the ASEAN, Brunei has agreed with the concept of "omni-enmeshment," i.e., the process of engaging with an actor to draw it in all-encompassing deep involvement, as a strategy in responding to great power politics in Southeast Asia (Putra 2021). In the frame of an increasing US–China competition, Brunei is a major proponent of approaches that lead states to become involved in a multi-faceted net of initiatives and programs that pivot on multi-lateralism. Brunei's trust towards ASEAN's regional norm construction rests upon the idea that the organisation incarnates the voices of small and middle powers amid the presence of great power politics in the IP. However, despite its interests in boosting multi-lateral co-operation, Brunei has shown a propensity towards an alignment with China. Brunei's decision to develop closer ties with China stems from the growing interdependence of the Brunei economy on China's future-oriented development plans like the BRI and prospects of Chinese FDIs in the years to come. Moreover, the recent increase in the bilateral trade between China and Brunei can be seen as an alignment of Brunei's "Wawasan Brunei 2035" strategy to China's BRI, the former embodying Brunei's strategic goal to implement by 2035 extraordinary reforms in the field of education, sustainable economy and labour. Indeed, in recent years Xi Jinping and Sultan Hassanal Bolkiah have coordinated closely on how to connect "Wawasan Brunei 2035" and the BRI and on how to establish greater co-operation among the two countries (Putra 2021). In this sense, China has supported the idea of implementing a Brunei-Guangxi Economic Corridor, a Land-Sea Trade Corridor and some thorough plans of investment in order to secure Brunei's loyalty and allegiance.

In conclusion, as Brunei acknowledges that the rise of China as superpower in the IP is inevitable, the sultanate has decided to neglect maritime geopolitical disputes in favour of building stronger trade, economic and infrastructural ties with Beijing. In this frame, Brunei seems to have adopted a strategy based both on bandwagoning and buck-passing. A behaviour inspired by bandwagoning is evident when considering the role that Brunei attributes to China for its future development, while back-passing may be seen in Brunei's strategy aimed at trying to get other regional states to deter or contrast China – especially in reference to geopolitical disputes and claims in the IP – while remaining on the side-lines.

Papua New Guinea

Papua New Guinea (PNG) is a country in the Pacific Ocean that comprises the eastern half of the island of New Guinea and its offshore islands in Melanesia with a population of approximately 9 million people. While the country enjoyed a relatively calm epoch in the last decades, the sudden Chinese rise has opened a spectrum of new challenges. Along with most of Melanesia, PNG has been placed on the "greater periphery" of Chinese grand strategy (Connolly 2020). However, since 2006 China expressed the intention to increase its engagement with Oceania and the Pacific Islands. While the region experienced a steady growth in Chinese interest over the past two decades, the official arrival of the BRI in 2018 encouraged local countries to focus their attention on Beijing.

In the case of PNG, the signing of the Memorandum of Understanding (MoU) with China in 2018 represented a turning point for the country's foreign policy strategy, linking it formally to the frame of the BRI. Actually, in 2018 PNG was not the only Pacific country to sign a MoU for the BRI with China, since Timor-Leste and all eligible PICs, including Vanuatu and Fiji, that upheld Beijing's "One China" policy and did not recognise Taiwan had done the same. Since 2018, China and PNG agreed to align the BRI with the PNG National Strategy, shifting China–PNG relations from a "Strategic Relationship" to a "Comprehensive Strategic Relationship" (Connolly 2020). Concretely, the linking of the BRI to PNG would imply an implementation of the so-called "Five Connectivities," i.e., stronger China–PNG liaisons in the sectors of trade, infrastructure, policymaking, people-to-people interaction and finance.

From PNG's perspective, the BRI is viewed as a source of opportunity but also as a challenging project: while Port Moresby is aware of the importance of cheap and rapidly produced critical infrastructure and of trade and business prospects, it is also concerned about the significant risks that the initiative could entail in terms of geoeconomic and geostrategic dependence. While the BRI may well bolster economic development, the costs of tying a country's economy to another's may be detrimental in the long run. In the case of PNG, given its relatively fragile growth and leadership, strong ties with China could unveil the shadow of vassalisation.

From a theoretical viewpoint, PNG's strategy *vis-à-vis* the rise of China in the IP resembles somewhat an example of bandwagoning combined with an official alignment with Beijing, as shown by the signature of the MoU in 2018.

Pacific Island Countries

Pacific Island Countries (PICs) comprise a variety of scarcely populated insular independent states or autonomous entities scattered in the Pacific Ocean. The group of countries includes the Commonwealth of the Northern Mariana Islands, the Federated States of Micronesia, Fiji, French Polynesia, Kiribati, the Marshall Islands, Nauru, New Caledonia, Palau, Solomon Islands, Tonga, Tuvalu, Vanuatu and Wallis and Futuna. Characterised by small populations, remote locations, high telecommunications and transportation costs and poor infrastructure, PICs suffer from structural weaknesses. However, the PICs so-called "Blue Pacific" strategy should be able to tackle some of the difficulties that the region faces, shaping a new long-term pan-Oceanic identity for these relatively isolated nations (see Box 22.2).

Unlike many other regional actors, according to PICs the single greatest security threat to the IP region is not China but climate change (Köllner 2021). This idea was confirmed in the 2018 Boe Declaration on Regional Security, which also affirmed that the concept of "security" implied not only traditional security but also environmental security and human security. From a military point of view, PICs do not perceive concrete threats. In this sense, they tend to reject the logic of China–US competition that underscores the idea that smaller states are to be treated as objects of great power rivalry. Also, China's increasing presence is generally viewed with optimism, believing that it may provide concrete opportunities for political and economic engagement beyond what traditional regional powers have to offer (Köllner 2021). In this sense, PICs do not fear to engage with both traditional and new regional powers, as well as on the global stage.

While sharing geographic proximity, PICs are unique within the wider IP region in terms of culture, language and economies (Naupa 2017). Most countries of the region have relied on several public diplomacy efforts to bridge the geographic and cultural distances, although diplomatic regional interactions are still scarce overall. Some "soft" diplomatic relations are promoted mainly through cultural exchange programs, short-term training and people-to-people exchanges.

In the last decades, PICs have been promoting the idea of "New Pacific Diplomacy" consisting of collective action in the pursuit of shared interests across a range of issue areas that include ocean governance, seabed mining, sustainable development, decolonisation and trade. In this perspective, an important diplomatic initiative promoted by PICs to enhance their "New Pacific Diplomacy" was the establishment in 1971 of the Pacific Islands Forum (PIF) (see Box 22.3). This platform has been used in time as the paramount tool to implement Pacific diplomacy, supporting development and trade, environmental, climate and sports diplomacy, and ocean diplomacy (Naupa 2017). PIF countries have complicated diplomatic relations with China, since some adhere to the "One China" policy – e.g., Vanuatu and Fiji – while others upkeep diplomatic ties with Taiwan – e.g., Kiribati, the Marshall Islands, Nauru, Palau, Tuvalu and the Solomon Islands. Also, each PIF member maintains a distinctive relation with other countries of the greater IP region like Japan, India, Indonesia, Malaysia, the Philippines, Russia, South Korea, Thailand, Canada and the United States. PICs could increase their chances of visibility by strengthening their relations in the larger IP through institutional arrangements like ASEAN and APEC, and the PIF Secretariat (PIFS). Specifically, while being an observer to the APEC, PIFS should foster stronger technical and diplomatic relations with the ASEAN. PICs tend to use network diplomacy in the frame of international institutions as a tool for bolstering political, security, economic and cultural ties with major actors of the IP. At the same time, they tend to utilise multi-lateral fora to leverage wider diplomatic networks and overcome structural deficiencies.

From a conceptual framework, unlike the previous case studies, overall, the PICs adopted a strategy that is closer to non-alignment. Instead of bandwagoning or overtly aligning with China, they decided to prioritise aspects such as climate change and enhance strategies aimed at pursuing autonomous interests in the Pacific Ocean.

Box 22.3 The Pacific Islands Forum

The Pacific Islands Forum (PIF) is an international organisation that aims at fostering co-operation between the insular countries of the Pacific Ocean. Founded in 1971 as South Pacific Forum (SPF), the name was changed in 2000 to better reflect the correct geographical location of its member states lying both in the North and South Pacific. Currently, the PIF member states are Australia, Cook Islands, Fiji, French Polynesia, New Caledonia, New Zealand, Niue, Papua New Guinea, Samoa, Solomon Islands, Tonga, Tuvalu and Vanuatu. In February 2021, Palau decided to leave the Forum and several other participant countries have indicated their intention to review their membership, raising concerns about the future of the organisation. The Forum's decisions are implemented by the Pacific Islands Forum Secretariat (PIFS) which developed from the South Pacific Bureau for Economic Cooperation (SPEC). In addition to its role as a harmoniser of the region's point of view in relation to policy issues, the PIFS implements plan in the fields of economic development, transportation and trade, and chairs the CROP. The main goal of the PIF is to work in support of member states, to enhance the economic and social well-being of the South Pacific population by encouraging cooperation between governments and international agencies and representing the interests of the Forum members in the international community.

Suggested reading:

- The Pacific Islands Forum, "The Pacific Islands Forum," https://www.forum-sec.org/who-we-arepacific-islands-forum/.
- United Nations, "Intergovernmental and Other Organizations," https://web.archive.org/web/20210610015003/https://www.un.org/en/about-us/inter-governmental-and-other-organizations.
- The Guardian, "Future of Pacific Islands Forum in doubt as Palau walks out," 5 February 2021. https://www.theguardian.com/world/2021/feb/05/future-of-pacific-islands-forum-in-doubt-as-north-south-rift-emerges.

Conclusion

This chapter has examined the role of small powers in the contemporary frame of IP great power rivalry. As China increases its presence in the IP through several projects including the BRI, and as US-led initiatives like the QUAD and the AUKUS embody efforts to counter China's rise, small regional powers need to reprioritise their strategic agenda. In deciding whether to balance, bandwagon, stay non-aligned, hedge, buckpass or engage, small states need to assess the costs and benefits that these strategies would entail. As highlighted in the last section and epitomised in **Table 22.1**, the evidence

Table 22.1 Small states' strategies in the Indo-Pacific

IP Small state	Strategy	Objective
Laos	Bandwagoning	Bandwagon with rising China to counter regional challenges, increase international visibility and foster domestic development
The Maldives	Hedging	Keep a swinging behaviour to gain the maximum benefits from the co-operation with India and China, while maintaining India as key security provider and China as crucial commercial and economic partner
Brunei	Bandwagoning and buck-passing	Bandwagon with rising China while buck-passing geopolitical disputes and claims *vis-à-vis* Beijing to other regional actors
Papua New Guinea	Bandwagoning and alignment	Bandwagon and align with rising China to bolster economic development and international visibility
Pacific Island Countries	Non-alignment	Autonomous strategy in relation to rising China, while prioritising key sectors like climate change and diplomatic dialogue in multilateral fora

suggests different trends. While for Laos the alignment and bandwagoning with China represents the rational choice in order to counterbalance dynamic neighbours, in the case of the Maldives the national strategy envisions an "India-first" policy in reference to security and defence but also the building of deep commercial ties with China, which underscores an approach close to hedging. Furthermore, while Brunei – unlike other IP countries – opted for side-lining its claims on the disputed SCS in favour of developing closer economic relations with Beijing in a strategy that combines aspects of bandwagoning with aspects of buck-passing, PNG has established since 2018 – like other neighbouring countries – through the MoU a concrete co-operation with China with important long-term implications for the Oceanian and Melanesian region that embodies a fully fledged example of bandwagoning. Finally, while focusing on the implementation of the "Blue Pacific" strategy and the "New Pacific Diplomacy" based on ocean governance and sustainable development, PICs have manifested divergent policies *vis-à-vis* China: some have adhered to the "One China" policy and others have opted to maintain the allegiance with Taiwan, thus manifesting an explicit stance close to non-alignment.

With the increase of great power rivalry in the IP, future previsions predict that small states in the region – neglected until few decades ago – will play an ever-growing role. In order to gain a more incisive international weight, small states of the IP should invest more in those regional sectors that have been depicted as strategic by the literature (Köllner 2021).

- *Trade policy*: Regional trade should be encouraged and promoted especially in multi-lateral and intergovernmental organisations. At the same time, small states should not rely only on one exclusive producer, but instead diversify the suppliers of resources.
- *Climate policy*: Small states should implement strategies aimed at contrasting climate change and environmental degradation, paying specific attention to the safeguard of the Indo-Pacific natural habitat.

- *Ocean governance*: Effective ocean governance requires solid forms of governance to maintain the ocean for its various uses in a sustainable manner. In this sense, small states should encourage the negotiations of international agreements and treaties that pursue more sustainable relations with the ocean.
- *Digital governance*: Small states should foster the shaping of norms, institutions, standards, regimes and regulations that aim at improving global digital governance. Investment in digital technology can help to increase the importance of a small state, while making it more competitive in the international system.
- *Connectivity*: The key to a successful IP strategy is to promote projects that aim at creating connectivity bonds throughout the region. In this frame, small states should adhere to those initiatives that wish to create intense infrastructural interconnections among regional countries, including the BRI.
- *Defence*: Due to the rising great power rivalry in the IP, small states should invest more in their security and defence apparatus. Particular attention should be paid in tackling potential asymmetric threats stemming from the cybernetic realm and the sphere of disinformation.
- *Human security*: The safeguard of the fundamental rights of human beings should be paramount in forging national security strategies. The protection of human security should cover the spheres of economic security, food security, health security, environmental security, individual security, collective security and political security. Small states could boost their prestige and credibility if they show they are capable of protecting human security.

While it is too early to provide an overall assessment of the future strategic weight of these countries, it is undoubtable that they will incarnate indispensable actors for the implementation of projects like the BRI. At the same time, their foreign policy strategies, inclinations and alignments will be crucial to determine whether the United States is losing grip on the IP in favour of China or whether it can still consider itself as the hegemonic power.

To conclude, in addressing the guiding research questions raised at the beginning of the chapter, the current strategic importance of small powers in the IP rests on the key role they can play in the frame of the increasing rivalry between major powers. Despite their size, small powers can adopt strategies that may affect great powers. While they cannot be seen as absolute protagonists in the international arena, their foreign policy strategies can exploit greater powers' rivalry for their own benefit in a win-win scenario. The adoption of bandwagoning, buck-passing, hedging or non-alignment strategies shows that small powers do not embody mere passive agents or buffers in the hands of major powers, but can shape a consistent foreign policy approach that impacts on the major powers' objectives. In this sense, small powers may be considered, albeit partially, gamechangers in the IP.

References

Alapuro, Risto (ed.), *Small States in Comparative Perspective: Essays for Erik Allardt*, (Oslo: Norwegian University Press, 1985).

Archer, Clive and Nugent, Neill, "Introduction: Small States and the European Union," *Current Politics and Economics of Europe*, 11(1), 2002: 1–10.

Chazan, Naomi (ed.), *Irredentism and International Politics*, (London: Adamantine Press, 1991).

Chun, Chae-Sung, "Theoretical Approaches to Alliance: Implications on the ROK-US Alliance," *Journal of International and Area Studies*, 7(2), 2000: 71–88.

Connolly, Peter, "The Belt and Road Comes to Papua New Guinea: Chinese Geoeconomics with Melanesian Characteristics?" *Security Challenges*, 16(4), 2020: 41–64.

Crowards, Tom, "Defining the Category of 'Small' States," *Journal of International Development*, 14(2), 2002: 143–179.

Fiori, Antonio and Passeri, Andrea, "Hedging in Search of a New Age of Non-alignment: Myanmar between China and the USA," *The Pacific Review*, 28(5), 2015: 679–702.

Fox, Annette B., *The Power of Small States: Diplomacy in World War II*, (Chicago, IL: University of Chicago Press, 1959).

Handel, Michael, *Weak States in the International System*, (London: Frank Cass, 1981).

Hansen, Lise B., *Småstaters Indflydelse i Den Europæiske Union*, (Copenhagen: Copenhagen Research Project on European Integration, 1997).

Heiduk, Felix and Wacker, Gudrun, "From Asia-Pacific to Indo-Pacific: Significance, Implementation and Challenges," SWP Research Paper, Berlin: Stiftung Wissenschaft und Politik-SWP-Deutsches Institut für Internationale Politik und Sicherheit, 2020.

Heraclides, Alexis, *The Self-Determination of Minorities in International Politics*, (London: Frank Cass, 1991).

Jung, Sung Chul, Lee, Jaehyon and Lee, Ji-Yong, "The Indo-Pacific Strategy and US Alliance Network Expandability: Asian Middle Powers' Positions on Sino-US Geostrategic Competition in Indo-Pacific Region," *Journal of Contemporary China*, 30(127), 2021: 53–68.

Kang, David C., "Between Balancing and Bandwagoning: South Korea's Response to China," *Journal of East Asian Studies*, 9(1), 2009: 1–28.

Katzenstein, Peter J., *Corporatism and Change: Austria, Switzerland and the Politics of Industry*, (Ithaca, NY: Cornell University Press, 1984).

Keohane, Robert O., "Lilliputians' Dilemmas: Small States in International Politics," *International Organization*, 23(2), 1969: 291–310.

Knudsen, Olav F., "Analysing Small-State Security: The Role of External Factors," in Werner Bauwens, Armand Clesse and Olav F. Knudsen (eds.), *Small States and the Security Challenge in the New Europe*, (London: Brassey's, 1996): 3–20.

Knudsen, Olav F., "Small States, Latent and Extant: Towards a General Perspective," *Journal of International Relations and Development*, 5(2), 2002: 182–198.

Köllner, Patrick, "Beyond 'Indo-Pacific': Understanding Small Pacific Powers on Their Own Terms," GIGA Focus Asien, 5, Hamburg: German Institute for Global and Area Studies (GIGA), Leibniz-Institut für Globale und Regionale Studien, Institut für Asien-Studien, 2021. https://nbn-resolving.org/urn:nbn:de:0168-ssoar-75926-5.

Korolev, Alexander, "Shrinking Room for Hedging: System-unit Dynamics and Behaviour of Smaller Powers," *International Relations of the Asia-Pacific*, 19(3), 2019: 419–452.

Labs, Eric J., "Do Weak States Bandwagon?" *Security Studies*, 1(3), 1992: 383–416.

Murphy, Anne M., "Beyond Balancing and Bandwagoning: Thailand's Response to China's Rise," *Asian Security*, 6(1), 2010: 1–27.

Naupa, Anna, "Indo-Pacific Diplomacy: A View from the Pacific Islands," *Politics and Policy*, 45(5), 2017: 902–917.

Neumann, Iver B. and Gstöhl, Sieglinde, *Lilliputians in Gulliver's World?: Small States in International Relations*, (Reykjavík: Centre for Small State Studies, 2004).

Ørvik, Nils, *The Decline of Neutrality 1914–1941: With Special Reference to the United States and the Northern Neutrals*, (Oslo: Johan Grundt Tanum Forlag, 1953).

Pang, Edgar, "Same-Same But Different: Laos and Cambodia's Political Embrace of China," *ISEAS, Yusof Ishak Institute*, 66, 2017: 1–7.

Papadakis, Maria and Starr, Harvey, 'Opportunity, Willingness and Small States: The Relationship between Environment and Foreign Policy,' in Charles Herman, Charles Kegley and James Rosenau (eds.), *New Directions in the Study of Foreign Policy*, (London: Allen and Unwin, 1987): 409–432.

Pape, Robert A., "Soft Balancing against the United States," *International Security*, 30(1), 2005: 7–45.

Paul, Thazha V., "When Balance of Power Meets Globalization: China, India and the Small States of South Asia," *Politics*, 39(1), 2019: 50–63.

Plagemann, Johannes, "Small States and Competing Connectivity Strategies: What Explains Bangladesh's Success in Relations with Asia's Major Powers?" *The Pacific Review*, 35(4), 2021: 736–764, DOI: 10.1080/09512748.2021.1908410.

Putra, Bama A., "Comprehending Brunei Darussalam's Vanishing Claims in the South China Sea: China's Exertion of Economic Power and the Influence of Elite Perception," *Cogent Social Sciences*, 7(1), 2021: 1–14.

Ramachandran, Sudha, "The China-Maldives Connection," *The Diplomat* [Online], 25 January 2018. https://thediplomat.com/2018/01/the-china-maldives-connection/.

Rosenau, James N., "Pre-theories and Theories of Foreign Policy," in Robert B. Farrell (ed.), *Approaches to Comparative and International Politics*, (Evanston, IL: Northwestern University Press, 1966): 27–92.

Rothstein, Robert L., *Alliances and Small Powers*, (New York: Columbia University Press, 1968).

Schweller, Randall L., "Bandwagoning for Profit: Bringing the Revisionist State Back In," *International Security*, 19(1), 1994: 72–107.

Scott, David, "Small Island Strategies in the Indo-Pacific by Large Powers," *The Journal of Territorial and Maritime Studies*, 8(1), 2021: 66–85.

Spykman, Nicholas J., *America's Strategy in World Politics*, (New York: Harcourt, Brace and Company, 1942).

The World Factbook, Central Intelligence Agency, 2022. https://www.cia.gov/the-world-factbook/countries/laos/.

Theys, Sarina and Rietig, Katharina, "The Influence of Small States: How Bhutan Succeeds in Influencing Global Sustainability Governance," *International Affairs*, 96(6), 2020: 1603–1622.

Thorhallsson, Baldur, "The Size of States in the European Union: Theoretical and Conceptual Perspectives," *Journal of European Integration*, 28(1), 2006: 7–31.

Thorhallsson, Baldur and Steinsson, Sverrir, 'Small-state Foreign Policy,' in Cameron Thies (ed.), *The Oxford Encyclopaedia of Foreign Policy Analysis*, (Oxford: Oxford University Press, 2017): 1–21. DOI: https://doi.org/10.1093/acrefore/9780190228637.013.48

Thorhallsson, Baldur and Wivel, Anders, "Small States in the European Union: What Do We Know and What Would We Like to Know?" *Cambridge Review of International Affairs*, 19(4), 2006: 651–668.

Vandenbosch, Amry, "The Small States in International Politics and Organization," *The Journal of Politics*, 26(2), 1964: 293–312.

Väyrynen, Raimo, "On the Definition and Measurement of Small Power Status," *Cooperation and Conflict*, 6(1), 1971: 91–102.

Vital, David, *The Inequality of States: A Study of the Small Powers in International Relations*, (Oxford: Clarendon Press, 1967).

Wæver, Ole, "Identity, Communities and Foreign Policy: Discourse Analysis as Foreign Policy Theory," in Lene Hansen and Ola Wæver (eds.), *European Integration and National Adaptations: The Challenge of the Nordic States* (London: Routledge, 2002): 20–49.

Walt, Stephen M., "Alliance Formation and the Balance of World Power," *International Security*, 9(4), 1985: 3–43.

Walt, Stephen M., *The Origins of Alliances*, (Ithaca, NY: Cornell University Press, 1987).

Walt, Stephen M., "Testing Theories of Alliance Formation: The Case of Southwest Asia," *International Organization*, 43(2), 1988: 275–316.

Waltz, Kenneth N., *Theory of International Politics*, (New York: Random House, 1979).

Waltz, Kenneth N., *Realism and International Politics*, (London: Routledge, 2008).

Index

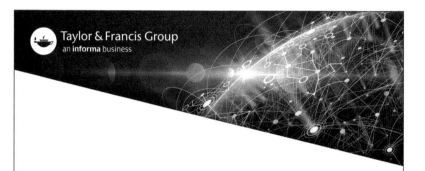